FROM CUSTER
TO MACARTHUR

TURNER PUBLISHING COMPANY

TURNER PUBLISHING COMPANY
Publishers of Military History

Publisher's Editor: Robert J. Martin
Writer: Edward L. Daily
Designer: Luke A. Henry

Copyright © 1995
Turner Publishing Company

Library of Congress Catalog Card No.95-60659

ISBN: 978-1-68162-288-0

Books available from the publisher.

TABLE OF CONTENTS

THE GARRYOWEN

Blazon of the Regimental Insignia of the 7th U.S. Cavalry, USA

A cavalry horseshoe, or, heels upward, with crease, sabre and seven nail heads, white. Above and joining the heels of the shoe, a scroll, azure, bearing the words, "GARRYOWEN," or ...

At the base and emerging from sinister side of the shoe, a dexter arm embowed, vested azure, the hand in the buckskin gauntlet, proper, grasping an old style U.S. Army sabre, or hilted, or blade extended to center or scroll gripe, sabre threaded or ...

Explanation of Design

The horseshoe is symbolic of the Cavalry. Its color, gold (yellow in heraldic tincture), is the color of the old uniform facings of the United States Cavalry, in existence when the Regiment was organized and still is retained as the color of the Cavalry Arm.

The words, "GARRYOWEN," are the title of an old Irish (sic) war song known and used as the Regimental song since the days of General Custer. Its rollicking air symbolizes the esprit de corps for which the Regiment is noted.

The arm, taken from the crest of the Regimental Coat of Arms, symbolizes the spirit of the Cavalry Charge. At the time of the organization of the Regiment, this position of the arm and sabre was known as "Raise Sabre" and was taken at the command, "Charge." The sabre itself is of the old Cavalry type used in the Indian campaigns. The gauntlet also is symbolic of

those times. The blue of the sleeve is the blue of the old Army uniform. The twisted emblem at toe of the shoe is symbolic of Indian days.

For many years, the Regimental song was accepted as being of Scottish origin, however, it has been definitely established that the song is of Irish origin. It had been used by several Irish regiments as their quick march; the Fifth Royal Irish Lancers stationed in the suburb of Limerick called "GARRYOWEN," (the Gaelic word, meaning "Owen's Garden") used it as their drinking song. The words hardly can be called elevating, but depict the rollicking nature of the Lancers while in town on pay day in search of their peculiar style of "camaraderie."

Authority: Boosey: London: (no date, presumably about 1800) "Songs of Ireland."

The Song of GARRYOWEN

It was an Irish quick marching or drinking song adopted by the 7th Cavalry Regiment in 1867. Its first introduction to war was at the Battle of the Washita, on Nov. 17, 1868. After that, all 7th Cavalry troopers were known as GARRYOWEN.

We are the pride of the Army and a Regiment of great renown
Our names in the pages of history from 66 on down
If you think we stop or falter while into the fray we're goin'
Just watch our step, with our heads erect when our band plays
"GARRYOWEN"

ESPRIT de CORPS TO THE GARRYOWEN

To somewhat clarify the existence or absence of esprit de corps in a military unit, one must perhaps focus on traditions and heritages of an organization and its historical past. To better understand esprit, it is necessary to look beyond the immediate unit and consider the men, events, incidents and battles that are connected to its history as a whole.

The term "Cavalry" has been synonymous with esprit de corps in the military profession throughout the ages. Such terms as Dragoons, Lancers, Hussars, Horse Guards and Cavalry suggest a colorful mounted soldier dashing toward his enemy with sword raised at the charge. And from the earliest times, every battle has had its lessons and has left its mark on the particular unit involved. Weapons and tactics change, but the men who fight the battles and the principles for which they are fought remain much the same. However, a unit enriched with a glorious past history could so imbue an officer or soldier to feel duty-bound to maintain the unit's high reputation in the face of overwhelming odds.

In the case of the GARRYOWEN, 7th U.S. Cavalry Regiment and its modern Army units, the continuance existence of this indefinable enthusiasm, inspiration and spirit cannot be

attributed to any single event or individual in the history of the regiment. A combination of legends and traditions have kindled this esprit.

The adopted of the regimental song "GARRYOWEN" in 1867 by Gen. George Armstrong Custer, did much to enhance the prestige of the 7th Cavalry among its sister regiments serving within the frontier. The Battle of the Little Big Horn, publicized out of all proportion to its military importance, has served to focus worldwide attraction on the 7th Cavalry Regiment.

GARRYOWEN troopers always have been and are today, the custodians of a personal pride in self and unit that is exceeded by no other unit in the Armies of the World. This blood bond to the glories of the past, coupled with the heroism and devotion to duty exemplified by deeds from Custer to MacArthur and beyond, have given 7th Cavalry troopers a stubborn determination to endure to the utmost.

The famous GARRYOWEN Esprit — an intrinsic part of the reputation of the regiment. Of the other old historic regiments in the Army, the GARRYOWEN Esprit stands very unique and distinctive, and has won the admiration of soldiers throughout the world.

THE AUTHOR

Edward L. Daily

Edward L. Daily enlisted directly into the 1st Cavalry Division in 1948. After completing Armored-Infantry basic training at Fort Knox, KY, he was sent immediately to the Far East Command in Japan. Arriving in Tokyo, Japan, in February 1949, he was assigned to Company H, 2nd Battalion, 7th Cavalry Regiment.

He soon found himself learning his new trade as a machine gunner in the 1st Platoon. But, at that particular time, most of their training consisted of occupation duty that existed within the Eighth Army. A major influence soon appeared in his life and military career, which came from his company commander, Capt. Melbourne C. Chandler. Chandler attempted to instill in every trooper a dedicated effort to become a better soldier, and he further emphasized the strict guidelines of the heritage and tradition of the famous GARRYOWEN regiment.

When the Korean War started, the 7th Cavalry Regiment departed from Japan in July 1950, to fight against communist aggression from the North Korean Army. Fighting a savage enemy, the 2nd Battalion experienced many battle casualties during the early stages of combat. This created a very serious condition because there was a shortage of replacements and, in some instances, there were none at all! Because of this desperate situation, promotions within the ranks came to those capable survivors. From the recommendations of Lt. Robert M. Carroll, Capt. Mel Chandler and Maj. Omar Hitchner, Commander, 2nd Battalion, he received a battlefield commission to temporary 2nd Lieutenant on Aug. 10, 1950.

Assuming leadership of the same 1st Platoon, it was a very proud time in his life and military career. However, two days later, on Aug. 12, 1950, during a vicious battle on the Naktong River, the forward elements of his platoon were overrun, and he could not evade capture.

With the grace of God, he managed to escape from the enemy on Sept. 12, 1950, and was held captive only 32 days. Receiving the appropriate medical treatment, he volunteered to return to his previous unit and active duty on Sept. 23, 1950. This time, conditions had changed greatly in favor of the United Nations Forces, because the United States Marines and the 7th Infantry Division previously had made an amphibious landing at Inchon, South Korea, thus cutting off the entire supply line of the North Korean Army.

Nonetheless, he would face many struggles and hardships as he remained in combat with the 7th Cavalry Regiment. On May 10, 1951, he returned to the United States. He was honorably discharged from the Army on May 27, 1952.

Among the medals awarded to him were: the Distinguished Service Cross; Silver Star Medal; Bronze Star Medal (V); Purple Heart w/2 Oak-leaf Clusters; Army Commendation Medal; Korean Campaign Medal w/5 Bronze Battle Stars; South Korean Presidential Unit Citation; Combat Infantryman Badge and the Army Parachutist Badge. In June 1988, he was awarded the American Ex-Prisoner of War Medal by the Department of Defense.

He is a life member of the 1st Cavalry Division Association and the 7th U.S. Cavalry Association; and over the years, he has remained loyal and dedicated to both organizations. Currently, he is a member of the Boards of Governors of the 1st Cavalry Division Association. The 1st Cavalry Division is stationed at Fort Hood, Texas. He is past president of the 7th U.S. Cavalry Association and current president of the Korean War Veterans Chapter, 7th U.S. Cavalry Association.

PREFACE

The 7th U.S. Cavalry Regiment is now within its 127-year history and is etched in the glittering pages of American history. The first 30 years of its history is presented in detail in the pages which follow. The material upon which this history is based has been taken from the official documents on file in the National Archives and the Department of the Army. Furthermore, the descriptions of major events, names of individuals, place names, dates, and figures are exactly as they appear in these records. Many of the incidents described have been related by former members of the regiment and are so identified. Also, the material used as a basis for the period 1866-1909 was taken from the *Illustrated Review* of the 7th United States Cavalry Regiment, which was published by the regiment in 1910. Actually, this first regimental history was initiated as a result of the following directive:

Camp McGrath, Batangas, P.I.
19 Sep 1906
Headquarters 7th U.S. Cavalry

Major Loyd S. McCormick,
7th U.S. Cavalry Camp

Sir:

The regimental commander desires you to get up the history of the Regiment as required by General Orders, No. 1, War Department, dated 4 Jan 1905. He has intended to prepare the manuscript himself in great part but he finds he cannot do the work under the constant interruptions his great variety of duties subject him.

To the end in view you will be excused from such duties as may prove incompatible with a prosecution of this work; such clerical assistance as you may need and can be supplied will be furnished you; and you shall have access to all returns, records, etc., from the organization of the regiment. There are now on file histories of each and every troop down to include 1904, since when the yearly history has been forwarded.

Very respectfully,
(Signed) E. Anderson
Captain and Adjutant,
7th Cavalry

The history directed above was barely started when the regiment was ordered back to the United States and took station at Fort Riley, Kansas, and it was not until late 1907 that it got underway. In November 1907, Brigadier Generals Edward S. Godfrey and Winfield S. Edgerly, and Colonels Luther R. Hare and Charles A. Varnum met at Fort Riley and reviewed the rough manuscript for accuracy and completeness.

During this period, the late Corporal Edward S. Luce was detailed on special duty (in addition to his regular duties as troop clerk of Troop A) to type the final manuscript. Later in life he became superintendent of the Little Big Horn Battlefield, and he was a past historian of the 7th U.S. Cavalry Association. He was always dedicated and loyal to the GARRYOWEN and is credited with making many contributions to the early history of the 7th U.S. Cavalry Regiment and to the 7th U.S. Cavalry Association.

The early records of the regiment were all handwritten, usually in perfect spencerian script, but through the years the original records have become faded and cracked when unfolded. Many names are illegible and frequently misspelled. For example, General Custer's adjutant was William Winer Cooke. For several years his middle name appears in the records as "Winner" and his last name was spelled as Cook, without the "e."

Detailed Records of Events were submitted for each troop during the period 1866-1909. Histories covering activities of the regiment for an entire year were submitted annually until 1914. Regulations were then changed and monthly regimental strength reports only were submitted until about 1941 with no entries made as to the activities of the individual troops. The entries on individual troop morning reports for the period 1923-1942 are brief and describe only the minimum required official activities of the period covered. The few official historical accounts of the regiment's activities during this period are not uniform and apparantly depended upon the whims of the regimental commander at the time. The periods during which the regiment was engaged in combat is covered in detail in periodic operations reports, after actions reports, and daily unit journals.

The original records of the regiment have suffered from many disasters throughout the years and has made research exceptionally difficult. In 1915, the storage tent containing many of the old records burned at Columbus, New Mexico. In 1940, a cloudburst at Fort Bliss flooded a basement where many records were stored and damaged them beyond future use. Coupled with these disasters, from time to time over-zealous adjutants and "record administrators" have destroyed valuable records in an effort to comply with orders or accomplish what they thought was "cleaning out useless files."

It will be noted that GARRYOWEN, the name of the regiment, is spelled both as one word and two words throughout this history. While its original spelling was probably one word, it is spelled both ways in the regiment's records and is used throughout this text as it appears in the official records for the period covered.

Many contemporary reports, letters, etc., have been quoted freely and often verbatim so as to give a faithful picture to the reader, not only of events but how members of the regiment viewed their adversaries, allies, and those aspects of our national history in which they participated. Due to the incomplete and often inaccurate records, the pages which follow are based upon all known official existing records and accurately reflect the activities of the regiment during its existence. The author of this book offers his sincere apologies for any terminology used within this text that should inadvertently give offense to any group or organization. *Ed Daily, author.*

FOREWORD

As the author of this book, I would like to emphasize a few brief comments that are of historical significance. During June 23-25, 1994, a Wolakota-peace ceremony was conducted between the Lakota and the 7th U.S. Cavalry Association. This successful event was culminated over a period of fourteen months, which involved extensive traveling, discussions and careful planning, between both parties.

Much credit must be given to numerous individuals, who devoted and dedicated their time, and energy to ensure the overall success of the event. The initial initiation from Francis Whitebird who at the time was Commissioner of Indian Affairs, State of South Dakota, must be recognized with sincere appreciation and gratitude. And to the Honorable Walter Dale Miller who at the time was Governor of South Dakota; Major General Harold J. Sykora, Adjutant General of the State of South Dakota National Guard; Peter Henry, Director, VA Medical Center, Fort Meade; Major Bob Meier, Training Administrator, South Dakota Military Academy; Becky Sutton, Director, Cavalry Museum, Fort Meade; the entire Staff, VA Medical Center, Fort Meade; the entire Staff, Cavalry Museum, Fort Meade; Lt. Gen. (RET) Harold G. Moore, Honorary Colonel, 7th Cavalry Regiment; Sherman Haight, appointed First Sergeant to the Horse Troopers; Bob Cooper, Honorary Member, 7th U.S. Cavalry Association; Bob "Snuffy" Gray, Master of Ceremonies; Lynas End of Horn, Lakota who gave his full support; to all the members of the 7th U.S. Cavalry Association and Korean War Veterans Chapter; to all the Lakota people who participated and gave us their overwhelming support.

I was greatly honored during the ceremony and within those very critical fourteen months prior to the scheduled event, which gave me the opportunity to personally meet many Native Americans whose culture, and heritage I knew very little about. Nevertheless and without hesitation, I quickly attempted to educate myself of the Lakota who expressed a proud heritage and dedication of their nature, and keeping to the traditions and beliefs of their ancestors. Noteworthy to this, is when I was invited in October 1993, as a guest to the council meeting at Pine Ridge Reservation. During that particular meeting, I was introduced to Chief Oliver Red Cloud (4th generation to Chief Red Cloud), and Alex White Plume. Both are of the Oglala band of Sioux. Immediately, they both expressed their feelings of grief concerning the making and breaking of peace treaties, for the Great Sioux Reservation. An expression and true example of the agony within their hearts, and souls of the prolonged struggles and suffering endured by the Lakota people.

After that trip I returned to my home in Tennessee and I quickly started to research, and learn of the Treaty of April 29, 1868. This is when the Commission met Chief Red Cloud with his Oglala and Brule Sioux, at Fort Laramie, and concluded the signing with them. During that summer, this same Treaty was submitted and accepted by the head men of the Hunkpapa, Upper and Lower Yanktonais, Blackfeet, Two Kettle, Sans Arc, and Minniconju Sioux, at various places along the Missouri River.

Then in March 1994, I travelled to Pierre, South Dakota, to meet with Francis Whitebird and Bob "Snuffy" Gray. From there, Bob and I travelled on northward by automobile to Fort Peck Reservation in Montana. We were scheduled to meet with Chauncey Whitright, Chairman of the Native American Strong Heart Society and Gary Moe who is the Administrator for the Missouri Valley Development Corporation.

Shortly after our arrival, we also had the opportunity to meet with Merle Lucas a Native American who was a highly decorated veteran of the Vietnam War. However, I am very saddened to say that he suddenly passed away, this past June 1994. A tremendous loss to his family, the Fort Peck Reservation, and to America. Furthermore, he had made plans to attend the Wolakota-peace ceremony on June 25, 1994, with a veterans delegation from Fort Peck Reservation. His sudden death prevented this from happening.

Also, he was instrumental on the day that we met him in recommending Bob and myself to personally meet Caleb Shields, Tribal Chairman for the Assiniboine and Sioux Tribes at Fort Peck Reservation. When Bob and I left the office of Caleb, he had assured both of us that there was a better understanding between both parties, and a step forward in the right direction. It should be noted that Chauncey Whitright and Lois Red Elk also attended this meeting. Lois is a reporter for their local newspaper, the "Wotanin Wowapi."

As I continue, I would like to bring forth a further important fact. Arvol Looking Horse (keeper of the sacred pipe), gave us his support and blessing during the start of the Wolakota-peace ceremony on June 23, 1994. Those of us who had the opportunity to 'smoke the pipe' with him were greatly honored of this tribute toward peace. And several were descended from men who fought against each other, during the Battle of the Little Big Horn. Also present, were the four races of mankind and under the vision of a bald eagle, which circled overhead. From this phenomenal sighting, all of us had the motional feeling that the spiritual world was observing us.

Committed to enlighten the reader with factual knowledge rather than speculation, I will further exploit the Lakota Indian who shared a very important part of the early military history of the 7th U.S. Cavalry Regiment.

It is not to be doubted that the Black Hills were exploited, not only by individuals, but under official direction by the United States Government. In 1874, General Custer with the 7th U.S. Cavalry Regiment, was sent on the Black Hills Expedition for thorough exploration. The expedition brought out the report that there was gold in the Hills. Suddenly, the Hills were invaded by white men and a formal complaint, and objection was filed by Chief Red Cloud. This continued on until December 1875, when the Indians were notified to report to their reservation before the end of the following month.

In early February 1876, General Crook took to the field with 883 troops of the 2nd and 3rd Cavalry, to force all Indians to live on their reservation. Through driving snow and temperatures as low as 50 degrees below zero, Scout Grouard literally felt his way along the trail that led to the Powder River. On March 17th, and twenty-six days after its departure, the entire force returned to Fort Fetterman - worn, weary and defeated by the warriors under the leadership of Crazy Horse.

A few months later and with the defeat of the 7th U.S. Cavalry Regiment during the Battle of the Little Big Horn on June 25, 1876, another change in government policy would follow. In September, a Commission of which Right Reverend Henry B. Whipple of Minnesota was a member, negotiated a Treaty with the Sioux, which opened the Black Hills, though not materially changing the conditions of the 1868 Treaty, except in so far as it required all Indians to live on their reservation.

It was a notorious fact that the government did not comply with the stipulations and conditions of the 1868 Treaty. The making of unfair Treaties and the violation of Treaty rights are the two important things of which the Indian has most right to complain.

Nevertheless, history is history and we can't change it. However, we should constantly attempt to put it in the right perspective and make sure that it is properly interpreted for future generations to come. We can definitely win if we judge people on what they do today, and not on what people did in the 19th Century. I firmly believe that the success of the Wolakota-peace ceremony on June 25, 1994, was a positive and important step forward of symbolic peace between the 7th Cavalry and the Lakota people. *Ed Daily, author.*

SELAH R.H. TOMPKINS

Two regimental commanders stand out as the most colorful in the entire history of the 7th U.S. Cavalry Regiment, George Armstrong Custer and Selah R.H. Tompkins. To the latter goes the honor of having served longer in the regiment than any other person, and his fame was known equally in all the regiments of cavalry throughout the Army.

Selah R.H. Tompkins (whose ancestors had been cavalrymen for seven generations) was born in Washington, DC, 17 Jul 1863, the oldest son of General and Mrs. C.H. Tompkins. In 1862 his father was awarded the Medal of Honor, when in the most daring and successful cavalry engagements in the Civil War, he led his troops of Dragoons into Fairfax, Virginia, inflicted severe losses, secured valuable information, and won for himself the name of "Fairfax Charlie." Selah R.H. Tompkins was the grandson of Colonel Daniel D. Tompkins, graduate of the West Point class of 1820, and a great-grandson of Major Charlie Stockton of the British Army, a cavalry leader in the Revolutionary War. His two brothers (Colonels Frank and Daniel D. Tompkins) also cavalrymen, served in almost every cavalry regiment in the Army. Both were in the chase of Villa into Mexico and later with the AEF in World War I. Colonel Frank Tompkins also served as chairman of the Military Affairs Committee in the Vermont Legislature.

Selah R.H. Tompkins came into the service from civil life in 1884 as a second lieutenant, 7th Infantry, then stationed at Fort Laramie, Wyoming. In the spring of 1886, he was transferred to the 7th Cavalry and assigned to Troop D, then stationed in Wyoming. It was during this period in American history that the Indians were causing the government unceasing trouble, and Lieutenant Tompkins participated in the last major engagements against the Indians—the Battles of Wounded Knee and White Clay Creeks. In the former engagement he was cited for bravery and conspicuous valor in action.

In 1892 he was transferred to Troop B, 7th U.S. Cavalry Regiment, and remained in this same organization until his transfer to Troop G in 1901 when he received his captaincy. He served in Troop G until 1911 when he was promoted to major and assumed command of the 1st Squadron, 7th Cavalry.

In January 1914 Major Tompkins was transferred and commanded the 1st Squadron, 5th Cavalry, until his transfer back to the 7th Cavalry in March 1916. He was then a lieutenant colonel and joined his old regiment in Mexico during the Punitive Expedition where he was awarded the Silver Star for action. In July 1916 he was promoted to colonel and given command of the regiment he had joined as a "shave tail" in 1886. To this veteran cavalryman then goes the proud and unique record of being the only officer in the service to have held every grade from second lieutenant to colonel in one regiment for a period of over 32 years.

Out of Mexico marched the regiment in 1917, with Colonel Tompkins in the lead, across the bridge. From 1917 until February 1920, he was stationed at Fort Bliss commanding the 7th Cavalry Regiment; the 2nd Brigade, 15th Cavalry Division; and for two periods he was commander of the El Paso District, a key post on the Mexican border during World War I. In June 1919 he led a force of cavalry, artillery and engineers across the Rio Grande in a chase after Pancho Villa—the Mexican bandit.

The Mexicans were encountered in a small engagement at Zaragosa in the vicinity of Juarez.

In March 1920 he was relieved of command of the 7th Cavalry and attached to the 10th Cavalry at Brownsville. For a short while he was in command of the Ringgold sector, then transferred back to Brownsville, from whence he was transferred to Fort Sam Houston in May 1920. On 9 Sep 1920 he was given command of the Camp Stanley reservation.

After 43 years of service he retired at the age of 64, but still active, even though one of the oldest officers in are Army at the time. He died on 5 Feb 1939, at the age of 76.

Besides being an integral and vital part of the 7th Cavalry, Colonel Tompkins was one of the most picturesque and widely known figures in the U.S. Army. A man of magnetic personality and outstanding character, brusque but kind, Colonel Tompkins was known either personally or by reputation by every cavalryman. His army-wide popularity was evidenced when it required the services of an army truck to deliver his Christmas mail in 1926.

As a special favor to Colonel Selah R.H. Tompkins, the War Department ordered him back to his old regiment to assume command for one week prior to his retirement on 17 Jul 1927. On that day he issued the following General Order:

17 Jul 1927
General Orders
No. 17

After serving for nearly 43 years as an officer in the Army, 32 years of which were in the 7th Cavalry, I have this day reached the age of retirement from active service. The time has come for me to say good-bye to the members of the regiment in which I spent so many happy years. No one can understand what the 7th Cavalry means to me and to be retired as colonel of that gallant regiment is the realization of my boyhood ambition.

God bless you all. You will always have my love and affection and may the years to come bring increased happiness and honor to you all.

Good-Bye!
S.R.H. Tompkins
Colonel, 7th Cavalry
Commanding.

He was affectionately known among his troops and brother officers alike as "Colonel Tommy" and sometimes referred to as "Pink Whiskers" due to his flaming red beard. He always believed with the dictionary that the word "cavalry" meant "mounted troops" and strongly opposed motorizing cavalry units. His salty temperament and colorful language were well known and are illustrated by the story dealing with 400 cavalry recruits sent to him in the Philippines. He was ordered to mold them into a fighting unit. After a few weeks his superior wrote asking how the task was progressing to which he replied, "I have 400 men who have never seen a horse, and 400 horses that have never seen a man and 12 officers who have never seen man or horse. Now what the Hell can I do?"

Colonel Selah R.H. Tompkins' outstanding service to the regiment and fame as a cavalry officer account in large measure for the esprit so inextricably interwoven.

INTRODUCTION

The actual objective of this book is to provide the American public, and particularly those who have been fortunate enough to have served in the 7th United States Cavalry Regiment during its existence, with a complete and accurate history of that regiment. It is hoped that this regimental history will provide some insight as to the rich military heritage of the modern day Army battle units bearing the name of the 7th Cavalry.

The title part of this book is derived from Lt. Col. George Armstrong Custer, who created "immortal" controversy concerning his command of the 7th U.S. Cavalry Regiment during the Battle of the Little Big Horn. During World War II, one of General Douglas MacArthur's favorite Army divisions was the 1st Cavalry Division. The 7th Cavalry Regiment was one of the assigned infantry units of the division during the Pacific Campaign of World War II. Actually, the 7th Cavalry Regiment was first assigned to the 1st Cavalry Division on 15 Sep 1921. To this very day, it continues to be one of the organic regiments to that division. The 1st Cavalry Division is stationed at Fort Hood, Texas.

The winning of the West is a tale of high drama in American History. American Indians, pioneers and covered wagons, the building of transcontinental railroads and telegraph wires, herds of buffalo, cattle herds and ranchers, cowboys and cattle-drives, the discovery of gold and silver, are separate scenes in this drama of the stirring frontier days made possible by a thin thread of blue-the United States Army. The history of the 7th Cavalry Regiment-not the oldest or the most decorated-typically illustrates the part played by all the old Army regiments in building America since the end of the Civil War.

The 7th Cavalry Regiment's record during this era well illustrates the important role of the United States Army in the advance of frontier settlements. Stationed at remote and isolated army posts, it was called upon to protect settlers and guard emigrants, freighters, mail stages, and telegraph lines from the plains Indians. Sometimes it undertook exploring expeditions into little known regions, and sometimes it protected scientific expeditions into new territory. It shielded surveyors laying out the route for railroads to the Pacific and the construction crews who built the roads. Sometimes it evicted white trespassers from Indian reservations and frequently risked lives in heroic fights against overwhelming numbers of provoked Indians. It was called upon to assist civil authorities in the war-torn southern states by arresting violators of revenue laws and members of the Klu Klux Klan. It provided escorts to International Boundary Survey Commissions and Indian agents, pursued road agents, and patrolled the boundaries of the United States to prevent arms smuggling. It furnished entertainment for civic functions in the frontier towns to help ease the hardships of frontier life. These activities were not accomplished without toll.

The incomplete Records of Events for the regiment during the years 1866-1891 record a total of 181,692 miles marched by horse by all elements of the regiment through sun-parched deserts and blizzard-swept plains. These conditions on the frontier, coupled with low pay and poor subsistence, resulted in 10 suicides and 160 desertions-over half of them occurring in the first two years after the regiment was organized. Murders, accidental shootings, death by freezing and drowning, and disease-the most common one during the period-chronic diarrhea, cholera, typhoid, undiagnosed fevers, and pneumonia-took a toll of 208 lives during the period. Additionally, the regiment lost 324 killed and 148 wounded in actions against the plains Indians during this period of horsemen, horses, and hardships. The year 1891 generally marked the end of the Indian Wars and of the American frontier. The buffalo had disappeared, the transcontinental railroads completed, most of the Indians on reservations, and the good land had been turned by plow.

The pay of a private for fighting Indians under awful hardships and in lonely places was $16.00 per month of which $1.00 was deducted until the end of his enlistment and 12 1/2 cents was deducted each month for the Soldiers Home, leaving $14.87 1/2. For the thankless tasks of the forgotten Army, Congress even neglected to pass a pay bill for the Army for fiscal year 1876, and both officer and enlisted man subsisted on what they could borrow for one entire year while they fought and died on the plains.

During the next 25 years, the 7th Cavalry was involved in American wars beyond her borders-Cuba, the Philippine Islands, and Mexico. In accomplishing its duties at these far-flung outposts during the period 1892-1917, the Regiment's Record of Events records over 150,000 miles traveled, including 104,364 miles by horse. In addition to maintaining law and order in Cuba, two tours of duty in the Philippine Islands, and a campaign in Mexico during this period, the regiment was called upon to participate in numerous State functions, guard federal property from mobs during the great industrial strikes of 1894, and help train National Guardsmen. It participated in numerous horse shows and military tournaments and gave fancy exhibition drills at public festivals throughout the southern and mid-western states for the entertainment of the general public. The Records of Events record 41 desertions, 14 suicides and 108 deaths resulting from typhoid, yellow fever, malaria, drownings and miscellaneous accidents during the period. One member of the regiment was killed in action in Cuba while serving on detached service with the 1st U.S. Volunteer Cavalry (Rough Riders), and two were killed and eight wounded in action in the Punitive Expedition in Mexico.

The trench warfare of World War I, with its barbed wire and machine guns, found no place for mounted troops, and the regiment was stationed along the Mexican border to guard against the ever-present danger from the south.

The period following World War I found the United States with the smallest regular army in the world in relation to its population, wealth and area. Penny-wise foolishness coupled with Utopian peace dreams again forced the Army into the dark ages of hopelessness and despair. The underpaid, undermanned, obsoletely equipped, poorly trained Army barely existed during the period 1918-1942 on the paltry appropriations, much less provide protection to the nation's growing population and power.

Yet, with all these handicaps, the 7th Cavalry Regiment performed many public services and conducted limited training. During these "lean years," the regiment guarded American property and lives along the Mexican border to prevent depredations by bandits from across the Rio Grande. It was called upon to perform flood duty, fight forest fires, assist civil authorities in maintaining law and order, train National Guard and Reserve officers and supervise the Civilian Conservation Corps (CCC) camps. It participated in horse shows, polo games, and various worthwhile community activities. It conducted limited maneuvers, experimented with new vehicles, horse trailers and airplanes, underwent many reorganizations and countless inspections and reviews during the transition from "horses to horsepower." The regiment marched by horse some 40,747 miles, not counting those traveled while on maneuvers during this period.

The last chapter in the regiment's history began at the turn of the year 1942 and ended with the conclusion of World War II. As the war clouds gathered during the latter part of 1941, the regiment's training was increased and the mounted cavalry made its last appearance in the extensive Louisiana maneuvers. Pressure grew at higher quarters to eliminate the mounted service and the blow fell in early 1943 when all horse cavalry units began converting to dismounted units. The regiment's faithful mounts were turned in at Fort Bliss, Texas, as it prepared to join General MacArthur's strategic forces in the South Pacific area as an infantry unit. As a Standard Operating Procedure (SOP) to sentiment, the 7th Cavalry Regiment was permitted to keep its old name, but that was all. The next few years found the regiment fighting as a part of the U.S. forces which took part in the island-hopping campaigns which ultimately led to the capture of the Philippines and the crushing defeat of the Japanese Empire. These bloody battles, fought in the steaming South Pacific jungles, were won at a cost to the regiment of 300 killed and 1,000 wounded.

This history book is a genuine tribute to those former members of the 7th United States Cavalry Regiment who have served their country at home and abroad since 1866-whose heroic deeds and noble accomplishments have established a feeling of just pride in the traditions of the cavalry throughout the military service, and continue as a source of inspiration in today's modern Army. *Ed Daily, author.*

CHAPTER I

The Indian Wars (1866-1891)
Horses, Horsemen and Hardships

At the end of the Civil War in April 1865, the western frontier and the Mexican border were critical trouble spots. The Indians had taken full advantage of the distractions of the Civil War to undo most of the work the Army had earlier accomplished in securing the safety of the Western frontier. In Minnesota and the Dakota Territory, the Sioux conducted daily skirmishes of the white settlers. The Utes had gone on the warpath in Idaho, and the Navajo were on the rampage in New Mexico. The Apaches were conducting raids into the outskirts of San Antonio. As the Indians increased their raids on the frontier settlements and ambushes and skirmishes of small detachments of the dwindling Army, the problem of maintaining peace in the West became more acute.

In this inevitable struggle between the aborigines and an advancing civilization, many wrongs were committed by the whites but there were also atrocities committed by the Indians. Irrespective of the merits of any controversy, the sole duty of the Army in this situation was to protect the citizens of the United States who, as immigrants, settled upon Western lands their right to which was guaranteed by the government.

Added to these conditions, the armies of Maximilian, emperor of Mexico, placed on the throne by the French emperor, Napoleon III, threatened the entire border along the Rio Grande.

Following the peace at Appomattox, Congress focused attention on these distant troubles heretofore obscured by events closer to the nation's capital, and recognized the urgent need for a larger regular army — particularly additional cavalry — to restore order on the troubled frontiers.

1866

In July 1866, Congress authorized four more cavalry regiments, the 7th through the 10th. Recruits for one regiment of this newly authorized cavalry were concentrated at Fort Riley, Kansas, in August 1866. These recruits represented almost every strata of human society — young adventurers, professional frontiersmen, outcasts from society, fugitives from justice, refugees from the Civil War, both north and south alike, recently arrived immigrants to this county seeking to enlist in the Army to save enough money to get started in the new land, and professional soldiers who wanted to reenlist in a "new outfit." At least half of this heterogeneous collection of manhood were foreign born and many could barely speak the English language.

This was the beginning of the 7th Cavalry Regiment which was to be trained, welded into a fighting unit, and engage a craft foe and the best horsemen of the plains within a matter of months.

Note: Of the 45 Congressional Medals of Honor awarded members of the 7 Cavalry Regiment during the period of the Indian Wars, 26 were awarded to members of the regiment who were U.S. born and 19 were awarded to those who were foreign born (6 in Ireland, 7 in Germany, 2 in England, 1 in Scotland, 1 in France, 1 in Australia, and 1 in Sweden.

The initial organization was inaugurated by Maj. John W. Davidson, 2nd Cavalry, on the 10th of September. Maj. Davidson's orders for organizing the regiment read as follows:

Headquarters, Department of the
Missouri
St. Louis, Missouri, August 27, 1866

(SPECIAL ORDERS NO. 2)
• • • • • •

4. Bvt. Maj. General John W. Davidson, Maj. 2nd U.S. Cavalry is hereby detailed to take charge of and superintend the organization of the new Regiment of Cavalry at Fort Riley, Kansas. He will select from the subalterns of the 2nd U.S. Cavalry a suitable number of officers to assist in the organization but not to take such a number as to interfere with the efficiency of that Regiment. Not more than one of every seventy-five recruits should be detailed and their names forwarded to this office. They will be detailed

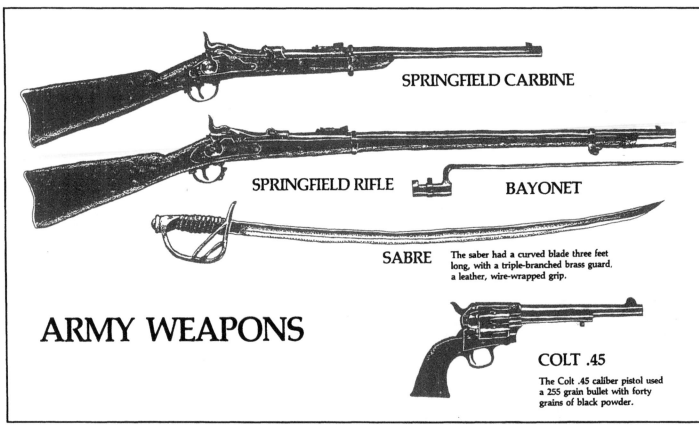

ARMY WEAPONS

SPRINGFIELD CARBINE

SPRINGFIELD RIFLE   BAYONET

SABRE   The saber had a curved blade three feet long, with a triple-branched brass guard, a leather, wire-wrapped grip.

COLT .45   The Colt .45 caliber pistol used a 255 grain bullet with forty grains of black powder.

The model 1873 Springfield became the basic gun for the Indian Wars. It was a .45 caliber trap-door, single-shot, breech-loading weapon, and used a centerfire reloadable cartridge with a 405 grain bullet backed by seventy grains of black powder. The gun was known throughout the West as the .45-70. Each trooper carried a total of 100 rounds of carbine ammunition, divided between their person and saddle bag. The other arm supplied in the 7th Cavalry was the colt single-action Army model of 1873 six-shot revolver of .45 caliber, which proved to be a reliable weapon. The troopers carried only 24 rounds for the revolver into battle June 25, 1876. First Lieutenant James Calhoun (Custer's brother-in-law) wrote in his diary on July 1, 1874, that "The new Springfield arms and ammunition were issued today. They seem to give great satisfaction. In fact, this expedition is as thoroughly equipped as to render it one of the most complete that ever moved West." (Artwork courtesy of Morgan Pennypacker.)

on this duty until the Regimental organization is announced from Washington and at least one officer per Company arrives to replace those retained.

• • • • • •

By Command of Maj. General Hancock:
/s/ Assistant Adjutant General

The following general order was later is- sued *(retroactively) which officially designated the newly authorized regiment:*

WAR DEPARTMENT
Adjutant Generals Office
Washington, November 23, 1866
General Order Number 92

Under the act of July 28, 1866, the designation of organization of regiments by which the military peace establishment is increased and fixed will be as follows. The provisions of this order are in accordance with the conditions of the Army on, and are of effect from, the 21st day of September 1866.*

1. The two additional regiments of Cavalry, composed of white men, will be the 7th and 8th Regiments of Cavalry. The field officers of these regiments are —

SEVENTH CAVALRY
Col.: Andrew J. Smith
Lt. Col.: George A. Custer
Maj.: Alfred Gibbs
Station: Division of the Missouri
• • • • • •

While the organization of the Seventh Regiment of Cavalry had begun in the autumn of 1866, it was not completed until December 22. Maj. Gibbs joined the regiment on October 6, 1866, but on October 25 was absent on an Examining Board at Washington, D.C., and the regiment was actually commanded by Maj. Davidson, 2nd U.S. Cavalry, until November 26, 1866.

The Regimental Return for September 1866 states: "The Regiment was organized by virtue of Special Orders No 2, CS, Headquarters, Department of the Mo., August 27, 1866." The same return lists the following troops as organized on the dates indicated:

Field and Staff	Sept. 10	Troop G	Sept. 17
Troop A	"	Troop H	"
Troop B	"	Troop I	"
Troop C	"	Troop K	"
Troop D	"	Troop L	"
Troop E	"	Troop M	"
Troop F	"		

By the end of September 1866, the above troops had been organized with a total enlisted strength of 882, and were all commanded by officers of the 2nd U.S. Cavalry.

The following named commissioned officers joined the regiment during November 1866:

Col. A.J. Smith — November 26

Lt. Col. G.A. Custer — November 16 — Assigned to Troop D but detailed Acting Regimental Adjutant

1st Lieutenant T.W. Custer — November 16 — Assigned to Troop A but detailed Acting Regimental Quartermaster Note: Lt. Col. G.A. Custer's brother — one of two persons in the entire Army ever to have been twice awarded the Congressional Medal of Honor. Lt. Custer's awards were both made for service during the Civil War.

Capt. W.P. Robeson — November 14 — Assigned to Troop B

1st Lt. M. Berry — November 16 — Assigned to Troop C

Capt. M.W. Keogh — November 16 — Assigned to Troop I

Capt. R.M. West — November 16 — Assigned to Troop K

Capt. M.V. Sheridan — November 26 — Assigned to Troop L

At the end of November only the Regimental Headquarters, and Troops A, D and H were

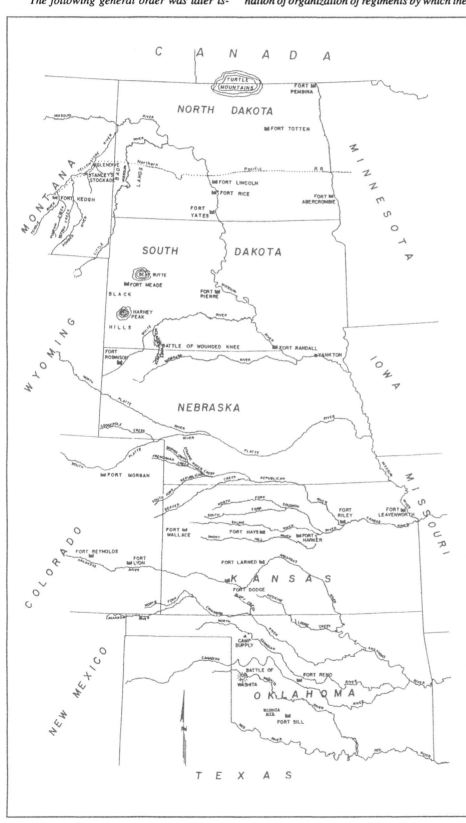

Frontier Posts occupied by units of the 7th U.S. Cavalry Regiment from 1866-1891.

at Fort Riley; the other troops had been ordered to take other stations during the month. Troops B and C were at Fort Lyon, Colorado Territory; Troop E at Fort Hayes, Kansas; Troops F and G at Fort Harker, Kansas; Troop I at Fort Wallace, Kansas; Troop K at Fort Dodge, Kansas; and Troop L at Fort Morgan, Colorado Territory.

During December, the following named commissioned officers joined the regiment:

Capt. A.P. Morrow — December 11 — Assigned to Troop E
1st Lt. O. Hale — December 29 — Assigned to Troop M
1st Lt. L.P. Gilette — December 29 — Assigned to Troop L
2nd Lt. H.J. Nowland — December 12 Assigned to Troop F
2nd Lt. H. Jackson — December 4 — Assigned to Troop G

By the end of the year the regiment had a total of 15 commissioned officers and 963 enlisted men. Since the beginning of the organization, 80 men had deserted, 13 had joined from desertion, one had died from wounds and 11 from disease. Many of the enlisted men had seen service in the Volunteers during the civil War. They found the great amount of drill incident to organization and training of the new regiment irksome, and life at frontier posts lonesome and monotonous. The long marches to the new stations, on the straight government rations, over the cold, bleak and barren plains, were so different from service with the limits of civilization, that some deserted rather than face the privations and hardships. However, the morale of the entire regiment was high in most instances.

1867

Since organization the different troops of the regiment had been stationed at posts from which only small commands could be sent into the field for service. However, on March 26, 1867, Headquarters and Troops A, D, H and M, under command of Lt. Col. Custer, left Fort Riley, Kansas to form a portion of Maj. General Hancock's expedition to the plains. The command arrived at Fort Harker on April 1st, where it was joined by Troops F and G. The command departed Fort Harker on April 3, and reached Fort Larned on April 7, where Troops E and K were added to the column.

The Cheyenne and Sioux encampments were located on the North Fork of the Pawnee River over 30 miles northwest of Fort Larned. General Hancock, then commanding the Department of the Missouri, had invited the chiefs to a council; however, he did not attain the desired results and on April 13, his entire command left all impedimenta at Fort Larned and started in pursuit of the Indians, chasing them in various directions for nearly 300 miles. The command finally crossed the Smoky Hill River west of Monument Creek and marched to camp near Fort Hays, Kansas on April 19. Since it was too early in the years for very much grass — only the forage for the horses — the animals were exhausted and in need of recuperation. Therefore, operations for the remainder of the month of April and the month of May were confined to scouting by detachments to keep the Smoky Hill route open.

On June 1st, Headquarters and Troops A, D, E, H, K and M, under command of Lt. Col. Custer, left camp and marched toward the Platte River. The command marched a distance of 225 miles and upon arrival camped near Fort McPherson, Nebraska on June 10. No hostile Indians were seen en route. The only incident of importance which occurred during the march was the melancholy suicide of Maj. (Brevet Col.) Wickliffe Cooper, 7th Cavalry, on June 8, while in camp on Medicine Lodge Creek. The command remained in camp near Fort McPherson until June 17, when it moved toward the Republican River, arriving near the north fork on June 22 after marching a distance of 129 miles. Maj. Elliott left the same evening with dispatches for Fort Sedgwick; and Troop D, under command of Lt. Robbins, left for Fort Wallace with a wagon train for subsistence stores. At daylight on the morning of June 24, the camp was surrounded by a large band of Sioux Indians who attempted to stampede the animals.

A detachment of 24 men of Troop A under Capt. Hamilton was attacked on June 24 by a bank of about 50 Sioux. Lt. Robbins, with Troop D returned with the train of provision on June 28. On June 26 he had a running fight near Black Butte Creek for three hours with about 500 Sioux and Cheyenne warriors, who were finally driven off. Losses during the engagement were five warriors killed, one government horse captured, one horse killed and three abandoned due to exhaustion.

On June 29, the command moved toward the Platte, camping on the south fork of the Republican River the next day. From July 1-14, the command scouted between the Smoky Hill and Platte River routes. At Riverside Station, on the Platte River, 40 miles west of Fort Sedgwick, instructions were received for the command to move to the Smoky Hill route, in the neighborhood of Fort Wallace The post was reached on July 14.

Cholera made its appearance in this camp, and only by the most exacting care and supervision did the command escape an epidemic. On July 12, the remains of Lt. Kidder, Second Cavalry, and party were found and buried on Beaver Creek, Kansas. Sometime during the month, Troop G joined the command, having completed its duty of escorting General Wright's Engineering party from Fort Hays, Kansas to Fort Lyon, Colorado Territory. The troop commander reports that on this trip the "water was deceitfully alkaline and the grazing not even suggestive of verdure."

The July Troop Return carried Lt. Col. Custer on detached service from the command since the 15; however, the authority is not shown. Maj. Elliott was in command during the absence of Lieutenant Col. Custer. Actually, Lieutenant Col. Custer had been relieved of command and ordered to report to Fort Leavenworth, Kansas, pending charges that during his expedition he had set such a killing pace that his men deserted in droves and that he had issued the order to shoot them on sight. Additionally, he was charged with absenting himself from his command without proper authority during which he had visited his wife, then at Fort Riley, Kansas. He was courtmartialed at Fort Leavenworth on September 16. Extracts of the actual charges and specifications follow:

"Charge I ... Absence without leave from his command:
   1. At or near Fort Wallace on or about the 15 of July 1867, absent himself from his command without proper authority, and proceeded to Fort Riley, a distance of 200 miles, this at a time when his command was expected to be actively engaged against hostile Indians.

"Charge II ... Conduct to the prejudice of good order and military discipline:
   1. ... immediately after the troops of his command had completed a long and exhausting march, and when the horse belonging thereto had not been rested and were in an unfit condition for said service, did select a portion of such command, consisting of three commissioned officers and about seventy-five men with their horses, and did set out upon and execute a rapid march from Fort Wallace, Kansas to Fort Hays, the said march being upon private business and without proper authority or any urgency or demand of public business; and in so doing did seriously prejudice the public interest by overmarching and damaging the horse belonging to the said detachment of his command.
   2. While executing an unauthorized journey on private business from Fort Wallace to Fort Harker, in the same state, did procure at Fort Hays, on or about the 17 of July 1867 two ambulances and eight mules belonging to the U.S. and did use such ambulances and mules for the conveyance of himself and part of the escort from said Fort Hays to Fort Harker.
   3. When near Downer's Station on or about the 16th of July, 1867, after having received information that a party of Indians had attacked a small party detached from his escort near said Station, did fail to take proper measures for the repulse of said Indians, or the defense of relief of said detachment; and, further after the return of such detached party of his command with report that two of their number had been killed, did neglect to take any measures to pursue such party of Indians, or recover or bury the bodies of those of his command that had been killed as aforesaid.

Additional Charge ... Conduct prejudicial to good order and military discipline:
   1. While en route commanding and marching a column of his regiment, six companies of thereabouts strong, from the valley of the Platte River to the valley of the Smokey Hill River, did when ordering a party of three commissioned officers and others of his command in pursuit of supposed deserters who were then in view leaving camp, also order the said party to shoot the supposed deserters down dead, and to bring none in alive. This on "Custer's Cavalry Column Trail," while traveling southward about fifteen miles south of Platte River and about fifty miles southwest of Fort Sedgwick, Colorado, on or about the 7th day of July, 1867.
   2. Did order the following names and designated soldiers of his regiment, viz (3 men) and other enlisted men of his com-

mand, to be shot down as supposed deserters, but without trial, and did cause three men to be severely wounded. This on "Custer's Cavalry Column Trail," while traveling southward between fifteen and forty miles south of Platte River, and between fifty and seventy miles southwest from Fort Sedgwick, Colorado on or about the 7th day of July, 1867.

3. Did after the following named and designated soldiers of his regiment, viz (3 soldiers) had been summarily shot down and severely wounded by the order of him, did order and cause the said soldiers to be placed in a government wagon, and to be hauled eighteen miles, and did then and there neglect and positively and persistently refuse to allow the said soldiers to receive any treatment or attention from the Acting Assistant Surgeon with his command or any other medical or surgical attendance whatever.

4. While commanding and marching a column of his regiment, six companies or thereabouts strong, did on or about the 7th day of July, 1867, at a point about fifteen miles south of Platte River, and about fifty miles southwest from Fort Sedgwick, Colorado, order and cause the summary shooting, as a supposed deserter, but without trial, of one Private ......, of Company K, a soldier of his Command, whereby he, the said ...., was so severely wounded that he soon after, —to wit; on or about the 17th day of July, 1867, at or near Fort Wallace, Kansas — did decease; he, the said Custer, thus causing the death of him, the said ...."

• • • • • •

As a result, Lt. Col. Custer was suspended from rank and command for one year and forfeited his pay proper for the same time.

The reviewing officer, in examining the testimony in the case, stated that he was convinced that the Court, in warding so lenient a sentence from the offenses of which the accused was found guilty, must have taken into consideration his previous services. The court-martial Order was signed "by Command of General Grant."

Until August 12, the entire command, consisting of Troops A, D, E, G, H, K and M, was commanded by Maj. Elliott, engaged in routing camp duties with frequent scouts by troops and small parties. however, on this date the command departed camp on a scout for Indians by way of the headwaters of the Saline River to Fort Hays, Kansas, arriving there during the night of August 28 on Little Beaver Creek, northeast of the post, where a deserted Indian camp was found. From this point the command marched toward Fort Wallace, and on August 31 was camped on a fork of the Solomon River. The Troop Return for this period states "the horses were much jaded, men weary and exhausted, weather hot, water scarce and unwholesome and grass sparse." Troop G August muster roll reports "but little water and clouds of grasshoppers — men worn out and exhausted, horses unhappy looking and feebly endeavoring to sustain life on the parched and sun-bleached buffalo grass; many horses barefooted, their hoofs worn to the quick

and encased in moccasins of buffalo rawhide. Since the last muster the troop has marched 797 miles and has suffered severely on account of extreme heat, want of good water, and inability to obtain vegetables."

On September 1, Troops A, D, G and M left for Fort Wallace — 74 miles — remaining there in camp until the 19th, and then marched to new Fort Hays, where they remained three days, and then marched to Fort Harker. On September 1, Troops E, H and K left camp with the he other four troops and accompanied them to new Fort Hays where they remained for stations. Since August 12, Maj. Elliott's command had marched about 850 miles. All troops were constantly called on for escorts, and little time was actually spent at their stations. On October 8, Troops G and M, under command of Maj. Elliott, were detailed as escort to the Indian Peace Commission and marched from Fort Harker to Medicine Lodge Creek (153 miles from Fort Harker and 73 miles southeast of Fort Larned), arriving there October 14 and camping near the Indian villages. The mission was completed on October 28, and the escort marched to Fort Larned, arriving there October 30 en route to Fort Harker, having marched a total distance of 478 miles during September and October. The muster rolls of Troop G for the month of October states "...until October 29 when the Commission, having concluded the customary peace and the benevolent Indian Agents having distributed the annuities, including 74 new revolvers, many cases of butcher knives, a large number of files for making arrow heads, and a wagon load of powder and lead — Troop broke camp and marched with command and Commission for Fort Larned."

The frequent skirmishes with the Indians, the problems incident to the rugged frontier duty and other events of interest, are indicated in more detail in the following extracts of the individual Troop Returns for the year.

Troop A — Accompanied Lt. Col. Custer's command until the end of September performing frequent scouts throughout the operation. The troop returned to Fort Leavenworth, Kansas, in November, where they were stationed at the end of the year. The troop marched approximately 1,877 miles during the year.

Troop B — At the beginning of the year the troop was stationed at Fort Lyon. From January 19-27, Capt. Robeson with 50 men of the troop and Lt. Berry and 50 men of Troop C marched a distance of 250 miles in pursuit of deserters. The troop moved to Fort Dodge, Kansas, during the period April 3-10, where it remained for the rest of the year. On June 12, while the troop horses were grazing about two miles from the post, they were stampeded by a large body of Kiowa Indians who succeeded in running off 71 head of them. In attempting to rescue the herd, Private James Spillman received several arrow wounds and died the next day. While stationed at Fort Dodge, detachments from the troop were constantly required for detached service as escorts and guards. The troop marched approximately 315 miles during the year.

Troop C — Since the troop remained at Fort Lyon, Kansas, during the entire years, it devoted most of its attention to the pursuit and arrest of deserters and to the recovery of stolen horses.

Many of the deserters took horses, arms and equipment, however 15 deserters were apprehended and six horses recovered during the year. The troop marched approximately 515 miles during the year.

Troop D — Accompanied Lt. Col. Custer's command until the end of September, performing frequent scouts throughout the operation. The troop returned to Fort Leavenworth, Kansas, in November where they were stationed at the end of the year. The troop marched approximately 2,046 miles during the year.

Troop E — Accompanied Lt. Col. Custer's command until the end of September, performing frequent scouts throughout the operation. On April 13, the troop marched 31 miles from Fort Larned to the South Pawnee Fork on the Arkansas River, surrounded a Cheyenne village at midnight and on the 14th started in pursuit of the Indians for 250 miles. The troop returned to Fort Leavenworth, Kansas in November where they were stationed at the end of the year. The troop marched approximately 2,105 miles during the year.

Troop F — Accompanied Lt. Col. Custer's command until the end of April, performing frequent scouts and escorts throughout the operations. The troop remained at Monument Station from July to November when it returned to Fort Leavenworth, Kansas, and remained until the end of the year. The troop marched approximately 2,000 miles during the year.

Troop G — Accompanied Lt. Col. Custer's command until mid-April, when it returned to Fort Hays. While at Fort Larned (about April 7), excessively cold weather was experienced, As the change was sudden and unexpected both men and horses were injuriously affected. The pursuit having been prosecuted with much energy and determination, with but little time for rest, and limited forage (the grass not having started yet) the horses were very much reduced in vitality. On May 13-14, a rapid forced march with other troops was made to beyond Lookout Station to attack Indians; however, they had disappeared when the command arrived. On June 7-8, the entire camp was submerged to a depth of two feet by a sudden and unprecedented flood in Big Creek. The entire command narrowly escaped drowning and several men of detachments from other troops were drowned. On the morning of June 26, Indians were reported to have run off the stock from the Pond Creek Station, three miles distant. The troop hastily pursued the Indians and after a short but desperate fight with severe loss to the Indians, routed about 200 of the remainder. It is believed that their famous chief, Roman Nose, was among those killed. The command behaved with great gallantry, Sergeants Gordon, Haines and Williams, and Corporals Harris, McDermott, Douglas and Ludlow being especially noticeable. Some attached men of the regiment were killed and wounded. The troop remained in camp near Fort Wallace until July 8, when General Wright resumed his survey of the railroad route to the Pacific, via Fort Lyon; the troop escorting him through the "arid, waterless, heat-oppressed and grasshopper abounding region" to the Arkansas River, thence along the left bank to Fort Lyon, where the troop was relieved as escort by a detachment of the Third Cavalry. The troop returned to Fort

Leavenworth, Kansas, in November, where it was stationed at the end of the year, having marched approximately 1,691 miles during the year.

Troop H — Accompanied Lt. Col. Custer's command until the end of September, performing frequent scouts and escorts throughout the operation. The troop returned to Fort Harker, Kansas, in November, where they were stationed at the end of the year having marched approximately 1,518 miles during the year.

Troop I — Remained at Fort Wallace, Kansas, during the entire year. On eight different occasions in June, the men of the troop were attacked by Indians while escorting stages, and on two occasions the post was attacked. The most important attack occurred on June 11, when 2nd Lt. J.M. Bell, with two privates of the troop and one private from Company E, Third Infantry, were attacked by 25 Indians while escorting a stage four miles west of Big Timbers. After fighting for four miles, they succeeded in reaching the stage station; however, the infantryman was killed during the engagement. On June 21, one sergeant and twelve men were engaged in a fight near the post, in which one private was killed and one wounded. On June 26, ten men were engaged three miles from the post and one corporal and three privates were wounded. In all these engagements, the men behaved most gallantly. During the year the troop was constantly on scouting and escort duty.

Troop K — Accompanied Lt. Col. Custer's command until the end of September, performing frequent scouts and escorts throughout the operation. The troop returned to Fort Leavenworth, Kansas, in November where they were stationed at the end of the year, having marched approximately 2,000 miles during the year.

Troop L — From January 1 until sometime in July, the troop was stationed at Fort Morgan, Colorado Territory, and from July until the end of the year at Fort Reynolds, Colorado Territory. The troop had no field service with the other troops of the regiment during the year, as the two posts at which it was stationed had no other garrison troops. It was a section of the country, however, offering many inducements to the deserter, and detachments were out in pursuit of them much of the time. During the year 75 men deserted from this troop alone, most of them fully equipped and many of them mounted as well. The most notable case of desertion that has ever taken place in the regiment was on January 14, when the 1st Sergeant detailed himself, two sergeants, five corporals and 21 privates for detached service, mounted and fully equipped. At the appointed hour in the evening the detail was formed and marched out of the garrison. After marching nearly all night the detail went into camp, where the 1st Sergeant calmly informed the others that they were all deserters, no authority for the detail having existed. It is believed that few, if any, of the men had any previous notion of conditions under which they had left the post.

Troop M — Accompanied Lt. Col. Custer's command until the end of September, performing frequent scouts and escorts throughout the operations. The troop returned to Fort Harker, Kansas, in November, where it was stationed at the end of the year, having marched approximately 1,500 miles during the year.

1868

The Headquarters and all troops remained in garrison during the remainder of the winter. Those troops stationed further west than Fort Leavenworth were called upon for a great deal of scouting and escort duty. This arduous duty was performed under the most difficult conditions and resulted in much individual suffering and hardship. There was constant danger from roving bands of Indians who lost no opportunity to attack whenever they felt that they could inflict a loss without great risk to themselves. There was no doubt in the minds of the federal authorities that the Indians would resume their operations against the white man on a more extended scale as soon as spring arrived and grass appeared in sufficient abundance for the nourishment of the Indians' herds of ponies. To subsist these herds through the winters the plains Indians always moved their villages south and established themselves in such sheltered localities as were best suited to their needs — many tribes and bands usually selecting the same stream and extending their villages along its banks for 20 or 30 miles.

The following unpublished account of the fight of "The Washita" described the Indian situation and the movements of the regiment during the greater part of the year so accurately, that it is inserted in its entirety. It was written by 2nd Lt. F.M. Gibson, who was then on duty with Troop A and took part in the battle.

"THE WASHITA"

"To write a narrative of the Battle of the Washita without entering to some extent into its causes and effects, would be to leave an hiatus at the beginning and end which the narrative itself could not supply, so in order to give as comprehensive a view of the whole situation as may be, I shall touch, though but lightly, upon the causes that led to the Washita campaign and its immediate results.

"I desire to express my indebtedness to the able pen of the late General George A. Custer, U.S. Army, for a great deal of the data used in this narrative, and to the memory of him who fought and won the Battle of the Washita, I respectfully dedicate my story.

"The previous winter had been a quite one for the Troops, nothing having occurred in the war of Indian hostilities to disturb their tranquillity, but the Department Commander having a thorough knowledge of the habits and dominant characteristics of nomadic tribes, felt reasonably sure they would be astir in the early spring, bent upon their usual evil designs, which were annually anticipated with dread forebodings by the border settler.

"Therefore, to avert these yearly occurrences if possible, five of the six Troops of the Seventh Cavalry stationed at fort Leavenworth, A, D, E, G and K, were ordered into the field in April, under command of Major Elliott, and marched westward nearly three hundred miles to Ellis Stations, on the Kansas Pacific Railroad. There being, however, no necessity to engage in active operations for the present, the camp here established became one of cavalry instruction. The Troops remained in this vicinity until the warpath demonstrations of the young bucks of the Cheyenne, Arapahoe, Comanche and

Cheyennes captured at the Washita, are Far Bear, Big Head and Dull Knife. Courtesy of Battlefield Museum.

Charging Hawk was scout for Custer during 1868 Washita Campaign. Photo by O.S. Gott.

Kiowas, who were thirsting for fame, made it expedient to shift our base to Fort Larned.

"A word upon our Indian policy might interest the reader. Of course, the Indian Commissioner at Washington was changed with each change of administration, and upon entering on the duties of his office, the new incumbent was invariably confronted with the same old knotty problems of Indian policy that had been left unsettled by all his predecessors; therefore, it was always a matter of speculation with the military, who generally got hold of the 'hot end of the poker' whether the new Commissioner would adopt a rigorous and just policy, and acquiesce, at least with the Indians being brought to book for their misdeeds and infractions of law and order, or whether he would assent to the conciliatory and pampering course so urgently recommended and insisted upon by the eastern philanthropist, whose humanity was always tempered with enough sagacity to suggest their remaining themselves well within the bounds of civilization, and thereby keeping their skins whole and heads covered. While the civil and military authorities were working with the same end in view, i.e., peace between the whites and

Indians, the methods employed to bring about this desirable result were so conflicting and pursued on lines so diametrically opposed, that their efforts proved abortive. The former, who never even go a 'sniff of the battle from afar,' were comfortably ensconced well out of harm's way, in luxuriously appointed offices, racking their brains and devising ways and means to reach the Indian's heart through his stomach, by flattering his vanity, and by catering to his love for gaily colored vestments and trumpery with which to cover his unwashed skin; and the army was taking the hard knocks incident to active campaigning in fair weather and foul, in order to bring the Indian down to a peace footing by meeting our well merited chastisement to those disposed to resist the power and supremacy of the government and disregard the majesty of the law.

"This yielding policy on the part of the Indian Bureau resulted only in exorbitant and constantly increasing demands, until it became necessary for the army to step in and effect a settlement. At the very time that the Indian Department and its agents were busy doling out annuities and presents, protesting that peace and quiet reigned and that the Indians were all on their reservations, the young warriors of the Sioux and Northern Cheyenne were raiding the settlements of the Republican, Saline, Solomon and Smoky Hill Rivers, and those of the Kiowas, Comanche and Southern Cheyenne were industriously at work committing all kinds of depredations in the country south of the Arkansas. [Author's note: The Department of the Interior governing Indians' affairs was frequently at odds with the War Department, as indicated in the following letter:

Fort Larned, Kansas
August 10, 1868
Department of Interior

Sir:
I have the honor to inform you that I yesterday made the whole issue of annuity, goods, arms and ammunition to the Cheyenne Chiefs and people of their nation. They were delighted at receiving the goods, particularly the arms and ammunition, and expressed themselves as being so well contented, previous to this issue. I made them a long speech. They have now left for their hunting grounds, and I am perfectly satisfies that there will be no trouble with them this season and consequently with no Indians of my Agency.

Your obedient servant,
(signed) E.W. Wynkoop]

"As a natural sequence to this state of affairs, the air soon became pregnant with rumors of war, and the Troops in the Indian country were on the ragged edge of expectancy, and reports were daily received of attacks made by war parties from the very tribes whose chiefs were at the time professing the kindliest feelings for the whites. That the fact of these raids was well known to them, and that they were practicing their well developed art of cunning, deceit, and deviltry will hardly admit of a doubt. The Indian Department now suggested that the innocent and peaceably inclined be protected, and that the guilty be turned over to the military for punish-

Custer and 7th U.S. Cavalry attack on Indian village at dawn on Washita River on November 27, 1868. Painting by James E. Taylor. Courtesy of National Park Service, Dept. of Interior.

Kiowa and Cheyenne scouts during the Wishita Campaign. Courtesy of Battlefield Museum.

7th U.S. Cavalry charging into Black Kettle's village at daybreak, November 27, 1868. (Harper's Weekly, 1868) U.S. Army photo.

ment. To this suggestion General Sherman strenuously objected on the ground that such a course as separating the good from the bad was neither feasible or expedient and that it was utterly impossible of accomplishment. The other part of the contract he was will to take, and did. It is quite possible that some of these Indians had not themselves been guilty of murder, rape and rapine, but neither had they attempted any restraining influence over those who had, nor did the chiefs comply with the agreement to surrender the criminals on demand. General Sherman considered that these Indians had flagrantly violated all treaty stipulations, and protested against any goods or clothing going to any portion of the tribes off their reservations, and solicited an order from the President declaring all such to be outlaws. [Author's note: The following letter from General Sherman in example of his frequent protests:

Headquarter, Military Division of
the Missouri, St. Louis, Mo.,
September 19, 1868
Major General Philip H. Sheridan, U.S.A.,
Hdqrs, Department of the Missouri in the
Field Depot on the Northern Canadian at the
Junction of Beaver Creak, Indian Territory.

Dear General;
I now regard the Cheyenne and Arapahoe at war and that it will be impossible to discriminate between the well disposed and the warlike parts of the band, unless an absolute separation be made. I prefer that the agents collect all the former and conduct them to their reservations within the Indian Territory, south of Kansas. So long as Agent Wynkoop remains at Fort Larned, the vagabond part of the tribes will cluster about him for support. The vital part of these tribes are committing murders and robberies from Kansas to Colorado, and it is an excess of generosity on our part to be feeding and supplying the old, young and feeble, while the young men are at war.

I am,
W.T. Sherman,
Lieut-General, Commanding]

"Facilities of communications in those days were not as good as now, and as the Indian question was absorbing the attention of the philanthropist in the east on the one hand, and by the military authorities in the west on the other, it was considered advisable to subdivide the military departments in which hostilities were apt to occur into districts, so that the Troops might be kept more closely in hand, and dispatched on field service with the least possible delay. The country in which the Seventh Cavalry was at this time serving was a part of the district of the Upper Arkansas, commanded by General Sully, U.S. Army, an officer who had long enjoyed a wide reputation as a successful Indian fighter. his district included besides the frontier of Kansas, those military posts more contiguous to the hostile tribes. He had concentrated a portion of his command at points on the Arkansas River, and caused scouting parties to be sent in pursuit of marauding bands; they, however, always managed to elude the Troops, and continued their raids and depredations without fear of substantial interference. The settlers of Kansas and Colorado, many of whom had suffered a total destruction of their homes and in many instances a desecration of their firesides at the hands of the wild and wily 'wards' of our government, had become enraged, desperate and determined that rigorous measures of a most aggressive nature should be taken to rid them and the country of this disturbing element whose ever recurring depredations were leaving death and destruction in their wake, and were so menacing to the welfare of the sparsely settled districts that husbandry was practically abandoned and self defense and the protection of property and happiness became necessary substitutes for yeomanry. So intense became the excitement among these people, so frequent the massacres, and so numerous the nameless atrocities committed upon their wives and daughters that the hatred existing between them and the Indians was characterized by deadly bitterness. The Governor of Kansas had appealed to the general government to give protection to the settlers, or if this could not be granted, authority was asked to permit the people to take the matter in hand themselves and institute retaliatory measures. [Author's note: In 1866-1867, a Peace Commission from Washington made treaties with the several tribes to end the depredations. In spite of concessions made, however, conditions were in such a state that the small regular army force operating in the West could not cope with the situation, and Governor Crawford of Kansas appealed to the Federal government either for additional protection or for permission to recruit troops within his state borders to aid the regular army troops. This permission was granted to the Governor when it was seen that the Peace Commission's effort had not remedied the situation. General Sherman, realizing that the Peace Commission was both helpless and useless, issued the authority for Governor Crawford to recruit a regiment of cavalry of regular army strength from the citizenry of Kansas. These troops would be equipped, armed, and paid by the Federal government. This regiment — the Nineteenth Kansas Volunteer Cavalry — was to assist the Seventh Cavalry. The movement of this regiment was not quick enough to join the Seventh Cavalry on the Canadian and Washita River, and when they arrived the battle was over. — Keogh, Comanche and Custer, by Edward S. Luce, 1939, pp. 30-31.]

"Between August and November, 1868, settlers of the borders of Kansas and Colorado sustained the following losses, viz: killed 117; wounded 16; women captured 4; children captured 2; horses and mules stolen 619; stock cattle stolen 958. With these unsettled scores rankling in their breasts, is it any wonder that the hardy yeomen grew impatient for the day of reckoning and the dawn of a brighter future?

II
"Matters had reached the stage previously described when General Sheridan, who commanded the Department of the Missouri with Headquarters at Fort Leavenworth, Kansas, and upon whom the responsibility of affairs in his department rested, decided to take an active part himself. This meant much to those who had never been in touch with General Sheridan in military matters and it was his guiding hand that led the move of the Seventh Cavalry to Fort Larned, within a few miles of which were also located large camps of Arapahoe, Cheyenne, Comanche and Kiowas. With these Indians we at first sustained quite cordial relations, interchange of visits being frequent between the two camps. But this apparent friendliness was short lived, and even its semblance ceased on the receipt of well-authenticated reports of raiding parties from their bands.

"The Indians were not slow to notice our changed manner and doubtless suspected the cause, but of course feigned innocence. Seeing, however, that ruse would not answer, they evidently concluded it would be wise to make themselves as 'scarce' as possible, and very soon 'evaporated.' Their disappearance was like the touch of the magician's wand — presto, they were gone. We tarried but a short time after their departure, for now war was practically declared and we were ordered to proceed to Fort Dodge to participate in an expedition there being fitted out under the personal supervision of General Sully to operate south of the Arkansas.

"After being thoroughly equipped and amply supplied, this expedition, composed of eight troops of the Seventh Cavalry, A, B, C, D, E, F, G and I, and three or four companies of the Third Infantry with General Sully in command, crossed the Arkansas River near Fort Dodge about September 1st, and directed its march southerly toward the Cimarron River, at which point the first encounter occurred. The Indians on this occasion manifested no desire for a general engagement, but seemed satisfied for the present to oppose our progress by vigorously harassing our flanks, advance and rear, and by keeping up a constant running fire which was more annoying than effective; but when the command got to Beaver Creek it became apparent that their forces had become considerably augmented, and that some daring spirits among them must have inspired the others with extraordinary boldness and courage, for they opened fire on our camp during the night, a procedure on their part quite out of the ordinary. Such an unusual occurrence, it must be admitted, took the Troops very much by surprise and as everybody except the camp guard, had turned in for the night, considerable confusion prevailed before the soldiers got down to business in the real army style. This nocturnal demonstration did not last long, and as nothing was accomplished on their side, this mode of attack was not repeated and it is supposed their paid a good price fore their temerity.

"Each morning after breaking camp and before the rear guard was well out of gun shot, a goodly number of warriors invariably dashed in to pick up the crumbs or any part of the equipment that might be found; and on one of these occasions two belated cavalrymen were cut off and fell into the hands of the Indians. The instant this became known, the rear guard and two Troops of Cavalry charged in pursuit, and after a long chase and hot fight, on of these prisoners was rescued badly wounded. The other might have been rescued had not the Troops been peremptorily ordered to rejoin the column, so he, poor fellow, fell a victim to the fate of all such captives.

"As we proceeded down the valley of Beaver Creek the ever increasing number of Indians and the stubbornness of their opposition, led to the conclusion that we must be in the vicinity of their villages, and on the afternoon of our fifth day out, and while penetrating a range of sand hills near the site where Camp Supply was located later, we encountered the combined resistance of several hundred Arapahoe, Cheyenne, Kiowas and Comanche. These hills were steep and sandy, and of such a character that mounted Troops could not be used to advantage, so, as the Infantry was in the rear with the train, we were dismounted to fight on foot, and had our attack been made with as much vigor and determination as the Indians displayed in their resistance, the hills could easily have been taken by the dismounted cavalry, and, leaving the Infantry to guard the train, we could have pushed on to their villages, which, we afterward learned, were but a short distance beyond, and the Washita campaign would in all probability never have been necessary.

"General Sully for some reason did not consider this plan feasible. He feared the train could not be pulled through such a country, opposed by so many Indians; but considering that not more than one half of our Cavalry was engaged in that fight and that the enemy was driven at every point, it is reasonable to suppose with all the cavalry taken into action, and what could be spared of the Infantry, we had quite an important victory within easy reach had we chosen to seize it. However, we were ordered to withdraw and retraced our steps to Bluff Creek. The casualty list was a short one and the loss sustained by the Indians was never learned. Our march back to Dodge could hardly be called a triumphal one, but we got there in fairly good condition. General Sully with the Infantry crossed the river to the post, and the Cavalry was ordered to proceed to Bluff Creek, some thirty miles southeast, and there establish a sort of observation camp; and thus our little campaign ended, quite barren of results.

"General Sheridan's idea was to have two expeditions in the field at the same time, so as to settle the Indian troubles, if possible, before the snow commenced to fly, a result much to be desires. The majority of the available Troops had been concentrated on the Arkansas River to take part in General Sully's expedition, thus leaving the valleys of the Republican, Solomon and Smoky Hill Rivers comparatively unprotected; as these were the favorite raiding places of the Sioux, Northern Cheyenne, Arapahoe, and Dog Soldiers. The latter was a band of warriors composed principally of Cheyennes, but made up of the most vicious and turbulent of all the tribes. They were the most warlike and troublesome of all the plains Indians, and at the same time the most attractive in appearance and resembled more closely than any others the ideal 'brave' as depicted by Cooper. These bands were quite in evidence in their favorite haunts, and as such large draughts had been made to increase the size of Sully' expedition, General Sheridan was without the necessary Troops to place in the field against them. Therefore, he decided to avail himself of authority granted by Congress for the employment of frontiersmen as scouts, and recruited them from among that class of daring adventurous spirits sure to be met on the border.

"Fifty men of this character were employed to operate against these unruly bands, and General George A. Forsythe was selected to command them. The choice was well made, for Forsythe was a zealous man and a hard worker, and while the task was difficult and the obstacles many, he had his men engaged and equipped for field service in remarkably short time. The object of this little command was to find the trail and follow it to camp as soon as possible, for it was supposed that when the issue was brought to a head, or in other words, when the Indians were well and severely punished, the settlers would be able, at least for a time, to enjoy the peace and quite so necessary to the farmer, and so highly prized by him. The Indian is a veritable 'artful dodger,' and in border parlance, 'if he aims not to be caught, you must rise earlier than the proverbial lark to catch him, but if on the other hand, he shows any indifference about it, you may look for a very large crop of Indians in the immediate neighborhood.'

"Forsythe's command we outfitted at Fort Hays, Kansas, and left that post August 28th, 1868, so his and General Sully's expedition took the field about the same time, just as General Sheridan had planned. Forsythe scouted the country between Fort Hays and Wallace, and leaving Wallace early in September, he headed for the town of Sheridan and from there proceeded northward to the Republican River, where he struck the trail of a small war party. As he followed this trail it grew in size rapidly and led to the Arickaree fork of the Republican. Here the indications were such as to convince these experiences plainsmen that they were in close proximity to their enemy, who were evidently well supplied with war path paraphernalia of all descriptions.

"On the 16th of September, Forsythe camped his men near a small island in the river, and at the crack of dawn on the following morning, all hands were suddenly aroused by the sentinel's loud and warning cry, 'Indians.' The little camp was wide awake in an instant, and the practices eye of each man soon saw that the best fighting of which he was capable and the most sterling qualities he possessed would be put to the test that day. I shall not go into the details of this stubborn and gallant fight further than to mention briefly the general results. Forsythe's killed and wounded numbered nearly half of his little band. He himself was severely wounded twice, Lieutenant F. H. Beecher, Third U.S. Infantry, was killed, and Acting Assistant Surgeon J.H. Moore was mortally wounded; hence the other sufferers were deprived of surgical or medical aid. All their animals were killed or captured and their supply of rations was about exhausted, and in this plight Colonel L.H. Carpenter, U.S. Army, who commanded the relief party from Fort Wallace, found what was left of Forsythe's scouts on the morning of September 25th. The loss to the Indians was large, but never accurately ascertained. This fight and the demonstrations made by General Sully's expedition, may be said to be the actual opening of the hostilities which inaugurated the Washita campaign.

III

"At Bluff Creek, where we left the Cavalry, there was little to break the monotony and hum-

drum of every day camp life, except the daily visits of the aborigines; these were no longer of that friendly nature which for a while characterized their visits to our camp near Larned, but on the contrary, were marked by an entirely different tone and manner. They now contented themselves with simply sending us their compliments from harmless distances in the shape of leaden missiles with which a considerate government kept them generously supplies. Their wonderful scattering ability and the apparent fewness of their numbers made it next to useless to send Troops in pursuit and furthermore, they not only did no damage, but they furnished a little daily diversion to what would otherwise have been a very dull camp, and we rather enjoyed their diurnal displays of good riding and poor marksmanship. The fall was coming on apace, and we began to wonder if we had been forgotten and what the next move would be or lead to, upon which subject many wagers were made and a great deal of random speculation indulged in.

"Our suspense was soon dispelled, for before the end of September it was rumored that General Custer, who had not been in the field that year, would join in a few days and resume command of the Seventh Cavalry in camp on Bluff Creek. These rumors proved to be based on facts as shown by the following telegram:

In the Field, Fort Hays, Kansas
September 24, 1868
General G.A. Custer,
Monroe, Michigan.

General Sherman, Sully and myself and nearly all the officers of your Regiment have asked for you, and I hope the application will be successful. Can you come at once? Eleven companies of your Regiment will move about the first of October against the hostile Indians from Medicine Lodge and towards the Wichita Mountains.

(Signed) P.H. Sheridan,
Major General, Commanding

"It was in response to the application mentioned in this dispatch that General Custer joined on Bluff Creek about the 6th day of October. His arrival seemed to infuse new life in the command. We had unconsciously fallen into a state of inertia, and appeared to be leading an aimless sort of existence, but with his coming, action, purpose, energy and a general strengthening of the loose joints was the order of the day. Everybody was alert and ready to meet any emergence, and it was well that it was so, as all our resources were called into requisition the very afternoon of his arrival. The Indians had evidently concluded to treat us to a surprise, for an hour before sunset they made the boldest dash into camp they had yet attempted and one of a character so threatening that it necessitated instant action.

"General Custer was in his element now; nothing could have happened more opportunely or more to his taste — even though he had squared himself to pay his respects to an ample meal after a thirty mile ride. We turned out and formed a dismounted skirmish line in much less time that it takes to tell it. The warriors were more numerous and displayed much more courage than usual, by keeping within range of our carbines. Their purpose doubtless was to encourage pursuit by a party of about equal strength, and when their pursuers were well out of reach of succor, to fall upon them with a largely augmented force and destroy them if possible; but this was too old a game to be worked successfully and finding their efforts in that direction futile, they disappeared in their customary rapid and mysterious manner.

"After this initiation and insight into the prevailing condition, Custer decided that the camp should be held in check no longer and that aggressive action should commence at once. In accord with this decision he ordered four mounted detachments, each one hundred strong and fully armed, to be ready to move immediately after dark. They scouted the country thoroughly in all directions but discovered no trace of Indians, their camps or belongings. But these scouting trips were not fruitless, for the face of penetrating the enemy's country inspired the Troops with confidence and convinced the Indians that they were not yet the masters of the situation.

"The many obstacles in the way of successful operations against hostile Indians in the summer months are obvious; for instance, the tribes can move their families hither and on with comparative ease and safety and practically without hindrance; they are at home wherever they find themselves; they live entirely upon the country; their needs are few and easily supplied; grass and game are abundant; wood and water sufficient; the weather just to their taste and most favorable to their nomadic tendencies. In the winter all these conditions are changed; the moving of a village is then attended with great deal of trouble and discomfort, and these are factors despised quite as much, if not more, by the Indian than by the white man; grass is very scarce and game not at all plenty; and to have a needful supply of water and wood it is necessary to locate their villages for the winter on the banks of some timbered stream, and after locating they find it most conducive to their comfort and happiness to remain there if possible until spring opens.

"For these and other reasons a winter campaign against Indians is considered more satisfactory than one undertaken when the conditions would be more favorable to them than to us. So, as the facilities for fitting out a winter campaign were near at hand, and such a move seemed to promise good results, we on Bluff Creek had to reconcile ourselves to a prospect of a winter in the saddle and a canopy for a roof. There were many men in the Seventh Cavalry at this time who were not familiar with this, or indeed any kind of warfare and were inexperienced in nearly everything pertaining to their duties as soldiers; and while the encounters they had already had under General Sully, together with some that followed his expedition, were unimportant and without definite result in themselves, yet they served a good purpose as a training school in practical and realistic methods, and were of great benefit in preparing these raw men for service.

"We eventually broke camp at Bluff Creek and wended our way to Medicine Lodge Creek, thoroughly scouting the country en route; and during the few days we camped on Medicine Lodge we ransacked every nook and cranny in that vicinity, but found nothing except old weather-beaten Indian trails; nothing to indicate the presence of anything animate; so, concluding our search we returned first to our old camp on Bluff Creek, and thence to camp on the north bank of the Arkansas, a few miles below Fort Dodge. By this time the year 1868 had nearly spent itself, it being then the tail end of October, and Jack Frost soon became a very prominent factor in every plan considered and in every calculation made. He was hailed with delight, yet detested for his presence; he was considered necessary to our success, yet regarded an obstacle in the way of it; he was welcomed as a harbinger of peace, yet utilized as an element of war. The hostiles regarded Jack Frost as their natural protector, yet he was their real enemy; with him in their midst they felt that peace was assured, yet he was a traitor to their cause and a spy in their camp; and upon such reconcilable terms, who could tell whether he would serve as friend or foe? We were not yet prepared to face winter weather in the field, but commenced our preparations at once with that end in view, for it was now pretty well understood that we were going to fight it out regardless of time. Everything was now bustle and activity. Everybody was busy getting his command and himself ready for a winter campaign. Prices at the traders' establishments went up even more rapidly than the mercury traveled in the opposite direction. The trader himself was the jolliest fellow about, he was busy as a beaver day and night, but cheerful withal, and everybody thought it was very considerate and obliging in him to accommodate us with blue flannel shirts at $9.00 apiece, and cotton socks at $1.00 a pair. The command was being newly organized, re-equipped, and generally brushed up; the halt, lame, and the blind, both man and beast, were culled out, and everything and everybody not of vital value to a fighting column was eliminated.

"These preparations had been made on a scale indicative of a long campaign, and finally, everything being in readiness the entire Seventh Cavalry, save one Troop (L), broke into the ice covered Arkansas on the 12th day of November, 1868, and having turned our backs upon the border outskirts of civilization, we faced boldly towards the Wichita Mountains with an abiding faith in our ability to achieve success, and entirely unmindful of the discomforts, sufferings and privations which we were to experience. Our eleven Troops made a total strength of about eight hundred men and out of these, forty sharpshooters were selected and organized as a separate Troop, so that twelve organizations were made out of the eleven. At Mulberry Creek, we made our first camp from Dodge, and here were joined by the Infantry and the supply train, and here also the District Commander, General Sully, assumed command of the combined forces. Our march to the north fork of the Canadian River on Beaver Creek, where Camp Supply was then established, was an uneventful one.

"Upon our arrival at Camp Supply the Infantry immediately went to work to make themselves as comfortable as circumstances and appliances would permit, in contemplation of being more or less permanently located there. We of the Cavalry contented ourselves with the ordinary camp discomforts, for being but "birds of passage" we knew our stay would be short. While lying in camp at Supply, helping the Infantry cut and haul logs with which to build abiding places for their occupancy, and winding Micawber-like for 'something to turn up,' we were very much surprised one day by the unexpected arrival of General Sheridan and staff. Being a restless spirit, full of action, impatient of delay, and anxious for the success and welfare of the Troops, General Sheridan came, no doubt, to be more closely in touch with the purposes of the expedition, and in case of necessity, to personally direct and arrange the details of the campaign. However, whatever his motives, he was there, and his presence was no sooner known that felt. He had not been in camp long when he arranged to send the Cavalry off to 'do or die' and as our movements contemplated a field of operations extending beyond the jurisdiction to General Sully's command, he was ordered to return to his headquarters at Fort Harker, that he might devote his personal attention to matters of importance in his district.

"Camp supply now became, as its name would indicate, a base of supplies. In many respects this turned out to be a misnomer, for while there was a partial supply of everything, there was not an adequate supply of anything, at least for such a prolonged and far reaching campaign, as this one proved to be. There was sufficient for present needs, or perhaps enough for any prospective demands, as far as was known or contemplated; but long before we headed for home many suffered the pangs of hunger, our raiment was distressingly ragged, and our animals were dying by the score from exhaustion, begotten of toil and starvation. These facts are not alluded to in a spirit of complaint or censure, neither would I presume to place the blame if blame existed; but for the information of those who have so severely and in the main criticized the conduct of the Washita campaign, I wish to state emphatically they if there were any omissions that could have been avoided, and that resulted in the intense hardships, suffering and bitter privations experienced by both officers and men, they cannot be laid to the charge of any officer of the Seventh Cavalry, and with these few words of explanation I drop the matter.

"As we were eager and ready for active work, it did not take long to prepare for leaving Camp Supply. Rations and forage for thirty days were soon loaded on the wagons, and as we were to cut loose from all communication with the outside world, most of us scribbled off a few lines to our friends in the far away east, not knowing when, if ever, another such opportunity would present itself, and for some of our number they were the lines of farewell forever.

"As our preparations were few and quickly made, orders were issued on November 22nd, directing the Cavalry to move at daylight the following morning.

IV

"Reveille was the signal for the Cavalry to be up and doing, for in compliance with General Sheridan's orders issued the day before, the Seventh was to resume its march and penetrate a region of country heretofore practically unknown. Out exact destination was problematical, the location of the hostile villages was purely a matter of conjecture, and while we all knew we were operating on a "war path" basis, our movements seemed to be enveloped in an impenetrable cloud of mystery. Being perfectly convinced we were not booked for a frolic, we were entirely "at sea" as to whether we were to fight or make terms of peace. At least, this was the question among the subordinates who were not admitted to the war councils or taken into the confidence of the councilors. A cloud of uncertainty hung over all that concerned us, and the mysterious air of the knowing ones or those who thought or wanted it to appear that they knew, only served to quicken the curiosity of the youngsters, who perforce had to take what little satisfaction they could find in the old mythical adage, 'Everything comes to those who wait.'

"Everybody was in prime condition as regards health and spirits, and the whole outfit was in for it, whether it turned out to be a fight, a fluke or a frolic. We dispatched a very hasty and early breakfast that morning, so early in face that it was like taking it the night before, and for all the good it did it might as well have been left for the crows. At the proper intervals the different signals for breaking camp and packing up were sounded, and finally everything being in readiness, the men mounted, the sharp notes of the advance cracked through the crisp air and the column moved forward to that old tune whose inspiring strains have cheered the heart of many a weary soldier, 'The Girl I Left Behind Me.' If each one had a girl, there were upward of eight hundred of them left behind on that occasion.

"Emerging from our camp in the woods on the bank of Beaver Creek, we entered upon a scene so impressively grand and picturesque that it has fixed itself indelibly in the memory. A snowstorm had set in during the night, and our camp being in the midst of massive sheltering cottonwoods, its magnitude was not fully realized until we broke camp and rode out into it. Looking towards the west, the appearance of the country, with its pure white coverlet extending much further than the eye could penetrate, for the snow still falling was far too beautiful to admit of faithful description. To the south the tall sand hills which ordinarily were most unattractive were now clad in a snow garment which seemed to give them an air of stateliness and importance wholly foreign to them in their natural state. As we rode by them they seemed to be passing us in review with silent approval, and with an air of 'Bless you, my children,' and a wish of 'God speed.' It was a kind of a morning when everything was sharp and fresh, when every breath inhaled was invigorating, when every sound was clear cut and well defined and when the twittering chorus of the snow birds filled the air with melody, and our hearts with gladness. Our hearts were not only light, but in some cases free, for in those days, there were but few benedicts in the Seventh Cavalry, therefore, the great majority being free from that stress of responsibility that absorbs the thought and involves the affectionate solicitude of husband and father, they never burdened their heads with more care than their heels could kick off, consequently a state of semi-indifference regarding personal welfare prevailed. All, however, were more than anxious for the success of the expedition and bent every energy toward its accomplishment. The firm friendships formed in the early days among these officers have never been broken except when the grim specter of death has stepped in and severed the bond formed by affectionate regard and intimate association.

"It is not intended, however, to indulge in fulsome praise of the old officers of the Regiment; but those who had the privilege of knowing them will agree that they were an exceptionally fine lot of men — fine in character, in physique and in almost everything that goes to make up true manhood — and it is a matter of congratulation among their surveying associated that their lot was cast with that of these noble fellows, most of whom have met death of the field of action in the services of their country. It is pleasant to reflect that theirs and one's own interests were identical, and that we and they were a part of the same unit. At the time of which I write, both those who have already rendered their last account and those who have yet to answer that last roll call, were a band of loyal brothers, bound together by ties of such genuine affection that it was deemed a privilege to make a sacrifice for each other's benefit.

"We must not, however, burden our hearts and weary the reader with sad recollections but move on as swiftly as may be to the Washita River. With the collars of our great coats upturned and heads well protected from from the storm, we rode forth into its blinding fury under the guidance of our Osage Indian scouts. These Indians had been friendly with they whites for years, but it was war to the knife between them and the hostile tribes that were now engaging our attention. They were well posted as to the country which was entirely unknown to us, so they were allied to the government service, that we might have the benefit of their experience and native craftiness in locating the winter retreats of our common enemy. Our scouts were ordered to direct us to a point on Wolf Creek about fifteen miles distant, for as a rule the first march is always a short one; but the topography of the surrounding country was completely obscured by the storm, which was so dense that even the eagle eye of the Osage could not penetrate it. He was therefore useless as a guide for that day at least, for as he travels purely by sight, sometimes, however, like a dog, by scent, and as neither of these faculties were now available, we found ourselves like a ship at sea without a rudder. In this emergency as in many others, General Custer rose to the occasion, guiding the column himself and by the aid of his compass conducted us with as much dispatch as the circumstances would permit, to a camping place on Wolf Creek close to the point at first designated. Everybody was glad to reach a place to spend the night; it could hardly be called a camp just yet, for the equipage necessary to construct one was in the wagon train, still far in the rear, moving its weary length along slowly through a good foot of snow and in the midst of an unabated storm.

"Everyone was busy and kept his blood in circulation by helping to gather a needful supply of fuel, for our hurried breakfast and fatiguing march had given all an imperative appetite; so after doing full justice to a bountiful dinner, we enjoyed the cheering glow of the camp fire, over which we smoked our pipes, while the soft warm waves of calming heat induced a comfortable feeling of drowsiness, soon to be followed by 'Tired nature's sweet restorer, balmy sleep.' At four o'clock the next morning the unwelcome notes of the reveille recalled us from the blissful 'Land of Nod.' The storm fortunately had abated and when old 'Sol,' who had not risen as early as we, shone upon us, he disclosed a clear blue sky and an expanse of snow.

"The two succeeding days, during which our march continued up the valley of Wolf Creek, nothing worthy of note occurred, save the appearance of buffalo in large numbers. They had separated into bunches and sought shelter from the storm in the clumps of trees skirting the creek and its tributaries. This opportunity was improved by laying in a needed supply of fresh meat and that night found the camp stocked with an abundance of it. After the storm passed, the Indian scouts of course resumed their duties as guides, and being told to conduct the command to a point on the Canadian River in the neighborhood of the Antelope Hills, they changed our course on the fourth day to nearly due south, and at the end of a long and tiresome march we made camp after darkness had overtaken us, on the north bank of the Canadian. From information collected by General Custer, he had every reason to believe that the hostile villages were located not very far south of the Canadian and that the trail of a war party discovered some time before would lead to them. He also naturally concluded that if they had remained absent from their camps long enough to be overtaken by the storm, their trail could easily be found and followed and therefore decided to send a reconnoitering party to look for it. In order to carry into effect this plan, he directed Major Joel H. Elliott to proceed with three Troops to a point about fifteen miles up the north bank of the river. His orders were to follow any trail he discovered and to send back to General Custer every item of information.

"Elliott's command left us before dawn the following morning and we commenced our preparations for crossing this treacherous stream. The current was strong and the water filled with immense cakes of ice, so considerable time was spent before a suitable ford for wagons was found. Fording a river of this character is, at best, attended with more or less danger, as its bed is quicksand; so the obstacles to be overcome under the present trying circumstances can be better imagined that described; however, at the end of about three hours the rear guard following closely upon the heels of the last wagon, found itself on the south bank and the crowing had been successfully made. Just as the command, which had halted on the high ground waiting to see the last wagon safely over, was about to resume the march, General Custer, who had been eagerly and anxiously scanning the country in the direction from which tidings might be hoped for from Major Elliott, was at that instant rewarded. Contrary to the old saying, 'A watched pot never boils,' the General discovered in the distance, a lone horseman was approaching as rapidly as his overtaxed beast could carry him through the heavy snow. Before the arrival of this messenger there was plenty of time for conjecture and the vague guesses and tumbled thought, which doubtless flashed

Thousands of Buffalo roamed throughout the Dakota territory. Courtesy of Battlefield Museum.

Custer with his scouts on the Yellowstone Expedition of 1873-1874. Lt. Col. Custer holds a map at which his chief scout, Bloody Knife is pointing. Courtesy of Battlefield Museum.

In the western movement, thousands of Buffalo were slaughtered. Courtesy of Battlefield Museum.

L-R Dandy and Vic, both Custer's horses. Dandy was his favorite and Vic survived the battle of the Little Big Horn. He was acquired by one of the Indian warriors. Dandy was later presented to Custer's father by the members of the 7th U.S. Cavalry. Courtesy of Battlefield Museum.

Lt. Henry J. Nowlan was in the Battle of the Washita. Courtesy of Battlefield Museum.

through General Custer's busy brain during these moments of suspense, have most likely never been recorded. The man turned out to be 'Corbin,' on the the scouts who had accompanied Major Elliot. In broken and hurried sentences and in a manner indicative of great achievement, he reported that Elliott had stuck a trail of a war party of probable a hundred strong, about ten miles up the river, that it was less than a day old, that it crossed to the south

bank, taking from there a southerly direction, and that Elliott was following it as rapidly as possible. At last, then, the trail was found; now, at least, there was something tangible upon which to base future action. Corbin's excitement was communicated in a modified degree to others. He was asked if, provided with a fresh mount, he could overtake Elliot, and upon replying that he could, was sent after him with instructions for him to push the pursuit vigorously, while Custer

would cross lots, as it were, and strike the trail further along. Elliott in the meantime was to keep Custer informed of any change of direction on the part of the Indians. In case we did not overtake him before, Elliott was to halt his command not later than eight o'clock and await our arrival.

"After starting Corbin off, General Custer instantly turned his attention to stripping the command of every hindrance to rapid transit, as we were now to take part in the chase ourselves. We were to cut loose from the wagon train and take with us just as little in the way of rations, forage, blankets and the like, as it was possible to get along with. An ample supply of ammunition of course was necessary, for there was no doubt of our being on a 'hot trail,' which would certainly lead to battle in a very few hours.

"The train, which was to follow in our tracks as rapidly as it could, was abandoned to the charge of Lieutenant E.G. Mathey, and experienced officer, with a detail of men sufficiently strong to afford it proper protection, and in less than half an hour after Corbin's departure, our hurried preparations were completed; and we were in our saddles and gone. Certainly the definite purpose now took the place of partial doubt and questionable wisdom. In all large commands are to be found 'many men of many minds,' consequently there is generally a conflict of opinion as to the best way of accomplishing the greatest good, but just now, all were of one mind, all were eager to hurry on. The manifold discomforts incident to a very limited larder, single robe and the sky as a covering, in the midst of a severe winter, will every linger in the memories of the surviving participants of that memorable march, and the cheerfulness with which these discouraging conditions were accepted by everyone in the command, only serves to intensify the strong bond of unity that characterized the officers and men of the Seventh Cavalry.

The march was a long and rough one, every horse was urged to the top notch of his endurance, and as we hurried on hour after hour without a halt, without the slightest slackening of the forced pace, through the unbroken snow, which had now commenced to soften under the powerful rays of a midday sun, every eye and ear were strained and every faculty alert for some fresh development. The column was riding hard for Elliott's trail, and on and on it pushed itself. Yet nothing occurred to indicate to the weary rider that he had lessened the distance between himself and this desired goal. The shades of night found us still moving along at the same unchecked gait, seven o'clock came and a feeling of suppressed anxiety seemed to prevail, for there was still no sign of the trail. Some expressed the belief that the Indians had discovered that they were pursued and hence had separated into small bands to elude their pursuers, thus leaving Elliott to choose between the horns of a dilemma, and in such an event there was no telling which direction either he or the Indians had taken; but as we heard nothing further from him, we continued to urge our tired steeds on in their wearisome tramp. The scouts and guides had been kept well out from the column in search of the trail, and about eight o'clock, when weary, disappointed and somewhat depressed, we almost despaired of news, we saw one of them making frantic gyrations to attract attention, this being his mode of signaling that he had found the trail. We were not long reaching it, and upon examination, it turned out to be not only the trail of the war party, but also that of Elliott's command in pursuit.

"The discovery of this long looked for road to 'ruin or renown,' lightened our hearts, and encouraged wearied men and jaded horses to renewed effort. The traveling was easier now,

for the trail was well broken down, and it was like changing from a heavy to a compact road. Not a rein had been drawn since morning, not a moment of rest taken, not a morsel of food had passed our lips. But we were 'on the trail,' which largely compensated for a great deal of suffering endured in our fatiguing chase. We had now but one thought, and that was to overtake Elliott's command. The night was clear, the country nearly level and we could see over the snow covered surface for several miles, but nothing of Elliott, who must be still far in the lead. Finally, as we rounded the crest of a 'rise,' we saw in the distance a strip of timber, probably a couple of miles away, and upon nearer approach found Elliott's command carefully tucked away under its leafless branches, seeking much needed refreshment and rest on the banks of a stream of clear water.

"The joy and satisfaction of knowing that rest was at hand, can no more be expressed in words than can the hardships our small army frequently experience be appreciated by the general public in whose interest they are borne. The hand on the dial pointed to the hour of nine when

we arrived. One hour was the time allotted for food and rest, and at its expiration we were to be up and off again. To climb on top of a horse again with only one short hour's rest after such an exhausting ride was not the pleasantest thing imaginable. Personally, I would just then have given all I possessed for permission to sleep till 'Doom's day.'

"The horses had been unsaddled and given every care and attention possible. Our repast consisted of hard bread washed down by boiling hot coffee, drunk out of red hot tin cups that blistered the lips every time they came in contact. Much of our hour had been consumed before the coffee was prepared, so we had to drink it more or less hastily. Many of my readers I know have had a hard 'tussle' with a tin of hot coffee after the 'general' has sounded, and finally had to dilute it almost beyond recognition with cold water if they hoped to drink it at all. That was our experience here. 'Hard luck,' but there was no help for it at such a time. At ten P.M. we were again on the move, but we took things a little more quietly now, for it was necessary to exercise much caution. The trail grew fresher as we

MILITARY DIVISION OF THE MISSOURI

DEPARTMENT OF DAKOTA
DEPARTMENT OF THE PLATTE
DEPARTMENT OF THE MISSOURI
DEPARTMENT OF TEXAS

Department of Dakota, Commanded by BRIG. GEN. Alfred H. Terry. Department of the Platte, Commanded by Colonel Christopher Augur. Department of the Missouri, Commanded by MAJOR GEN. Philip Sheridan. Department of Texas, (Added later on) Illustration courtesy of Research & Review, The Journal of the Little Big Horn Associates.

progressed and it might at any time terminate at the threshold of an Indian village. It would not do to flush the game now, for that would certainly spoil the hunt. Not trumpet signals were used, and no talking permitted except in suppressed whispers; even the tramp of the horses as they broke through the top crust that had formed on the snow since sundown, made a noise that caused dismay in the command lest the hostiles should be aroused by it. The Osage scouts had been dismounted and sent ahead on foot that we might have timely warning of the proximity of the village. It now became necessary to 'make haste slowly'; frequently short halts were made, necessitated by the very deliberate, stealthy and cautious progress of the scouts in advance, who had evidently no intention of walking into a trap or an ambush. It was their peculiar knowledge of Indian traits and trails, together with their native cunning, caution and sagacity, that made their services particularly valuable at this time. About midnight we came to a more sudden halt than usual and all exchanged inquiring glances, for ever since we had left our temporary bivouac all seemed to be conscious of an air of mystery in regard to our movements. Of course, there was no real mystery, but those who have never been in a position where it was their duty to follow blindly the one in authority, can form no conception of how the imagination can discount the judgment under extraordinary circumstances such as these. As to this last halt, our suspense was short lived. General Custer had found the two Osage scouts who had been about half a mile in advance, halted, and apparently rooted to the spot. He quickly sent back word for the Cavalry to halt, and the Indians in the best English they could muster, told him they smelt fire. All present 'sniffed the air,' and failed to detect the odor, but the scouts stood firm in their belief, and upon intimation from General Custer reluctantly resumed the trail.

"In less than a mile beyond, they again came to an abrupt halt, this time to vindicate the perceptive powers of their nasal organs, for there, near at hand were the remains of what was originally a very small fire. This the Indians explained had not been made by the war party we were following, but by the boy herders from the village who had been tending the ponies. Upon closely examining the ground about the fire, it was found to be covered by innumerable pony tracks in all directions, so the Indian's theory was accepted as correct, and as a natural sequence, also the fact that we were now very near to the hostile camp. Absolute silence was enjoined upon all, so no word was to be spoken except in a whisper, and only when necessary to communicate an order.

"Much fear was entertained lest some of the horses should neigh or the dogs commence to bay at the moon, whose light was intensified by the great expanse of snow surrounding us, and might thus disclose our presence to the enemy. The crest of each hill was cautiously approached and the surrounding country critically examined before the command was permitted to pass over it, and finally the scout who first detected the odor of fire, was seen to flatten himself in the snow a short distance in front on top of a slight rise and after gazing long and intently,

crawled back to where General Custer awaited. He reported the hostile village down in the valley near by. The General dismounted, and accompanied by the scout hastened to the top of the hill to satisfy himself in regard to the matter, and though unable to see anything but heavy timer, he heard the barking of a dog and the tinkling of a bell supposed to be on the neck of a pony and coming back from the direction indicated by the scout. But the sound that reached his ear most distinctly and convinced him that the village had practically been reached was, to use his own words, 'the distant cry of an infant.'

"The command had been halted and all officers were ordered forward to report to General Custer. He informed them briefly of what he had seen and heard, and suggested that they should all proceed as noiselessly as possible to the crest with him and he would point out the location of the village and the features of the country surrounding it. This was done and the general plan of attack was explained. The design was to surround the village as completely as it was possible for eight hundred men to do so, and at daylight at a given signal to make a simultaneous attack from all sides. There were still several hours before daylight and ample time for the attacking columns to get in position. The dispositions were made as follows:

"Major Elliott commanded the battalion composed of G, H and M Troops, which was to move well around to the left, to a position as near the rear of the village as possible. The officers with this column besides Major Elliott were Brevet-Colonel Albert Barnitz, Brevet-Colonel F.W. Benteen and Lieutenant Owen Hale, Troop Commanders, and Lieutenants T.J. Marsh and H.W. Smith.

"Colonel William Thompson commanded B and F Troops, which were to march to a corresponding position to the right, to connect if possible and cooperate with Elliott's battalion, but the distance necessary to be covered made it impracticable to get within communicating distance, and furthermore it could not have been accomplished without disclosing the presence of Thompson's command to the Indians. The officers of this command were Brevet-Lieutenant-Colonel William Thompson and Captain Geo. W. Yates, Troop Commanders, and Lieutenants D.W. Wallingford and F.M. Gibson.

"E and I Troops were commanded by Colonel Meyers, and were posted down in the woods along the valley, about three-quarters of a mile to the right of the center. With this command were Brevet-Lieutenant-Colonel Edward Meyers and Brevet Captain Charles Brewster, Troop Commanders, and Lieutenant J.M. Johnson, but the latter before the close of the engagement was ordered to succeed Colonel Meyers in the command of E Troop, he having been incapacited by snowblindness.

"The center column consisted of the Osage scouts, Brevet-Lieutenant-Colonel W.W. Cook, with his detachment of sharpshooters, and Troops A, C, D and K, commanded respectively by Captain Louis McLane Hamilton [grandson of Alexander Hamilton — Auth.], Brevet Captain M. Berry, Brevet Lieutenant-Colonel T.B. Weir, and Brevet Colonel R.M. West; the Lieutenants were Brevet Lieutenant Colonel T.W. Custer, S.M. Robbins, E.S. Godfrey, and Edward

Law. Brevet Captain A.E. Smith, who was Acting Regimental Commissary, also went into action with this portion of the command. General Custer accompanied by Lieutenant M. Moylan, the Regimental Adjutant, personally conducted this column into the fight. The medical officers present were Assistant Surgeon Henry Lippencott, U.S. Army, and Acting Assistant Surgeon William H. Rennick, and both had their hands full soon after the first shot was fired, and rendered efficient and valuable services. The different columns reached their respective positions in due season, and there silently awaited the coming of the morn. The weary vigil of that night left an impression that can never be effaced by the lapse of time. Daylight never seemed so long coming, and the cold never so penetrating. It was an infraction of orders to talk or move about, so there was nothing left to do but remain perfectly quiet and immovable, thus maintaining a deathlike silence, while spending the night, in moody meditation, broken occasionally by spasmodic shivers and involuntary shakes. At break of day, the band, which was with the main column, was to strike up 'Garry Owen,' the signal for each command to charge into the village. At last the first faint signs of dawn appeared while the morning star still shone in majestic splendor like a beacon light, as if to warn the silent village with its sleeping 'braves' of approaching danger.

"And now we listened intently for the signal notes of 'Garry Owen,' our charging call, and the death march as well of many a comrade and friend. At last the inspiring strains of this rollicking tune broke forth, filling the early morning air with joyous music. The profound silence that had reigned through the night was suddenly changed to a pandemonium of tumult and excitement; the wild notes of 'Garry Owen,' which had resounded from hill to hill were answered by wilder shouts of exultation from the charging columns. On rushed these surging cavalcades from all directions, a mass of Uncle Sam's Cavalrymen thirsting for glory, and feeling the flush of coming victory at every bound, and in their impetuous eagerness, spurring their steeds to still greater effort, and giving voice to their long pent up emotions. There was no hope of escape for the surrounded Indians. Their pony herd had been effectually cut off, and their slumbering village entered from all sides before they had time to realize the extent of their peril; but they fought with courage and desperation.

"After charging into the village and taking possession of it, the battle began. The Troops were quickly dismounted, the horses sent to the safest place of shelter, and a desperate hand to hand battle ensued. The command had practically changed places with the Indians. Now it was our camp, and they were the surrounding party, but victory was surely ours, while death and destruction were inevitably the lot of the Indians. They sought cover behind every available tree, along the steep river banks, indeed behind anything that would afford the slightest protection, and as we were at very close quarters, and had exchanged places with them, the soldiers were in constant danger from hostile bullets fired from all directions. Every man was kept as busy as a bee, and every one knew that he was fighting for his life. The repeated caution to the new

Brig. Gen. Alfred Terry, Commander - Department of the Dakota. Courtesy of Battlefield Museum.

Colonel John Gibbon, Commander - Department of the Dakota. Courtesy of Battlefield Museum.

Brig. Gen. George Crook, Commander - Southern Column. Courtesy of Battlefield Museum.

men not to waste their ammunition had no effect at all in the excitement of such a hazardous conflict, and had it not been for the timely arrival of Brevet Major J.M Bell, the Regimental Quartermaster, who gallantly fought his way to the battle field about an hour after the fight began, with a fresh supply, the Troops might have been required to husband their ammunition greatly to their disadvantage. The rattle of the constant fusillade, and the din of its answering chorus, as it echoed through hill and dale, and across the open plain, seemed to infuse new ardor and enthusiasm into the already fired souls of these zealous Cavalrymen, and as the desperate fight progressed, its fury increased, and wilder and wilder grew the intense excitement, while louder and louder sounded the crack of our bullets as they sped on it their unerring flight, like a shower of hail into the very midst of our enemy. The desperation displayed by both sides in this bloody conflict beggars description, and the marked bravery of both friend and foe was beyond the need of praise.

"And so the battle raged with relentless and overwhelming fury, until its death-dealing hand had sent to the 'Happy Hunting Ground,' their chief 'Black Kettle,' and the great majority of his ill-fated band of Cheyennes. This victory was as complete as it was possible to make it. Black Kettle's band had been swept from the face of the earth, the remnant being too small a nucleus upon which to rebuild it. His village happened to be at the extreme west end of a number of hostile camps that had located for the winter on the banks of the Washita River, the remaining portion of the Cheyennes, and large bands of Arapahoe, Comanche, and Kiowas, and a small contingent of Apaches, occupying those further down the stream. Just as we were taking a respite from our day's hard work, it was found necessary to resume hostilities and meet the combined attack of the other bands, made for the supposed purpose of retaliation, and incidentally to rescue the survivors of their conquered allies, and also to recapture the large and valuable pony herd, in addition to numerous supplies of all kinds that had fallen into our hands. Their idea

evidently was, that after such success, and the capture of so much booty, our vigilance would be somewhat relaxed and they could take us unawares, but the eagle eye of watchfulness had marked their every move, and when they made their daring rush upon our lines they found the Troops more than ready to give them the warmest kind of a reception, and were soon convinced that it was too hot a place to tarry in; so quickly scattering as only Indians can, they retreated in ignominious haste and perched themselves on top of the high hills overlooking the valley, and watched intently our preparation for departure. After the failure of this bold attack they were no doubt much sadder, but possibly wiser men, and the experience it afforded should have furnished them with abundant foot for reflection. The last shot was fired, the battle was over, the victory ours. The iron hand of death had claimed as its victims two officers who had made brilliant records for themselves on many a hard fought field, and with them others who had but a few hours before been in the prime of vigorous healthy manhood. Many a joyous heart turned sad, and after the wild tumult of bloody conflict had ceased, there came a peaceful lull, and an impressive and solemn silence prevailed, as we turned our backs upon that deserted valley of death. The battle of the Washita had been desperately fought and fairly won, and its recital forms a fitting close to this narrative, which shall be prolonged only in order to give some final details, together with official reports.

V

"The herd captured numbered in all between eight and nine hundred animals, and after selecting a sufficient number of the best upon which to mount our prisoners, and to replace our own broken down horses, the reminder had unfortunately to be shot, as General Custer deemed it impracticable to take them along, especially as the Indians simply swarmed on the hill tops over which we had to pass, and as the ponies were more or less unmanageable, he did not care to incur the risk of their recapture. By four o'clock in the afternoon, or possible some-

what earlier, everything that could not be put to immediate use having been destroyed, we left the charred remains of Black Kettle's village, with every reason to expect a harder fight than the one just ended, but to our great surprise, as we approached the positions occupied by this overwhelming mass of savages, they disappeared like 'chaff before the wind,' a few shots were exchanged, but no damage was done.

"On leaving the site of the battle our march was directed down the valley toward the other hostile camps, or rather toward where they had been, for it was afterwards learned that those villages finding discretion 'the better part of valor,' had decamped and gotten their women and children well out of harm's way while the fight was going on.

"We proceeded down the valley until after dark; this was a 'blind' I think on General Custer's part, his purpose being most likely to mislead the Indians as to his real intentions, for as soon as darkness covered our movements, we turned back on our tracks, passed by our field of strife, and on to our trail made the day before.

"Our return march was necessarily slow, for besides Captain Hamilton's remains, we had a number of wounded, including Colonel Barnitz, who it was supposed had received his death wound. These were put in the three or four wagons, with which, as before stated, Major Bell so opportunely arrived early in the fight. We reached our wagon train during the forenoon of the second day of march, and making camp early that afternoon, got a little breathing spell and time to attend to such bodily comforts as were possible under such unfavorable circumstances; ample time also to sum up the results of the battle, which briefly stated, and from the best information attainable, are as follows, viz: The total destruction of Black Kettle's village and all it contained, including the eight or nine hundred animals before mentioned. One hundred and three warriors including their chief, Black Kettle, were killed, and fifty-three women and children were made prisoners. Our own casualties were: *Major Joel H. Elliott, Captain Louis M. Hamilton and twenty-one enlisted men killed,* and the wounded were Brevet Lieutenant-Colonel Albert Barnitz, seriously, and Brevet Lieutenant-Colonel T.W. Custer, and 2nd Lieutenant T.J. March, slightly, and eleven enlisted men. The circumstances attending the loss of Major Elliott, Sergeant Major Kennedy, and the seventeen enlisted men who accompanied them, have never, to my knowledge, become a matter of official record; the details have never been known, only surmised. The cause which led to their separation from the main command, was attributed to the fact that a number of Indians were seen escaping from the village, through the gap between the left of his squadron and the right of Thompson's squadron, and that Elliott and his party who went in pursuit, were cut off and killed by the hostiles from the villages below. In the excess of commotion and consequent excitement incident to a desperate hand to hand conflict such as this, their absence was not noticed for a long time, and when the bodies of these brave fellows were found some time later, there was every evidence that they had made a gallant stand against vastly superior odds. So perished this gallant

little band. Hamilton was shot through the heart while gallantly leading his squadron into the hostile village, and it is said of him, that he remained mounted and rode many yards after death ensued. The death of Captain Hamilton was particularly sad, for aside from the fact that he was a thorough soldier and exceedingly popular, he should not have been a participant in the battle of the Washita, and was there only through courtesy, as I shall explain. When it was decided to abandon our wagon train, it became necessary to detail an officer to remain with it, and General Custer well knew there was not an officer of the Regiment who would be left behind if he could avoid it, so realizing the futility of calling for a volunteer for this duty, he very naturally decided that the officer of the day and his guard, with and additional detail, should remain with the wagons. When the Adjutant, Lieutenant Moylan, communicated this order to Captain Hamilton, who happened to be the officer of the day, it simply crushed him. He was in command of the squadron composed of A and D Troops, and the thought of going into action without him

was a blow to his soldierly pride and sensitiveness that almost stunned him, so he hastened to General Custer, and made such a strong and manly appeal to be permitted to lead his squadron, that the General acquiesced, provided he could find some other officer willing to take his place. As these were the best terms he could make, he hurried off to Lieutenant Mathey, who he remembered was suffering from snow-blindness, and pled and reasoned with him until Mathey very unwillingly, and entirely out of consideration and respect for Hamilton, consented to relieve him as officer of the day, and take charge of the wagon train. Thus Hamilton through the courtesy and kindness of a brother officer, rode to his death. Both Elliott and Hamilton were able and gallant officers, devoted to their profession and zealous and thorough in discharging every duty devolving upon them. Colonel Barnitz, who it was supposed had received a fatal shot, dispatched two warriors before he fell, and bravely killed the 'buck' who so seriously wounded him. He was later retired from active service in consequence of the disabling

Major Gen. Philip Sheridan. Courtesy of Battlefield Museum.

From General to President, Ulysses S. Grant. Courtesy of Library of Congress.

Lt. Col. George A. Custer. Courtesy of Battlefield Museum.

Lt. Col. George A. Custer. Courtesy of National Archives.

Lt. Col. George A. Custer in his only civilian clothes.

Lt. Col. George A. Custer. Courtesy of National Archives.

Lt. H.M. Harrington was assigned to Company C, and he was killed in the battle on Custer Hill. He was one of Custer's favorite officers. Courtesy of Lawrence A. Frost.

Lt. Algernon E. Smith was Commanding Company E, and he was killed in the battle on Custer Hill. His body was found behind a dead horse on Custer Hill, and not with the other troopers of Company E. Courtesy of Battlefield Museum.

Lt. Benjamin H. Hodgson was killed in the battle during the Major Reno retreat at the river ford. He had been assigned to Company M. Courtesy of Lawrence A. Frost.

Lt. Winfield S. Edgerly was assigned to Company D, and he survived the battle. He and Captain Weir attempted to advance toward Custer's position, were driven back by the Indians. Courtesy of Lawrence A. Frost.

Lt. James E. Porter was assigned to Company I, but his body was never found. His buckskin coat with a bullet hole in it was later found in the Indian village. Courtesy of Battlefield Museum.

Lt. James G. Sturgis was assigned to Company M, and he was killed in the attack on the Indian Village. Courtesy of Battlefield Museum.

effects of that wound.

"It was originally intended in narrating this story to depict at some length the special part played by each of the different columns in this engagement, and to describe some of the many personal encounters that took place, wherein great courage on the part of both friend and foe were conspicuously displayed, but, so many years have rolled by since then, and so many of those who fought there have since 'fought their last battle,' that it is impossible now to collect the data necessary to a faithful account of such details; besides, after the columns had converged and charged into the village, they were all confronted by the same elements of danger, and all called upon to face the same peril, and therefore, the conditions being so nearly identical in all parts of the field, there was nothing to distinguish the success and good fighting qualities of one column from those of another, and where all

did so well, comparison would be not only odious but unjust.

"One incident of courage and coolness on the one side, and plush and impudence of the other, of which General Custer speaks in his book, is, I think, well worthy of repetition here. He says in effect, that Colonel Benteen, while leading his squadron to the attack, encountered an Indian boy, well mounted, and about fourteen years of age, who rode toward him in a a very threatening manner, and drawing a revolver fired twice at him. Benteen, on account of the boy's youth, was disposed to regard him as a noncombatant, and made signs of peace, but these were rejected with scorn, and the plucky little fellow dashed at Benteen to shorten the distance, and fired the four remaining shots, the bullet of the third discharge passing through the neck of Benteen's horse. After this Colonel Benteen made a final appeal to the youngster to surrender, but seeing him draw a second revolver, he was forced

in self defense to dispatch him. The opportune arrival of the Regimental Quartermaster, Brevet Major J.M. Bell, with an ambulance, two or three wagons, and a supply of ammunition, is worthy, I think, of further mention. He was not expected to come to the battle field, but he boldly pushed on to it, thinking that an additional supply of ammunition, which he had thoughtfully collected, might be useful, and he reckoned wisely, and luckily for himself and us, he reached us in the 'nick of time' for had he delayed a few moments longer, he would have been effectually cut off by the hordes of Indians who took possession of the surrounding hills, and doubtless he and his little escort would have met the fate of Elliott and his party; as it was, he had to fight his way through the timber skirting the Washita River, and had a number of mules killed before he reached us.

"From the camp where we resumed our wagon train, General Custer forwarded his report of the fight to General Sheridan, who was

Captain George W. Yates was Commander of Company F, but he did not die with them. His body was found on Custer Hill. Courtesy of Battlefield Museum.

Captain Thomas H. French was Commander of Company M and he survived the battle. Courtesy of Battlefield Museum.

Captain Thomas B. Weir was Commander of Company D and he survived the battle. Courtesy of Lawrence A. Frost.

Captain Myles Moylan was Commander of Company A and he survived the battle. Courtesy of Lawrence A. Frost.

Lt. William Van W. Reily was assigned to Company F, but his body was not with that Company. He was killed in the battle on Custer Hill. Courtesy of Battlefield Museum.

Sergeant Daniel A. Kanipe was assigned to Company C, and he had carried the first message ordering up the Pack Train. He survived the battle. Courtesy of Battlefield Museum.

still at Camp Supply; this he entrusted to two scouts who had repeatedly shown their worth and reliability since our departure from Supply, California Joe and Jack Corbin.

"This mission necessitated a ride of some sixty miles through the heart of a hostile country, but the risk and danger it entailed, made the journey a pleasure rather than a duty to these two plainsmen.

"In order that the reader may have the details of this battle from the 'point of view' also of our commanding officer, who is in a position to have a more thorough and accurate knowledge of it than any others present, the full report of General Custer is here subjoined.

Headquarters, Seventh U.S. Cavalry,
In the Field on the Washita River,
November 28th, 1868,
Major General P.H. Sheridan,

Commanding Dept. of the
Missouri General:

General:

On the morning of the 26th inst., this command, comprising 11 Troops of Seventh Cavalry, struck the trail of an Indian war party, numbering about 100 warriors. The trail was not quite twenty-four hours old, and was first discovered near the point where the Texas boundary line crosses the Canadian River. The direction was toward the Southeast. The ground being covered by over twelve inches of snow, no difficulty was experienced in following the trail. A vigorous pursuit was at once instituted. Wagons, tents, and all other impediments to a rapid march were abandoned. From daylight until nine o'clock at night the pursuit was unchecked. Horses and men were then allowed one hour for refreshment and at ten P.M., the march was resumed and contin-

ued until 1:30 A.M., when our Osage trailers reported a village within less than a mile from our advance. The column was countermarched and withdrawn to a retired point to prevent discovery. After reconnoitering with all the officers of the command, the location of the village, which was situated in a strip of heavy timber from below the village; the second column under Lieutenant-Colonel Myers, was to move down the Washita and attack in the timer from above; Brevet Colonel Thompson in command of the third column, was to attack from the crest north of the village; while the fourth column was to charge the village from the crest overlooking it on the left, back of the Washita. The hour at which the four columns were to charge simultaneously, was the first dawn of the day, and not withstanding the fact that two of the columns were compelled to march several miles to reach their positions, three of them made the attack so near together as to make it appear like one charge. The other column was only a few minutes late. There never was a more complete surprise. My men charged the village and reached the lodges before the Indians were aware of our presence. The moment the charge was ordered the band struck up "Garry Owen," and with cheers that strongly reminded me of scenes during the war, every Trooper led by his officer, rushed toward the village. The Indians were caught napping for once, and the warriors rushed from their lodges and posted themselves behind trees, and in deep ravines, from which they began a most determined defense. The lodges and all their contents were in our possession with a few minutes after the charge was ordered; but the real fighting, such has rarely if ever been equaled in Indian warfare began, when attempting to clear out of kill the warriors posted in ravines or under brush; charge after charge

was made, and most gallantly, too; but the Indians had resolved to sell their lives as dearly as possible. After a desperate conflict of several hours, our efforts were crowned with the most complete and gratifying success. The entire village numbering 47 lodges in all, under command of their principal chief, "Black Kettle," fell into our hands. By a strict and careful examination after the battle the following figures give some of the fruits of our victory: The Indians left on the ground and in our possession, the bodies of 103 of their warriors, including "Black Kettle" himself.

We captured in good condition, 875 horses, ponies, and mules; 241 saddles, some of very fine and costly workmanship; 523 buffalo robes; 210 axes; 140 hatchets, 35 revolvers, 47 rifles, 535 pounds of powder, 1050 pounds of lead, 4000 arrows, 90 bullet molds, 35 bows and quivers, 12 shields, 300 pounds of bullets, 775 lariats,

940 buckskin saddle bags, 470 blankets, 93 coast, 700 pounds of tobacco. In addition, we captured all their winter supply of dry buffalo meat, all their meal, flour and other provision, and if fact, everything they possessed, even driving the warriors from the village with little or no clothing. We destroyed everything of value to the Indians, and we now have in our possession as prisoners of war, 53 women and their children. Among the prisoners are the survivors of "Black Kettle" and the family of "Little Rock." We also secured two white children held captive by the Indians. One white boy held captive, about 10 years old, when about to be secured was brutally murdered by a woman, who ripped out his entrails with a knife. The Kiowas under "Santana" and the Arapahoe under "Little Raven," were encamped six miles below "Black Kettle's" village and the warriors from these two villages came to attempt the rescue of the Chey-

Lt. Charles C. DeRudio was temporarily assigned to Company A, and was with Reno in the attack on the Indian village. He survived the battle. Courtesy of Battlefield Museum.

Lt. Charles A. Varnum was assigned to Company A, and he survived the battle. Courtesy of Battlefield Museum.

Lt. Thomas M. McDougall was assigned to Company B, and was in charge of the Pack Train. He survived the battle. Courtesy of Battlefield Museum.

Trumpeter John Martini was the last trooper to see Custer alive. He carried Custer's last message to Captain Benteen, which had been written on a scrap of paper by W.W. Cooke. Courtesy of Battlefield Museum.

Trumpeter Charles A. Windolph was wounded during the battle, received the Medal of Honor for courageously holding a position on Reno Hill that assisted in procuring water for the besieged command. Courtesy of Battlefield Museum.

Sergeant Jeremiah Finley was assigned to Company C, and he was killed in the battle on Custer Hill. Courtesy of Battlefield Museum.

ennes. They attacked my command from all sides about noon, hoping to recover the women and herds of the Cheyennes. In their attack they displayed great boldness and compelled my force to repel them, but the counter charge of the Cavalry was more than they could stand; by three o'clock we drove them in all directions, pursuing them several miles. I then moved my entire command in search of the village of the Kiowas and Arapahoe, but after a march of 8 miles discovered they had taken alarm at the fate of the Cheyenne village and had fled. It was then three days march from where I had left my trains of supplies and knew that wagons could not follow me, as the trail had led me over a section of country that Cavalry could with difficulty move over it. The supplies carried from the train on the persons of the men were exhausted.

My men from loss of sleep and hard service were wearied out; my horses were in the same condition for want of forage. I therefore began my return march about 8 P.M., and found my train of supplies at this point (it having accomplished only 16 miles since I left it). In the excitement of the fight, as well as in self defense, it so happened that some of the women and a few of the children were killed and wounded. They latter I have brought with me, and they received all the needed attention the circumstances of the case permit. Many of the women were taken with arms in their hands, and several of my command are known to have been wounded by them.

The desperate character of the combat may be inferred from the fact that after the battle the bodies of 38 dead warriors were found in a small ravine near the village in which they had posted themselves. I have now to report the loss suffered by my own command. I regret to mention among the killed, Major Joel H. Elliott, and Captain Louis M. Hamilton, and 19 enlisted men; our wounded includes three officers and 11 enlisted men; in all, 35 men. Of the officers, Brevet Lieutenant-Colonel Albert Barnitz, Captain Seventh Cavalry, is seriously if not mortally wounded. Brevet Lieutenant Colonel T.W. Custer, and 2nd Lieutenant T.J. March, Seventh Cavalry, are slightly wounded. Brevet Lieutenant-Colonel F.W. Benteen had his horse shot under him by a son of Black Kettle, whom he afterwards killed. Colonel Barnitz, before receiving his wound, killed two warriors. I cannot sufficiently commend the admirable conduct of the officers and men. This command has marched constantly five days amid terrible snow storms, and over a rough country covered by more than 12 inches of snow. Officer and men have slept in the snow without tents. The night preceding the attack, officers and men stood at their horses heads for hours, awaiting the moment of attack, and this, too, when the temperature was far below the freezing point. They have endured a very privation and fought with unsurpassed gallantry against a powerful and well-armed foe, and from first to last, I have not heard a single murmur; but on the contrary, the officers and men of the several squadrons and companies seemed to vie with each other in their attention to duty and their patience and perseverance under difficulties. Every officer, man, scout, and Indian guide, did their full duty. I only regret the loss of the gallant spirits who fell in the "Battle of the Washita."

Respectfully subscribed,
(signed)
G.A. Custer,
Lieutenant-Colonel, Seventh Cavalry,
Brevet Major General, U.S. Army

"Upon our arrival at Camp Supply we were received like conquering heroes, and were the recipients of numerous ovations. On the day following our return, the following General Order was published to the command:

Headquarters Department of the
Missouri, in the Field, Depot on the
North Canadian at the Junction of
Beaver Creek, Indian Territory,
November 29th, 1868.
General Field Orders, No. 6

The Major General Commanding announces to this command the defeat by the Seventh Cavalry of a large force of Cheyenne Indians under the celebrate Chief Black Kettle, reinforced by the Arapahoe under Little Raven and the Kiowas under Santana, on the morning of the 27th inst., on the Washita River, near the Antelope Hills, Indian Territory, resulting in a loss to the Indians of one hundred and three warriors killed, including Black Kettle, the capture of fifty-three women and children, eight hundred and seventy-five ponies, eleven hundred and twenty-three buffalo robes and skins, five hundred and thirty-five pounds of lead, four thousand arrows, seven hundred pounds of tobacco, besides rifles, pistols, saddles, bows, lariats, and immense quantities of dried meat and other winter provision, the complete destruction of their village and almost total annihilation of this Indian band.

The loss to the Seventh Cavalry was two officers killed, Major Joel H. Elliott and Captain Louis M. Hamilton, and nineteen enlisted men; three officers wounded, Brevet Lieutenant-Colonel Albert Barnitz (badly), Brevet Lieutenant Colonel T.W. Custer, and 2nd Lieutenant T.J. March (slightly), and eleven enlisted men.

The energy and rapidity shown during one of the heaviest snow storms that has visited this section of the country, with the temperature below freezing point, and the gallantry and bravery displayed, resulting in such signal success, reflects of the highest credit upon both officers and men of the Seventh Cavalry; and the Major General Commanding, while regretting the loss of such gallant officers at Major Elliott and Captain Hamilton, who fell while gallantly leading their men, desires to express his thanks to the officers and men engages in the battle of the Washita, and his special congratulations are tendered to their distinguished Commander, Brevet Major General George A. Custer, for the efficient and gallant services rendered, which have characterized the opening of the campaign against Indians south of the Arkansas.

By command of
MAJOR GENERAL P.H. SHERIDAN
(Signed) J. Schuyler Crosby,
Brevet Lieutenant Colonel, A.D.C.
A.A.A.General
"We find ourselves at the close of this

narrative again at Camp Supply, the point from which we started for the Washita, and here w part company with the patient reader who can not be expected to be further interested in th fortunes or misfortunes of this Cavalry colum

"Our stay at Supply was just long enoug to re-equip for the other operations which were much too extensive and far-reaching to be embraced in this story, but the following communication, which may properly find place here, was received and published the latter part of December. (Viz)

War Department, Washington City,
December 2nd, 1868.
Lieutenant General Sherman,
St. Louis, Missouri

I congratulate you, Sheridan, and Custer, on the splendid success with which your campaign is begun. Ask Sheridan to send forward the names of officers and men deserving of special mention.

(Signed) J.M. Schofield,
Secretary of War.

"In commenting upon this in his work, General Custer says, "It was impractical to comply with the request contained in the closing portions of the dispatch from the Secretary of War, for the gratifying reason that every officer and man belonging to the expedition had performed his full part in rendering the movement against the hostile tribes a complete success.'

"In concluding this story, which is much longer than intended, and yet largely abbreviated, it only remains to mention briefly some of the good results of the labors of the troops during the trying winter of 1868-1869. The Seventh Cavalry in the first place, destroyed a band of Indians, and with them all their property, as has already been told. It kept the other tribes of that section constantly moving from place to place with their entire possessions and in a state of trepidation and uncertainty all winter long, and thus through the discomforts, exposure and suffering to which the warriors and their families were incessantly subjected several of the bands were forced to sue for peace. The campaign also resulted in bringing to the border settlers, who had suffered incalculable misery at the hands of the Indians, an era of comparative peace, such as had never existed before. But the crowning achievement of the troops and the one which was the most gratifying to the Seventh Cavalry, was the rescue from the Cheyennes of the two white women whom they had held captive for many months. The joy of these women at their deliverance was boundless, but the story of their cruel captivity was too full of horror to relate, and their return to their homes from which they had been ruthlessly torn, was as speedy as it was possible to make it.

"A week later, General Sherman sent the following telegram to the Commanding Officer at Fort Hays, Kansas, for delivery to General Sheridan:

Headquarter, Department of the
Missouri, in the Field, Camp on
Canadian; December 9th, 1868.
Commanding Officer,
Fort Hays, Kansas.

If a courier be going out to General [Sh]eridan write him for me that his letter of Nov. [tw]enty-third and his dispatch of Nov. twenty-[ni]nth giving the result of Custer's attack are [re]ceived and have been repeated to Washing-[to]n. I congratulate all the parties for their great [s]uccess which I regard as decisive and conclu-[s]ive. I have no doubt by Christmas he will have [t]he Indians begging for their lives, when he can [t]urn them over to the management of General [H]azen, after having executed those Indians who [b]egan this War. I feel deeply the loss of two such good officers as Major Elliott and Captain Hamilton.

Tell the General I will represent him at Chicago, and hope he will be in Fort Leavenworth before the twenty-second of February, and that he will see General Grant inaugurated as President at Washington on the fourth of March.

(Signed) W.T. Sherman,
Lieutenant-General, U.S.A.

"The Washita campaign was a success from 'start to finish,' and if the writer has been fortunate enough in the portrayal of its main features, to make it even momentarily interesting to the reader, he will be amply rewarded for his effort."

The above account by Lieutenant Gibson left the entire regiment, except Troop L, at Camp Supply, November 30th. It had but a brief rest, for on December 7th it marched toward Fort Cobb, Indian Territory, arriving there December 18th, a distance of 195 miles. While no Indians were encountered, the march was very wearing on men and horses, as it was over exceedingly barren and broken country, and was without rest and recuperation so much needed after the Washita trip.

On December 11th camp was made on the Washita River, six miles below where the fight had taken place. General Sheridan, Lieutenant Colonel Custer, and several officers with an escort of 100 men of the regiment visited the field and recovered the bodies of Major Elliott and 16 enlisted men. They also found the bodies of one white woman and child who had been killed by the Indians during the fight. Sometime in the 1880's 1st Lieutenant Hugh L. Scott, of the regiment, later major of the Fourteenth Cavalry, visited the battlefield, and with loose stones built a rude monument to mark the spot.

The Regimental Record of Events for the year 1868 indicated that the regiment remained at Fort Leavenworth until August 18th, when station was changed to Fort Dodge (by rail to Fort Hays, then marched to Fort Dodge, 91 miles); where it remained until October 9th, when, with troops H, K, and M marched down the Arkansas River 16 miles, crossed the river and marched across country to Bluff Creek where Major Elliott's command (Troops A, B, C, D, E, F, G, I) joined. On October 12th the entire command left Bluff Creek on a scout in the big bend of the Arkansas where an unimportant skirmish with the Indians took place. The regiment continued scouting until October 18th when, being out of rations, started for Camp Sandy Forsythe, arriving there and going into bivouac October 28th. The regimental headquarters marched a distance of 941 miles during the year.

Detailed events of each troop are indicated in the following extracts from troops returns.

Troop A—Under Command of Major Elliott, left Fort Leavenworth on April 10th with Troops D, E, G, and K and arrived at Fort Hays on April 25th, and then changed station to a camp near Fort Larned. The troop formed a portion of General Sully's expedition, leaving camp near Fort Dodge August 31st and engaged with the Indians on September 11th, 12th and 13th; arrived at Bluff Creek September 15th. Beginning October 12th, the troop, as part of the command, took part in the scout of the big bend of the Arkansas, Medicine Lodge Creek, Rattlesnake Creek and adjoining sections, arriving at Camp Sandy Forsythe October 28th. The troop marched 1,619 during the year.

Troop B—Remained in garrison at Fort Dodge, performing the usual post duties and much escort and scouting duty until July 22nd, when it marched to camp near Fort Larned, arriving July 23rd and returning to Dodge August 15th. On August 20th, Lieutenant Wallingford, with 38 men of the troop, marched to the assistance of a wagon train, near Pawnee Fork, corralled by Indians who were driving the livestock away. The troop returned August 23rd, bringing the wagon train to the post. Thereafter the troop formed a part of General Sully's expedition. (See Record of Events of Troop A, above.) The troop marched 1,193 miles during the year.

Troop C—Remained in garrison at Fort Lyon performing usual post duties until August 28th, when the troop joined General Sully's expedition. (See Record of Events of Troop A, above.) The troop marched 1,133 miles during the year.

Troop D— (See Record of Events of Troop A, above.) The troop marched a distance of 1,619 miles during the year.)

Troop E— (See Record of Events of Troop A, above.) The troop marched a distance of 1,558 miles during the year.

Troop F—Remained at Fort Leavenworth until April 27th performing usual post duties. Captain George W. Yates and 28 men of the troop were on detached service as an escort to the Indian Peace Commission visiting the Osage reservation from April 27th to June 6th. Upon return, the troop resumed post duties until August 18th, when it was ordered to Fort Harker by rail, where it joined General Sully's expedition on August 28th. (See Record of Events of Troop A, above.) The troop marched 1,161 miles during the year.

Troop G— (See Record of Events of Troop A, above.) The troop marched a distance of 1,561 miles during the year. [Author's note—The actual record of events of each troop for the year are in much detail and were hand-written under field conditions. Only the highlights from each troop's record of events are normally shown herein; however, the Record of Events of Troop G for this period are so complete and detailed that they are copied in full, beginning with the August return. These records and notes were made by Captain Albert Barnitz, severely wounded at the Washita.]

"After date of last return Troop remained encamped with detachment of Seventh Cavalry under Major Elliott in vicinity of Larned, changing camp twice in the meantime, until August 19th, when it broke camp and marched with detachment 25 miles in a northeast direction to Walnut Creek, and the following day marched 3 miles further down the stream and camped with the detachment, where it remained until the morning of August 29th, when it broke camp during a temporary cessation of a heavy rain storm, and marched with detachment towards Dodge crossing on Walnut Creek, 35 or 40 miles west of our camp, where we arrived on the evening of August 30th, and went into bivouac for the night to await the arrival of mud-bound train, August 30th, will resume march this evening for Dodge Crossing of the Pawnee Fork in quest of Indians; most of the baggage of the Troop has been sent to Hays and stored; distance, 73 miles.

"September Return—September 1st, Troop started at 6 A.M. from camp of detachment at Dodge Crossing on north fork of the Pawnee with 3 days rations and 3 days forage on saddles and marched on a scout in search of Indians to the source of the middle fork of the Pawnee, returning to camp of detachment at point of departure on evening of September 3rd, having marched during the three days, 95 miles; September 4th, Troop broke camp and marched with detachment 26 miles in a southwesterly direction to 'Sawlog,' crossing on the south fork of the Pawnee; September 7th, Troop broke camp and marched with detachment 12 miles to Fort Dodge and joined command under Brevet-Brigadier General Sully for a contemplated expedition against the Indians south of the Arkansas, Troop crossed the Arkansas the same evening with command and marched with it until past midnight in a southwesterly direction 24 miles to some stream which flows southward, and went into bivouac; September 8th, continued the march in a southerly direction, bearing a few points to westward, followed down the right bank of same stream 20 miles and went into bivouac; September 9th, continued the march in a southerly direction 8 miles and went into bivouac, Major Elliott with part of command continuing on to the Cimarron same evening; September 10th, continued the march 8 miles in a southerly direction and crossed the Cimarron (where we found Major Elliott awaiting us, he having found a trail leading eastward, and then continued the march 18 miles eastward along the stream following Indian trail; in the afternoon and evening skirmished occurred with a small party of Indians; a few of the Troop engaged; grass good all the way along the Cimarron; evidences of many animals having been recently grazed along the stream; September 11th, as we were breaking camp, a party of Indians dashed down and captured and carried off on their ponies at full speed, two men of F Troop, one of whom was severely wounded, they were obliged to drop in consequence of immediate and vigorous pursuit, but with the other they effected their escape, although pursued three or four miles. The Indians also succeeded in driving off at the same time 3 public horses of F Troop and one private horse, which were not recovered; continued the march, skirmishing 10 miles eastward along the stream to deserted Indian village which was found at point where some stream from south unites with the Cimarron; here we had an exciting engagement of several hours duration with a force of two or three hundred Indians, who charged repeatedly but were disconcerted and driven off among the bluffs, with apparent loss, by the superior range and accuracy of our guns; continued the march, following Indian trail and skirmishing constantly, for 14 miles in southeasterly direction to north fork of the Canadian, which we crossed and then went into camp on the right bank; camp fired into the night; September 12th, continued the march 20 miles in a direction nearly due east (bearing a little south) along the right or south bank of the stream, which is timbered and contains an abundance of water; about 11 o'clock as we approached Wolf Creek, a timbered tributary of the north fork of the Canadian, the Indians appeared in force in our front and made a vigorous and determined charge on the Troop, which had the advance, but were repulsed by a volley at close range (the Troop acting on foot and occupying the crest of a ridge), and dispersed among the sand hills, but soon reappearing in front and on our flanks; the action became general and lasted for half or three quarters of an hour, when the command moved on, skirmishing continually; crossed Wolf Creek and continued down north fork of the Canadian and camped on right bank of stream; camp fired into at night; September 13th, continued the march 20 miles in easterly direction to the middle fork of the Canadian, where crossing the stream and becoming involved in the sand hills, the fighting which had been kept up all the day, became more determined on the part of the Indians; Private Corbet of F Troop was killed here; train unable to proceed; command recrossed the stream and marched 3 miles in a northerly direction and camped on the north fork of the Canadian; September 14th, crossed north fork of the Canadian and continued the march 20 miles in a northerly direction, the Indians continually harassing our rear for 10 miles of the march until we had arrived on the summit of a mountain, when the Indians made a great smoke on a summit in our rear, assembled their forces and withdrew; camped this morning of right, south, bank of Buffalo Creek, a wide shallow stream which flows through red earth and sand amid bluffs composed of gypsum. A few Indians appeared while the last files were descending from the bluffs to the stream and some shots were exchanged, when the Indians withdrew. Having crossed the Cimarron our course (still north 10 degrees west) lay for 3 miles among sand hills covered with wild sage, and then 21 miles along high divides through an exceedingly broken red earth country, abounding with grass and buffalo, many of which were killed. We camped in the evening on some unknown stream which flows southeast and contains little water but much sand at present, and which is bordered by a few cottonwood trees; September 16th, rested in same camp; September 17th, General Sully started for Dodge, leaving Major Elliott in command; September 18th, 19th, 20th, 21st, 22nd, command remained in same place, having changed camp half a mile eastward, grass fair; ice formed on night of 22nd; September 23rd, Troop marched with command 12 miles northwest to a small stream which flows southwest, and next day, September 24th, continued the march 6 miles further in same direction to a fine timbered stream which flows southward, and which is now

known as Cavalry Creek; September 25th, Troop marched on a scout 20 miles up stream and back; September 28th, Troop marched 9 miles up same stream to encampment, where it remained until October 5th. Grass excellent, water good, fuel plentiful, weather fine. During September the Troop march 484 miles.

"During October the Troop marched as follows:

October 5th, in changing
             2 miles
And in escorting mail 18 miles on road toward Dodge and return
           36 miles
October 9, chasing Indians and skirmishing with same   *15 miles*
October 10th, Troop had skirmish with Indians in front of our camp
October 11th, on scout with C Troop and return
           12 miles
October 12th, 13th, from camp on east fork of Cavalry Creek to "Medicine Lodge" on Medicine Lodge Creek   *48 miles*
October 14th, 15th, 16th, on scout under Captain Myers along stream which flows parallel to and south of Rattlesnake Creek, and back to camp of Regiment on Medicine Lodge Creek 12 miles west of point of departure   *70 miles*
October 17th, westward along Medicine Lodge Creek 18 miles and then south 5 degrees west 14 miles to encampment *32 miles*
October 18th, to a point 1 mile west of our camp of October 11th on Cavalry Creek 16 miles
October 22nd, broke camp and marched to a point on the Arkansas River below the mouth of Mulberry Creek *35 miles*
October 23rd, crossed Mulberry Creek and camped   *2 miles*
October 27th, marched to vicinity of Dodge and camped (the Regiment still remaining at the mouth of Mulberry Creek) *12 miles*
Total distance during October *280 miles*

"1st Sergeant William W. Harris and Private Dennis Coughlin also carried the mail to Dodge on the night of October 5th, returning to camp on Cavalry Creek on the morning of October 7th, having marched 90 miles and had a skirmish with a small party of Indians.
"During the month of November the Troop marched as follows:
November 6th, from camp 1 mile east of Dodge to camp of Seventh Cavalry on Arkansas River, direction E.S.E. *9 miles*
November 12th, with command under General Sully to Mulberry Creek,   *direction south*   *5 miles*
November 13th, crossed Mulberry Creek and marched to Bluff Creek, direction a few points east of south   *24 miles*
November 14th, marched in a southerly direction 2 miles, then crossed to south bank of Cavalry Creek and marched 14 miles in a southerly direction to Bear Creek 16 miles
November 15th, marched in a southerly direction 4 1/2 miles, continued the march in a southeast direction to Cimarron River, and one mile S.S.W.   *11 1/2 miles*
November 16th, marched 8 miles south, continued the march 10 miles a few points east of

south and then S.S.W. to Beaver Creek
           25 miles
November 17th, marched east from Beaver Creek and camped on north fork of the Canadian
           15 miles
November 18th, followed down stream 15 miles and camped on middle fork of Wolf Creek at its confluence with north fork of the Canadian   *15 miles*
November 19, 20th, 21st, 22nd, remained in this camp now known as Camp Supply, refitting for a contemplated expedition against Indians
November 23rd, resumed the march with command under Lieutenant-Colonel Custer up stream, direction south   *14 miles*
November 24th, continued the march up stream and camped on left bank   *16 miles*
November 25th, left Wolf Creek on our right, marched through south to Canadian River   *18 miles*
November 26th, marched to north fork of Washita River, where we found Indian encampment; rested until daybreak and then broke in upon Black Kettle's band of Cheyenne Indians, killing a large number of warriors together with their stock; captured their women and children and a large amount of arms and ammunition and utterly destroying their village and winter supplies
           30 miles
November 27th, Left the Washita, returning northward and camped on north fork of the Washita   *10 miles*
November 28th, proceeded in northerly direction, crossed Canadian River, and camped on Washita   *10 miles*
November 29th, marched northward to Wolf Creek   *22 miles*
November 30th, marched to Camp Supply
           10 miles
Total distance during November 260 1/2 miles
"During the month of December the Troop marched as follows:
December 7th, from Camp Supply to Wolf Creek
           10 miles
December 8th, to Turkey Creek   *30 miles*
December 9th, to Canadian River 15 1/2 miles
December 10th, to branch of Washita 17 miles
December 11th, remained in camp
December 12th, on Washita River 17 1/4 miles
December 13th, on Washita River 9 1/2 miles
December 14th, on Washita River *12 miles*
December 15th, on Washita River 15 1/2 miles
December 16th, on Washita River 19 1/2 miles
December 17th, on Washita River 15 1/2 miles
December 18th, to Fort Cobb, Indian Territory
         21 1/2 miles
Total distance marched during December
        183 1/4 miles"
Troop H— (See Record of Events of Troop A, above.) The troop marched 976 miles during the year.

Troop I—Remained in garrison at Fort Wallace, performing the usual post duties and much escort and scouting duty until June 15th when it marched to Camp Alfred Gibbs, near Ellis Station, arriving June 22nd. From that date to the end of the year, events are the same as for Troop A. The troop marched 1,371 miles during the year.

Troop K— (See Record of Events of Troop

A, above.) The Troop was detailed as body guard to General Sully on his expedition leaving Fort Dodge August 31st and took part in the engagements of September 11th, 12th, 13th. The date of General Sully's return to Fort Dodge is not recorded; however, on October 9th, the troop, with Headquarters and Troops H and M under command of Lieutenant-Colonel Custer, left Dodge for Bluff Creek, where it joined the reminder of the regiment. The troop marched 1,241 miles during the year.

Troop L—Troop L did not form a part of the regiment engaged in the Battle of the Washita; however, it had by no means remained idle. It remained at Fort Reynolds, Colorado Territory, until some time in August when its station was changed to Fort Lyon, Colorado Territory. Civilians were not employed in any capacity at Fort Reynolds, and all post work was performed by the garrison, therefore, the troop was engaged in cutting and storing 700 tons of hay for use on the post.

During September, while on a scout from Fort Lyon the troop had a fight with a band on Cheyenne Indians on Rule Creek, Colorado Territory, in which four Indians were killed.

On November 11th, the troop accompanied four troops of the Tenth Cavalry, all under the command of Captain William H. Penrose, Third Infantry, on a scout for Indians south of the Arkansas. By the end of the month the troop had marched 265 miles. Grass was very scarce and the horses had suffered greatly. Two horses died from exhaustion. The march was continued, however, until December 11th, when the command reached Fort Lyon, having traveled 204 miles during the last eight days of the march. In addition to a scarcity of grass for the horses, only three days rations were provided for the men. The troops were forced to subsist on mule meat to a great measure. Twelve horses died in these last eight days. The troop remained at Fort Lyon until December 30th, when it left as guard to a wagon train enroute to the command of Major E.A. Carr, Fifth Cavalry, on Skull Creek in the northern part of Texas. The troop marched 469 miles during the year.

Troop M— (See Record of Events of Troop A, above.) The troop marched 976 miles during the year.

1869
Although the regiment had been in the field under canvas for the past year, it was destined to repeat the experience during the forthcoming year with no interval of post life. The comforts in garrison at that time were few, luxuries were out of the question, and a short relief from field work would have been welcomed by all. As Colonel Custer was determined to give the Indians no rest until they were ready to comply with the demands of the War Department, he lost no time in getting the regiment in condition to resume field operations and continue the pursuit of any band of Indians he could find. With this in view, Headquarters and Troops A, B, C, D, E, F, G, H, J, K, and M left Fort Cobb on January 6th, and marched over General Grierson's trail to the foot of the Wichita Mountains, 32 miles due south, where camp was established on Medicine Bluff Creek. Leaving the command in camp, Colonel Custer with Captain Rovvins, Lieutenant Custer, Lieutenant Cooke, Assistant Surgeon Rennick and 55 enlisted men, left camp January 22nd and marched west, crossing the north fork of the Red River about ten miles north of Camp Radzminski.

After marching 80 miles they struck the middle fork of the Red River, where a village of Arapahoe was found, numbering 65 lodges, under Little Raven, who was directed to proceed to the camp on Medicine Bluff Creek. After waiting three days for supplies the detachment marched 12 miles up Clear Creek and camped again.

Supplies being very short, the detachment remained in camp for two days while scouts were sent 50 miles in advance to search for the Cheyennes. The following day the detachments returned to the camp on Clear Creek, and then proceeded toward the regiment's camp on Medicine Bluff Creek. Lieutenant Johnson, with supplies, was met where the Arapahoe village had been found and Colonel Custer's detachment rejoined the regiment February 8th, having marched 408 miles.

Troop L, the only troop not with the regiment, returned to Fort Lyon, February 19th, from San Francisco Creek, having marched 200 miles.

The regiment remained in camp on Medicine Bluff Creek until March 2nd, when it left, via Camp Radzminski, for the north fork of the Red River a few miles above the mouth of the Salt Fork River. There the command was divided into two columns. The column under Captain Myers was to proceed on March 5th to the Washita River, where the fight of November 27th, 1868 had occurred, and to await further orders. (The Troop Returns for this period indicate that this division was not made by troops, but that men were detached from all troops for Colonel Custer's column. Probably Captain Myers had the dismounted men and the horses least able to stand a hard trip. The other, under Colonel Custer, marched west the same day in search of the Cheyennes.) On March 7th Colonel Custer's column followed a trail of one lodge and 14 animals and on the 9th the Indians were surprised but escaped, leaving 11 ponies and all of their provisions with the column.

On March 11th, an old trail was followed, and on the 15th, the column struck a village of 260 lodges. Colonel Custer's command was too exhausted to engage in a fight on which so much depended. It was known that these Indians had as prisoners two white women — Mrs. Morgan and Miss White — and every effort was to be made in getting possession of them. Negotiations were therefore begun and during their progress two chiefs and one warrior were captured and held as hostages for the safe return of the two white women.

Note: The sister of Chief Black Kettle, Mahwiss-a, and Chiefs Medicine Arrow, Dull Knife and Big Head as hostages for the return of the white women.

On the afternoon of March 18th, the Indians surrendered their prisoners and disappeared. (The return does not show that the hostages were given up; but the regimental return for April shows that two chiefs, one warrior and one woman were turned over on April 17th as prisoners to the commanding officer of Fort Hays, the post to which the regiment had marched.)

Two-thirds of the men were dismounted; therefore, it was impossible to pursue the Indians. As the main object of the trip — the rescue of the two white women — had been accomplished, the march to the rendezvous was begun and on the 24th, the two columns were joined at the Washita. During Colonel Custer's return march nearly all the train had to be burned because the mules were dying from starvation and exhaustion. For four days the men subsisted almost entirely on mule meat. On March 26th, the march to Camp Supply was begun, and on the 29th the column began the march to Fort Dodge. The regiment marched 444 miles during the month of March.

There was no more fighting Indians, but fighting cold, hunger and obstacles with which nature barred the routes of travel was even more wearing and destructive to the efficiency of the command. On the march from Supply to Fort Dodge the Regiment lost 128 horses and the "19th Kansas Volunteers" lost 148 horses.

Through the capture of Santana and Lone Wolf, head chiefs of the Kiowas, and a threat to hang them at sunset on a certain day, that tribe was forced to come in and camp on the reservation near Fort Dodge.

By extraordinary efforts of Lieutenant Colonel Custer with a detachment of two officers and 55 men, and a march of 350 miles, the Arapahoe had been located and brought back to their reservation where they remained at peace with the whites. The Cheyennes alone had remained obdurant to the peaceful efforts of the Government. They were finally located in Northern Texas and by a well-conceived and successfully executed plan, the detachment had captured three of their principal chiefs, the two white captives held by them were released, and an agreement entered into on the part of the Indians to return to their reservation, and on the part of Custer to restore to their people the three chiefs and the women and children captured at the Washita. The Indians complied with their part of the contract; and the Government, as far as it was able, fulfilled its stipulation. (Viz: the return of the women and children captured at the Washita — see Return for Troop D.)

The extreme severity of this winter's campaign will be appreciated when it is remembered that Lieutenant Colonel Custer's column left Camp Supply on the 7th of December 1868, with 1,400 cavalrymen, and on the 5th of March, 1869, his mounted effective strength was reduced to 650 men. However, with the return of the Cheyennes to their reservation, the work of the expedition south of the Arkansas was done. The regiment was withdrawn and the "19th Kansas" mustered out of the service.

During March Troop L changed station to Fort Leavenworth, marching 158 miles to Sheridan, thence by rail for 414 miles.

Troop H was left at Fort Dodge for station and the reminder of the column marched to Fort Hays, arriving April 8th, and camping on Big Creek about two miles below the post. For about a month the command remained in this camp, drilling and performing the usual camp duties, and furnishing many escorts and scouting parties. No regimental operations were undertaken during the reminder of the year, but nearly all the troops were located at detached points so as

Early western Army post as 7th U.S. Cavalry troopers eat while standing. Courtesy of Battlefield Museum.

Visitation at the Custer home at Fort Lincoln. L-R In the front row is Captain Tom Custer, Emma Wadsworth and Lt. Col. Custer. Courtesy of the J.C. Custer family.

Grizzly bear killed at Bear Butte Creek by Custer. L-R Scout Bloody Knife; Custer; Private Noonan and Captain Wm. Ludlow. (Illingworth photo) Courtesy of National Archives.

Seventh Cavalry Officers in front of Custer home at Fort Lincoln. Custer is third from the left in photo. Courtesy of Lawrence A. Frost.

to provide as much protection as possible to the settlers of southern and western Kansas. In the performance of these duties there is no record of distance marched except when a troop was out as a single unit.

Additional highlights of troop activated for the year, in addition to that described for the regiment, are indicated in more detail in the following extracts from individual troop returns:

Troop A—Accompanied the regiment through July. On July 30th the troop left Fort Hays as escort to the Indian Peace Commissioners, arriving at Camp Supply, August 7th and returned to Fort Hays on August 19th. It remained in camp near Fort Hays until October 12th, when it left under telegraphic orders for Fort Scott, Kansas, and camped on Limestone Creek near Girard, Kansas, October 29th, where it remained until the end of the year. The troop marched 1,299 miles during the year.

Troop B—Accompanied the regiment through May 31st. On June 1st, a detachment of

13 men of the troop under the command of 1st Lieutenant D.W. Wallingford, left on a scout along Walnut Creek to notify woodchoppers of existing Indian hostilities and returned June 5th. On June 7th a detachment of 40 men under command of 1st Lieutenant H.J. Nowlan, left on a scout along the Solomon and Saline Rivers and returned June 19th. On June 25th, the troop under command of 2nd Lieutenant E.G. Mathey, left for Fort Wallace, arriving July 1st and left Fort Wallace July 8th and on the 16th camped three miles beyond Denver, Colorado Territory. The troop left his camp August 1st and on the 3rd camped near Monument Wells, where the troops remained until August 23rd and then scouted along the Bijou Basin, arriving at Redman Station August 31st. The troop returned to Fort Lyons on October 31st, having marched 1,210 miles during the year; in addition, detachments of the troop marched 505 miles.

Troop C—Accompanied the regiment through May 31st. On June 4th, a detachment of

28 men under the command of Captain Berry, left Fort Dodge as escort to a government train and returned June 10th. The troop remained in this camp, performing the duties usually pertaining to camp life and making frequent marched on scouts and escort duty until October 13th, when it left for Fort Leavenworth, having marched 874 miles during the year.

Troop D—Accompanied the regiment until April 30th. On May 29th, the troop left camp near Fort Hays on a scout to the Solomon and Saline Rivers in search of hostile Indians and returned on June 1st. On June 13th, the troop left camp as escort to the Indian women and children captured at the Washita, en route to camp Sully for the purpose of turning these women and children over to their tribe. The troop marched 1,061 miles during the year.

Troop E—Accompanied the regiment until April 30th. The troop marched to Fort Wallace in May (date not recorded), and was divided into detachments as escorts to surveying parties; this duty continued until June 1st, when the entire troop left camp at Cheyenne Wells via Fort Lyon, Reynolds, Denver and arrived at Reeds' Springs June 30th. During July the troop marched to a camp near Fort Wallace. During August, the troop escorted surveyors for the Union Pacific Railroad. During September, the troop marched from Big Sandy to Fitz Meadows and during October it marched to a camp on the Smoky Hill River. In November, the troop went into winter quarters at Fort Wallace. (Note: The original returns of this troop are missing; therefore, only general accounts of the troop's activities can be obtained from the regimental returns.) The troop marched 1,852 miles during the year.

Troop F—Accompanied the regiment until May 31st. On June 25th, the troop left their camp near Fort Hays en route to Fort Wallace (date of arrival not recorded). The July return states that during the month the troop was escorting Major

L-R Lt. Charles Varnum; Lt. Nelson Bronson; Captain Benteen and Captain Thomas French. Courtesy of Battlefield Museum.

General Schofield, and had marched 259 miles. The end of the month indicated the troop was in camp near Denver, and it is supposed that the escort duty terminated there. The troop left camp near Denver August 1st and marched along the Denver and Santa Fe Stage road, camping on the 3rd at the source of Monument Creek and remained there until October 1st, scouting in the vicinity of Bijou Basin and Russelville. The troop then marched to Sheridan, Kansas, and on October 26th proceeded by rail to Fort Leavenworth, having marched 1,244 miles during the year.

Troop G—Accompanied the regiment until April 30th. On May 27th, the troop left camp near Fort Hays on a scout to the Saline and Solomon Rivers, and camped on the latter stream near the mouth of Asher Creek on May 31st. The camp was attacked three times the next day; however, the troop suffered the loss of only one horse which the Indians succeeded in taking when the herd was stampeded. During the month of June, 15 scouting parties were sent out from this camp, but only two of the parties had skirmishes with the Indians. During July, five scouting parties were sent out. The troop remained in this camp until November 22nd when it left for Fort Hays, arriving there on November 28th and going into quarters for the winter. The troop marched 714 miles during the year, and detachments marched an additional 990 miles.

Troop H—Accompanied the regiment until April 30th. The returns of this troop are very incomplete for the remainder of the year. The troop was left at Fort Dodge on the return march from Medicine Bluff Creek some time in April, having marched 547 miles during the year.

Troop I—Accompanied the regiment until May 31st. On June 8th, 1st Lieutenant Cooke and 39 men of the troop left camp near Hays for Camp Supply as escort to Brevet Major General Hardie, returning June 25th. It remained in camp performing the usual duties of field service until October 12th, when it marched with the command to Fort Leavenworth, having marched 1,154 miles during the year.

Troop K—Accompanied the regiment until April 30th. On May 10th, the troop left camp

near Fort Hays for Camp Beecher, 160 miles, and arriving there on May 20th. On the 28th it left for Fort Harker via Marion Center scouting the outskirts of the settlements between the Arkansas and Smoky Hill Rivers, arriving at Fort Harker on June 14th. From June 23rd to 29th the troop was escorting Major Merrill to the camps of Troops G and L. On July 10th, the troop left camp near Fort Harker on a scout for Indians who had been committing depredations along the Saline River; however, swollen streams delayed the march. On July 13th the troop was joined by a detachment of Troop L and one from Troop G on the 14th. On July 17th, the command camped on the south fork of the Solomon River, where it remained performing scouting and escort duties. On November 15th, the troop returned for winter quarters at Fort Harker. On December 13th, a detachment of 20 men under Lieutenant Godfrey left for a scout to Bunker Hill Station on the Kansas Pacific Railroad, thence to the Saline River, through the settlements to investigate a report that Indians were in the vicinity. The detachment marched 100 miles; however, the report proved groundless, and the detachment returned December 17th. The troop marched 1,067 miles during the year in addition to marches made by the detachments.

Troop L—Remained in the field as a portion of the command of Brevet-Brigadier General Penrose near San Francisco Creek, and engages in scouting and escort duty, until February 10th. The troop marched for Fort Lyon to take station, arriving there February 19th. Some time during March the troop changed station to Fort Leavenworth, marching to Sheridan, Kansas, and thence to Fort Leavenworth by rail. The troop left Fort Leavenworth June 2nd and went by rail to Fort Harker. Upon arrival the next day, it was ordered to the Saline River 25 miles north of Harker to scout that section and protect the settlers from the Indians. The troop remained there until August 24th, when it marched to the Republican River, 120 miles to a point near Lake Sibley and relieved a detachment of Artillery which had been on duty there. The troop scouted along the Republican River until the early part of November, and was camped at New

Typical noontime rest period in the Heart River Valley. Courtesy of the South Dakota Historical Society.

Wagon train with four columns ready for day's journey during 1873-1874 Expedition. (Illingworth photo) Courtesy of National Archives.

Scandinavia, Kansas. The troop returned to Fort Leavenworth for winter station on November 22nd, having marched 603 miles during the year.

Troop M—Accompanied the regiment until May 31st. On June 7th, 30 men of the troop, with detachments of Troops A and D, left camp near Fort Hays on a scout along the Saline River and towards Fort Harker; thence, along the Smoky Hill River, returning to camp June 19th. On July 17th, the troop left for Fort Dodge as an escort to public animals, arriving there July 21st and returned to camp August 5th. The troop remained in camp near Hays until October 13th performing scouting, escorting, and other duties incident to field service. The troop returned to Fort Leavenworth, Kansas, for winter quarters on October 25th, having marched 1,096 miles during the year.

1870

The troops of the regiment were destined to have but little rest during the year, although the determined policy which had been followed for the preceding year and a half had so subdued and scattered the various Indian tribes that regimental operations were not neccessary.

Small roving bands, with no following of women and children, were always ready to strike the settlements along the Saline, Solomon and Republican Rivers, and any unguarded wagon train traveling across the plains. In order to protect such a vast expanse of open, unsettled country, the troops of the regiment were nearly always moving independently, and many weary miles were marched with no apparent objective. This type of service had a much more depressing effect of the officers and men than the more exciting service of the two preceding years.

The year was spent performing the usual escorts, scouts and garrison duties. Of interest at the regimental headquarters was the great deal of social life, entertaining visitors from the East who were anxious to know General Custer, the now famous Indian fighter. The entertainment usually consisted of showing the visitors what life on the western plains was like. This included riding and hunting, camping in the open, and charades and parties in the officers' quarters at the post. General Custer and his charming young wife soon had a reputation for their hospitality. Their most famous guest during the winter of 1869-70 was the youthful Grand Duke Alexis of Russia, the son of the reigning Czar. Officially, he was the guest of the United States Government, but General Custer was appointed to be his escort on a buffalo hunt arranged by Colonel William F. Cody, better know as "Buffalo Bill." The details of that hunt and of the grand ball given later in Louisville, Kentucky, filled the newspapers of the day, and were on the tongues of socialites and plainsmen alike, all over the country.

The following are details of field service extracted from the Records of Events for each troop and will indicate the extensive scouting, patrol, and escort duties performed during the year:

Troop A—Remained in camp on Limestone Creek near Girard, Kansas, performing scouting and escort duty by detachment until September 11th, when the entire troop began a 229 mile march via the following route: Osage Mission; Little Labette Creek; Montgomery; the Verdigris River; Ennisville; Turkey Creek, Indian Territory; Big Cania; Elgin, Kansas; Beaver Creek; Elgin; Beaver Creek; to Walnut Creek near Arkansas City; Grouse Creek; Beaver Creek; Elgin; First Creek, Indian Territory; Ennisville, Kansas; Parker; Chetopa; Neosho River; Columbus, Kansas, return to station near Girard, Kansas. The troop marched 416 miles during the year.

Troop B—Remained at Fort Lyon, Colorado Territory, performing garrison, scout and escort duty until May 19th. The troop then marched to Kit Carson, Colorado Territory, on a scout north of the Republican River, and returned May 29th. The troop left on June 2nd as a part of Major Reno's command and scouted above the headwaters of the south fork of the Republican River, thence to and down the main branch to the mouth of the South Fork, thence to and down Beaver Creek, across Fox Creek to the Republican River and down same to the mouth of Fox Creek. From this camp a scouting party was sent out, leaving on June 16th, and followed an Indian trail across the Republican River, thence to Thick Woods, beaver Creek, Smoky Hill River and returned to Fort Wallace June 22nd. The troop then left Fort Wallace en route to Kit Carson on June 29th. The next record indicates that the troop left Cheyenne Wells, July 2nd, marched through Kit Carson and along the K.P.R.R. (Kansas Pacific Railroad) and arrived at Willow Springs July 5th. The next record indicates that the troop was at Hugo Station, Colorado Territory, September 30th. The troop left Hugo Station, October 12th, en route to Fort Leavenworth for winter station, where it arrived November 11th, having marched 1,259 miles during the year.

Troop C—Remained at Fort Leavenworth performing the usual garrison duties until April 27th, when it proceeded by rail to Fort Wallace and remained there until May 14th. It then marched for Kit Carson, Colorado Territory, and from there to the Republican River and then back to Fort Wallace, arriving on May 31st. On June 2nd it returned to Kit Carson by rail and on June 4th, joined the command of Major Reno. The troop returned to Fort Wallace, June 22nd by rail. The troop departed for Kit Carson the following day by marching, and on September 2nd, marched to Fitz Meadows, Colorado Territory, arriving there September 7th. The troop returned to Fort Harker via Fort Wallace, and arrived October 27th where it remained for the rest of the year, having marched 1,236 miles during the year.

Troop D—Remained at Fort Harker until February 22nd, when it marched to Lake Sibley, Kansas, arriving there February 26th. The troop marched to Scandinavia, Kansas, April 26th. During May the troop was out five days hunting for Indians in the vicinity of White rock and Beaver Creeks, and returned to New Scandinavia at the end of May. At the end of June the record shows the troop in camp near Fort Hays, but no dates of distances are recorded. The troop departed Fort Hays October 25th via Detroit, Kansas, arriving at Fort Leavenworth for winter station November 11th, having marched 471 miles during the year. The total distance marched was probably greater, however this is all that is recorded in the troop record for the period.

Troop E—Remained at Fort Wallace until January 27th, when it formed a part of an expedition under command of Lieutenant Colonel Custer against the Indians. It returned to Fort Wallace February 10th. The troop scouted for Indians until April 29th, when it left Wallace to protect citizens and railroad employees in the vicinity of Cheyenne Wells and Cedar Point, Colorado Territory. During May, the troop scouted in different directions from Cedar Point and Cheyenne Wells for Indians were reported to have committed depredations along the K.P.R.R. During the month of June the troop scouted the country adjacent to the K.P.R.R. for over 630 miles. The troop left camp at River Bend, Colorado Territory July 3rd on a scout to recover stock which had been stolen from the troop, and arrived in Denver July 6th. The troop returned to camp at River Bend on July 11th and departed August 12th in pursuit of horses stampeded by a hail storm. During the remainder of the year the troop marched via Fort Lyon, Willow Springs, where the troop reported to Captain Thompson, Seventh Cavalry, and scouted in different directions and was camped at Hugo Station until September 30th. On October 12th, the troop left for Fort Leavenworth for its winter station via Fort Hays, Abilene, Kansas, Fort Riley, and Topeka, having marched 2,965 miles during the year.

Troop F—Remained at Fort Leavenworth performing usual garrison duties until May 3rd, then marched to camp near Fort Hays, arriving there May 18th. On May 31st the troop left camp on a scout in the vicinity of the Solomon, Saline and the republican Rivers. The troop returned to its winter station at Fort Leavenworth, Kansas, in November. During the time the troop was stationed at Fort Hays, scouts were made to Saline River, Big Creek, Fossil Creek, Wilson Station, Fort Harker, Saline River, Dry Creek, Solomon River, Jewel City, White Rock Creek, Republican River, Lake Sibley, Clyde, Peace Creek, Moral Creek, Fort Riley, and to Three-mile Creek. During the year the troop marched 1,037 miles.

Troop G—Remained at Fort Hays performing the usual garrison duties, scout, and escort duties until February 18th when it marched to the forks of the Solomon River. During March, six scouting parties were sent out from this camp. On April 20th, a detachment of one sergeant, one corporal, one trumpeter and 19 privates moved to Spellman Creek and established a camp. The date on which this detachment rejoined the troop is not recorded. During May scouting parties marched 465 miles. The troop left camp at the forks of the Solomon River June 10th and marched to Camp Sturgis, near Fort Hays, and left camp September 5th, and marched to settlements on the Solomon River. One corporal and four men were stationed at Well's Stockade, 18 miles northwest of camp from September 11th to 28th. One corporal and four men were stationed near Bullock's Ranch, 22 miles southwest of camp from September 11th to 28th. One corporal and four men patrolled the country and escorted a wagon train from camp to the Saline River and returned. One sergeant and four men patrolled the country (carrying mail) from camp to the Saline River and return. One sergeant and two men patrolled 12 miles along Oak Creek and return. One sergeant and four men patrolled the country (carrying mail) from camp to Saline River and return. The troop left camp on the Solomon River October 14th and marched en route to Lyon via Harker, Hays, Wallace, and arrived at Fort Lyon, Colorado Territory, November 4th where it remained until the end of the year. The troop marched 720 miles during the year in addition to 1,222 miles by separate detachments.

Troop H—Remained at Fort Hays performing the usual garrison, scout, and escort duties until April 23rd and then marched to camp on the Saline River, arriving on April 29th. A detachment of the troop remained in camp on Beaver Creek, near Saline River, until May 12th when it proceeded to camp on Asher Creek, Solomon River, arriving there May 15th, scouting the country in various directions, until May 25th when it proceeded to hays, arriving there the same day. The entire troop left Hays May 25th by rail for Kit Carson, arriving there May 26th. The troop left Kit Carson July 2nd and left the same day and arrived at Willow Springs July 5th. It left Troops B and L at that place and proceeded to River Bend, Colorado Territory joining Troop E. The next day Troop L rejoined, and Troops H and L left for Denver and returned and joined Troop E on the 15th. All three troops returned to camp at River Bend July 16th and left on October 22nd, where Troop H resumed garrison duties until the end of the year, having marched 820 miles during the year.

Troop I—Remained at Fort Leavenworth performing the usual garrison duties until May 3rd and then, as a part of the command of Lieutenant Colonel Custer's command (F, I, L, M), left for Fort Hays and arrived there May 19th. Thirty men under Captain Keogh scouted the country between Fort Hays and Harker, returning to camp June 12th. The troop, with the command of Lieutenant Colonel Custer, left camp near Fort Hays July 13th and marched to the Saline River, returning to Fort Hays July 16th. After numerous scouts to the vicinity of the Saline River, the troop returned to Fort Hays for winter quarters on October 24th, having marched 480 miles during the year.

Troop K—Remained at Fort Harker until February 22nd, when it marched to Wolf Creek, arriving there February 24th. A permanent camp was established near the junction of Wolf Creek and the Saline River. On April 11th, the troop left camp in pursuit of thieves who had stolen a large number of mules from a government train on Bluff Creek on April 6th. The troop arrived at Bluff Creek April 17th and took up the trail the next day and followed it through the Sand Forks of the Arkansas River, Timber Mountain Fork, the headwaters of the Shanacospah, Little Medicine Lodge Creek, Medicine Lodge Creek (passed through the camp of the Indian Peace Commissioners of 1867), Pahoba Creek, headwaters of Bluff Creek. The total distance marched on this scout alone was 534 miles. The troop left on May 1st for Fort Harker arriving there May 8th and left Fort Harker on May 11th for camp on Wolf Creek, Beaver Creek, and Saline River, and returned to Fort Hays on June 11th. The troop with the command of Lieutenant Colonel Custer left Fort Hays on July 12th for the Saline River and returned July 15th; it

then left camp August 8th to scout the valleys of the Saline, Solomon, and Republican Rivers returning on August 22nd. The troop left Camp Sturgis near Fort Hays on October 25th en route to Fort Leavenworth for its winter quarters, arriving there on November 11th, having marched 1,545 miles during the year.

Troop L—Remained at Fort Leavenworth performing the usual garrison duties until May 3rd, then as a part of Lieutenant Colonel Custer's command (F, I, L, M), marched to Camp Sturgis, near Fort Hays, arriving there May 18th. The troop left camp May 18th by rail for Kit Carson, Colorado Territory, under orders to report to Brevet Major General Woods for active field service. The troop left Kit Carson May 21st on a scout to the Republican River, returning May 29th, and left again on June 1st as a part of the command of Major Reno and scouted the forks of the Republican River and the Big and Little Beaver Rivers. The troop arrived at Fort Wallace June 23rd and remained there in camp until the 28th and then marched for Kit Carson. It then left Cheyenne Wells for Kit Carson July 1st, and on the 2nd moved to five miles from Carson and went into camp until July 4th, when it moved again to Willow Station, remained there one day and on the 6th moved to River Bend on the 14th (no distance recorded). The following is entered on the August Return: "During the month of August the Troop has been in camp on the Big Sandy at a point between Carson and Denver cities, called River Bend. On the 7th of August the camp was visited by a severe hail storm, the coming of which was so sudden as to render it impossible for the men to repair to the herd in time to prevent a stampede; though as soon as the storm had ceased and it was deemed safe for the men to leave their tents, they were at once hurried to the herd when they found that all the horses had stampeded. The few stable guards succeeding in bringing in a sufficient number of horses to be the line to mount parties to be sent out the check the stampede. 1st Sergeant Murphy, one corporal and two men were immediately sent in a westerly direction with orders to strike the Bijou Basin and search the country and bring in all stray stock. The Sergeant having traveled all night and a part of the next day without discovering any tracks of the lost stock, prepared to return to the camp which he reached on the morning of the 9th. Another detail under Sergeants Abrams and Young also left camp the evening of the stampede traveling southwest following the Big Sandy a distance of about 52 miles. Not finding anything, the detail returned to camp at noon the 9th. On the 10th Sergeants Marlette and Young and eight men with four days rations were sent from camp across to the Arkansas, searching all the country between camp and that river. After traveling a distance of 250 miles the party returned home with the same success as the previous parties. From the 10th to the 22nd of August, at different time 14 horses returned to camp, leaving a deficiency of 14 horses yet to be accounted for. On the 22nd Sergeant Murphy and ten men were again sent out to patrol the Little Sandy with a view to capture a band of horse thieves supposed to be keeping government horses. Their camp was found but it had been evacuated. The stock being nearly exhausted and the Sergeant seeing no prospect of finding any-

thing, returned to camp on the 26th, having traveled over 150 miles."

During September scouting parties were sent out at different times to protect the line of the Denver Pacific railroad. The troop left River Bend on October 27th en route to Fort Wallace for winter quarters, arriving there November 3rd. On November 25th, Lieutenant Braden with 34 men left on a scout and returned the next day. During the entire month of December, a picket on non-commissioned officers and three men were out daily patrolling on the bluffs for the safety of the post herd. The troop marched 1,740 miles during the year and detachments of the troop marched an additional 814 miles.

Troop M—Remained at Fort Leavenworth, Kansas, performing the usual garrison duties until May 2nd, and then as a part of Lieutenant Colonel Custer's command (F, I, L, M) left for Camp Sturgis, near Fort Hays, arriving there on May 18th. On June 1st, five sergeants, four corporals, and 31 privates joined a detachment under Captain Yates and marched to the Solomon and Saline Rivers to protect settlers from Indian depredations, returning to camp on June 9th. On June 11th, Lieutenants Custer and McIntosh with 33 men joined the detachment under Captain Keogh and proceeded by rail 35 miles east to protect the railroad from Indians and returned by marching on June 13th. The troop scouted along the Saline, Solomon, and Republican Rivers from August 8th to 23rd. On October 5th, the troop left camp to relieve Troop G on the Solomon River, arriving there October 12th. On October 24th the troop returned to Fort Hays for winter quarters. The troop marched 760 miles, and troop detachments marched an additional 275 miles during the year.

1871

The tour of the regiment in the Department of the Missouri terminated early in the year. The following order was published upon transfer of the regiment from the Department of the Missouri:

HQRS. DEPT. OF THE MISSOURI

Fort Leavenworth, Kansas, March 8, 1871
General Orders No. 4.

Orders transferring the 7th Cavalry from this Department having been received from Headquarters of the Army, the Commanding General deems it his duty to express to the officers and soldiers of the regiment his high appreciation of their soldierly qualities and of the conspicuous services performed by them in this department.

The regiment carries with it a noble record of faithful services and gallant deeds. During the four years which it has been in this Department it has experienced all the hardships, dangers, and vicissitudes attendant upon military operations on our wild frontier. It has made many long and toilsome marches exposed to the severest storms of winter, and has gone for days in that inclement season without shelter and almost without food for man or animal.

It has been engaged in many bloody combats with the Indians in which its valor has been thoroughly tried and proved. It has met all dangers and privations with firmness and intrepid-

ity and has been distinguished throughout for steady discipline and efficient performance of duty.

The present soldierly condition and high state of discipline of the regiment give assurance that in the new field to which it is ordered it will be distinguished for the same high qualities which have so justly earned for it its brilliant reputation in this command.

With sincere regret the Commanding General sees this regiment leave this Department. It is needless to say that it will carry with it his hearty good wishes and his confident hope that its future will be as successful as its past history.

It will be long remembered in the Department as a model of soldierly discipline and efficiency.

By command of Brigadier General Pope:
(signed) W.G. Mitchell,
Brevet Colonel, U.S.A.
Acting Assistant Adjutant General

By the end of March, headquarters and all but four troops had changed to stations in the Department of the South, as follows:

Headquarters, Band, and Troops A and F, Louisville, Kentucky; Troop B, Unionville, South Carolina; Troop C, Chester, South Carolina; Troop d, Mount Vernon, Kentucky; Troop E, Spartanburg, South Carolina; Troop I, Bagdad, Kentucky; Troop K, Yorkville, Carolina. By the end of May the remaining four troops were stationed as follows: Troop G, Columbia, South Carolina; Troop H, Nashville, Tennessee; Troop L, Columbia, South Carolina; Troop M, Louisville, Kentucky.

Smaller towns were occupied by detachments from the troops, and very soon the regiment was scattered over an extensive section of the southern states. Its principal duties were in assisting United States Marshals to arrest violators of the internal revenue laws. This very unpleasant duty continued during the remainder of the year.

Since regimental operations were not conducted, all information pertaining to the regiment is found in the following extracts from the Records of Events of each troop:

Troop A—Remained in camp near Girard, Kansas, protecting settlers and performing the usual guard and camp duties until March 14th, when it proceeded by rail to Fort Leavenworth, arriving there the next day, and on the 19th embarked on the steamer. "Glasgow" with Headquarters and Troop F for Louisville, Kentucky, arriving there and taking station March 29th. The troop left Louisville April 3rd by rail for its new station, Elizabethtown, Kentucky, arriving there during the afternoon of the same day, and remained at this station until the end of the year, assisting in the execution of the internal revenue laws.

Troop B—Remained as part of the garrison at Fort Leavenworth until March 13th, when it embarked on the steamer, "McDonald," with Troop E and K, for Louisville, Kentucky, arriving there March 22nd, thence by rail to Unionville, South Carolina, arriving there for station on March 29th. On July 18th, Lieutenant Mathey and 25 men of the troop left for its new station at Spartanburg, South Carolina, on No-

vember 9th, and remained there until the end of the year, assisting in the execution of the internal revenue laws.

Troop C—Remained as part of the garrison at Fort Harker until March 12th, then proceeded by rail with Troop I to Fort Leavenworth, arriving there the next day. On March 14th, the troop embarked on the steamer, "Nile," with Troops D and I, for Louisville, Kentucky, arriving there on the afternoon of March 23rd. The troop then proceeded by rail to Chester, South Carolina, arriving there for stations on March 29th. On May 19th, Lieutenant Porter, with 20 men, left for temporary duty at Winnsboro, South Carolina, and the balance of the troop left for their new station, Rutherfordton, North Carolina, arriving there on June 27th. The troop remained at Rutherfordton until the end of the year, assisting in the execution of internal revenue laws.

Troop D—Remained as part of the garrison at Fort Leavenworth until March 14th, when it embarked on the steamer "Nile," with Troops C and I for Louisville, Kentucky, and was temporarily quartered at Taylor Barracks upon arrival. The troop left on the Louisville and Nashville Railroad on the afternoon of the 25th for station at Mount Vernon, Kentucky, arriving there on the morning of the 26th, where it established camp a quarter of a mile north of town. The troop then marched for its station at Chester, South Carolina, via Columbia and Yorkville, South Carolina, where it assisted in the execution of internal revenue laws for the reminder of the year.

Troop E—Remained as part of the garrison at Fort Leavenworth until May 13th, when it embarked on the streamer, "McDonald," with Troops B and K for Louisville, Kentucky, arriving at St. Louis March 19th, and at Louisville March 22nd, thence by rail on March 26th to Columbia, S.C., and to Spartanburg, S.C., for station, arriving on March 29th. On June 27th a detachment under Lieutenant McDougall left on a a scout after disguised men commonly know as "Ku Klux," returning the next day after a 32 mile march. A detachment of ten men under Lieutenant McDougall left in pursuit of the "Ku Klux," returning July 6th after a 60-mile march. On August 18th, Lieutenant McDougall and a detachment of 20 men, with 30 days rations, left for Greenville, S.C., as escort to the U.S. Marshal, afterwards marching to Gowansville on the same duty. Lieutenant McDougall and 15 of his party rejoined the troop on September 18th. On the night of September 26th, Lieutenant McDougall and 24 men marched to the vicinity of the "Cowpens Battlefield" to act as a posse for the U.S. Marshal and deputies in the arrest of men against whom warrants had been issued. The detachment returned on the night of September 29th with six prisoners. During November, the following scouting parties were out to assist U.S. Marshals in making arrests:

November 3rd, two officers and 12 men, returned November 5th with 12 prisoners.

November 12th, Lieutenant Craycroft and 10 men, returned next day with four prisoners.

November 30th, Lieutenant Craycrost and 20 men, returned December 1st. The troop left Spartanburg December 15th for station at Unionville, S.C., and remained at that station until the end of the year assisting in the execution of internal revenue laws.

Troop F—Remained as a part of the garrison at Fort Leavenworth until March 19th, when it embarked on the steamer, "Glasgow," with Headquarters and Troop A for Louisville, Kentucky, arriving there and taking station at Taylor Barracks on March 29th. The troop left Taylor Barracks July 20th by rail for Meridian, Mississippi, arriving there on July 25th for station. Its duties at Meridian were to assist the Civil authorities in the execution of laws. The troop returned to Taylor Barracks, Kentucky, on November 20th for station and remained there until the end of the year.

Troop G—Remained as part of the garrison of Fort Lyon, Colorado Territory, until April 5th, when it marched via Fort Wallace for camp near Fort Hays, Kansas, arriving there on April 18th. It left Fort Hays by rail with Troops H, L, and M, under command of Major Reno, for Louisville, Kentucky, arriving there on May 24th. On May 28th, the troop proceeded by rail to Columbia, S.C., and on June 7th left here and marched to its new station, at Sumter, S.C., arriving there on June 10th. The troop left Sumter by rail on August 8th for its new station at McPherson Barracks, Atlanta, Georgia, arriving there on August 9th. Lieutenant Hodgson and 12 men left on August 11th as an escort to assist U.S. Marshal Martin in the northern counties of the state of Georgia and returned on August 26th, after marching 300 miles. Lieutenant Hodgson and 12 men left by rail on August 28th for Tallahassee, Florida, as escort to Special Assessor Grant. Lieutenant Waring, Eighteenth Infantry, with ten men of the troop left on August 29th to protect and assist Deputy Collector Wood in Madison County, Georgia. Sergeant Patton and four men left on August 30th to protect and assist Deputy U.S. Marshal Martin in his duties. Lieutenant Waring and party returned September 6th, having traveled by rail 200 miles and marching 180 miles. Sergeant Patton and party returned September 1st and thereafter departed on four similar missions during the remainder of the month of September. The troop left McPherson Barracks by rail on October 14th, for a new station at Columbia, S.C. arriving there the next day. Lieutenant Hodgson and party returned from Florida October 20th, having traveled 1,112 miles by rail and marching 40 miles. Ten men under Sergeant Vickory left October 5th to protect civil officers in Coweta and Harralson Counties, and returned October 13th after marching 140 miles. The troop guarded "Ku Klux" prisoners in the county jail for its new station at Spartanburg, S.C., where it remained until the end of the year, arresting and guarding persons accused of being members of the "Ku Klux." The troop marched 295 miles during the year, and separate detachments marched an additional 970 miles.

Troop H—Remained as part of the garrison at Fort Hays until March 16th, when it left on a scout in the Saline River Valley, returning to Fort Hays March 28th. The troop scouted up the Saline and Solomon Valleys from April 13th to 27th. It left Fort Hays by rail on May 23rd with Troops G, L, and M, for Louisville, Kentucky, arriving there on May 28th, and left Louisville on May 31st by rail for station at Ash Barracks, Nashville, Tennessee, arriving there on June 1st. On June 17th, Lieutenant DeRudio and

25 men left for Tullahoma, Tennessee, to protect and assist internal revenue officers. On July 12th, a detachment of 11 men were sent out to assist internal revenue officers, returning on the 17th after marching 200 miles. Lieutenant DeRudio returned from Oxford with a part of this detachment on August 12th, the remainder proceeding to Humbolt, Tennessee. On September 19th, ten men were detailed to assist internal revenue officers, returning October 3rd after marching 200 miles. The troop left Ash Barracks December 29th for its new station at Huntsville, Alabama, arriving there the next day where it remained until the end of the year, having marched 500 miles during the year, with separate detachments marching an additional 400 miles.

Troop I—Remained as part of the garrison at Fort Harker until March 12th, then proceeded by rail with Troop C to Fort Leavenworth arriving there the next day. On March 14th, the troop embarked on the steamer, "Nile," with Troops C and D for Louisville, KY., arriving there on the afternoon of March 23rd and proceeded by rail to its station at Bagdad, Kentucky, arriving there on March 26th. The troop left Bagdad on September 25th for its new station at Shelbyville, KY., arriving there the same day, where it remained until the end of the year. There is no mention of any detached service on the troop record; however, it is unlikely that the troop did not perform duties outside the post.

Troop K—Remained as part of the garrison at Fort Leavenworth until March 13th, when it left on the steamer, "McDonald," with Troops B and E for Louisville, KY., arriving there March 21st and leaving the next day by rail for its station at Yorkville, S.C., arriving there on march 27th. The troop served there as part of the garrison until the end of the year. One note on the returns indicates that the troop engages in assisting U.S. Marshals in making arrests; however, no details of the service are given.

Troop L—Remained as part of the garrison at Fort Wallace. On February 18th, a detachment from the troop captured two horse thieves and their outfit consisting of five head of stock, a light wagon, arms and ammunition, all the property of settlers along the line of the K.P.R.R. On May 23rd, the troop left Fort Wallace by rail for Louisville, KY., joined Troops G, H, M at Fort Hays en route. The troop arrived at Louisville on May 28th. The next record states that the troop left Nashville, Tenn., June 1st by rail en route to Winnsboro, S.C., arriving at Columbia, S.C., June 4th, and remained in camp until June 9th, when it marched to Winnsboro for station the same day and went into camp a quarter of a mile from that city. The September return reports the general health of the troop as poor, most of the men having chills and fever. The troop left Winnsboro, October 12th and marched to Yorkville, S.C. for new station, arriving there October 14th where it was stationed for the reminder of the year assisting U.S. Marshals in making arrests. Thirty prisoners were taken during the month of October alone.

Troop M—Remained as part of the garrison at Fort Hays. From March 16th to 28th, the troop scouted through the country along the south and north branches of the Solomon River from the forks to the headwaters of those streams.

From April 13th to 29th the troop scouted the country between the Solomon and Republican Rivers and along the Republican River from the mouth of Prairie Dog Creek to the most remote settlements 301 miles away from the nearest white settlement. On May 23rd, the troop left Fort Hays by rail, with Troops G, H, L, for Louisville, KY., arriving there May 28th. It left Louisville by rail on May 31st en route to Darlington, S.C., for station, arriving there June 14th. The troop left Darlington by rail October 18th and arrived at its new station, Spartanburg, S.C., October 20th, and left November 7th and marched to Unionville, S.C. the same day. The troop must have performed duties similar to those performed by the other troops of the regiment in assisting U.S. Marshals in making arrests; however, there is no record made of any detached service. The troop marched 597 miles during the year.

1872

During the year, the regiment, except Troop L, continued on duty in the Department of the South for the purpose of protecting and assisting the civil officers of the Government in the arrest of illicit distillers and members of the "Ku Klux."

In December, Troop L was ordered to the Department of the Gulf and took station at Jackson Barracks, Louisiana. There were no regimental operations undertaken during the year, and all troops remained at their stations of the previous year and performed essentially the same duties unless mentioned below:

Troop C—Remained as part of the garrison at Rutherford, N.C., until March 12th, and then marched to new station at Lincolnton, N.C., arriving there March 13th after marching 44 miles. The troop left Lincolnton October 31st by marching and arrived the same day at the new station in Charlotte, N.C., a distance of 32 miles where it remained until the end of the year.

Troop D—Remained as a part of the garrison at Chester, S.C., until March 19th and then left by rail for its new station at Opelika, Alabama, where it arrived at midnight March 21st. On requisition from the Governor of the State of Alabama and of the Sheriff of Montgomery County, the troop moved by rail on November 28th to Montgomery, Alabama, leaving a detachment at Opelika to guard public property and returned to station by rail December 22nd and remained there until the end of the year.

Troop G—Remained as part of the garrison at Spartanburg, S.C., until August 19th, when it marched to its new station at Laurensville, S.C., where similar duties were performed until the end of the year.

Troop H—Remained as part of the garrison at Huntsville, Alabama. On February 15th, the troop moved by rail to its new station at Nashville, Tennessee, arriving there February 18th. On February 26th, a detachment left under Lieutenant DeRudio to assist internal revenue officers in the middle district of Tennessee, returning March 7th. On March 24th, a detachment left for the same purpose under command of 1st Lieutenant M. Barber, Sixteenth Infantry, returning April 18th, after marching 300 miles. On May 27th, a detachment under Lieutenant DeRudio left for the same purpose, and on the same day

23 men left with 44 horses for General Harding's farm, where the horses were grazed until July 10th, subject to charges incident to the service. Numerous other detachments went out from station until the troop left on October 16th for Ash Barracks, Nashville, Tennessee, via Livingston, Alabama, arriving there on November 19th, where it remained until the end of the year.

Troop I—Remained as a part of the garrison at Shelbyville, KY., until December 30th, when it proceeded by rail to its new station at Lebanon, KY., where it remained until the end of the year.

Troop L—Remained as part of the garrison at Yorkville, S.C., until December 17th, when it moved by rail to New Orleans, La., and took station at Jackson Barracks, arriving there on December 23rd where it remained until the end of the year.

Troop M—Remained as part of the garrison at Unionville, S.C., until December 24th, when it left by rail for its new station at Oxford, Mississippi. (Apparently troop trains were the same then as today, for the records of events for midnight December 31st indicates that the troop was still on the cars en route.)

1873

The regiment was ordered from the Department of the South to the Department of Dakota by General Orders No. 2, War Department, February 8th, 1873. A short time prior to this, orders had been issued for the regiment to proceed to the Department of Texas; however, the restless and threatening attitude of the Sioux Indians made it necessary to send cavalry request from General Sheridan, the regiment's destination was changed.

The troop was assembled by rail during March as follows: Headquarters, Band, and Troops A, F, H and I at Louisville, KY.; Troops B, C, D, E, G, K and M at Memphis, Tenn.; Troop L at New Orleans, La. On April 2nd all troops were transported to Cairo, Illinois by steamboat where they proceeded to destination shown below by rail.

At Sioux City, Iowa, the Regimental Headquarters, 1st Major (Major Joseph G. Tilford) and Troops D and I separated from the regiment and proceeded by train for Fort Snelling, Minnesota, for station. The Band and the other troops proceeded to Yankton, Dakota Territory, under command of Lieutenant Colonel Custer, arriving there on different trains from April 10th to 13th. The 2nd Major (Major Lewis Merrill) remained on duty in the South for a short time, and the 3rd Major (Major Marcus Reno) was sent on detached service to New York City.

While detained at Yankton waiting the wagon transportation and for the ice to clear the river, the regiment was introduced to a genuine Dakota blizzard beginning on April 14th. The blizzard was the worst experienced by the regiment during its fourteen years service in the Territory and is sometimes referred to as "Custer's Blizzard."

The following are newspaper accounts of the regiment's stay in Yankton during this period:

Dakota Herald (published Yankton, D.T., Tuesday, April 15, 1873).
"Now having a great blizzard (Sunday and

Monday) 7th Cavalry fare the worst, as they had not got their camp arranged ... Put horses in warehouses and stables in cities, some lost in timber. Officers to St. Charles Hotel, soldiers in numerous hotels and saloons. Rumor that some soldiers in going to and from camp strayed off and were frozen to death, others in exposed camp. Storm subsiding Tuesday."

Dakota Herald (April 22, 1873, Tuesday)

"Lieut. J. Aspinwell, Jas. W. Bell of 7th Cavalry are at St. Charles Hotel.

"The 'Key West' left Saturday with a large cargo, will proceed up Yellowstone. Col. Forsythe took passage ... government posts will have charge of all affairs pertaining to the military during the trip. Soldiers will be taken on at Ft. Rice.

"The 7th Cavalry stationed in this city have been under orders to take up their march for the upper Missouri posts on the 25th inst., and unless this order is revoked, Gen. Custer will start with the regiment at the appointed time. However, it is expected that other orders will be given and the regiment will remain at this place until there is sufficient grass to maintain stock while on the march.

"On Thursday there was a reception for the 7th Cavalry at Stone's Hall on Capital Street by the people at Yankton."

Dakota Herald (April 29th, 1873, Tuesday)

"The reception of the 7th Cavalry was a brilliant affair. Officers were in full dress uniform.

"It is rumored that Professor Vinitieri connected himself with the band of the 7th Cavalry.

"The 7th Cavalry will be paid off before leaving Yankton. Time is now set on the 12th of May."

Springfield Times (published in Springfield, D.T., of Bon Homme County, Thursday, May 8, 1873, L.C.F. Poore, Publisher).

"The 7th Cavalry are encamped on Snatch Creek, three miles below town. (Snatch or Plum Creek is west of the Bon Homme cemetery—the location pointed out by pioneers as the location of Custer's camp—Author's note.)

"A grand review of the 7th Cavalry took place in Yankton on Saturday last, Governor Burbank being invited by Gen. Custer to review the troops. The affair was quite a novelty for the Capital city and everybody turned out to witness the display.

"We were gratified to meet at Yankton on Saturday evening with Brevet Maj. Gen'l G.A. Custer in command of the 7th Cavalry. We served with him in the war for the Union and know him to be one of the bravest and most gallant officers of the Army."

Dakota Herald (May 13, 1873, Tuesday)

"The 7th Cavalry which left this place on Wednesday last have not yet arrived at Ft. Randall.

"17 invalid soldiers of the 7th Cavalry in the hospital in the city were taken on board the 'Katie P. Kountz' yesterday and will be conveyed to Ft. Rice."

Springfield Times (May 15, 1873, Thursday)

"The 7th Cavalry passed through this place about noon last Sunday, on their march to Ft. Rice. They went into camp just across Emanuel Creek, and a large number of our townspeople

and others visited them paying respects to Gen'l Custer."

Dakota Herald (Tuesday, June 17, 1973)

"The 'Miner' arrived on Sunday evening from her trip to Ft. Rice and the crossing. She went to accompany the 7th Cavalry and supply them along the route with forage, etc. Capt. J.L. Kelley, commander of the 'Miner' made the trip a successful one. T.B. Burleigh, clerk, gives the following memoranda of the trip:

"Left Yankton May 7, loaded with freight for 7th Cavalry. At Bon Homme there laid three days, and one day at Choreau Creek. Arrived at Yankton Agency on the 13th, remained 1/2 day. On 14th tied up at Ft. Randall, stayed until 16th ... Ft. Thompson 18."

According to pioneers of Bon Homme, South Dakota, and records on file there, six members of Custer's command (names unknown) died while in camp at Snatch Creek, and were later buried in the Bon Homme Cemetery. The records of Bon Homme Cemetery Association states, "Meeting held June 3, 1893. On motion a committee of three be appointed to take up and remove to cemetery soldiers bodies lying outside the cemetery within 30 days, Committee consisting of J.H. Emmons, F.W. Harrison and Fred Wells." /s/ J.H. Emmons, Sec'y, W.C. Bardwell, Pres. [Author's note: The above information, as well as the extracts of newspaper accounts of the regiment's stay in Yankton and Bon Homme were furnished by Miss Hazel B. Abbott, Yankton College, Yankton, S.C. There are no entries in the Regimental Record of Events indicating any deaths occurring during this period.]

On May 7th, the entire command—Band, and Troops A, B, C, E, F, G, H, K, L, and M, under Lieutenant Colonel Custer—marched for Fort Rice, Dakota Territory, 495 miles, arriving there on June 10th. Upon arrival, Lieutenant Colonel Custer reported to General D.S. Stanley for duty with the expedition was designed for the protection of engineering surveyors of the Northern Pacific Railway. The entire expedition consisted of about fifteen hundred men and two pieces of light artillery.

The column left Fort Rice June 20th. On July 16th, Troops C and H were left on the Yellowstone River, 25 miles below the mouth of the Powder River, to establish and guard the supply camp of the expedition. They remained there until picked up by Lieutenant Colonel Custer September 10th on his return march to Fort Lincoln, and for this reason did not participate in either fight of the regiment during the summer. The Little Missouri River was crossed July 11th and the Yellowstone reached July 15th, and crossed July 24th. The regiment camped near the mouth of the Powder River July 31st and left here August 2nd and marched up the Yellowstone. On August 4th, Custer, who, according to his usual custom, had gone ahead of the main column with 90 men, was attacked by 300 Indians on the north bank of the Yellowstone River about four miles above the present site of Fort Keogh, Montana. The Indians were well armed with breech-loading rifles and fought with great stubbornness for three and a half hours. The ammunition of the troops was about exhausted when, by a well directed charge, the Indians were driven from the field.

One trooper was missing and one wounded in this engagement while the loss among the Indians was heavy. The troops fought dismounted and under cover while the Indians charged gallantly within very short range. The same day the Regimental Sutler, the Veterinary Surgeon and one private were killed by a small party of Indians while trying to join Custer from the main column.

The trail of a large village was discovered on August 8th, and Custer was detached with his cavalry (Troops A, B, E, F, G, K, L, and M), and a company of scouts under Lieutenant D.H. Brush, Seventeenth Infantry, to follow and strike the Indians. The pursuit began as soon as night fell and was continued with great vigor. On the morning of the 11th, the Indians attacked Custer's camp on the Yellowstone, opposite the mouth of the Big Horn River, and a spirited engagement ensued. Lieutenant Braden, while holding a prominent point on the left flank with a small detachment, while Custer made his dispositions, was charged by 100 warriors, the Indians riding to within 30 yards of the dismounted line. Although shot through the thigh bone, Lieutenant Braden's exhibition of cool nerve maintained his position and repulsed the daring Indians.

On the bluffs south of the river, old men, women, and children were seen in large numbers evidently waiting in anticipation the time for their part in the drama; however, their dusky braves could not face the vigorous charge of the "pony soldiers." The Indians finally broke in complete route, the cavalry pursuing them for eight miles, when they escaped by crossing the Yellowstone.

In this engagement, the regiment lost one officer, Lieutenant Charles Braden, and two enlisted men wounded; and one enlisted man killed. Several officers had horses shot from under them. The Indians' losses were estimated by Custer to be 40 killed and wounded on the north side of the river, while several were known to have been hit on the south bank. As later verified by Indians who were present, there were 900 engaged in the attack. General Custer's official report of the fight states, "I desire *to bear testimony to the good conduct of every man connected with my command, including officers, men and scouts. Where all did so well no special mention can be made."*

No Indians were seen during the remainder of the season. The expedition left the Yellowstone at Pompey's Pillar and continued its march as far as the Mussel Shell River, arriving there August 19th, and leaving there August 27th. On August 29th, Custer's command was detached from the main expedition and ordered to march to Fort Lincoln, Dakota Territory, by way of the supply camp. The command crossed the Yellowstone on the steamboat "Josephine," September 9th, and on September 12th left the supply camp en route to Fort Lincoln, Dakota Territory, directly opposite the town of Bismarck, arriving there September 21st. The regiment had marched over 1,500 miles since leaving Yankton, on the 7th of May.

In the meantime, Troops D and I, under command of Major Reno who had rejoined from detached service in New York City, left Fort Snelling by rail June 3rd, and arrived at

William H. Illingworth was the 1873-74 Black Hills Expedition photographer. Courtesy of South Dakota Historical Society.

Horatio N. Ross was one of Custer's two miners to first discover gold in the Black Hills near French Creek and near Custer City, on July 30, 1874. Courtesy of Battlefield Museum.

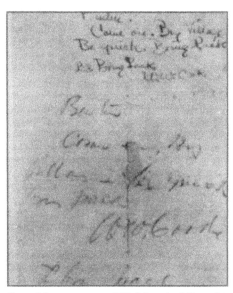

Custer's last message scribbled down by Adjutant Lt. W.W. Cooke for Private Martini to carry it to Capt. Benteen. It read: Benteen, Come On, Big Village, Be Quick, Bring Packs. W.W. Cooke, P.S. Bring Packs. Courtesy National Archives.

Breckenridge, Minnesota on June 5th. From here they marched to Fort Abercrombie, Dakota Territory, arriving there June 22nd, after marching 189 miles. This squadron (During this period, two troops constituted a squadron.) had been detailed as escort to the International Northern Boundary Survey Commission and reached the Mouse River, 250 miles west of Fort Pembina, on August 3rd. Camp Terry, a supply depot, was established on the bank of that stream and continued until October 14th, when the work of the Commission was suspended for the season. On that day the squadron began the return march for Fort Totten, Dakota Territory, 260 miles, arriving there October 22nd for winter station.

General Order No. 102, A.G.O., of this year published the Amnesty Proclamation of President Grant. Under this order, a large number of deserters surrendered to the military authorities.

1874

The usual round of garrison duties, with occasional escorts, occupied the different troops during the winter and until well into the spring of 1874. On April 23rd, a band of Indians stampeded and drove off 85 mules belonging to the citizens in the vicinity of Fort Lincoln. Lieutenant Colonel Custer, with his command, pursued the Indians for 20 miles and recovered the stolen stock. The command galloped for 4 1/2 hours (20 miles) and several troop horses died of exhaustion. On May 30th, Troops D and I, under command of Major Reno, again left Fort Torten for field duty as escort to the International Northern Boundary Survey Commission.

General Sheridan, in his annual report of 1873, had recommended the establishment of a large military post near the base of the Black Hills in order "to secure a strong foothold in the heart of the Sioux Country, and thereby exercise a controlling influence over the Indians people." Pursuant to his directions an expedition was organized at Fort Lincoln in June 1874, for the purpose of reconnoitering the route from that post to Bear Butte in the Black Hills and to explore the country south, southeast and southwest of that point, and to study the question of estab-

lishing army posts to control the Indians. Custer was detailed to command the expeditionary force, which consisted of ten troops of the Seventh Cavalry, two companies of Infantry, a detachment of scouts, and a group of scientists. This force was directed to return to Lincoln within sixty days.

Troops A, B, C, E, F, G, H, K, L and M, of the Seventh Cavalry Regiment, moved into camp two miles south of Fort Lincoln on June 20th. The senior Major (Major Joseph G. Tilford) and Troops C, H, K and M had marched from Fort Rice the same day, preparatory to taking part in this expedition. The expedition began its march July 2nd. The command camped at Harney's Peak, near the present site of Custer City, South Dakota, 416 miles southwest of Fort Lincoln, on July 30th. The return march was begun on August 1st; however, some of it was not over the same route. Fort Lincoln was reached August 30th. The expedition had marched 949 miles since July 2nd, but did not engage any Indians during the entire march.

The well-equipped scientific party with the expedition gathered much valuable information as to the geology, zoology and paleontology of the Black Hills region explored; however, the presence of precious metals in large quantity appears to have been doubted by the members of the scientific party, but not by the practical miners in or with the command. General Custer reported that gold was found "in the grass roots," creating considerably newspaper comments, criticisms, and controversy. Indeed, this was the first real exploration and report upon the Black Hills by an authorized party. The maps then existing gave only an outline of the foothills, and Harney's Peak was located by intersections within the interior of the region mark "unexplored."

The Black Hills territory had been specifically reserved for the Sioux Indians by the treaty of 1868. Notwithstanding this treaty, the report of gold in paying quantities by the Custer expedition served to increase the public pressure on the government to open the Black Hills region

for development. Having been moved five times, the Sioux Indians refused to renounce their rights to their sacred and private hunting ground of the Great Spirit. Frequent clashes occurred between the Indians and hunters and prospectors who killed the great herds of buffalo and brought back stories of gold and ignored the treaty rights of the Indians. It was due to this growing trouble with the Sioux nation that the Custer expedition was ordered into the field. It may be said that these continuous invasions by the white men of the Sioux Indians' territory marked the beginning of the rise of the Sioux against the white which finally made necessary the expedition of 1876 and culminated in the Seventh Cavalry's Battle of the Little Big Horn.

The following winter an expedition under command of Captain Guy V. Henry, Third Cavalry, was sent from Camp (later Fort) Robinson, Nebraska, to rescue prospectors at French Creek (now Custer City) from suffering starvation. Hardly a member of the command escaped frostbite from the severe weather, including Captain Henry who lost some of his fingers.

On September 29th, six Troops (A, B, E, G, H and K) of the Seventh Cavalry, under Major Merrill, left Fort Lincoln by rail for duty in the Department of the Gulf. They were assigned to station at different points in Louisiana and Alabama, where they remained, performing constabulary duty, until the spring of 1876.

In the meantime, Troops D and I had marched 429 miles by way of Forts Stevenson and Buford and arrived at Dry Porcupine or Lime Creek, Montana Territory, on June 30th; and at Sweet Grass Hills, Montana Territory, on July 26th, 346 miles further. This latter camp remained the base of operations for the Commission during the balance of the season, and on August 13th the two troops began their return march to Fort Totten. On August 31st they were camped near the Missouri River between Old Fort Peck and Fort Buford, having marched 347 miles. On September 14th they arrived at Fort Totten for winter station, having marched 1,471 miles as a command since May 30th.

Buffalo Bill was once a scout for Custer.

Major Gen. Winfield S. Hancock, Commander of the Department of Missouri. Courtesy Ed Daily.

Lonesome Charlie Reynolds was one of the finest scouts in the west. Greatly respected by Custer and died with him at the Battle of Little Big Horn. (Barry photo) Courtesy of Smithsonian Institute.

Highlight from selected Troop Records of Events follow:

On the night of May 27th, Captain Hale, Lieutenant Godfrey and 100 men (22 of them from Troop K) and three Indian scouts, scouted toward the Cannon Ball River in search of a trail reported made by Indians form the Missouri River Agencies on their way north to attack the Berthold Agency near Fort Stevenson. The detachment marched to Dog Teeth Buttes but failed to find the trail, and returned at noon on May 29th. On May 31st, Captain Hale and 26 men of Troop K were a part of Captain Hart's detachment of 120 officers and men from the post ordered to report to Lieutenant Colonel Custer at Fort Lincoln for further field duty in pursuit of the Indians mentioned above. The detachment returned to its station on June 3rd.

On December 12th, Lieutenant Tom Custer (General Custer's brother), temporarily commanding Troop L, and 26 men marched to the Standing Rock Indian Agency and arrested the Sioux chief, "Rain-in-the-Face," who was the principal in the murder of the Sutler and the Veterinary Surgeon in August, 1873. Rain-in-the-Face subsequently escaped from the guard house at Fort Lincoln and is reputed to have killed Lieutenant Tom Custer in the Battle of the Little Big Horn in 1876. The detachment returned to its station on December 17th.

On May 31st, Captain French and 31 men of Troop M were a part of Captain Hart's detachment of 120 officers and men from the post ordered to report to Lieutenant Colonel Custer at Fort Lincoln for duty in scouting for a band of Indians reported to be en route from the Missouri River Agencies to attack the Berthold Agency near Fort Stevenson. The detachment went as far as the Heart River, 140 miles, without finding signs of the Indians and returned to station of June 3rd. Troop M left for Fort Rice of November 14th and marched to the Standing Rock Agency to assist the U.S. Marshal in arresting certain Indians and returned November 16th. On December 13th, Captain French and 25 men of Troop M and 75 men of Troops C, F, and L, all under command of Captain Yates, marched to the Standing Rock Agency to arrest certain Indians suspected of murder and returned

on December 16th. On December 19th Captain French and 40 men of Troops C and M marched to the Standing Rock Agency to protect it against the Indians located there who were "bent on doing mischief"; and returned on December 24th.

1875

During the winter and spring of 1875, the headquarters and troops remained at their respective winter stations and performed the usual garrison duties together with considerable escort duty. Troops D and I changed station from Fort Totten to Fort Lincoln in April. Troops A, E, and H changed stations from the Department of the Gulf to the Department of Dakota in May, and were stationed temporarily in camp opposite Fort Randall, Dakota Territory, near the town of White Swan. Until September these troops were engaged in ejecting miners and other unauthorized persons from the Black Hills. Highlights from individual Troop Records of Events follow:

Troop A—Remained as part of the garrison at Livinston, Alabama, until May 18th, then left by rail and arrived at Yankton, Dakota Territory, on May 22nd. Troops E and H were already there. The three troops left Yankton May 26th and arrived at Fort Randall on May 30th. Lieutenant Varnum with 20 men of the troop were on a scout from June 15th to 17th for Indians reported to have stolen horses from the settlements. From June 25th to 29th, the troop searched the Little Platte River, Nebraska, for a war party of Indians reported to be in that vicinity. The troop left Fort Randall on July 26th for operations in the vicinity of the White River, Dakota Territory, and arrived at the first crossing of that stream and took temporary station there on August 2nd. From August 9th to 16th, Lieutenant Varnum with 35 men were absent from camp in search of miners who were endeavoring to enter the Black Hills between the camp and Wounded Knee, Dakota Territory. Captain Moylan with 40 men searched for miners attempting to enter the Black Hills, between September 4th and 10th. The troop left camp on September 11th and arrived at Fort Randall September 17th. Troops A, E, and H left Fort Randall on September 20th, and arrived at Fort Rice on October 7th. The next day Troops A and E marched to Fort

Elizabeth Clift Bacon (Libbie), was Custer's wife. Courtesy of the J.C. Custer family.

Lincoln for station. On October 19th, Troops A and D left for temporary duty as Fort Stevenson and arrived there October 23rd. Troop A left Fort Stevenson October 25th and arrived at Fort Lincoln October 28th.

Troop B—Remained as a part of the garrison at Shreveport, Louisiana, during the entire year.

Troop C—Remained as part of the garrison at Fort Rice during most of the year. On March 17th, Captain Hart, Lieutenant Harrington and 19 men of Troop C with 17 men of Troop M, marched to the Standing Rock Agency to capture an escaped Indian prisoner and returned on March 19th. On August 24th, Lieutenant Harrington and 14 men of Troop C with 11 men of Troop M, left for the Cannon Ball River in pursuit of Indians who were reported to have 30 mules that had been stolen from the troops in the Black Hills, and returned of August 26th. From August 25th to 27th, 10 men of Troop C with 12 men of Troop M were in pursuit of a party of Indians who had driven off the horses of the hay contractor whose camp was about five

Emanuel H. Custer, Custer's father. Courtesy Battle-field Museum.

Boston Custer was Custer's brother, who was a civilian. He was killed in the Battle of the Little Big Horn. Courtesy of Battlefield Museum.

Harry (Autie) Armstrong Reed was Custer's nephew. He was killed in the Battle of the Little Big Horn. Courtesy Battlefield Museum.

Lieutenants W.W. Cooke and Tom Custer with the Wadsworth sister. Courtesy of Lawrence A. Frost.

Custer and wife Libbie with brother Tom. The three were almost inseparable. Courtesy of the National Archives.

miles from the post. The troop left Fort Rice on October 9th, and arrived at Fort Lincoln for new station the same day.

Troop E—Remained as part of the garrison at Opelika, Alabama, during the early part of the year. On January 14th, Lieutenant McDougall and ten men marched to Chambers County to assist the civil authorities in serving a warrant of John B. Rutland. Not finding him, the detail returned on January 15th. On January 14th, Lieutenant Craycroft and 15 men left for a trip through the northeastern counties of Alabama in search of illicit distillers. On January 28th, a detachment of 16 men went to assist the civil authorities in serving warrants in Chambers and Tallapoosa Counties; eight men returned January 30th with three prisoners. On February 3rd, a detail of eight men assisted in arresting three citizens of Lee County, charged with intimidation, and returned on February 16th. Lieutenant McDougall with 13 men left on April 19th to assist in the arrest of illicit distillers in Chambers, Lee, Randolph and Tallapoosa Counties and returned April 28th with five prisoners. The troop left Opelika by rail on May 14th and arrived at Yankton, Dakota Territory of May 19th.

Troop F—Remained as part of the garrison at Fort Lincoln during the entire year. On September 25th, Captain Yates with 36 men of Troop F (and 24 men from other organizations) left in pursuit of a band of Indians believed to have killed a cattle herder near Bismarck. The Indians were trailed to Standing Rock Agency. The detail returned to Fort Lincoln on September 30th (the return does not indicate whether the murderer was captured).

On February 9th, Captain French and 24 men of Troop M marched to Standing Rock Indian Agency to return two men of Company D, Seventeenth Infantry, who were charged with killing an Indian the previous night. The detail returned of February 11th.

1876

The most colorful and important phase in the history of the settlement of the western United States involved the continuous struggles

At Fort Lincoln from left to right. Top row: Agnes Bates, Lt. James Calhoun, Custer's sister Margaret. Center: Custer's wife Libbie, Lt. Col. Custer, Col. Wm. Thompson. Front: Lt. Fred Calhoun. Courtesy of Battlefield Museum.

Major Marcus Reno had Companies A, G, and M assigned to him with orders to cross the Little Big Horn River and charge the Indian Village. He survived the battle. Courtesy of the Smithsonian Institute.

Captain Thomas W. Custer was commander of Company C, but died very near his brother on Custer Hill. His body was severely mutilated, but did not have his heart torn out. He was 31 years of age. Courtesy of Battlefield Museum.

Captain Frederick Benteen had Companies D, H, and K assigned to him with orders to scout the left of the trail approaching the Little Big Horn River. He survived the battle. Courtesy of the Smithsonian Institute.

Captain Myles W. Keogh was Commander of Company I and was killed in the battle. His horse Comanche was the only survivor of the battle on Custer Hill. Courtesy of Battlefield Museum.

Lt. W.W. Cooke was the Adjutant to Custer and scribbled the last message to Captain Benteen. He was killed in the battle on Custer Hill. Courtesy of the E.S. Luce family.

Lt. James Calhoun was married to Custer's sister Margaret. Assigned to Company C and was killed in the battle. Courtesy of the J.C. Custer family.

between the white man and the Indian. The year 1876 is probably the most memorable year in the history of the 7th U.S. Cavalry Regiment and represents the climax in this struggles. From 1865 to 1891 there were 13 different campaigns and at least 1,067 separate engagements between the Indians and the United States troops; however, none stand out in the history of the entire United States Army as does the bloody event which took place between the 7th U.S. Cavalry regiment and the Indian tribes on the heights above the Little Big Horn River in southeastern Montana on that hot Sunday afternoon in June 1876. No other battle in the history of the United States Army has excited so much interest, criticism, or controversy as the "Battle of the Little Big Horn—Custer's Last Stand." More has been written about this one battle—much of it pure fiction—than any other single battle except pos-

sible Gettysburg. Indeed more ink has been spilled over this battle than blood, for the regiment has suffered many more casualties in subsequent actions in its history with much less publicity.

The purpose of this history is to present the events pertaining to the regiment as they actually occurred as supported by entries in the official Records of Events of the regiment during this period. Accordingly, no attempt has been made to affix blame for the events leading up to that infamous battle, or for individual actions during the actual battle itself. However, it is considered appropriate to review the events which set the stage for the outbreak which occurred in 1876.

The injustices of the preceding years were clinched by the growth of fraudulent practices against the Indians living on the reservation. The

administration of Indian affairs was in the hands of a governmental bureau. Indian agents, obtaining their positions through appointment, were growing rich overnight by fleecing the Indians of their clothing and rations. It was the lucky man who could manage an appointment as one of these agents, and frequently the appointee paid a handsome price for the extremely lucrative position. Much of the supplies sent for issue to the Indians were actually, through the connivance of the post trader, sold to them, although they could ill afford to pay the prices demanded. Much of the flour and grain sent to the agencies was mixed with sand, and the meat unfit for human consumption. Taken all in all, the conditions of the reservations were not such as to make the Indians satisfied with living there, especially when their nomadic customs are considered.

The more peaceable members of the tribes

who had gone on the reservations were half starved due to the failure of the agencies to provide them with proper food. The tribes were enraged at the building of railroads across the plains; the wanton destruction of their herds of buffalo by white hunters, and the constant encroachment by the whites into the Black Hills, their sacred tribal lands. The following are but a few of the examples of the mistreatment of the Indians.

During the winter of 1874-1875, it was reported to General Custer that the Indians at the Standing Rock Agency were without food. Supplies had been sent to the rail depot a hundred miles away, but the Indians agency had no means of transporting the supplies across the snow-covered country. General Custer telegraphed for authority to divide his surplus supplies with the Indians until the Indian Bureau could get the supplies through to they agency; however, his offer was refused by the Department of Interior saying that the Indians would be fed by their own agents. As a result, there were many deaths from starvation at the Standing Rock Agency before the spring thaws.

Similar conditions were reported at other agencies, and General Hatch reported from New Mexico that the Indians were leaving their agencies because they could not get food or supplies and added "There is no *game in the country and the military are prohibited from issuing provisions to the Indians. The Cavalry are in the field, but they have only power to force the Indians to starve peaceably or be killed violently. Unless food is furnished and furnished promptly, to these Indians, one of two results is inevitable."*

General Crook reported that the Indians at Red Cloud and Spotted Tail agencies were very hungry, and asked if he might be permitted to loan the agency some beef cattle; however, his request was also refused.

For some time the troops had been active in keeping miners and prospectors out of the Black Hills region. All efforts were futile and when the troops seized the trespassers, escorted them out of the restricted area and turned them over to the civil courts, they were promptly released, and returned to the area. In November, 1875, General Sheridan sent a confidential letter to General Terry stating that "President Grant

Blacksmith Henry A. Bailey was assigned to Company I, and was killed in the battle on Custer Hill. Courtesy of Battlefield Museum.

George B. Herendeen was a scout for Custer and he survived the Little Big Horn Battle. Courtesy of the Montana Historical Society.

Encampment of 7th Cavalry during the 1973-74 Black Hills Expedition. Courtesy of Battlefield Museum.

Survivors from the Battle of Powder River in March 1876. Under the command of Brig. Gen. George Crook, he failed to destroy the Indian village which historians thought to be that of "Crazy Horse." It became to be known as the 'horsemeat march' of 1876, because both troopers and equipment were worn out. Many of their horses had been destroyed for food. Courtesy of the National Archives.

Wagon train of 7th Cavalry during the 1873-74 Black Hills Expedition. Courtesy of Battlefield Museum.

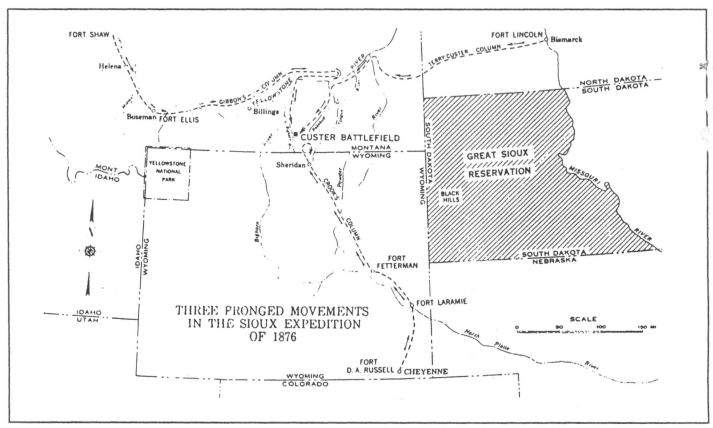

THREE PRONGED MOVEMENTS
IN THE SIOUX EXPEDITION
OF 1876

Three Pronged Movements in the Sioux Expedition of 1876. Courtesy of the National Park Service.

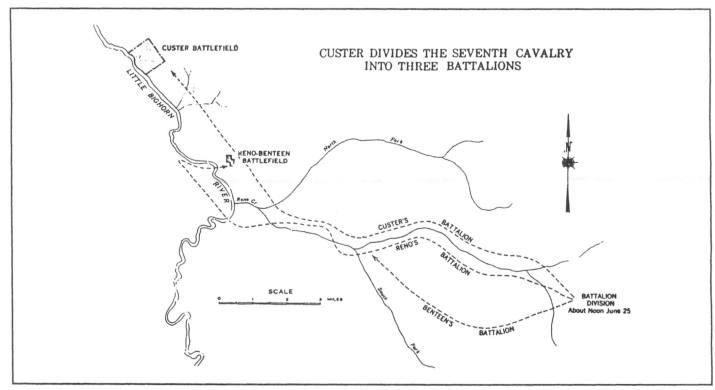

CUSTER DIVIDES THE SEVENTH CAVALRY
INTO THREE BATTALIONS

Custer Divides the Seventh Cavalry into Three Battalion. Courtesy of the National Park Service.

had a small conference in Washington on November 3rd, and that while the orders forbidding miners to go into the Black Hills should not be revoked, the troops should make no efforts to keep them out ... therefore quietly cause the troops of your Department to assume such attitude as will meet the views of the President in this respect." Within four months after the troops were withdrawn, the prospectors and settlers had poured into the area—Custer City alone had a population of over eleven thousand.

As one outrage after another was committed against the Indians and their treaties, small bands of the young men from various tribes began to slip off their reservations to join the bands gathering under Sitting Bull, the great Sioux chief and medicine man, far to the West. As time went by, the crafty medicine man received constant accessions to his growing band. He became more and more defiant, until in December of 1875, the Indian Bureau issued the infamous order that all Indians must be on their reservations by January 31st, 1876, or be considered hostiles and subject to action by the the military.

Because of the severe winter, few of the couriers sent out with the ultimatum arrived in the villages of the hostiles before the deadline. By then it was impossible for the Indians to comply because of the weather; however, it is doubtful that many would have complied with the order under any circumstances. The Indians had reached the limit of their patience. The Indian Bureau then admitted defeat and turned the problem over to the Army, under whose jurisdiction the whole affair should have been placed in the beginning, rather than entrusting it to civilians who were interested mainly in lining their own pockets at that time. Because of this situation, the army officers were practically powerless. The Army functioned under the War Department, while the corrupt Indian agents were under the Department of the Interior.

Thus, the events of the past few years made the expedition of 1876 inevitable, since the Government was determined to return the Indians to their reservations. The plans for the Black Hills expedition called for three columns to come from different directions—General Crook's from the south, General Gibbon's from the west, and Generals Terry and Custer from the east. The three columns were to cooperate in driving the roaming Indians back to the agencies, and if the Indians should resist, it was believed that any one of the columns could handle them. General Sheridan wrote to General Sherman from Chicago on May 29th as follows:

"As no very correct information can be obtained as to the location of the Indians, and as there would be no telling how long they would stay at any one place if it were known, I have given no instructions to Genls. Crook or Terry, preferring that they should do the best they can under the circumstances, ... as I think it would be unwise to make any combinations in such a country as they will have to operate in, as Indians, in any great numbers, can not keep the field as a body, or at most ten days. I therefore consider, and so do Terry and Crook, that each column will be able to take care of itself, and of chastising the Indians should it have the opportunity...

"I presume the following will occur: General Terry will drive the Indians towards the Big Horn Valley and General Crook will drive them back towards Terry; Colonel Gibbon moving down on the north side of the Yellowstone, to intercept if possible such as may want to go north of the Missouri to Milk River. The result of the movement of these three columns may force many of the Indians back to the agencies on the Missouri River and to Red Cloud and Spotted Tail agencies."

As winter blended into spring, more and more Indians slipped off their reservation. The Indian Bureau reported to the Army that they could expect to find about 1,000 to 1,500 warriors opposing them. Little did the Generals realize that even then the village of Sitting Bull were being joined by those of the brilliant Crazy Horse, the followers of fierce Gall, Hump, Crow King, and the Northern Cheyennes under Two Moons. The Indian agents reported only a small number of Indians unaccounted for, and pocketed the receipts from the supplies sent for the large number that were actually off their reservations. Thus, was the foundation laid, for to this misinformation, in itself, can be attributed in

large part the massacre which occurred the following spring.

On the first day of March, 1876, General George Crook opened the campaign which was to consume all of the following spring, summer, autumn, and winter. Marching northward from Fort Fetterman, Wyoming, his command numbered about 800 soldiers of the 2nd and 3rd Cavalry and the 4th and 9th Infantry.

Scouting the headwaters of the Tongue and Rosebud Rivers, he then turned southeast to the Powder River. On March 16th, at the head of Otter Creek, Crook sent Colonel J.J. Reynolds and six companies of cavalry to follow a recently discovered trail. Reynolds was to join Crook the next evening at the mouth of Lodge Pole Creek on the Powder River. Early on the morning of March 17th, a bitterly cold day with the thermometer standing far below zero, the cavalry charged into a sleeping camp of Indians. The Sioux and Cheyennes were driven out of their tepees, but took their position on the rocky bluffs bordering the village, where they poured a hot

fire into the cavalry troopers. The Indian village was burned and the ponies driven off, but the warriors rallied and inflicted severe losses on the troops who were performing the work of destruction. Reynolds, for some reason, suddenly ordered the village to be abandoned. A great deal of loot which had been captured in he initial charge, and which had not yet been destroyed, was left in the hands of the Indians, as were the dead bodies of some of the troopers. That evening the warriors recaptured some 700 ponies which had been taken at the beginning of the battle. The loss of these ponies would have been a crippling blow to their savage might. Reynolds and Crook joined, and the command returned to Fort Laramie. The failure of the Battle of Powder River, coupled with the severe cold and deep snow, rendered further prosecution of this campaign useless.

Note: Most historians insist that this village belonged to "Crazy Horse," but the Indians are most emphatic in denying it. They claim it was a village of Cheyennes with a visiting band of

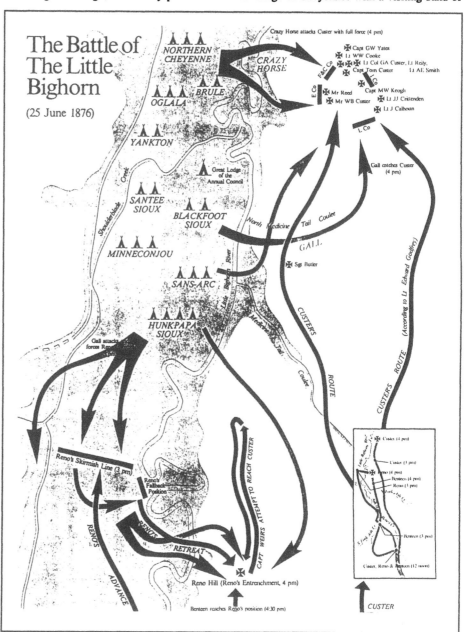

This map illustrates Custer's route, according to Captain E.S. Godfrey. Courtesy of Ed Daily.

Sitting Bull was the Hunkpapa Sioux leader, perhaps the most famous of all North American Indians, who inspired the Sioux in their defense of the Powder River country; and Battle of the Little Big Horn. In 1890, he embraced the Ghost Dance and as a result was killed (shot in the back) by Indian policemen shortly before the massacre of Wounded Knee. Courtesy of Battlefield Museum.

Chief Joseph of the Nez Percés was one of the ablest statesmen the North American Indian ever produced. Courtesy of Battlefield Museum.

Indian scaffold burial - photo by Barry. Courtesy of Burdick Collection.

Red Cloud the Oglala Sioux war leader who took charge of the Indian forces during the three-year campaign (1866-68) against the Bozeman Trail and Fort Phil Kearny. After 1868, he became a champion for peace and made frequent trips to Washington. Courtesy of Battlefield Museum.

Oglala Sioux under "He Dog" and that "Crazy Horse" was not present.

Crook, his command reorganized, then left Fort Fetterson for the second time on May 29th. This time he was to take part in a three-pronged advance into the hostile country. General John Gibbon, Colonel of the 7th Infantry, had left Fort Ellis, Montana Territory, early in April with six companies of his own regiment and was later joined by four troops of the 2nd Cavalry. His command was to move down the north bank of the Yellowstone River to effect a junction with the eastern column from Fort Lincoln, which was to move up the south bank of the Yellowstone. With Crook to the south, it was hoped that the three columns would trap the hostiles, and that they would be defeated and driven back to the Indian agencies. With Crook and Gibbon now in the field, we shall turn out attention to events transpiring at Fort Lincoln.

General Custer, who was in command of the important post at Fort Lincoln, was to have led the eastern column. During the spring, however, he had been called to Washington to testify in the impeachment trial of Secretary of War Belknap, who was accused of selling the post tradership at Fort Sill, Indian Territory. The Congressional Committee was groping into every act of the delinquent Secretary, and Custer had indicated that he would be willing to testify with regard to irregularities at posts along the Missouri River. His only piece of real knowledge was based on an honest mistake, and he immediately acknowledged his error when it was pointed out to him. However, during the course of his testimony, Custer implicated President Grant's brother (Orville Grant) in some shady dealings of the frontier. While he had no proof, his statements were undoubtedly true, and as a result President Grant took personal offense, and removed Custer from command (Custer was in Washington at the time), replacing him with General Terry, then commanding the Department of the Dakota. General Terry, a kind, generous, and efficient officer, was without experience in Indian warfare and desired Custer's services. Thoroughly alarmed, Custer went to General Sherman, who was now reestablished in Washington, and Sherman agreed to see that he was allowed to leave Washington by the following Monday, but Custer was to see the President before leaving. however, Grant would not see Custer, and Sherman had gone to New York City; therefore, Custer could not see either of them. Upon obtaining authority from the Adjutant General, Custer left by train for his regiment in the West. At Chicago, he was stopped by orders from Sherman, by direction of the President, that he was not justified in leaving Washington, and that he was to remain in Chicago to await further orders. When these orders arrived he was permitted to proceed to Fort Lincoln, "But not to accompany the expedition." Custer then sent a personal telegram (through General Terry) to the President as follows:

Headquarters, Dept. of Dakota
St. Paul, Minn., May 6, 1876

"The Adjutant General Division of the Missouri, Chicago.
I forward the following:

To His Excellency, the President:
(Through Military Channels)
I have seen you order transmitted through the General of the Army directing that I be not permitted to accompany the expedition to move against the hostile Indians. As my entire regiment forms a part of the expedition and I am the senior officer of the regiment on duty in this department I respectfully but most earnestly request that while not allowed to go in command of the expedition I may be permitted to serve with my regiment in the field. I appeal to you as a soldier to spare me the humiliation of seeing my regiment march to meet the enemy and I not share its dangers.

/s/ G. A. Custer"

General Terry endorsed the request as follows:

"In forwarding the above I wish to say, expressly, that I have no desire whatever to question the orders of the President or my military superiors. Whether Lieutenant Colonel Custer shall be permitted to accompany the column or not, I shall go in command of it. I do not know the reasons upon which the orders given rest: but if these reasons do not forbid it, Lieutenant Colonel Custer's services would be very valuable with his regiment."

/s/ Alfred H. Terry
Commanding Department

Sheridan, in Chicago, supported the recommendation and immediately forwarded the request with the following endorsement:

"Brig. General E.D. Townsend
Washington, D.C.

The following dispatch from General Terry is respectfully forwarded. I am sorry Lieutenant Colonel Custer did not manifest as much interest in staying at his post to organize and get ready his regiment and the expedition as he now does to accompany it. On a previous occasion in eighteen sixty-eight I asked executive clemency for Colonel Custer to enable him to accompany his regiment against the Indians, and I sincerely hope if granted this time it may have sufficient effect to prevent him from again attempting to throw discredit on his profession and his brother officers.

/s/ P.H. Sheridan,
Lieutenant General"

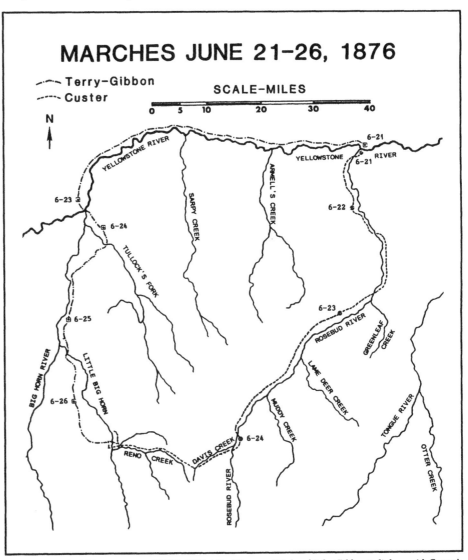

MARCHES JUNE 21-26, 1876

-·-·-·- Terry-Gibbon
-·-·-·- Custer

SCALE-MILES

0   5 10   20   30   40

N

YELLOWSTONE RIVER

YELLOWSTONE RIVER

6-21
6-21
6-22

6-23
6-24
6-23
6-25

SARPY CREEK
ARMELL'S CREEK
ROSEBUD RIVER
GREENLEAF CREEK
LAME DEER CREEK
MUDDY CREEK
TONGUE RIVER
OTTER CREEK

TULLOCK'S FORK

BIG HORN RIVER
LITTLE BIG HORN
6-26

RENO CREEK
DAVIS CREEK
6-24
ROSEBUD RIVER

The June 21-26, 1876 movements of BRIG. GEN. Alfred Terry and Colonel John Gibbon to link-up with Custer's 7th U.S. Cavalry.

Low Dog was the Oglala Sioux Chieftain who fought in the Custer Battle. Courtesy of Battlefield Museum.

Gall was a Hunkpapa Sioux Chief, who led the main attack against Custer, after having routed Reno and his troops. Courtesy of the National Archives.

Rain-In-The-Face was the Hunkpapa Sioux Chief who boasted that he had cut out the heart of Tom Custer. Courtesy of Battlefield Museum.

Custer's leadership of his regiment was well known to Grant, and either unwilling to imperil the success of the expedition, or moved by Custer's plea, Grant telegraphed approval for Custer to accompany the expedition in command of his regiment —the Seventh U.S. Cavalry.

Early in the spring orders were issued for the regiment to concentrate at Fort Lincoln and report to Lieutenant Colonel Custer for duty with the expedition.

Troops E and L arrived from Fort Totten on April 17th and were placed in quarters. Troops B, G and K arrived from the Department of the Gulf on May 1st, and Troops H and M arrived from Fort Rice on May 5th. As each troop reported, except Troops E and L, it was placed in a camp about two miles south of Fort Lincoln. On May 15th, Lieutenant Colonel Custer, Field Staff, Band, and Troops A, C, D, E, F, I and L, joined the rest of the regiment in this camp.

The expedition left Fort Lincoln at 5 a.m. on May 17th. Marching anywhere from ten to forty miles a day, according to the weather and the nature of the terrain, the column marched across the western part of what is now North Dakota and arrived at the Little Missouri River on May 29th, where it remained in camp until May 30th. On May 31st, the column marched 10 miles from that river and camped, remaining there June 1st and 2nd due to a severe snow storm. The column arrived at the Powder River on June 7th.

While the expedition was encamped on June 1st, General Terry went down the river to communicate with the supply steamer "Far West," Captain Grant Marsh commanding. The "Far West," hired by the government for $360 a day to perform the work of supply steamer, ferry, and courier boat, had come up from the lower river. She was a light draft boat, and was to play a conspicuous part in the ensuing campaign. Captain Grant Marsh was the most famous of the upper river pilots, and had done considerable work for the army on previous occasions. On her way up, the "Far West" had stopped at Fort Buford, where Captain Stephen Baker and

Crazy Horse was the great leader of the Oglala Sioux and played an important part in the Custer Battle. This photo is perhaps one of the only pictures taken of him. Photo by Lt. Thomas Wilhelm, 8th U.S. Infantry, 1874. Courtesy of the National Archives.

Company B of the 6th Infantry came aboard as escort. Three other companies of the 6th Infantry, under Major O. H. Moore, had already marched overland to Stanley's Stockade, at the mouth of Glendive Creek. It will be remembered that this was the supply depot established three years previous during the Yellowstone Expedition for the Northern Pacific. On June 7th, the steamer tied up at the mouth of the Powder River. That afternoon, Major Brisbin and others from Gibbon's command floated down to the "Far West" on skiffs with dispatches for General Terry, who arrived the next morning.

Terry, after reading Gibbon's dispatches, sent couriers with word for Gibbon to leave his command and come down the Yellowstone to meet the boat, which was to steam upriver until he was encountered. The next morning, about fifteen miles below the mouth of the Tongue

John Grass was Chief of the Blackfeet that engaged in the Custer Battle. Courtesy of Battlefield Museum.

Spotted Eagle was Chief of the Sans Arc Sioux, who were in the Custer Battle. Courtesy of Battlefield Museum.

Sitting Bull was the Hunkpapa Sioux spiritual leader of the Sioux. He was not a warrior and did not fight in the battle. Courtesy of Lawrence A. Frost.

Arikara scouts were known as the "Ree" scouts for Custer. L-R Red Star, Boy Chief, and Red Bear. Courtesy of the North Dakota Historical Society.

Lone Wolf was a Kiowa Chief, and he was held hostage along with Chief Satanta, by Custer. Courtesy of National Archives.

Strikes Two was one of Custer's Arikara scouts. Courtesy of the North Dakota Historical Society.

Two Moon was Chief of the Northern Cheyennes that attacked Custer and his troops. Courtesy of Battlefield Museum.

River, Terry and Gibbon met. The boat then carried the two generals on up to the site where Gibbon's command was camped. After a reunion of all the officers, Gibbon and his staff went ashore and the "Far West" returned to the Powder, where Terry left to return to the 7th Cavalry camp.

By June 15th, following Terry's orders, Major Moore and Captain Marsh had moved the supplies from Stanley's Stockade to the mouth of the powder River where the new supply depot was to be located. Major Moore's battalion was detailed to garrison this new supply base.

Upon General Terry's return to the 7th Cavalry camp on June 10th, preparations were made for Major Reno to take Troops B, C, E, F, I and L, comprising the right wing of the 7th Cavalry, and to scout up the Powder River for signs of Indians. He was to follow that river to its forks, then cross over to the Tongue and follow it down to its mouth, where he was to meet the rest of

the regiment. Major Reno's command left camp on the afternoon of June 10th. On June 11th, the Headquarters, Band, and the remaining six troops under General Custer, which formed the left wing of the regiment, marched to the junction of the Powder and Yellowstone Rivers—the present site of Miles, City, Montana—arriving there the same day and went into camp to wait for Major Reno's command.

Major Reno discovered a large Indian trail on the Tongue River, and followed the trail into the valley of the Rosebud River. On the very day that Reno reached the farthest point up the Rosebud, General Crook, not over 40 miles away, was fighting the Battle of the Rosebud. The fight was with a very large war party under Crazy Horse. The fierce battle was a draw, and Crook withdrew, falling back to Goose Creek, near the present site of Sheridan, Wyoming. He reported that more Indians were in the hostile country than previously supposed, and asked for more reinforcements. Although Crook discovered at this point that the Indian Bureau's reports were incorrect as to the number of Indians absent from the agencies, the information had to go by way of Chicago to reach Terry's column, and arrived too late to prevent the tragedy which occurred a few days later.

On June 15th, Headquarters, Band and Troops A, D, G, H, K and M, under the command of Lieutenant Colonel Custer, left the junction of the Powder and Yellowstone Rivers, where the permanent camp and supply depot had been established, and marched up the Yellowstone River to the mouth of the Tongue River, arriving on the 18th. The column remained in camp during the 19th, and in the afternoon scouts reported Reno's command eight or ten miles up the Yellowstone. General Terry immediately sent a communication to Reno ordering him to halt and await the arrival of the rest of the command. Custer's column left camp at 8 a.m. on the 20th and reached Reno's camp at 11:30 a.m. on the 21st, where the regiment reunited and went into camp at the confluence of the Rosebud and the Yellowstone Rivers. The Band

Little Raven, a Chief of the Arapahoes who was peacefully inclined as the result of a conference with Custer. Courtesy of the National Archives.

and wagon train were left behind at the Powder River base.

Soon after the regiment was reunited, the steamboat "Far West" arrived, and on the evening of June 21st, a conference was held aboard the "Far West" between Generals Terry, Gibbon, and Custer to plan the operation for trapping the Sioux.

Major Reno's scouting trip had proven that the trail of the Indian village led toward the valley of the Little Big Horn. It was agreed that Custer should march up the Rosebud valley and then into the Little Big Horn valley from the south, while Generals Terry and Gibbon would journey up the Yellowstone, thence up the Big Horn, and finally the Little Big Horn, catching the village from he north. It was further agreed that the two commands would strike the village on the 26th of June. Gibbon's four troops of the 2nd Cavalry were offered to Custer to add to his own 7th, but he refused, saying that to throw the two regiments together might promote discord. General Terry agreed with him. Custer also refused the offer of the Gatling Gun detachment commanded by Lieutenant Low because he feared it could not negotiate the rough country through which the command was to traverse. General Terry wished an examination of Tullock's Creek to be made, and George Herendeen, a scout of Gibbon's command, was furnished for the purpose of taking the information through to Terry. Six Crow scouts were transferred from Gibbon's column to guide Custer, as the Ree Scouts were not familiar with the country. The officers then went ashore, and Custer had officer's call sounded. The basis for the subsequent voluminous controversy arose over the question as to whether Custer disobeyed his orders, and stems from the written instructions handed Custer as the regiment marched out of camp the next day. Although they have been quoted in many histories of this action, it is not thought out of place to insert them here.

Camp at Mouth of the Rosebud River
Montana Territory
June 22, 1876
Lieutenant-Colonel Custer
7th Cavalry

Colonel:
The Brigadier-General Commanding directs that, as soon as your regiment can be made ready for the march, you will proceed up the Rosebud in pursuit of the Indians whose trail was discovered by Major Reno a few days since. It is, of course, impossible to give you any definite instructions in regard to this movement, and were it not impossible to do so the Department Commander places too much confidence in your zeal, energy and ability to wish to impose upon you precise orders which might hamper your action when nearly in contact with the enemy. He will, however, indicate to you his own views of what your action should be, and he desires that you should conform to them unless you shall see sufficient reason for departing from them. He thinks that you should proceed up the Rosebud until you ascertain definitely the direction in which the trail above spoken leads. Should it be found (as it appears almost certain that it will

be found) to turn towards the Little Horn, he thinks that you should still proceed southward, perhaps as far as the headwaters of the Tongue, and then turn towards the Little Horn, feeling constantly, however, to your left, so as to preclude the possibility of the escape of the Indians to the south or southeast by passing around your left flank. The column of Colonel Gibbon is now in motion for the mouth of the Big Horn. As soon as it reached that point it will cross the Yellowstone and move up at least as far as the forks of the Big and Little Horn. Of course its future movements must be controlled by circumstances as they arise, but is is hoped that the Indians, if upon the Little Horn, may be so nearly enclosed by the two columns that their escape will be impossible.

The Department Commander desires that on your way up the Rosebud you should thoroughly examine the upper part of Tullock's Creek, and that you should endeavor to send a scout through to Colonel Gibbon's column with information of the result of your examination. The lower part of this creek will be examined by a detachment from Colonel Gibbon's command. The supply steamer will be pushed up the Big Horn as far as the forks if the river is found to be navigable for that distance, and the Department Commander, who will accompany the column of Colonel Gibbon, desires you to report to him there not later than the expiration of the time for which your troops are rationed, unless in the meantime you receive further orders.

Very respectfully,
Your obedient servant,
(signed) E.W. Smith
Captain, 18th Infantry
Acting Assistant Adjutant General

The regiment left camp around noon on June 22nd and marched up the Rosebud 93 miles and then crossed the divide into the valley of the Little Big Horn on June 25th, where it found the Indian village and at once attacked. The engagement lasted, with intervals, until the next evening, when the Indians withdrew. The battle was disastrous, the regiment losing 13 officers and 237 enlisted men killed, and 44 enlisted men wounded, five of whom died later from the effects of their wounds.

The brief tragic incident in the history of the 7th U.S. Cavalry Regiment has been the subject of more controversy and speculation than any other single event in the history of the American frontier. The endless accounts and descriptions have all been disputed to some degree, and many are no doubt the endeavor of writers and artists more gifted with imagination than historical accuracy. However, in keeping with the practice of inserting personal experiences throughout this book, even at the expense of some repetition, the following account of the Battle of the Little Big Horn is the most accurate and reliable known to exist. This account, published in the "Century Illustrated Monthly Magazine," of January 1892, was written by (then) 1st Lieutenant Edward S. Godfrey, who commanded Troop K at the time of the battle, and is reproduced herewith in its original test by special permission of Appleton-Century-Croft, Inc.

"CUSTER'S LAST BATTLE"
By One of His Troop Commanders

On the 16th of April, 1876, at McComb City, Missouri, I received orders to report my troop ("K," 7th Cavalry) to the commanding General of the Department of the Dakota, at St. Paul, Minnesota, at the latter place about twenty-five recruits fresh from civil life joined the troop, and we were ordered to proceed to Fort Abraham Lincoln, Dakota, where the Yellowstone Expedition was being organized. This expedition consisted of the 7th United States Cavalry, commanded by General George A. Custer, 28 officers and about 700 men; two companies of the 17th United States Infantry, and one company of the 6th United States Infantry, 8 officers and 135 men; one platoon of Gatling Guns, 2 officers and 32 men (of the 20th United States Infantry); and 40 "Ree" Indian scouts. The expeditionary forces were commanded by Brigadier-General Alfred H. Terry, the Department Commander, who with his staff arrived several days prior to our departure.

On the 17th of May, at 5 A.M., the "general" (the signal to take down tents and break camp) was sounded, the wagons were packed and sent to the Quartermaster, and by six o'clock the wagon train was on the road escorted by the Infantry. By seven o'clock the Seventh Cavalry was marching in column of platoon around the parade ground at Fort Lincoln, headed by the band playing "Garry Owen," the Seventh's battle tune, first used when the Regiment charged at the battle of Washita. The column was halted and dismounted just outside the garrison. The officers and married men were permitted to leave the ranks to say "good bye" to their families, General Terry, knowing the anxiety of the ladies, had assented to, or ordered, this demonstration, in order to allay their fears and satisfy them, by the formidable appearance we made, that we were able to cope with any enemy that we might expect to meet. Not many came out to witness the pageant, but many tear-filled eyes looked from the windows.

During this halt the wagon-train was assembled on the plateau west of the post and formed in column of fours. When it started off the "assembly" was sounded, and absentees joined their commands. The signals "Mount" and "Forward" were sounded, and the Regiment marched away, the band playing "The Girl I Left Behind Me."

The 7th Cavalry was divided into two columns, designated right and left wings, commanded by Major Marcus A. Reno and Captain F.W. Benteen. Each wing was subdivided into two battalions of three troops each. After the first day the following was the habitual order of march: one battalion was advance-guard, one was rearguard and one marched on each flank of the train. General Custer, with one troop of advance-guard, went ahead and selected the route for the train and the camping places at the end of the day's march. The other two troops of the advance-guard reported at headquarters for pioneer or fatigue duty, to build bridges and creek crossings. The rearguard kept behind everything; when it came to a wagon stalled in the mire, it helped to put the wagon forward. The battalions on the flanks were to keep within five

Curly was one of Custer's Crow Indian scouts, who many think was the last one to see Custer alive. The Indian scouts had no other duty than to find the enemy, (the Sioux). It was the troopers job to do the fighting and not theirs. Custer advised them to leave once he had found the Indian village; and they followed his advice. Courtesy of Battlefield Museum.

White-Man-Runs-Him was one of Custer's Crow scouts. The Crows were mortal enemies to the Sioux. Courtesy of the National Archives.

Goes Ahead was one of Custer's Crow scouts. Courtesy of Battlefield Museum.

The Sioux celebrate. Fiske photo.

Hairy Moccasin was one of Custer's four Crow scouts. Courtesy of the National Archives.

hundred yards of the trail and not to get more than half a mile in advance or rear of the train. To avoid dismounting any often than necessary, the march was conducted as follows: one troop marched until about half a mile in advance of the train, when it was dismounted, the horses unbitted and allowed to graze until the train had passed and was about half a mile in advance of it, when it took up the march again; each of the other two troops would conduct their march in the same manner, so that two troops would be alongside the train all the time. If the country was much broken, a dozen flankers were thrown out to guard against surprise. The flankers regulated their march so as to keep abreast of their troop. The pack-animals and beef herd were driven alongside the train by the packers and herders.

One wagon was assigned to each troop, and transported five days' rations and forage and the mess kit of the troop; also the mess kit, tents,

Indian Buffalo hunt - painting by Schreyvogel. Courtesy of Battlefield Museum.

and baggage of the troop officers and ten days' supplies for the officer's mess. The men were armed with the carbine and revolver; not one, not even the officer of the day, carried the saber. Each troop horse carried, in addition to the rider, between eighty and ninety pounds. This additional weight included all equipment and about one hundred rounds of ammunition. The wagon-train consisted in all of about one hundred and fifty wheeled vehicles. In it were carried thirty days' supplies of forage and rations (excepting beef), and two hundred rounds of ammunition per man. The two-horse wagons, hired by contract, carried from fifteen hundred to two thousand pounds; the six mule government wagons carried from three to five thousand pounds, depending on the size and condition of the mules. The Gatling guns were each hauled by four condemned Cavalry horses and marched in advance of the train. Two light wagons, loaded with axes, shovels, pickaxes and some pine boards and scantling, sufficient for a short bridge, accompanied the "pioneer" troops. The "crossings," as they were termed, were often very tedious and would frequently delay the train several hours.

During this time the Cavalry horses were unbitted and grazed, the men holding the reins. Those men on duty at the crossing slept, or collected in groups to spin yearns and take a whiff at the "dingy dundeens." The officers usually collected near the crossing to watch progress, and passed the time in conversation and playing practical jokes. About noon the "strikers," who carried the haversacks, were called, and the different messes had their luncheon, sometimes separately, sometimes clubbing together. When the haversacks were opened, the horses usually stopped grazing and put their noses near their rider's faces and asked very plainly to share the hardtack; if their polite request did not receive attention they would paw the ground, or even strike their riders. The old soldier was generally willing to share with his beast.

The length of the day's march, varying from ten to forty miles, was determined in a great measure by the difficulties or obstacles encountered, by wood, water, grass, and by the distance in advance where such advantages were likely to be found. If about two or three o'clock in the afternoon, a column of smoke was seen in the direction of the trail and a mile or two in advance, it was a pretty sure indication that a camp had been selected. The Cavalry, excepting the rearguard, would then cut loose from the train and go directly to camp. The rearguard would send details to collect fuel and unpack their wagons. The adjutant showed the wing commanders the general direction their lines of tents were to run, and the latter then directed the battalion or troop commanders to their camping-places. Generally one flank of each line would rest near the creek. The general form of the camp was that of a parallelogram. The wings on the long side facing each other, and the headquarters and guard were located at one end nearest the creek; the wagon train was parked to close the other end and was guarded by the infantry battalion. The troops, as they arrived at their places, were formed in line, facing inward, dismounted, unsaddled, and, if the weather was hot and the sun shining, the men rubbed the horses' backs until dry. After this the horses were sent to water and put out to grass, with sidelines and lariats, under charge of the stable guard, consisting of one non-commissioned officer and three or six pri-

An Indian Army Scout firing a .50 caliber Sharps rifle. Courtesy of Battlefield Museum.

A typical Sioux Indian village in the 1870s. Courtesy of Battlefield Museum.

The .45-70 Gatling Gun troopers of the 7th U.S. Cavalry in 1876. Custer had left them at Fort Lincoln because they were too heavy and cumbersome for the Cavalry. Courtesy of Battlefield Museum.

Steamer "Far West" in 1876, which transported supplies on the Missouri River to the 7th U.S. Cavalry. Courtesy Battlefield Museum.

Curley, a Crow Indian scout with his pony. He escaped the Battle of the Little Big Horn to ride to the Steamer "Far West," and report the massacre of Custer and his troops. Courtesy of Battlefield Museum.

Captain Miles Keogh as a young Papal Guard in 1861. Courtesy of Battlefield Museum.

Comanche held by attendant at Fort Meade, SD, in 1887. Courtesy of Battlefield Museum.

vates. The men of the troop then collected fuel, sometimes wood, often a mile or more distance from the camp; sometimes "buffalo chips." The main guard, consisting, usually, of four or five non-commissioned officers and twelve or fifteen privates, reported mounted at headquarters, and were directed to take posts on prominent points over-looking the camp and surrounding country, one non-commissioned officer, and three privates. The officer of the day, in addition to his ordinary duties in camp, had charge of the safety of the cavalry herds. sometimes this latter duty was performed by an officer designated as "Officer of the Herd." To preserve the grazing in the immediate vicinity of the camp for evening and night grazing, all horses were required to be outside the camp limits until retreat. When the train arrived, the headquarters and troop wagons went directly to the camping place of their respective commands. The officers' baggage and tents were unloaded first; then the wagons went near the place where the troop kitchen was to be located, always on the flank of the troop farthest from headquarters. The teamsters unharnessed their mules and put them out to graze. The old stable guard reported to the troop commander for fatigue duty to put up the officers' tents and collect fuel for the mess. The troop officer's tents were usually placed twenty-five yards in rear of the line of men's tents and facing toward them. Their cook or mess tent was placed about ten or fifteen yards farther to the

rear. The "striker" made down the beds and arranged the "furniture," so to speak, which generally consisted of a camp-stool, tin washbasin, and a looking-glass. The men put up their tents soon after caring for their horses. The fronts of their tents were placed on a line established by stretching a picket-rope. The first sergeant's was on that flank of the line nearest to the headquarters. The horse equipment were placed on a line three yards in front of the tents. The men were prohibited from using their saddles as pillows. A trench was dug for a mess fire, and the grass was burned around it for several yards to prevent prairie fires. After this the cooks busied themselves preparing supper. Beef was issued soon after the wagon train came in, and the necessary number of beeves were butchered for the next-day's issue; this was hauled in the wagons. Stable call was sounded about an hour before sunset. The men of each troop were formed on the parade and marched to the horse herds by the first sergeant. Each man went to his own horse, took off the sidelines and fastened them around the horse's neck, then pulled the picket-pin, coiled the lariat, noosed the end fastened to the head halter around the horse's muzzle, mounted, and assembled in line at the place indicated by the first sergeant. The troop was then marched to the watering place, which was usually selected with great care because of the boggy bona fide mire beds of the prairie streams. After watering, the horses were lariated outside but in the immediate vicinity of the camp. The ground directly in rear of the troop belonged to it, and was jealously guarded by those concerned against encroachment by others. After lariating their horses, the men got their currycombs, brushes, and nose bags, and went to the troop wagon, where the quartermaster-sergeant and ferrier measured, with tin cups, the forage to each man, each watching jealously that he got as much for his horse as those before him. He then went at once to feed and groom his horse. The officer whose duty it was to attend stables and the first sergeant superintended the grooming, examining each horse's back and feet carefully to see if they were all right. When a horse's back got sore through the carelessness of the rider, the man would generally be compelled to lead his horse until the sore was well. Immediately after stables, the cook announced in a loud tone "supper." The men with haversack and tin cup went to the mess fire and got their hardtack, meat, and coffee. If game had been killed the men did a little extra cooking themselves.

The troop officers' mess kits consisted of a sheet-iron cooking-stove, an iron kettle, stewing, frying, baking, and dishpans; a small Dutch oven, a camp-kettle, a mess-chest holding tableware for four persons, and a small folding-table. The table in fair weather was spread in the open air. The early part of the meal was a matter of business, but after the substantials were stowed away, the delicacies were eaten more leisurely and time found for conversation. After supper the pipes were lighted, and the officers, if the weather was cold, went to the windward side of the campfire. Each man as he took his place was sure to poke of kick the fire, turn his back, hitch up his coattail, and fold his hands behind him.

Retreat was sounded a little after sunset and

Pawnee Killer was a southern Oglala warrior who fought against Custer. Courtesy of Battlefield Museum.

Spotted Tail the great Brule Chief. He was the uncle to Crazy Horse and was the most fearless of all Sioux warriors. Courtesy of Battlefield Museum.

Lazy White Bull was a Mininconju Sioux Chief who fought against Custer. Courtesy of Battlefield Museum.

He Dog was the Chief Lieutenant to Crazy Horse and remained loyal to him to the end. They were related by marriage. Photo taken in 1879. Courtesy of Battlefield Museum.

He Dog at old age - he lived to be over ninety years of age at death.

Crow was the Sioux Chief who gave the first battle cry that opened up the Battle of the Little Big Horn, against Major Reno and his forces. Courtesy of Battlefield Museum.

Short Bull was one of the principle leaders of the Ghost Dance, and was a Brule Sioux Medicine Man. Courtesy of Battlefield Museum.

Kicking Bear a Miniconjou Sioux along with Short Bull was a prime leader of the Ghost Dance among the Indians at Pine Ridge. This led to the death of Sitting Bull and led to the Massacre at Wounded Knee. Photo by William Dinwiddie 1896.

Chief Sitting Bull was killed by Red Tomahawk of the Indian Police in 1890. Photo by David F. Barry in 1884.

the roll was called, as much to insure the men having their equipment in place as to secure their presence, for it was not often we were near enough to any attraction to call the men away. (In 1876 there was not a ranch west of Bismarck, Dakota, nor east of Bozeman, Montana). The stable guards began their tours of duty at this time. The non-commissioned officer reported to the troop commander for instructions for the night; these usually designated whether the horses were to be tied to the picket-line or kept out to graze, and included special instructions for the care of sick or weak horses. At dusk all horses were brought within the limits of the camp. The picket-line was stretched over three wagons in front of the men's tents, or three posts were used when remaining in camp over a day.

During the evening the men grouped about the fires and sang songs and spun yarns until "taps." The cooks prepared the breakfast, which usually consisted of hard bread, bacon, and coffee. If beans or fresh meat were to be cooked the food was put into the Dutch ovens or camp-kettles, which were placed in the fire trench, covered over with hot ashes and coals, and a fire built over them. If the wind blew hard all fires were extinguished to prevent prairie fires. The cooks were called an hour or an hour and a half before reveille. At the first call for reveille, usu-

ally 4:20 A.M. the stable guard awakened the occupants of each tent and the officer whose duty it was to attend the roll-call. Stable call followed reveille and was superintended by an officer. This occupied about three-quarters of an hour. Two hours after reveille, the command would be on the march. Of course there were incidents that occasionally relieved the monotony.

Antelope were very plentiful, and the men were encouraged by troop commanders to hunt. General Custer had a number of staghounds, which amused themselves and the command in their futile attempts to catch them. One morning they started up a large buck near where the column was marching; Lieutenant Hare immediately followed the hounds, passed them, drew his revolver, and shot the buck. Nothing of special interest occurred until the 27th of May. when we came to the Bad Lands of the Little Missouri River. On the 30th General Custer was sent with four troops to scout up the Little Missouri, for about twenty miles. He returned the same day, without having discovered any recent "Indian signs." On the 31st we crossed the Little Missouri without difficulty. On the 1st and 2nd of June we were obliged to remain in camp on account of a snow-storm.

We remained in camp on the Powder River for three days. General Terry went to the

Yellowstone to communicate with the supply steamer Far West, which was at the mouth of the Powder River. He also went up the Yellowstone to communicate with General Gibbon's command, known as the "Montana Column," composed of four troops of the 2nd Cavalry and several companies of the 7th Infantry. Before General Terry left it was given out that the 7th Cavalry would be sent to scout up the Powder River, while the wagon-train, escorted by the Infantry, would be sent to establish a supply camp at the mouth of the Powder.

Eleven pack-mules, saddles, and aparejos (Packsaddles), were issued to each troop for this scout. This was a new departure; neither officers, men, nor mules had any experience with this method of transportation. There were a few "packers" (civilian employees) to give instructions. Short, compactly built mules, the best for the purpose were selected from he teams. A non-commissioned officer and four men of each troop were detailed for packers. After some instructions had been given by the professionals, especially how to tie the "diamond hitch," we concluded to make our maiden attempt by packing two empty water-casks. The mule was blinded and he submitted, with some uneasiness, to the packing. We supposed the packs were securely fastened and did not anticipate any trouble; but it is always the unexpected that happens with a mule. The blind was lifted; the mule gave a startled look first to one side, then to the other, at the two casks bandaged to his sides. He jumped to one side, causing to rattle a bung-plug that had fallen inside one of the casks. This startled him still more, and with head and tail high in the air he jumped again. He snorted and brayed, bucked and kicked, until the casks fell off. One was fastened to the saddle by the sling-rope. He now began to run, braying and making such a "rumpus" that the camp turned out as spectators. The affair excited serious concern lest all the animals in camp would be stampeded. When the cask was loose we got him back and made a second attempt with two sacks of grain. These he soon bucked off and then regaled himself with the spilt grain. As a final effort we concluded to try the aparejos, and pack two boxes of ammunition. This done, the mule walked off with as little concern as if he had been a pack-mule all his life.

General Terry having returned, orders were

Red Tomahawk (center) of the Indian Police at Standing Rock Reservation. He shot Sitting bull in the back of the head in 1890. Courtesy of Battlefield Museum.

Troopers of 7th Cavalry and dead Indians at Wounded Knee in December 29, 1890. Courtesy of Battlefield Museum.

Troopers of 7th Cavalry and dead Indians at Wounded Knee in December 29, 1890. Courtesy of Battlefield Museum.

Troopers of 7th Cavalry and dead Indians at Wounded Knee in December 29, 1890. Courtesy of Battlefield Museum.

issued on the 10th for the right wing, six troops, under Major Reno, to make a scout up the Powder, provided with twelve days' rations.

The left wing was ordered to turn over all forage and rations; also the pack-mules, except four to each troop. Major Reno left at 3 P.M., and the next day the rest of the command marched to the mouth of the Powder. My troop was rearguard, and at times we were over three miles in rear of the wagon-train waiting on the packers, for we had taken this opportunity to give them practical instruction.

Up to this time we had not seen an Indian, nor any recent signs of them, except one small trail of perhaps a half dozen tepees, evidently a part of agency Indians on their way to join the hostile camps. The buffalo had all gone west; other game was scarce and wild. The indications were that the Indians were west of the Powder, and information from General Gibbon placed them south of the Yellowstone. some of the officers of the right wing before they left expressed their belief that we would not find any Indians, and were sanguine that we would all get home by the middle of August.

Major Reno was ordered to scout to the forks of the Powder, then across the Mizpah Creek, follow it down to near its confluence with the Powder; then cross over to Pumpkin Creek, follow it down to Tongue River, scout up that stream, and then rejoin the Regiment at the mouth of the Tongue by the time his supplies were exhausted; unless, in the meantime, he should make some discovery that made it necessary to return sooner or make preparations for pursuit. A supply depot was established at the mouth of the Powder, guarded by the Infantry, at which the wagon train was left.

General Terry, with his staff and some supplies, took passage on the steamer "Far West" and went up the mouth of the Tongue. General Custer with the left wing, marched to the mouth of the Tongue, where we remained until the 19th waiting tidings from Reno's scout. The grounds where we camped had been occupied by the Indians the previous winter. (Miles City, Montana, was first built on the site of this camp.) The rude shelters for their ponies, built of driftwood, were still standing and furnished fuel for our camp fires. A number of their dead, placed upon scaffolds, or tied to the branches of trees, were disturbed and robbed of their trinkets. Several persons rode about exhibiting trinkets with as much gusto as if they were trophies of their valor, and showed no more concern for their desecration that if they had won them at a raffle. Ten days later I say the bodies of these same persons dead, naked, and mutilated.

On the 19th of June tidings came from Reno that he had found a large trail that led up the Rosebud River. The particulars were not generally known. The camp was full of rumors; credulity as raised to the highest pitch, and we were filled with anxiety and curiosity until we reached Reno's command, and learned the details of their discoveries. They had found a large trail on the Tongue River, and had followed it up the Rosebud about forty miles. The number of lodges in the deserted village was estimated by the number of camp fires remaining to be about three hundred and forty. The indications were that the trail was about three weeks old. No Indians had

been seen, nor any recent signs. It is not probable that Reno's movements were known to the Indians, for on the very day Reno reached his farthest point up the Rosebud, the battle of the Rosebud, between General Crook's forces and the Indians was fought. The two commands were then not more than forty miles apart, but neither knew nor even suspected the proximity of the other.

We reached the mouth of the Rosebud about noon on the 21st, and began preparations for the march and the battle of the Little Big Horn.

There were a number of Sioux Indians who never went to an agency except to visit friends and relatives. They camped in and roamed about the Buffalo Country. Their camp was the rendezvous for the agency Indians when they went out for their animal hunts for meat and robes. They were known as the "Hostiles," and comprised representatives from all the different tribes of the Sioux nation. Many of them were renegade outlaws from the agencies. In their visits to the agencies they were usually arrogant and formenters of discord. Depredations had been made upon the commerce to the Black Hills, and a number of lives taken by them or by others, for which they were blamed. The authorities at Washington had determined to compel these Indians to reside at the agencies—hence the Sioux War. Sitting Bull, an Hunkpapa Sioux Indian, was the chief of the hostile camp; he had about sixty lodges of followers on whom he could at all times depend. He was the host of the Hostiles, and as such received and entertained their visitors. These visitors gave him many presents, and he was thus enabled to make many presents in return. All visitors paid tribute to him, so he gave liberally to the most influential, the chiefs, i.e. he "put it where it would do the most good." In this way he became known as the chief of the hostile Indian camp, and the camp was generally known as "Sitting Bull's Camp." Sitting Bull was a heavy set, muscular man, about five feet eight inches in stature, and at the time of the battle of the Little Big Horn was forty-two years of age. he was the autocrat of the camp—chiefly because he was the host. In council his views had great weight, because he was known as a great medicine man. He was a chief, but not a warrior chief. In the war councils he had a voice and vote the same as any other chief. A short time previous to the battle he had "made medicine," had predicted that the soldiers would attack them and that the soldiers would all be killed. He took no active part in the battle, but, as was his custom in time of danger, remained in the village "making medicine." Personally he was regarded as a great coward and a very great liar. "a man with a big head and a little heart." The command passed the remains of a "Sundance" lodge which took place about June 5th, and to which I shall refer again. This was always a ceremony of great importance to the Indians with the graduation or commencement exercises of our civilized communities. In anticipation of this event, the Indians from the agencies had assembled at this camp.

Major James McLaughin, United States Indian Agent, stationed at the Devil's Lake Agency, Dakota from 1870 to 1881, and at Standing Rock Agency, Dakota, from 1881 to the present time (1892-Author), has made it a point

to get estimates of the number of Indians at the hostile camp at the time of the battle. In his opinion, and all who know him will accept it with confidence, about one-third of the whole Sioux nation, including the northern Cheyennes and Arapahoe, were present at the battle; he estimates the number present as between twelve and fifteen thousand; that one out of four is a low estimate in determining the number of warriors present; every male over fourteen years of age may be considered a warrior in a general fight such as was the battle of the Little Big Horn; also considering the extra hazards of the hunt and expected battle, few women would accompany the recruits from the agencies. The minimum strength of their fighting men may be put down as between twenty-five hundred and three thousand. Information was dispatched from General Sheridan that from one agency alone about eighteen hundred lodges had set out to join the hostile camp; but that information did not reach General Terry until several days after the battle. The principal warrior chiefs of the hostile Indians were: "Gall," "Crow King," and "Black Moon," Sans-arc Sioux; "Hump," of the Minneconjous, and "White Bull" and "Little Horse," of the Cheyennes. To these belong the chief honors of conducting the battle, of whom, however, "Gall," "Crow King," and "Crazy Horse" were the ruling spirits.

Generals Terry, Gibbon, and Custer had a conference on board the Steamer "Far West." It was decided that the Seventh Cavalry, under General Custer, should follow the trail discovered by Reno. "Officers Call" was sounded as soon as the conference had concluded. upon assembling, General Custer gave us our orders. We were to transport on our pack mules fifteen days' rations of hard bread, coffee, and sugar; twelve day's rations of bacon, and fifty round of carbine ammunition per man. Each man was to be supplied with 100 rounds of carbine and 24 rounds of pistol ammunition, to be carried on his person and in his saddlebags. Each man was to carry on his horse twelve pounds of oats. The pack mules sent out with Reno's command were badly used up, and promised seriously to embarrass the expedition. General Custer recommended that some extra forage be carried on the pack mules. In endeavoring to carry out this recommendation some Troop commanders foresaw the difficulties, and told the General that some of the mules would certainly break down, especially if the extra forage was packed. He replied in an excited manner, quite unusual with him, "Well, gentlemen, you may carry what supplies you please; you will be held responsible for your companies. The extra forage was only a suggestion, but bear this fact in mind, we will follow the trail for fifteen days unless we catch them before that time expires, no matter how far it may take us from our base of supplies; we may not see the supply steamer again."; and, turning as he was about to enter his tent, he added, "You had better carry along an extra supply of salt; we may have to live on horse meat before we get through." He was taken at his work and an extra supply of salt was carried. "Battalion" and "wing" organization were broken up, and Troop commanders were responsible only to General Custer.

The written instructions he received were

explicit, and fixed the location of the Indians very accurately. Of course as soon as it was determined that we were to go out, nearly every one took time to write letters home, but I doubt very much if there were many of a cheerful nature. Some officers made their wills; others gave verbal instruction as to the disposition of personal property and distribution of mementos; they seemed to have a presentiment of their fate.

At twelve o'clock noon, on the 22nd of June, the "Forward" was sounded, and the Regiment marched out of camp in columns of fours, each Troop followed by its pack mules. Generals Terry, Gibbon and Custer stationed themselves near our line of march and reviewed the Regiment. General Terry had a pleasant word for each officer as he returned the salute. Our pack trains proved troublesome at the start, as the cargoes began falling off before we got out of camp, and during all that day the mules straggled badly. After that day, however, they were placed under the charge of an officer, who was directed to report at the end of each day's march the order of merit of the efficiency of the Troop packers. Doubtless General Custer had some ulterior design in this. It is quite probable that if he had had the occasion to detach troops requiring rapid marching, he would have selected those troops whose packers had the best records. At all events, the efficiency was much increased, and after we struck the Indian trail the pack trains kept well closed.

We went into camp about 4 P.M., having marched twelve miles. About sunset, "Officers Call" was sounded, and we assembled at General Custer's bivouac and squatted in groups about the General's bed. It was not a cheerful assemblage; everybody seemed to be in a serious mood, and the little conversation carried on, before we all had arrived, was in undertones. When all had assembled the General said that until further orders trumpet calls would not be sounded except in an emergency; the marches would begin at 5 A.M. sharp; the troop commanders were all experienced officers and knew well enough what to do, and when to do what was neccessary for their Troops; there were two things that would be regulated from his headquarters, i.e. when to move out of and when to go into camp. All other details, such as reveille, stables, watering, halting, grazing, etc., on the march would be left to the judgment and discretion of the troop commanders; they were to keep within supporting distance of each other, not to get ahead of the scouts, or very far to the rear of the column. He took particular pains to impress upon the officers his reliance upon their judgment, discretion and loyalty. He thought, judging from the number of lodge fires reported by Reno, that we might meet at least a thousand warriors; there might be enough young men from the agencies, visiting their hostile friends, to make a total of fifteen hundred. He had consulted the reports of the Commissioner of Indian Affairs as to the probable number of "Hostiles" (those who had persistently refused to live or enroll themselves at the Indian agencies), and he was confident if any reliance was to be placed upon those reports, that there would not be an opposing force of more than fifteen hundred. General Terry had offered him the additional force of the battalion of the Second Cavalry but

he had declined it because he felt sure that the Seventh Cavalry could whip any force that would be able to combine against him; that if the Regiment could not, no other Regiment in the service could; if they could whip the Regiment, they would be able to defeat a much larger force, or, in other words, the reinforcement of this battalion could not save us from defeat. With the Regiment acting alone there would be harmony, but another organization would be sure to cause jealousy. He had declined the offer of the Gatling guns for the reason that they might hamper our movements or march at a critical moment, thirty miles a day. Troop officers were cautioned to husband their rations and the strength of their mules and horses, as we might be out for a great deal longer time than that for which we were rationed, as he intended to follow the trail until we could get the Indians, even if it took us to the Indian Agencies on the Missouri River or in Nebraska. All officers were requested to make to him, then or at any time, any suggestions they thought fit.

This "talk" of his, as we called it, was considered at the time as something extraordinary for General Custer, for it was not his habit to embosom himself to his officers. In it he showed a lack of self-confidence, a reliance on somebody else; there was an indefinable something that was not Custer. His manner and tone, usually brusque and aggressive, or somewhat rasping, was on this occasion conciliating and subdued. There was something akin to appeal, as if depressed, that made a deep impression on all present. We compared watches to get the official time, and separated to attend to our various duties. Lieutenants McIntosh, Wallace (killed at the Battle of Wounded Knee, December 28th, 1890) and myself walked to our bivouac, for some distance in silence, then Wallace remarked, "Godfrey, I believe General Custer is going to be killed." "Why, Wallace," I replied, "What makes you think so?" "Because, said he, "I have never heard Custer talk in that way before."

I went to my Troop and gave orders what time the "silent" reveille should be and as to other details for the morning preparations; also the following directions in case of a night attack: the stable guard, packers, and cooks were to go out at once to the horses and mules to quiet and guard them; the other men were to go at once to a designated rendezvous and await orders; no man should fire a shot until he received orders from an officer to do so. When they retired for the night they should put their arms and equipment where they could get them without leaving their beds. I then went through the herd to satisfy myself as to the security of the animals. During the performance of this duty I came to the bivouac of the Indian scouts. "Mitch" Boyer, the half-breed interpreter, "Bloody Knife," the chief of the Ree scouts, "Half-Yellow-Face," the chief of the Crow scouts, and others were having a "talk." I observed them for a few minutes, when Boyer turned toward me, apparently at the suggestion of "Half-Yellow-Face," and said, "have you ever fought against these Sioux?" "Yes," I replied. The he asked "Well, how many do you expect to find?" I answered, "It is said we may find between one thousand and fifteen hundred." "Well, do you think we can whip that many?" "Oh, yes, I guess

so." After he had interpreted our conversation, he said to me with a good deal of emphasis, "Well I can tell you we are going to have a _____ big fight."

At five o'clock, sharp, on the morning of the 23rd, General Custer mounted and started up the Rosebud, followed by two Sergeants, one carrying the Regimental standard and the other his personal or headquarters flag, the same kind of flag as used while commanding his Cavalry division during the Rebellion. This was the signal for the command to mount and take up the march. Eight miles out we came to the first of the Indian camping places. It certainly indicated a large village and numerous population. There were a great many "wickiups" (bushes stuck in the ground with the tops drawn together, over which they placed canvas or blankets). These we supposed at the time for dogs, but subsequent events developed the fact that they were the temporary shelters of the transients from the agencies. During the day we passed through three of these camping places and made halts at each one. Everybody was busy studying the age of the pony droppings and tracks and lodge trails, and endeavoring the determine the number of lodges. These points were the all-absorbing topics of conversation. We went into camp about five o'clock, having marched about thirty-three miles.

June 24th we passed a great many camping places, all appearing to be of nearly the same strength. One would naturally suppose these were the successive camping places of the same village, when in fact they were the continuous camps of the several bands. The fact that they appeared to be of nearly the same age, that is, having been made at the same time, did not impress us then. We passed through one much larger than any of the others. The grass for a considerable distance around it had been cropped close, indicating that large herds had been grazed there. The frame of the large "Sundance" lodge was standing and in it we found the scalp of a white man, probably one of General Gibbon's command who had been killed some weeks previously. It was whilst here that the Indians from the agencies had joined the Hostiles camp. The command halted here and "Officers Call" was sounded. Upon assembling we were informed that our Crow scouts, who had been very active and efficient, had discovered fresh signs, the tracks of three of four ponies and of one Indian on foot. At this time a stiff southerly breeze was blowing, as we were about to separate, the General's headquarters flag was blown down, falling toward our rear. Being near the flag, I picked it up and stuck the staff in the ground, but it fell again to the rear. I then bored the staff into the ground where it would have the support of a sage-bush. This circumstance made no impression on me at the time, but after the battle an officer asked if I remembered the incident; he had observed it, and regard the fact of its falling to the rear as a bad omen; and felt sure we would suffer a defeat.

The march during the day was tedious. We made many long halts so as not to get ahead of the scouts, who seemed to be doing their work thoroughly, giving special attention to the right, toward Tulloch's Creek, the valley of which was in general view from the divide. Once or twice signal smokes were reported in that direction.

Little Big Man who fought with Crazy Horse. Courtesy of Battlefield Museum.

Touch the Clouds was a seven foot tall Mininconju war chief who fought with Crazy Horse. He was feared by his enemies. Courtesy of Battlefield Museum.

Young Man Afraid-Of-His-Horses was an Oglala Sioux Chief. Courtesy of Battlefield Museum.

The Army returned a year later to Custer Battle site and found the field scattered with bleached bones. Courtesy of Battlefield Museum.

Troop C, 7th Cavalry, at San Carlos Indian Agency, 1896. Courtesy of the National Archives.

pliments and wants to see all the officers at headquarters immediately." So we gave up our much needed rest and groped our way through horse herds, over sleeping men, and through thickets of bushes trying to find headquarters. No one could tell us, and as all fires and lights were out we could not keep our bearings. We finally espied a solitary candle-light, toward which we traveled, and found most of the officers assembled at the General's bivouac. The General said that the trail led over the divide to the Little Big Horn; the march would be taken up at once, as he was anxious to get as near the divide as possible before daylight, where the command would be concealed during the day, and give ample time for the country to be studied, to locate the village and to make plans for the attack on the 26th. We then returned to our Troops, except Lieutenant Hare, who was put on duty with the scout. Because of the dust it was impossible to seen any distance, and the rattle of equipment and clattering of the horses' feet made it difficult to hear beyond our immediate surroundings. We could not see the trail, and we could only follow it by keeping the in the dust cloud. The night was very calm, but occasionally a slight breeze would waft the cloud and disconcert our bearings; then we were obliged to halt to catch a sound from those in advance, sometimes a whistling or hallooing, and again getting a response we would start forward again. Finally troopers were put ahead, away from the noise of our column, and where they could hear the noise of those in front. A little after 2 A.M., June 25th, the command was halted to await further tidings from the scouts; we had marched about ten miles. Part of the command unsaddled to rest the horses. After daylight some coffee was made, but it was almost impossible to drink it, the water was so alkaline that the horses refused to drink it. Sometime before eight o'clock, General Custer rode bareback to the several troops and gave orders to be ready for march at eight o'clock, and gave information that scouts had discovered the locality of the Indian villages or camps in the valley of the Little Big Horn, about twelve or fifteen miles beyond the divide. Just

The weather was dry and had been for some time, consequently the trail was very dusty. The Troops were required to march on separate trails so that the dust clouds would not rise so high. The valley was heavily marked with lodge-pole trails and pony tracks, showing that immense herds of ponies had been driven over it. About sundown we went into camp under the cover of a bluff, so as to hide the command as much as possible. We

had marched about twenty-eight miles. The fires were ordered to be put out as soon as supper was over, and we were to be in readiness to march again at 11:30 P.M. Lieutenant Hare and myself lay down about 9:30 to take a nap; when comfortably fixed we heard some one say, "He's over there by that tree." as that described our locality pretty well, I called out to know what was wanted, and the reply came. "The General's com-

Indian Troops - Troop L, 7th Cavalry in 1891, at Fort Sill Oklahoma Territory. Courtesy of Ed Daily.

Sitting Bull and Buffalo Bill Cody in 1885. Photo by David Notman.

before setting out on the march I went to where General Custer's bivouac was. The General, "Bloody Knife," and several Ree scouts and a half-breed interpreter were squatted in a circle having a "talk," after the Indian fashion. The General wore a serious expression and was apparently abstracted. The scouts were doing the talking, and seemed nervous and disturbed. Finally "Bloody Knife" made a remark that recalled General Custer from his reverie, and he asked in his usual quick, brusque manner, "What's that he says?" The interpreter replied, "He says we'll find enough Sioux to keep us fighting two or three days." The General smiled and remarked, "I guess we'll get through with them in one day."

We started promptly at eight o'clock and marched uninterruptedly until 11:30 A.M. when we halted in a ravine and were ordered to preserve quite, keep concealed, and not do anything that would be likely to reveal our presence to the enemy; we had marched about ten miles.

It is a rare occurrence in Indian warfare that gives the commander the opportunity to reconnoiter the enemy's position in daylight. This is particularly true if the Indians have a knowledge of the presence of Troops in the country. When following an Indian trail the "signs" indicate the length elapsed since the presence of the Indians. When the "signs" indicate a "hot trail," i.e., near approach, the commander judges his distance and by a forced march, usually in the nighttime, tries to reach the Indian village at night and make his disposition for a surprise attack at daylight. At all events his attack must be made with celerity, and generally without knowledge of the numbers of the opposing force than that discovered of conjectured while following the trail. The dispositions for the attack may be said to be "made in the dark," and successful surprise to depend upon luck. If the advance to the attack be made in daylight it is next too impossible that a near approach can be made without discover. In all our previous

The famous Budweiser painting of Custer's Last Battle. There probably have been more discussions over this painting than any other in military history. Courtesy of author's collection.

experiences, when the immediate presence of the Troops was once known to them, the warriors swarmed to the attack, and resorted to all kinds of ruses to mislead the Troops, to delay the advance toward their camp or village, while the squaws and children secured what personal effects they could, drove off the pony herd, and by flight put themselves beyond danger, and then scattering made successful pursuit next to impossible. In civilized warfare the hostile forces may confront each other for hours, days, or weeks, and the battle may be concluded with a tolerable knowledge of the numbers, positions, etc. of each other. A full knowledge of the immediate presence does not imply immediate attack. In Indian warfare the rule is, "touch and go." These remarks are made because the firebrand nature of Indian warfare is not generally understood. In meditating upon the preliminaries of an Indian battle, old soldiers who have participated only in the battles of the Rebellion are apt to draw only upon their own experiences for comparison, when there is no comparison.

The Little Big Horn, River, or the "Greasy Grass" as it is known to the Indians, is a rapid mountain stream, from twenty to forty yards wide,

with pebbled bottom, but abrupt, soft banks. The water at the ordinary stage is from two to five feet in depth, depending upon the width of the channel. The general direction of its course is northeasterly down to the Little Big Horn battle field, where it trends northwesterly to its confluence with the Big Horn River. The other topographical features of the country which concerns us in this narrative may be briefly described as follows: Between the Little Big Horn and Big Horn Rivers is a plateau of undulating prairie; between the Little Big Horn and the Rosebud are the Little Chetish or Wold Mountains. By this it must not be misunderstood as a rocky upheaval chain or spur of mountains, but is a rough, broken country of considerable elevation, or high precipitous hills and deep narrow gulches. The command had followed a trail up a branch of the Rosebud to within, say, a mile of the summit of these mountains, which for the "divide." Not many miles to our right was the divide between the Little Big Horn and Tulloch's Fork. The creek that drained the watershed to our right and front is now called "Sundance," or Benteen's Creek. The trail, very tortuous, and sometimes dangerous followed down the bed and

An Osage Scout for Custer. Courtesy of Herb Peck, Jr.

Kiowa Chief, was one of the head tribesman with Black Kettel's Village. Courtesy of Herb Peck, Jr.

Sly Fox was a Kiowa Chief. Courtesy of Herb Peck, Jr.

Satanta a Kiowa Chief was held hostage by Custer. Courtesy of the National Archives.

A rare photo of Moses E. Milner - "California Joe." Courtesy of Nebraska State Historical Society.

Captain Michael Smith was the 1873-74 Expedition Wagonmaster. (Illingworth photo) Courtesy of the South Dakota Historical Society.

Custer's four trusted scouts. Left to right: Will "Medicine Bill" Comstock, Chief of Scouts; Ed Guerrier, a half-blood Cheyenne; Thomas Adkins, a courier; "California Joe" (Moses E. Milner), Chief of Scouts, prospector and Indian fighter. Courtesy of C.W. Brice family.

valley of this creek, which at that time was dry for the greater part of its length. It was from the divide between the Little Big Horn, somewhere about twelve or fifteen miles away. It was to their point of view that General Custer had gone while the column was halted in the ravine. It was impossible for him to discover more of the enemy that had already been reported by the scouts. In consequence of the high bluffs which screened the village, it was not possible in following the trail to discover more. Nor was there a point of observation near the trail from which further discoveries could be made until the battle was at hand.

It was well known to the Indians that the Troops were in the field, and a battle was fully expected by them; but the close proximity of our column was not known to them until the morning of the day of the battle. Several young men had left the hostile camp on that morning to go to one of the agencies in Nebraska. They saw the dust made by the column of Troops; some of their number returned to the village and gave warning that the troops were coming, so the at-

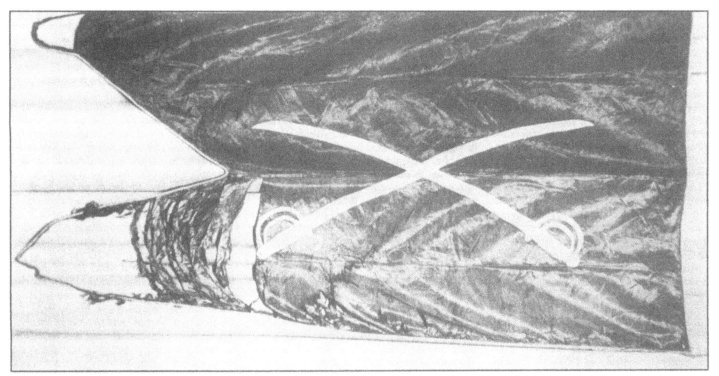

Personal Headquarters Flag of General Custer, which was 36 inches high and 5 ¹/₂ feet long. The center of the swallow tail cutting back about 22 inches. The crossed white sabers were the actual length of Civil War sabers, and both sides were stitched on. The top half was red silk and the bottom half blue. The whole outer edge was bound in a ¹/₄ inch woven silk cord. It had two ties each at the top and bottom corners. As a previous General, Custer retained the right to carry a personal flag. Courtesy of Dr. Lawrence Frost.

Corporal Dan Ryan was assigned to Company C and was killed in the battle. Courtesy of Battlefield Museum.

Sergeant John Ryan was assigned to Company M, and he survived the battle. In the 7th Cavalry, he was noted for his marksmanship with a rifle. Courtesy of Battlefield Museum.

Chief Big Foot laying dead in the snow at Wounded Knee. Courtesy of the National Archives.

tack was not a surprise. For two or three days their camp had been pitched on the site Where the were attacked. The place was not selected with the view to making that the battle field of the campaign, but whoever was in the van on their march thought it a good place to camp, put up his tepee, and the others as they arrived followed his example. It is customary among the Indians to camp by bands. The bands usually camp some distance apart, and Indians of the number then together would occupy a territory of several miles along the river valley, and not necessarily within supporting distance of each other. But in view of the possible fulfillment of Sitting Bull's prophecy the village had massed.

Our officers had generally collected in groups and discussed the situation. Some sought solitude and sleep, or meditation. The Ree scouts, who had not been very active for the past day or two, were together and their "medicine man" was anointing them and invoking the Great Spirit to protect them from the Sioux. They seemed to have become satisfied that we were going to find more Sioux than we could well take care of. Captain Yates' Troop had lost one of its packs of hard bread during the night march from our last camping place on the 24th. He had sent a detail back on the trail to recover it. Captain Keogh came to where a group of officers were, and said this detail had returned and reported that when near the pack they discovered an Indian opening of the boxes of hard bread with his tomahawk, and that as soon as the Indian saw the soldiers he galloped away to the hills out of range and then moved along leisurely. This information was taken to the General at once by his brother, Colo-

nel Tom Custer. The General came back and had "Officers Call" sounded. He recounted Captain Keogh's report, and also said that the scouts had seen several Indians moving along the ridge overlooking the valley through which we had marched, as if observing our movements; he thought that the Indians must have seen the dust made by the command. At all events our presence had been discovered and further concealment was unnecessary; that we would march at once to attack the village; that he had not intended to make the attack until the next morning, the 26th, but our discovery made it imperative to act at once, as delay would allow the village to scatter and escape. Troop commanders were ordered to make a detail of one non-commissioned officer and six men to accompany the pack; to inspect their Troops and report as soon as they were ready to march; that the Troops would take their places in the column of march in the order in which reports of readiness were received, and that the last one to report would escort the pack train.

The inspections were quickly made and the column was soon en route. We crossed the dividing ridge between the Rosebud and Little Big Horn valleys a little before noon. Shortly afterward the Regiment was divided into battalions. The advance battalion, under Major Reno, consisted of Troop M, Captain French; Troop A, Captain Moylan and Lieutenant DeRudio; Troop G, Lieutenant McIntosh and Wallace; the Indian scouts under Lieutenants Varnum and Hare and the interpreter Girard: Lieutenant Hodgson was acting Adjutant and Doctors De Wolf and Porter were the medical officers. The battalion under General Custer was composed of Troop I, Captain Keogh and Lieutenant Porter; Troop F, Captain Yates and Lieutenant Reily; Troop C, Captain Custer and Lieutenant Harrington; Troop E, Lieutenants Smith and Sturgis; Troop L, Lieutenants Calhoun and Crittenden; Lieutenant Cook was the Adjutant, and Dr. G.E. Lord was medical officer. The battalion under Captain Benteen consisted of Troop H, Captain Benteen and Lieutenant Gibson; Troop D, Captain Weir and Lieutenant Edgerly, and Troop K, Lieutenant Godfrey. The pack train, Lieutenant Mathey in charge, was under the escort of Troop B, Captain McDougall.

Major Reno's battalion marched down a valley that developed into the small tributary of the Little Big Horn, now called "Sun-dance," or Benteens Creek. The Indian trail followed the meandering of this valley. Custer's column followed Reno's closely, and the pack train followed their trial. Benteen's battalion was ordered to the left and front, to a line of high bluffs about three or four miles distant. Benteen was ordered if he saw anything to send word to Custer, but to pitch into anything he came across; if, he arrived at the high bluffs, he could not see any enemy, he should continue his march to the next line of bluffs and so on, until he could see the Little Big Horn Valley. He marched over a succession of rough, steep hills and deep valleys. The view from the point where the Regiment was organized into battalion did not discover the difficult nature of the country, but as we advanced farther it became more and more difficult and more forbidding. Lieutenant Gibson was sent some distance but saw no enemy, and so signaled the result of his reconnaissance to Benteen. The obstacles threw the battalion by degrees to the right until we came in sight of and not more than a mile from the trail. Many of our horses were greatly jaded by the climbing and descending, some getting far to the rear of the column. Benteen very wisely determined to follow the trail of the rest of the command, and we got into it just in advance of the pack train. During this march on the left we could see occasionally the battalion under Custer, distinguished by the Troop mounted on gray horses, marching at a rapid gait. Two or three times we heard loud cheering and also some few shots, but the occasion of these demonstrations is not known.

Some time after getting on the trail we came to a water hole, or morass, at which a stream of running water had its source. Benteen halted the Battalion. While watering we heard some firing in advance, and Weir became a little impatient at the delay of watering and started off with his Troop, taking the advance, whereas his place in column was second. The rest of the battalion moved out very soon afterward and soon caught up with him. Just as we were leaving the waterhole, the pack train was arriving, and the poor thirsty mules plunged into the morass in spite of the efforts of the packers to prevent them, for they had not had water since the previous evening. We passed a burning tepee, fired presumably by our scouts, in which was the body of a warrior who had been killed in the battle with Crook's troops on the Rosebud on the 17th of June.

The battalion under Reno and Custer did not meet any Indians until Reno arrived at the burning tepee; here a few were seen. These Indians did not act as if surprised by the appearance of the Troops; they made no effort to delay the column, but simply kept far enough in advance to invite pursuit. Reno's command and the scouts followed them closely, until he received orders to move forward at as rapid a gait as he thought prudent, and charge the village afterward, and the whole outfit would support him. The order was received when Reno was not very far from the Little Big Horn River. His battalion then moved at a trot to the river, when Reno delayed about ten or fifteen minutes watering the horse and reforming the column on the left bank of the stream Reno now sent word to Custer that he had everything in front of him and that the enemy was strong. Custer had moved off to the right, being separated from Reno by a line of high bluffs and the river. Reno moved forward in column of fours about half a mile, then formed the battalion in line of battle across the valley with the scouts on the left, after advancing about a mile further he deployed the battalion as skirmishers. In the meantime the Hostiles, continually reinforced, fell back, firing occasionally, but made no decided effort to check unmanageable and carried them into the Indian camp. The Indians now developed great force, opened a brisk fire, mounted, and made a dash toward the foothills on the left flank where the Ree scouts were. The scouts ignominiously fled, most of them abandoning the field altogether.

Reno, not seeing the "whole outfit" within supporting distance, did not obey his orders to charge the village, but dismounted his command to fight on foot. The movements of the Indians around the left flank and the flight of the scouts caused the left to fall back until the command was on the defensive in the timber and covered by the bank of the old river bed. Reno's loss thus far was one wounded. The position was a strong one, well protected in front by the bank and the fringe of timber, somewhat open in the rear, but sheltered by timber in the bottom. Those present differ in their estimates of the length of time the command remained in the bottom after they were attacked in force. Some say "a few minutes"; others, "about an hour." While Reno remained there his casualties were few. The Hostiles had him nearly surrounded, and there was some firing from the rear of the position by Indians on the opposite bank of the river. One man was killed close to where Reno was, and directly afterward Reno gave orders to those near to "mount and get to the bluffs." This order was not generally heard or communicated; while those who did hear it were preparing to execute it, he countermanded the order, but soon afterward he repeated the same order, "to mount and get to the bluffs," and again it was not generally understood. Individuals observing the preparations of those on the left, then gave orders to mount. Owing to the noise of the firing and to the absorbed attention they were giving to the enemy, many did not know of the order until too late to accompany the command. Some remained concealed until the Indians left, and then came out. Four others remained until night and then escaped. Reno's command left the bottom by troop organizations in column. Reno was the foremost in this retreat, or "charge," as he termed it in his report, and after he had exhausted the shots of his revolvers he threw them away. The hostile strength pushed Reno's retreat to the left, so he could not get to the ford where he had entered the valley, but they were fortunate in striking the river at a fordable place; a pony trail led up a funnel-shaped ravine into the bluffs. Here the command got jammed and lost all semblance of organization. The Indians fired into them, but not very effectively. There does not appear to have been any resistance, certainly no organized resistance, during this retreat. On the right and left of the ravine into which the pony path led were rough precipitous clay bluffs. It was surprising to see what steep inclines men and horses clambered up under the excitement of danger.

Lieutenant Donald McIntosh was killed soon after leaving the timber. Dr. De Wolf was killed while climbing one of the bluffs a short distance from the command. Lieutenant B.H. Hodgson's horse leaped from the bank into the river and fell dead; the Lieutenant was wounded in the leg, probably by the same bullet that killed his horse. Hodgson called out, "For God' sake, don't abandon me." He was assured that he would not be left behind. Hodgson then took hold of a comrade's stirrup-strap and was taken across the stream, but soon after was shot and killed. Hodgson, some days before the battle, had said that if he was dismounted in battle or wounded, he intended to take hold of somebody's stirrup to assist himself from the field. During the retreat Private Dalvern, Troop F, had a hand-to-hand conflict with an Indian; his horse was killed; he then shot the Indian, caught the Indian's pony, and rode to the command.

Reno's casualties thus far were three officers, including Dr. J.M. De Wolf, and twenty-nine enlisted men and scouts killed; seven enlisted men wounded; and one officer, one interpreter, and fourteen soldiers and scouts missing. nearly all the casualties occurred during the retreat and after leaving the timber. The Ree scouts continued their flight until they reached the supply camp at the mouth of the Powder, on the 27th. The Crow scouts remained with the command.

We will now go back to Benteen's battalion. Not long after leaving the waterhole a sergeant met him with an order from Custer to the commanding officer of the pack-train to hurry up. The sergeant was sent back to the train with the message; as he passed the column he said to the men, "We've got 'em boys." From this and other remarks we inferred that Custer had attacked and captured the village.

Shortly afterward we were met by a trumpeter bearing this message signed by Colonel Cook, Adjutant: "Benteen, come on. Big village. Be quick. Bring packs," with the postscipt, "Bring packs." The column had been marching at a trot and walk, according to whether the ground was smooth or broken. We now heard firing, first straggling shots, and as we advanced the engagement became more and more pronounced and appeared to be coming toward us. The column took the gallop with pistols drawn, expecting to meet the enemy which we thought Custer was driving before him in his effort to communicate with the pack-train, never suspecting that our force had been defeated. We were forming in line to meet our supposed enemy, when we came in full view of the valley of the Little Big Horn. The valley was full of horsemen riding to and fro in clouds of dust and smoke, for the grass had been fired by the Indians to drive the troops out and cover their own movements. On the bluffs to our right we saw a body of troops and that they were engaged. But an engagement appeared to be going on in the valley too. Owing to the distance, smoke, and dust, it was impossible to distinguish if those in the valley were friend or foes. There was a short time of uncertainty as to the direction in which we should go, but some Crow scouts came by, driving a small herd of ponies, one of whom said, "Soldiers," and motioned for the command to go to the right. Following his directions, we soon joined Reno's battalion, which was still firing. Reno had lost his hat and had a handkerchief tied about his head, and appeared to be very much excited.

Benteen's battalion was ordered to dismount and deploy as skirmishers on the edge of the bluffs overlooking the valley. Very soon after this the Indians withdrew from the attack. Lieutenant Hare came to where I was standing and, grasping my hand heartily, said with a good deal of emphasis: "We've had a big fight in the bottom, got whipped, and I am ... glad to see you." I was satisfied that he meant what he said, for I had already suspected that something was wrong, but was not quite prepared for such startling information. Benteen's battalion was ordered to divide its ammunition with Reno's men, who had apparently expended nearly all in their personal possession. It has often been a matter of doubt whether this was a fact, or the effect of imagination. It seems most improbable, in view of their active movements and the short time the command was firing, that the "most of the men" should have expended one hundred and fifty rounds of ammunition per man.

While waiting for the ammunition pack-mules, Major Reno concluded to make an effort to recover and bury the body of Lieutenant Hodgson. At the same time he loaded up a few men with canteens to get water for the command; they were to accompany the rescuing party. The effort was futile; the party was ordered back after being fired upon by some Indians who doubtless were scalping the dead near the foot of the bluffs.

A number of officers collected on the edge of the bluff overlooking the valley and were discussing the situation; among our number was Captain Moylan, a veteran soldier, and a good one too, watching intently the scene below. Moylan remarked, quite emphatically: "Gentle-men, in my opinion General Custer has made the biggest mistake of his life, by not taking the whole regiment in at once in the first attack." At this time there were a large number of horsemen, Indians, in the valley. Suddenly they all started down the valley, and in a few minutes scarcely a horseman was to be seen. Heavy firing was heard down the river. During this time the questions were being asked: "What's the matter with Custer, that he doesn't send word what we shall do?" "Wonder what we are staying here for?" etc., thus showing some uneasiness; but still no one seemed to show great anxiety, nor do I know that any one felt any serious apprehension but that Custer could and would take care of himself. Some of Reno's men had seen a part of Custer's command, including Custer himself, on the bluffs about the time the Indians began to develop in Reno's front. This party was heard to cheer, and seen to wave their hats as if to give encouragement, and then they disappeared behind the hills or escaped further attention from those below. It was about the time of this incident that Trumpeter Martini left with Custer's last orders to Benteen, viz: "Benteen, come on. Big village. Be quick. Bring packs. Cook, Adjutant. P.S. Bring Packs." The repetition in the order would seem to indicate that Cook was excited, flurried, or that he wanted to emphasize the necessity for escorting the packs. It is possible, yes probable, that from the high point Custer could then see nearly the whole camp and force of the Indians and realized that the chances were desperate; but it was too late to reunite his forces for the attack. Reno was already in the fight and his (Custer's) own battalion was separated from the attack by a distance of two and a half to three miles. He had no reason to think that Reno would not push his attack vigorously. A commander seldom goes into battle counting upon the failure of his lieutenant; if he did, he certainly would provide that such failure should not turn into disaster.

Captain Weir and Lieutenant Edgerly, after driving the Indians away from Reno's command, on their side, heard the firing, became impatient at the delay, and thought they would move down that way, if they should be permitted. Wier started to get his permission, but changed his mind and concluded to take a survey from the high bluffs first. Edgerly, seeing Wier going in the direction of the firing, supposed it was all right and started down the ravine with the troop. Weir, from the high point, saw the Indians in large numbers start for Edgerly, and signaled for him the change his direction, and Edgerly went over to the high point, where they remained, not seriously molested, until the remainder of the troops marched down there; the Indians were seen by them to ride about what afterward proved to be Custer's battlefield, shooting into the bodies of the dead men.

McDougall came up with the pack-train and reported the firing when he reported his arrival to Reno. I remember distinctly looking at my watch at twenty-minutes past four, and made a note of it in my memorandum-book, and although I have never satisfactorily been able to recall what particular incident happened at that time, it was some important event before we started down the river. It is my impression, however, that it was the arrival of the pack-train. It was about this time that thirteen men and a scout named Herendeen rejoined the command; they had been missing since Reno's flight from the bottom; several of them wounded. These men had lost their horses in the stampede from the bottom and had remained in the timber; when leaving the timber to rejoin, they were fired upon by five Indians, but they drove them away and were not again molested.

My recollection is that it was about half-past two when we joined Reno. About five o'clock the command moved down toward Custer's supposed whereabouts, intending to join him. The advance went as far as the high bluffs where the command was halted. Persons who have been on the plains and have seen stationary objects dancing before them, now in view, and now obscured, or a weed on top of a hill, projected against the sky, magnified to appear as a tree, will readily understand why our views would be unsatisfactory. We could see stationary groups of horsemen, and individual horsemen moving about; from their grouping and the manner in which they sat their horses we knew they were Indians. On the left of the valley a strange sight attracted our attention. Some one remarked that there had been a fire that scorched the leaves of the bushes, which caused the reddish-brown appearance, but his appearance was changeable; watching this intently for a short time with field-glasses, it was discovered that this strange sight was the immense pony-herds of the Indians.

Looking toward Custer's field, on a hill two miles away we saw a large assemblage. At first our command did not appear to attract their attention, although there was some commotion observed among those nearer to our position. We heard occasional shots, most of which seemed to be a great distance off, beyond the large groups on the hill. While watching this group the conclusion was arrived at that Custer had been repulsed, and the firing was the parting shots of the rearguard. The firing ceased, the groups dispersed, clouds of dust arose from all parts of the field, and the horsemen converged toward our position. The command was now dismounted to fight on foot. Weir's and French's troops were posted on the high bluffs and to the front of them; my own troop along the crest of the bluffs next to the river; the rest of the command moved to the rear, as I supposed to occupy other points in the vicinity, to make this our defensive position. Busying myself with posting my men, giving directions about the use of ammunition, etc. I was a little startled by the remark that the command was out of sight. At this time Weir's and French troops were being attacked. Orders were soon brought to me by Lieutenant Hare, Acting-Adjutant, to join the main command. I had gone some distance in the execution of this order when looking back, I saw French's troop come tearing over the bluffs, and soon after Weir's troop followed in hot haste. Edgerly was near the top of the bluff, trying to mount his frantic horse, and it did seem that he would not succeed, but he vaulted into his saddle and then joined the troop. The Indians almost immediately followed to the top of the bluff, and commenced firing into the retreating troops, killing one man, wounding others and several horses. They then started down the hill side in

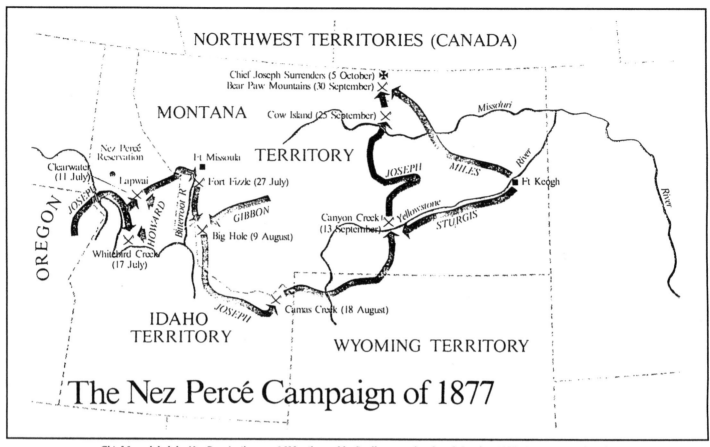

Chief Joseph led the Nez Percé tribe over 1600 miles and he finally surrendered on 5 October 1877. Courtesy of Ed Daily.

pursuit. I at once made up my mind that such a retreat and close pursuit would throw the whole command into confusion, and, perhaps, prove disastrous. I dismounted my men to fight on foot, deploying as rapidly as possible without waiting for the formation laid down in tactics. Lieutenant Hare expressed the intention of staying with me, "Adjutant or no Adjutant." The led horses were sent to the main command. Our fire in a short time compelled the Indians to halt and take cover, but before this was accomplished, a second order came for me to fall back as quickly as possible to the main command. Having checked the pursuit we began our retreat, slowly at first, but kept up our firing. After proceeding some distance the men began to group together, and to move a little faster and faster, and our fire slackened. This was pretty good evidence that they were getting demoralized. The Indians were being heavily reinforced, and began to come from their cover, but kept up a heavy fire. I halted the line, made the men take their intervals, and again drove the Indians to cover; then once more began the retreat. The firing of the Indians was very heavy; the bullets struck the ground all about us; but the "ping-ping" of the bullets overhead seemed to have a more terrifying influence than the "swish-thud" of the bullets that struck the ground immediately about us. When we got to the ridge in front of Reno's position I observed some Indians making all haste to get possession of a hill to the right. I could now see the rest of the command, and I knew that that hill would command Reno's position. Supposing that my troop was to occupy the line we were then on, I ordered Hare to take ten men and hold the hill, but, just as he was moving off, an order came

from Reno to get back as quickly as possible; so I recalled Hare and ordered the men to run to the lines. This movement was executed, strange to say without a single casualty.

Indians now took possession of all the surrounding high points, and opened a heavy fire. They had in the meantime sent a large force up the valley, and soon our position was entirely surrounded. It was now about seven o'clock.

Our position next to the river was protected by the rough, rugged steep bluffs which were cut up by irregular deep ravines. From the crest of these bluffs the ground gently declined away from the river. On the north there was a short ridge, the ground sloping gently to the front and rear. This ridge, during the first day, was occupied by five troops. Directly in rear of the ridge was a small hill; in the ravine on the south of this hill our hospital was established, and the horses and pack-mules were secured. Across this ravine one troop, Moylan's, was posted, the packs and dead animals being utilized for breastworks. The high hill on the south was occupied by Benteen's troop. Everybody now lay down and spread himself as thin as possible. After lying there a few minutes I was horrified to find myself wondering if a small sage-bush, about as thick as my finger, would turn a bullet, so I got up and walked along the line, cautioned the men not to waste their ammunition; ordered certain men who were good shots to do the firing, and others to keep them supplied with loaded guns.

The firing continued till nearly dark (between nine and ten o'clock), although after dusk but little attention was paid to the firing, as everybody moved about freely.

Of course everybody was wondering about

Custer — why he did not communicate by courier or signal. But the general opinion seemed to prevail that he had been defeated and driven down the river, where he would probably join General Terry, and with whom he would return to our relief. Quite frequently, too, the question, "What's the matter with Custer?" would evoke an impatient reply.

Indians are proverbial economists of fuel, but they did not stint themselves that night. The long twilight was prolonged by numerous bonfires, located throughout their village. The long shadows of the hills and the refracted light gave a supernatural aspect to the surrounding country, which may account for the illusions of those who imagined they could see columns of troops, etc. Although our dusky foes did not molest us with obtrusive attentions during the night, yet it must not be inferred that we were allowed to pass the night in perfect rest; or that they were endeavoring to soothe us into forgetfulness of their proximity, or trying to conceal their situation. They were a good deal happier than we were; nor did they strive to conceal their joy. Their camp was a veritable pandemonium. All night long they continued their frantic revels; beating tom-toms, dancing, whooping, yelling with demoniacal screams, and discharging firearms, we knew they were having a scalp-dance. In this connection the question has often been asked "if they did not have prisoners at the torture?" The Indians deny they took any prisoners. We did not discover any evidence of torture in their camps. It is true that we did find human heads severed from their bodies, but these probably had been paraded in their victory during that terrible night.

Our casualties had been comparatively few

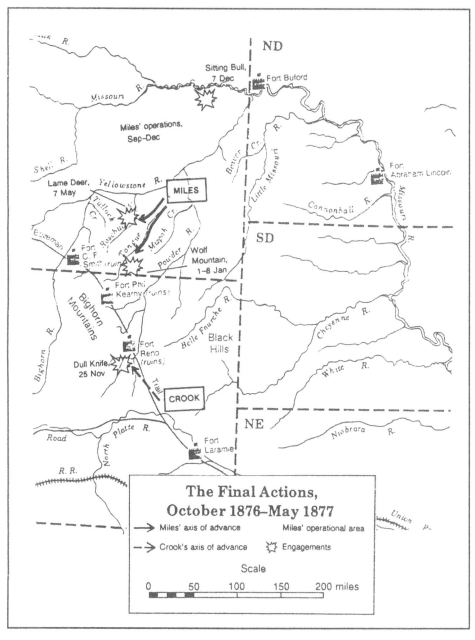

The Final Actions,
October 1876–May 1877

→ Miles' axis of advance   Miles' operational area

⤍ Crook's axis of advance   ✺ Engagements

Scale

0   50   100   150   200 miles

since taking position on the hill. The question of moving was discussed, but the conditions coupled to that proposition caused it to be indignantly rejected. Some of the scouts were sent out soon after dark to look for signs of Custer's command, but they returned after a short absence saying that the country was full of Sioux. Lieutenant Varnum volunteered to go out, but was either discouraged from the venture or forbidden to go out.

After dark the Troops were arranged a little differently. The horses were unsaddled, and the mules were relieved of their packs; all animals were secured to lariats stretched and picketed to the ground.

Soon after all firing had ceased the wildest confusion prevailed. Men imagined they could see a column of Troops over the hills or ridges, that they could hear the tramp of horses, the command of officers, or even the trumpet-calls. Stable-call was sounded by one of our trumpeters; shots were fired by some of our men, and familiar trumpet-calls were sounded by our trumpeter immediately after, to let the supposed marching column know that we were friends. Every favorable expression or opinion was received with credulity, and then ratified with a cheer. Somebody suggested that General Crook might be coming, so spoke one, a civilian packer, I think, mounted a horse, and galloping along the line yelled: "Don't be discouraged, boys, Crook is coming." But they gradually realized that the much-wished for reinforcements were but the phantasm of their imaginations, and settled down to their work of digging rifle pits. They worked in pairs, in threes and fours. The ground was hard and dry. There were only three or four spades and shovels in the whole command, axes, hatchets, knives, table-forks, tin cups, and halves of canteens were brought into use. However, everybody worked hard, and some were still digging when the enemy opened fire at early dawn, between half past two and three o'clock, so that all had some sort of shelter, except Benteen's men. The enemy's first salutations were rather feeble, and our side made scarcely any response; but as dawn advanced to daylight their lines were heavily reinforced, and both sides kept up a continuous fusillade. Of course it was their policy to draw our fire as much as possible to exhaust our ammunition. As they exposed their persons very little we forbade our men, except well known good shots, to fire without orders. The Indians amused themselves by standing erect, in full view for an instant, and then dropping down before a bullet could reach them, but of that they soon seemed to grow tired or found it too dangerous; then they resorted to the old ruse of raising a hat and blouse, or a blanket, on a stick to draw our fire, we soon understood their tactics. Occasionally they fired volleys at command. Their fire, however, was not very effective. Benteen's Troop suffered greater losses than any other, because their rear was exposed to long-range fire from the East.

Benteen came over to where Reno was lying, and asked for reinforcements to be sent to his line. Before he left his line, however, he ordered Gibson not to fall back under any circumstance, as this was the key of the position. Gibson's men had expended nearly all their ammunition, some men being reduced to as few

A .50 caliber Gatling gun. Drawing by Lisle Reedstrom.

as four or five cartridges. He was embarrassed, too, with quite a number of wounded men. Indeed, the situation here was most critical, for if the Indians had made a rush, a retreat was inevitable. Private McDermott volunteered to carry a message from Gibson to Benteen urging him to hasten the reinforcements. After considerable urging by Benteen, Reno finally ordered French to take M Troop over to the south side. On his way over, Benteen picked up some men with the horses. Just previous to his arrival an Indian had shot one of Gibson's men, then rushed up and touched the body with his "coup-stick," and started back to cover, but was killed. He was in such close proximity to the lines and so exposed to the fire that the other Indians could not carry his body away. This, I believe, was the only dead Indian left in our possession. This boldness determined Benteen to make a charge, and the Indians were driven nearly to the river. On their retreat they dragged several dead and wounded warriors away with them.

The firing almost ceased for a while, and then it recommenced with greater fury. From this fact, and their more active movements, it became more serious than a mere fusillade. Benteen came back to where Reno was, and said if something was not done pretty soon the Indians would run into our lines. Waiting a short time, and no action being taken on his suggestion, he said rather impatiently, "You've got to do something here pretty quick; this won't do, you must drive them back." Reno then directed us to get ready for a charge, and told Benteen to give the word. Benteen called out, "All ready now, men. Now's your time. Give them hell. Hip, hip, here were go!" and away we went with a hurrah, every man, but one who lay in his pit crying like a child. The Indians fired more rapidly than before from their whole line. Our men left the pits with their carbines loaded, and they began firing without orders soon after we started. A large body of Indians had assembled at the foot of one of the hills; intending probably to make a charge, as

Benteen had divined, but they broke as soon as our line had started. When we had advanced 75 or 100 yards, Reno called out, "Get back, men, get back," and back the whole line came. A most singular fact of this sortie was that not a man who advanced with the lines was hit; but directly after every one had gotten into the pits again; the one man who did not go out was shot in the head and killed instantly. The poor fellow had a premonition that he would be killed, and had so told one of his comrades.

Up to this time the command had been without water. The excitement and heat made our thirst almost maddening. The men were forbidden to use tobacco. They put pebbles in their mouths to excite their glands; some ate grass

roots, but did not find relief; some tried to eat hard bread, but after chewing it a while would blow it out of their mouths like so much flour; a few potatoes were given out and offered some relief. About 11 A.M. the firing was slack, and parties of volunteers were formed to get water under the protection of Benteen's lines. The parties worked their way down the ravines to within a few yards of the river. The men would get ready, make a rush to the river, fill the camp-kettles and return to fill the canteen. Some Indians stationed in the copse of woods, a short distance away, opened fire whenever a man exposed himself, which made this a particularly hazardous service. Several men were wounded, and the additional danger was then incurred of rescuing their

A few of the Indian survivors at Wounded Knee. Courtesy of the National Archives.

Personal items of an officer. Bible, ink bottle, mirror, folding knife, spoon, binoculars, folding cup, matches, reading glasses, plug of tobacco, tin match container, razor, 10 inch black hunting knife with bone handle, German imported playing cards. Courtesy of E. Lisle Reedstrom.

In this Indian beaded bag they found Custer's Stars and Bars swallow tail guidon. The pouch and guidon were taken from Indians at Slim Buttes. Courtesy of Brady Collection.

Crow King was a Sioux Hunkpapa. Courtesy of Brady Collection.

White Swan was one of Custer's scouts. Courtesy of Battlefield Museum.

Dull Knife was a Cheyenne and said "It was a good day to die." Courtesy of Brady Collection.

A Sioux and Cheyenne Village. Courtesy of Brady Collection.

wounded comrades. I think all these men were awarded with medals of honor. By about one o'clock the firing had ceased altogether.

Late in the afternoon we saw a few horsemen in the bottom apparently to observe us, and then fire was set to the grass in the valley. About 7 P.M. we saw emerge from behind this screen of smoke an immense mass crossing the plateau, going toward the Big Horn Mountains. A fervent "Thank God" that they had at last given up the contest was soon followed by grave doubts as to their motive for moving. Perhaps Custer had met Terry, and was coming to our relief. Perhaps they were short of ammunition, and were moving their village to a safe distance before making a final desperate effort to overwhelm us. Perhaps it was only a ruse to get us on the move, and then clean us out.

The stench from the dead men and horses was now exceedingly offensive, and it was decided to take up a new position nearer the river. The companies were assigned positions, and the men were put to work digging pits with the expectation of a renewal of the attack. Our loss on

the hill had been eighteen killed and fifty-two wounded.

During the night Lieutenant DeRudio, Private O'Neal, Mr. Girard, and an interpreter, and Jackson, a half-breed scout came to our line. They had been left in the bottom when Reno made his retreat.

In 1886, on the tenth anniversary, an effort was made to have a reunion of the survivors at the battlefield. Captain Benteen, Captains McDougall and Edgerly, Dr. Porter, Sergeant Hall, Trumpeter Penwell, and myself met there on the 25th of June. Through the kind efforts of the officers and of the ladies at Fort Custer our visit was made as pleasant as possible. Through the personal influence of Major McLaughlin, Indian Agent at Standing Rock Agency, Chief Gall was prevailed upon to accompany the part and describe Custer's part in the battle. We were unfortunate in not having an efficient and truthful interpreter on the field at the reunion. The statements I have used were, after our return to the agency, interpreted by Mrs. McLaughlin and Mr. Farribault, of the agency, both of whom are

perfectly trustworthy and are familiar with the Sioux language.

It has been previously noted that General Custer separated from Reno before the latter crossed the Little Big Horn under orders to charge the village. Custer's column bore to the right of the river (a sudden change of plan, probably), a ridge of high bluffs and the river separated the two commands and they could not see each other. On this ridge, however, Custer and staff were seen to wave their hats, and heard to cheer just as Reno was beginning the attack; but Custer's Troops were at that time a mile or more to his right. It was about this time that the trumpeter was sent back with Custer's last order to Benteen. From this place Custer could survey the valley for several miles above and for a short distance below Reno; yet he could only see a part of the village; he must, then, have felt confident that all the Indians were below him; hence, I presume, his message to Benteen. The view of the main body of the village was cut off by the highest points of the ridge, a short distance from him. Had he gone to this high point he would have understood the magnitude of the undertaking, and it is probable that his plan of battle would have been changed. We have no evidence that he did not go there. He could see, however, that the village was not breaking away toward the Big Horn Mountains. He must, then, have expected to find the women and children fleeing to the bluffs on the north, for in no other way do I account for his wide detour to the right. He must have counted upon Reno's success, and fully

Jack Red Cloud wearing silver peace medal which was given to his father Chief Red Cloud, by President Ulysses S. Grant in 1871. Photo was taken in 1909 by Warren K. Moorhead, at Pine Ridge Agency, South Dakota. Courtesy of R.S. Peabody Museum.

American Horse, Oglala Sioux Chief (1840-1908). He was a great warrior, orator and diplomat. Photo by David Barry, 1898. Courtesy of Denver Public Library, Western History Department.

Katie Roubideaux Blue Thunder at the age of 8, and she lived to be 101 years old. (1890-1991). She was the daughter of Louis Roubideaux, the official interpreter on the Rosebud Reservation in the late 1880s and at one time Captain of the Indian Police. Photo by John A. Anderson, 1898. Courtesy of the Nebraska State Historical Society.

expected the "scatteration" of the non-combatants with the pony herds. The probable attack upon the families and the capture of the herds were in that event counted upon to strike consternation in the hearts of the warriors, and were elements for success upon which General Custer fully counted in the event of a daylight attack.

When Reno's advance was checked, and his left began to fall back, Chief Gall started with some of his warriors to cut off Reno's retreat to the bluffs. On his way he was excitedly hailed by "Iron Cedar," one of the warriors, who was on the high point, to hurry to him, that more soldiers were coming. This was the first intimation the Indians had of Custer's column; up to the time of this incident they had supposed that all the Troops were in at Reno's attack. Custer had then crossed the valley of the dry creek, and was marching along and well up the slope of the bluff forming the second ridge back from the river, and nearly parallel to it. The command was marching rapidly in column of fours, and there was some confusion in the ranks, due probably to the unmanageableness of some excited horses.

The accepted theory for many years after the battle, and still persisted in by some writers, was that Custer's column had turned the high bluffs near the river, moved down the dry "Reno's" creek, and attempted to ford the river near the lowest point of these bluffs; that he was there met by an overpowering force and driven back; that he then divided his battalion, moved down the river with the view of attacking the village, but met with such resistance from the enemy posted along the river bank and ravines that he was compelled to fall back, fighting, to the position on the ridge. The numerous bodies found scattered between the river and the ridge were

Little Big Horn Battlefield Monument very near where Custer made his last stand. Photo by David Barry in 1881. Courtesy of Denver Public Library, Western History Department.

Fort Abraham Lincoln, Dakota Territory - officers living quarters of the 7th Cavalry Regiment. Courtesy of Battlefield Museum.

supposed to be the first victims of the fight. I am now satisfied that these were men who either survived those on the ridge or attempted to escape the battle.

Custer's route was as indicated on the map and his column was never nearer the river or village than his final position on the ridge. The wife of Spotted Bull Horn, when giving me her account of the battle, persisted in saying that Custer's column did not attempt to cross at the ford, and appealed to her husband, who supported her statement. On the battlefield in 1886, Chief Gall indicated Custer's route to me, and then it flashed upon me that I myself had seen Custer's trail. On June 28th, while we were burying the dead, I asked Major Reno's permission to go on the high ridge east or back of the field to look for tracks of shod horses to ascertain if some of the command might not have escaped. When I reached the ridge I saw this trail, and wondered what could have made it, but dismissed the thought that it had been made by Custer's column, because it did not accord with the theory with which we were then filled, that Custer had attempted to cross at the ford, and this trail was too far back, and showed no indication of leading toward the ford. Trumpeter Penwell was my orderly and accompanied me. It was a singular coincidence that in 1886 Penwell was stationed at Fort Custer, and was my orderly when visiting the battlefield. Penwell corroborated my recollection of the trail.

The ford theory arose from the fact that we found numerous tracks of shod horses, but they evidently had been made after the Indians had possessed themselves of the Cavalry horses, for they rode them after capturing them. No bodies of men or horses were found anywhere near the ford, and these facts were conclusive to my mind that Custer did not go to the ford with any body of men.

As soon as Gall had personally confirmed Iron Cedar's report he sent word to the warriors battling against Reno, and to the people in the village. The greatest consternation prevailed among the families, and orders were given for them to leave at once. Before they could do so the great body of warriors had left Reno, and hastened to attack Custer. This explains why Reno was not pushed when so much confusion at the river crossing gave the Indi-

ans every opportunity of annihilating his command. Not long after the Indians began to show a strong force in Custer's front, Custer turned his column to the left, and advanced in the direction of the village to near a place now marked as a spring, halted at the junction of the ravines just below it, and dismounted two Troops, Keogh's and Calhoun's to fight on foot. These two Troops advanced at double time to a knoll, now marked by Crittenden's monument. The other three Troops, mounted, followed them a short distance in the rear. The led horses remained where the Troops dismounted. When Keogh and Calhoun got to the knoll the other Troops marched rapidly to the right; Smith's Troop deployed as skirmishers, mounted, and took position on a ridge, which, on Smith's left, ended in Keogh's position (now marked by Crittenden's monument) and, on Smith's right, ended at the hill on which Custer took position with Yates and Tom Custer's Troops, now known as Custer's Hill, and marked by the monument erected to the command. Smith's skirmishers, holding their gray horses, remained in groups of fours.

The line occupied by Custer's battalion was the first considerable ridge back of the river, the nearest point being about half a mile from it. His front was extended about three-fourths of a mile. The whole village was in full view. A few hundred yards from his line was another but lower ridge, the further slope of which was not commanded by his line. It was here that the Indians under Crazy Horse from the lower part of the village, among whom were the Cheyennes, formed for the charge on Custer's Hill. All Indians had now left Reno. Gall collected his warriors, and moved up the ravine south of Keogh and Calhoun. As they were turning this flank they discovered the led horses without any other guard than the horse-holders. They opened fire upon the horse-holders and used the usual devices to stampede the horses—that is, yelling, waving blankets, etc.; in this way they succeeded very soon, and the horses were caught up by the women. In this disaster Keogh and Calhoun probably lost their reserve ammunition which was carried in the saddle-bags. Gall's warriors now moved up to the foot of the knoll held by Calhoun. A larger force dismounted and advanced up the slope

far enough to be able to see the soldiers when standing erect, but were protected when squatting or lying down. by jumping and firing quickly, they exposed themselves only for an instant, but drew the fire of the soldiers, causing a waste of ammunition. In the meantime Gall was massing his mounted warriors under the protection of the slope. When everything was in readiness, a signal from Gall the dismounted warriors rose, fired, and every Indian gave voice to the warwhoop; the mounted Indians put whip to their ponies, and the whole mass rushed upon and crushed Calhoun. The maddened mass of Indians was carried forward by its own momentum over Calhoun and Crittenden down into the depression where Keogh was, with over thirty men, and all was over on that part of the field.

In the meantime the same tactics were being pursued and executed around Custer's Hill. The warriors, under the leadership of Crow King, Crazy Horse, White Bull, "Hump," and others, moved up the ravine west of Custer's Hill, and concentrated under the shelter of the ridges on his right flank and back of his position. Gall's bloody work was finished before the annihilation of Custer was accomplished, and his victorious warriors hurried forward to the hot encounter then going on, and the frightful battle was completed.

Smith's men had disappeared from the ridge, but not without leaving enough dead bodies to mark their line. About twenty-eight bodies of men belonging to this Troop and other organizations were found in one ravine nearer the river. Many corpses were found scattered over the field between Custer's line of defense, the river, and in the direction of Reno's Hill. These, doubtless, were of men who had attempted to escape; some of them may have been sent as couriers by Custer. One of the first bodies I recognized and one of the nearest to the ford was that of Sergeant Butler of Tom Custer's Troop. Sergeant Butler was a soldier of many years' experience and of known courage. The indications were that he had sold his life dearly, for near and under him were found many empty cartridge shells.

All the Indian accounts that I know of agree that there was no organized close-quarters fighting, except on the two flanks; that the annihilation at Custer's Hill the battle was virtually over. It does not appear that the Indians made any advance to the attack from the direction of the river; they did have a defensive force along the river and in the ravines which destroyed those who left Custer's line.

There was a great deal of firing going on over the field after the battle by the young men and boys riding about and shooting into the dead bodies.

Tuesday morning, June 27th, we had the "reveille without the morning guns," enjoyed the pleasure of a square meal, and had our stock properly cared for. Our commanding officer seemed to think the Indians had some "trap" set for us, and required our men to hold themselves in readiness, to occupy the pits at a moment's notice. Nothing seemed determined except to stay where we were. Not an Indian was in sight, but a few ponies were seen grazing down in the valley.

About 9:30 A.M. a cloud of dust was observed several miles down the river. The assembly was sounded, the horses were placed in a protected situation, and camp-kettles and canteens were filled with water. An hour of suspense followed; but from the slow advance we concluded that they were our own Troops. "But whose command is it?" We looked in vain for a gray-horse Troop. It could not be Custer; it must then be Crook, for if it was Terry, Custer would be with him. Cheer after cheer was given for Crook. A white man, Harris, I think, soon came up with a note from General Terry, addressed to General Custer, dated June 26th, stating that two of our Crow scouts had given information that our column had been whipped and nearly all had been killed; that he did not believe their story, but was coming with medical assistance. The scout said that he could not get to our lines the night before, as the Indians were on the alert. Very soon after this Lieutenant Bradley, Seventh Infantry, came into our lines, and asked where I was. Greeting most cordially my old friend, I immediately asked, "Where is Custer?" He replied, "I don't know, but I suppose he was killed as we counted 197 dead bodies. I don't suppose any escaped." We were simply dumb-founded. This was the first intimation we had of his fate. It was hard to realize, it did seem impossible.

General Terry and staff, and officers of General Gibbon's column soon was greeted with prolonged, hearty cheers. The grave countenance of the General awed men to silence. The officers assembled to meet their guests. There was scarcely a dry eye; hardly a word was spoken, but quivering lips and hearty grasping of hands gave token of thankfulness for the relief and grief for the misfortune.

During the rest of that day we were busy collecting our effects and destroying property. The wounded were cared for and taken to the camp of our new friends of the Montana column. Among the wounded was saddler "Mike" Madden of my Troop, whom I promoted to be Sergeant on the field for gallantry. Madden was very fond of his grog. His long abstinence had given him a famous thirst. It was necessary to amputate his leg, which was done without administering any anesthetic; but after the amputation the Surgeon gave him a good stiff

drink of brandy. Madden eagerly gulped it down, and his eyes fairly danced as he smacked his lips and said, "M-ed, Doctor, cut off my other leg."

On the morning of the 28th, we left our entrenchments to bury the dead of Custer's command. The morning was bright, and from the high bluffs we had a clear view of Custer's battlefield. We saw a large number of objects that looked like white boulders scattered over the field. Glasses were brought into requisition, and its was announced that these objects were the dead bodies. Captain Weir exclaimed, "Oh, how white they look!"

All the bodies, except a few, were stripped of their clothing. According to my recollection nearly all were scalped and mutilated, but there was a notable exception, that of General Custer, whose face and expression were natural; he had been shot in the temple and in the left side. Many faces had a pained, almost terrified expression. It is said that "Rain-in-the-Face," a Sioux warrior, had gloried that he had cut out and eaten the heart and liver of one of the officers. Other bodies were mutilated in a disgusting manner. The bodies of Dr. Lord and Lieutenants Porter, Harrington, and Sturgis were never found, at least not recognized. The clothing of Porter and Sturgis was found in the village, and showed that they had been killed. We buried, according to my memoranda, 212 bodies. The killed of the entire command was 265, and of wounded we had 52.

The question has often been asked, "What was the cause of Custer's defeat?" I should say:

First: The overpowering numbers of the enemy and their unexpected cohesion.

Second: Reno's panic rout from the valley.

Third: The defective extraction of the empty cartridge shells from the carbines.

Of the first, I will say we had nothing conclusive on which to base calculations of the numbers—and to this day it seems almost incredible that such great numbers of Indians should have left the agencies, to combine against the Troop, without information relative thereto having been communicated to the commanders of Troops in the field, further than heretofore mentioned. The second has been mentioned incidentally. The Indians say if Reno's position in the valley had been held they would have been compelled to divide their strength for the different attacks, which would have caused confusion and apprehension, and prevented the concentration of every able-bodied warrior upon the battalion under Custer; that, at the time of discovery of Custer's advance to attack, the chiefs gave orders for the village to move, to break up; that, at the time of Reno's retreat, this order was being carried out, but as soon as Reno's retreat was assured the order was countermanded, and the women were compelled to return with the pony herds; that the order would not have been countermanded had Reno's forces remained fighting in the bottom. Custer's attack did not begin until after Reno had reached the bluffs.

Of the third we can only judge by our own experience. When cartridges were dirty and corroded the ejectors did not always extract the empty shells from the chambers, and the men were compelled to use knives to get them out.

When the shells were clean no great difficulty was experienced. To what extent this was a factor in causing the disaster we have no means of knowing.

A battle was unavoidable. Every man in Terry's and Custer's commands expected a battle; it was for that purpose, to punish the Indians, that the command was sent out, and with that determination Custer made his preparation. Had Custer continued his march southward—that is, left the Indian trail—the Indians would have known of our movements on the 25th, and a battle would have been fought very near the same field on which Crook had been attacked and forced back a week before; the Indians never would have remained in camp and allowed a concentration of the several columns to attack them. If they escaped without punishment or battle Custer would undoubtedly have been blamed.

E.S. Godfrey,
Captain, Seventh Cavalry

The author has attempted to research various documents on the Battle of the Little Big Horn and discovered some interesting statements in the book, "MY FRIEND THE INDIAN," which was published in April 1910. The author was James McLaughlin, a United States Indian Inspector, who had previously served as Agent to the Sioux at Devils Lake and Standing Rock Agencies. For over thirty-eight years he had the opportunity to share friendships with many of the prominent Indians who participated in that particular battle. Some of the Indians were: Gall; Crow King, Spotted Tail; and many others.

Also included herewith, are statements from Mrs. Spotted Horn Bull, a Hunkpapa Sioux woman who witnessed the battle from the Indian village. Strangely within the interview by McLaughlin, she completely ignored all questions as to the whereabouts of Sitting Bull during the battle. The missionaries held her in high esteem as to the accuracy and verity of the incident.

In her view of the tragedy, there were about ten thousand Indians, including women and children in the village, which was along the Greasy Grass by the Big Horn River. The total number of warriors was unknown. With the evidence of so many women and children, actually proves that the Indians were not inviting an attack nor "spoiling" for a fight. When the Indians left the agencies to join Sitting Bull, they took their families with them. They expected and desired to keep away from the soldiery.

She further commented that her people first saw the soldiers of Long Hair (Custer), at a long distance to the east. They were several miles away and on the little hills between the Greasy Grass and the Rosebud River. From the position of Long Hair and his soldiers, they could not see the large ravine around a small butte nor down to the banks of the river. Soon hundreds of warriors were in the river and running up into the ravine to hide and attack Long Hair from both sides as they marched down to the river and village. However, she had not seen the soldiers (Reno's) approaching with their surprise attack at her end of the village. Through the tepee poles of the Blackfeet, the bullets rattled from the soldiers carbine fire. The tepees were empty and the bullets were coming from a strip of timber on the west river bank of the Greasy Grass. The soldiers of the white chief (Reno) had been stopped and soon the young men of our people, forced the soldiers back across the river where they moved up into the hill (Reno Hill). And she said that the Indians lost 22 dead and many wounded, which no one knew the actual total wounded, because they were all carried away. (With the exception of one who fell in the hands of Benteen's men).

Chief Gall the principal Indian leader during the battle, was regarded as a close friend to Indian Inspector McLaughlin. He considered Gall to be one of the finest, strong in council and natural leader of men. Concerning the battle, Gall stated that he did not know how many warriors were present during the fighting. He further mentioned that the location of the village or camp, was not decided upon in advance. Because it had no military advantage!

Of noteworthy is the most interesting comment from Mrs. Spotted Horn Bull: "If the white chief (Reno) and his soldiers had not fired until all of them were ready to attack, and if they had rode their horses into the village of the Sioux, the power of the Dakota nation might have been broken, and our young men killed in the surprise, for they were watching Long Hair only and had no thought of an attack from anywhere else. But the Great Spirit was watching over his red children."

The following personal accounts of the Battle of the Little Big Horn were compiled by Colonel Henry Hall, for the Tepee Book, 1926, Sheridan, Wyoming, published on the fiftieth anniversary of the Battle of the Little Big Horn.

John Sivertsen, a member of Troop M, commanded by Captain Thomas E. French, which formed a part of Reno's detachment, gave the following account of the battle in which he took part:

"After we had forded the Little Big Horn, above the Indian village, Major Reno gave the command, 'Right front into line! Load Pistols! Gallop!' And away we went down the valley, the men shouting like Indians, 'Hi-Yah! Hi-Yah!' Reno yelled, 'That's right, boys!' We rode until we got pretty close to the Indian camp. By this time we saw Indians on every side, the bluffs on the left being crowded with them. The command was given, 'Dismount and fight on foot!' and we did so, forming in skirmish line, five feet apart. The Indians were shooting at us form all sides. Then we went into a clump of timber. I was the tallest man in the troop—they called me 'Big Fritz'—and I was Number One in the line. When we dismounted in the timber I gave my horse to Number Four, who held it with his own and two others.

"The fight in here was very hot and men were falling fast. We could not see the Indians, but they were signaling all the time to each other with their little bone whistles, and they seemed to be on all sides. Major Reno got alarmed about the horses and ordered a retreat, but Captain French changed the command to 'Fall back with faces to the enemy!' I could find neither my horse nor the horse holder when this order to fall back to the river was given, and so, with about twelve or fourteen others, I stayed in the woods. Lieutenant DeRudio was with us and took command. Firing was still going on all around us, and we could hear the shots and shouts in the pursuit of our comrades to the river and up the bluffs. We hid ourselves in the timber as best we might and succeeded in keeping out of sight of the Indians, but they kept on firing and were whistling all around us. Later, I can't tell you how long afterward, things got quieter, and Lieutenant DeRudio said we must try to get upon the bluffs to the command. So we crept down to the river.

"It looked rather deep, and as I was the tallest man there, I was ordered to cross first and show the way. Sergeant White, who was done out, asked me to take his gun, which I did, and waded the stream carrying two guns and two canteens. I got over all right and was the first to reach the other shore.

"A short distance up the hill I came across the body of an Indian. He was lying on his back with a carbine in one hand and a whip in the other. I felt his head and found that he had been scalped, so I suppose he was one of the Crow scouts that had joined us some days before, as none of our men had time to scalp a Sioux if they had killed one in their flight up the bluffs. The first man I met on top of the bluffs was Captain French. He was very much astonished an pleased. They had had a roll call when they got on the bluff, and all who were not present were marked dead or missing. He shook my hand and said, 'Fritz, I'm glad to see you, You were on the list of dead and here you are back to life again. You're wet from fording the river. Go to the sergeant and get a blanket and sit down by the camp fire.' So I found my troop, got a blanket and some good, partly dried my clothes, and got straightened out a little.

"The men knew nothing about Custer, but they had heard heavy fighting after reaching the bluffs. I was put on the firing line. With my butcher knife I dug a little hole behind a sage-brush and fought from there. The bush wasn't two feet high and I was the biggest man in the troop, but somehow that bush seemed to be a protection.

"We were attacked many times that night and the next afternoon, but we held them off and once charged and drove them down the bank with a hurrah. The second day about noon, perhaps, we saw a body of men coming up the river valley. At first we though it was more Indians, but as they came nearer we saw that they marched in order like soldiers, and soon the cry arose, 'It's Terry! It's Terry!' The few Indians that were still hanging around went off in a hurry, and in a little while General Terry and his command were up on the bluffs beside us. He came forward and Reno's regiment formed a circle around him and his staff and gave him three cheers. The gray-haired commander took off his hat and wept like a child.

"Well, of course, that ended the fighting there, and we were soon making friends with the relief party. And, one thing more: after we left the battlefield and went into camp, I say my horse out on the prairie and went and caught him. He was just as I had left him when I dismounted in the woods, the first day of the fight. My blouse was still strapped across the saddle and the saddle pockets were filled with ammunition. Evidently the Indians had not got hold of him. I tell you I was glad to see him."

James Wilber, also a member of Troop M who was with Reno and was partially paralyzed from a wound received on the second day of the battle, stated the following:

"When we left the woods to cross the Little Big Horn and reach the bluffs on the other side, I was lucky enough to get my horse. It was a wild rush for the river with the Indians on all sides, yelling like devils, shooting into our ranks, and even trying to drag men from their horses. One big Sioux rode along side of me as we went along at full gallop, and tried to pull me from the saddle. He had been shot in the shoulder, and every jerk he made at me the blood gushed from the wound and stained my shirt and trousers. He was a determined devil and hung on to me until we almost reached the river. Right at the Little Big Horn a trooper was shot down in front of me and Lieutenant Hodgson got his first wound. My horse stumbled over Hodgson and went over the bluff into the stream, but got to his feet again and carried me across and up the hill. Lieutenant Hodgson hung on to the stirrup of Bugler Myers and got over the river and part way up the hill, but received another wound there and was killed."

June 28th was devoted to burying the dead. Camp was moved 4 1/2 miles as progress was slow and tedious, the river was crossed and the command was mustered. The 29th was devoted to destroying the enormous amount of camp equipment and supplies left behind by the Indians, making litters for the wounded, and to scouting up the Little Big Horn. The march was resumed that night, with the wounded, and camp was made at the mouth of the Little big Horn at 2:30 a.m. on July 1st. Hand litters proved so unsatisfactory that mule litters were constructed for transporting the wounded. The regiment left the same day and marched 20 miles down the Big Horn; and on the 2nd reached and crossed the Yellowstone and camped on Pease Bottom. On July 3rd the steamboat "Far West," with Captain Stephen Baker's company of the Sixth Infantry as escort, and having on board the wounded and Colonel E.W. Smith, A.D.C., with dispatches, left down the river and on to the Missouri. Bismarck was reached at 11 p.m. on July 5th, a journey of over 700 miles in 54 hours which established a record never equaled again by packet boats on the Missouri River. At dawn the next day the families at Fort Lincoln were notified of the disaster at the Little Big Horn.

One lone survivor who had served under Custer's immediate command was found amid the havoc on the battlefield. This was "Comanche," Captain Keogh's horse. While the last rites for the victims were being performed on June 27th, a lone horse was observed by First Lieutenant Henry J. Nowlan. The horse had been wounded in seven places and was so weak and emaciated that it was at first though wise and humane to put him out of his misery; however, it was decided otherwise and he was slowly led with the column to the junction of the Little Horn and the Big Horn Rivers and put aboard the

L-R White Man Runs Him and Brig. Gen. E.S. Godfrey (Army retired) pose in 1926 at the battle site to propose a monument to the 7th Cavalry Regiment. When the monument was completed, many Indians participated in the ceremony and Godfrey emotionally moved, and had to wipe tears from his eyes. Courtesy of the National Archives.

steamer "Far West" with the other battle wounded. Captain Grant Marsh, of the "Far West," saw that Comanche lacked no attention, and a specially prepared stall, softly bedded with grass was made for him at the extreme stern of the vessel. Upon arrival at Fort Lincoln, Comanche was nursed back to health and placed on the retired list by regimental order. A special "belly band" sling was made upon which he was suspended for nearly a year. With the daily care of Veterinarian Stein, and of Blacksmith Gustave Koran and John Burkman (Old Nutriment) who were detailed on special duty as his personal attendants, Comanche was able by the spring of 1878 to move around without assistance. At the age of 30 Comanche died at Fort Riley, Kansas, where the regiment was then stationed. The horse's body was prepared by Professor L.L. Dyche, of the University of Kansas, and is now displayed in the Dyche Museum at the University of Kansas, Lawrence, Kansas.

Old Nutriment was the nickname applied to Burkman by General Custer. Burkman was for many years (since the Civil War days)

Custer's personal orderly, and on campaigns when food was scarce Old Nutriment always seemed able to find sufficient quantities for General Custer's table. He survived the encounter due to the fact that on June 25th, the General sent him back with his two additional mounts (Vic and Dancy) to stay with the pack train. Burkman died by his own hand at the age of 88. After his separation from the Army, he lived close to the battlefield and died only a few miles from the site. (From Keogh, Comanche and Custer, by E.S. Luce, 1939)

The regiment left Fort Lincoln on August 8th and marched 35 miles up the Rosebud, where a column under General Crook joined General Terry's command on August 10th. As no other command was known to be in the immediate vicinity, the dust raised by Crook's column was supposed to be caused by Indians moving to attack. Chief Trumpeter Hardy was sent down the column on a dead run to warn the command, and in a few moments the entire command was in a position to receive whatever was in store for them. The surprise, however, was a pleasant one

when it developed that the opposing force w[as] composed of friends. The combined forces [of] Generals Crook and Terry left the next day a[nd] marched to the Powder River, crossing it 40 mi[les] above its mouth, thence to the supply depot a[t] its junction with the Yellowstone River, arrivin[g] there on August 17th. On August 24th, Genera[l] Crook's command left the depot and marche[d] toward the Black hills, and at Slim Buttes ha[d a] severe fight with Indians.

General Terry's command crossed the Yellowstone River August 27th, marched in a northerly direction, and on August 31 was camped on Fox Creek, about 45 miles from Fort Buford. Between September 1st and 9th, the regiment scouted in the vicinity of the Yellowstone. On September 10th, the regiment started for the Missouri River and reached the stream opposite Wolf's Point September 13th. It crossed and left Wolf's Point on September 16th, arrived at Fort Buford on September 18th, Fort Berthold on the 22nd, Fort Stevenson on the 23rd, and Fort Lincoln at noon on September 26th. The Band and Troops A,C, D, E, F, and L occupied quarters, and Troops B, G, H, I, K, and M went into camp below the post in anticipation of a movement down the Missouri River to disarm and dismount the Indians at the Standing Rock and Cheyenne Agencies.

The regiment was increased to 1,244 men by the arrival of 503 recruits. More than 500 new horses were also received and assigned to the troops. With further field work soon to be undertaken, there was little time in which to reorganize the shattered troops, draw, issue and repair equipment and give the new men and horse enough training and drill to smooth the rough edges. The absence of 16 officers from the regiment,a and five inexperienced ones who had joined by transfer and assignment, made a very noticeable shortage of qualified officers. However, by steady application and long hours of training, the regiment was soon put in shape.

On October 17th, Headquarters and Troops B, E, F, H, I K, L and M with Companies A and H, Seventeenth Infantry; Company D, Twentieth Infantry; a section of Parrott guns; and 28 Indian scouts, under command of Colonel Sturgis, crossed the Missouri and went into camp. The command left on October 20th and marched down the left bank of that stream and arrived opposite the Standing Rock Agency on October 22nd. In the meantime, Major Reno with Troops A, C, D, and G, had left Fort Lincoln October 21st and marched to Fort Rice and thence the next day to Standing Rock Agency on the right bank of the river, the two forces arriving the same day. Upon accomplishing the required duty - disarming and dismounting the Indians - Reno's command arrived back at Fort Lincoln on November 3rd, having in charge about 900 ponies. Sturgis' command left the Standing Rock Agency on October 26th and arrived nearly opposite the Cheyenne Agency on October 30th. After disarming and dismounting the Indians here, arrangements were made for locating the regiment at its winter station. Troop F left this camp on November 4th with 1,000 ponies and arrived at Fort Abercrombie for station on November 14th after a 265 mile march. The rest of Sturgis' column began its return march on November 4th. Troops H and M were left at Fort Rice for station the same day. Troop C left Fort Lincoln on November 18th and arrived at Fort Totten for station on November 24th. A number of men were badly frozen on this march. The other six troops took station at Fort Lincoln.

Note from the author of this book: *For dramatic intensity, "Custer's Last Stand" can hardly be surpassed because of the complex and intriguing puzzle it created. For over a century the Little Bighorn had fueled controversy which has caused a prolific source of legend and myth. However, it also awarded Custer immortality.*

Questions central to a convincing explanation of the battle elicit no answers on which me can agree. Did Custer disobey orders? Did he commit tactical blunders? What circumstances motivated his decisions? Did he perish because of the failure of subordinates? How did he and his troopers meet death? Did he take his own life? He was the first to fall. He was the last to fall. Each new generation continues to study, ponder and debate these questions. Where history withholds answers, legend and myth flourish.

Actually no one knows when Custer fell. His remains, stripped of clothing, were not scalped of mutilated, but others were left undisturbed too. Neither of the two bullet holes in his body exhibited powder burns to support a suicide thesis. No "only survivors" story has withstood critical scrutiny. The Indians did not even know they were fighting Custer, much less could they identify the warrior who killed him.

George Armstrong Custer and the 7th Cavalry commands both universality and the appropriate symbolic association. The universality is valid, the legacy of a dramatic and controversial career capped by one of the grandest denouncements in American history. The associations are less valid, the legacy not a record or a conception of Indians that sets him apart from contemporaries, but rather of the mysterious interaction of history, legend, and myth in the natural consciousness.

1877

The regiment carried out the usual garrison routine during January, February, and March. Early in April, Troops A, D, H and M marched to Fort Lincoln from Fort Rice and went into camp preparatory to the 1877 campaign, the whole regiment being present except Troop C. From May until the end of the year different detachments of the regiment, seldom smaller than three troops, marched an aggregate of 6,887 miles, in pursuit of Indians. The different engagements and expeditions were so diversified that highlights are given in the following from individual Troop Record of Events.

Troop A — Remained in garrison at Fort Rice until April 21st, when it marched to Fort Lincoln preparatory to taking the field. In May the troop marched by way of Bismarck to Cedar Creek, thence to Sunday Creek and the Tongue River. July and August were spent in scouting the vicinity of Cedar and Sunday Creeks, and by the end of that period they were in camp near the mouth of the Tongue River. In September, the troop formed part of the command of Colonel Nelson A. Miles, Fifth Infantry, and participated in the attack, September 30th, on the Nez Perce camp on Snake Creek near the Bear Paw Mountains. The command charged the camp mounted. Five men were killed and one officer and eight men were wounded. From October 1st to 5th, the troops were constantly on the skirmish line around the Indian village. On October 5th, Chief Joseph surrendered and during the remainder of the year Troop A formed a part of the escort with Troops C, F, G, H, I, K, L, and M guarding the captured Indians on their way back to their reservation. Fort Lincoln was reached on December 30th.

During the latter part of this year, 2nd Lieutenant E.B. Fuller made one of the most daring and celebrated rides in the history of Indian warfare, carrying dispatches through the heart of Indian country and performing the duty in a conspicuously able manner.

The following letter, containing an official report of the action at Snake Creek, M.T., September 30th, 1877, is included here due to its accuracy and detail.

Camp J.G. Sturgis, D.T.
August 16th, 1878

Lieutenant E.A. Garlington,
Adjutant, Seventh Cavalry

Sir:
In compliance with letter of the Colonel, commanding the Regiment, of the 14th inst., directing me as senior surviving officer of that portion of the Seventh Cavalry which took part in the action at Bear Paw Mountain, M.T., September 30th, 1877, to submit a report of the operations of the companies of the Seventh Cavalry during the engagement, I have the honor to submit the following:
On the morning of September 30th, 1877,

the battalion of the Seventh Cavalry Company A, Captain Moylan; Company D, Captain Godfrey, and the 1st Lieutenant E.P. Eckerson; Company K, Captain Hale; and 2nd Lieutenant J.W. Biddle; all under command of Captain Owen Hale, Seventh Cavalry, and constituting a part of the force under command of Colonel N.A. Miles, Fifth Infantry, moved from its camp near the northeast end of Bear Paw Mountain, M.T., at 2:30 o'clock A.M. The column moved as follows: battalion of the Second Cavalry in advance, Seventh Cavalry center, Fifth Infantry in rear. The march was continued until about 8 o'clock A.M. as near as I can recollect, when the trail of the Nez Perces Indians was discovered pointing in a northerly direction; it was pronounced by the Cheyenne Indian scouts who accompanied the command, to be two days old. After a short halt on the trail the march was resumed in the same order as above mentioned. The command had marched about five or six miles from the point where the halt was made on the trail when information was received from the Cheyenne scouts that the Nez Perces' village was located on a creek about seven miles in front. The command was immediately given for the column to take the trot, and subsequently the gallop was taken up. About this time, an order was brought to me from captain Hale, Commanding battalion, that the Seventh Cavalry would, by order of Colonel Miles, charge the village, mounted with pistols. After passing over the divide which separated us from the Indian village, the battalion was formed in line about 1 1/2 miles from the village. Company K on the right, Company D in the center, Company A on the left. The line being formed, the battalion moved forward at the trot, then the gallop and the charge. During the movement to the front in line, Company

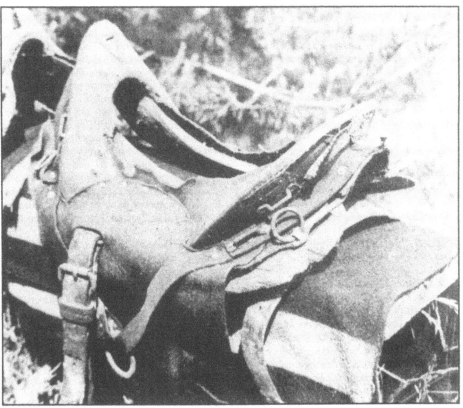

McClellen saddle. Oil and lamp black helped to prevent rawhide from cracking. Courtesy of E. Lisle Reedstrom.

K, under Captain Hale, diverged to the right and struck at the Indians almost at right angles to the direction which Companies A and D charged. Company K struck the Indians first and was repulsed with some loss. The Company retired to a distance of about 250 or 300 yards, dismounted and deployed as skirmishers. After repulsing Company K, the Indians turned their attention to the other two Companies (A and D), which charged in front. These two Companies charged up to within twenty yards of a line of Indians that was concealed behind a high bank which overlooked their village (the village being situated in a deep ravine through which Snake Creek ran), and owing to the fact that this bank was at the point charged by the companies almost perpendicular, they could not dislodge the Indians, neither could they charge through them owing to the nature of the ground. Taking in the situation at once and seeing the hopelessness of being able to do anything at this point mounted, I gave the order for the Companies to fall back; the movement was executed by "fours left about." In the execution of this movement some confusion occurred for the very good reason that the men were under a heavy fire from the Indians and that the large majority of them had never been under fire before, being mostly all recruits. The loss of the Companies in the action thus far was not so great as might have been expected for the reason that a heavy depression in the ground between them and the Indians protected them somewhat, the Indians over-shooting them. The movement was executed, however, and the Companies reformed on the right of the line occupied by the Fifth Infantry, some 200 or 300 yadrs to the rear. The loss thus far in Companies A and D was three men killed and four wounded. During the movement to the rear, Captain Godfrey, who was riding in rear of his Company and watching the Indians, had his horse killed under him. The fall of the horse was so sudden that Godfrey was thrown heavily to the ground, falling upon his shoulder and was partially stunned for a moment. Captain Godfrey would most certainly have lost his life at this time, as the Indians were advancing in his direction, but for the gallant conduct of Trumpeter Thomas Herwood, Company D, Seventh Cavalry, who, seeing Captain Godfrey's danger, separated himself from his Company and rode between where Captain Godfrey was lying and the Indians, thereby drawing the attention of the Indians to himself till Captain Godfrey was sufficiently recovered from the effects of his fall to get upon his feet and join his Company. In his gallant attempt to save his officer, Trumpeter Herwood was wounded through the body, and I believe, since discharged from the service on Surgeon's Certificate of Disability.

An order was at that time received from Colonel Miles to dismount the Companies and that they be deployed to the right and make connection with Company K, that Company being at this time severely handled by the Indians. The Indians, not being particularly engaged at any other point, concentrated most of their force upon it and succeeded in driving back it's skirmish line, also in driving the horse-holders who were dismounted, from their lead horses. Having thus far been successful in driving the men away from their horses, the Indians attempted

to lead into their village several of the horses of Company K, and were only prevented from accomplishing their purpose by the rapid advance of Companies A and D on foot at the double time. It was during this movement that Companies A and D suffered their heaviest loss. The Indians poured heavy cross fire into them as they advanced, killing and wounding a great many of the men. It was in this advance that Captain Godfrey was wounded, he having mounted another horse, was gallantly cheering on his men to the assistance of their comrades of Company K. Being mounted, he was a conspicuous mark for the Indians to shoot at.

It is but proper that I should here mention the gallantry and coolness of Captain Godfrey throughout the action up to the time of his being wounded and taken from the field. His conduct was brave, cool and soldierly throughout and added very materially to the success of the movement of the companies to the assistance of Captain Hale's company. The connection with Company K was made with considerable loss. Having established my line, I reported to Captain Hale for further instructions and was in the act of receiving orders from his when I was shot through the upper part of the right thigh and had to be taken from the field. Farther than this I have no personal knowledge of the part taken by the Companies of the Seventh Cavalry in action.

The conduct of officers and men up to the time of my being taken from the field was superb. I am unable to mention any particular men for individual acts of gallantry when all did so well, except in the case of 1st Sergeant Chas. R. Miller, Company A, Seventh Cavalry, who has already been recommended for Certificate of Merit, and Trumpeter Thomas Herwood, Company D, Seventh Cavalry, who, I believe, is now out of the service.

I am unable to give the loss the battalion sustained at the time I was wounded. From what I was able to observe of Captain Hale in the action, his conduct was such as might be expected of him - cool and gallant. When I reported to him after connecting my line with his, I found him in the skirmish line encouraging his men by words and acts. The line of all three companies of the Seventh Cavalry was at this time not more than 100 yards from the enemy. I would further state, that, to the best of my recollection, the whole time I was engaged in the action, from its opening to the time I was wounded, was not more than 45 minutes. I may be somewhat in error as to time and distance, but what I stated on these points is my best recollection of them.

Below is the loss sustained by the battalion in the action:

Company A, 5 men killed, 1 officer (Captain Moylan), 8 men wounded;

Company D, 4 men killed, 1 officer (Captain Godfrey), 11 men wounded;

Company K, 2 officers (Captain Hale, Lieutenant Biddle), and 9 men killed, 12 men wounded.

Making a total of 53 officers and men killed and wounded out of 115 officer and men engaged. All of which occurred during the first day's fight.

I am sir,

Very respectfully,
Your obedient servant,
(signed) M. Moylan,
Captain, Seventh Cavalry

Troop B - remained at Fort Lincoln until the regiment took the field in May. Until October it remained in the cantonment on the Tongue River engaged in the onerous duties of escort to wagon and supply trains. To prove that the troop was not idle it is shown by the records that during November and December the troop and its detachments traveled 715 miles.

Troop C - Remained in garrison until August when it proceeded to Fort Lincoln and scouted the country for miles around. It remained until December 9th detached from the rest of the regiment and did not see its post again until December 26th. The troop marched 1,575 miles from August 14th to December 26th.

Troop D - Performed the usual garrison duties at Fort Totten until the regiment took the field, and did its full share of the scouting until September when it took part in the fight against the Nez Perce Indians under Chief Joseph on September 30th. Captain Godfrey and 10 men were severely wounded in this fight. The Indians aimed for "shoulder straps and chevrons" and that their aim was true is evidenced by the casualty list. The remainder of the year was spent in getting the Indians back on their reservation.

Troop E — Performed garrison duty at Fort Lincoln until May, thence to the cantonment on the Tongue River on June 19th. The troop marched 415 miles during May and June. July and August were spent in hard scouting work in the vicinity of Cedar and Sunday Creeks and in the Yellowstone country, marching 843 miles during this period along. From September 30th to December 30th, the troop was constantly on the move, traveling 1,732 miles.

Troop I - Remained on garrison duty at Fort Lincoln until April 30th, and then marched to the camp on Cedar Creek, M.T., arriving May 29th. On June 5th the troop was ordered to the Little Big Horn battlefield to remove the remains of officers who were killed there, and did not rejoin the regiment until July 19th, having marched 564 miles. With Headquarters and Troops F, G, H, L and M, it marched to the Upper Yellowstone country to intercept hostile Nez Perce Indians having marched 645 miles. The troop returned to Fort Lincoln November 19th, but from December 6th to the 27th were again out guarding the stage route having marched 837 miles.

1878

The troops of the regiment did not all arrive at their winter stations until January 16th, when Troop F took station until January 16th, when Troop F took station at Fort Totten, D.T., on Devil's Lake. The remainder of the winter, and until a portion of summer had passed, was spent in garrison duty and in preparing for field service. This came as a result of orders directing a summer camp to be established at Bear Butte, about ten miles from where the town of Sturgis, South Dakota, is now located. This was on the route of Indian travel between the Nebraska Agencies and those on the Yellowstone and Upper Missouri Rivers. The authorities considered it necessary to have troops stationed along this route so as to readily intercept their travel. On July 4th, the Headquarters and Troops A, C, D, E, G, I, K and M left Fort Lincoln and marched to Bear Butte, arriving there July 18th, and established, the summer camp at the base and north of the Butte on Spring Creek. Troop B remained in garrison at Standing Rock Agency (Fort Yates), and Troop F at Fort Totten, and Troops H and L remained at Fort Lincoln until July 25th when, under Lieutenant Colonel Otis, with Major Tilford attached, were left in charge of the Cheyenne Indian prisoners of war en route to the Indian Territory. They arrive at Bear Butte (later Camp J.G. Sturgis), August 8th. The prisoners of war were turned over to the new escort, Troop K, and Troops H and L joined the regiment in camp. Troop K left with the prisoners August 11th and arrived at Sidney barracks, Nebraska, September 13th.

In the meantime the ordinary duties of observation in the field were performed by the troops at Bear Butte. Troops C and G, under Colonel Sturgis, scouted through the Spearfish, Red Water and False Bottom Valleys July 21st to 23rd; and Troops A and I, under Captain Moylan, scouted toward Slim Buttes July 21st to 24th. Troop E escorted Lieutenant General Sheridan, July 25th and 26th. On August 2nd, Troops D and M, under Captain T.H. French, left for Stanley's Crossing on the Little Missouri River at the mouth of Davis Creek, arriving there August 13th, as escort to a party of surveyors for the Northern Pacific railroad supposed to be at that point. A considerably portion of this march was through a section of country about which nothing was known. An alleged guide was employed at Deadwood, D.T., but his guesses were not nearly so much to be depended upon as was the judgment of Captain French, who was an exceptionally good plainsman. The two troops returned to camp August 23rd as the surveyors were not met at the designated point.

On August 29th, Troops E and M were transferred from Camp J.G. Sturgis to Camp Ruhlen for station, arriving there the same day. As no quarters or barracks could be built before winter, it became necessary to provide such shelter for officers and men as could be built with temporary material. By digging into the side of the hill, and the use of slabs from the saw mill, in connection with tents, the troops made themselves and their families fairly comfortable, although a Dakota winter under such conditions cannot be expected to afford much real enjoyment. The Construction Quartermaster, Colonel George Ruhlen (then 1st Lieutenant, Seventeenth Infantry), was soon on the ground with a number of mechanics and laborer, and did all he could to assist in preparation for the winter, but his principal efforts had to be devoted to sawing lumber and arranging for work on the new post - later Fort George Meade, South Dakota.

Troops H and I had left camp August 22nd, on a scout to French Creek, returning August 31st.

Troop B at Fort Yates was suddenly called for on August 27th, to overtake a party of Indians who had left Standing Rock Agency without authority. After an exciting and rapid chase the Indians were overtaken 12 miles west of old Fort Rice and brought back to the agency.

On September 26th, camp was moved about five miles, to the valley of Bear Butte Creek, two miles below Camp Ruhlen.

On September 27th Troops C and G, under command of Captain Jackson, left camp on a scout toward Slim Buttes; and on September 29th, Troops A and I left to scout the Fort Pierre stage road and the Cheyenne River Valley. Smaller parties were continually out scouting.

Troops C and G returned from their scout October 3rd; but Troops A and I were still absent on October 6th, when the camp at Bear Butte was broken up. Upon receipt of telegraphic orders, the remainder of the command (to which Troops E and M from Camp Ruhlen were added), under Major Tilford, started for the New Red Cloud Agency, then being established on White Clay Creek - later designated Pine Ridge Agency, South Dakota. Troops A and I returned from their scout October 7th and the next day started to overtake the regiment, which was accomplished on the 12th by hard marching.

This movement was made necessary by the fact that in September the Cheyenne Indians had left their reservation in the Indian Territory and had crossed Kansas evading all pursuers, and were apparently heading for the large Dakota agencies. A junction was to be prevented at all

Captain Grant Marsh, of the supply ship Far West, who played a very important part in the campaign of 1876, that culminated in the Battle of the Little Big Horn. Photo Courtesy of Ed Daily.

hazards, and the Seventh Cavalry was to reach this new agency as soon as possible and, in connection with other troops in the field, to frustrate the intentions of the Cheyennes and capture them if possible. The agency was reached October 15th, and the next day the command moved to old Camp Sheridan, Nebraska, as a better point from which to accomplish its mission.

The judicious distribution of all troops in the field showed the Cheyennes the futility of attempting to reach the Red Cloud Agency. They then divided into small parties and in that way endeavored to evade the troops and reach the agencies on the Upper Missouri River. An example of an Indian's ability to endure is the case of one party of Cheyennes which made three efforts to break through the line, each time reaching a point 60 miles north of the Union Pacific railroad, when they were compelled to return for water. One small band did escape by passing to the west of the Black Hills. When the Indians separated into smaller bands, the troops had to follow suit. The troops of the Seventh Cavalry were sent on scouts as follows:

Troops A and I, October 29th, toward Camp Robinson; Troop C, October 25th, along Ash Creek; Troops D and E, October 19th, to Wolf Creek three miles from the agency; Troop G,

October 26th along Ash Creek; Troop H, October 26th along Ash Creek; Troop K, October 27th, between Ash Creek and Niobrara River; Troop L, October 28th, to Niobrara River; Troop M, October 25th, to Niobrara River.

Another band of Indians was captured by a squadron of the Third Cavalry under Captain J.B. Johnson. While in the first camp after their surrender, the Indians had a change of heart, and positively refused to accompany Captain Johnson any further, and by burrowing in the ground they constructed a most skillful system of defense. Troops C and G, of the 7th Cavalry, with a piece of artillery, were sent to Captain Johnson's assistance, and participated in the second surrender which took place October 27th, when the Indians saw the effective preparations for immediate action. This ended the necessity for keeping the regiment in the field, and orders were soon given for it to assemble at Camp Ruhlen. Headquarters and Troops L and M left Camp Sheridan on November 5th and arrived at Camp Ruhlen November 10th. The next day Troops A, C, D, E, G, H, I, and K reached the same point. Leaving Troops E and M at their winter station, Camp Ruhlen, the command left on November 12th and arrived at Fort Lincoln on November 20th, where Troops A, C, D, G, I and L occupied winter quarters. On November 23rd, Troop D left for its winter station, Fort Yates, arriving there on November 25th. On November 22nd, Troop K left for Fort Totten, its winter station, arriving there on December 2nd.

1879

Nothing occurred during the year to very the ordinary garrison routine except one or two short scouts to investigate alleged Indian outbreaks, none of which proved of any great importance. On September 27th-28th, Troop C was on duty at Deadwood, D.T., fighting a prairie fire. Between February 23rd and 28th, Troop E with Troop M, scouted between the Belle Fourche and Cheyenne Rivers after hostile Indians. Between December 15th and 17th Troop E scouted to the mouth of White Wood Creek on the trail of stolen cattle. In June, Headquarters, Band, and Troops A, C, G, and H changed station to Fort Meade, D.T.

1880

From May until December troops of the regiment were engaged primarily in guarding construction parties on the Northern Pacific railroad.

Troop A - Scouted to the Little Missouri River June 7th to 28th, and performed the usual garrison duties at Fort Meade, D.T., during the remainder of the year. The following remarks on the muster rolls by the mustering officer were usually found: "Everything pertaining to this company is in admirable shape," or "This troop is the equal of the best I have seen in nearly forty years of cavalry service."

Troop B - Performed the usual garrison duties at Fort Yates until June 1st, when the Troop took to the field for the cantonment of the Little Missouri River. Numerous scouts were engaged in by small detachments under Lieutenants Gresham and Barry.

Troop C - Remained in garrison at Fort Meade without any occurrence of importance until August 14th when Lieutenant Sickel with 50 men took to the field and was absent for one month in the vicinity of the Belle Fourche and Little Missouri Rivers.

1881

The year proved uneventful except for numerous small scouts as described in the individual troop narratives. During the month of September, 171 men were discharged due to their expiration of term of service. These were men known as "The Custer Avengers," and had enlisted immediately following the Battle of the Little Big Horn.

On July 9th, Troop C with Troop M, left for Fort Pierre, D.T., for the purpose of protecting teams which were hauling government stores between Fort Meade and Fort Pierre. The troops returned on August 8th, having marched 355 miles.

Troop E - performed garrison duty at Fort Meade until June 18th, when it proceeded to a camp on the Little Missouri River and scouted the country in the neighborhood of the Belle Fourche River and through the Bad Lands, returning to Fort Meade on October 25th.

On January 2nd, while in camp near Fort Buford, Troop F participated in the capture of a band of Sioux and took the captives back to Fort Buford. Many men were badly frozen due to the extremely cold weather. During March, Lieutenant Robinson, with five men of Troop F marched to the Big Muddy River, M.T., and returned March 30th, having captured 13 Indians and 10 ponies. In April, Lieutenant Robinson and ten men of Troop F proceeded to the Popular River and brought in Crow Dog's band of 136 hostile Indians, which had surrendered. During August, September and October, Troop F guarded working parties of the Northern Pacific railroad and returned to Fort Buford on October 29th.

1882

Except for some changes of station noted in troop narratives, the year was spent in scouting and protecting the working parties on the Northern Pacific railroad.

Troops A and C remained at Fort Meade until April 27th, when they marched 412 miles to Fort Sisseton, D.T., arriving May 23rd. On August 5th, the return march of 422 miles was begun, and Fort Meade was reached August 29th.

Troop F - Remained in garrison at Fort Buford until July 1st, when the troop marched 335 miles to camp near Billings, M.T. The troop remained there as part of an escort to working parties of the Northern Pacific railroad until November 1st, and returned to Fort Buford on November 13th, where it performed the usual garrison duties for the remainder of the year.

Troop H - Remained in garrison at Fort Meade until May 16th, when the troop took to the field to protect working parties on the Northern Pacific railroad until September 24th, having marched 500 miles.

Troop I - Performed garrison duty at Fort Totten until August 22nd, when the troop marched 213 miles to Turtle Mountain, D.T., and returned on the 31st.

Troop K - Performed garrison duty at Fort Totten until October 14th, when the troop changed station to Fort Meade, D.T., arriving November 21st, having marched 431 miles.

Troop L - Remained in garrison at Fort Lincoln until June 24th. The troop then took to the field and scouted along the Cedar, Grand, and Little Missouri Rivers and the Bad Lands until October 18th. The troop arrived at Fort Buford and performed the usual garrison duties there the remainder of the year, having marched 1,1[?] miles during the entire year.

Troop M - Performed garrison duty at Fort Meade until June 3rd, when the troop took to the field as escort with the U.S. Geodetic Survey, returning to the post on October 8th, having marched 1,246 miles during the period.

1883

Except for several scouts by detachments to return wandering Indians to their reservations, there were no important occurrences in the regiment to vary the routine garrison duty.

The Records of Events for all troops show garrison duty at their respective stations during the entire year.

1884

Except for a scout in pursuit of road agents by Troop F, there were no important occurrences in the regiment to vary the routine garrison duty throughout the year.

The Records of Events for all troops show garrison duty at their respective stations during the entire year, except for Troop F which performed garrison duty at Fort Buford, D.T., until May 14th, when the troop took to the field in search of road agents who had attempted to rob Paymaster Whipple between Glendive, M.T., and Fort Buford, D.T. The troop remained out until May 23rd, having marched 275 miles. While acting as paymaster's escort, Sergeant Coonrad and Blacksmith Morrow were engaged in a fight with road agents about eight miles above Scott's Ranch, M.T., in which the Sergeant was killed. Sergeant Coonrad's conduct was most gallant, as he kept up a fire on the robbers after he was mortally wounded and as long as he had strength to raise his carbine.

1885

Except for numerous small scouts sent out to patrol the boundary line between the United States and the Northwest British Provinces in order to prevent arms and ammunition from crossing to the aid of the insurgents in those provinces, the year was spent quietly in garrison at the respective stations of the troops. On June 3rd, Troop G changed station, by rail, from Fort Leavenworth, Kansas, to Fort Keogh, M.T., arriving on June 9th. The Records of Events for all troops show usual garrison duties at stations indicated, except as follows:

Troop F - Performed garrison duty at Fort Buford, D.T., during the year, except for a 56 miles scout made by Captain Bell and a detachment of 35 men northwest of the post on May 1st, returning the same day. The detachment recovered a contractor's herd of beef cattle which had been run off by Cree Indians.

Troop G - Remained in garrison at Fort Leavenworth, Kansas, until June 3rd, when it proceeded by rail to Fort Keogh, M.T., for station. The troop arrived on June 9th, and performed garrison duties until November 22nd, when the troop left for Indian camps on the Tongue and Rosebud Rivers and returned to Fort Keogh on November 27th where it performed garrison duty for the remainder of the year.

Troop I - Performed garrison duties at Fort Totten, D.T., until April 1st, when Lieutenant Waterman and a detachment of ten men of the troop proceeded 94 1/2 miles to the Turtle Mountain, D.T. From then until July small parties were continuously scouting along the Northwest Boundary Line, traveling a total distance of 587 miles, and returning to Fort Totten on July 7th where the troop performed garrison duties for the remainder of the year.

1886

There were no unusual occurrences in the regiment during the year, until October. Troops A, B, D, E, G and H changed stations as indicated. All other troops performed garrison duty during the entire year.

Troop A - Performed garrison duty at Fort Meade, D.T., until October 19th, when the troop changed station by marching 221 miles to Fort Keogh, M.T., arriving on November 3rd.

Troop B — Performed garrison duty at Fort Yates, D.T., until October 5th, when the troop changed station by marching 211 miles to Fort Meade, D.T., arriving on October 17th.

Troop D - Performed garrison duty at Fort Yates, D.T., until October 18th, when the troop changed station by marching 200 miles to Fort Meade, D.T., arriving on October 27th.

Troop E - Performed garrison duty at Fort Meade, D.T., until October 5th, when the troop changed station by marching 204 miles to Fort Yates, D.T., arriving on October 15th.

Troop G - Performed garrison duty at Fort Keogh, M.T., until October 4th, when the troop changed station by marching 223 miles to Fort Meade, D.T., arriving on October 15th.

Troop H - Performed garrison duty at Fort Meade, D.T., until October 5th, when the troop changed station by marching 204 miles to Fort Yates, D.T., arriving on October 15th.

Troop L - Performed garrison duty at Fort Buford, D.T., until June 28th, when the troop scouted up the Yellowstone Valley in search of Poplar River Indians and returned on July 2nd having marched 140 miles.

1887

Except for numerous small scouts as indicated for each troop, there were no significant occurrences in the regiment during the year. During July, Headquarters, Band, and Troops C, D, G, and M, changed station from Fort Meade, D.T., to Fort Riley, Kansas; Troop F and L changed station from Fort Buford, D.T., to Fort Meade, D.T; and Troop I changed station from Fort Totten, D.T., to Fort Meade, D.T.

Troop A - Marched to the Cheyenne Indian Agency, arriving on October 31st, and then marched to the Crow Indian Agency, M.T., arriving on November 1st, where it participated in an engagement with the Crow Indians on November 5th. The troop scouted to a point on the Little Big Horn River about 20 miles from the Agency, and arrested the Crow Chief "Deaf Bull," returning to the Cheyenne Agency, arriving on November 14th and remained in camp

until the 25th and returned to Fort Keogh on November 28th.

Troop F - Scouted along the line of the St. Paul, Minnesota, and Manitoba R.R., relieving Troop L at Milk River, M.T., on June 29th. The troop remained in camp until July 22nd and then proceeded 120 miles by marching and by rail to Fort Buford, D.T., arriving on July 23rd and left Fort Buford, D.T., on August 7th and marched 316 miles to Fort Meade, D.T., for station, arriving on August 20th.

1888

During the year, the entire regiment was reunited at Fort Riley, Kansas, for a short time - Troops B, E, I and L arriving on July 12th, and Troops A, F, H and K of July 13th. On July 21st, Troops E, F, H and K left Fort Riley for Fort Sill, Indian Territory (I.T.), arriving on August 14th. On September 29th, Troops C, D, G, and M made a practice march to Topeka, Kansas, returning to Fort Riley on October 10th.

1889

The only event of note during the year was the participation of Headquarters and eleven troops of the regiment in the field maneuvers at Camp Schofield, I.T., during the period September 20th to October 11th.

1890

The year was uneventful until September when one squadron (Troops A, B, C, D, G and I) took a practice march to Lawrence, Kansas, and returned. Troops D and G participated in a Grand Army of the Republic (G.A.R.) reunion at Manhattan, Kansas, during the same month. Troops E and K change station from Fort Sill, I.T. to Fort Riley, Kansas during September. On September 9th, in compliance with General Orders No. 79, AGO, dated July 25th, 1890, Troops L and M were skeletonized, and the noncommissioned officers were attached, and the privates transferred to the other troops in the regiment.

the Battle of Wounded Knee occurred at the end of this year, marking the end of the Indian Wars, and the last major engagement in which the regiment participated against the Indians. It is believed appropriate, therefore, that a brief review of the events leading up to the battle should be inserted.

After the Battle of the Little Big Horn, Sitting Bull and a small band of Sioux escaped into Canada. After five years, the diminishing band was no longer able to endure the starvation, disease, and freezing in the Canadian wilds. Therefore, Sitting Bull led his small band of followers across the border in the summer of 1881, and surrendered to the United States Government at Fort Buford Montana. Sitting Bull and his band were then placed on the reservations near the South Dakota Bad Lands and at the Standing Rock Agency, near Fort Yates, North Dakota.

By 1890, all hopes of driving the whites from the sacred lands of the Sioux had vanished, and the Indians had turned their attention to a fanatical religion which took the form of a distinctive "ghost dance" in which a "messiah" was to appear, and rid the Indians' land of the white man. A new world was to return in which the ancestors of the Sioux were to live again among their descendants, and the buffalo were going to

return to provide a plentiful livelihood for the Indian. The white man's bullets could no longer harm the Indian, as the "messiah's" new medicine was to make the bullets harmless.

The Government became alarmed at the number of Indians who were participating in this new worship, and fearful that the Indians would be excited into a frenzy and take the warpath against the whites, ordered troops into the region in the fall of 1890.

Major McLaughlin, the agent of the Standing Rock Agency, advised against sending troops into the territory, as he thought this new craze would fail when the miracles which it was to produce did not materialize.

Sitting Bull was a prime leader in the "ghost dance" ritual. Hoping to gain some of his former power, he sold cheese cloth shirts which would "turn the white man's bullets." Upon rumor that he planned to leave the reservation taking a large number of warriors with him, Colonel Drum and Agent McLaughlin ordered his arrest. Forty Indian policemen, under command of a Lieutenant Bull Head, were ordered to arrest Sitting Bull, as it was believed that the Indians would be more effective in accomplishing this delicate mission than troops. On December 15th, the Indian contingent arrested Sitting Bull in his cabin without a struggle. However, a large crowd had gathered and began to taunt the old chief for giving up so easily. Seeing his prestige being strained, Sitting Bull suddenly began to scream for help, and Red Tomahawk, one of the Indian policemen, shot Sitting Bull in the head, killing him instantly. The agency Indians immediately opened fire on the Indian policemen killing a large number of them, including Lieutenant Bull Head and Red Tomahawk who had killed Sitting Bull. A detachment of the 8th Cavalry, under command of Captain Fetchet, were waiting nearby and dispersed the crazed Indians.

A number of young die-hard warriors escaped and joined Big Foot's band of Sioux who had broken away from the Pine Ridge Agency and were heading for the Dakota Bad Lands.

These disturbances then account for the following actions of the regiment which are reflected in the Records of Events for this period.

On November 24th, Headquarters, and Troops A, B, C, D, E, G, I, and K, left Fort Riley by rail, en route to the Pine Ridge Agency, S.D. The troops left the train at Rushville, Nebraska, November 26th, and marched to the Pine Ridge Agency, arriving there on November 27th. They remained in camp until December 27th, when Troops A, B, I and K, under command of Major S.M. Whitside, marched 18 miles and camped at the crossing of Wounded Knee Creek, S.D., on the same date. On December 28th, the troops marched 9 miles toward Porcupine Creek, S.D. It was here that Big Foot's band of Sioux Indians was captured. The troops returned with them to the camp on Wounded Knee Creek on the same date.

Headquarter, N.C.S. (non-commissioned staff), Troops C, D, E, and G of the Seventh Cavalry Regiment and four Hotchkiss guns of Battery E, 1st U.S. Artillery, under command of Colonel J.W. Forsythe, left camp on December 28th, marched 18 miles, and joined Major Whitside's command at the crossing on Wounded Knee Creek on the same date.

On December 29th, while disarming Big

Foot's band of Sioux Indians, a battle ensues in which the Indians were defeated with a loss to the regiment of one officer (Captain Wallace who had fought with Reno at the Little Big Horn), and 24 enlisted men killed, and two officers and 32 enlisted men wounded. The command returned to camp at the Pine Ridge Agnency the same date.

On December 30th, the entire command left camp and marched about eight miles below the Agency on White Clay Creek, S.D., and were engaged in a skirmish with hostile Sioux Indians during the day with a loss to the regiment of one enlisted man killed and one officer and six enlisted men wounded. The regiment returned to camp the same day.

The foregoing was taken from the Regimental Return for December 1890. It is regretted that a more detailed account of this engagement is not preserved in the records of the regiment. From statements from those who participated with the regiment, it is known that as the troops advanced with the intention of searching the warriors of Big Foot's band, a signal was given (from Yellow Bird, an old medicine man), and each warrior dropped his blanket which had been previously held up about his face, and opened fire. This was when most of the casualties occurred among the troops. After the first volley from the Indians, they dropped to the ground, hoping that the surrounding troops would fire into one another. The presence of many officers and soldiers of experience, however, prevented this and it was a matter of only a short time until the Indians were driven from their camp and took shelter in a nearby ravine. Many women and children were shot during the melee. Indeed,

many women took as active a part as the warriors themselves, and more than one casualty among the troops was the result of a woman's knife, tomahawk, or rifle. The Indians would not surrender, and treacherously fired upon every flag that was sent in. The affair, therefore, resulted in the practical extermination of the band, numbering some 106 men and the usual percentage of women and children. Note from the author of this book: To this very day, the Wounded Knee Affair continues to reflect a very serious controversy. To the Lakota Nation (Sioux), it is called the Wounded Knee Massacre.

1891

In January, Headquarters, and Troops A, B, C, D, E, G, I and K, left their camp at the Pine Ridge Agency, S.D., and marched to Rushville, Nebraska, entraining there for Fort Riley, Kansas. While en route, the section of the train carrying Troops C, D, E, and G was in a serious collision near Florena, Kansas, and Captains Ilsley and Godfrey were seriously injured, one enlisted man killed and fifteen injured. Captain Godfrey never fully recovered the use of his right leg. In February, Headquarters, and Troops B, D, E, G, I, and K, embarked by rail for St. Louis, Missouri, where they took part in the funeral ceremonies of General W.T. Sherman, U.S.A. During the remainder of the year, several small expeditions were made by different troops which are noted in the individual troop narratives. It is worthy of comment that the horse, "Comanche," the only survivor of the Custer command at the Battle of the Little Big Horn, died at Fort Riley, Kansas, on November

6th of colic. In July, Indians were enlisted in Troop L, under the provisions of General Orders No. 28, AGO, dated March 9th. Troop L, designated as an Indian Troop, was stationed at Fort Sill, Oklahoma Territory (O.T.).

Troops A and B - Performed garrison duty at Fort Riley, Kansas, until September 2nd, when they marched to Hope Kansas, to take part in a G.A.R. reunion and returned to Fort Riley on September 6th.

Troop C - Performed garrison duty at Fort Riley until August 14, when it proceeded to the Pottawatomie and Kickapoo Reservations in Kansas for the purpose of removing intruders, arriving on August 17th. The troop left the reservations for Fort Riley on September 17th, and arrived on September 20th, having marched 153 miles.

Troop F - Performed garrison duty at Fort Sill, O.T., until April 6th, when the troop marched 47 miles to Little Beaver Creek, O.T., for the purpose of making a survey for the proposed wood reservation, and returned to the post on April 23rd. The troop performed garrison duty until July 19th, when it marched to the Chickasaw Nation, I.T., marching 186 miles to different points and returned to the post on July 16th.

Troop H - Performed garrison duty at Fort Sill, O.T., until April 29th, when the troop marched to the Texas Cattle Trail Crossing on the North Fork of the Red River, returning to Fort Sill, May 12th, having marched 136 miles. It performed garrison duty at Fort Sill until September 6th, when the troop again marched to the Texas Cattle Trail Crossing on the North Fork of the Red River, and returned on September 13th, having marched 136 miles.

CHAPTER II
South and Beyond the Borders (1892-1917) Cuba, The Phillipines and Mexico

1892

The year was uneventful with all troops performing the usual garrison duties at their respective stations except for the following activities noted in the Record of Events for individual troops.

Troops B and K—Performed garrison duty at Fort Riley, Kansas, until October 8th, when the troops left by rail for Fort Sheridan, Illinois, arriving on October 9th at their new station. The troops participated in the opening ceremonies of the World's Columbian Exposition from October 17th to 22nd, and then performed garrison duty at Fort Sheridan for the remainder of the year.

Troops C, D, and G—Performed garrison duty at Fort Riley, Kansas, until December 24th, when they proceeded by rail to Fort McIntosh, Texas, arriving on December 27th. The troops remained in camp at Fort McIntosh until December 29th, then marched 69 miles to Carrizo, Texas, and established a permanent camp on December 31st. This camp was established in connection with the "Garcia" outbreak along the Mexican border.

Troop F—Performed garrison duty at Fort Sill, O.T., until April 2nd, when the troop marched 58 miles to Minco, O.T., and proceeded by rail to its new station at fort Myer, Virginia, arriving on April 7th, where troop performed garrison duty for the remainder of the year.

Troop H—Performed garrison duty at Fort Sill, O.T., until March 29th, when the troop left for a month's duty at the Cheyenne and Arapahoe Reservations, returning on April 23rd having marched 116 miles. The troop performed garrison duty until. October 8th, when it marched 28 miles to Rush Springs, I.T., thence by rail to its new station at Fort Riley, Kansas, arriving on October 11th.

Troop L—Performed duty at Fort Sill, O.T., until April 14th, when the troop marched 94 miles to the Cheyenne Reservation and performed duty in connection with the opening of the reservation, arriving back at the post on April 24th. The troop then performed garrison duty at Fort Sill for the remainder of the year. (Note—the Troop Record shows Private Burgess (Mo-ne–wer–to–qua) died on August 16th at Fort Sill, O.T., phthisis, pulmonolis, haemoptysis).

1893

The year was uneventful with all troops performing the usual garrison duties at their respective stations, except as noted. Troops C, D, and G remained on duty patrolling the Mexico border until July, when the changed station from their permanent camp at Carrizo, Texas, to Fort Hancock, Sam Houston, and Clark, Texas, respectively. Troops B and K—stationed at Fort Sheridan, Illinois—were busily engaged per-

forming escort duty for thedifferent dignitaries arriving to take part in the dedication ceremonies and to attend the World's Columbian Exposition. On April 29th, the troops proceeded by rail to Chicago, Illinois, where they acted as escort to the President of the United States (Grover Cleveland) and the Duke of Veragua at the opening of the World's Columbian Exposition, returning to the post on the same day.

Troop L—Performed garrison duty at Fort Sill, O.T., during the entire year/ (Note—The Troop Record shows Private Nas–cha–na–ni (Yellow Buffalo) died February 10th at Fort Sill, O.T., of pneumonia; and Private Wirt Davis (Nole–quo–quo–Curing Scalps) died October 5th at Fort Sill, O.T., of laryngal tuberculosis).

1894

The year passed with few events of interest except for the changes in station and the various duties noted in the following extracts from Record of Events for individual troops. Except as noted, all other troops performed garrison duty at their respective stations.

Troops B and K—Performed garrison duty at Fort Sheridan, Illinois, until July 3rd, when the troops proceeded by rail to Chicago, Illinois, to guard and protect public property form their violence of strikers and mobs. They returned to their post on July 21st and performed garrison duty until August 13th, when they marched 14 miles to Evanston, Illinois, and went into camp for field maneuvers, remaining until September 3rd, and returned to Fort Sheridan to perform garrison duty for the remainder of the year. On July 16th, while the troops were marching with several other organizations through Chicago, a caisson of Light Battery F, Second Artillery, exploded. Farrier Joseph Galler was instantly killed and Sergeants George Hoffman and Anthony A. Kane, and Trumpeter Herbert Antis were wounded. All were from troop B. Lieutenant Selah R.H. Tompkins (later Regimental Commander—See 7th Cavalry Organization) had a narrow escape from death when a fragment of shell barely missed his head and killed a man immediately behind him.

Troop F—Performed garrison duty at Fort Myer, Virginia, until August 10th, when the troop proceeded by rail to Gettysburg, Pennsylvania, and went into camp with the National Guard of Pennsylvania, returning to Fort Myer on August 19th where it performed garrison duty. On October 4th, the troop proceeded by rail to its new station at Fort Sam Houston, Texas, arriving on October 7th, where it performed garrison duty for the remainder of the year.

1895

During the year Headquarters and nine troops of the regiment changed their stations to New Mexico and the Arizona Territory.The troops at Fort Grant, Arizona Territory (A.T.) alternated in tours of one month's duty at the San Carlos Indian Agency, A.T. During the later part of the year many scouting expeditions were sent out after Indians who were terrorizing the adjacent country.

To indicate the necessity for moving the Seventh Cavalry Regiment to the southwest during this period, the following narrative and documents describing the raids from across the Mexi-

can border by Indians into Arizona over a period of years are included.

Since 1892 numerous raids had been made by a few Apaches, headed by on "Kid," resulting in the killing of people, stealing of livestock and property. Immediately after these depredations the Indians found their way into Mexican territory and their hiding place in the Sierra Madre mountains in Mexico. These exploits brought about an agreement between the Government of the United States and that of Mexico, in which it was stipulated that its duration should be for one year from the date of its promulgation. The provisions of this agreement, published in General Orders No. 85, A.G.O., December 22, 1892, expired on the 25th of November, 1893.

On February 23, 1893, the commanding General, Department of Arizona, telegraphed to the Adjutant General from Los Angeles, California, that on the 22nd at 6:45 P.M. Indians had reported that "Renegade Kid" had stolen a woman about four miles north of the sub–agency; that parties were started in pursuit, and that all posts would be notified as soon as the wire line, then broken, could be repaired.

On February 24th, 1893, the Commanding General, Department of Arizona, repeated the dispatch from the commanding Officer, San Carlos, A.T., in which is was stated that Lieutenant G.L. Byram, 1st Cavalry, reported that he had lost "Kid's" trail in the mountains between Rock Canyon and Ash Creek Canyon, 35 north of the subagency; made "Kid" drop the woman; and would scout north and east to cut the trail again.

On December 8th, 1893, the Govenor of Arizona addressed the Secretary of war, requesting that Lieutenant C.P. Johnson, 10th Cavalry, be specially detailed with power to take such action as might, in his judgement, be necessary for the purpose of running down the Indian known as "The Kid," and stated that this Indian with a small band of followers had continuously for the past three years kept the frontier settlers of Southeastern Arizona, Southwestern New Mexico, and northern Sonora and Chihuahua, Mexico, in a constant state of unrest, had killed many people and destroyed and stolen a large amount of property. He deemed this a most propitious time to start out on this work due to the abundance of grass, water, etc. In suggesting Lieutenant Johnson, it was understood that the officer consented and the citizens had requested him to do so, knowing that he was well acquainted with the region of country infested by "The Kid" and his band, and as he was one of the best Indian trailers ever engaged in the military service in that territory, and that he believed, therefore, that Lieutenant Johnson could and would run down the Indians.

This request was referred to the Commanding General, Department of the Colorado, who returned it, remarking as follows:

"No man can truthfully say that during the year 1893, nearly at its close, that outrage of any character has been committed at the hands of Apaches—by kid—or any other individual Apache, upon the white inhabitants within the borders of the Territory of Arizona. Commanding Officers, with the troops on duty there, are vigilant and on the lookout for Kid. He has no band or following. Kid is now in hiding sup-

posed to be in the northwestern corner of the White Mountain reservation.

We have on duty in Arizona many officers who are fully as competent and ambitious for this work as Lieutenant C.P. Johnson, 10th Cavalry. Lieutenant Johnson's services are not desired or deemed necessary for Indian service in the Department of Colorado."

The Major General Commanding the Army, in submitting the case to the Secretary of War, concurred in the views of the Department Commander and the Major General Commanding the Army, and they were communicated to the Govenor of Arizona in a War Department letter of January 4, 1894.

On May 13th, 1895, the Commanding General, Department of Colorado, telegraphed to the Lieutenant General Commanding Officer, Fort Grant, Arizona, in which it was reported that the signal sergeant at Wilcox had reported that several miners had come in from mines about 25 miles southwest of Wilcox and near Old Fort Bowie, and had reported that about 12 Indians were seen in that vicinity at that the miners were fired upon. Mr. Morgan, a merchant in Wilcox, vouched for the reliability of the miners. The commanding Officer, Fort Bayard, was ordered to send out a troop of cavalry to investigate, follow the trail and arrest the Indians if overtaken; and report the action.

The foregoing action of the Department Commander was approved by the Lieutenant General Commanding, and on May 16th, 1895, the Department Commander telegraphed the Adjutant General that Colonel Bacon, commanding at Fort Apache, reported that he would start part of his troops direct to Clifton, and part southwest in search of Indians supposed to be stealing horses; also that the Acting Indian Agent—Captain Myer—at San Carlos reported that from best information attainable he believed there were no Indians off his reservation. The same date Department Headquarters informed that the Adjutant General that the Acting Indian Agent at San Carlos has telegraphed that a Indian —from description, probably Massi—killed one Indian woman, wounded another and carried off a third, ten miles south from that agency. Police and troops were sent immediately in pursuit of the trail of the murderer which led directly south.

On May 18th, 1895, the Department Commander telegraphed the Adjutant General, repeating a dispatch from Captain Pitcher, 1st Cavalry, then at Lordsburg, New Mexico, stating that he had arrived at that point on the 17th, with his troop; went to Wilcox by train the previous night, and investigated the reported Indian trouble; that these Indians were seen near the southern end of the Dragoon mountains, and that they were probably in Mexico bythat time.

On May 17th, 1895, the Department Headquarters informed the Adjutant General that Lieutenant Rivers, 1st Cavalry, had reached Clifton on that date. He reported that he was unable to obtain any definite information about Indians, or of their having stolen horses.

The following messages ensued which directly involved the 7th Cavalry and necessitated the numerous scouting expeditions as described in the Individual Troop Records during the next three years.

Telegram
Department of Colorado
Denver, Colo., Dec. 6, 1895
Adjutant General of the Army
Washington, D.C.

Telegram just received 3p.m. from Commanding Officer, Apache, reports Indian killed in Cibicu yesterday by party of five armed white men. Left pack mule in hands of Indians by which expect to identify party. Lieut. Fenton with Troop G, Seventh Cavalry, sent to investigate.

F. WHEATON, Brig. Gen. Comdg.

Telegram
Department of Colorado
Denver, Colo., Dec. 6, 1895
Adjutant General of the Army
Washington, D.C.

Commanding Officer, Grant, reports: "Had a round–up at San Carlos yesterday and find six warriors absent from Nosey's band of white Mountain Apaches on Gila River. Bell is acting in the matter and will catch them if possible."

F. WHEATON, Brig. Gen. Comdg.

Telegram
Department of Colorado
Denver, Colo., Dec. 6, 1895
Adjutant General of the Army
Washington, D.C.

Commanding Officer, Fort Apache, telegraphs that old George who camps on Turkey Creek and was away hunting in direction of Solomonville, is suspected of killing Mr. Merrill and daughter. Officer, ten men and interpreter ordered to George's camp first, thence over the divide toward Solomonville by Gila Bonita. Have also sent out Indian police to ascertain if any strangers are on reservations. 2:45p.m.

Telegram
Department of Colorado
Denver, Colorado, Dec. 10, 1895
Adjutant General of the Army,
Washington D.C.

Commanding Officer, Apache, reports that Lieut. Fenton, commanding Troop G, Seventh Cavalry, found dead Indian, as reported, on Cubicu; secured pack–mule and murderers' outfit; found calf killed; belonged to Indian. Indians reported to be looting ranches cause of trouble. Authority of the President is requested to employ troops to assist in apprehending such Indians, when necessary.

THOS. WARD, Ass't Adj't Gen'l
In absence of Dept. Commander.

Telegram
Adjutant General's Office
Washington, December 13, 1895
Commanding General
Department of Colorado
Denver, Colorado

Major General Miles, commanding the Army, directs that, concerning outbreak and depredations by Indians from San Carlos and reports to public press, you be instructed that when outbreaks and hostilities of this character occur it will be considered of minor importance that the troops scout the country and investigate the crimes committed; that you will, therefore, give directions as to these movements and such instructions to troops that they will make it their chief and imperative duty to pursue, intercept, capture or destroy the Indians; that it is expected and ordered that the troops move for this purpose and continue in the field until it shall have been accomplished. He further directs that you have troops fully equipped for this service and report by telegraph as to what is required to equip each command , in addition to what it now has, with scouts, trailers, pack and wagon transportation, tents, camp equipage, and all necessary appliances; that you report action and all important information of events as they transpire.

RUGGLES,
Adjutant General

Telegram
Fort Grant, Ariz., Dec. 13, 1895
Adjutant General
Washington, D.C.

Your dispatch of this date received. Reports just received from Lieutenant Colonel Powell, commanding Fort Apache, indicate no immediate danger of serious trouble with White Mountain or San Carlos Apaches as the four white men against whom Indians at cibicu are especially incensed for the killing of an Apache on fifth instant have been turned over to the civil authorities at Globe, Arizona, by Lieutenant Fenton from that post to whom these men surrendered for protection. Colonel Sumner, commanding Fort Grant, ;has detachments out from this post on the trail of a small band of Indians supposed to be from south of the boundary, not more than six in number, who are believed to have been the murderers of the white man Merrill and his sixteen year old daughter, killed near Ash Springs on road between Solomonville and Duncan, Arizona, on the third instant. The moment it was learned that Indians supposed and believed to be Indians were deprecating and killing citizens, detachments from Fort Apache, Bayard, San Carlos and Grant wer ordered out for the purpose of pursuing, capturing and destroying the offenders.

Hope to be able to report this accomplished at an early date. As there are no indications of any general uprising among different Apache tribes, I anticipate no difficulty in speedily quieting the disturbed region with means at hand. Arrived here last evening and had no facts to report until I reached here from Fort Huachuca. I have not seen , but infer from your dispatch, that very much exaggerated reports of an Indian uprising have been published. This, of course, without my knowledge or approval.

F. WHEATON, Brig. General Comdg.

Telegram
Fort Bayard, N.M., Dec 18, 1895
Adjutant General, U.S.A.,
Washington, D.C.

Captain McCormick with his troop, I, Seventh Cavalry, from Fort Grant got on trail on the 11th inst. of the little party of Indians that had been pursued by Sheriff Wight and his posse shortly before in an exceptionally rough country west of Ash Springs. The troop kept up the pursuit with difficulty, mostly on foot in rocky mountains. I ordered a troop First Cavalry commanded by Captain Crane, 24th Infantry, on 12th instant to move from Clifton to near Duncan to co-operate with the Fort Grant force. Colonel Sumner joined them yesterday south of Solomonville and reported to me that hostile party were heading north. I at once directed Lieutenant Colonel Powell, 11th Infantry, commanding Fort Apache to move two detachments, 7th Cavalry, under Lieutenant Fenton, 7th Cavalry, and battalion 11th Infantry, south to intercept the Indians. The country is perhaps the most broken and the roughest anywhere, and a small party of not more than six Indians difficult to overtake. The troops have been indefatigable and have made earnest efforts to catch the Merrill murderers. They are ordered to destroy them when found. Grehsam's Troop A, 7th Cavalry, moved east from Fort Grant yesterday and will be in position today to aid the other troops in case this party of Indians should turn south and attempt to re-cross the border to Mexico. Am glad to report no truth whatever in published statements that three cowboys had been killed near Sampson's Ranch, Arizona. Within thirteen minutes after report reached Grant troops were making a forced march to that point, some ninety miles distant. On reaching ranch they learned the report was false, as is also published report that German family had been murdered by Indians thirty-five miles south of Bowie, Arizona. The German referred to denounced the report as utterly groundless.

F. WHEATON, Brigadier General

Telegram
Denver, Colorado, Dec. 20, 1895
Adjutant General of the Army
Washington, D.C.

Department Commander telegraphs from Deming, New Mexico: "Following dispatch just sent to Colonel Sumner at Solomonville, Arizona; `Continue the search for the murderers of the Merrill family as long as there is the least hope of destroying them; when this is hopeless patrol the region of country between Ash Springs, Sheldon and Solomonville, using one troop for this purpose, relieving it every month until further orders.' I have authorized Captain Crane to be withdrawn to Bayard on twenty-fifth."
THOMAS WARD, Ass't Adj't General

Telegram
Washington, D.C., December 21, 1895
Commanding General
Department of Colorado
Denver, colorado

Telegrams signed by Assistant Adjutant General, December 20th and 21st, have been received. The Major General Commanding the Army is perfectly well aware of the character of the country in which the depredations have been committed, and in which the Indians have been pursues. It must be fully understood that the troops will continue this pursuit until the Indians are found and either destroyed or captured. This pursuit will be continued indefinitely. If the

trails are lost, the troops will continue the hunt until they are found, again, and no cessation of effort will be admitted until the end is accomplished. Simply patrolling a district is neither giving proper protection to its settlements, nor punishing the hostile Indians who have committed crimes.
SAMUEL BRECK,
Assistant Adjutant General

Telegram
Denver, Colo, Dec. 21, 1895
Adjutant General of the Army
Washington, D.C.

Department Commander directs me to telegraph the following situation to–day twentieth as follows: Troop I, Seventh Cavalry, at Whitlock Cienega, Troop A, Seventh Cavalry at Ash Springs, Troop I, First Cavalry, commanded by Capt. Crane twenty–fourth Infantry at Eagle Pass on Gila River. On the sixteenth hostile Indians were surprised by the troops that had been following them since the eleventh. They abandoned their pony and took to the rocks regardless of trail, the troops followed on foot and their efforts to find the murderers though aided by guides and trailers have been unavailing. If the band of Indians was larger they might be caught. Country is so rough they probable will be able to elude their pursuers. I have ordered pursuit continued until hopeless. If not successful will have menaced locality patrolled by one troop of Cavalry from Fort Grant to be relieved monthly. I have been in constant personal telegraphic communication with post commanders whose troops are in the field and am confident that officers and men have made every possible effort.
THOMAS WARD, Assistant Adjt. General

The incidents described above are routinely described in the Record of Events of the troops concerned, as well as similar incidents which are contained in the Record of Events for the other troops of the regiment engaged in such scouting activities during the same period. It is interesting to note that such incidents were usually considered as a part of the "usual garrison duty" and seldom described in very much detail by the troop concerned. Other incidents are described as follows:

Troop A—Performed garrison duty at Fort Riley, Kansas, until May 17th when the troop proceeded by rail to Wilcox, a.T., then marched 28 miles to their new station at Fort Grant, A.T. arriving on May 23rd. During the remainder of the year the troop performed garrison duty at Fort Grant, except as follows:

Practice march to San Pedro Valley, A.T., June 26th to 28th, distance marched 152.7 miles

Tour of duty at San Carlos Indian Agency, A.T., September 3rd to October 7th, distance marched 348 Miles;

Left Fort Grant, December 16th and established a base at Solomonville, A.T., for operations against Indians, distance marched 42 miles; this duty was performed for the remainder of the year.

Troop B—Performed garrison duty at Fort Sheridan, Illinois, until May 29th, when the troop marched 78 miles to Chicago, Illinois, taking part in the funeral of Secretary of State, Walter Q. Gresham, and returned to the post on the fol-

lowing day. The troop performed garrison duty at Fort Sheridan until July 5th, when the troop marched 220 miles to Camp Douglas, Wisconsin, arriving on July 18th. The troop performed camp duty until August 26th, when it returned to Fort Sheridan by marching 220 miles.

Troop C—Performed the usual garrison duty at Fort Hancock, Texas, until October 5th, when the troop proceeded by rail for its new station at Fort Grant, A.T., arriving on October 6th. The troop marched 28 miles from Wilcox, A.T., and performed garrison duty at Fort Grant for the remainder of the year, except as follows:

Practice march to Hot Springs, A.T., December 1st to 3rd, distance marched 82 miles.

Tour of duty at San Carlos Indian Agency, A.T., December 6th, where troop remained until the end of the year; distance marched 174 miles.

Troop D—Performed garrison duty at Fort Sam Houston Texas, until April 16th, when the troop took a practice march to Kerrville, Texas, returning April 25th, having marched 150 miles. The troop performed garrison duty until October 5th when it left by rail for its new station at Fort Bayard, New Mexico, arriving on October 7th, and performed garrison duty for the remainder of the year, except for a detachment on a 200 mile scout for Indians December 4 to 14th.

Troop E—Performed garrison duty at Fort Riley, Kansas, until May 17th, when the troop proceeded by rail to Wilcox, A.T., then by marching 28 miles to its new station at Fort Grant, A.T., arriving on May 23rd. During the remainder of the year, the troop performed garrison duty at Fort Grant, except as follows:

Tour of duty at San Carlos Indian Agency, A.T., August 3rd to September 8th, distance marched 348 miles;

Practice march December 1st to 3rd to Wilcox, A.T., distance marched 66 miles;

Left Fort Grant December 23rd for a base of operations against Indians at Solomonville, A.T., where the troop remained until the end of the year; distance marched 42 miles.

Troop F—Performed garrison duty at Fort Sam, Houston, Texas, until April 16th when the troop took a practice march to Kerrville, Texas, and returned April 25th, having marched 150 miles. The troop performed garrison duty until October 5th, when it proceeded by rail to its new station at Fort Grant, A.T., arriving on October 8th, after marching 28 miles from Wilcox A.T. The troop performed garrison duty for the remainder of the year, except as follows:

Tour of duty at San Carlos Indian Agency, A.T., November 3rd to December 11th, distance marched 348 miles.

Troop G—Performed garrison duty at Fort Clark, Texas, until May 18th, when the troop took a practice march of 151 miles, returning on May 28th and performed garrison duty until October 5th. The troop then proceeded by rail to its new station at Fort Apache, A.T., arriving on October 12th, having marched 100 miles. The troop performed garrison duty at Fort Apache during theremainder of the year except as follows:

Scouts for Indians by detachments December 6th to 13th, distance marched 250 miles;

December 6th to 15th, distance marched 300 miles;]

December 17th to 26th, distance marched 300 miles;

Troop H—Performed garrison duty at Fort Riley, Kansas, until May 17th, when the troop proceeded by rail to Wilcox, A.T., then by marching 28 miles to its new station at Fort Grant A.T., arriving on May 23rd. During the remainder of the year the troop performed garrison duty at Fort Grant except as follows:

Tour of duty at San Carlos Indian Agency, A.T., July 3rd to August 8th, distance marched 348 miles;

Practice march to Fort Huachuca, A.T., and return october 15th to 28th, distance marched 333 miles;

Practice march December 1st to 3rd, distance marched 84 miles.

Troop I—Performed garrison duty at Fort Riley, Kansas, until May 17th, when the troop proceeded by rail to Wilcox, A.T., then by marching 28 miles to its new station at Fort Grant, A.T., arriving on May 23rd. During the remainder of the year the troop performed garrison duty at Fort Grant, except as follows:]

Tours of duty at San Carlos Indian Agency,A.T., June 3rd to Jul;y 9th and October 3rd to November 7th, distance marched 696 miles;

Left Fort Grant December 4th for a base of operation against the Indians at Solomonville, A.T., where the troop remained until the end of the year. Distance marched 42 miles.

Troop K—Performed garrison duty at Fort Sheridan, Illinois, until May 29th, when the troop marched 78 miles to Chicago, Illinois, taking part in the funeral of Secretary of State, Walter Q. Gresham, and returned to post the following day. The troop performed garrison duty at Fort Sheridan until July 5th when it left for Camp Douglas, Wisconsin, arriving on July 18th, having marched 220 miles. The troop performed camp duty and returned to Fort Sheridan on August 26th, again marching 220 miles on the return.

Troop L—Performed garrison duty at Fort Sill, O.T., during the entire year.

Troop M—Remained a skeleton troop with station at Fort Grant, A.T., since May 23rd.

1896

During this period the entire regiment, except Troop I stationed at Fort Sill, O.T., continued to engage in small expeditions against the Indians in the southwest and along the Mexican border. The most notable among these Indians were "Massai" and the "Apache Kid," both Chiricahua Apaches who conducted raids against the ranches on the United States side of the border, killing the ranchers and their families and stealing their livestock. The troops were hampered in their efforts to these Indians since they could not pursue them across the border into Mexico. In order to alleviate this situation, General Miles, Commanding the Army, sent the following request to the Secretary of War:

HEADQUARTERS OF THE ARMY
Washington, D.C.
April 14, 1896

Respectfully submitted to the Honorable the Secretary of War, to assist in guarding, as far as possible, against the practice of using the international boundary line as a means of protection

for raiding parties, it is recommended that arrangements be made with the Government of Mexico to furnish to our officers along the border, through its officers nearest the boundary line, such information as they may obtain of impending raids from that territory, or escape of raiders from it to our side—we on our side in return undertaking to do the same thing for them—this information to be used in capturing the marauders. It is believed a cooperation of the officials of the two nations along the border in this way will be a great aid in protecting those who live in the section of country involved.

NELSON A. MILES,
Major General Commanding.

As a result of this request, the agreement of 1892 was renewed between the Governments of the United States and Mexico as shown below. This agreement permitted our troops to cross the border into Mexico when in close pursuit of Indians. When such crossing were to be make, however, it was necessary to notify the Mexican authorities in advance whenever possible. This frequently caused some delay and permitted the Indians to escape before authority was received by our troops to continue the pursuit.

GENERAL ORDERS}
No. 85}
HEADQUARTERS OF THE ARMY
Adjutant General's Office,
Washington, December 22, 1892

By direction of the Secretary of War the following is published for the information of all concerned:

The agreement entered into by the Government of the United States of America and of the United Mexican States, as published in General Orders, No. 71, July 2, 1890, Headquarters of the Army, is renewed under the following terms:

The undersigned, duly authorized thereto by their respective Governments,

In view of the wish of the Government of the United States of America, manifested by its Honorable Secretary of State, under date of the 17th of the current month, through its Legation, to the Secretary of Foreign Affairs of Mexico, for a renewal of the agreement signed at Washington on the 25th of June, 1890, to allow federal troops of each of the two countries to cross over to the territory of the other in pursuit of savage hostile Indians, such renewal having become necessary by reason of the raids which, according to advices from the War Department of the United States, are being committed by some Apaches headed by the Indian called "KID" along the dividing line between Arizona and New Mexico, it being feared that they seek to evade pursuit made by troops of the United States, by crossing the frontier of Mexico.

And, considering that the understanding between the two interested Governments to avoid the continuation of the evils consequent upon the uprising of the said Indians is urgent.

They have agreed, in name and representation of their respective Governments, to renew the aforesaid agreement of June 25, 1890, of which a printed copy in English and Spanish is hereto attached, to the end that its effects may

prevail for all such time as said uprising may exist for their pursuit by an armed force, provided that, in no case, may the duration of the agreement thus hereby renewed, be extended beyond one year from this date.

Done in two copies, signed and sealed in the city of Mexico, this twenty–fifth day of November, the year one thousand, eight hundred and ninety–two.

(SEAL) C.A.DOUGHERTY
(SEAL) IGNO MARISCAL

BY COMMAND OF
MAJOR GENERAL SCHOFIELD:
R. WILLIAMS,
Adjutant General.

OFFICIAL:
Assistant Adjutant General.

AGREEMENT
Between James G. Blaine, Secretary of State of the United States of America, and Matias Romero, Envoy Extraordinary and Minister Plenipotentiary of the United Mexican States.

Signed at Washington, June 25, 1890.

Agreement entered into in behalf of their respective Governments, by James G. Blaine, Secretary of State of the United States of America, and Matias Romero, Envoy Extraordinary and Minister Plenipotentiary of the United Mexican States, providing for the reciprocal crossing of the international boundary line by the troops of their respective governments, in pursuit of Indians, under the conditions hereinafter stated.

ARTICLE I.

It is agreed that the regular federal troops of the two Republics may reciprocally cross the boundary line of the two countries when they are in close pursuit of a band of Indians, upon the conditions stated in the following articles:

ARTICLE II.

It is understood for the purpose of this agreement, that no Indian scouts of the Government of the United States of America shall be allowed to cross the boundary line, unless they go as guides and trailers, unarmed, and not exceeding in any case, two scouts for each Company or each separate command.

ARTICLE III.

The reciprocal crossing agreed upon in Article 1, shall only occur in the unpopulated or desert parts of said boundary line. For the purpose of this agreement the unpopulated or desert parts are defined to be all those points which are at least ten kilometers distant from any encampment or town of either country.

ARTICLE IV.

No crossing of troops of either country shall take place from Capital Leal, a town on the Mexican side of the Rio Bravo, eighty–four kilometers (52 English miles) above Piedras Negras, to the mouth of the Rio Grande.

ARTICLE V.

The Commander of the troops which cross the frontier in pursuit of Indians, shall, at the time of crossing, or before if possible, give notice of his march to the nearest military com-

mander, or civil authority, of the country whose territory he enters.

ARTICLE VI.

The pursuing force shall retire to its own territory as soon as it shall have fought the band of which it is in pursuit, or have lost its trail. In no case shall the forces of the two countries, respectively, establish themselves or remain in the foreign territory, for any time longer than is necessary to make the pursuit of the band whose trail they follow.

ARTICLE VII.

The abuses which may be committed by the forces which cross into the territory of the other nation, shall be punished by the government to which the forces belong, according to the gravity of the offense and in conformity with its laws, as if the abuses had been committed in its own territory, the said government being further under obligation to withdraw the guilty parties from the frontier.

ARTICLE VIII.

In the case of offenses which may be committed by the inhabitants of the one country against the foreign forces which may be within its limits, the government of said country shall only be responsible to the government of the other for denial of justice in the punishment of the guilty.

ARTICLE IX.

This being a provisional agreement it shall remain in force until both governments negotiate a definite one, and may be terminated by either government upon four months notice to the other to that effect; but in no case shall this agreement remain in force for more than one year from this date.

ARTICLE X.

The Senate of the United Mexican States, having authorized the President to conclude the present agreement, it shall have its effect from this date.

In testimony whereof we have interchangeably signed this agreement this 25th day of June, 1890.

JAMES G. BLAINE. (L.S.)
M. ROMERO. (L.S.)

The following messages and extracts of correspondence indicate the regiment's activity along the border in pursuit of the Indians as a result of this renewed agreement. As is often the case, the more minor an operation, the greater the direction from higher headquarters. This was particularly true in the pursuit off these Indians. The frequent harassment and interference in an otherwise routine operation by each higher echelon of command was of little assistance in capturing the Indians. Additionally, the information frequently reported to the troops by the excited citizens was more often based on rumor than fact, and caused many extra miles of hard riding without results.

Telegram
Headquarters Department
of the Colorado,
Denver, Colo.,June 8,1896
Colonel E.V.Sumner, 7th Cavalry,
Bisbee, Arizona.

Two–forty–five p.m. Your dispatch five–ten

p.m. seventy received ten o'clock Monday morning. You acknowledge receipt of only one telegram of June sixth. Four were sent you at one–fifteen, eight–fifteen, eight–thirty and ten o'clock p.m., the last gave the International Agreement....

Department Commander renews his repeated oral instruction that in all these operations you use no larger bodies than necessary, but divide the cavalry troops into small detachments, so as to cover a large area, as Indians are not likely to be found in large parties.

Avoid marching by daylight when equally practicable at night, so that approach of columns may not be betrayed by dust to Indians occupying high points of observation.

See Army Regulations four–fifty–seven, four–fifty–eight, four–fifty–nine. General Wheaton directs that every officer commanding a detachment keep a daily diary and itinerary of his march, make simple sketches of his routes, noting all points of valuable information, turn them over to these headquarters at frequent intervals showing the regions traversed.

Should you find it necessary to change your field depot General Wheaton desires you to promptly notify these headquarters so that Department staff may be fully prepared to fill requisitions.

Report by telegraph when you leave Bisbee. Mail from there report of your immediate plans for the future.

Acknowledge receipt of these instructions as well as of the other three telegrams sent you June sixth.

WM. J. VOLKMAR,
Assistant Adjutant General.

Telegram
Headquarters Department of the Colorado,
Denver, Colorado, June 9, 1896.
Colonel E.V. Sumner,
7th Cavalry,
Bisbee, Arizona.

Eleven a.m. General Wheaton has no further instructions for you this morning other than to notice carefully how very strict are the limitations of the International Agreement and to caution all your officers accordingly. He wishes you all success in operations of your command. Telegraph when you leave Bisbee and your destination.

VOLKMAR,
Assistant Adjutant General

Letter
Headquarters Department of the Colorado,
Denver, Colo., June 15, 1896.
Colonel E.V. Sumner,
Seventh U.S. Cavalry,
San Bernardino, Arizona.

Sir:

Your personal letters of May 27th (Fort Grant) and of June 13th (Bisbee), addressed to me by name, and your official letter of June 6th (San Bernardino) to the Adjutant General of the Department, have all been received and attentively read by General Wheaton....

Referring to your personal letter dated Bisbee, June 9th, the Commanding General directs me to say that neither he nor you have any latitude in the matter of the conditions of the International Agreement for crossing the border. That instrument is based upon negotiations between the highest authorities of the two Governments, and if violated in the slightest particular by any officer, whomsoever,—no matter what his individual views,—he places himself and his Government in grave peril of a misunderstanding perhaps not easy to satisfactorily explain.

...In reporting any engagements that may occur, you will also please definitely state the locality with reference to some well–known point, the War Department having just called for specific report upon the places of the recent fights of the detachments commanded by Lieutenants Rice and Averill.

Very respectfully,
WM.J. VOLKMAR,
Assistant Adjutant General.

Telegram.
Headquarters Department of the Colorado,
Denver, Colo.,June 16, 1896.
Colonel E.V. Sumner,7th Cavalry,
Care J.H.Slaughter, Slaughter's Ranch,
San Bernardino, Arizona, via Bisbee.

One–fifty p.m. Your cipher dispatch of sixteenth received ten–fifty–five this morning.

General Wheaton directs me to say you have already received most explicit and distinct orders based upon War Department instructions received by him.

The Mexican Government has been requested by ours to permit our troops to cross the boundary into Mexico as a favor. You have been furnished with the terms of the International Agreement and you will, under no circumstances, depart from them or permit your subordinates to do so. Important letter to this effect mailed you yesterday. If, under these terms, Indian scouts decline to cross the line, in pursuing a trail of Indians, do the best you can without Indian scouts.

If Article two, reported by you to be fatal, should embarrass your operations, you will remember that you are not responsible for an International Agreement made by higher authority.

Acknowledge receipt stating place and hour.
By command of Brigadier General Wheaton:

VOLKMAR,
Assistant Adjutant General.
DEPARTMENT OF STATE
Washington,July 17, 1896.

The Honorable
The Secretary of War.
Sir:

I have the honor to enclose herewith, for your consideration and reply, copy of a note from the Mexican Charge d' Affaires, calling attention to a press dispatch published in the Washington Post of June 24, 1896, touching the expedition of Lieutenants Averill and Rice to the State of Sonora for the purpose of Capturing the Apache Kid and his band.

If the newspaper report is correct, the Mexican Government is of the agreement of June 4th last, and asks that proper steps be taken for its precise observance.

I have the honor to be, Sir,
Your obedient Servant,
RICHARD OLNEY

Enclosure:
From the Mexican Legation, July 15, 1896.
Translation.

Mexican Legation,
Washington, July 15, 1896.
Received July 16, 1896.

Mr. Secretary:

I have the honor to state to you that the "Post" of this city of the 24th of June last published the annexed telegram dated the previous day in Tucson, Arizona, in which it is said that Lieutenants Averill and Rice of the Army of the United States, with two companies of cavalry comprising some 70 Indian scouts, in union with Mexican forces, were going south from the State of

Sonora for the purpose of carrying out a plan having for its object the capture of the Apache Kid and his band. As this proceeding would contravene the stipulation of the agreement signed in this city of the 4th of June last, especially as to its first and second articles, seeing that the hot pursuit of the aforesaid band is not involved but a concerted plan probably designed by the aforesaid officers, and the number of Indian scouts is considerably larger than that fixed by the; agreement in question, the Government of Mexico gives me instruction to ask that of the United States that if, after having investigated the facts, it appears that there be in effect infraction of the aforesaid agreement, it will be pleased to take the proper steps for its precise observation.

Be pleased to accept, Mr. Secretary, the assurance of my distinguished consideration—

M. COVARRUBIAS.

THE WASHINGTON POST
June 24th, 1896

OUR TROOPS ON MEXICAN SOIL

Two Cavalry Companies Co-operating With Mexican Troops in Sonora.

Tucson, Arizona, June 23,—Advices from San Bernardino ranch says that Lieuts. Averill and Rice with two companies of cavalry, and sixty scouts, including White Mountain, Yuma and Papago Indians, have been joined by Mexican troops, and are now going south through Sonora.

The plan is first to go to Yequi village, where the Apache Kid is supposed to be, then the troops will separate or deploy in squads and move northward with the hope of forcing the Indians to seek shelter on this side of the line where they will be met by troops in the vicinity of San Bernardino Cloverdale.

———

Official copy respectfully referred to the Commanding General, Department of the Colorado, with instructions to ascertain and report the; facts in the case, and who will see that the agreement of June 4th, 1896, is complied with.

By command of Major General Miles:
J.C. GILMORE
Assistant Adjutant General.
A.G.O.,
July 23, '96.

———

1st Indorsement,
Headquarters, Department of the Colorado,
Denver, Colorado, July 27, 1896.

Respectfully referred to Colonel E.V. Sumner, 7th Cavalry, commanding Fort Grant, A.T., inviting attention to the enclosed extracts from various telegrams from these Headquarters.

With return of these papers and without delay Colonel Sumner will please render a full and complete report of all operations of any troops under his command that have at any time crossed the border into Mexico. The report shall include the names of officers commanding detachments, the number of enlisted men and the number of Indian scouts with each detachment.

Referring to enclosed extract from telegram of June 8, from these headquarters, requiring every officer commanding a field detachment to keep a careful itinerary of his daily marches and to furnish a sketch thereof, the field notes and sketches of the following named officers, especially should be forwarded, viz:

Captain H.G. Sickel, 7th Cavalry, commanding detachment, which left Guadalupe Canyon, June 16, 1896.

Captain P.S. Bomus, 1st Cavalry, commanding detachment, leaving San Bernardino, June 16, 1896.

1st Lieutenant S. Rice, 7th Cavalry, commanding detachment leaving San Bernardino, June 16, 1896.

2nd Lieutenant Wm. Yates, 1st Cavalry, commanding detachment leaving San Bernardino, June 16, 1896.

1st Lieut. W.J. Nicholson, Adjutant 7th Cavalry, leaving SanBernardino, July 1, 1896.

By command of Brigadier General Wheaton:

W.M. J. VOLKMAR,
Assistant Adjutant General.

———

Sir:

Acknowledge the receipt of your letter of 17th ultimo, enclosing translation of a letter from the Mexican Charge d'Affairs, calling attention to a press dispatch published in the Washington Post of June 26, 1896, touching the expedition of Lieutenants Averill and Rice to the State of Senora for the purpose of capturing the Apache Kid and his band, and stating that if the newspaper reports are correct, the proceeding contravenes the stipulations of June 4, 1896, I have the honor to transmit, herewith, copy of a report from Col. E.V. Sumner, which it is thought affords a full and satisfactory explanation.

Very respectfully,
Acting Secretary of War

The Honorable
The Secretary of State.

———

Fort Grant, A.T.
August 1, 1896.

Adjutant General
Department of the Colorado.
Denver, Colorado.

Sir:

Referring to letter dated Department of State, Washington, July 17, 1896, addressed to the Hon. Secretary of War and signed Richard Olney, enclosing the translation of a letter dated Mexican Legation Washington, July 15, 1896, inviting attention to a newspaper article published in Tucson, Arizona, June 23, 1896, also in the Washington Post, June 24, 1896, which publication is in words as follows:

"Tucson, Ariz., June 23—Advices from San Bernardino ranch says that Lieuts. Averill and Rice with two companies of cavalry, and sixty scouts, including White Mountain, Yuma, and Papago Indians, have been joined by Mexican troops, and are now going south through Sonora.

The plan is first to go to Yuqui village, where the Apache Kid is supposed to be, then the troops will separate or deploy in squads and move northward with the hope of forcing the Indians to seek shelter on this side of the line where they will be met by troops in the vicinity of San Bernardino and Cloverdale."

I have the honor to report that this publication is false from beginning to end, that the force described was never organized, moved in any direction, or even thought of, and further that in conducting military affairs on the Mexican border I have strictly complied with every article of the agreement entered into between the Republic of Mexico and the United States, a copy of which was sent me for my information and guidance. The Civil and Military authorities of the States of Chihuahua and Sonora were duly notified of the crossing of United States troops into the territory of Mexico and a military representative of the Mexican Government Lt. Colonel Kosterlitzky, was in my camp, was duly informed and fully consulted about all movements, and signified his approval both as to what had been done and was being done.

Very respectfully
Your obedient servant,

/s/ E.V. Sumner
Colonel 7th Cavalry, Commanding

A general description of the conditions along the border and some of the various measures to cope with the situation are indicated in the following messages:

Telegram:
Department of Colorado,
Denver, Colo., January 13, 1896.

Adjutant General of the Army,
Washington, D.C.
Following from Captain Godfrey, Seventh Cavalry, commanding San Carlos, is repeated

for the information of the Major General Commanding the Army:

"Am satisfied Capt. Myer, Indian agent, has done all in his power in a quiet way to determine if the Merrill murderers have been on the reservation, or if the murder was committed by the reservation Indians. He is convinced that Massai was the murderer. If Massai has been on the reservation, Capt. Myer is satisfied it has not been known to the agency Indians. His letter on this subject mailed today." Quotation ends.

FRANK WHEATON,
Brig. Gen. Comdg.
Fort Grant, A.T.
April 27, 1896.

Adjutant General,
Department of the Colorado.
Denver, Colorado.

Sir:

Having returned from the Southern part of this District of observation, I have the honor to submit the following report. The few Indians left in this country from the Chiricahua band, have a camp in Mexico not far from our Southern border. From necessity for food, or from a malicious desire to plunder and murder citizens of the United States the different members of this band cross the border periodically when they think it is safe to do so, waylay any defenseless citizen on their route, steal horses and plunder ranches. It is supposed that; they cross the border on foot and at night, hide in the mountains on our side of the line for days and when an opportunity presents itself they gather a sufficient number of animals to carry their plunder and return to Mexico.

That portion of our border lying between the Bernardino and the Animas Valley to the East is like a door left wide open, and the carelessness of the citizens, in their defenseless condition, is simply an invitation to these Indians to plunder and murder them.

The murder committed, the plunder packed on stolen animals, it is but a step for them to recross the border and be in safety. To prevent these raids this district of country must be at all times under surveillance of troops and in sufficient force to make it hazardous for these Indians to come North of the line with any hope of returning in safety, and if they cross the line either East or West of the limits named the troops will still be in position to head them off. To prevent these raids, troops at Grant or Bowie might as well be in New York, communication is slow and even if a raid could be anticipated the troops could not do more than follow the trail of the raiders to the performance in the way of supplies and destruction of property with no chance of success.

It is therefore imperative, in my opinion, that troops should be stationed near the border line, and I believe when these camps are made permanent they can be supplied at very reasonable rates. I am informed by citizens living West of San Bernardino that no sign of Indians has been seen in their vicinity for several years although several trails once frequented by them are known. This is accounted for by the number of wire fences lately built through that section and the fear of the Indians of such obstruction.

It has occurred to me that some additional wire fencing East of San Bernardino, to be built by the Government, might be serviceable as a preventive, or a more certain way of discovering a raid by any soldier or cowboy riding the line, who would be apt to pass a footprint without noticing it. This fence would also reduce the number of troops necessary to guard the country and consequently reduce the expense account.

There is an organization being effected between the Cattle owners on the border and the Mexicans, all of whom suffer from these Indians, for the purpose of routing them out of their stronghold in the Sierra Madre Mountains and forcing them across the line. In view of having received this information I have left part of Bell's troop and all the Indian Scouts available, under Rice, with Lieut. Bullock, Commanding Troop "E".

At present the main camp is at Rucker. Rice with a party of soldiers and scouts is at San Bernardino and Lieut. Averill with a like party is at Guadaloupe Canyon.

They have orders to keep parties out in all directions and to be on the alert. Rice will get prompt information through Mr. Slaughter, the overseer of the San Bernardino Ranch, of any movement and they are all prepared to act quickly.

I am fully convinced that, there being no sign of trouble at San Carlos; or elsewhere within this District of Observation, the only way to prevent depredations in future by Indians from Mexico is to guard the line so closely that they cannot pass without being observed and pursued.

Lieut. Rice (with his Scouts) has done wonderful work in trailing and pursuing the last band of Indians and driving them across the border. His report in detail will be forwarded as soon as possible but in the meantime I desire to recommend him to the Department Commander for favorable mention.

Very respectfully,
Your obedient servant,
/s/ E.V. SUMNER
Colonel 7th Cavalry, Commanding

1st Indorsement
HEADQUARTERS DEPT. OF
THE COLORADO
Denver, Colo., May 2, 1896

Respectfully forwarded to the Adjutant General, U.S. Army

A Camp of troops at old Camp Rucker, or in that vicinity, I feel will accomplish the best results.

From personal observation, I know that the Animas Valley, San Bernardino and the Guadaloupe Pass should, for some time, be covered by frequent scouting parties and I know of no better place than the vicinity of Camp Rucker for headquarters for such parties.

/s/ Frank Wheaton
Brigadier General,
Commanding

The following is a report to the Adjutant General of the Army of the initial operations conducted shortly after the agreement with the Government of Mexico. The individual reports referred to by the Department Commander are in greater detail under the Record of Events for the troops concerned.

HEADQUARTERS DEPARTMENT OF
THE COLORADO
Denver, Colorado,
May 28, 1896.

To the
ADJUTANT GENERAL
Of the Army
Washington, D.C.

Sir:

Referring to the telegrams forwarded by letter of May 13th from these headquarters, I have the honor to transmit a copy of Lieutenant Averill's official report of his fight with Indians on the morning of the 8th instant. I also enclose copies of official reports of Lieutenants Rice and Averill of their concerted attack upon another party of Indians on the morning of the 17th instant.

It is much to be regretted that the last mentioned affair did not result more successfully. From the circumstances that the single Indian in the party had no less than three women, was equipped with a field glass and had five horses, it is inferred he was an Indian of some consequence —possibly either Massai or the Kid. This warrior was badly wounded and I am greatly disappointed that he was not successfully pursued and captured after the fight. However, I have already l;had occasion to repeatedly commend Lieutenant Rice for his energetic work in command of the scouts and invite attention to his successful pursuit of the band of Indians whom he drove across the border after their murder of Mr. Hands on March 28th, 1896. In any complimentary action that may hereafter be taken by the Major General Commanding the army, I request that 1st Lieutenant Sedgwick Rice, 7th Cavalry, be included, and invite attention to a recommendation by his Regimental Commander, for favorable mention. The communication containing it was forwarded by my endorsement on May 2, 1896.

In transmitting these reports, I invite attention to Lieutenant Rice's commendatory language regarding Lieutenant Averill, and I heartily concur in the following remarks of the Regimental Commander, Col. Sumner, 7th Cavalry, who says in his letter of transmittal of Lieutenant Averill's report of his fight on the 8th instant.

Fort Grant, A.T.,
May 15, 1896.

Adjutant General,
Department of the Colorado,
Denver, Colorado.

Sir:

Accompanying Lieut. Averill's report I respectfully ask to submit the following remarks:

I trust work like this will be appreciated by higher authority and that this young officer will receive suitable commendation for his untiring efforts in the field. He has, I think, found the only road to success in this kind of warfare and if we are to pursue this road in the future, we must be better prepared for it.

* * * *

According to the same letter from Colonel Sumner, Troops A, C, E, F and I, 7th Cavalry, stationed at Fort Grant, have marched, as separate troops, from December 1st to April 30th, last, 3,423 miles, and by detachments, 11,609 miles, a record of great activity.

As the troops of Forts Grant, Bayard, and Huachuca will be employed very actively for ;a considerable time to come, in scouting by small detachments the Southern parts of Arizona and New Mexico near the Mexican border, I earnestly request that the number of Indian scouts allotted to this Department be temporarily increased from the present number of forty, to seventy, and that authority be granted me to hire three or four interpreters and guides, until the officers serving in the three Southernmost Districts of Observation shall have become sufficiently acquainted with the country and its very scant water supply.

Furthermore, in view of the small number of vacancies that will probably exist for the graduating class of West Point, this year, I earnestly recommend that as many as possible additional 2nd Lieutenants be attached to the 7th Cavalry and to the two troops (I and A), of the 1st Cavalry stationed at Bayard and Huachuca, respectively. These gentlemen should be well selected from those best fitted physically in temperament and by natural taste for the very active work they will find in this Department, and which would be an admirable training for them as future leaders of cavalry.

Very respectively,
/s/ Frank Wheaton
Brigadier General
Commanding.

1st Indorsement.
Adjutant General's Office.
June 4th, 1896.
Respectfully submitted to the Major General Commanding the Army.
/s/ Ass't Adjutant General.

2nd Indorsement.
Headquarters of the Army.
Washington, June 6th, 1896.

In view of the excellent and successful work now being done and the great difficulty of hunting down individual Indian bands in this difficult country, which seems to be the only course to follow, the Major General Commanding recommends that the number of Indian scouts allotted to the Department of Arizona be increased from forty (40) to seventy (70) and that four competent interpreters and guides be authorized for the troops operating against the Indians.

/s/ Assistant Adjutant General

3rd Indorsement.
War Department
Adjutant General's Office.
Washington, June 9, 1896.

Employment of four competent interpreters and guides, approved by the Acting Secretary of War for a period not exceeding four months,—to be discharged within that period as soon as their services can be dispensed with.

In view of the careful consideration extended to the subject of scouts for the entire army prior to the reduction in November, 1894, (Colorado, on the recommendation of the Department Commander, being allowed 16 instead of 48) and the saving of expense resulting therefrom, the Acting Secretary of War is not prepared to approve the increase of 30 as now asked for.

If the Department Commander, through a careful distribution of the present authorized number (40) cannot efficiently meet the wants of the service, it is desired that he shall report specifically and fully the reasons for a further increase; also the distribution contemplated of the entire number, particularly with reference to the number needed at Forts Grant, Bayard, and Huachuca, respectively.

The foregoing has been made known to the Major General Commanding the Army, who directs that the Department Commander be informed, by telegraph, accordingly.

(s)Acting Adjutant General.

On May 8th, a detachment of eight men from Troop I, under command of 2nd Lt. N.K. Averill, Seventh Cavalry, surprised a party of Indians near Lang's Ranch, A. T., killing one warrior and capturing one girl and the entire camp outfit.

The following is the complete report of this scout rendered by Lt. Averill:

San Bernardino, A.T.
May 9, 1896.

The Adjutant 7th Cavalry,
Fort Grant, A.T.
(through proper military channels.)

Sir:

I have the honor to report that on the night of May 5th, I received a report about 8:30 P.M. from Mr. Slaughter saying that his men had found an Indian camp which had apparently been abandoned only a few days before, and saying he would show me the place.

I left camp at 9:00 P.M. with 8 men and a packer, with what rations I could get on 3 mules. Arrived at San Bernardino at 12:15 A.M. and sent a courier to Lieut. Bullock with message to send some men to Guadalupe to watch it. We left San Bernardino early in the morning and marched into the Guadalupe Mountains till dark. May 7 we found the Indian camp at about 8:00 A.M. It was on ;the highest peak in the country and a solid almost perpendicular wall of rock on 3 sides from the south. It could be gotten to only by a narrow winding trail. There were two lookouts where the Indians had evidently posted men during the day and which commanded the entire country for miles. Where the rocks did not naturally form a wall they had built small fortifications of rock and where they; would not be noticed from the outside from even a few feet away so it would have been absolutely impossible to get to them by day. The Scouts said there were three or four men, seven women and child and about ten ponies and that they left only about seven days before. I sent them to circle around till they cut the trail, and we followed till noon, where we found the only water in that section, far up a canyon. We halted there and I sent the Scouts on foot to try to find a fresh trail and to locate the camp if possible, or to find water for the next halt. They came back at dark, had evidently run all the way, and reported that they

had found a trail a day or two old and had followed it to the top of a mountain about 8 miles off and had seen from there some ponies several miles further but had not been able to find or locate the camp. We started at once, had to leave two men with the packs, and rode till about midnight, it was very dark and rough and the men's clothing was pretty well torn to pieces! The Scouts then said we should walk so at about 10 A.M. we started and walked till nearly four, when the Scouts said they were near where they had seen the horses. We could not move further as no one knew where the camp was and we might run onto it accidentally when they would hear us and all would get away. About daylight the Scouts saw a small fire about a quarter of a mile away. We only had 13 men, as I had to leave two more with the horses that night, leaving us Mr. Slaughter and two men, the five Scouts, 4 men and myself. I left the soldiers in ;the vicinity of where we were and started to get around them. They were located on a rocky hill where four deep canyons ran almost together so we could not hope to get entirely around them. Mr. Slaughter and one man took one canyon, Mr. Fisher and myself crossed to the other, and I sent the Scouts round to get on the other side and drive them if possible our way. Two of them went a little way and then would go no further but the other three weren't getting around nicely when suddenly all the Indians came out together and made a break. The Scouts say they saw some of the Soldiers. They ran like deer to the canyon away from us. We all fired as soon as they made the break but only one fell and he never got up, but before we could get to him he rolled down into the canyon where we could hear him yelling and then the Indians stopped long enough for the women to get him off. They were firing every little while. The Scouts chased them a little way but as we could never climb the hill fast enough, they soon came back. The Scouts also said one woman was hit but this I cannot vouch for. Mr. Slaughter thinks the Indian very severely wounded, if not dead, and says he will die anyway from blood poisoning, that 9 out of 10 do here at this season of the year when they are wounded. We then climbed up to their camp, where we found they had evidently left everything except their guns. They fired from 15 to 20 shots at us form the top of a very steep hill about 600 yards off but did no damage, and a heavy gun of Mr. Slaughter's with one of the new carbines which I had soon drove them off. We knew there was no good trying to follow them up the mountain on foot, and it was miles around, so we turned our attention to the camp. We found a little girl, about two years old, and everything else they had in the world, four or five wickies full, a large supply of dried meat, mesquite corn, a little sugar and salt, bags full of acorns and large hides full of water. Many large canteen and several hides, etc. and a great deal of the food packed up as if they were just going to start on a long trip, 7 saddles and bridles in good shape, a large quantity of plunder in Indian saddle bags and bags the women carry, most of which was evidently American with a few Mexican things. A complete reloading outfit for a 45–75 Winchester with powder and balls, shoeing outfits, hatchets, needles, thread, scissors, everything that one could think of, blankets, parts of carpets, fresh leather, etc. also

$1.25 in U.S. coin. We took what we could, threw everything else into the wickies, with the straw, and burnt it up, so that they were left without a thing in the world but what they had on. We then caught their ponies, 9 in number, and rode back to the horses. As we had no rations or grain and some of the horses were unshod, we started back and I sent a courier ahead. If it had not been for Mr. Slaughter and his man Fisher we would have never been able to do anything as they knew all the water and country, and took us by the canyons, as the Indians could have seen the horses if we had attempted to cross the hills. The Scouts did magnificently on the trailing and night work and all but two of them in the skirmish. Four of the ponies belonged to Mr. Slaughter, the Scouts have the other five which I will bring in, also the saddles, etc. Mr. Slaughter wishes to adopt the child which is at the ranch now, most of the outfit is here also.

I do not think that the ordinary soldier is much good for this work, especially when mounted on white horses, which can be seen for miles. The Indian Scouts and Cowmen were worth twice as much, and I fully believe if we had had 10 to 15 more men along so we could have gotten around the camp, especially if they had been Scouts, we could have killed or captured every Indian, and I do not believe that the detachment of Scouts, of say 25, would have a great deal of trouble in getting these small bands. It can never be done in the day time and if they ever get surrounded in the day time only a mountain howitzer would get them out for no man could get to them, they take the highest peaks and carry plenty of water. The first camp had evidently been occupied for a long time and only left on account of water failing. The band was evidently not the one Lieut. Rice followed for they had none of the goods taken from the last ranches attacked. Mr. Slaughter who probably knows more about them than any man living thinks there are several bands, so it will take some time to get them. I would suggest if any more troops come down here that either of his two men, Mr. Fisher or Mr. Hildreth, be employed and have plenty of nerve, working all the time right in the Indian country. I expect this band to come North to get some supplies and will keep as good a lookout as is possible.

Very respectfully,
/s/ N.K. Averill
2nd Lieut. 7th Cavalry

On May 17th another party of Indians was surprised by a detachment under Lieutenants Rice and Averill. The following are the complete reports as rendered by these officers:

San Bernardino, A.T.,
May 18, 1896

The Adjutant,
Fort Grant, A.T.

Sir:

I have the honor to submit the following:

Pursuant to verbal orders form Captain J.M. Bell, 7th Cavalry, I left San Simon Station May 11, with a detachment of 3 Indian Scouts and four troopers and proceeded south through the Peloncillo Mountains in search of hostile Indians.

About 6:30 o'clock p.m., the 12th instant, the Scouts discovered a trail of 5 horses 4 of which were shod with raw hide and one with iron shoes, one warrior and two women of the party. I took this trail on the following morning at day light and followed it south through the mountains until about 1 p.m., the 14th inst., when I met some troopers which Lieut. Averill had posted at a point where the trail left the mountains for the Animas Valley. These men informed me that Lieut. Averill had discovered the trail ahead of me that day and knowing that he would follow it to the line I proceeded to his camp in the Guadalupe Canyon. Lieut. Averill overtook me before reaching this camp and informed me that the trail had crossed the border about 3 miles west of Cloverdale Ranch. I sent a courier with this information to the Commanding Officer that evening.

Believing that the Indians were not far distant I determined to scout the mountains in the vicinity of Guadalupe Canyon and for this purpose I applied to Lieut. Bullock, 7th Cavalry, who had come to Averill's camp on the 13th, for re-enforcements. On the 15th inst., I left camp with a detachment of Lieut. Averill and 10 Indian Scouts, 1 enlisted man of Troop E, 7th Cavalry, and proceeded to the mountains, sending the Scouts out at dusk to locate the camp if possible. This they did at daylight on the 16th. I then moved camp as near as was possible to the camp of the Indians and at dark that night I proceeded to surround there camp which was located in an exceedingly difficult position in a ledge of very steep mountain. I ordered Lieut. Averill with all of the troopers but Private L'Estocq, Troop I, and 3 Scouts and requested Mr. Slaughter with his party to approach the camp from the north, or the foot of the mountain, and take up a position from, which they could receive the Indians should they break in their direction. This route was a difficult one and required four and a half hours in which to cover it. With Private L'Estocq and seven Scouts I proceeded to a position on the mountain above and overlooking their camp and distant from it about 250 yards, this position we reached at 4 o'clock a.m., on the 17th inst., after travelling all night on foot. This position was all that could be desired and commanded the camp from three sides. I could plainly see all that was taking place within the camp after daybreak and watched for nearly two hours for the only warrior of the party to arise from his bed, but the three women were up and preparing breakfast for about an hour and could easily have been killed, but believing, after consultation with the scouts, who assured me that it was quite certain that if we could succeed in killing the warrior, the women would surrender I had given positive orders to all members of the detachment that they were in no case to fire upon a squaw unless it became necessary in self defense. At 6:50 a.m., the warrior make a squaw, who from her actions had, I believe, discovered Lieut. Averill's presence. I then opened fire on the warrior, who, with the squaw disappeared in a narrow defile through the rock leading directly down the mountain, leaving all of their possessions behind them, where I expect Lieut. Averill and Mr. Slaughter to meet them; these gentlemen how-

ever had had the misfortune to be misled by the Scouts and found when it was unfortunately too late they were not near enough to cut off the escape of the party. Their work was exceedingly energetic and deserving of better results, but not being possessed of the knowledge of the exact location of the camp we were all too muck at the mercy of the Scouts which fact in this case proved disastrous. The Indians, then broke in ;the canyons on either side of their camp and although we made every effort to follow them it was without success except in the case of the warrior whose very bloody trail was followed until his gun, which was a Springfield rifle cut off to carbine length, model of 1873, field glasses, moccasins, and part of his clothing, all of which were abandoned in his flight, were recovered. This trail was followed by three Scouts who assured me that the man was dead, however they did not find his body. Owing to the fact that the Scouts had been without rest or food for nearly 48 hours, and the men for about 20 hours, I determined to abandon the search for the body. (It will be made by Lieut. Averill however in a day or two, who will also make an attempt to discover the body of the warrior who was undoubtedly killed by his detachment on the morning of the 8th inst.) I then returned to my horses and packs which I had left in a canyon several miles to the rear, and today returned to Bullock's camp where I left the detachment and came on to this point. I am of opinion that this party of Indians were not a part of that which was struck by Lieut. Averill, for the following reasons:

1st. They had evidently been in the mountains for three days, north of the point where I found their trail on the 12th inst., and as that was at least two days march from the camp Lieut. Averill destroyed, they could not possibly have been there on the 8th inst.

2nd. Lieut. Averill captured all of the possessions of the party he found, while this camp was comparatively well equipped and had five horses, two of which had been stolen from the San Simon Co.

Mr. Frank Hands is here today and has identified many articles captured by Lieut. Averill as belonging to himself and his brother who was killed on the 28th of March and had failed to identify any articles from the camp captured yesterday.

I send by this courier some female garments captured yesterday which I hope may serve as a clue by which to identify the murderers of the Merrill family at Ash Springs last December.

Every effort was made to induce the women to surrender; they were told that we were soldiers and would not harm them but they would not come in. The work of the scouts was untiring and most skillful and is, in my opinion, deserving of the highest praise, excepting in the case of those with Lieut. Averill and Mr. Slaughter, who I think from fear failed to take them within striking distance of the camp. I desire also to commend the energy of Lieut. Averill and the troopers of the detachment to the special consideration of the Regimental Commander. The demands made upon them were very great but they met them in a manner which reflected much credit upon themselves and the organizations to which they belong.

I enclose report of Lieut. Averill.

I am of opinion that the gun captured from the; warrior was the only one in the camp for the reason that the women in their flight were sure to be without arms and there were none found in the camp. It seems possible that their surrender might have been prevented owing to their excitement in the fight and that they may conclude to make their way to the reservation.

Unless I receive orders to the contrary I will proceed to Camp Rucker on the 21st for rations. The horses of the Scouts and the troopers who left Grant with me as well as the pack mules are completely worn out and will require a little rest before any more work can be done with them.

In this connection I desire to state that I was much handicapped for the want of an interpreter and urgently request that one may be employed and assigned to the detachment who is physically able to accompany me in the field.

Very respectfully,
/s/ SEDGWICK RICE,
1st Lieut. 7th Cavalry
San Bernardino, A.T.
May 18, 1896

1st Lieut. Sedgwick Rice,
7th Cavalry

Sir:

I have the honor to submit the following report of the action of my detachment on the night of the 16th. and morning of the 17th of May:

The Scouts having located the camp, the entire command under Lieut. Rice make a night march from the top of a mountain to a high ridge on the north of camp. From here arrangements were made to entirely surround camp, Lieut. Rice taking the most difficult portion of the work viz, getting in rear of camp on the mountain.

My detachment was to take the East canyon and the front, Mr. Slaughter and party to take the West canyon.

The camp was pointed to us and both Mr. Slaughter and myself understood it to be back of a certain high ledge, or pinnacle, of rocks on the other side of the canyon. It was very indistinct and there were several of these pinnacles and, as it turned out afterwards, we had both missed the right one. I left at about 2:30 a.m. with 6 men leaving 2 with Mr. Slaughter. The Scout with me did not want to go at all but started as I thought, to get into the proper canyon. He would stop every little way and say "camp right here, we sit down, Chericahuas hear us, etc." but I made him go on, but he went so slowly, evidently either through fear for himself or through fear of alarming the Indians, that it was about light before we had even got to the bottom of the canyon and then he refused to go further saying we were right there. I did not know exactly where the camp was but I knew it wasn't there, so I went on, sending Sergt. Rice with two men around in the canyon which I supposed to be to the East of camp, going myself up to the peak behind which I supposed the camp to be and distributed the men so as to be sure and catch anyone coming that way down the ridge. Some time after daylight I saw someone on a high pinnacle on the next ridge, calling the Scout he said it was an Indian squaw and this was the first that I knew, even approxi-

mately, where the camp really was. I watched these for a short time with field glasses when I saw several persons. I decided it was Lieut. Rice and the Scouts, and started down into the canyon between the ridges with the intention of getting up that ridge. I started with but one man as the rest were too much scattered to gather them. Before leaving I told the Scout explicitly not to fire until I did for fear of alarming the women if they came our way. We had just gotten to the bottom of the canyon when a volley was fired over us and the three women came tumbling down the side of the ridge directly toward me. I stepped behind a rock so as to let them get right down to us, but when they were about half way down the Scout on the hill behind us jumped up, fired his piece into the air and began yelling, of course the women turned and ran behind some rocks and I only saw one after that. We could have killed them easily but wanted to capture them. We went up there as soon as we could but never saw them again. We could hear the Scout shooting into the air and yelling for the next half hour, while the one supposed to go with Mr. Slaughter was doing the same on the other side of the first canyon. It seems he had had almost the same experience with his Scout. As it turned out afterwards we could have ridden down into the last canyon with no danger in the world of their hearing us, and easily have crept right up to the camp if the Scouts had only taken us, and without their hearing us. In the darkness I thought I had to trust the Scout and when he wouldn't go—my misunderstanding as to the proper ridge—caused me to post my men on the wrong ridge and in the wrong canyon entirely.

I believe the Scouts will go fairly well when there are several of them together as shown by those with Lieut. Rice but when alone they do not seem to work at all. The men under me did splendid work this time and though the trip was a very hard and difficult one they all wanted to go and never grumbled at all, and if we could only have gotten to the right place I believe they would have all done as well there.

Very respectfully
/s/ N.K. Averill
2nd Lieut. 7th Cavalry

Troop G—Performed garrison duty at Fort Apache, A.T., during the entire year except for numerous scouts made by the troop or detachments. One such scout is described as follows:

Headquarters, Fort Apache, A.T.
February 18th, 1896

Special Orders No. 29:—

I:—2nd Lieut. Charles W. Fenton, and twenty (20) men of Troop "G" 7th. Cavalry, and two Indian Scouts, will proceed at 9 o'clock a.m. tomorrow to scout the country between this post, by the way of Cibicu and Canyon Creek, and the western border of the Indian reservation, as far as Ellison's Ranch, thence to Salt River and up Salt River by such trails as may be found practicable in returning to this post. Lieut. Fenton will examine as far as practicable within a few miles on either side of the trail, the banks of Caruixo and Canyon Creeks, with the view of determining the practicability of making a wagon road through that country.

He will take such notes as will enable him

on his return to make a correct map of the country passed over, giving the location of any Indian camps coming within his observation.

A written report will also be submitted with the map.

He will endeavor to ascertain if Massai or any other Indians have been visiting that section of the country.

The detachment will be armed and equipped for field service, provided with six pack mules and rationed for ten days.

By order of Lieut. Col. Powell
/s/ John S. Battle
2nd Lieut. 11th Infantry
Adjutant

It is of interest to note that during this period a separate drill regulation for cavalry troops was written which expanded the old regulations. The board of officers selected by the War Department to revise the cavalry regulations was composed of members of the regiment. The following order prescribes these new regulations.

War Department, Washington,
May 18, 1896.

A board of officers consisting of Lieut. Col. Louis H. Carpenter, Seventh Cavalry; Capt. Edward S. Godfrey, Seventh Cavalry; and Capt. Ernest A. Garlington, Seventh Cavalry; with First Lieut. Tyree R. Rivers, Third Cavalry, as Recorder, having revised the Drill Regulations for Cavalry, and the same having been further revised by Maj. Gen. Thomas H. Ruger, United States Army, under special instructions of the War Department, the regulation is approved by the President and is published for the information and government of the Army, and for the observance of the Militia of the United States.

To insure uniformity throughout the Army, all Cavalry exercises and maneuvers not embraced in this system are prohibited, and those herein prescribed will be strictly observed.

Daniel S. Lamont,
Secretary of War

1897

The year was uneventful except for the continued small expeditions against Indians, practice marches, and scouts. All troops performed garrison duties at their respective stations throughout the year. Troop G—Marched 346 miles to the Zuni Indian Reservation, N.M., for the purpose of protecting civil authorities, returning October 11th.

Troop H—Marched 329 miles to Fort Wingate, New Mexico, and assisted at the post during cavalry competition, returning to Fort Apache on October 11th.

Troops I and K—Participated in the Independence Day Celebration at Bisbee, A.T., July 2nd to 6th, distance marched 84 miles.

Troop L—Performed garrison duty at Fort Sill, O.T., until September when the troop was transferred to Fort Grant, A.T., for station. The experimental Indian Troop did not prove successful and all enlisted personnel of the troop were discharged per instructions from Headquarters, Department of the Missouri (See 7th Cavalry Organization).

Pvt. William F. Foy of Troop F, as mounted messenger, in Cuba 1898. Courtesy of Ed Daily.

Troop F, 7th Cavalry, Huntsville, Alabam en route to Cuba, 1898. Courtesy Ed Daily.

Mast of Battleship "Maine" in Havana Harbor, Cuba 1898. Courtesy of Ed Daily.

1898

The troops of the regiment continued to engage in scouting for Indians and actively patrolled the Mexican border until August of this year. The troops at Fort Grant, A.T., alternated in tours of one month's duty at the San Carlos Indian Agency, A.T. Many troops ordered for active duty in Cuba at the outbreak of the Spanish American War. However, the regiment was concentrated at Huntsville, Alabama, in October and remained in camp there until December, and then changed station to Macon, Georgia, where it remained until the end of the year. The following is the record of individual Troops.

Troop A—Performed garrison duty at Fort Bayard, N.M., until April 21st, when the troop changed station to Fort Duchesne, Utah. The troop traveled by rail to Pine, Utah, arriving there on April 24, and marched 95 miles to Fort Duchesne, arriving on April 29th, and then proceeded by rail to Huntsville, Alabama, to join the regiment in camp there, arriving on October 9th. The troop remained at Huntsville until December 8th, when it changed station, with the entire regiment by rail, to Macon, Georgia, arriving on December 9th.

Troop B—Performed garrison duty at Fort Grant, A.T., until January 3rd when the troop

7th Cavalry mules and wagons in foreground. Maro Castle across the mouth of Havana Harbor, Cuba 1898. Courtesy of Ed Daily.

Pvt. Albert H. Koch, Troop M, 7th Cavalry, near Camp Columbia, Cuba, 1900. Courtesy of Ed Daily.

7th Cavalry Bandsman Will Crawford, Havana, Cuba, 1899. Courtesy of Ed Daily.

Formal Guard Mount, 7th Cavalry, Fort Riley, Kansas, 1894. Courtesy of Ed Daily.

7th Cavalry Horse Show, Atlanta, Georgia, 1902. Courtesy of Ed Daily.

7th Cavalry Band at General Garcia's funeral, Havana, Cuba, Feb. 11, 1899. Courtesy of Ed Daily.

7th Cavalry Rough Riders, Atlanta, Georgia, 1902. Courtesy of Ed Daily.

performed a tour of duty at San Carlos Indian Agency, A.T., until February 3rd, distance marched 140 miles. The troop then performed garrison duty at Fort Grant until April 24th, and marched 56 miles to Fort Sill, O.T., arriving at Rush Springs, O.T., on April 24th, and marched 56 miles to Fort Sill on the same day. The troop performed garrison duty until May 26th, when it marched 180 miles to Fort Reno, O.T., and return on June 19th. Garrison duty was performed until October 1st, when the troop proceeded to Huntsville, Alabama, to join the remainder of the regiment. (Same as Troop A for remainder of the year)

Troop C—Returned from a tour of duty at San Carlos Indian Agency, A.T., to Fort Grant, A.T., on January 4th, distance marched 70 miles. The troop then performed garrison duty, except for additional tours of duty at San Carlos Indian Agency, A.T., April 3rd to May 4th, and July 2nd to August 6th, having marched 280 miles. The troop left by rail to join the regiment at Huntsville, Alabama, on October 1st, arriving on October 9th, and remained at Huntsville until December 8th, when it changed station with the entire regiment. (Same at Troop A for remainder of the year)

Troop D—The record of events is the same as that of Troop A, except that the troop scouted 269 miles to Routt County, Colorado, and return, in quest of Indians from August 3rd to 14th.

Troop E—Performed garrison duty at Fort Grant, A.T., except for tours of duty at San Carlos Indian Agency, A.T., February 3rd to March 4th, May 3rd to June 4th, and August 3rd to September 6th, total distance marched 420 miles. The troop left for Huntsville, Alabama, on October 1st, arriving October 9th. It remained at Hunts-

ville, Alabama, until December 8th, when the troop changed station with the entire regiment. (Same as for Troop A for remainder of the year)

Troop F—Performed garrison duty at Fort Grant, A.T., except for a tour of duty at San Carlos Indian Agency, A.T., March 3rd to April 4th, distance marched 140 miles. On May 13th, the troop marched 92 miles to its new station at Fort Huachuca, A.T., arriving on May 16th. It performed garrison duty at Fort Huachuca, A.T., until October 4th, when the troop changed station to Huntsville, Alabama, with the remainder of the regiment. (Same as Troop A for the remainder of the year)

Troop G—Performed garrison duty at Fort Apache, A.T., except for a tour of duty of a detachment at San Carlos Indian Agency, A.T., May 28th to July 7th, distance marched 170 miles. On September 27th, the troop proceeded by rail to Huntsville, Alabama. (Same as for Troop A for the remainder of the year)

The above routine entry in the Troop Return pertaining to a march to the Papago Indian Reservation does not, of course, indicate why such a march was necessary. It is believed of interest, therefore, to insert here, copies of correspondence —typical of the reports, many of them false— which had sent the troops of the regiment on the hundreds of scouts and marches along the Mexican border during the past three years.

EXECUTIVE DEPARTMENT,
TERRITORY OF ARIZONA,
OFFICE OF THE GOVERNOR,
PHOENIX.

Phoenix, Arizona
Apr.22nd, 1898.

To the President,
Washington, D.C.

Sir:

I would respectfully request and strongly urge, for the reasons hereinafter set forth, that the First Regiment of Infantry, N.G.A., consisting of ten Companies of fifty men each be called into the service of the United States, and that a call be issued for a Regiment of Volunteer Cavalry to consist of eight Troops of a maximum strength of sixty each, organized in two Battalions. Both of these Regiments, so organized, to be used entirely for the purpose of home defense of the Territory of Arizona. The Cavalry to be used entirely in patrol duty, and the Infantry stationed at important points on the border. The mobilization of the regular Troops has left only 13 organizations of the regular Army within the borders of the Territory,—four troops of Cavalry and two Companies of Infantry at Fort Grant, two troops of Cavalry and two Companies of Infantry at Fort Huachuca, and two troops of Cavalry and one Company of Infantry at Fort Apache. I represent to you that this force is entirely inadequate to insure the citizens of the Territory against a possible uprising of the numerous Indian tribes within our borders, and at the same time to protect the inhabitants of the towns and ranches situated near the borders of Mexico. A glance at the map of the Territory will show how much exposed the inhabitants of the counties of Pima and Cochise are to raids by bands of Indians.

There is not the slightest doubt in my mind, but that during a state of war, Spanish sympathizers in Mexico, knowing the comparatively unprotected state of our borders, would make frequent raids into the Territory; and that cattle thieves and desperados would also embrace the opportunity to plunder and steal, making sudden raids upon the towns and ranches lying close to the borders and then retiring beyond the international line into haunts that are almost inaccessible. It would profit nothing to follow such a class of outlaws and attempt to punish them after the depredations had been committed. The only way in which our citizens can be guaranteed immunity from such attacks is by constant watchfulness and guarding of the points which such people would be most inclined to attack. We have 37,000 Indians within our borders, who are doubtless at the present moment apprised of the partial withdrawal of the regular troops from the Territory. Some Indians of these tribes would probably take advantage of the situation, and give the small number of Troops left sufficient employment to keep them out of mischief. In addition to our own Indians it should be borne in mind that there are numbers of Indians living in the State of Sonora right at our gates who would also give trouble. The attack upon the town of Nogales, Arizona in 1896, is in evidence of that fact. Only yesterday I was in receipt of information to the effect that the Papago Indians from this Territory had crossed the line into Mexico and had attacked the mining camp of El Plomo, some 80 miles west of Nogales. These Indians are of thievish habits and very mischievous, and are constantly stealing cattle from our cattle men in the southern part of Pima County.

Our legislature is not in session and there is no way of calling it together to make any appropriation for the Territorial defense. Moreover, as this is a Territory and not a State, and therefore directly under the Federal protection, it seems only right that the Federal Government should look after the protection of its citizens. Should the Nation require it, it would be found that our citizens would respond liberally and patriotically to the call for Volunteers to leave the Territory and fight the Nation's battles: but this request is upon different lines, and is only made after mature deliberation and consideration upon my part and the firm belief that the number of men asked for will be found none too many to preserve law and order in this Territory. When the call for Volunteers is made the quota allotted to us might be taken from the troops already so organized. The 500 carbines for which I made requisition the 9th inst could be used to equip the Cavalry forces asked for. Again requesting that this matter be given your earnest and careful consideration and that action be taken thereon at the earliest possible convenient moment, I remain,

Very respectfully,
/s/ MYRON H. McCORD
Governor of Arizona

P.S.
I enclose a copy of a letter just received from Colonel Willis P. Harlow, of Nogales, Arizona, as indicative of the situation.

M.H. McC.

Nogales, A.T., April 21st, 1898.
Hon. Myron H. McCord,
Phoenix, A.T.

Dear Sir:
I confirm my wire today as follows:

April 21st, 1898.
"Myron H. McCord, Governor,
Phoenix, A.T.
On the fourteenth forty Papagos attacked El Plomo Camp, and fired from a distance. Fire returned by people. Indians left and camped twelve miles distant from El Plomo until the sixteenth, when they moved fifteen miles further north and crossed the line into Arizona on the twentieth about seventy–five miles west of this point. No casualties reported as yet."

"W.P.Harlow".

Which information I obtained form Colonel Juan Fenochio, who is the Commander of the Federal troops on the other side; he also said that he would furnish me with the names of the leaders of the Papagos if possible, at which time, I shall again communicate with you. While talking with the Colonel, he wanted to know whether or not he could make some sort of an arrangement whereby, in case of the rougher element 'shooting up the town', as he expressed it, he would be permitted to catch them if the chase

Troop C, 7th Cavalry, Columbia Barracks, Cuba, 1900. Courtesy of Ed Daily.

Troop M, 7th Cavalry, Camp Columbia, Cuba, 1900. Courtesy of Ed Daily.

7th Cavalry Fancy Drill Team, Atlanta, Georgia, 1902. Courtesy of Ed Daily.

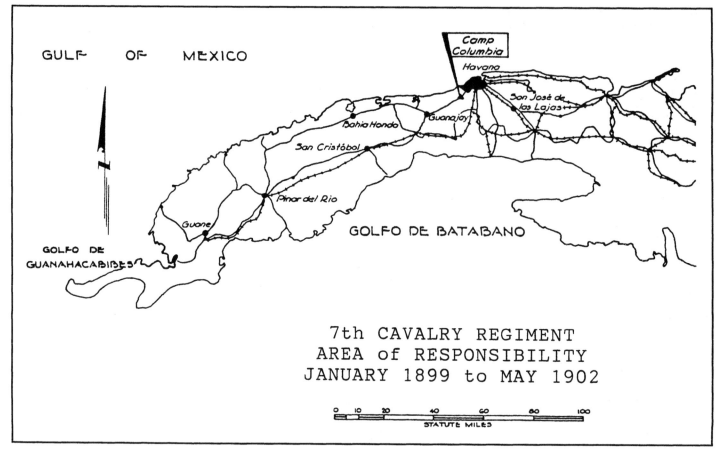

GULF OF MEXICO

GOLFO DE GUANAHACABIBES

Guane

Pinar del Rio

San Cristóbol

Bahia Hondo

Guanajay

GOLFO DE BATABANO

Havana

Camp Columbia

San José de las Lajas

7th CAVALRY REGIMENT
AREA of RESPONSIBILITY
JANUARY 1899 to MAY 1902

0 10 20   40   60   80   100
STATUTE MILES

led into our country. I explained to him your liberal views on such matters as I understood them, and I told him I thought that if he would grant us the same privilege, that there would be no trouble if he happened to step onto Arizona soil, in hot pursuit. To this he answered that if we were troubled by the rougher element, or marauders, or Indians, while endeavoring to keep the peace in our town, to forget there was a line dividing the two towns, or that there was a line between the United States and Mexico. In this connection, I requested the privilege, in case things got warm, of posting a few men upon Mexican soil about half a mile south of Nogales, to act as pickets and warn the citizens, in case of attack on the town in the night time. To this he replied that we could go ahead and do this as far as he was concerned, and that he would communicate with his superiors and have the matter arranged; he asked me for the same privilege, and I told him I would communicate with you, but that if before I received your answer, he deemed it necessary to send out such men, that I would send a man or two along with them, which he could make look like an American crowd with a few Mexican helpers, in case we were criticized in Washington. I deem it of the first importance that something of that kind should be done, and that at once; as, I am informed by reliable men, that there are a great many lawless people within reaching distance of this town. For instance, I am informed by an American who is heavily interested in Sonora, that he made a trip to Hermosillo last week for the purpose of ascertaining the feeling among the officials, and he informs me that to a man, the better class, (which in Mexico means the people that have the dollars and official positions) favor Spain, and that

his cow boys, and such people as they, are constantly talking of the amount of "fun" they could have on the line in case war is declared, and the troops taken from Huachuca. This man's name, you can have if you want it, but he specially requested me not to divulge his name until he could settle up his business interests in Sonora, and get back, which will be about the tenth of next month. If it is possible for you to do so, I wish you would write me a letter to the effect that the International Law, and the treaties between Mexico and the United States would be very liberally construed, for the purpose of quelling riots, etc., and in the letter, requesting me to wait upon Colonel Juan Fenochio and make some arrangements with him to this effect, which I will show to the Colonel and then return to you. In this connection, I think that later on, we will have to have some sort of an understanding between Washington and Mexico. I do not care to pose as an alarmist, but you remember the old saw, a stitch in time saves nine.'

Yours very truly,
/s/W.P. Harlow

P.S. Rumor has it that the Indians who crossed the line yesterday are heading this way, but I have private information to the contrary. At least, it was not known sixty miles west of here yesterday noon.

W.P.H.
Fort Huachuca, A.T.
May 10, 1898.

The Adjutant
Sir:
In obedience to S.O.No.46, Fort Huachuca, A.T., April 29, 1898 issued in compliance with telegraphic orders from Department Headquar-

ters same date, I left the post at 1:15 p.m., April 30, 1898 and arrived at Nogales, A.T.,May 1st, 1898, to investigate the reported attack on El Ploma, Mexico, by Papago Indians alleged to be from the United States.

The report of attack on El Ploma was telegraphed by Jesus McZepeda, a citizen of Mexico, and who I understand has large cattle interests in the vicinity of El Ploma in Sonora, Mexico. In the course of my investigation I learned that a Papago Indian named Grover Ramon and other reliable authorities stated that forty Papagoes fully armed and equipped had gone to Sonora, Mexico from the United States for the purpose of attacking El Ploma to avenge the killing of four Papagoes about a year ago. The attack on El Ploma was made by some fifty Indians who rode up close to the town and commenced firing while about twenty others collected cattle estimated at about six hundred after which all started for the United States, and to which point they were followed by soldiers and vaqueros. The Indians were reported to have separated into three parties, one party crossing near Meguel's going up to a village back of Barboquavari Peak, one farther west to Siervita village where fearing they would be followed by Mexican troops they moved to Fresno village, and the third west of Cobita at La Lesna. No cattle if any was driven over by the third. It took the Papagoes two days after the attack to reach the line, as they retreated to Cobita on April 15th, and on the 16th crossed into the United States.

About seventy men formed a party in El Ploma to follow the Papagoes, and these followed by fifty soldiers of the 4th Mexican Cavalry, who arrived after the attack are reported to have followed the trail to the line.

The report from El Ploma does not show that anyone was killed or wounded during the attack or during the subsequent pursuit.

In a letter from Mr.C.F. Nesler, United States Indian Inspector to United States Consul, Nogales, Mexico, he stated the following to be the result of his investigation:

I found these Indians to be Sonora Papagoes and properly under the jurisdiction of Mexico. The recent raid was made by a band of thirty–two Indians under the leadership of El Gato, Cachora, Napoleon and Two Days. This band of Indians until a year or two ago were residents of Mexico and at this time claim to be Mexican Indians. In 1889 or 1890 members of this same band murdered two Mexicans and fled to the American side. They were then under the charge of Senor Manuel Zepeda who now resides at Altar, 45 miles south of El Ploma. Mexican authorities offered a reward for the apprehension of the murderers and paid the then sheriff of Pima County, Arizona, F.M.Shaw, $500 for capture. The Indians then returned to Mexico and resided there until a year or so ago. About one year ago they attempted another raid and lost two or three men. Their identity as Sonora Indians I can establish by the testimony of any number of responsible citizens of this Territory, and while I can readily see the necessity of preventing a recurrence of these troubles along our borders, I am unable to take any action in this matter as these people are the wards of the Mexican Government, and not under the jurisdiction of the United States.

From a consideration of these facts which were learned chiefly from letters on the subject to and from the United States officials and also from information gathered from conversation with men who had traveled through part of the Papago country in the United States and its continuation in Sonora, I would conclude that the Papago Indians reside part in the United States and part in Mexico; that the Indians who attacked El Ploma were Mexican Indians who had to leave Mexico on account of trouble, and had taken refuge in the United States; that these might have been assisted by some roving American Indians, who were induced to cross by a prospect of stealing cattle and smuggling them into the United States where a ready sale for them appears to be found to other Indians chiefly on the Pima Phoenix, Sacaton, Tempi, Maricopa and other points.

I have been unable to learn of any hostile disposition at any time of the Papagoes towards settlers in any place in, or bordering on their country. Therefore, there appears to me only two conditions to be guarded against; one an attack on Mexican territory from the United States; the other, smuggling cattle from Mexico into the United States.

I think the Mexican border would be safe from attack if a detachment of Mexican troops were kept at El Ploma or some point near the line to guard against incursions of Indians who left Mexico, and who may be aided by sympathizers from the United States; such a detachment, for instance, as is now kept by the United States at San Bernardino, A.T., to guard the line against American Indians who have crossed into Mexico. As the country from Buenos Ayres, Arizona to Yuma is a desert where water can be

found only at long distances in wells varying from 400 to 700 feet deep, and in some few places in the mountains which rise up here and there out of the plains, and are known only to the Papagoes who roam through that country, it is difficult and almost impossible for the; officials and inspectors of the Custom House stationed at the sub–port at Buenos Ayres to guard the line to Yuma. If a station were established at San Domingo from which Inspectors could ride the line to meet those from Buenos Ayres, cattle could not be smuggled in at a point so far west from the station as to make it impossible for the Inspectors to intercept them after information had been received. With the possibility of smuggling cattle into the United States thus removed, and Mexican territory protected by its own authorities I think the Papago trouble as between the United States and Mexico would be settled.

Very respectfully,
/s/ JOHN O'SHEA
2nd Lieut. 7th Cavalry

TO: Hdqtrs. Dept. of the Colorado,
Denver, Colorado, May 16, 1898.

Official copy respectfully furnished the Adjutant General of the Army, for the information of higher authority, in connection with previous report on this same subject by Lieutenant Edward Lloyd, 15th Infantry, forwarded by indorsement May 11, 1898.

/s/E.V.SUMNER
Colonel,7th Cavalry,
Commanding.

Fort Huachuca, A.T.
May 12, 1898.

The Adjutant,
Fort Huachuca, A.T.
Sir:

In compliance with instructions contained in Special Orders No. 51 dated Fort Huachuca, A.T., May 10, 1898, I have the honor to report that I left this post on the morning of the 11th instant and proceeded by rail to Nogales, A.T. Upon arrival at that place on the morning of the same day I at once called upon the U.S.Consul and U.S. Collector of Customs and most of the leading citizens of Nogales, A.T., with a view of ascertaining the truth or falsity of the reports and rumors of unauthorized movements of Papago Indians in that vicinity. I found the general consensus of opinion to be there was no foundation in fact for the reports (which had been started by the talk of an old Yaqui Woman in Mexican Nogales, who in trying to persuade her warrior to leave the town had told him it was going to be attacked).

Since the attack on the Custom House last year by a small band of Yaquais., the people of this town appear to be very easily stamped by any report, no matter how groundless or absurd, of an Indian attack, which naturally spreads to our side of the line. The report that Indians were leaving the town was also without foundation.

I found everything peaceable and quiet, and, on our side of the line, all appeared to be satisfied that there was no cause for any alarm. I also called upon the Commanding Officer of the Mexican Troops - Colonel Fenoque - now stationed in Mexican Nogales, who informed me

that he believed there was no foundation for the reports which had been circulated, and kindly offered to telegraph to his posts along the border west of Nogales, and let me know if all was quiet in that direction. I enclose a copy of the reply to Colonel Fenoque"s telegram which he politely furnished for my information.

Very respectfully,
/s/ H. G. NOLAN
Major 7th. Cavalry.

Troop K - Performed garrison duty at Fort Huachuca, A.T., except for a 305 - mile scout to the Mexican border and return. May 14th. to June 6th. On October 4th., the troop proceeded by rail to Huntsville, Alabama, to join the remainder of the regiment. (Same as for Troop A for the remainder of the year.

Troop L - Organized at Fort Grant, A.T., during the month of June, where it performed garrison duty until October 1st. The troop proceeded by rail to Huntsville, Alabama, to join the remainder of the regiment, arriving October 9th. (Same as for Troop A for the remainder of the year) (Note - the Troop Record of Events shows 2nd. Lieutenatn Allyn K;. Capron killed in action at the Battle of Las Gusimas, Cuba, while seving as a Captain, 1st. U.S. Volunteer Cavalry, June 24th. Captain Capron, a member of Troop L, had volunteered for service with the 1st. U.S. Volunteer Cavalry - Lieutenant Colonel Theodore Roosevelt's famous Rough Riders).

Troop M - Organized at Fort Grant, A.T., on May 21st, and, performed garrison duty, except for a tour of duty at San Carlos Indian Agency, A.T., September 2nd to 23rd, distance marched 140 miles. On October 1st, the troop proceeded by rail to Huntsville, Alabama, to join the rest of the regiment, arriving on October 9th. (Same as for Troop A for the remainder of the year)

1899

Headquarters, Band, and Troops A, C, E, G, I and L left Savannah, Georgia, under the command of Lieutenance Colonel Cooney, 7th Cavalry, on the transport "Manitoba" for Havana, Cuba,. January 13th, 1899. The command arrived in Havana on January 16th, and went into camp at Vedado, Cuba, about three miles west of Havana, on January 17th. On January 19th, the 3rd Squadron, consisting of troops C, G, E, and I, under command of Major Godfrey, 7th. Cavalry, proceeded by rail to Pinar del Rio, Cuba, arriving and taking station there the same date. Troops B, D, F, H, K,and M, under command of Major Hayes, 7th Cavalry, left Savannah, Georgia, on the transport "Manitoba" on January 25th, 1899. Troops K and D went into camp with Headquarters at Vedado, while the 1st Squadron, consisting of Troops B, F, H and M, under command of Major Hayes, 7th Cavalry, established Camp Columbia, near Mariano, Cuba. Camp Vedado was abandoned April 25th, when the troops marched to Camp Columbia and took station there. Columbia Barracks was established and occupied on July 29th, by Headquarters, Band, and Troops A, B, D, F, H, K, L, and M.

Upon the appearance of Yellow Fever at Pinar del Rio - the station of the 3rd. Squadron - these troops were ordered into a Quarantine Camp, three miles from Pinar del Rio on July 23rd.

During the remainder of the year the regiment as a whole was engaged largely in provost duty, practice marches, and in scouting the country in the vicinity of Havana and Pinar del Rio for the purpose of suppressing the numerous bandits who began their operations immediately upon departure of the Spanish Troops from the Island of Cuba.

1900

Due to an outbreak of Yellow Fever at Pinar del Rio, Troop I was ordered to take station at Guanajay, Cuba, on July 27th. This troop was followed by the rest of the squadron (Troops C, E and G), on August 8th. Upon their arrival at Guanajay the order was changed, designating Columbia Barracks as their station. Troops C, E, and G arrived there on August 7th and Troop I followed on August 8th.

By this movement, the entire regiment was concentrated for the first time in many years. The regiment served at Columbia Barracks continuously, until the evacuation of Cuba by the United States Troops in May, 1902.

Yearly practice marches were made by the troops, lasting from ten days to six weeks. By these marches the entire western part of the Island was covered, and maps were made of much of the area. The troops were instructed in the duties of a soldier in the field - every precaution being taken to make the instruction as profitable as possible, both to officers and men.

There was no suitable place to hold target practice near Columbia Barracks during the target season of 1900; thererore the troops, in turn, marched 36 miles to Guanajay, and while in camp there held their regular practice. This range was also used by the troops from Pinar del Rio.

Troops D and F performed garrison duty at Columbia Barracks until March 1st, when they proceeded to Gunajay, Cuba, for target practice, remaining until March 5th, when they returned to the post for a review of the Secretary of War (Elihu Root).

1901

The regiment spent the entire year in garrison at Columbia Barracks, Cuba. Individual troops continued their garrison duties, practice marches and scouts throughout the island.

1902

The beginning of the year found the entire regiment stationed at Columbia Barracks, Cuba, performing routine garrison duty. In April, the 1st Squadron changed station to Chickamauga National Park, Georgia; Troop C and a detachment of 24 enlisted men from the regiment had charge of the horses of the regiment. In May, the remainder of the regiment, after participating in the inauguration ceremonies of the first President of the Republic of Cuba, joined the 1st Squadron at Camp George H. Thomas, Chickamauga National Park, Georgia. On September 7th, the regiment was reviewed by the President of the United States - Theodore Roosevelt - at Camp George H. Thomas, and then participated in the parade in his honor at Chattanooga, Tennessee, the following day. In October a detachment of 48 enlisted men of the regiment, under command of Captain Edward Anderson, 7th Cavalry, gave exhibition drills at the Horse Show at Atlanta, Georgia. The detachment received the highest praise from the press and the people. A silver loving cup was presented from the citizen's committee. The garrison duties of the new camp were exceedingly strenuous- building roads , clearing and leveling parade grounds, and in the general preparation of what evolved into a model permanent field camp. The regiment completed the year under canvas at this camp.

1903

The regiment remained at Camp George H. Thomas, Chickamauga National Park, Georgia, for the entire year. The regiment, except Troop C, marched to Waco, Georgia, for target practice during the summer season. On May 4th, and 9th, the entire regiment paraded at Chattanooga, Tennessee, in connection with the Spring Festival held in that city. A detachment of the regiment also gave exhibition drills. During the latter part of July and the first part of August, Troop C participated in a camp of instruction for the first Georgia Cavalry at Savannah, Georgia, where they had their annual target practice at the State Rifle Range near thar city. During September and October, the regiment, except Troops A, B, and C, participated in the annual fall maneuvers at West Point, Kentucky. In October, Troop C made an extended tour through the principal cities of the South, giving exhibitions of fancy drill and horsemanship at horse shows, expositions and carnivals in Nashville, Tennessee; Birmingham, Alabama; Jacksonville, Florida; and Macon and Augusta, Georgia, returning to the regiment with a great number of silver loving cups. In December, Troop C again gave exhibition drills at Alabany, Georgia, in connection with the Red Men's carnival being held there.

7th Cavalry Rough Riders, Atlanta, Georgia, 1902. Courtesy of Ed Daily.

7th Cavalry Horse Show, Atlanta, Georgia, 1902. Courtesy of Ed Daily.

The 2nd and 3rd Squadrons, 7th Cavalry at Fort Oglethorpe, Georgia, Dec. 20, 1904. Courtesy of Ed Daily.

Cavalry Camp of Instruction, Camp Young, West Point, KY, 1903. Courtesy of Ed Daily.

7th Cavalry Band, Spring Festival, Chattanooga, TN, 1903. Courtesy of Ed Daily.

7th Cavalry Pack Train, Chattanooga, TN, 1903. Courtesy of Ed Daily.

1904

Except for marches to Waco, Georgia, for tartget practice, the regiment remained at Camp George H. Thomas, Chickamauga National Park, Georgia, until July. During July and August, Troop E marched to Birmingham, Alabama, for duty at a camp of instruction for the Alabama National Guard. Troop I proceeded by rail to Columbia , South Carolina, for similar duty with the National Guard of South Carolina. In August and September, Headquarters, Band, and Troops A, B, C, D, F, G, H, K, and L participated in annual fall maneuvers at Thoroughfare, Virginia. Upon completion of the maneuvers. Headquarters, Band, and Troops A, B, C, and D changed station to Fort Myer, Virginia, separating from the remainder of the regiment at the maneuver camp. The remainder of the troops returned to Camp George H. Thomas, Georgia, and moved into new barracks (Fort Oglethorpe) the following month. During October, a detachment of Troop C commanded by Second Lieutenant John C. Montgomery gave exhibition drills at Lynchburg, Richmond, and Norfolk, Virginia. Similar exhibition drills were given as the various horse shows and carnivals by Troop H at Savannah, Georgia, and Jacksonville, and Tampa, Florida; and by Troop I at Athens, Macon, and Columbus Georgia. All three troops reflected great credit upon the regiment during these public exhibitions.

1905

At the beginning of the year, the Headquarters, Band and 1st Squadron of the regiment were stationed at Fort Myer, Virginia, and the 2nd and 3rd Squadrons at Fort Oglethorpe, Georgia. The winter at Fort Myer was one of the most severe for years and it was impossible to have much outdoor drilling, as the drill ground was frozen and covered with snow, or muddy between the times of thawing. Athletic exercises were held daily during the week in the splendid gymanasium. Riding exercises were also held daily in the large riding hall, built for that purpose, with a seating capacity for one thousand spectators. There, was great rivalry among the different troops to excell in skill and the variety of features in there exercises. A public exhibition drill was given each Friday afternoon, the troops drilling by turn. The hall was crowded with spectators for practicaly every drill, and many times hundreds were turned away. There spectators included high ranking cabinet officers, ambassadors, senators, and respectable citizens from all walks of life, many coming several hundred miles expecially to see the remarkable feats in horsemanship, and the trained horses.

One prominent feature of the service at Fort Myer was escort duty for funerals and burials at the Arlington National Cemetary. This duty occurred from two to three times a week with as many as three occuring in a single day. While many of these were original internments from Washington, D.C. and throughout the country, others were from the Phillipines and elsewhere. Not one was from the regiment.

General Orders No. 176, War Department, series, 1904, ordered the regiment for its first tour of duty in the Phillipine Islands. This required practically a reorganization of all the enlisted men of the regiment. Every troop was to be at its maximum strength upon departure, each man with at least two years and three months to serve, or two years and seven months at date of reorganization (February 18th, for the Non-commissioned staff and Band and troops of the 1st Squadron; January 18th, for the 2nd Squadron, and March 18th. for the 3rd).

Except for Non-commissioned officers, all personnel with less than the minimum time to serve who desired to reenlist at once for three years were reenlisted. Those of the regiment at Fort Myer who did not desire to reenlist were transferred to the 13th Cavalry, the relieving regiment; those at Fort Oglethorpe to the 12th Cavalry, that was to occupy the station.

The Band lost eight of its capable musicians by these transfers, and the regiment lost many of its very best horsemen. The regiment's loss was the other two regiments' gain, for each of the latter received a nucleus sufficient to carry on and impart to others there own excellent training and skill, which, it is learned, they did with great credit to themselves and satisfaction to others. The most severe and discourging blow was the loss of all the trained horses, for every horse had to be left behind. Nearly every officer and man lost a long intimate friend and companion whose will had been bent and sometimes subdued by him through long patient care and kindness. The gain was shared by two regiments but the loss all fell upon the 7th Cavalry Regiment.

Four hundred and fourteen men were discharged and reenlisted under the order and two hundred and five were transferred.

The Band and 1st. Squadron (Troops A, B, C, D) participated in the procession at the inaugral ceremonies of President Theodore Roosevelt on March 4th. The mounted dress uniform, prescribed in general orders from the War Department, was worn. The uniform consisted of dark blue dress cap and coat, olive drab breeches, khaki leggings and russet leather shoes. The press claimed that the President was disgusted with its appearance. It is admitted that it was a mongrel dress, and an order from the War Department immediately followed, prohibiting the wearing of this mixture of uniform in the future.

The 2nd Squadron of the regiment left Fort Oglethorpe, Georgia, on the afternoon of April 20th with one passenger and one baggage train. The men traveled in six tourist cars and the officers and their families in a Pullman sleeping coach. Transportation was furnished by the Queen & Cresent line. The squadron - commanded by Major L. S. McCormick - passed through Vicksburg, Shreveport, Fort Worth, El Paso; over the Southern Pacific railroad to San Francisco, California, where it arrived the morning of April 26th, and went into camp at the Presidio.

The 2nd. Squadron embarked at San Francisco, California, on the U.S.A. Transport "Sherman," and sailed at noon on May 2nd, arriving at Honolulu on the 10th and departed at 11 a.m. on the 12th. About two hours out of Honolulu it was found that a member of the steward's department had developed a case of small-pox and the transport put back to Honolulu and left the patient at that port, renewing its voyage the same day. The transport arrived at Guam on the 27th and departed on the same date, and arrived at Hariveles (Quartantine station for Manila) from 7 p.m., June 1st. Two cases of small-pox had occurred among the crew of the transport before reaching Manila, but there were no cases among the troops. The next day it went to Manila, discharged the mail, and returned to Hariveles, where it remained in quarantine for two days. On the 5th it returned to Manila, where it remained two days more; however, no one was permitted to go ashore. The transport left Manila on the afternoon of June 7th, arriving at Batangas Harbor the next morning. The squadron disembarked and took station at Camp McGrath, whre it remained quarantined for ten days.

The regiment Headquarters, Staff, Non-Commissioned Staff and Band, and the 1st Squadron left Fort Myer, Virginia, about 9 a.m. May 20th, by street car transportation to the Baltimore and Ohio Railroad Station, and entrained, leaving at noon. Traveling over that railroad on a mixed train - baggage, tourist cars for men, and two Pullman sleeping coaches for officers and their families- by way of Chicago, thence over the Atchison, Topeka and Sante Fe Railroad, through Kansas City and Alburquerque, to San Francisco, they arrived at the latter place on May 27th under the command of Major W. J. Nicholson. This part of the regiment went into camp at the Presidio to await sailing of the U.S.A. Transport "Sheridan".

The Regimental Headquarters and Band remained in camp at the Presidio of San Francisco when the 1st. Squadron boarded the Transport "Sheridan" and sailed from San Francisco for Manila at noon on May 31st. The "Sheridan" arrived at Honolulu at 6 a.m. June 7th, and departed at 4 p.m. June 8th. It arrived at Guam on June 10th and departed June 21st, and arrived at Manila early in the morning of the 26th. On the evening of the 28th, the "Sheridan" sailed for Batangas where it arrived early in the morning of the 29th. The squadron disembarked, Troop B took station in the town while Troops A, C, and D, took station at Camp McGrath with the 2nd Squadron. On July 16th, Troop A left Camp McGrath to take station at Calmba, on the Laguna, and arrived at that station July 17th, and remained there until the end of the year.

The 3rd Squadron, under command of Major E. P. Brewer, left Fort Oglethorpe, Dodge, Georgia, on June 20th, with tourist cars for men and Pullman sleeping coach for officers and their families on the Queen and Cresent Railroad to Kansas City, thence over the Atchison, Topeka and Santa Fe Railroad to San Francisco, California. It arrived there on June 26th, and went into camp at the Presidio with the Regimental Headquarters and Band. The Headquarters, Band and 3rd Squadron embarked on the U.S.A. Transport "Logan" and sailed from San Francisco at noon on June 30th, with the 1st Squadron of the 8th Cavalry; Companies A and B, Engineer Corps; Companies L and M, 10th Infantry; and many officers and men casuals, and arrived at Honolulu in the forenoon of July 7th. The two companies of the 10th Infantry, Major Robert Van Vliet Commanding, disembarked at Honolulu, and the "Logan" sailed 4 p.m., July 8th, and arrived at Guam in the forenoon of July 20th. It sailed on the afternoon of the 21st, and, passing through the San Bernadino Straits, it arrived at Manila early in the morning of the 26th. The 3rd Squadron disembarked on the 27th and proceeded by rail to Camp Gregg, in the Province of Pangasinan, where it was stationed at the end of the year.

The Adjutant and Band left Manila on the evening of July 28th on the Coaster "Lall-Loc," arriving at Batangas on the morning of the 29th, taking station at Camp McGrath. The Regimental Headquarters left Manila on the cable transport "Liscuim," on the evening of the 29th, arrived at Bantangas on the morning of the 30th and took station at Camp McGrath. Troop B changed quarters in Batangas to Camp McGrath on the 31st and the Headquarters, Band, and Troops B, C, D, E, G and H remained at the camp until the end of the year.

The entire regiment made the journey across the continent and the voyages across the Pacific without loss by death or desertion, and only one man (of the 2nd Squadron) was left enroute - he having walked off the train in his sleep a short distance west of Kansas City, had received some bruises but no serious injuries. He made his way back to the recruiting rendezvous at Kansas City and joined before the squadron sailed from San Francisco. One man of the Band was left sick in the hospital at the Presidio of San Francisco when the Headquarters sailed.

The regiment arrived in the Phillipines in the rainy season, and took the old horses and equipment left by the 12th Cavalry - the unit which it relieved. Some of the horses were recognized as those that had served with the 4th Cavalry in the campaigns of 1899, 1900 and 1901, and from the 1st and 6th Regiments, of a later date, many were blind in one or both eyes. The youngest animals were largely mares, many of the equipments were old and worn and had been repaired many times. Leather in this climate deteriorates rapidly from moisture and heat, and soon molds. Much of the equipments had been stored for several months without care during the dampest season.

The garrison school season in the Philippine Division is from June 1st to October 31st. The school began in August for officers of the regiment at the various stations, and the time was extended for the school at Camp McGrath until Novemver 30th.

The regiment did not have its annual target practice prior to leaving the states, and began in August and continued until November 7th. It rained every day of the season but five or six, and the practice was conducted under the worst of conditions. The ground was low and necessarily level, men wallowed in the mud whenever they had to lie down. The figure of merit was consequently very low.

The garrison school had been suspended during the target season, but was renewed in November, and as the rain subsided, regular drilling was resumed. Orders from Headquarters, Department at Luzon, required a course of mounted reconnaissances to be taken up and a district of country lying east of the camp to be mapped. Each detachment or troop was to make accurate topographical sketches of its allotted territory on a scale of two inches to the mile. These sketches were consolidated later into one map by the post intelligence officer. Troop E was absent on this duty (two platoons) from December 2nd to 11th. One platoon worked up the territory in the vicinity of Conde, Batantgas; and the other platoon in the vicinity of Talahib. Troop C mapped the zone near San Isidro, December 3rd to 12th; Troop F mapped Mt. Bubihan, December 3rd to 12th; Troop D mapped Mt. Mapagon, December 12th to 21st; and Troop H mapped Nabato, December 12th to 21st. Troop B mapped Laya, December 13th to 22nd; Troop G that of Abung, December 13th to 22nd. Troop E made a topographical reconnaissance from December 26th to 31st, passing around Lake Taal from the East. Troop F made a similar trip December 26th to 31st, to Nasigbu, returning around Lake Taal, from the west. These operations closed the year.

A rather unusual matter of interest to the regiment and the service on the part of the citizens of Chattanooga, Tennessee, is worthy of record. The citizens of that city, on learning of orders for the regiment to go to the Phillipines, ordered purchased and presented to the regiment a handsome set of silken colors, and for each troop a similar guidon, with appropriate letters and a silver band on the staff of each color and guidon with the following inscription:

"PRESENTED BY THE CITIZENS OF
CHATTANOOGA, TENNESSEE,
April 1905."

On the 30th of May the presentation was

made in the City of Chattanooga with appropriate ceremonies. The presentation being made by the Mayor of the City and received by Lieutenant Colonel D. C. Pearson, of the regiment. Since the 1st and 2nd Squadrons were not present at the ceremonies, the colors and guidons were turned over to Major E. P. Brewer of the 3rd Squadron for delivery to the regimental headquarters in the Philippines, where they were distributed to the troops. The following acknowledgement was made by the regimental commander:

"Headquarters Seventh U.S. Cavalry,
Camp McGrath, Batangas, P.I.,

September 25, 1905
To the
Hon. Alex. W. Chambliss
Mayor of Chattanooga,
Chattanooga, Tenn.
My dear Sir:

As regimental commander of the Seventh Cavalry, I desire to make acknowledgement on my part, and that of the entire regiment, of the receipt from the commander to Third squadron, Major E. P. Brewer, of a most beautiful set of regimental colors and a guidon for each of troops "A," "B," "C," "E," "G," and "H," that were brought by him, due to the absence of the headquarters and these troops from the foreman presentation at Chattanooga, by the citizens of your city, of a complete set of colors for the regiment and a guidon for each of its troops. In making this acknowledgement it is impossible for me to find words to express the emotion that this most gracious presentation has kindled in my own heart, or even to convey vaguely to you the deep and sincere appreciation, I may say election, of every member of the regiment over the event, for it seems to them and to me far more than simply a manifestation of the cordial feelings that obtained between the citizens of your city and the Seventh Cavalry.

Written history, and still stronger stories handed down by tradition, tell us how standing armies have been used by monarchs in the past as engineers of oppression to the masses, not only in depriving them of their rights, but by the weight of expense in maintaining them. Quartering troops upon us in colonial days, the bitter expriences of our forefathers in the wars of the revolution and independence, have endowed Americans with an inherited prejudice and bitter antipathy against a standing army.

Forgetting that this nation is not a monarchy, that our President is not a monarch, that our standing or regular Army is simply a trained Army, differing from the militia only in the manner of its maintenance, this prejudice has never been eradicated from the popular mind, and the regular army had been endured and maintained rather as a necessary evil than as a desirable national institution, much less one to be proud of. Yet, never has its valor been questioned on its thousand of battle fields, and search history as carefully as you may, there cannot be found an incident where the regular Army has proved a menace or unfaithful to the people of our institutions, while it has countless times proved itself the safeguard and bulwark of our democratic-republican government. Still this deep seated seemingly irradicable prejudice has pre-

vailed and supposedly the strongest in what is called the "South". Now to have the citizens of your city, located in the heart of the south, who have demonstrated their superior intelligence, enlightenment and foresight, by the beautiful and prosperous city they have created and are developing on such broad lines, to have the Citizens of Chattanooga, I say, break the bonds of inherited prejudice by such an act of the heart makes that act of double weight to the recipents not only as a demonstration of good will and friendship to us as a regiment but kindles the hope that, in time, the regular Army will be taken to the heart of the poeple, as it deserves, and will be considered, what it really is, a republican institution. I cannot find words to express our thanks and gratitude, and trust you will convey them in better words that I can, to the people of your city.

Very respectfully,
/s/ CHAS. MORTON
Colonel, Seventh U.S. Cavalry,
Commanding the Regiment."

The duties at Camp McGrath were ardous for the officers and men, as they were employed early and late. The absence of a large number of officers on detail was a hardship upon the regiment. Officers had to be constantly attached to and detached from troops to equalize the duties and to have at least one officer for duty with each troop. Frequent changes of this kind were not good for the officers, bad for the troops, detrimental to discipline and added to the annoyances and responsibilities of a command officer.

A condition existed in the regiment at this time which is not entirely foreign to a historical sketch, in that 14 officers in the regiment were closely related by blood or marriage. The Colonel had a son-in-law in the regiment, a major had a son, and among the captains and lieutenants there were two brothers, and four sets of two officers had married sisters. These two brothers had two brothers-in-law, making four officers in one family in the regiment at the same time.

1906

The year will long be remembered as one of the most strenous in garrison service in the history of the regiment. General Orders No. 19, Philippine Division, series 1906, prescribed all drills and exercises to be conducted with troops fully armed and equipped for the field. It also prescribed practice marches, night operations, and target practice, all to take place simultaneously. In order to comply with the terms of this order, the troops of the command would fire on the rifle range one morning, take a practice march that afternoon, fire with the pistol the next morning, go on practice marches in the afternoon, and engage in a night maneuver after dark. Several months of this strenous life reduced the horses to mere bags of bones and put many of the men on the sick list; however, those who remained were fit for any duty called upon to perform.

At the beginning of the year, the Headquarters, Non-commissioned Staff, Band and Troops B, C, D, E, F, G, and H were stationed at Camp McGrath, Batangas Province. The 3rd Squadron (Troops I, K, and M) at Camp Gregg, Pangasinan Province, and Troop A at Calamba, Laguna Province, all on the Island of Luzon, Philippines.

At all stations of the regiment the target season was during the months of January, February and March. There were a marked improvement in target practice over the year before, due to dry weather and the improved conditions of the ranges. At Camp McGrath the use of the siding target in lieu of the Laidley, materially improved range practice firing.

Early in January, confidential instructions were received from the Division and Department Commander to hold the 2nd Squadron and the pack train in readiness for active service in the field. The Manila press was aflame with sensational headlines of "War with China!" While there was no apparent cause for war on the part of China, in a sensitive nation, the papers were creating a cause on our own part. This preparation, however, involved only requisitions for partly worn-out material - fit for garrison duty only and not for extended active service, due to the rapid deterioration of leather, canvas and iron in this climate.

The theoretical instruction of non-commissioned officers continued by troop commanders throughout the year at Camp McGrath, and the regular garrison school for officers at all stations from June 1st to October 31st.

To show in a measure the number of duties performed and variety of instruction given daily, the following lists of calls are included in this history:

Camp McGrath, Batangas, P.I.,
April 7th, 1906.
GENERAL ORDERS,
No. 15
I. The following drills and exercies are announced to take effect Monday the 9th instant, to continue until further notice and all orders conflicting herewith are revoked. All exercises will be conducted strictly in accordance with General Orders No. 19,
Headquarters Phillipines Division, c.s.
PRACTICE MARCHES - Mondays and Thursdays.
NIGHT OPERATIONS - Alternate Tuesdays, beginning the 17th
instant.
FIELD PROBLEMS - Wednesday.
EXTENDED ORDER DRILLS - Alternate Tuesdays, beginning the 10th instant, and every Friday. On Tuesdays the drill will be by troop, on Fridays by squadron.
PACK DRILLS - Tuesdays and Fridays, both squadrons.
SIGNAL DRILLS - Tuesdays, Wednesdays and Fridays.
SWIMMING DRILLS - At river near stables for men needing instruction. At beach for horses, under qualified swimmers.
TROOP "B" - Mondays;
TROOP "C" - Tuesdays;
TROOPS "D" and "E" - Wednesdays;
TROOP "F" - Thursdays;
TROOPS "G" and "H" - Fridays.
Troops will be excused from afternoon stables on days they attend swimming drill. Horses will be rubbed until dry upon being placed in stables after returning there-from.
MACHINE GUN DRILLS - Each troop, commander will detail one sergeant, two corporals and eight privates, under charge of

an officer, as a machine gun detachemnt for his troop. The drills will be as follows:

TROOP "H" - Mondays;
TROOP "G" - Tuesdays;
TROOP "F" - Wednesdays, first drill hour;
TROOP "C" - Wednesdays, second drill hour;
TROOP "E" - Thursdays;
TROOP "B" - Fridays, first drill hour;
TROOP "D" - Fridays, second drill hour.

These drills will not begin until the machine gun arrives at post.

II.The following list of calls and duties are announced to take effect the 9th instant…

Reveille, except Mondays and Thursdays,
1st call, 5:15 a.m.; Reveille, 5:25 a.m.; Assembly, 5:30 a.m.

Mess call, breakfast, immediately after reveille.

Fatigue call, 6:30 a.m.

Drill call, followed by boots and saddles, 6:45 a.m.

Alternate Tuesdays, beginning 10th inst., extended order; Wednesdays, field problems; Fridays, extended order.

Assembly, 6:50 a.m.

Recall, Fridays and alternate Tuesdays, beginning 10th instant, 8:15 a.m.

Water and stable call, alternate Tuesdays, beginning 10th instant, Wednesdays and Fridays, immediately after return of troops from drill.

Pack drill Signal drill Trumpet practice — Tuesdays and Fridays — 1st call, 9:45 a.m. Assembly, 9:50 a.m. Recall, 11:00 a.m.

Recall from Fatigue, daily, 11:30 a.m.

Mess call, dinner, daily, 12:00 noon.

Fatigue call, Sundays excepted, 12:30 p.m.

Sick call, daily, 1:00 p.m.

Swimming drill, daily, except Saturdays and Sundays, 1st call, 3:15 p.m.; Assembly, 3:20 p.m.; Recall, 4:45 p.m.

Water and stable call, except Sundays, 4:00 p.m. Assembly, 4:05 p.m.

Machine gun drill, Wednesdays and Fridays, 1st call, 4:55 p.m.; Assembly 5:00 p.m.; Recall, 6:00 p.m.

Guard mounting, daily, 1st call, 5:25 p.m. Assembly, 5:30 p.m.

1st Sergeants' call, daily, immediately after guard mounting.

Recall from fatigue, except Sundays, 5:45 p.m.

Retreat, 1st call, 6:10 p.m. Assembly, 6:15 p.m.

Mess call, supper, immediately after retreat.

Tattoo, 9:00 p.m.

Call to quarters, 9:45 p.m.

Taps, 10:00 p.m.

MONDAYS AND THURSDAYS

Reveille, 1st call, 4:15 a.m.

Reveille, 4:25 a.m.; Assembly, 4:30 a.m.

Mess call, immediately after reveille.

Drill call followed by boots and saddles (practice march), 5:25 a.m.

Assembly, 5:30 a.m.

Alternate TUESDAYS, beginning 17th instant.

Drill call, followed by boots and saddles (night operations), 7:10 p.m.

WEDNESDAYS

Signal drill, 1st call, 7:10 p.m.

Assembly, 7:15 p.m.; Recall, 8:15 p.m.

SATURDAYS

Troop inspection, followed by saber drill and exercise:

1st call, followed by boots and saddles, 7:25 a.m.; Assembly, 7:30 a.m.; Recall, 8:45 a.m.

SUNDAYS

Water and stable drill, 6:55 a.m.

Assembly, 7:00 a.m.

Water call, 4:00 p.m.

Assembly, 4:05 p.m.

Church call, 9:45 a.m.

Church call 7:30 p.m.

III. In addition to the signal drills herein prescribed, troop commanders will cause all officers and non-commissioned officers of their organizations to be instructed until they become proficient in visual signaling both day and night.

IV. All men detailed on special duty from this office, except chief baker; also troop cooks, farriers and blacksmiths belonging to the 1st Squadron, will attend the swimming drill and Saturday inspection with their troops, beginning on the 10th of each month; those of the 2nd Squadron will perform the same duties beginning on the 20th. All officers and other men, except the sick, guard, prisoners and room orderly, will attend all drills and exercises prescribed herein with their respective organizations unless especially excused in advance from this office.

BY ORDER OF COLO-
NEL MORTON:
(Sgd.) E.
Anderson,
Capt. and Adjt., 7th
Cavalry, Adjutant

In operations and all field work, blank cartridges were used in carbines and pistols and all conditions were made to approximate as nearly as possible those of actual war. Both officers and men attained great proficiency in this work, particularly in the collection and transmission of information, locating the enemy and developing his positions and strength. Reports were required by all officers on the topographical sketches of positions and the operations of troops on both sides in minor tactics problems. Discussions of the details of the solutions were held immediately or soon after each problem.

Practice marches of nine miles out and return were made, and bivouacs established at their terminal, from which reconnaissance parties were sent three miles in as many dirrerent directions. The marches were conducted under the assumed conditions of a hostile region, with advance and rear guards, flankers and patrols. Practical instruction was given in security and information and outpost duty. Reports and sketches were required. Officers and men became familiar with and proficient in all these various duties.

After the close of the officers' school in October, mounted reconnaissance parties with pack mules were sent out in charge of lieutenants to report upon and make sketches of trails leading to different points in the Province of Batangas. Most of the officers became very adept in this work and a great many of the non-commissioned officers and men developed considerable proficiency.

Both day and night signaling was kept up by detachments from all the troops under a number of lieutenants, and as men acquired proficiency they were replaced by others. This was is addition to the regular signal instruction conducted by the different troops.

One half hour was devoted, five days in the week, to dismounted athletics and some extra time to mounted gymnastics, though much of the latter subject was covered in the regular drills. For men who put in several hours in a day riding at a trot, galloping and charging, vaulting on, off, and over horses at the run, and jumping hurdles and ditches, it was particularly annoying to require them afterwards to hop, skip and jump afoot for exercise. Normally, the regular training of the cavalry soldier gave him all the physical exercises necessary to keep up his vigor.

At the Department Meet in December, which was participated in by all regiments in the department, mounted and dismounted, the regimental team won first prize in athletic events, in very spirited contests. It failed by a small number of points in winning the prize for cavalry events. The team from the pack train attached to the regiment also won first place in the pack train events.

An hour's practical instruction each week in swimming for men and horses was given each troop for most of the year, as well as instruction in packing mules.

The great amount of work with field equipment was hard upon the old horses in a tropical climate. Some of them had seen duty in the States before the declaration of the Spanish-American War, and the percentage of disabled became very large. The amount of effort required of them was more severe than ordinary campaigning, except on raids and forced marches. As a result, instead of hardening them for endurance for field work, it broke them down.

Instruction was given for five months of the year in the first aid to the wounded. The efficiency of each troop was tested by the inspectors of the division by calling men out of each troop at random at inspection and giving them different kinds of cases of injury, to render the proper aid, and then requiring them to explain the object of the details in their work.

Indeed, the condition found by the numerous inspectors and their comments thereon show in a measure the high degree of efficiency the regiment had attained. No serious fault or irregularity was reported or found by inspectors during the year. At the inspection made by the Inspector General of the Division at the first of the year, he remarked that Camp McGrath was more like a regular military post than any he had inspected in the Philippines. The Division Commander, with three inspectors, inspected again in April and he expressed himself as highly pleased with everything — and members of his party said of the twelve posts inspected on the tour, none compared with the efficiency and excellence found at Camp McGrath. It was inspected again in May by the Department Commander, who was enthusiastic and profuse in his praise. The officers who went into the minutia of the inspection said they had inspected all the cavalry commands in the department and "the Seventh Cavalry had skinned them all." It was inspected again in October by a division inspector, who spoke in warm praise of the conditions found, and that they were so excellent that he was two and one-half days less time in making his inspection than he had expected it would require.

The new Springfield rifles, model of 1903, were received at Camp McGrath in early December, and about the same time at Camp Gregg. They were immediately issued and the Krag-Jorgensen carbines turned in to the Manila Ordnance Depot. Though there was little time to test the new rifle before the end of the year, all troops were favorably impressed with its superiority as a service arm over all other patterns issued in the Army, in addition to establishing a uniform arm for all branches of the service.

The health of the regiment was excellent throughout the year for the tropics, due no doubt to: (1) the table fare, for besides the regular ration and subsistence stores to be purchased at the Commissary, a superior quality of fish could be procured cheaply throughout the year from the natives, as also eggs, chickens and a variety of vegetables and fruits; (2) excellent sanitary condition of barracks and environment; (3) abundant supply of good water for drinking and bathing; (4) judicious ample exercise to keep up the physical vigor.

There were no deaths in the regiment from disease, the four that occurred resulted from accident or encounters. The sick cases were generally venereal diseases or the results of excessive use of alcoholic drinks, particularly the native "Bino." The old canteen supplied beer and light wines under restrictions that prevented excessive use and intoxication. However, since the prohibition of all traffic in liquors at military stations, poisonous liquors were sold without restraint around each military post by depraved characters whose only object was to fleece money from the soldiers. The great bulk of the offenses against dicipline were the result of drinking. The lack of a variety of social diversion made a soldier's life exceedingly monotonous, particularly so when far away from home and in an inhospitable land without affiliations and in an enervating climate. It is belived that the climate also had a bad effect upon the nervous system, which, combined with effects of excessive use of poisonous liquors, not only weakened the physical but mental and moral stamina of the men. In any event, the number of cases of absence from roll calls and breaches of discipline increased during the year.

The post was enlarged during the year to accommodate a full regiment of cavalry and complete water and sewer systems installed and surface drainage perfected. The healthy condition of the regiment may be attributed to this, and most certainly added to the conveniences and comforts of the station; however, they added much additional work upon the regiment. The manual labor was performed principally by natives and garrison prisoners. A very excellent telephone system, with a twelve-phone switch board, was installed during the year by the officers and men of the regiment. Also a system of sliding targets and many improvements of the target range and the grounds of the camp.

On May 15th, the province was visited by a terrific wind and rain storm. The streams became swollen within a very few hours to an unprecendented height. The Calumpan River went out of its banks and burst in the walls of the reservoir at the camp pumping and ice plant, involving some three weeks' constant work in day time of about all of the available strength of the command to clean away the debris, and caused a cost of $1,000 in labor and material to repair the damage. It also washed out about a hundred yards of sewer pipe that was buried eight and ten feet, involving a heavy expense for repairs and reconstruction.

During the year, the regiment was called upon to report, make surveys, and submit maps and data upon the feasibility and practicability and cost of land to make the camp a brigade post, and for field artillery, and also for a new target range; and for an enlargment of the military tract of land for the purpose of military maneuvers.

The duties of all the officers present were largely increased by the great number of others absent throughout the year. Of the 21 absent at the end of the year, one was on leave, two were sick and 18 were on detached services. Due to these absences, frequent changes of officers from one troop to another had to be made to provide troops with officers to properly handle them, and to equalize as far as possible the duties.

Troop A—Was relieved from Calamba when that station was broken up in September and joined its squadron at Camp McGrath on September 25th, by marching 40 miles. 1st Lieutenant Thomas H. Jennings—the only officer serving with the troop—was ordered to Manila on October 1st, for duty in connection with the approaching Department Athletic Meet, and was still absent of that duty at the end of the year.

Troop D—Was ordered to the Department of the Visayas and left Camp McGrath on December 10th to take station at Tanauan, Leyte, where it remained throughout the rest of the year. The Troop embarked on the U. S. C. T. "Minao de Battan" and proceeded to Tacloban, Leyte, arriving on December 18th. It then marched 12 miles to Tanauan, Leyte, arriving on December 20th. Before its departure, men of other troops were attached to it to bring it up to a strength of 65. Its duty included the escorting of trains, supplies and parties to and from interior points on that turbulent island. Its duty was arduous and trying, as it was constantly employed in rainy weather, in country boggy and without roads, and all communications over bad, tortuous trails through brushland and jungles.

Troop H—Took a practice march of 87 miles through Batangas Province, May 21st to 30th. Troop M took one practice march of 62 miles through the surrounding country, May 26th to 30th, and one of 73 miles, December 27th to 30th.

With the foregoing exceptions, the regiment performed garrison duty at the same stations throughout the year.

1907

This year concluded the first tour of Philippine service for the regiment. In February, Troop E, the Machine Gun Platoon, a pack train of 32 mules, and the Regimental Athletic Team marched 80 miles to attend the Division Athletic meet at Manila, where they carried off the majority of the individual trophies, including the Division Silver Cup for general athletics.

Troop D remained in Leyte, being charged with the safe conduct of supplies between Tanauan, Dagomi and Barauen and the reconnaissance of the country as far south as Abuyog and north to Tacloban, penetrating to the mountains in the interior. In April the troop returned from Leyte, having marched over 944 miles during the month of March along. That it performed its duties to the entire satisfaction of the District and Department Commanders is evidenced by the following letters:

"Headquarters, 2nd Dist., Island of Leyte, Burauen, Leyte, P.I., April 16, 1907.
Captain Robert,
Tanauen, Leyte.
Congratulate you upon obtaining what you desire, but am very sorry to see you and your troop leave us, as the work of all has been loyal and most efficient in every way and at all times. Another troop may replace yours, but none can do better work.
/s/ Bell
Commanding 2nd District."

"Headquarters, U.S. Troops in the Field, Island of Leyte
Camp Bumpus, Tacloban, Leyte, April 29, 1907.
Captain Thomas A. Roberts,
Troop "D," 7th Cavalry,
Camp McGrath, Barangas, Luzon, P.I.
Sir:
I take pleasure in expressing to you, and through you to the officers and men of your troop my appreciation of the excellent services rendered while on duty at Tanauan, Leyte, O.I., both in the field and performing the arduous escort duty of supplies to stations in the interior.

A greater part of the service was performed during the rainy season when the roads and trails were in a deplorable condition but the promptness and willingness with which this duty was performed has always excited the commendation of all who knew of your service.

You always disposed of the work in hand with great good judgment and it will be difficult to fill your place with such satisfactory results. I very much regret the necessity for losing your services and hope that the early prospect of the transfer of your regiment to the United States will compensate for your faithful services in Leyte. With best wishes, I am,

/s/ Fred A. Smith
Colonel, 8th Infantry,
In Charge of Field Operations,
Island of Leyte."

"Headquarters Department of the Visayas, Iloilo, Panay, P.I., April 27, 1907.
The Adjutant General,
Philippines Division,
Manila, P.I.

Sir:
In connection with the departure from this department of Troop "D," 7th Cavalry, commanded by Captain Thomas A. Roberts, and its return to duty at its proper station at Camp McGrath, Batangas, P.I., I wish to make a special report of the exceptionally efficient service Captain Roberts, his officers and his Troops have

A Cavalry Soldiers bunk and equipment, circa 1907. Courtesy of Ed Daily.

7th Cavalry escort to Brig. Gen. E.S. Godfrey, Fort Riley, Kansas, Nov. 22, 1907. Courtesy of Ed Daily.

Troop F, 7th Cavalry, Fort Riley, Kansas, 1907. Courtesy of Ed Daily.

7th Cavalry on parade, St. Joseph, Missouri, 1907. Courtesy of Ed Daily.

7th Cavalry Three-Horse Roman, Fort Riley, Kansas, 1907. Courtesy of Ed Daily.

7th Cavalry Bareback Squad, Fort Riley, Kansas, 1907. Courtesy of Ed Daily.

rendered in the field operations in progress in the Island of Leyte.

Captain Roberts' troop has been stationed at Tanauan, and has been charged especially with forwarding and safeguarding supplies from the beach at that town to the troops operating in the interior from Dagami and Burauen. In addition, The Troop has been constantly called on to perform other escort duty and to scout the country East of the mountains to the Coast.

All the many demands made on Captain Roberts and his command have been met in so cheerful and prompt a way that I believe all connected with the troop are worthy of thanks and commendation.

Very respectfully,
/s/ A.L. Mills,
Bragadier General, I.S.A.,
Commanding."

"Philippine Constabulary,
Headquarters Third Division,
Iloilo, Iloilo, P.I.
June 30, 1907.

Colonel F. A. Smith, 8th U.S. Infantry,
In Charge of Field Operations,
Tacloban, Leyte.
Sir:

The Constabulary Officers in Leyte in rendering their annual report mention with gratitude the great assistance given the constabulary in transporting articles and men for them on Military launches and otherwise by yourself and the officers serving under you, especially Major Bell, Captains Roberts and Conrad, and the Quartermaster, Lieut. Frissell at Tacloban.

I would like to add my thanks and appreciation for your courtesy and that of the officers serving under you, not only those just named by extending to the officers serving in the various

columns and posts, to the Constabulary in the matter of trasportation as well as in various other ways.

Very repectfully,
/s/ W.C. Rivers,
District Director."

The troops performed usual routine duties at their post until June 2nd, when the 9th Cavalry arrived on the U. S. A. T. "Logan." Property was transferred and the regiment embarked on June 11th and sailed to Mariveles the same night. It went into quarters at the Quarantine Station, where all property was disinfected. The 3rd Squadron was relieved at Camp Gregg by the 5th Battalion, Philippine Scouts on June 12th, and left the post on June 13th, by rail, arriving in Manila the same date and embarked on the "Logan" for Mariveles, where it disembarked for

Troop A, 7th Cavalry, Aug. 18, 1907, Fort Riley, Kansas. The only troops left remaining after mustering out of service, and all had enlisted for the tour in the Philippines. Courtesy of Ed Daily.

Inspecting Thanksgiving Dinner by General Kerr, at the Troop A Mess Hall, Fort Riley, Kansas, 1907. Courtesy of Ed Daily.

Saber Drill, Troop B, 7th Cavalry, Fort Riley, Kansas, 1907. Courtesy of Ed Daily.

disinfection on June 14th. On the 15th all the troops embarked on the "Logan" and proceeded to Woosung, China, where a quantity of flour was unloaded for the relief of famine. The command remained there until June 21st and then proceeded to Nagasaki, Japan, arriving on June 23rd. At Nagasaki, the ship was refueled and sailed on June 26th for San Francisco, by way of Honolulu.

The "Logan," with the entire regiment on board, crossed the 180th Meridian about 6:00 a.m. July 5th. While at sea, the regimental band played ocncerts regularly, and boxing and wrestling bouts were held for the amusement of the men. The transport arrived at Honolulu at 6:30 p.m. on July 8th; however, shore leave was not granted the men because of the prevalence of bubonic plague in the city. The regiment sailed from honolulu at 11:30 a.m. on July 9th and arrived in San Francisco at 9:30 a.m. on July 17th, and proceeded to the Folsom Street dock and unloaded property until 1:30 p.m. on July 18th. The entire regiment then marched to the Oakland Ferry and left Oakland in two sections at 9:40 p.m. the same date. The first section (Headquarters, Band, and Troops A, B, C, D, and H) was under command of Lieutenant Colonel John F. Guilfoyle, 7th Cavalry; and the second section (Troops E, F, G, I, K, L, and M) under Major E. P. Brewer, 7th Cavalry, left at 10:00 p.m.

During the journey, the first section was delayed by a broken car and the second section passed it, arriving at Fort Riley, Kansas, at 5:30 p.m., on July 25th; while the first section arrived at 11:00 p.m. on the same date. Thus, the regiment returned to the post where it was organized 41 years before.

Both trains were met by many officers from the post, among whom were Brigadier General E. S. Godfrey and Colonel F. K. Ward, the latter having been assigned to the regiment. After unloading, the regiment marched to the post, passing by General Godfrey's quarters, and formed on the parade ground, where it was presented to Colonel Ward. The squadrons were assigned ot quarters alphabetically from right to left.

On September 21st, Troop L proceeded by rail to St. Joseph, Missouri, to participate in a military tournament and returned to Fort Riley on September 30th.

On October 1st, the 1st Squadron (Troops A, B, C, D), Major William J. Nicholson, 7th Cavalry, Commanding, left for Hastings, Nebraska, camping at Wakefield, Clay Center, Clyde, Concordia, and Scandia, Kansas, and Hardy, Guide Rock, and Blue Hills, Nebraska. It remained at Hastings during the Frontier Festival, October 9th to 12th, and returned to Fort Riley, Kansas, on October 21st, having marched 400 miles. On October 24th, Headquarters, Band,

Troops E, F, G, I, K, L and M, Lieutenant Colonel John F. Guilfoyle, 7th Cavalry, Commanding, proceeded on an annual practice march of 287 miles to Fort Leavenworth, Kansas, and return, camping at Ogden, Manhattan, Wamego, Rossville, Topeka, and Ozawkie, Kansas.

On October 9th, Brigadier General Edward S. Godfrey, U. S. A., reached the statutory age for retirement. At noon, all officers of the regiment, attended by the regimental Band, paid their respects to General Godfrey. "GarryOwen" was played and after greeting the General all sang "The Wild Missouri." General Godfrey, Colonels Ward and Macomb made short addresses and all showed the deep feeling of the regiment for an officer who had served so many years in the 7th Cavalry, including the Battle of the Little Big Horn.

While the 1st Squadron (Troops A, B, C, D) performed usual garrison duties at Fort Riley, Kansas, the Regimental Headquarters, Band, 2nd and 3rd Squadrons took a practice march of 188 miles as follows: Ozawkie, November 1st; Winchester, November 2nd; Fort Leavenworth, November 3rd, 4th, and 5th; Big Stranger, November 6th; Lawrence, November 7th; Topeka, November 8th; Rossville, November 9th; Wamego, November 10th, Manhattan, November 11th and 12th; and returned to Fort Riley, Kansas, at noon November 13th.

The regiment performed the usual garrison duties at Fort Riley, Kansas for the remainder of the year.

1908

The regiment was in garrison at Fort Riley, Kansas, during the entire year. The year was properly begun by the Regimental Commander making the usual formal calls on the Commanding Officer of the Post, Cavalry and Artillery units, and on all the families of the post.

The routine of garrison service during this year was broken by the maneuvers held at Pawnee Flats on the post during the period August 8th to September 7th. During the period September 9th to October 7th, the regiment marched 329 miles to St. Joseph, Missouri, and return. During this period, the regiment formed a part of division, commanded by Brigadier General Charles Morton, consisting of two regiments of cavalry, two regiments of infantry, one battalion of field artillery, and one battalion of engineers.

Due to a ruling that the entire organization,

or teams from separate organizations, only could compete in the different events, there were no representatives of the regiment in the annual military tournament. This caused some unfavorable comment, but the comparison of the total number of recruits received since January with the total enlisted strength of the regiment, and a consideration of the further fact that the regiment had been actively engaged in target practice since the first of May, not only explains why no fancy drill squads were formed, but caused speculation as to how even the ordinary recruit instruction could have been given.

The regiment returned from St. Joseph, Missouri, on October 7th. Troops I and L preceded the regiment on leaving St. Joseph and participated in a carnival at Nortonville, Kansas, rejoining the regiment at that place.

On October 5th, Troop A left Fort riley on its annual practice march, proceeded to Wichita, Kansas, and took part in the carnival at that place, returning on the 22nd. From that date, for the first time since May 1st, the entire regiment was at the post.

During November the weather was favorable and drills were taken up viogrously and the improvement to morale and instruction became more apparent. For about two weeks, the troops commanders had their troops exclusively, but thereafter the morning instruction was divided into three periods—troop, squadron and regimental drills. By the end of November, the regiment again was able to give a spririted and accurate regimental or squadron drill.

During the month of October, 45 ponies were sent to the regiment and put under charge of Captain Williams and 1st Lieut. Lee for a systematic course of training before being used for polo or other purposes. This instruction continued during the month with specially selected men detailed under these officers and provided a fine school for the men as well as for the horses. This was probably the beginning of a regimental school of equitation under graduates of the Mounted Service School.

Since the beginning of this year the regiment had lost 412 of the old men who had enlisted for Philippine service, and had received 550 new recruits. During the year 122 men deserted. With rifle and pistol practice to conduct, the problem of training and instructing the new men was one that taxed the energies of the officers and old soldiers to the limit. All were busily engaged from reveille to retreat, and even with every effort that could be made, the regiment had to go to the maneuvers in August largely a recruit organization. From the first of May to October, there was no time when at least half of the regiment was not under canvas. The remainder of the year was spent in hard work instruction the new men in the manifold duties of the cavalry soldier.

1909

The beginning of the year found the entire regiment still at Fort Riley. The New Year was properly ushered in by the Commanding General and the Commanding Officers of the 7th Cavalry and the 8th Field Artillery, calling at the quarters of all officers, to wish the families a Happy New Year.

The usual routine duties were performed

7th Cavalry Band on Parade, Junction, Kansas, Memorial Day, 1908. Courtesy of Ed Daily.

1st Squadron, 7th Cavalry, Picket Line, Fort Riley, Kansas, 1908. Courtesy of Ed Daily.

during January. The open weather permitted many out-of-doors drills and the officers' class in equitation continued daily.

In this connection, it seems well to record the fact that the scheme of instruction in this respect, as prescribed by the War Department, had been outlined and put into effect by Colonel Ward, the Regimental Commander, several weeks before the orders of the President were promulgated or known, thus showing that the regiment was well up the mark in energy and desire to excel.

Instruction in pointing and aiming and in gallery practice was actively taken up during April, as well as the usual 3-day's marches made by squadron—the 1st Squadron, April 5th, 6th, 7th; the 2nd Squadron, April 14th, 15th, 16th; the 3rd Squadron, April 22nd, 23rd, 24th.

Target practice on the range began in May and continued during the month. Keen interest was taken in this work, all other duties were, as far as practicable, put in the background, and all energy concentrated on teaching the young cavalryman how to shoot. As will be seen later, the labor had its reward in a marked increase in the several figures of merit and in the number and kinds of insignia worn by both officers and men.

Target season ended in July and the monthly practice marches by squadron were resumed. The 1st Squadron was absent July 18th, 19th, 20th; the 2nd Squadron, July 24th, 25th, 26th; and the 3rd Squadron, July 13th, 14th, 15th. The country within two-day's march of the post was alive with troops during a large part of July.

During the month, Major Nicholson was absent for several days at Wichita, Kansas, arranging for the annual practice march of the regiment, to be taken in September.

In August the regiment started in with renewed zeal to drill and prepare for the Military Tournament to be held at Des Moines, Iowa, in September. The 2nd Squadron and Machine Gun Platoon had been designated to attend. The regimental commander decided to retain Troops D and I at the post while Headquarters, Band and six troops were at Wichita, and the 2nd Squadron at Des Moines.

An arrangement of the saber exercises was set to music and a portion of each drill hour was taken up by it, also drill was held just before retreat. Marked improvement in the general appearance of the men became apparent in a short time.

During the month of August, Captains Pow-

7th Cavalry Dress Parade, Fort Riley, Kansas, 1908. Courtesy of Ed Daily.

U.S. Army Transport "Sheridan," 1908. This troop transport carried the 7th Cavalry Regiment to the Philippines and return on both tours of duty of the islands prior to 1915. Courtesy of Ed Daily.

ers and Williams and 1st Lieutenants Casteel, Kendrick and Brown were on duty with the National Guard of Kansas from the 17th to the 26th, inclusive. During the encampment, at the request of the regimental commanders, Color Sergeant Trometre and Chief Trumpeter Clancy took the National Guard bands and field music in charge and instructed them. Letters of thanks were received by the regimental commander, which were in the highest degree commendatory of the work of officers and men.

Troops D and I, under Captain R. B. Powers, returned from their annual march on September 5th. Due to Captain Powers having been on duty with the Kansas National Guard in camp, 1st Lieutenant Thomas P. Bernard commanded the provisional squadron until its arrival at Fort Leavenworth. Only two officers (Lieutenants Bernard and Herr) were with the troops when they left the post, and, on arrival at Topeka, Lieutenant Herr was disabled by an infected wound and threatened with blood poisoning; he was sent back to the post and Lieutenant Bernard was left alone with the provisional squadron.

On September 15th, the 2nd Squadron and Machine Gun Platoon, under Captain S. R. H. Tompkins; left by rail for Des Moines, Iowa.

They were played out of the post by the band and sent away with heartiest wishes for success.

On September 17th, Headquarters, Band, and six troops, under Lieutenant Colonel John F. Guilfoyle, left for Wichita. Exhibition drills were given at nearly every town where the regiment camped, and horses and men arrived in Wichita on the 23rd. Headquarters, Band, and three batteries of the 6th Field Artillery, under Lieutenant Colonel Eli D. Hoyle, were in camp there, and as Lieutenant Colonel Guilfoyle was the senior officer present, he assumed command of the camp, as required by Army Regulations. The town was thrown open to the soldiers and the men rose to the occasion, for there were no cases of disorder and the people generally spoke in terms of high praise of the discipline of the command. The 25th. was announced an "Military Day" of the carnival known as the "Peerless Prophets." In the morning there was a parade of the battalion of the Kansas National Guard and two regular regiments, all under command of Lieutenant Colonel Guilfoyle. In the afternoon the National Guard drilled in the bayonet drill and manual of arms. They were followed by a well executed battery drill under Captian J. W. Kilbreth, 6th F. A., and a fancy drill under

Captain C. R. Loyd, 6th F. A. On the conclusion of the artillery drills, the 7th Cavalry marched in review at a gallop before the packed grandstand, after with Troop A, under 2nd Lieutenant J. A. Shannon, gave a spirted and beautifully executed troop drill. When the troop, in almost perfect alignment, charged and jumped a long, 3-foot hurdle, roars of applause went up from the crowd. Troop A's drill was followed by a lively squadron drill by Troops K, L, and M, under Captain F. Beach; both extended and close order movements were given and a dismounted attack was made. This drill, to judge from the applause, was very well executed. Following the squadron, the saddle squad of Troop C, under 1st Lieutenant D. T. E. Casteel, put up a showy and accurate exhibition of fancy movements. From the first moment to the end of the drill a continuous roar from the spectators testified to their satisfaction with and admiration of the skill of the riders and the intelligence and training of the horses. The bareback squad then made its appearance, under command of 2nd Lieutenant H. E. Mann, and capped the climax. The men had been selected from all six troops and carefully and thoroughly trained for the occasion. It seemed to be the psychological moment, for during the whole drill not a man failed to do his part perfectly, nor did a horse shy or balk. In the opinion of the officers who watched, all of whom had seen many similar exhibitions, it was one of the finest in the experience of any of them. The citizens had never seen anything of the kind and the immense crowd, estimated at 35,000, cheered the men to the echo. As soon as the bareback drill was over, a number of men assembled for a half-mile Roman race. After a false start or two, they were off. Private Caylor, of Troop A, won and received a handsome watch. Corporal Dare, Troop B, second, received a handsome dressing case, both donated by citizens of Wichita. The day's entertainment was brought to a close by a mounted parade of the entire six troops. During the ceremony the musical saber drill was given with much success. Not until the rear of the regiment was passing through the gate of the Fair Grounds did the crowd start to disperse, notwithstanding the fact that they had begun to gather at 8:00 a.m. The roofs of all buidings were covered with people and many perched for hours on the sharp tops of board fences.

On returning to camp, a telegram from Des Moines announced the winning of several first prizes in the tournemnt at that place. The following was sent: "Congratulations. Hit 'em again. By order Lt. Col. Guifoyle: Roberts, Adjutant."

While at Hervington, on September 19th, and order was received to send Lieutenant Blair back to the post to train for the International Horse Show, at Madison Square Garden, New York. Lieutenant Blair was acting Regimental Quartermaster and Commissary and his loss in that capacity was severely felt, while all missed his genial and cheerful face in camp. While at Lindsborg, word was received of the accident that finally caused his death.

The regiment broke camp on September 27th, and started on its return march. The monthly muster was held at Lindsbourg.

Headquarters, Band and Troops, A, B, C, K, L, and M returned to the post on October 7th

The 7th Cavalry Band, 1909. Courtesy of Ed Daily.

The 7th Cavalry Trumpet Corps, Courtesy of Ed Daily.

Regimental Non-Commissioned Officer Staff, 7th Cavalry Regiment, Fort Riley, Kansas, 1909. (L to R standing) Robert J. Napier, 1st Squadron Sergeant Major; Claude B. Clarke, 2nd Squadron Sergeant Major; William H. Bauer, 3rd Squadron Sergeant Major. (L to R seated) Max Weimann, Color Sergeant; Napier Nunns, Regimental Quartermaster Sergeant; Walter E. Powers, Regimental Sergeant Major; Hubert W. Ketchum, Regimental Commissary Sergeant; Carl Trometre, Color Sergeant.

and were greatly welcomed by Troops D and I, who had a weary three weeks on guard and fatigue duty.

The usual routine was followed during the rest of October, with only one break, this occuring on the 26th, when the victorious 2nd Squadron and Machine Gun Platoon returned from the Des Moines tournament and the later carnival at Omaha.

All the field officers and Troops D and I were in the field in connection with the annual field officers' physical test, so Captain George W. Read had the remaining six troops and the band saddle up and go out near Morris Hill to welcome the conquerors home. The sight was inspiring as Captain Tompkins approached at a lively trot, swung into line smartly and the two commands saluted and then cheered each other. Each organization that left Fort Riley for the tournemant brough back at least one blue ribbon fluttering from the guidon. It was not only in the competitive events that the men had excelled, but also the saddle and bareback squads, under 2nd Lieutenant S. M. Williams, covered themselves with glory and displayed drills that

were seldom equalled and never surpassed during the tournament. Although deprived of the Band, the musical saber drill of the squadron did not suffer. Chief Trumpeter Clancy trained a corps of trumpeters in special airs, to the music of which the squadron executed the many movements like one man and elicted hearty applause and commendation when the drill was given. A peculiarly pleasing feature of the reception of the homecomers was the courtesy shown by them to Battery E, 6th Field Artillery, under Captian Edward Hill, 6th. F. A., which was with them during the entire time. The battery was saluted by the squadron and then put in column immediately after the regiment and thus escorted into the post. The best of feeling prevailed between the men of the two organizations.

Colonel Ward, Lieutenant Colonel Guilfoyle, and Major Nicholson returned from their 90-mile ride and reported that the distance was too short to be really interesting. The two last-named had just returned from a 300-mile march, which the first did not take due to his pressing duties as Commandant of the Mounted Service School.

While in camp at Salina, Kansas, on October 2nd, telegraphic orders were received from Fort Riley to send to that post 1st Lieutenant Lee and 2nd Lieutenants Shannon and Nicholson, the first named to go into training for the horse show at Madison Square Garden, New York, to fill the place of Lieutenant Blair, and last two to enter the class of the Mounted Service School.

The conduct of the troops of the regiment, while away from the post, was so remarkably good that it elicted the following commendatory orders and letters.

Headquarters, Fort Riley, Kansas,
November 1, 1909.
GENERAL ORDERS
No. 57
The following letter and resolution from the Wichita Commercial Club, Wichita, Kansas, is published for the information of this command:

Wichita, Kansas, Saturday,
October Thirtieth, Nineteen-nine,
Commanding Officer, Fort Riley, Kansas.

Dear Sir:
It is a matter of great pleasure to me to enclose a copy of resolution unanimously adopted by the WICHITA COMMERCIAL CLUB *at a meeting held on October twenty-six, nineteen-nine.*

It will be appreciated if you will transmit this resolution to the officers and men comprising these organizations that visited here during Jubilee week, that they may know how high a regard they have established in the minds of the people of the City of Wichita and contiguous territory as a result of that visit.

Yours sincerely,
John McGinnis, Secretary.

A RESOLUTION ADOPTED BY THE
WICHITA COMMERCIAL CLUB
AT A MEETING HELD
OCTOBER TWENTY - SIXTH,
NINETEEN-NINE.

RESOLVED: *That it is the sense of this meeting, representing the spirit and purpose of the* WICHITA COMMERCIAL CLUB, *that the Commanding Officers and Enlisted men of the Seventh Cavalry and Sixth Field Artillery, United States Army, who participated in the exhibition of military drills in this city on September twenty-fifth, nineteen-nine, Military Day of the Peerless Prophets Jubilee, be extended the sincere thanks and hearty congratulations of this body for their splendid display of training and proficiency on that occasion, and especially for the uniform conduct of both commands while in this City.*

That their visit has been productive not only by enlightening the people of this section of the splendid condition in which the Army is maintained, but by enhancing public regard for the United States Soldier, with the conviction that the physical and moral quality of the troops marks them as fine Soldiers, Gentlemen and good citizens, such as to stir with pride every patriotic-minded person.

That is is a great source of satisfaction that we should have had this opportunity to come so pleasantly in touch with such worthy represen-tatives of the regular Military establishment of our country, and that it is our sincere wish and hope that the future may afford similar opportu-nities for renewing and cementing the cordial acquaintanceship that had been formed.

By Order of Colonel Ward:
William J. Kendrick,
1st Lietuenant, 7th Cavalry,
Acting Adjutant General.

Headquarters Department
of the Missouri,
Omaha, Nebraska, October 9, 1909.

CIRCULAR,
No. 18.
The Department Commander takes plea-sure in publishing the following communications. The organizations who participated in the mili-tary tournament at Des Moines and who are re-ferred to in these letters are as follows:

Company "A," Hospital Corps; Company "D" and Baloon Detachment, Signal Corps; Company "K," 3rd Battalion of Engineers; 2nd Cavalry; 1st Gun Platoon, 7th Cavalry; 2nd Squadron, 15th Cavalry; a platoon of Battery "C," 4th Field Artillery; Battery "E," 5th Field Artillery; Battery "E," 6th Field Artillery; 13th Infantry (less 1st Battalion); detachment Bak-ers and Cooks and Quartermaster's Pack Train No. 24; and 16th Infantry (less 1st battalion).

By Command of Brigadier General
Morton:
W.P. Burnham
Major, General Staff,
Chief of Staff

THE COMMERCIAL CLUB,
Office of the Secretary,
Des Moines, Iowa,
October 2, 1909.
General Charles Morton, U. S. A.,
Department of the Missouri,
Omaha, Nebraska.

Sir:
As secreatry of the Des Moines Commer-cial Club, it affords me great pleasure to enclose to you the accompanying resolution, together with the information that it received the unani-mous endorsement of the Club with its member-ship of over 750 business and professional men and that it is but a mild expression of the esteem in which the poeple of this city hold the officers and soldiers of the Army.

The resolution inadequately expresses our appreciation of the great honor conferred upon us by the Army in giving to Des Moines such a splendid tournament and for our people I want to assure you that we are at your service and desirous at any time to cooperate with you for the good of Fort Des Moines, your Department and the Army.

Respectfully,
Geis Botsford,
Secretary,

BE IT RESOLVED: —That the Commer-cial Club of Des Moines, Iowa, hereby express hearty congratulations to General Charles Morton, commander of the Department of the Missouri, U.S.A., and in command of the Mili-tary Tournament at Des Moines, for the success of the military tournament.

The Commercial Club wishes to comment especially on the conduct of the soldiers while in the city. They acquitted themselves in every respect as gentlemen, polite, courteous and af-fable, and in every way demeaning themselves as worthy American soldiers.

There was not a single act done in the city by a soldier that was in any way derogatory to their standing as citizens or to their positions in the Army of the United States.

Jerry R. Sullivan,
B.F. Kauffman,
Geis Botsford,
Committee.

Adopted by unanimous vote at meeting of September 29, 1909,

Geis Botsford,
Secretary.

CITY OF DES MOINES,
DEPARTMENT OF PUBLIC SAFETY,
Des Moines, Iowa, October 4, 1909.
General Morton,
Commanding General,
Department of the Missouri,
Fort Omaha, Neb.

Dear Sir:
Several important happenings of local sig-nificance have prevented me from writing you before. I therefore take the first opportunity to congratulate you on the success of the military tournament in this city and thank you in the name of the Department for the splendid discipline maintained by the soldiery while in this city, and the conduct of the soldiers in the city was most exemplary and they have made innumerable friends. I must unhesitatingly state that never before was so large a number of people present in the city with so little disorder and so few ar-rests.

Hoping that we again have the pleasure of witnessing your entertainment, I am,

Very respectfully yours,
A.G. Miller,
Chief of Police.

HEADQUARTERS PROVISIONAL
DIVISION
Camp Corse, Des Moines, Iowa
September 25, 1909.
GENERAL ORDERS,
No. 7.
At the closing hour of this tournament and before the departure of the troops, the Command-ing General wishes to express to the command his congratulations over the success upon all lines of this largest military tournament ever held in the United States; and to express his appre-ciation of and gratification over the interest, energy, and zeal displayed by every organiza-tion, thus causing the whole affair to move from start to finish without hitch, friction, or jar, and with uniform good feeling throughout, though the contest were spirited and executed with great determination.

There is equal satisfaction over the condi-tions that obtained in the camp. The ground be-

ing contracted for camping such a large com-mand made it too condensed for comfort, and made necessary the enforcement of the strictest sanitary measures, which was accomplished with gratifying results with hardly a complaint from the vigilant Sanitary Inspector.

The Commanding General's interest in these military tournaments is based almost wholly upon the conviction that the better the Army is known and understood by the people the better it is for the people and the Army. He is convinced that this encampment with its exhibi-tions of Army life and many of the features of its training, has a revelation to many thousands of people, and of mutual benefit.

But the best feature of all has been the bear-ing and conduct of the command, which have evoked the highest terms of praise from people and press, and demonstrate not only the high standard of character of the personnel of the Army but its equally high order of training and discipline.

By Command of Brigadier General
Morton:
W.P. Burnham,
Major, General Staff,
Chief of Staff.

OFFICIAL
D.B. Devore,
Major, 11th Infantry,
Adjutant General.

HEADQUARTERS PROVISIONAL
DIVISION,
Camp Thayer, Fort Omaha, Nebraska,
October 9, 1909.

GENERAL ORDERS,
No. 5.
The Commanding General of the Provi-sional Division takes this opportunity to express his appreciation of the excellent showing and good conduct of the troops during this encamp-ment.

By Command of
Brigadier General Smith:
D.B. Devore,
Major, 11th Infantry,
Adjutant General.

Upon return of all troops to the post, much time was spent in getting rid of the rust that al-ways accumulates during practice marches. Men and horses returned in fine condition and by the end of November, when the winter set in, the regiment was able to put up splendid troop, squadron and regimental drills and was well in-structed in the other manifold branches that are required of good cavalrymen.

In November, marksmanship insignia were received and distributed. The effectiveness of the hard training conducted the previous spring is evidenced by the following decorations, in ad-dition to several bars awarded for continued qualifications:

26 Expert Riflemens Badges;
67 Sharpshooters' Badges;
114 Marksman's Pins.

Winter closed down on the regiment with a vengeance and during the entire month of De-cember the ground was covered with thick ice and snow, rendering it almost impossible to have even exercise for the horses except at rare intervals. However, the schools were conducted and the riding hall was in use during every hour of daylight.

Captain Fitzhugh Lee and 1st Lieutenant George M. Lee were placed in charge of the school of equitation for officers, and Captain George Williams and 2nd Lieutenant J.V. Spring, Jr., of that for non-commissioned officers. Good progress was made during the month.

On the 12th, the regiment and the garrison at large were shocked to learn of the death of 2nd Lieutenant Winn Blair. Lieutenant Blair had many friends and was very highly thought of professionally as well as socially. The orders of the Regimental Commander announcing his death are quoted below in full:

HEADQUARTERS SEVENTH U.S. CAVALRY,
Fort Riley, Kansas, December 13, 1909.
GENERAL ORDERS, No. 81.

With the deepest regret, the Regimental Commander announces the death of 2nd Lieutenant Winn Blair, 7th Cavalry, at the Army and Navy General Hospital, Hot Springs, Arkansas, at 10:30 a.m., December 12, 1909.

This young officer joined the Regiment October 22, 1904, having graduated from the Military Academy in June of the same year. The exigencies of the service caused his attachment to and service with four troops of the regiment, in each of which faithful performance of duty, loyalty to his commanding officers and consideration for those under him were characteristic.

He served as Squadron Quartermaster and Commissary of the Third Squadron from May 18, 1907, to June 23, 1909, and on more than one occasion was selected to act as Regimental Quartermaster and Commissary of the Regiment in the field, to the eminent satisfaction of the Regimental Commander. He represented the Regiment in Pistol Competitions in 1906 and 1909, each time winning a place on the team. He entered the Mounted Service School in 1908 and completed the course with such credit that he was detailed, upon application by the School, to take a post graduate course.

To his proficiency as a horseman was due the accident that brought about his untimely end, as he suffered a fracture of the leg while training a horse for the International Horse Show, at Madison Square Garden, New York, and during an operation that subsequently became necessary, he died from heart failure while under an anasthetic.

In all the manifold duties that fall to a subaltern serving with his Regiment, Lieutenant Blair gave evidence of a high order of military and executive ability. As a man, he was of a singularly lovable character, endearing himself both to his associates and those under his command.

The Entire Regiment mourns with his bereaved family, and regrets that the Array must be deprived of the services of so promising a young officer. Winn Blair will always be a cherished memory in the Seventh Cavalry.

The officers of the Regiment will wear the badge of mourning for thirty days.

By Order of Lieut. Colonel Guilfoyle:
T.A. ROBERTS,
Captain and Adjutant, 7th Cavalry,

Christmas Day was celebrated by splendid dinners and many Christmas trees throughout the post. As most of the troop messes were run by the Bakers and Cooks School, the dinners were even more elaborate than usual. All troop dining rooms were decorated, but that of Troop F surpassed anything before seen in the regiment.

1910

The regiment was stationed at Fort Riley, Kansas, for the entire year.

During the first three months of the year, the organizations of the regiment availed themselves of the open winter for outdoor instruction, both mounted and dismounted. The usual routine garrison duties, including the garrison schools for officers and non-commissioned officers, were continued and completed by the end of the theoretical period (March). In April the real work started with outdoor drills and maneuvers in anticipation of the fall maneuvers.

The regiment was inspected, drilled and maneuvered on April 19th, 1910, by Major J.B. Irwin, Inspector General's Department. At these formations the regiment was commanded for the first time by its new Colonel, George K. Hunter.

Target practice, both rifle and pistol, began early in the month of May. All troops took their regular turn on the rifle range, and Troops F, I, K and L were given the entire range in order to complete their practice before the opening of the camp of instruction for National Guard officers of cavalry and field artillery. These four troops were designated as a provisional squadron, under the command of Captain Ewing E. Booth, 7th Cavalry, for duty as troops of instruction. On May 29th, the provisional squadron went into camp on the "Hogback," Fort Riley Military Reservation, Kansas, and remained there until June 30th, engaging in field work of every description incident to the instruction of the National Guard officers from the several States and Territories. The remaining troops of the regiment completed pistol practice before the end of May, and completed rifle practice during the months of June and July.

Upon orders from the War Department to test the relative endurance of cavalry and field artillery with the present equipments, the 3rd Squadron (Troops I, K, L and M), Captain Ewing E. Booth, 7th Cavalry, Commanding, and the 2nd Battalion, 6th Field Artillery, Major J.E. McMahon, 6th Field Artillery, Commanding, left the post July 18th and marched 143 miles in five days.

On August 2nd, Troops A and B marched to the Camp of Instruction at Pawnee Flats (Fort Riley Military Reservation, Kansas), and went into camp as Headquarters Guard for the Commanding General, Brigadier General Frederick K. Ward, U.S.A., and Staff. On the 12th of August, Headquarters, Field and Staff, Band, Troops E, F, G, H, I, K, L and M, and the Machine Gun Platoon marched to the Camp of Instruction and went into camp on Pawnee Flats. Troops C and D remained at Fort Riley as guard for post and property, and prepared for a military tournament to be held at Des Moines, Iowa. The troops at the Camp of Instruction (Except Troops A and B) performed the usual duties incident to a camp of this kind from the date of arrival to September 15th. The Band, Machine Gun Platoon, and

Troops A and B left the Camp of Instruction and returned to Fort Riley on September 16th, to prepare for the military tournament at Des Moines, Iowa.

Headquarters, Field and Staff, and Troops E, F, G, H, I, K, L and M, under command of Colonel George K. Hunter, 7th Cavalry, left the Camp of Instruction on September 16th, on the annual practice march, scheduled for Beatrice, Nebraska, and return. The column was escorted from the camp by the regimental band, and, with a minimum of confusion incident to breaking camp and preparing for the march, the regiment started on the longest march it had made in many years.

The marches made were as follows:
September 16, to Riley Center, Kansas, 18.9 miles.
September 17th, to Randolph, Kansas, 17.25 miles.
September 18th, to Blue Rapids, Kansas, 22.5 miles.
September 19th, to Marysville, Kansas, 14 miles. At this point, instructions were received from Headquarters, Department of the Missouri, to extend the march to Omaha, Nebraska, instead of to Beatrice, as originally intended, in order that the troops might participate in the Ak-Sar-Ben Carnival to be held in Omaha. The troops were hard pressed for suitable clothing and equipment for a trip of this nature, since they had taken the field in their field uniforms and carried no clothing suitable for parading purposes. Nevertheless, the troops resumed the march the following day, September 20th, to Barneston, Nebraska, 19.5 miles, and to Beatrice, 25 miles, on September 21st. The command remained in camp here on September 22nd in order to test the animals. The following day orders were issued at reveille for the command to remain in camp that day due to the failure of the railroads to deliver supplies at the next point on the itinerary. However, two hours later word was received that the supplies would be delivered by the time the command could reach the next point. The command immediately broke camp and marched 20 miles to Cortland, Nebraska. The first half of the march was made in a driving rain. On September 24th, the command marched to Lincoln, Nebraska, 22 miles. The command remained in camp at Lincoln on September 25th, and among other pleasant features of the day's stay was the visit and talk given the officers and men by Captain Jack Crawford, a former Indian scout of the frontier days, who scouted with the regiment when its history was young and General Custer was making his name as an Indian fighter on the western plains. On September 29th, the command arrived at Fort Omaha, Nebraska, where it went into camp at Camp Ak-Sar-Ben on the reservation, having marched 232 miles.

The Band, Machine Gun Platoon, and Troops A, B, C, and D, under command of Major William J. Nicholson, 7th Cavalry, left Fort Riley, Kansas, by rail, for Des Moines, Iowa, on September 21st and arrived at Camp John A.T. Hull, Des Moines, Iowa, The following day, where they participated in the military tournament held there until September 30th. This squadron won many honors for the regiment throughout the contests, which were held in connection with the tournament. On October 1st, this command left by rail for Omaha, Nebraska, arrived the following day and marched to Camp Ak-Sar-Ben, Fort Omaha, Nebraska, where they joined the remainder of the regiment in camp. This date is marked conspicuously in the annals of the regiment as one on which the entire regiment as a unit took to the field. The march that followed is the only one that the regiment has ever made with all organizations serving in the same column.

The entire regiment remained in camp at Camp Ak-Sar-Ben, engaging in parades, drills, and exhibitions incident to the carnival until October 8th. In addition to the carnival in the city of Omaha, a military tournament was held at Fort Omaha, in which the regiment took part and earned considerable distinction, winning in a majority of the events in which it was entered. On October 9th, the entire regiment, Major William J. Nicholson, 7th Cavalry, commanding, left the camp at Fort Omaha, Nebraska, on the return march. On October 18th, the command arrived at Fort Riley, Kansas. The total distance marched on the return trip to the post was 224 miles, and the total distance marched during the trip was 454.8 miles. The regiment was commanded on the march during the last three days by Captain Selah R.H. Tompkins, 7th Cavalry, as Major William J. Nicholson was taking the field officers' test ride.

The remainder of the year was spent in garrison performing the usual duties incident thereto and in preparing for the coming change of station to the Philippine Islands. An early and cold winter prevented any extended outdoor instruction, although every opportunity was taken to further the mounted instruction of the command.

On March 13th, 1st Lieutenant George M. Lee, 7th Cavalry, was seriously injured during a practice polo game. The pony ridden by another officer became unmanageable, ran away and collided with Lieutenant Lee's pony just as the latter was making a goal. Lieutenant Lee's pony fell, knocked over the goal post and rolled over Lieutenant Lee, who was rendered unconscious for nearly two weeks. A long sick leave followed, and this officer was incapacitated for full duty during the remainder of the year. Polo received a severe handicap in the temporary loss of the team captain.

Until February 8th, the strength of the troops at Fort Riley was authorized at 85. For troops from which a machine gun platoon was detailed, the strength was authorized at 92. General Orders No. 21, War Department, February 8th, 1910, reduced the strength of these troops to 65 and 72, respectively. This resulted in men being assigned to the regiment in excess of the authorized strength, and orders were received to transfer a total of 229 enlisted men to the 6th and 11th Cavalry and 4th Field Artillery. Unsuccessful efforts were made to retain these men in the regiment to fill vacancies to be caused by the discharge of men due to expirations of terms of service. Due to the large number of men transferred and the very large number discharged, the regiment was short-handed during the season of the year when men were most urgently required for the summer instruction period and the maneuvers in the fall. A detachment of 79 recruits arrived and were assigned to the troops of the regiment while in the Camp of Instruction. These recruits, although barely started in their recruit instruction, helped to fill the ranks on the annual practice march later in the fall.

1911

The beginning of the year marked the closing days of the regiment's second tour of duty at Fort Riley, Kansas, as it had been ordered to its second tour of Philippine service by General Orders No. 204, War Department, series 1910.

A fairly open winter permitted much outdoor instruction. During inclement-weather indoor drills were held in the riding hall and gymnasium, following the existing regulations as closely as possible. Schools of equitation were held for both officers and non-commissioned officers and selected privates. Captain Fitzhugh Lee and 1st Lieutenant Lewis Brown, Jr., 7th Cavalry, were instructors in the officers' school, and Captain George Williams, 7th Cavalry, instructor in the school for non-commissioned officers and selected privates. Garrison school work was interrupted by the change of station, and resumed during the month of June in the Philippines.

About the middle of January, final preparations for the change of station to the Philippines began in earnest. Much of the work incident to the change had been accomplished during the winter months, and this materially helped in the trying period of transferring property and public mounts and closing all records and accounts.

Troops E and F were designated to remain at Fort Riley in charge of property and animals until the arrival of the 13th Cavalry—the relieving regiment. A detachment of 52 enlisted men was transferred to the 13th Cavalry from the 7th Cavalry to assist these organizations in the manifold duties.

On January 30th, at about ten o'clock in the morning, the freight section carrying the troop's baggage left Fort Riley for San Francisco, California, in charge of 2nd Lieutenant Allen F. McLean, 7th Cavalry, and a detachment of enlisted men from the various troops.

The Field Staff and Band, Machine Gun Platoon, Troops A, B, C, D, G, H, I, K, L and M marched to the railroad station, after being inspected by the post commander (Brigadier General Walter S. Schuyler, U.S.A.), and entrained. The entire command traveled in one section. The demonstration from the commands left at the post and the many townsfolk from the surrounding country was touching, and showed in a measure the esteem in which the regiment was held during its tour of over three years and a half at Fort Riley. At about eleven o'clock, the section moved out and the familiar sights were soon lost to view. Due to the slow-train, together with long sidings, it was noon on January 31st before Denver, Colorado, was reached, where a stop of two hours or more was made. Lengthy stops were made, at the principal cities throughout the trip. The Union Pacific and Southern Pacific systems, over which the trip was made, offered a better schedule after leaving Denver. Cheyenne, Wyoming, was reached late the same night, where a lengthy stop was made, as was also done at Ogden, Utah, on the following night (February 1st), and Reno, Nevada, on the night of February 2nd. The troop section overtook the freight section at Sacramento, California, about noon on February 3rd. The troop section continued in advance to San Francisco, California, and reached the Oakland Mole about 5:00 p.m. on February 3rd, where the regiment transferred to the ferry, crossed to San Francisco, and again embarked on the U.S.A.T. "Sheridan," in dock at the foot of Folsom Street. February 4th and 5th were spent in loading property and preparing for the long sea voyage.

Promptly at noon on February 6th the transport cast off and proceeded down San Francisco Bay and through the Golden Gate. The transport was speeded on her way by the whistles of her sister craft and the Artillery station boat, which was loaded with officers and the Artillery band from the Presidio of San Francisco and kept abreast of the transport until the Gate was reached.

The trip to Honolulu was a trifle rough for the cavalrymen-landsmen, but from Hawaii to the Philippines the weather was calm. Honolulu was reached at 1:00 p.m. on February 13th, and the transport sailed at 12:35 a.m. in the 15th. A full day and a half afforded an opportunity for sightseeing, which was well utilized by all.

Guam was reached after a pleasant though warm trip, at 11:22 p.m. on February 26th. The transport laid outside the harbor all night and entered about six o'clock the following morning, due to the dangerous entrance to the harbor. At 3:21 p.m. on the same day-after unloading mail and supplies for the Marine Corps garrison—the transport cast off from the anchorage buoy and the last lap of the 9,881 mile trip began. Nothing of note happened during the voyage, except the inevitable quarantine for measles and mumps.

Manila was reached at 10:00 a.m. on March 4th. Quarantine inspection was passed, property unloaded, and the regiment disembarked and encamped on the Luenta Fill (Camp Egbert), awaiting the departure of the 13th Cavalry from Fort William McKinley, Rizal, P.I., on March 14th. On the morning of the 14th of March, the troops proceeded to Fort William McKinley, by electric transportation, and after reporting to the post commander (Colonel Daniel Cornman, 7th Infantry), marched to their assigned barracks and proceeded to settle down for its second tour of duty in the, Philippine Islands. The strength of the regiment was increased by 129 enlisted men, who were transferred from the 13th Cavalry and reported for duty on the date the regiment arrived at Port William McKinley.

The distances traveled in the change of station were Fort Riley, Kansas, to San Francisco, California, by rail, 1,880 miles; San Francisco, California, to Manila, P.I., by U.S.A. Transport, 7,997 miles; Manila, P.I., to Fort William McKinley, P.I., by electric cars, 6 miles; for a total distance of 9,881 miles traveled.

The remainder of the month of March and the months of April and May were devoted to settling down, preparing for and engaging in rifle and revolver practice. No exceptional firing results were obtained by the organizations, due to the large percentage of recruits and the new firing regulations which were new to many of the seasoned men. However, the regiment was well represented at the Division Rifle and Pistol Competitions, held at Fort William McKinley, Rizal, P. I., in May.

Early in the month of April, the Division Commander called on the regiment for the detail of one Veterinarian and 13 enlisted men, to be well instructed in farriery, for duty with the civil government in connection with the extermination of rinderpest, a disease raging among cattle in the north central provinces of Luzon. Veterinarian William C. Van Allstyne, 7th Cavalry, and a detachment of 13 enlisted men (one from each troop and the Machine Gun Platoon)—for the most part non-commissioned officers and graduates from the Farriers and Horseshoers School at Fort Riley, Kansas—left Fort William McKinley on April 13th and proceeded to Camp Gregg, Pangasinan, from where they were assigned to duty in the adjoining provinces. Veterinarian Van Allstyne returned to his station on May 1st, and the men of the detachment at the end of the year. Both the military and civil governments praised the efficient work performed by this detachment of the regiment.

The provisional squadron, Troops E and F, under command of Major E.P. Brewer, 7th Cavalry, remained at Fort Riley, Kansas, after departure of the regiment, to care for property and animals. Transferred men and incoming recruits for the 13th Cavalry were organized into detachments to help care for public animals and for the police of barracks, stables and grounds. Troop E and a detachment of 13th Cavalry, unassigned, had charge of property and mounts turned over by Troops A, B, C, D and G; and Troop F and a similar detachment those turned over by Troops H, I, K, L and M. These duties were performed from January 30th to April 19th, when the 13th Cavalry arrived at Fort Riley and took over property and mounts. From April 20th to 30th, the provisional squadron completed packing property, loading and prepared for departure. On April 29th, they entrained at Fort Riley enroute to the Philippines by way of the same route traveled by the regiment in January and February. The squadron arrived at San Francisco, California, on May 3rd, and embarked on the U.S.A.T. "Sheridan" on the same date, leaving San Francisco on May 5th. They arrived at Honolulu at 9 a.m. on May 13th, and left at 3 p.m. on May 14th. They arrived at Guam at 5 p.m. on May 27th, and left at 4 p.m. on May 28th; and arrived at Manila on June 3rd. Here they proceeded by electric cars to Fort William McKinley the same day.

Troops E and F had target practice during the months of June and July, and the remainder of the regiment completed theirs in June.

Early in the month of June, the periods of instruction—in compliance with General Orders No. 7, War Department, series 1911—were designated from Headquarters Philippines Division in General Orders No. 32, series 1911. This order prescribed the garrison and theoretical period from June to November and the field and practical period from December to May. The order prescribed subperiods of instruction: June to August for troops as units, September for squadrons, October for regiments and November for all arms of the service serving at a post. In addition to the usual garrison drills in close and extended order, instruction was held in fencing, both mounted and dismounted, swimming, signaling, equitation for noncommissioned officers and selected privates (in charge of 1st Lieu-

tenant John V. Spring, Jr., 7th Cavalry), and in the various forms of garrison school, viz: post graduate work, regular garrison school subjects for subalterns, and non-commissioned officers' school. Particular attention was given to map reading and topographical work, all officers below the grade of lieutenant colonel attended for the month of June, and it formed one of the two Subjects in the school for non- commissioned officers.

The schedule of instruction was carried out for the different periods to include October 22nd. On October 23rd, and continuing until November 15th, the regiment experimented in double-rank formation for mounted drill, in compliance with letter, The Adjutant General's Office, Washington, D. C, dated September 8th,-1911. In order to have a troop of 96 enlisted men in ranks, the troops were consolidated for drill purposes, Troops A, B and C forming one troop; Troops D, E and F; Troops G, H and I; and Troops K, L and M the others. These consolidated troops were commanded at the experimental drills by the senior officers present with the troops. At the completion. of the drills on November 15th, 1911, reports of officers who had commanded consolidated troops (Captains Matthew C. Butler, Thomas A. Roberts, George Williams, Evan H. Humphrey and James C. Rhea, 7th Cavalry) were enclosed in a report to the Adjutant General of the Army. Drill regulations for double rank drill were not available and the only aid was a pamphlet from the War Department General Staff, entitled "Cavalry Notes," compiled by Major H.T. Allen, General Staff; consequently, the drills were for the most part composed of improvised movements conforming as closely as possible to the regulations for single rank.

The remainder of the month of November was devoted to combined instruction which two regiments of infantry (7th and 12th); 7th Cavalry; 1st Battalion, 1st F.A.; Company L, Signal Corps; and Ambulance Company No. 4, Hospital Corps, participated.

During the month of November the regiment was considerably stirred over prospects of field service in China. There was some concern for the safety of foreign interests there from the combatants of the revolution then in progress for the establishment of a republican form of government. The entire regiment was prepared for field service, with a minimum of surplus equipment. All equipment was placed in shape for hard field service, and requisitions submitted for clothing and tentage for a winter campaign. Unfortunately, the regiment was not called to serve; however, one battalion of the 15th Infantry was ordered to China before the end of the year for duty in connection with guarding the railroad from Peking to the sea.

The month of December marked the opening of the field and practical period and was devoted to the instruction of troops as units. Field instruction in extended order exercises and maneuvers, swimming of horses, and individual cooking, were held throughout the month. Practice marches totaling 717 3/4 miles were made through Rizal Province by all troops of the regiment.

The Machine Gun Platoon was temporarily disbanded the first of the year, and changed from the 2nd to the 1st Squadron. Upon arrival at Fort

William McKinley, the platoon was assembled and given barracks (part of Troop D) and stables, for the first time since the organization of the platoon. Until that time, the men of the platoon had been rationed and quartered with the respective troops from which detailed. The strength of the platoon was increased from three non-commissioned officers and 18 privates to four non-commissioned officers and 20 privates, in March, and remained the same throughout the year. Instruction in platoon work was carried on throughout the year and the platoon trained with the 1st Squadron and the regiment in their respective periods. On October 26th, the platoon, under command of 1st Lieutenant James A. Shannon, 7th Cavalry, and Sergeant R. Anderson, Troop C, attached, with 23 enlisted men, 20 riding horses, nine pack mules and two machine guns left for Camp Stotsenburg, Pampanga, for machine gun target practice. The platoon embarked on a lighter and proceeded to Guagua, Bataan, 50 miles away and marched 20 miles overland to Camp Stotsenburg. The following day, upon arrival in camp of the other machine gun platoons of the division, they engaged in target practice until December 14th, when they marched 20 miles to Guagua, Bataan, and embarked on a lighter and returned 50 miles to Fort William McKinley arriving on December 15th.

The health of the regiment was good throughout the year with two exceptions. In July and August an epidemic of dengue fever broke out in several of the troops. Troop I had the most cases. Investigation seemed to prove that the prevalence of this fever was due to neglect on the part of most of the men to use the mosquito bar, and the cases became few and scattered when stringent orders on the subject of the mosquito were issued and enforced. In October the majority of Troop H were admitted to the hospital suffering from ptomaine poisoning, the cause of which was never determined. Men of the troop that ate one, two and three meals of the day were taken sick, while other men who ate the same meals were not. One fatality occurred from this poisoning.

Polo was the premier sport of the regiment; the officers' team (composed of Captains Williams and Rhea, 1st Lieutenants Brown, Spring and Shannon and Lieutenants Whiteside and Chapman) competed at Camp John Hay, Benguet, and Camp Storsenburg, Pampanga, making a creditable showing at both tournaments. In December they won the championship of the Philippine Islands and Manila.

1912

During the year the entire regiment was stationed at Fort William McKinley, Rizal, Philippine Islands.

The regiment was inspected January 4th and 5th, by Major Tyree R. Rivers, Inspector General's Department, in regard to equipment, drill and instruction, and administration.

The month of January was devoted to practical field training in all its forms, including squadron practice marches totaling 120 miles.

On January 24th, the regimental and squadron headquarters detachments were organized. Due to the inability of these detachments to be quartered and messed separately, the composition of the detachments was effected by placing capable men of the various troops on special duty in the capacities required; i.e., Regimental Headquarters Detachment: one wagoner, one saddler, one' farrier and horseshoer, two orderlies: Squadron Headquarters Detachments: (one for each squadron): one wagoner and two orderlies. In addition to their duties as members of the detachments, the enlisted men were required to become proficient in map reading and general all around knowledge of the routine of their headquarters. The detachment performed all duties pertaining to their respective positions in a manner that greatly facilitated the work of the headquarters office and especially so while in the field during the Department Field Inspection.

From February 1st to 12th, the regiment, at its station, prepared for the Department Field Inspection. On the 13th and 14th of February, the entire regiment—less Band-left for Field Inspection. Colonel George K. Hunter, 7th Cavalry, commanded the Northern Detachment during the maneuvers, Lieutenant Colonel William J. Nicholson 7th Cavalry, commanding the regiment. During the month of February, at the Department Field Inspection, the regiment marched and maneuvered as follows:

February 13th, Headquarters and 1st and 2nd Squadrons marched to and went into camp at Camp Malecon, Manila, seven miles.

February 14th, 3rd Squadron and Machine Gun Platoon marched seven miles to Manila and, with the rest of the regiment, embarked on launches, with horses on lighters, and proceeded 65 miles to Guagua, Pampanga, and encamped.

The entire regiment then marched and maneuvered as follows:

February 15th, to Porac, Pampanga,
12 miles.
February 16th, to Camp Stotsenburg, Pampanga, 12 miles.

At Camp Stotsenburg the entire Northern Detachment (7th Cavalry, 8th Cavalry, 14th Cavalry, one battalion each of 1st and 2nd Field Artillery, Engineers, Signal and Sanitary Troops) was assembled and thenceforth marched over 100 miles as one command.

Headquarters and 2nd and 3rd Squadrons and Machine Gun Platoon returned from the Field Inspection to Fort William McKinley, Rizal, by marching 67 miles.

The 1st Squadron, Major S.R.H. Tompkins, 7th Cavalry, commanding, was detached from duty with the regiment at the Field Inspection on March 1st, for the purpose of receiving 273 public riding horses and horse equipments from the 14th Cavalry at Camp Stotsenburg. This squadron marched over 75 miles.

The Band left Fort William McKinley on April 9th for Camp John Hay, Benguet, and remained there as part of that garrison, until June 1st, when it returned to its proper station.

The organizations of the regiment while present at their station during March and April engaged in target practice, both rifle and mounted and dismounted revolver.

General Orders No. 8, War Department, March 30th, 1912, designated the 8th, 13th, 15th, 24th Infantry Regiments and the 7th and 8th Cavalry Regiments as Colonial Regiments for service in the Philippine Islands. The tour of duty for officers was set at three years, with the privilege of remaining longer on application. The tour of enlisted men to be three years or longer, at the discretion of the man, who could reenlist for additional service if his physical condition warranted. The strength of troops was raised to 100 men each, which with the non-commissioned Staff and Band, made the strength of the regiment 1,236 men. The men of the Machine Gun Platoon (25) and Headquarters Detachments (14 were included in the strength of troops and deducted prorata to form these organizations). While the officers of these Colonial Regiments were transferred to regiments in the United States at the expiration of their tour, provisions were not made for deserving non-commissioned officers. Non-commissioned officers in all grades had the alternative of remaining indefinitely in the Philippines with their regiments, or returning to regiments in the United States to start as privates. For old and worthy non-commissioned officers of the Non-Commissioned Staff and 1st Sergeants, and other old non-commissioned officers, this plan worked hardships. Later, the Act of Congress of August 24th, 1912, was passed, which cut out the travel pay to be paid on discharge to two cents per mile, or in kind, and abolished the computation of foreign service after current enlistment as double time toward retirement; thus, all incentive for remaining on foreign service with a Colonial Regiment passed. Only one inducement was held out to tempt men to remain —the 20% increase in pay—which, according to the majority, did not offset the increased prices for commodities over those in the United States. The seven-year enlistment, provided for in this Act meant—to the old soldier with a view to retirement-only one year added to each enlistment period, with a corresponding cut in his cumulative reenlistment pay. However, to the younger soldier, who did not continue soldiering as a vocation, it meant much more. During the year, the regiment lost few men by discharge per expiration of terms of service. In 1913 and early 1914 practically the entire regiment would be eligible for discharge. A canvass of the regiment indicated few, if any, reenlistments would be made in the Philippines among the younger soldiers, and the only reenlistments that could be assumed were those among the higher ranking non-commissioned officers, who wanted to make at least one effort to remain identified with the regiment they had served so long. This Act also contained legislation that affected officers to a marked degree. An officer on detached service had to serve two of every six years actually on duty with a tactical unit of the arm of service in which he was commissioned. This law returned to a duty status several officers from detached service.

During the month of May troops took practice marches totaling 562 1/2 miles.

From June to November, inclusive, the organizations engaged in garrison training. At times, much instruction was held indoors due to heavy rains, and mounted work was confined to beaten trails and roads, due to wet ground.

On June 19th, Troops I, K and L left of the "Liscum" for Camp McGrath, Batangas, to escort horses of the 8th Cavalry Regiment, left there on departure of six troops of that regiment for the Southern Islands. These troops traveled a total distance of 70 miles, marching, and 115 miles by water, and received 213 public riding horses on transfer from the 8th Cavalry.

During November, troops of the 1st and 2nd Squadrons took practice marches totaling 520 miles.

The health of the command remained good during the year, without sickness of an epidemic or general nature appearing. The provisions of the law whereby sickness occasioned through misconduct on the part of the soldier, (i.e. venereal disease) caused loss of pay, served to clear the hospitals of all but the most deserving patients.

Sports for off-duty hours were encouraged. Polo remained the sport supreme for the officers; the teams excelled as ever. Baseball for enlisted men easily took first place. In the regimental league, Troop I won the pennant. The Post League (13th Infantry, 8th Cavalry, 1st Field Artillery, Staff Corps, 7th Cavalry) was won handily by the regimental team.

During the year 1913, the entire regiment was stationed at Fort William McKinley, Rizal, Philippine Islands.

Except for periods when the regiment, in whole or in part, took the field for field inspection and maneuver, the year was passed in the performance of the usual routine incident to garrison duties. The period January 1st to May 31st and November 1st to December 31st, included field inspection and maneuvers, preparation for and annual target practice, and training which embraced all features for field work. The period June 1st to October 31st included garrison training for troops and the schools of equitation for officers and non-commissioned officers and selected privates. During this period the usual schools were held for officers, including postgraduate work and regular preliminary courses, and schools for non-commissioned officers and selected privates in subjects of service manuals and topography. Schools for enlisted men in common branches of education were held at the post during this period.

During January the regiment was inspected by the Inspector General (Lieutenant Colonel J.B. Erwin, I.G. Dept.), beginning on January 13th and lasting for about ten days. The report of his inspection revealed no serious irregularity or non-compliance with existing orders.

During January, practice marches totaling 114 1/2 miles were made by each squadron.

On February 14th, the Band left for Camp John Hay, Mountain Province, where it remained until June 1st, when it returned to its proper station. It engaged in the usual garrison duties incident to service of Bands during its stay at Camp John Hay.

On February 10th, the regiment—less Band-Major S.R.H. Tompkins, 7th Cavalry, commanding, left for the annual Department (District) of Luzon Field Inspection, marching to Cabanatuan, Nueva Ecija, the point of concentration of the Northern Detachment. A semi-permanent field camp was established at Cabanatuan (Colonel William J. Nicholson, Cavalry, attached to 7th Cavalry, commanding) and included in the Detachment the following troops: 7th Cavalry, less Band; two Troops of 8th Cavalry; 1st Battalion, 1st Field Artillery; Company L, Signal Corps; Provisional Regiment of Philippine Scouts, and Hospital Corps.

The Southern Detachment, concentrated at Sibul Springs, Bulacan, was composed largely of dismounted troops.

For the period February 14 to 25th, the Northern Detachment engaged in maneuvers in the country about Cabanatuan on a progressive schedule, troop regiment and active detachment. Much hard work was done by all in the preparing for combined maneuvers with the Southern Detachment to follow. The camp afforded an excellent opportunity for such work, being adjacent to large tracts of country well adapted to maneuvering. Camp was broken on Febraury 27th, and the detachment moved out to engage the Southern Detachment in combined maneuvers. The 3rd Squadron, Major Peter E. Traub, 7th Cavalry, commanding, constituted the advance cavalry, and preceded the command far to the south of the Penaranda River. The command moved south to the Penaranda River, with no actual contact with the enemy, and went into camp on the bank of the river opposite the town of Penaranda, Neuva Ecija, for the night. The advance cavalry returned to camp after dark for rations and forage—the pack train carrying them for the squadron had gone astray. The main command had marched 14 miles. On February 28th, the detachment gained contact with the Southern Detachment and maneuvered with it to the south of and along the bank of the Penaranda River. At the conclusion of the maneuver, the Northern Detachment went into camp on the bank of the Penaranda River at the town of Papaya, Nueva Ecija—the Southern Detachment camped at Penaranda, Nueva Ecija. The main command marched four miles. On March 1st, the detachment remained in camp Fat Papaya. On March 2nd, the Northern and Southern Detachments maneuvered in the country south of the Penaranda River along the Bardies-Penaranda trail, taking two positions. At the conclusion of the day's maneuver, all mounted troops of the detachment proceeded to camp at San Miguel de Mayumo, Bulacan. The main body of the command marched 18 miles. Early on the morning of March 3rd, the troops left camp at San Miguel de Mayumo and proceeded to a position near Bardies, Nueva Ecija, held by dismounted troops of the detachment. During the day, it engaged the Southern Detachment in two positions and upon completion returned to camp at San Miguel de Mayumo. The main command marched 15 miles. On March 4th, the detachment was discontinued as such and organizations left San Miguel de Mayumo for their proper stations.

During the period of inspection, including marches to and from concentration, the main body of the regiment marched 190 miles, exclusive of the distance marched by the regiment and units thereof during the progressive schedule of instruction while in camp at Cabanatuan.

During the maneuvers good practical instruction was received by the regiment as a unit and by individual officers and troops. The scheme involved two separate armies, which served to increase the individual interest and good results were accomplished in scouting, patrolling and security and information. The camps selected, and especially the camp of concentration at Cabanatuan, were as good as could be secured but mostly rice fields. Wood and water

for troops were in abundance at all camps. In every camp made, water for animals was especially plentiful and watering places ample, except at San Miguel de Mayumo, Bulacan, where the river sank between high banks and allowed only two or three units to water at the same time. Artesian well water was obtained at all camps and pure enough for cooking and drinking purposes without filtering. The supply departments rendered good work and rations and forage followed the command with no shortage reported. While the weather was hot and the roads dusty, travel was good due to the nature of the roads which for the most part were well made and in good repair. There was no rain during the entire inspection, except two very slight showers while at the camp of concentration at Cabanatuan. The health of the command was excellent throughout and the regiment lost very few men from duty. The animals, mounts and field transportation, returned to the post in good condition, hardened and a little lean due to hard constant work under saddle and in train. Very few horses or mules were disabled and rendered unfit for duty except for a few old horses which were lost through complete exhausion and killed to prevent further suffering.

During the months of March, April and May the regiment engaged in and completed target practice. The results obtained were sufficiently good to repay the hard work spent on the range in coaching and developing the many men engaged in their first range practice.

During May and June the regiment, in parts, took the field at different times. The talk of trouble with Japan increased the interest in this work.

Troop F, on May 21st, was ordered to prepare for field service, dismounted. The troop left the post that afternoon, embarked on lighters and crossed Manila Bay to Guagus, Pampanga, where it received animals of the 1st Batallion, 1st Field Artillery, 24th Infantry, and Medical Corps, ordered from Camp Stotsenburg, Pampanga, to duty on Corregidor Island. The troop marched overland to Camp Stotsenburg, Pampanga, in charge of these animals (total distance by lighter and march, 99 miles) and remained at this station, caring for the animals, until June 23rd. On June 24th, the troop returned by rail to its proper station.

The 3rd Squadron (I, K, L, and M), Captain George Williams, 7th Cavalry, commanding, left the post on May 28th for a reconnaissance of the country surrounding Laguna de Bay, and marched 122 miles. A thorough reconnaissance was made of the country for ten miles and each side of the main road was covered.

On June 14th, upon short notice, Headquarters, Field Staff, Non-commissioned Staff, Band, Machine Gun Platoon, and Troops A, B, C, D, E, G, and H left the post as a part of the Cavalry Detachment (six troops, 8th Cavalry, remainder of detachment) under command of Lieutenant Colonel D.H. Doughton, 8th Cavalry, and proceeded in the direction of Batangas Province operating against a supposed hostile force from that point, The hostile force was represented by the remainder of the 8th Cavalry, which had been relieved from duty in the Department of Mindanao and stationed at Camp McGrath, Batangas, and had been ordered to proceed over-

land to its new station at Camp Stotsenburg, Pampanga, by way of Fort William McKinley, Rizal. The detachment marched 85 1/2 miles.

During the period June 14th-17th, the 3rd Squadron (Troops I, K, L and M) patrolled the country south and west between Fort William McKinley, Rizal, and Alabang, Cavite, establishing patrols on roads and sending scouting parties through the country to the south of Alabang. Aerial scouting was performed by student officers attached to the Aviation School at Fort William McKinley, and on July 17th, while troops were returning to the post, an aeroplane scout followed the command almost the entire morning, at times lost to sight of the command by clouds.

Due to activities on the part of native (Philippine politicians, and from information gained from the Secret Service of the Insular Governtment, it was known that certain native elements were urging an outbreak against the established government. It was generally believed that this outbreak would occur on Independence Day (July 4th) as this idea, "Independencia," was the object of the outbreak. Accordingly, as a preventive measure and precaution, the 2nd Squadron (Troops E, F, G, H), Major Francis H. Beach, 7th Cavalry, commanding, was ordered to Manila on the afternoon of July 3rd, and stationed above the city as follows: one troop at Land Transport Corral, one troop at Meisic Police Station, one troop at Depot Quartermaster and one troop at Department Headquarters, Fort Santiago. No trouble occurred and the reported outbreak did not develop. The squadron returned to its station on the morning of July 5th. Lieutenant Colonel George H. Sands, 7th Cavalry, was placed in command of all troops of the line in the city of Manila in the event of hostilities, and his command included regular infantry, cavalry, and Philippine Scouts.

On October 15th, the Machine Gun Platoon left the post en route to Camp Stotsenburg, Pampanga, for annual target practice. During November and December all troops took practice marches totaling over 500 miles covering all parts of the Island of Luzon.

The health of the command throughout the year was excellent and the sick rate low.

The mounts of the regiment averaged about 75 per troop throughout the year. This number of mounts was sufficient to mount the strength of the regiment at all times. For the most part these mounts had been in service in the Philippine Islands for several years and were not up to the standard set for cavalry mounts. Few mounts were received during the year, and these by transfer from other posts. At the beginning of the year the regiment had 994 mounts, of which 37 were unserviceable, and at the end of the year 933 mounts, of which 48 were unserviceable. The loss shown was occasioned by condemning and destroying unserviceable mounts and by a few purchases of mounts by officers and transferring them to the Quartermaster Corps.

Polo continued to be the sport supreme of the officers, whose teams competed with success against all comers, although without the marked success evidenced in the preceding two years. This was due in part to the fact that the mounts of the teams of the regiment were in some cases disposed of by the officers, who were to be ordered to the United States for duty at the beginning of the new year. Also, the other teams, both military and civilian, were given new life by the arrival of new players and new mounts. The regimental baseball team again won the post pennant quite handily, competing with teams of the 13th Infantry; 1st Battalion, 2nd Field Artillery; and the Signal and Hospital Corps.

At the Department Rifle and Revolver Competition, held at Fort William McKinley, Rizal, during December, the regiment won one gold, one silver, and three bronze medals.

During the year many changes occurred in the enlisted personnel strength. In addition to the large number of enlisted men who usually sever their connection with the service after three years, the regiment lost heavily among the older and experienced non-commissioned officers. There was no longer any incentive for remaining with regiment they had been identified with for many years. Few of the older men desired to remain and reenlist only to look forward to four more years of tropical service with no inducement offered other than the 20% increase in pay. The loss of double time toward retirement for tropical service and indefinitely remaining on foreign service were given as the prime causes for leaving the regiment. Each transport leaving the Islands took its heavy toll of the seasoned, experienced men from the regiment, whose places were filled by the assignment of recruits, an exchange that worked ill, for the efficiency of the regiment as a whole.

1914

The year 1914 was one of considerable activity for the regiment both in the field and garrison. *Field detachment No. 2 consisted of the 7th and 8th Cavalry Regiments; Headquarters and 2nd Battalion 2nd Field Artillery; 8th Infantry; Provisional Regiment of Philippine Scouts and 1/2 Field Company L, Signal Corps — Colonel George K. Hunter, 7th Cavalry, commanding.*

From January 1st to 21st, inclusive, the entire regiment engaged in revolver and preliminary rifle practice in addition to the usual garrison duties.

Early on the morning of January 22nd, orders were received from Headquarters Field Detach ment No. 2 to prepare for field service at once and to be ready to leave the post at the earliest possible hour. The regiment was to take part in maneuvers in which nearly all of the troops of the line, including Philippine Scouts, participated. The plan of the maneuvers was an assumed invasion b hostile forces conveyed by warships, which were to land at Batangas, Batangas Province, Luzon, and march on the city of Manila. The defending force was represented by Field Detachment No. 2, and the hostile by Field Detachment No. 1. *Field Detachment No. 1 consisted of the 13th and 24th Infantry Regiments; 1st Battalion, 2nd Field Artillery; Troops G and H, 7th Cavalry; 1/2 Field Company L, Signal Corps and a Provisional Regiment of Philippine Scouts — Colonel William G. Buttler, 24th Infantry, Commanding.*

Shortly after mid-day, Headquarters, the Machine Gun Platoon, Troops A, B, C, D, E, F, I, K, L, and M (Lieutenant Colonel George H. Sands, commanding), and the wagon train fully armed and equipped for a long period of field service left the post en route for Batangas Province, marching 17 1/2 miles to, and going into camp, at Alabang, Rizal Province. Early the next morning the regiment was on the march as the advance cavalry of the repelling force. After a march of 20 miles, they camped at Calamba, Laguna Province. The following day—January 24th—a march of ten miles was made to Tanauan, Batangas Province, where camp was made and detachments of troops were sent on reconnaissance 16 miles to the front as far as San Jose, Batangas Province. Troops A and L had detached at Calamba and sent 20 miles to San Pablo, Lagtma, on the main road from Lucena, Tayabas Province—a possible landing place for the invaders. On January 25th, Troops A and D marched ten miles to Tiaong, Tayabas, and reconnoitered the country to the south in the direction of Lucena. The remainder of the regiment marched to Lipa, Batangas, where Field Detachment No. 2 was to concentrate. The concentration was practically completed the 25th and 26th of January. The Supply Departments took advantage of the Manila Southern Railroad and had supplies and materials on the ground promptly. On January 26th, the detachment sent strong parties to the south in an attempt to gain contact. A detachment under Lieutenant Hyatt penetrated as far as Camp McGrath, Batangas, the concentration point of Field Detachment No. 1, cut signal communication and returned safely to the command. Other parties, in-force, scouted the entire front from Lake Taal on the west to the mountains on the east, and gained contact in several places with the enemy's cavalry. Troops A and D returned to   S a n Pablo from Tiaong on January 26th, and on January 27th, marched by way of Alaminos, Batangas, and joined the command at Lipa (19 miles). On January 27th and 28th, the command continued scouting, with Lipa as the base, across the front and gained contact with small groups of the enemy. On January 29th, just south of San Jose, Batangas, contact was made by both sides with a considerable force. The line of resistance of Field Detachment No. 2 was withdrawn to the south of Lipa, where it remained through January 30th. The infantry and artillery held the line and the majority of the mounted troops were held in reserve at Lipa. Dismounted engagements were frequent by both 7th and 8th Cavalry units during the withdrawal of the line of resistance, and in almost every case enabled the infantry of Field Detachment No. 2 to establish its new lines in good order. The mounted troops covered the entire front and performed the service of information in a highly creditable manner, keeping the detachment commander informed at all times of the enemy movements which enabled him to make his dispositions in such a manner as to hinder successfully the progress of the superior invading force. On January 31st the, entire command evacuated the base at Lipa and withdrew ten miles to Tanauan, while the enemy's outposts reached three miles north of Lipa. On February 1st, the command advanced that distance and engaged the enemy and retired 14 miles to Tanauan. On February 2nd, the command again advanced toward Lipa and engaged the enemy at Papay, Batangas, until finally forced to retire 14 miles to Biga, Batangas. On February 3rd, it held defensive positions at Biga until forced to retreat toward Calamba, maintaining contact with the enemy until 11:15 a.m., when the maneuver was concluded. The regiment then marched 11 miles to Cabuyao, Laguna. On February 4th, it began the return march to its station, marching that day to Alabang, 14 miles, and 13 miles on February 5th to Fort William McKinley.

Upon the departure of the regiment from its station on January 22nd, Troops G and H remained at the post under orders to join Field Detachment No. 1. On January 23rd, both troops marched six miles to Manila, embarked on U.S.A.T. "Warren" and proceeded 70 miles to Batangas Bay. On the following day, they disembarked and marched three miles to Camp McGrath, Batangas, the concentration point of Field Detachment No. 1. From January 25th to 28th, with a base at Camp McGrath, Batangas, Troops G and H scouted the country to the north toward San Jose and Ibaan, Batangas. On January 29th, they gained contact at San Jose, and camped at Banay Banay II, 20 miles distant. On January 30th, they engaged the enemy toward Lipa and returned 15 miles to their former camp. On January 31st, they acted as an advance cavalry in pushing the line of attack 15 miles to Lipa. On February 1st, they engaged troops to the north of Lipa and returned ten miles to that town. February 2nd, they advanced 15 miles to Santo Tomas, Batangas, as flank guards for the advance to the north. On February 3rd, they engaged the enemy until the close of the maneuver, and then marched 13 miles to camp at Calamba. On February 4th, they began the return march to their station, camping that night at Alabang (20 miles), and arrived at Fort William McKinley (13 miles) on February 5th

The benefits of the maneuver as a training for the eventualities of active service were many and varied. Not the least of these was the actual preparation and departure of the regiment for field service in about six hours from the receipt of the order, which came as a surprise to all (particularly since previous instructions had been issued for a garrison inspection by officers of the Inspector General's Department). The regiment left the post with its full equipment, prepared for hard and long field service, and withstood the test well. The troops were worked hard, especially in reconnaissance, scouting and in gaining contact, and fulfilled all expectations, with regard to these and other duties in a manner highly creditable to themselves and the army. The character of the maneuver involved separating the individual troops from the main body to' so great an extent that at times not more than one troop was with the headquarters of the regiment. This introduced a phase of field training which the regiment had not been called upon to perform heretofore and from which good results were obtained. It was generally conceded by all that the maneuver, in plan and execution, was the most successful of recent years as the entire maneuver closely simulated what was then believed would be actual wartime conditions in the field. The country was rolling and wooded and admirably adapted to offensive and defensive tactics. The weather was fair throughout the maneuver period with only one or two slight showers—sufficient to lay the top dust—to the advantage of the cavalry. The services of supply were well planned and efficient. The health of the command was excellent.

From February 6th to 17th, the regiment performed the usual garrison duties and engaged in rifle and revolver practice.

On the afternoon of February 18th, on short notice, the entire regiment, less the Band, which remained at Fort William McKinley, left the post (Major Arthur Thayer, 7th Cavalry, commanding), fully armed and equipped for prolonged field service. They marched 22 miles to Marilao, Bulacan, arriving and going into camp late that night. On February 19th, they marched 28 miles to Calumpit, Tarlac, 28 miles, and on February 20th they marched 26 miles to Florida Blanca—the point of concentration of a Provisional Cavalry Brigade (7th and 8th Cavalry, Colonel Eben Swift, 8th Cavalry, Commanding).

The plan of this maneuver was an operation against Corregidor Island by a hostile force of infantry with siege artillery. The enemy were to land on the west coast and operate in the mountains of Bataan and in the country eastward. The invading force was represented by regular infantry which had embarked on transports. They disembarked on the coast at a point south of Olongapo, from whence they operated east and south.

On February 21st, the entire command, except Troops E and F, marched 30 miles to Balanga, Bataan. Troops E and F were detached at Dinalupihan, Bataan, where they camped. On February 22nd, they remained in camp at Balanga. Troops G and H remained at Balanga, and on February 23rd, the command marched 13 miles to Limay, Bataan. On February 24th they marched 12 miles to Cabcaben, Bataan. On February 25th, the mand marched to the Pangolingan River, engaged the enemy, forced him to retire to the north side of the river, and placed outposts on the south bank. The main body of the command then returned two miles to camp at Cabcaben. On February 26th, the command advanced to the outposts and repulsed the attacks of the enemy until the close of the maneuver about 1:00 p.m., and returned two miles to camp at Cakaben. On February 27th, Headquarters, Machine Gun Platoon, and the 3rd Squadron remained in camp at Cakaben and the 1st Squadron marched 13 miles to camp at Alsasin Point. On February 28th, Headquarters, Machine Gun Platoon, and the 3rd Squadron marched 13 miles to Alsasin Point, where, on the same day, Headquarters, Machine Gun Platoon, 1st and 3rd Squadrons, embarked on the U.S.T.A. "Liscum" and "Warren," disembarked at Manila (28 miles), and marched six miles to Fort William McKinley. Troops E and F at Dinalupihan, Bataan, patrolled Olongapo Trail, covering about 20 miles daily, from February 21st to 28th, inclusive, and then remained in camp until March 1st. Troops G and H, at Balanga, Bataan, guarded trains and supplies and patrolled trails to the west coast, from February 23rd to 28th, inclusive. On March 1st, Troops G and H marched 15 miles from Balanga to Dinalupihan, Bataan, joining Troops E and F. On March 2nd, the 2nd Squadron with the field train of the regiment, began the march en route to their station, marching 21 miles that day to Guagua, Pampanga. On March 3rd, they marched 17 miles to Calumpit, Tarlac; on March 4th, 30 miles to Caloocan, Rizal; and on March 5th, 12 miles to Fort William McKinley.

The second maneuver of the year was as great a success as the first. It entailed more hardships, due to the use of water transportation, the mountainous character of the country, and the difficulty of supply in a region which, for the most part, was possible by trails only. However, the nature of the problems involved in the maneuver and their execution were the source of instructive training to the troops participating. The weather remained fair throughout the entire period, and the health of the command was remarkable, considering the hard service.

On February 25th, the Band, which had remained at its station during the absence of the regiment on the two maneuvers, proceeded by rail to Camp John Hay, Benguet, where it remained as part of the garrison of that station until May 4th, on which date it returned, by rail, to its proper station.

Target practice, both rifle and revolver, were resumed upon the return of the troops to their station from the second maneuver, and continued until they were concluded in the second week of April.

During the latter part of April and the month of May the usual garrison duties, were performed, except for the period May 1-23, inclusive, when the regiment was inspected by Major J.M. Jenkins, Inspector General's Department. Only minor irregularities and deficiencies, which were immediately corrected, were observed during the inspection. The results of the inspection were very gratifying to all concerned.

Colonel George K. Hunter, who had commanded the regiment since 1910, was transferred to the 1st Cavalry on June 1st, 1914, upon the expiration of his tour of duty in the Philippine Islands, and left station on leave May 15th. Colonel Cunliffe H. Murray, the new regimental commander, transferred from the 12th Cavalry, arrived on June 4th and assumed command of regiment.

On July 1st, new Tables of Organization went into effect in the regiment, which abolished the Machine Gun Troop and Regimental and Squadron Headquarters. Detachments and created the Machine Gun Troop (Provisional) and the Headquarters Troop (Provisional) composed of 48 and 12 men, respectively.

During the month of July, the horses of the regiment—mixed in color—were recolored (reassigned) according to troop as follows:

Troop A: black — Troop B: sorrel — Troop C: bay — Troop D: bay — Troop E: bay — Troop F: bay — Troop G: bay — Troop H: sorrel — Troop I: bay — Troop K: bay — Troop L: brown and dark bay — Troop M: bay — Machine Gun Troop: black — N.C.S., Band and Headquarters Troop: black.

From June 1st to September 14th, the usual garrison duties were performed, except that, in addition, during September, the regiment completed packing its property for a change of station to Camp Stotsenburg, Pampanga, and made arrangements for the march to and participation in the camp of instruction held at that station.

During the latter part of August and the first part of September the Islands were struck by the heaviest typhoon since 1899. The rainfall was so great that all rivers were flooded over their banks, roads were damaged and destroyed, railroad traffic suspended in some sections due to washouts, and the country generally flooded. To ascertain the best route of march, select camp sites and procure supplies, a detachment, under Captain Comly, Quartermaster, with Lieutenant Smith, three enlisted men and two wagons, marched from Fort William McKinley to Calumpit, Tarlac. At this town the detachment was detrained several days because of high water and impassible roads. About the 10th of September the storm abated and the detachment rejoined its station.

On September 15th, the entire regiment as part of a detachment of U.S. troops consisting of the 7th Cavalry; 1st Battalion, 2nd Field Artillery; and a Provisional Machine Gun Battalion (7th Cavalry, 8th, 13th and 24th Infantry)—commanded by Colonel Cunliffe H. Murray, 7th Cavalry-left Fort William McKinley en route to Camp Stotsenburg, Pampanga, and marched 12 miles to Caloocan, Rizal. Camp was made on the grounds of the Manila Golf Club. Considerable difficulty was experienced at this camp in procuring potable water for the animals. The camp grounds were largely tinder water, thereby making it necessary to transport cots for all. Supplies of hay and grain, as well as subsistence stores, for the day, were shipped from Manila by wagon transportation to this camp. Due to the flooded condition of all possible camp sites along the route, such supplies were shipped thereafter by rail to points along the line of march. On September 16th, the command marched 21 miles to Malolos, Bulacan. The detachment was scattered over the town, since there was no suitable site available to camp the entire command. For the remainder of the march, camps were made on the best available ground and the troops were scattered in several sites at Calumpit, while at San Fernando camp was made on the grounds of the Provincial Government. After the first camp, potable water was plentiful, and wood could be purchased. On September 17th, the regiment marched 7 3/4 miles from Malolos to Calumpit, Bulacan, and crossed the Rio Grande de Pampanga at the latter point. A detachment of the 37th Company, Philippine Scouts, had constructed a flying ferry just east of the Manila Railroad bridge on the Bagbag River. All troops of the detachment were crossed on this ferry. The Machine Gun Battalion remained at Malolos during September 17th, and the 1st Battalion, 2nd Field Artillery, camped on the south bank of the river during the ferrying of the 7th Cavalry, which consumed the greater part of the day and the night. The regiment crossed with few mishaps. Two escort wagons ran off the ferry into deep water but were recovered intact, and a few animals fell overboard in loading. On September 18th, the regiment marched 10 miles to San Fernanda, Pampanga. The road although passable for mounted men, was almost impassable for wagon transportation because of deep gumbo mud. By means of picket lines attached to the wagons, the troopers brought the trains into camp successfully, the last squadron arriving with its train after dark. On September 19th, a 17 mile march was made from San Fernando. to Camp Stotsenburg, Parnpanga. The regiment arrived after nightfall, and the 8th Cavalry entertained the regiment with a most welcome dinner and troop for troop shared stables and quarters for the night. The Machine Gun Troop, as part of the Provisional Machine Gun

Battalion, marched 12 miles from Malolos to San Roque, Pampanga, on September 18th; eight miles to Calalup, Pampanga, on September 19th; and 12 miles to Camp Stotsenburg, Pampanga, on September 20th, where it went into camp with the remainder of the Machine Gun Battalion for target practice until October 31st.

The remainder of the regiment pitched camp on the plain just east of the post of Camp Stotsenburg on September 20th and 21st. From this date to October 31st, the regiment, as part of a Provisional Cavalry Brigade (7th and 8th Cavalry and 2nd Field Artillery, commanded by Colonel Cunliffe H. Murray, 7th Cavalry), engaged in drill and instruction under the provisions of the Cavalry Service Regulations, Experimental, 1914.

The camp of the brigade was pitched in order of the 7th Cavalry, 8th Cavalry, 2nd Field Artillery, from west to east. It was a model camp on sandy soil, well laid out, well policed and had many comforts not usually found in camps of this period (viz, showers, and shelters for messing). With the exception of one severe rain storm on September 20th and several fairly hard rains thereafter, the weather was pleasant—the days hot and the nights quite cool. The health of the command remained excellent throughout. During November, the Department Commander, Major General Thomas H. Barry, U.S.A., visited the camp and observed the drill and instruction of troops.

The obstacle ride for officers and the field officers test ride were held during the period from November 1st to the 14th. On November 1st, the regiment, as part of a Combined Maneuver Brigade in camp at Camp Stotsenburg, Pampanga, was busy making preparations to take the field for combined maneuvers and field exercises. On November 2nd, the entire regiment, as part of the Combined Maneuver Brigade, marched to a camp near Angeles, Pampanga, camping on the east bank of the Abagan River. The regiment formed part of a Brown Detachment in an effort to intercept a White Army advancing south along the Manila-Dagupan Railroad. The regiment, in addition to the advance guard, outpost, patrolling, and reconnaissance work necessitated by the various phases of the problem, marched as follows:

On November 2nd, from Camp Stotsenburg Pampanga, to camp near Angeles, Pampanga—
6 1/2 miles.

On November 3rd, to camp near Bamban, Pampanga, on the banks of the Bamban River—
13 1/2 miles.

On November 4th, to camp near Capas, Pampanga—
13 miles.

On November 5th, to Camp Stotsenburg, Paimpanga—
15 miles.

During the period November 6th to 14th, the regiment was employed in maneuvers and field exercises, at the camp.

The 8th Cavalry left camp en route to its new station at Fort William McKinley, Rizal, on November 14th. On November 15th, camp was broken and the 7th Cavalry Regiment moved into quarters on the post. For the remainder of the year the regiment performed the usual garrison duties and settled itself to the conditions of a new garrison. Considerable activity was shown in taking advantage of the hunting that the country afforded, especially in the mountains to the west of the post. During the latter part of the year, at the holiday season, large parties availed themselves of the vacation period to bring in many trophies of deer and wild hog.

During the year, the order for the three-year tour for officers in the Philippine Islands began to effect changes in the regiment. The regiment lost 36 officers and one veterinarian by transfer to regiments in the United States, and gained 33 officers, two attached and one veterinarian by transfer from home regiments. The effect on the regiment of this wholesale changing of officers was shown in many ways. The new officers brought customs of other regiments which fuzed with those of the 7th Cavalry. It was a year in which the enlisted and commissioned personnel labored to acquaint themselves with one another, their peculiarities and abilities; to that end, the year closed with the regiment in splendid condition.

The beginning of the year found the regiment supplied' with 883 serviceable and 50 unserviceable horses and the end of the year with 768 serviceable and 19 unserviceable horses. The losses were occasioned by accident and ordered destruction. A few horses, unsuited for cavalry, were turned in to the Quartermaster Corps for use as draft animals. The supply of horses was not sufficient for the needs of the command. Troops could barely supply sufficient mounts for ordinary drills for the available men, even with the usual post absentees on duty, sick and in confinement. None of the troops had sufficient mounts to mount the entire troop when called upon to do so. For the most part the mounts were far below the average as the horses had been in the Philippine Islands for many years and handed down from one regiment to another. Many were old and unable to stand hard service. No new horses nor remounts were received during the year and only a small number turned to line service from service in the Quartermaster Corps.

A feat of daring and endurance was performed by an officer and a detachment of four enlisted volunteers of the regiment. This small group successfully made the ascent to the highest point of Mount Pinaruba—situated about seven miles due west of Camp Stotsenburg. It is a matter of record that Spanish explorers, Insular government and military parties failed in trying to reach the highest point. Therefore this feat, performed by men of the regiment, adds one more to the already long list of achievements. The following general order, issued to the regiment, commends those participating in the feat.

HEADQUARTERS SEVENTH U.S. CAVALRY
Camp Stotsenburg, Pamp., P.I.
Dec. 27, 1914.
General Orders, No. 96.

The Regimental Commander announces with pleasure that the ascent of Mount Pingtuba was made on the 28th of November, 1914, by 2nd Lieutenant Thomas J.J. Christian, Squadron Quartermaster and Commissary, 7th Cavalry, and Privates Edgar J. Eckton, Henry Huthmacher, William H. Sanderson and Howard F. Sitlet, Machine Gun Troop, 7th Cavalry. This great peak had defeated all known attempts of man to climb it and the final success of Seventh Cavalrymen was due to the skillful selection of the route, endurance and high order of fortitude. To Lieutenant Christian belongs the honor of planning the feat and of real leadership; to Private Eckton the distinction of gaining the highest point, slightly higher than the nearby second highest peak reached by his comrades.

BY ORDER OF COLONEL MURRAY:
J.C. PEGRAM
1st Lieut. & Sqdn. Adjt., 7th Cav.,
Asst. to Adjt.

Due to the field activities, outdoor sports in the regiment did not flourish as well in this as in past years. However, the officers continued their good work at polo throughout the year and after arrival at Camp Stotsenburg added golf and tennis. A department order, making daily physical exercise compulsory, helped swell the ranks of the latter players. Baseball continued the premier sport of the enlisted men and the troop teams of the regiment did very well. Field days were held once each month during the latter part of the year and the regiment usually excelled.

1915

Until November of this year the regiment performed the usual garrison and field duties incident to camp life in the Philippine Islands. In November the regiment began to pack property preparatory to a change of station to the United States. At 8:30 a.m. on November 14th, the regiment left Camp Stotsenburg on the Manila Railroad and arrived in Manila 55 miles distant at noon. The troops then boarded lighters which took them to Pier No. 1, where they again embarked on the Transport "Sheridan," which had twice before carried the regiment to and from the Philippine Islands. It was little realized at the time the Regiment left that it would return to Manila and Japan some 30 years later under considerably different circumstances. The many villages and landmarks in the Philippines so familiar during the practice marches and maneuvers during the period 1913-1915 became objectives won at the cost of many lives to the regiment during World War II. It is interesting to note that the scheme of maneuver used during many of the practice field exercises and maneuvers conducted during this period were used by the small Army garrison force against the Japanese invasion of the Philippines in early 1942.

The regiment left Manila at Noon on November 15th and arrived at Nagasaki, Japan, on November 20th. It left Nagasaki, Japan, on November 21st and by way of Honolulu, arrived at San Francisco on December 14th.

Upon disembarking at the Presidio of San Francisco, the regiment went into quarters and remained there until December 21st, when it left en route to Oakland Station by tugboat. At Oakland Station, the regiment entrained on the Coast Line of Southern Pacific Railroad for the Mexican Border. It arrived at Douglas, Arizona, about 1:30 p.m. on December 23rd and marched to its temporary station at Douglas, Arizona, arriving there about 4:00 p.m. The usual camp duties were performed until the end of the year.

Many lives were lost due to the Punitive Expedition. Military funerals became common in El Paso. Courtesy of John Hardmand collection.

Brig. Gen. John J. Pershing, Commander of the Punitive Expedition of 1916, crosses the Santa Maria River in pursuit of bandit Pancho Villa. Courtesy of the National Archives.

1916

The beginning of the year found the regiment, less the First Squadron, adjusting itself to a new camp and conditions at Camp Harry J. Jones, Douglas, Arizona, where it had arrived on December 23rd the previous year from its second tour of duty in the Philippine Islands.

It is believed appropriate to insert here international conditions between the United States and Mexico which caused the 7th Cavalry Regiment's concentration along the Mexican border at this time.

Since 1910, continuous bloodshed and disorders had marked the internal political quarrel in Mexico. Warring political groups in Mexico during the period 1910 to 1916 had generally embittered the entire Mexican population against the United States. This included the Carranza forces—the recognized government of Mexico—and the Villa forces, led by the bandit, Francisco (Pancho) Villa. During these years, the lives of Americans and other aliens were sacrificed, vast properties developed by American capital and enterprise were destroyed or rendered non-productive, bandits were permitted to roam at will throughout the territory contiguous to the United States and to seize the property of Americans without punishment or without effective attempt at punishment. The lives of citizens of the United States who ventured to remain in Mexican territory, or to return there to protect their interests, were taken, and the murderers were neither apprehended nor brought to justice. The conditions which existed in Mexico during this period were more deplorable than any other in the annals of history. *"Chasing Villa," by Col. Frank Tompkins, Military Service Publishing Company, 1934, pp. 37. (The Military Service Publishing Company is now the Stackpole Publishing Company, Harrisburg, PA.)*

The territory adjacent to our border towns soon became a favorite battle ground for Mexican revolutionists, as both sides knew our troops were forbidden to resist actively any damage to life and property which might result, and did result, from the wild firing of the battling forces. The bandits also knew that if defeated, they could find sanctuary on American soil. The many battles along our border resulted in our border towns being shot full of holes, and not only were buildings scarred, but many of our people were killed and wounded by stray shots from Mexico, some of them in their own homes.

"Depredations upon American persons and property within Mexican jurisdiction were still more numerous. The American Government repeatedly requested in the strongest terms that the Mexican Government safeguard the lives and homes of American citizens and furnish the protection, which international obligation imposes, to American interests in the northern states of Nuevo Leon, Coahuila, Chihuahua, and and also in the states to the south. For example: On January 3, 1916, the American requested the Mexican Government to send to punish bands of outlaws which had looted the Cusi mining property, 80 miles west of the city of Chihuahua, but no effective results came from this request. During the following week the bandit Villa with about 200 men was operating without opposition between Rubio and Santa Ysabel, a well known to Carranza authorities. Meanwhile a party of unfortunate Americans started by from Chihuahua to visit the Cusi mines, after having received assurances from the Carranzista authorities in the State of Chihuahua that country was safe, and that a guard on the train was not necessary. The Americans held or safe conducts issued by authorities of de facto Government. On January 10, 1916, the train was stopped by Mexican bandits and 18 of the American party were stripped of clothing and shot in cold-blood, in what is known as the Santa Ysabel massacre."

"Despite repeated and insistent demands military protection should be furnished to Americans, Villa openly carried on his operations, constantly approaching closer and closer to the border. He was not intercepted, nor were his move-

Francisco "Pancho" Villa, bandit chieftain. He was assassinated by fellow Mexicans in 1923. Courtesy of the Brown Brothers.

ments impeded by the de facto government and no effectual attempt was made to his hostile designs against Americans.

"While Villa and his band were slowly moving towards the American frontier in the neighborhood of Columbus, New Mexico, not a single Mexican soldier was seen in this vicinity. Yet the Mexican authorities were fully cognizant of his movements, for on March 6th, three days before the Columbus raid, as General Gavira publicly announced, he advised the American military authorities of the outlaw's approach to the border, so that they might be prepared to prevent him crossing the boundary.

"Villa's unhindered activities culminated in

the unprovoked and cold-blooded attack upon American soldiers and citizens in the town of Columbus on the night of March 9th. The invaders were driven back across the border with heavy casualties by American cavalry, and fleeing south within sight of the Carranzista military post at Casas Grandes, no effort being made to stop them by the officers and garrison of the de facto Government stationed there.

"These four years of humiliation for the States were accurately epitomized by Senator Henry Cabot Lodge before the Lynn, Massachusetts, Republican Club, March 17, 1916, eight days following the Columbus raid, when he said in part:

'The responsibility for the conditions in Mexico rests on the government of the United States. The administration found Mexico and Mexican relation in bad condition. They have made these bad infinitely worse.

'The result of the President's war against General Huerta was the destruction of the only government that offered any prospect of order or peace or responsibility. Out of this miserable tragedy one thing commands our attention above all others: Americans have been murdered in Mexico, soldiers wearing the American uniform have been shot on the soil of the United States. The Americans robbed and slain in Mexico were entitled to our protection for their property and their lives. They have had none. Within a week Mexicans have invaded the United States, attacked an American town, and killed American citizens and American soldiers. This the inevitable result of our failure to protect Americans in their rights both by land and sea.'

'We are told that the great cry of the Democratic party is to be that their President has kept peace. The virtue in keeping peace depends altogether on how it is kept. You can always keep the peace if you will submit to any wrong, to any outrage, to any oppression. The peace of this country would have been far better kept, we should have been in far less danger of war today, if we had kept it without humiliation, kept it in honor and without fear.

We all want peace. We are all against war if it can possibly be avoided; but we shall insist that American rights shall be protected at home and abroad.'"

At this time the 1st Squadron, 7th Cavalry was performing patrol duty on the stationed as follows:

Troop A—Hachita, New Mexico.
Troop B—Hachita, New Mexico.
Troop C—Culberson's Ranch, New Mexico.
Troop D—Slaughter's Ranch, New Mexico.

The entire regiment was under canvas during this period, and early in January troops at Douglas began to make adobe barracks. This work was interrupted on March 13th, when the regiment left the unfinished structures and took the field as part of the Punitive Expedition into Mexico under the command of Brigadier General John Pershing.

"While the State Department had notified the press that an adequate force would be sent at once in pursuit of Villa with the single purpose of capturing him, the final instructions General Pershing received were to pursue and disperse his band or bands. So it will be seen that the information given to the press by the State Department and the orders given to General Pershing by the War Department were quite different. General Pershing accomplished his mission. He dispersed the bands of Villa, scattered them leaderless to the four winds, and rendered them impotent as a menace to our border states, but he did not capture Villa, though he would have done so had not President Wilson interfered at the eleventh hour and called off the chase.

"The Punitive Expedition was organized in accordance with the following order:

HEADQUARTERS PUNITIVE EXPEDITION, U.S. ARMY,
Columbus, N.M., March 14, 1916. General Orders)
No.1)

1.   The forces of this command are orga-

7th CAVALRY REGIMENT'S ROUTE INTO MEXICO 1916-1917

Indian Scouts at El Valle, Mexico in 1916. Some 39 Apache Scouts dubbed "Pershing's Pets" were attached to the Expedition to track and provide intelligence on bandits. Courtesy of the National Archives.

7th Cavalry Headquarters and Officers tents in Mexico, 1916. Courtesy of Ed Daily.

nized into a provisional division to be called Punitive Expedition, U.S. Army.

2. *The following staff is announced: Chief of Staff: Lieut. Colonel DeR. C. Cabell, 10 Cavalry; Asst. to Chief of Staff: Capt. Wilson R. Burtt, 20th Infantry; Adjutant: Major John L. Hines, Adjutant General's Department; Intelligence Officer: Major James A. Ryan, 13th Cavalry; Inspector: Colonel Lucien G. Berry, 4th Field Artillery; Judge Advocate: Captain Allen J. Greer, 16th Infantry; Quartermaster: Major John F. Madden, Quartermaster Corps; Surgeon Major Jere B. Clayton, Medical Corps; Engineer Officer: Major. Lytle Brown, Corps of Engineers; Signal Officer: Captain Hanson B. Black, Signal Corps; Aides: 1st Lieut. James L. Collins, 11th Cavalry; 2nd Lieut. Martin C. Shallenberger, 16th Infantry.*

3. *The Provisional Division will consist of: (a) First Provisional Cavalry Brigade, Colonel James Lockerr, Commanding. Troops: 11th Cavalry, 13th Cavalry Battery "C," 6th Field Artillery (attached). (b) Second Cavalry Brigade, Colonel George A. Dodd, Commanding. Troops: 7th Cavalry, 10th Cavalry Battery "B," 6th Field Artillery (attached). (c) First Provisional Infantry Brigade, Colonel John H. Beacon, Commanding. Troops: 6th Infantry, 16th Infantry Cos. "E" &"H," 2nd Battalion Engineers (attached). (d) Ambulance Company No. 7, Field Hospital No. 7.. (e) Signal Corps Detachments, First Aero Squadron. Detachment Signal Corps.. (d) wagon Companies, Number 1 and 2.*

4. *Lieutenant Colonel Euclid B. Frick, Medical Corps, will report to the Commanding Officer (Major Sample) as surgeon in charge, Medical Group.*

11. (1) The following telegrams from Department Headquarters are quoted for the information of all concerned and compliance therewith is enjoined.

March 14, 1916.

The Department Commander directs that you inform all subordinates in your command that they will report promptly by wire to proper authorities, who will report to these headquarters the names of all officers and enlisted men accompanying your command who are wounded or killed in action or who die of sickness while in the field. Commanding Officers of base and cantonment hospitals will be instructed to make reports.

"Bundy"

March 14, 1916.

The greatest caution will be exercised after crossing the border that fire is not opened on troops pertaining to the de facto Government of Mexico as such troops are very likely to be found in country which you will traverse. The greatest care and discretion will have to be exercised by all.

"Bundy."

(2) It is enjoined upon all members of the command to make the utmost endeavor to convince all Mexicans that the only purpose of this expedition is to assist in apprehending and capturing Villa and his bandits. Citizens as well as soldiers of the de facto Government will be treated with every consideration. They will not in any case be molested in the peaceful conduct of their affairs, and their property rights will be scrupulously respected.

BY COMMAND
OF BRIG. GEN. PERSHING:
DeR. C. Cabell, Lieutenant Colonel,
10 Cavalry,
Chief of Staff.

Under orders from Department Headquarters the Expedition was to enter Mexico in two columns. The west column consisting of the 7th and 10th Regiments of Cavalry and Battery "B" 6th Field Artillery, was to have its base at and move by way of Culberson's Ranch."

The regiment marched from Douglas, Arizona, to Culberson's Ranch, New Mexico, by way of Hudspeth's Ranch, Highlonesome Ranch, an approximate distance of 90 miles, arriving on 15th. Here the troops of the 1st Squadron the rest of the regiment.

On March 15th telegraphic orders were sent to Colonel Dodd at Culberson's Ranch to hold command in readiness to start upon arrival General Pershing, but owing to an accident the General did not arrive until midnight, the column having waited, ready to start, since 9:30 p.m., a poor preparation for a night's march. In view of the forced planned for this column their wagon transportation had been sent to Columbus, pack trains being only transportation to accompany the column.

This flying column led by General Pershing in person—crossed the border at 12:30 a.m. March 16th, and marched 25 miles in the dark to Geronimo Rock, where they arrived at 6:00 a.m. and went into bivouac. At noon they again took up the march and after a 30 mile march halted the

night at Ojitos. They bivouacked at Ojitos that night, and took up the march at 7:00 a.m. on the 17th for Colonia Dublan, where they arrived about 8:00 p.m., having marched 68 miles that day. Thus the column had marched approximately 125 miles since crossing the border which greatly surprised the Mexicans. It was a long grueling march when considering the long distances the Regiment had marched to reach Culberson's the heavy loads carried, the rough country covered, and the fact that neither men nor horses had any sleep the night of March 15-16.

Upon the arrival of the western force at Dublan, natives reported that Villa and his men were somewhere in the vicinity of San Miguel, gathering supplies, recuperating stock, and seizing new mounts from the people in that vicinity. It was at once determined to send three separate cavalry columns south with instructions to cooperate with each other to the fullest extent. It was believed possible, by moving these detachments, approximately parallel to each other, that Villa would be prevented from moving toward Sonora on the west, or toward the railroad on the east, with the additional chance of cutting his trail or getting ahead of him before he could move south of the railroad into the mountains back of Guerrero, where it was believed that he would probably go.

One of the three detachments, consisting of the 7th Cavalry Regiment (29 officers, 647 enlisted men, commanded by Colonel James B. Erwin), left Colonia Dublan on the night of March 17-18 (a few hours after reaching that place from their forced march from Culbersoffs Ranch) with orders to proceed without delay by way of Galeana to the southwest of El Valle, thence to ascend the eastern slopes of the Sierra Madre Oriental Mountains by trail to the eastern edge of the San Miguel plateau in the hope of striking Villa's band if there, or as he moved eastward with his spoils.

The second detachment, consisting of the Second Squadron and Machine Gun Troop of the 10th Cavalry, 14 officers and 258 enlisted men, under Command of Colonel W.C. Brown, was directed to proceed by rail and detrain at Rucio, and from there moved direct to San Miguel.

The third column, cosisting of the First Squadron of the 10th Cavalry, 8 officers and 204 enlisted men, under command of Major E.W. Evans, was also ordered to proceed by rail to Las Varas, near Madera, cover the territory to the south of Babicora plateau, prevent Villa from moving southwest, and cooperate with the other

Troop D Squad Tents at Colonia, Mexico, 1916. Courtesy of Ed Daily.

7th Cavalry Troop D, in bivouac area at Colonia Juarez, west of Dublan, Mexico, 1916. Courtesy of Ed

Pvt. Burke, a Bugler from Troop D, 7th Cavalry on march in Mexico, 1916. Courtesy of Ed Daily.

Lt. D.B. Leininger, Regimental Veterinarian with his mount "Ranger" in Mexico, 1917. Courtesy of Ed Daily.

two columns as far as practicable.

The first of these three columns to hit the trail was the 7th Cavalry-Regiment. This command had reached Colonia Dublan in the early evening of March 17th, after their memorable march from Culberson's Ranch. Before the animals had a chance to recover from this effort the regiment was ordered out, at about 3:00 a.m., March 18th, as one of the three flying columns in pursuit of Villa and his band.

On March 21st Colonel George A. Dodd was ordered to join the 7th Cavalry Regiment and take command of the overall operations. He had further instructions to cooperate with the l0th Cavalry Regiment, and in case of emergency or pressing expediency, to use that regiment or any part of it in the attainment of his objective. He joined the 7th Cavalry Regiment in its camp about six miles south of Galeana and assumed overall command of operations while Colonel Erwin retained immediate command of the 7th Cavalry Regiment.

On March 22nd the regiment proceeded southward, passing by El Valle about noon. Lieutenant Robert M. Campbell, 7th Cavalry, and Scout Tracy were sent with a message to the commander of the Mexican federal troops in that place, Colonel Salas, requesting an interview. Colonel Salas expressed a desire to see the American commander, but first sent his adjutant to meet the American troops, which had halted on the outskirts of the town. The trail followed by the 7th Cavalry Regiment led through a canyon whose sides were covered by Carranza troops. Colonel Salas met Colonel Dodd and asked by what authority the United States troops were in Mexico. The letter under which the United States troops were acting was interpreted to him, and he stated that he already had a copy of that letter, but that it had not been sent by his government.

Salas then confided that Villa was at Namiquipa with a large command; there three or four days before, Villa had beaten him

badly and had driven him back through Cruces to El Valle, where he had taken up a defensive position in expectation of further attacks. Salas detailed a staff officer to accompany the American troops through the canyon and the command pushed on as rapidly as conditions would permit, and bivouacked at Aqua Zarca.

On March 23rd camp was broken long before daylight between four and five o'clock, and the command followed the road to the crossing of the Santa Maria River about six miles north of Cruces. At El Valle, and during this day's march, assurances were received that Villa was still at Namiquipa, and that he had expressed his intention of remaining there until driven out. There were no troops in Cruces, though a strong anti-American sentiment prevailed there. Therefore, the regiment left the main road in order to keep its presence unknown in Cruces, and followed an arroyo eastward, striking an indistinct trail leading south to the foothills of the mountains east of Cruces and Namiquipa, and nearly parallel to the general course of the river.

Colonel Dodd intended to remain concealed about 12 or 13 miles from Namiquipa, then proceed to and surround the place and take it at daybreak the next morning, but before it was possible to act upon this plan, information was received that Villa was no longer at Namiquipa. Here it was learned that on March 20th, immediately after Colonel Salas' defeat, Colonel Cano, another Carranzista commander, had attacked Villa and driven him from Namiquipa. It was uncertain whether Villa had gone south, west, southwest or east, and Colonel Dodd, bitterly disappointed at learning that he was too late to catch Villa at Namiquipa, ordered the command to bivouac at the nearest source of water.

After a study of the scant and conflicting information, the commander sent a message to General Pershing the following morning advising him of the information just obtained, and also dispatched a note to Colonel Cano requesting him to guard certain passes, while the American column would swing westward in an endeavor to get south and west of Villa. This plan was based upon a report that Villa had passed through or near Oso Canyon, and gone to the south or southwest. Until the receipt of this report Colonel Dodd had believed that Villa had gone south or east, and had conducted his march accordingly.

The command swung into the saddle at 5:00 a.m., March 23rd and followed a good road for ten miles to the Santa Maria River, where good water was found. A few miles farther, opposite Cruces, a native stated that there were some Carranzistas at Ortega under Colonel Cano; some Villistas had come to Cruces, the day before to get provision to take to Villa, wounded in the hills just southeast of Cruces; no Villistas were in Namiquipa, and further stated that Villa had left Namiquipa and gone no one knew where, and that all Villistas had scattered from Namiquipa on March 19th or 20th, after a fight with the Carranzistas. It was further learned that there were two factions in Namiquipa, one friendly and the other which threatened to fight if American troops entered the town. Villa had made a speech here before going to Columbus saying he was going to hit a blow on the border, hurt Americans' pride and bring on intervention. The native also stated there were no troops in Namiquipa and that people in the town did not know American soldiers were present.

Namiquipa was considered the most revolutionary town in Mexico, and had a population of 3,000 to 4,000 people. At 5:00 p.m. Mr. Tracy (civilian scout and guide) was sent into Namiquipa for information.

The column then continued south five miles to a valley running east and west where water and food were found plentiful and made camp, at about 12:45 p.m. after a march of 20 miles.

At 8:15 on the morning of March 24th, three Carranzista soldiers—members of Colonel Cano's command-came into camp. They had been sent by Colonel Brown, 10th Cavalry Regiment at Babicora, with information that Villa had pretty surely gone south from Namiquipa to Santa Geronimo or south of there. They stated that Villa expected reinforcements from General

Banderas to reach him from the south, and the rendezvous was supposed to be Los Tanques, 23 miles east of the Namiquipa; that Villa had about 200 men, many of whom had been taken along by force. The Carranza people thought he could increase this number to about 800 by forcing more to accompany him. Colonel Cano had about 100 men near Babicora about 30 miles from Namiquipa, and that Colonel Brown with his command had arrived at Babicora on March 22nd and was to wait there for Colonel Dodd and his command. These soldiers also said that Santa Ana had been looted and that no supplies could be obtained there; and that Chavez or Babicora were the best places from which to operate, (Santa Ana, Chavez, and Babicora were properties of the American publisher, W.R. Hearst) as they had supplies, and Maximiliano Marquez, a Mexican agent for Mr. Hearst, had some 50 men, all good scouts.

These Carranzista soldiers were sent to find Cano and give him information of the American plan, which was to march to Chavez for supplies and to communicate with the l0th Cavalry Regiment at Babicora. From there two columns would go southeast, the 10th Cavalry Regiment to go farthest south, the 7th Cavalry to go southwest, and Cano to guard Villa's northern exit at El Oso. A Carranza column was to go to Santo Tomas (just north of Guerreo) and await directions, would be to march east and block Villa's southern exit. Cano was supposed to be at Santa Clara east of Namiquipa.

Colonel Dodd broke camp at 9:45 a.m. and marched into a cold gale, hard on man and beast. The command followed a trail for 12 miles going a little south of west across the hills, and arrived at Las Cruces where the horses were watered in irrigation ditches at the south end of

town. Mr. Tracy joined them here and confirmed Villa's fight with the Carranzistas on Sunday the 19th and his fight with Cano a couple of days later at Las Animas. Tracy stated that Cano was reported at Namiquipa on the 23rd and Villa at Los Tanques the same date. The command then continued the march, buffered by the gale winds all day and finally arrived in a canyon on the east slope of the Sierra Madre Oriental Mountains where camp was made at 5:30 p.m., having covered 20 miles in cruel weather.

The command broke camp at 6:20 a.m. Saturday the 25th, and travelled up the canyon, leading the horses up steep rocky trails and over the divide. The march continued for 20 miles through Chavez, halfway to Babicora, where the troops camped and secured supplies. Also messages were received from Colonel Cabell and Colonel Brown, and messages sent to Brown by courier and to General Pershing by wire. Colonel Maximiliano Marquez, caretaker of Babicora, was very hospitable and cordial. The command remained in camp until 4:00 a.m. the 26th.

About 5:00 p.m. on the 25th 1st Lieut. Emil Engel, 7th Cavalry, who had left Dublan the same evening as Colonel Dodd but at a later hour, caught up and delivered three messages: (1) Colonel Cabell to Major Frank Tompkins (13th Cavalry) directing him to establish a base at El Valle; (2) Colonel Cabell to Colonel Dodd, giving information we already knew of Colonel Brown's movements; (3) Colonel Brown to Colonel Erwin, addressed to San Miguel, stating he would move to Chavez.

Colonel Dodd here arranged to leave two troops of the 7th Cavalry Regiment to guard Jaral and Aramillo passes. Colonel Marquez got word about 5:00 p.m. that Carranza troops had moved

7th Cavalry Camp, Colonia Dublan, Mexico, 1917. Courtesy of the National Archives.

7th Cavalry Troop F camp near Colonia Dublan, Mexico, 1917. Courtesy of the National Archives.

7th Cavalry Horses on picket line at Colonia Dublan, Mexico, 1917. Courtesy of the National Archives.

7th Cavalry passing in review, Colonia Dublan, Mexico, 1917. Courtesy of the National Archives.

7th Cavalry on march into Mexico, 1916. Courtesy of Ed Daily.

to passes south of Los Tanques from the southeast, and that Carranza troops were in Santa Clara. The 10th Cavalry Regiment was reported by messenger, at 9:00 p.m., to be close to Los Tanques.

The 7th Cavalry bivouacked overnight at Santa Ana and late in the evening of the 26th, Lieutenant William C.F. Nicholson, 7th Cavalry, came with messages from Colonel Brown which had been sent from Namiquipa on the 25th. In one of them was stated: "Villa's whereabouts unknown, but it is thought possible he has gone through the mountains towards Bachineva." Colonel Dodd stated that this slight clue was somewhat in line with the conclusions he himself had arrived at, which was the probability of Villa striking for the Guerrero Valley.

From the Santa Maria plain two passes with good trails lead to the Guerrero Valley: the Piojo Trail direct from Providencia to San Isidro and Guerrero: and the Nahuerachic Trail from the same point, but farther west, through Nahuerachic Pass, leading southwest to Santo Tomas. In order to take either trail it would have been necessary for Villa to leave the mountains and at some point cross the plains. On March 27th, Colonel Dodd marched to Providencia, looking for signs of the passage of Villa. Finding nothing, he was satisfied that all reports that had reached him of western and southwestern movements of the bandit chief after the Namiquipa fight were false, and that Villa had not crossed the plain toward these passes.

Accordingly, without lingering at Providencia, the column took up the march to Bachineva, making bivouac at a place called Soledad. No water was available here for the horses, therefore the command resumed the march early on the morning of March 28th. At Delicia, the command was met by one of Cano's officers, Lieutenant Ismall Ontevera, and some of his men. Ontevera said that he had just driven off some of Villa's men who had been spying on the American Column. He also stated that Villa

had, on the previous night, passed toward the south some 25 miles farther to the east, and was now on the Mexican Northwestern Railroad near San Diego; however, Colonel Dodd did not attach much importance to this report.

A little later a native told Colonel Dodd that Villa had been in Bachineva two or three days before, had taken property and persons, and had made an inflammatory speech stating that the Americans were coming and urging everyone to join him; also that Villa had been in a fight at Guerrero the night just passed. Colonel Dodd gave some credence to this report and pushed on to Bachineva, where it was confirmed, and where it was also learned that Villa was wounded and was still, at last report, at Guerrero with 500 or 600 men. After receiving this information from the native and before reaching Bachineva, Lieut. Herbert A. Dargue, flying from the north, landed his plane alongside the marching column and delivered a message from General Pershing. This message acquainted Colonel Dodd with the fact that Major Robert L. Howze, 11th Cavalry Regiment, with a command of 240 officers and enlisted men of that regiment, had been sent out to take up the chase, and conveyed instructions that Colonel Dodd should turn over his pack animals to the fresh column, put his command in camp near Namiquipa, and allow it to recuperate until further orders.

Lieutenant Dargue returned with a reply which included information of the situation, and disclosed Colonel Dodd's plans for the immediate future. "I am now satisfied," he states "that Villa is not far distant." And added, "I shall proceed farther south, and shall continue in such touch as is possible to attain (and attack if possible) with Villa. At any rate, until fresh troops arrive."

Colonel Dodd was now satisfied for the first time that he was on the right trail, for every indication and new rumor indicated that the immediate objective of Villa was Guerrero, military center of the Guerrero district, or some other important point in the Guerrero Valley. The command was practically without supplies and had been living on fresh beef, frijoles, and parched corn for several days. The troops were very tired and had not only suffered severely from poor rations, but also from the intense cold that had been endured on the high Babicora plateau, where canteens of water froze solid and whiskers grew icicles. The horses of the command were nearly worn out and had also suffered from a lack of forage. From March 13th to March 28th the troops had marched 14 out of 15 days for a distance of approximately 400 miles under the most trying conditions, and with a shortage of rations and forage; and on top of this they had a night march ahead of them of about 36 miles over unknown mountainous trails, to be followed at dawn, as every man in the command hoped, by a battle with an enemy who not only knew the ground but outnumbered them at least two to one.

The weakest horses and men, quite a large number of the latter, and with them the only medical officer of the column, had been left at the base at Santa Ana, and all but a few of the pack mules had already been sent back to the base. Bivouac was made for a few hours south of Bachineva where the men were fed and horses grazed. Colonel Dodd consulted his maps and guides and made an estimate of the situation. The guides with the column knew nothing of the country, as they had never before gone beyond the limits of the territory familiar to them. Reliable native guides could not be secured, though large sums of money were offered, and none of the natives would state whether a certain designated trail led to Guerrero or not. The only reply to inquiries being the usual 'Quien sabe?' Mr. Barker, on whom the Colonel had greatly relied for information and as a guide, had been in Guerrero but once, some years before, but had entered from another direction. He had had a trail explained to him which led from Bachineva to Guerrero, a long way around, which could be taken, and which he believed could be followed. This trail, or what was believed to be the trail, was indicated on the map.

Realizing that this juncture was a critical one, Colonel Dodd resolved to follow a moderate certainty rather than an absolute uncertainty, and in doing so made a forced night march, hoping to reach Guerrero the next morning by or before daylight. After resting a few hours in bivouac the march was continued until dark, when bivouac was again made. At 11:00 p.m. the night march began. The uncertainty of the route caused many halts and delays, during which the men would lie down on the ground, and in spite of the bitter cold, go to sleep holding the reins. At the last bivouac two guides were impressed into service, who, as was feared, led the command the longest way around, though, as was known, in the correct general direction. Later, before daylight, the knowledge and the courage of these guides gave out simultaneously and others, probably equally unreliable, had to be found, all of which, together with the long circuitous route followed during the night, consumed much valuable time. Finally at about 6:30 a.m. a position was reached from which the town of Guerrero could be located, but it was probably 8:00 o'clock or later before the attack could be made, due to the treachery of the guides in leading the column into an impossible approach.

Guerrero, military center of the Guerrero district, is located in the lower plain of the Guerrero Valley, and is not visible from the east until one is directly over it. On the east side there are precipitous bluffs, high and in most places impassable, cut by deep arroyos running well back into the upper plain. These arroyos are also invisible until one is practically at their edges. The main road from the east follows a steep spur or 'hogback.' On the west side are bluffs, not quite so abrupt, and these extend back to the mountains. This edge of the valley is also cut by deep, partly wooded arroyos, difficult of passage.

Colonel Dodd says of the approach march: "Had the main road been struck and followed, disposition for attack would have been quickly and more advantageously made." "Finding myself misled, and being ignorant of the corrugated character of the ground between the column and the town along the bluffs, I endeavored to correct the doings of the guide by following the bluff, but was stopped by the arroyos. These had to be headed in many cases, which necessitated extra distance and consumption of much time."

Colonel Dodd's plan of attack was to detach one squadron and order it across the river to the west side, so that it might, unobserved if possible, gain the foothills west of the town and block the arroyos leading out from the valley on that side. The 2nd squadron, commanded by Major Edwin B. Winans, was selected for this mission. Its advance is described by Captain Samuel F. Dallam the commander of Troop E— the last troop in the squadron, and designated as rear guard — as follows:

"*Our squadron turned off to the left, descended the bluff, crossed the river, changed direction to the right and pushed on to get between the town and the hills. As the squadron went over the bluff, it naturally became elongated, and I saw it was drawing away from me, so I dismounted my men in order to go down the faster. Arriving at the base of the bluff, I halted to assemble my troop and moved forward some distance in the of the column. As I descended the bluff, looking to the right, I could see at the far end of the village, mounted men leaving it and galloping up the bluff on the same side that I was descending. I estimated that these men would encounter the head of the regimental column on that side.*

"*Pushing along the rear of the column, I saw one our troops had disappeared, then another, and finally I saw the third turn off to the left. Firing came from the hills on our left and not from the town. As our troops had evidently gone into action, and as the direction of the enemy was in my front toward the town, I pushed on to get between the town and our squadron. Just between me and the town was a ravine, and I mounted patrols. About this time the squadron commander rode up beside me and I gave him my plan, which he approved.*

"*Securing the ravine and some houses beside it, which were used as shelter for the horses, a squad was detached to reduce an annoying fire coming from our left and rear. Another squad was sent up ahead outside of the town, and the balance remained in hand near the houses.*

"*Shortly after we had taken this position, the commander, with the rear guard and train, tried to rush the ravine but was killed in the attempt, and his troops and train and some Carranza prisoners captured. About this time Lieutenant Pearson Menoher appeared on the opposite side of the ravine with a detachment.*

"*Lieutenant Albert J. Myer also appeared from that side of the ravine. He had been with the brigade commander on the bluff, and they had seen a large force of Villistas leave the town on our side before our arrival and feared we would he ambushed. Lieutenant Myer had offered to inform the squadron commander of the situation, and had descended the bluff and ridden along through the town and the Villistas for the purpose.*"

The Villista commander, General Hernandez, was killed by Captain Dallam's troop, which also captured two machine guns and other arms, and secured some Carranza prisoners, who were being held by the bandits.

No bandits escaped through the arroyo after Captain Dallam had attained this position, while those who had already passed were pressed and driven westward. The balance of the squadron, arriving at the arroyo, encountered a large body of Villistas moving in an orderly manner, not firing, and carrying the Mexican flag. They were consequently not molested, and this ruse undoubtedly saved the escaping party from annihilation. This same use of the national flag was resorted to elsewhere but without such favorable results to the bandits.

In the meantime the main body had been pushing along the eastern bluff. The arroyos caused much delay, and the command was still a distance from the town when it became evident that the bandits had been alarmed and were escaping. Therefore the attack had to be initiated at long range.

As a number of the bandits were seen escaping at the north end of town whence they then struck eastward, Lieutenant Colonel S.R.H. Tompkins, then with Troop C, was sent with that troop to intercept the escaping party. He was presently reinforced by Major A.L. Dade with Troops I, K, and L. Later, as the Villistas moved toward the hills about Colera, Troop B, under Captain William B. Corwin, and the Machine Gun Troop under Lieutenant Albert C. Wimberly, were sent as further reinforcements.

The pursuit of the bandits was pressed vigorously, in spite of the exhausted condition of the horses. Several stands were made by the retreating parties, and dismounted fire action was resorted to. A mounted pistol charge was planned, but had to be abandoned because it was found impossible to urge the horses into a rapid gait. The poor beasts had given all they had and could do no more.

The running fight continued until the Villistas entered the mountains, which were rough and difficult to traverse. Here they broke into small detachments and scattered. The engagement had started shortly after 8 a.m. on March 29th, and it was 11:30 a.m. before the regiment was reassembled.

The command that participated in this action consisted of 25 officers and 345 enlisted men, all of the 7th Cavalry Regiment, except Colonel Dodd and his staff. The only casualties were five men wounded, none seriously. Villa's command numbered between 500 and 600. Their losses are not known, but Colonel Dodd reported 30 killed and an unknown but large number wounded. The captured property included two machine guns, 44 rifles, 13 horses and 23 mules.

Francisco (Pancho) Villa, having been wounded twice in a fight with Carranzista troops several days previously, was not present with his band at Guerrero at the time of this action. His movements have not been accurately determined; but there was some reason to credit the report that he left Guerrero at two o'clock on the morning of the 29th, the day of the 7th Cavalry Regiment's attack. The doctor who had treated Villa in Guerrero was interviewed, and confirmed the report that Villa's leg was broken. The sought-for Pancho was, then, probably effecting his escape in a wagon, accompanied by a small escort, while the 7th Cavalry column was feeling its poorly guided, uncertain, but determined way through the night from Bachineva to Guerrero. In fact it was during this night march that the command, uncertain as to its route, halted at a road fork. The guide, Mr. J.B. Barker, preferred one route, while the advance guard commander, after consultation with some natives, desired to take the other. Later indications showed that if the column had taken the route preferred by the advance guard commander, it might easily have encountered Villa and his body guard. In any case, it is certain that Dodd's column missed the bandit chief at this time by not more than a few miles.

Villa's command at Guerrero was under orders to follow the commander, who knew of the near approach of the American troops and sought to avoid them. The bandit command was saddling up to leave when the 7th Cavalry struck them.

Colonel Dodd estimated that from March 22nd, when he took immediate command of the column, to the evening of the 29th after the engagement, the command had marched approximately 225 miles, an average of over 28 miles a day, much of it over very rough trails, on insufficient and at times practically no forage, without rest for a day; this marching, immediately following other marches from March 13th (for a portion of the command, and for the balance from March 9th), to the 20th of approximately 252 miles. And it might be well to add that much of this campaigning was at elevations around 7,000 feet above sea level with the accompanying hot days and freezing nights, a condition which soon consumed the vitality of man and horse.

After this engagement the command went into camp close to San Isidro until the afternoon of March 30th, when the entire body moved to Frijole Canyon, ten miles to the north. Here it rested over the 31st and while in camp endured a hail and snow storm. Scouting was continued in an effort to learn the movements of Villa and his adherents subsequent to their departure from Guerrero.

On April 1st the regiment left the 3rd Squadron at Frijole Canyon and marched to Providencia. Here the command received the first fresh supplies since leaving Galeana. Colonel Dodd visited General Pershing at the expedition headquarters at San Geronimo and received instructions to send two troops to occupy Bachineva and to block the Mazana and Naheurachic Passes, then to return with the balance of the command to Frijole Canyon. Lieutenant Colonel S.R.H. Tompkins was sent with the troops to Bachineva, Captain Dallam to guard Naheurachic Pass with Troop E, and Lieutenant Henry E. Mitchell with Troop F was sent to Mazana Pass, somewhat to the north of Troop E's station. Headquarters and two remaining troops returned to Frijole Canyon on April 3rd.

Just before the departure of the regiment from Rancho Frijole, word was received that a party of Mexican federal soldiers under the command of Major Erviso had mutinied at or near Matachic or Tejolocachic (on the railroad northwest of Guerrero) and intended joining the Villistas.

Troops K and M, under Captain William J. Kendrick, were ordered to those points to investigate and take appropriate action. At daybreak on the morning of April 8th, this command, while saddling up in their bivouac a few miles south of Tejolocachic, heard firing to the north. The troops mounted and rode to the sound of the guns to find about 30 Mexicans surrounding and firing upon two Americans and nine Carrianzista soldiers who were defending the Aqua Zarza ranch house. Both troops advanced and after a short engagement dispersed the attackers. The

detachment kept up the pursuit as far as Matachic, but the mutineers kept well concealed in the ravines and underbrush. It was believed that two of them were wounded. The detachment suffered no casualties.

The two Americans at the ranch, Mr. W. Henry Acklin and Mr. Wallace C. Mebana, as well as Major Erviso and eight soldiers of his command, were escorted to Matachic. The besiegers of the ranch turned out to be part of Erviso's force that had deserted from him a few days previously because of their hatred of the Americans, in which their commander apparently did not concur. Captain Kendrick, in reporting the incident, stated that, in his opinion, "The sentiment of the people of this section is growing stronger and more bitter against Americans on account of the presence of U.S. troops in Mexico."

The detachment returned to camp at Rancho Frijole on April 9th. In this little expedition Lieutenant T.K. Brown commanded Troop M, and Lieutenant E.B. Lyon commanded Troop K.

At about 5:00 p.m. on April 13th, the command left camp and marched continuously for 35 miles all night over rough trails, passing through arroyos and arrived at Ariseachic before daybreak. The command then proceeded to Aqua Caliente, where a fresh and heavy trail was struck, leading northeast. This was followed until it disappeared a little south and about ten miles west of Minaca. Leakage of the trail showed that small parties, usually no more than two, three or four, left it from time to time. This, from subsequent developments, was undoubtedly the trail of Julio Acusta and possibly the members of other bands many of whom left the trail going to the south and west, joining Cervantes command that later looted the town and mine of Yoquivo, and which Colonel Dodd afterward fought at Tomochic on April 22nd.

The command went into camp on the 15th near where the trail ran out, at a place called Tonachic, sending into Minaca for whatever much needed supplies as could be obtained.

In this night march Colonel Dodd rode, as was his custom, well forward with the advance guard. He was thus in a position to get the earliest information of any new developments, but jeopardized his personal safety, of which at all times he appeared completely careless. The presence of the commander, accompanied by the guides and the officer personnel of rather a large staff, intermingled with the advance guard, on difficult trails, and in the darkness, made the position of the advance guard commander an unenviable one.

At the other end of the long drawn out column was Captain Dallam, who says of this march:

"Once again I had the rear guard. The route through deep, wooded canyons, and along rough narrow trails. The moon was bright and the night was intensely cold, as usual. All that troop commanders knew was that we were off again on another night march. Neither distance, direction, nor destination was given. We had our place in the column and our duties to perform: to keep in place and be ready when called upon.

"Darkness came on quickly in the canyons, which were deep and narrow. The trails twisted and wound among the trees. At times we would

suddenly come to the head of a canyon where three or more possible trails or directions might be followed. At times it was necessary to dismount and look for tracks of the preceding troops. The moon threw fantastic shadows across the path and distorted all objects. The intense cold and weariness numbed the faculties, and the utmost vigilance was required to keep in place. Sometimes a glimpse would be caught of the horses ahead; they would disappear and then, strive as one would, it seemed that they never could be found again. The pace was a forced walk, the trail rough, the horses stumbled, and the cold grew more intense. One's legs became numb from the knee down but there was no halting. Not until nearly midnight did we make our second and last halt. The squadron was still complete. The small pack train was up and my rear platoon close behind it.

"A few minutes and we were off again, pushing all the time, pressing the horses to their fastest walk. Urgency required our arrival before dawn. The pack train fell behind, and each time as the necessity arose I dropped a connecting file behind until the first platoon was all but used up.

"Suddenly we stopped. We had reached our destination. Troops, were assembled. Orders went back to bring together Troop E. It seemed they would never arrive. The other three troops surrounded the town and advanced. The packmaster began to ring his bell to call the train together; the troop was assembled. The town was rushed—the enemy had gone. He had marched 30 miles. At daylight our scouts went out. We watered, fed, and slept until the arrival of further orders.

"This maintenance of contact is the problem of the rear guard commander. Hampered by the trains, pushing off into the unknown, assuming himself of contact out in front and in the rear, requires the utmost vigilance and efficient, reliant noncommissioned officers. Here were no roads, no sign posts, and no guides, nothing but rocky trails and thick woods, and a deceiving moonlight."

A rumor reached Colonel Dodd that the Villista force he had been tracking was at Yoquivo, had looted that place, and were holding a Frenchman named Seyffert, and an unnamed American for ransom.

Major Gonzales, commanding a federal detachment numbering some 40 men (most of whom were boys) offered to accompany the American force with his command on an excursion to Yoquivo. Colonel Dodd agreed to this enterprise, and Major Gonzales' detachment passed through the American camp about midnight of April 17th.

Without waiting for further supplies Colonel Dodd sent 17 men dismounted and the unserviceable horses into Minaca, and followed Gonzales early the following morning. Terrero on the Kansas City, Mexico and Orient railroad was reached at 10:45 a.m., and shortly afterwards the detachment struck off to the west of the railroad and traversed the Arroyo Ancho.

After traveling in a southwesterly direction all afternoon, bivouac was made toward nightfall in a pretty canyon that was very inviting after a long day's march of about 28 miles. The march was resumed at daylight on the 19th, and again the trail led southwest through the Sierra Madre Occidental Mountains over a difficult trail. Napuchic, a camp of log huts, was passed about midafternoon, and the command arrived at Aguachic just after 5:00 p.m. and bivouacked there, having marched an estimated 30 miles.

The command was up before dawn of April 20th, and in the saddle at 5:45. The direction of march now changed to the northwest, and at the end of some ten miles, junction was made with Major Gonzales. The two commands continued together along the very difficult trail until 1:00 p.m. when bivouac was made in a deep canyon at Basogachic, some eight or ten miles east of Yoquivo. Here the combined forces remained, well concealed it was thought, until the moon rose at 11:00 p.m. Then, instead of taking the shortest and most direct route to Yoquivo, in order to effect a surprise, the command marched over a little used steep and rocky trail which wound along the edges of precipices at a very high altitude in the piercingly cold wind.

Yoquivo was reached about an hour before dawn, and at the first sight of daylight the troops advanced to attack the place. The first sign of life was a bright light in a small stone house; it was Gonzales and his troops. Gonzales was stretched on a couch, resting, and a huge fire was going to keep him warm while half a dozen of his men were administering to his comfort. The Villista bandits had departed.

From the inhabitants and the released prisoners in Yoquivo it was learned that word of the approach of the combined American and Mexican forces had been received in the middle of the previous afternoon. It is not unlikely, and Colonel Dodd was convinced of the fact, that the march was betrayed by the Mexican "allies" themselves. The prisoners (the American and the Frenchman) had been released on partial payment of the ransom demanded. The Villista band, numbering about 200, commanded by Candelaro Cervantes and including among its leaders Manuel Baca, and Cruz Dominiguez, had vacated the place about 8:00 p.m. the previous evening, after having stayed there for five days.

Our troops bivouacked in the vicinity, and sprawled in the sun to warm up and rest, while some welcomed small supplies were gathered from the village. Colonel Dodd, instead of being discouraged and chagrined, felt an assurance that he was rather hot on a sure trail, and determined to follow it to the end.

He requested Major Gonzales to accompany him farther with the little detachment. The Mexican commander excused himself, however, and plans were made to continue the expedition without his assistance.

The troops loafed in the sun until it was too hot, and then hunted the shade hoping to remain there indefinitely after the hard cold ride. However, about 3:30 p.m., orders were given to march and the command took the trail shortly afterward heading northeast. The few pack mules were loaded with supplies of all kinds which had been purchased at Yoquivo. The trail proved to be the most difficult the command had yet encountered and it seemed as though the horses could not stand another day's march.

The trail wound through a rocky chasm, then turned about in the opposite direction, and corkscrewed up the steep, wooded slope of the mountain, the top of which was attained about midnight. Darkness prevented further travel and the tired column rested until dawn.

After a hasty breakfast at dawn the march was resumed following the tortuous trail as rapidly as possible until about 3:00 in the afternoon when, from the crest of a hill, a view was obtained of the valley of Tomochic with the little village nestling in its plain. Some 30 or 40 bandits were seen at the same time running into the hills north of the village. This first observation was made from what was really a high mountain, with an elevation of over 8,000 feet. The trail leading down to the valley was equally steep and difficult, so that considerable time was consumed in getting down to the level of the town, which was entered about 4:30 p.m.

Tomochic—a small, very old town rounded when the Spaniards first came into Mexico—consists of a dozen or so scattered buildings with a small mixed population of Mexicans, half-breeds, and Tarahumara Indians, all living in indescribable squalor. The town is located in a small valley or pocket (rincon) opening into the valley of the Tomochic River (locally so called, but noted on the maps as the Aros, and at some points the Rio Verde). It is approached from the southwest by the Yoquivo trail, while the Campo-Minaca trail passes through it nearly east and west. It is surrounded by high and rugged mountains, clothed with splendid pine forests, and scarred with battlemented canyons. Some points on the Yoquivo trail were found to be higher than 9,000 feet, and the town itself lies at an elevation of 6,625 feet.

The aneroid barometer carried by the command was found to be practically useless, as it registered no more than 6,000 feet. Over these high trails the command had marched in single file, sometimes mounted, often on foot with each man holding to the tail of the horse ahead of him. Horses and men alike were rapidly becoming unshod. Added to this suffering was the shortage of adequate rations and the high altitude which caused very noticeable difficulty in breathing, headache, and bleeding at the nose.

After leaving the summit the trail followed by the command from the southwest became concealed from the town by the ridges, one of which terminated at a point near the river. Level ground was reached in a clear space or pocket where the troops were massed and concealed. A machine gun was placed at this location to command the town and cover the advance of the attack.

From their position, Troop L, commanded by Captain William P. Moffet, closely supported by Troop E commanded by Captain Dallam, all under the command of Major Winans, were ordered to gallop rapidly around the point, charge into and take possession of the town.

The march-weary horses had to jump down from a high bank into the river bed, and when across the river, jump upon a rocky shelf to get out. The advancing troops drew fire from several directions, but continued on into the village which the bandits had completely evacuated. Their rear guard was seen to scatter. Some mounted and some on foot, they took to the nearby hills to the north and south of the village, from which they opened fire.

The balance of the command, less a platoon sent to the north to cover the plain, followed closely in support of Major Winan's Squadron, and patrols were sent out to dislodge or kill the enemy parties which had occupied the hills to the north and south. A considerable number of the bandits took flight toward the east along the Ocampo-Minaca trail.

From the first point of observation a large herd of horses and what appeared to be a column of troops were noticed in the distance. As it seemed probable that the enemy main body might be in this locality, Major Dade was sent with Troop H, Captain Rush S. Wells and Troop I with Captain A.C. Gillem and Captain E.M. Leary accompanying, to the east with orders to attack any forces found there and to capture or kill the herd. This force was accompanied by a machine gun. The herd proved to be brood mares, and no considerable force was encountered in this direction, however the troops did receive some fire from small parties or individual bandits in the hills. The absence of half of the command on what proved to be a useless mission was felt as a serious handicap when the principal resistance developed in another quarter.

A machine gun, under charge of Sergeant H.H. Rogers, was advanced to an abandoned adobe house in order to secure a more raking fire on the trail up which some of the enemy were fleeing. A platoon was sent in support, and later the remainder of Troop L, under Captain Moffet, was sent to the same position.

Until the departure of Major Dade with Troops H and I to the east the enemy firing had been rather light and scattered, and had ceased altogether from the nearby hills. But soon thereafter, a heavy fusilade was received from the circular hills to the east. This came from the enemy main body which, it was later learned, had advanced some three miles up the trail which could be plainly seen where it passed over the crest. Upon learning of the attack upon their rear guard, the bandits had returned and were now scattered along the crest and sides of the mountains, extending from about a point at the northeast to the southeast. They had a decided advantage from this position, and there was no way of getting around them in the short time remaining before dark.

Upon receiving this heavy fire, although dominated by fire from the hills, a dozen men of Troop E under Major Winans immediately occupied the knoll. The headquarters party advanced under fire to the knoll and joined them and from this point kept a well directed fire upon the head of the trail.

As darkness set in the enemy withdrew two or three miles along the trail from which they subsequently scattered. Pursuit was impossible after nightfall and the command was assembled and occupied the village.

Continuance of the action was half expected at daybreak, Easter Sunday, April 23rd, but nothing developed as the enemy force had put many miles behind them.

The regiments casualties were two killed: Saddler Ray of Troop L, and Private Bonshee of Troop H who died during the night from a shot in the abdomen, There were also three men wounded and several horses died from exhaustion.

At least 30 of the Villistas were killed and

wounded, and it is probable that their casualties were still larger. A number of their horses and mules and some arms were captured. Their defeat led to a thorough disintegration and demoralization of the Cervantes force. It had numbered between 150 and 200 on April 22nd, the date of the fight at Tomochic. A few days later Cervantes had scarcely a dozen men with him, according to reports.

A story was subsequently current at Matachic that the Tarahumara Indians, who had no love for the marauding Villista bands, found and gathered in one place all of the bandits, presumably wounded, and being unable to care for them, poured pitch over them and set them on fire.

After resting over April 23rd, the command returned by easy marches to its former camp (San Pedro) near Minaca.

The dead were taken along and interred in the cemetery at that place, and the wounded were sent through as rapidly as possible to Namiquipa. The squadron proceeded by easy stages to Providencia and Namiquipa, where it arrived April 28th, and joined the headquarters of the regiment.

During the absence of this squadron, a minor action had occurred on April 20th. A patrol of two enlisted men and a civilian guide, while scouting the country south of the camp of the 7th Cavalry Regiment, then established at Cocomorachic, encountered a band of ten Villistas, who were waiting in ambush behind the stone wall of a corral. The patrol opened fire at short range, upon discovering the bandits, and then retreated under sharp fire to shelter. Information was sent back to the regimental commander, Colonel James B. Erwin, who sent Troop M under Lieutenant Thoburn K. Brown to the scene. Before the arrival of the troop, however, the bandits had scattered, after losing four of their number mortally wounded by the fire of the patrol.

The regiment remained at Providencia, inactive except for patrolling, for more than a month, and, on June 3rd marched a short distance to the north and took station in Raspadura Pass, where much needed remounts were received. Two days later Colonel Dodd was ordered to El Valle. He assumed command of the large camp at that place, where troops of all arms of the service had been assembled. He was promoted to Brigadier General during his service at this camp, and left it and retired from active service due to his age (64) on July 28, 1916.

A high meed of praise must be accorded this officers, for the unflagging determination and energy with which he prosecuted the pursuit in the face of great difficulties that resulted in the rout of Villa's principal band at Guerrero, and the consummation of the task at Tomochic.

Where only a surmise was had as to the course taken by Villa, where every story contradicted the preceding one, and all reports and rumors were vague and misleading, where roads and trails were unknown, and the country rugged and difficult, where supplies were depleted, with small store in the looted countryside to draw upon, where horses gave out and men fell sick— he was not daunted nor drawn aside from a dogged, persistent determination to find the trail of the bandits and follow it.

For General Dodd no clue was too faint or improbable to follow down, or trail of pony tracks too slight to examine. No marches were too long and no way too rough for him to undertake. He scorned hardships, and was ever a splendid example of hardihood to officers and men. Red shirted Tracy, the invaluable guide and scout, said of this cavalry-man, whom he observed at close range for several weeks of vigorous campaigning: "Colonel Dodd ate less, slept less, and worked harder than any other man in the command."

Villa's forces had scattered in different directions under separate leaders and were still within the State of Chihuahua. It was believed that Villa was in hiding in the mountains to the south of San Borja. The territory infested by these bandits was divided into five districts, each to be patrolled by a regiment of cavalry supported by infantry and artillery. To carry out this plan, the following order was issued:

Headquarters Punitive Expedition, U.S. Army In the Field, Namiquipa, Mexico, April 29, 1916 General Orders)
No. 28)

1. As the result of the arduous and persistent pursuit of Villa by various columns of this command, his forces have suffered losses of approximately one hundred killed with unknown wounded, and have been broken into smaller bands and scattered to different sections of the State of Chihuahua and elsewhere. The situation had been changed to the extent that our troops no longer pursue a cohesive force of considerable size, but by surprise with small, swiftly moving detachment they must hunt down isolated bands, now under subordinate leaders, and operating over widely separated portions of the country. For this purpose the country to be covered for the present is accordingly divided into districts and apportioned to organizations available for such duty.

2. The commander of each separate district will organize his own agents and establish as far as possible his own service of information. Every assistance will be given from these headquarters in providing guides and interpreters and in furnishing information. It is also directed that this office and adjacent commanders be furnished with all information of importance that comes to the knowledge of district commanders, especially such as would influence operations of troops in adjacent districts. Each seems likely to lead to the capture of any of the participants in the Columbus raid, and will keep the Commanding General and, as far as practicable, the Brigade Commander, advised of all movements in his district.

3. All officers are reminded that this expedition is operating within the limits of a friendly nation, whose peaceful inhabitants should be treated with every consideration. It is also desirable to maintain the most cordial relations, and cooperate as far as feasible, with the forces of the de facto government. Experience so far has taught, however, that our troops are always in more or less danger of being attacked, not only by hostile followers of Villa, but even by

other who profess friendship, and precaution must be taken accordingly. In case of unprovoked attack, the officer in command will, without hesitation, take the most vigorous measures at his disposal to administer severe punishment to the offenders, bearing in mind that any other course is likely to be construed as a confession of weakness.

4. The following districts to be covered are embraced within the limits prescribed. The boundary lines are to be understood as indicating in general the territory over which district commanders are for the present to operate, but will not limit their efforts to secure information, often otherwise unobtainable, nor confine their activities when in actual pursuit of Viiiisle bands. In locating their headquarters, district commanders, under direction of the brigade commanders, will give due consideration to the question of supply.

Namiquipa District: Commencing at a point north of Alimo on the 13th parallel, thence east to the Mexican Central Railroad inclusive, south to Sauz, generally west through Tepehuanes, San Miguel Madera to Tio Chico, north to the 13th parallel, thence east to Alimo.

Bustillos District: Commencing at San Miguel, thence along southern boundary of Namiquipa district to Sauz, south to near Salas, west to San Andres and San Antonio, and excluding both towns, thence southwest to Mal Paso, thence north to Bachineva and San Miguel, including both towns.

Satevo District: Commencing at San Antonio, thence east through and including San Andres to Mapula, thence along the Mexican Central railroad to Jimenez, Partel to Santa Barbara, thence northwest to San Lorenzo and San Antonio.

San Borja District: Commencing at San Antonio, southeast to San Lorenzo and Santa Barbare, west to Guachochic, north to Garichic northwest to Ranoho de Bantiago, northeast to San Antonio.

Guerrero District: Commencing at San Miguel, thence south through Bachineva to Mal Paso, southwest to Ranoho de Santiago, southeast to Carichic, south to Guachochic, west to third meridian west of Chihuahua, north to a point west of Madera, thence east to Madera, thence southeast to San Miguel.

BY COMMAND
OF BRIG. GEN. PERSHING,
DeR. C. Cabell,
Lieutenant Colonel, 10th Cavalry
Chief of Staff

Official:
John L. Hines,
Major, Adjutant General,
Adjutant.

Pursuant to the plan laid down in this order, cavalry regiments were assigned to those districts where they had the most service, and with which the personnel was the most familiar, viz:

District	Cavalry	Commander
Namiquipa	10th	Major Elwood W. Evans
Guerrero	7th	Col. George A. Dodd
Bustillos	13th	Col. Herbert J. Slocum
Satevo	5th	Col. Wilber E. Wilder
San Borja	11th	Col. James Lockett

During the month of May, regimental headquarters remained at Providencia, sending out patrols and scouts and gathering information concerning the surrounding country and the hostile Villistas. At the end of the month the entire command was concentrated and preparations were made for taking up the march again.

On June 3rd, the regiment moved to Colonia Dublan, Chihuahua, stopping for rest and supplies at Raspadura Pass, Santa Maria River, Namaquipa, El Valle, Angosture, Galeana and Morman Lakes. The distance covered approximately 170 miles through the hot desert country.

From July until the end of the year the regiment remained in camp at Colonia Dublan, Chihuahua. Here an intensive period of training was entered into, which, coupled with outpost duties, scouting and patrolling, kept the command busy night and day. The men and animals suffered greatly from the heat and sand storms and, in the middle of November, it was necessary to send a detachment to Columbus, New Mexico, for remounts. This detachment left November 16th, and returned with the remoumts on the 29th.

On November 25th, the 1st Squadron was sent to Colonia Juraz, Mexico, for station, where it remained until December 1st.

During the latter part of the year the command suffered greatly from high winds and sand storms coupled with the severe cold at night. However, the men withstood these hardships well and a high standard of morale was maintained throughout the entire year.

1917

On January 6th, Troop E escorted Brigadier General Eben Swift, U.S. Army, on a hunting trip in the mountains surrounding Colonia Dublan, Mexico.

On January 8th, Troop C left in pursuit of deserters and returned with five deserters, having ridden 75 miles in 30 hours through bandit infested mountains and deserts.

On January 30th, the entire regiment, less Troops L and M, left camp at Colonia Dublan for its return to the United States. It camped at the Corralitas Ranch, 18 miles distant, at the end of the first day's march. Troops L and M remained at Colonia Dublan, leaving January 31st as escort to Mormon, Mexican and Chinese refugees.

The remainder of the march to Camp Steward, Texas, was made as follows:

January 31st, Ojo Federico, Mexico.
23 miles.
February 1st, Espia, Mexico,
28 miles.
February 2nd, Boca Grande, Mexico,
22 miles.
February 3rd, Las Palomas, Mexico,
23 miles.
February 5th, Columbus, New Mexico,
11 1/2 miles.

Here the command was reviewed by General Pershing who had commanded the punitive expedition into Mexico.

February 7th, Malpaio, New Mexico,
25 miles.

February 8th, Noria, New Mexico,
27 miles.
February 9th, Anapra, New Mexico,
24 miles.
February 10th, Camp Steward, Texas,
13 miles.

The regiment had marched a total of 215 miles since leaving Colonia Dublan.

On May 23rd the regiment moved to Fort Bliss, Texas, where the troops went into barracks for the first time after many hard days of campaigning. The section now known as the "New Post" was assigned to the regiment at that time. From here the troops were detailed to patrol the Rio Grande River as far as Ysleta and Fabens, Texas.

The 1st Squadron left Fort Bliss by rail for station at Fort Yellowstone, Wyoming, on June 22nd and arrived at its destination on the 27th. The squadron consisted of seven line officers, two medical officers, 436 enlisted men of the line, 13 enlisted men of the medical department, and 442 public horses and 37 mules.

Troops K, L, and the Regimental Band marched 41 miles to Las Cruces, New Mexico, on September 26th to participate in the Dona Ana County Fair and returned to Fort Bliss on October 1st.

Throughout the remainder of the year, the regiment, less the 1st Squadron, performed outpost and patrol duty along the Rio Grande, the troops alternating with each other in occupying the several different outpost positions at Ysleta, Fabens. and Fort Hancock, Texas, in this section. On December 26th, the 1st Squadron left Fort Yellowstone by rail and joined the regiment at Fort Bliss on the 31st.

7th Cavalry Regiment crossing border into the United States on return from Punitive Expedition into Mexico, 1917. Courtesy of Ed Daily.

CHAPTER III
The Army Lean Years
(1918-1941)
From Horses to Horsepower

1918

The entire year was spent in garrison at Fort Bliss, Texas. During the period the regiment continued its patrol of the border by troops.

The regiment participated in brigade maneuvers April 22nd to 24th, and from May 10th to 21st.

The 2nd Squadron with Regimental Headquarters and the Machine Gun Troop made a practice march of 106 miles to Fort Hancock, Texas, and return, during the period August 6th to 9th. This same practice march was made by the 1st and 3rd Squadrons during the period August 10th to 13th.

During the period September 9th to 16th, the entire regiment made a practice march of 134 miles to Diversion Dam, New Mexico, camping approximately 600 yards from the old ruins of Fort Selden, New Mexico, upon arrival. The regiment paraded through the streets of Las Cruces, New Mexico, on its return trip.

The entire command was quarantined due to the prevalence of Spanish Influenza during the period October 16th to November 23rd.

1919

The entire regiment was stationed at Fort Bliss, Texas, at the beginning of the year. The 3rd Squadron was temporarily stationed at Camp Cody, New Mexico, for patrol and guard duty during the period February 1st to March 20th.

During the month of April 48 horses and 17 mules in the regiment were killed to prevent suffering due to an epidemic of Glanders disease.

During the month of June the Villistas began threatening American lives and property along the Rio Grande river towns.

At 12:45 a.m. on June 15th, the entire regiment, less Troops E, G, and H, left Fort Bliss and assembled at San Lorenzo ford to protect American lives in this locality. The regiment returned to Fort Bliss about 9:00 a.m. the same day without locating the enemy. At 6:45 p.m., the command was again assembled at San Lorenzo ford and this time crossed the border into Mexico at 1:20 a.m. Here the Villistas were met and a sharp engagement ensued which lasted about two hours before the bandits were driven back with heavy losses. The following is an account of the engagement:

Headquarters Seventh U.S. Cavalry,
Camp at Fort Bliss, Texas
June 17, 1919

From: Commanding Officer, 7th U.S. Cavalry

To: Commanding General, El Paso District, El Paso, Texas, (Thru C.O. 2nd Cavalry Brigade).

Subject: Report of Operations.

1. Pursuant to verbal orders the Regiment proceeded to designated rendezvous, San Lorenzo Ford, arriving there at 7:45 p.m. the 15 inst. The river was crossed between 10:10 and 10:40 p.m.. The march toward Juarez was begun at 12:20 p.m. the 16th inst. The regiment furnished flanking patrols and rear guard. At 1:20 a.m. left flank patrol killed one Villista, captured one and two Mauser rifles, near the Agricultural College. From about 1:45 to 2:00 a.m. the First Squadron was dismounted facing north, on a road about onehalf mile south of the federal line of entrenchments. During this time there was considerable fire toward our direction. Sergeant Chigas, Troop L, received a serious bullet wound in the chest. Two horses were wounded. A search was made of the front of operations but no dead or wounded Mexicans were discovered.

2. The column returned to the Fords, the march beginning at 6:00 a.m., the Seventh Cavalry leading. After watering and feeding the march was taken up at 8:10 a.m. past San Lorenzo Church in the general direction of the Alberto Stephenson Ranch. En route four prisoners were captured and information obtained as to the location of the Villista main body.

3. The advance guard and patrols located the Villista main body in camp in the fields and foothills along the south side of the Rio Grande Valley about due west from the Cinecue Church. Prisoners stated his strength to be about 500 men.

4. Pursuant to instructions from Commanding Officer, 2nd Cavalry Brigade, this regiment proceeded to lead the attack. Line of troop columns was formed facing south, preceded by officer patrols. The advance guard (Troop L) was directed to cooperate in the attack. Two troops of the 3rd Squadron dismounted to fight on foot and opened fire at 1100 yards against masses of the enemy, who were plainly seen mounting up in considerable confusion. The Machine Gun Troop on the left of these two troops also opened fire. The 2nd Battalion of the 82nd Field Artillery prepared to go into action on our right. The 1st Squadron was directed to proceed to our left mounted to intercept the enemy. The enemy mounted up and made for the hills south, out of range of small arms, our artillery came into action. I requested permission of and obtained permission from Commanding Officer of the Brigade to proceed to the support of the 1st Squadron. The ground between the position and the enemy was intersected by deep irrigation ditches, impossible to cross except at great intervals and then only with difficulty. The ground was muddy and soft from cultivation. Horses sank to their fetlocks at every step and speed was impossible. The 1st Squadron caught up with the Villistas near the edge of the mesa south of the valley and there engaged them. Three dead Villistas were discovered. The 1st Squadron continued the pursuit until the Villistas were out of sight beyond the hills on the southern sky line. The 1st Squadron then halted and it was here that I with the rest of the regiment joined shortly after 11:00 a.m. The 8th Engineers also joined my command. The Villistas appeared to have retreated in 3

general directions—one to south east down the Rio Grande, one to south of my positions, and one to southwest from 5th Cavalry front about a mile from my right (north) flank.

5. I considered that the instructions of the Brigade Commander to pursue and disperse the Villistas had been complied with. This was further confirmed by an order received from the Brigade Commander to return to the position to which the attack was started. The position farthest south of the regiment was about 4 miles due south of the Cinecue Church. The return from the position was begun at 12:15 p.m., the position of the Brigade Commander being reached at 1:20 p.m.

6. Everywhere that the Villistas had been there was evidence of great precipitance in their flight. Probably 50 horses and mules were found abandoned, some of them completely saddled and bridled. 4 horses and 5 mules were brought in with the regiment. 26 horses and mules were found dead on the hills immediately south of the regiment's position. Numerous saddles were found scattered about and without making a complete search 32 rifles were recovered.

7. There was but one casualty in the regiment, that of Sergeant Chigas above reported. The regiment is known to have killed 5 Villistas. The number of wounded is not known as most of them were probably carried off, however three wounded men were observed who were left behind. The regiment turned in 8 Villista prisoners.

8. The regiment, as part of the Brigade, resumed the march to San Lorenzo Ford at 2:00 p.m., crossing on the pontoon bridge at 3:45 p.m. proceeding to and arriving at Camp at 4:30 p.m.

9. Strength of the regiment was 22 officers and 435 men and about 450 horses and 14 mules.
/s/HOWARD R. HICKOK
Lieut. Col. 7th Cavl. U.S.A.

On July 28th, the regiment less Troops E, F, G, H, and K left Fort Bliss, on a practice march of 88 miles to Cloudcroft, New Mexico, and returned on August 10th. Troops F and K were detailed as guards at Camp Wagner, New Mexico.

The remainder of the year was spent in patrolling the border and the usual camp duties at Fort Bliss.

1920

This year was devoted to the usual duties incident to garrison duty at Fort Bliss, Texas, and to patrolling the Mexican border. During the period July 23rd to August 6th, the Headquarters and Troops A, B, C, D, and Machine Gun Troop made a practice march from Fort Bliss to Camp Dickman, near Elephant Butte Dam, New Mexico, and return. During the period August 6th to 26th, Troops E, F, G, and H made the same practice march, and Troops I, K, L, and M followed during the period August 22nd to September 10th.

1921

The regiment spent the entire year perform-

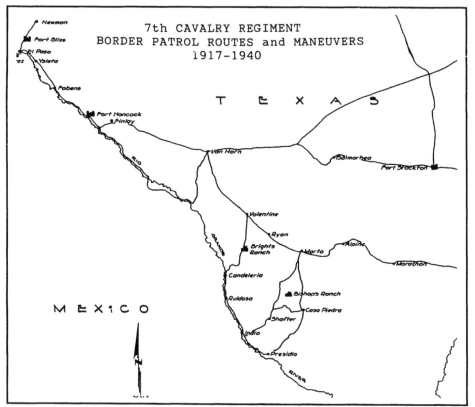

7th CAVALRY REGIMENT
BORDER PATROL ROUTES and MANEUVERS
1917-1940

ing the usual garrison duties at Fort Bliss, Texas. During the period September 4th to 5th, field maneuvers and an inspection were held by the Commanding General, 8th Corps Area.

During the period September 20th to 29th, the 1st Squadron made a practice march of 205 miles from Fort Bliss, Texas, to Marfa, Texas, and return.

On October 17th, 1st Lieutenant Charles H. Bryan and four enlisted men left Fort Bliss on a 172 mile patrol along the international boundary. Messages were sent to the post from the patrol by carrier pigeon.

During the month of November three officer patrols — each using pack transportation — were made along the international boundary as follows:

Captain A.W. Roffe, 7th Cavalry, and four enlisted men, left Fort Bliss by marching on November 4th, following the route: Matra to Childus Tanks, to Shafter, to Indio, to Ruidoso, to Candelaria, to El Cornedor, to Everetts Ranch, to Hollands Ranch, to Brites Ranch, to Marfa. Total distance 216 miles. The patrol returned on November 15th.

1st Lieutenant Charles H. Martin, 7th Cavalry, and four enlisted men left Fort Bliss by marching on November 18th, following the route: Marfa to Bishops Ranch, to Red Wind Mill, to Jacksons Ranch, to LaJitas, to Santa Helena, to Glenn Springs to Tornilia Creek, to Water Hole, to Marathon, to Alpine, to Marfa. Total distance 311 miles. The patrol returned on November 30th.

1st Lieutenant Alan L. Fulton, 7th Cavalry, and four enlisted men, left Fort Bliss by marching on November 18th, following the route: Marfa to Bishops Ranch to Casa Piedres, to Redford, to Presidio, to Indio, to Ruidosa, to Candelaria, to El Cornedor, to Everetts Ranch, to Hollands Ranch, to Valentine, to Ryan, to

Marfa. Total distance 273 miles. This patrol returned on November 30th.

In the fall of this year, when the reorganization of the Army took place, Troops D, H, I, K, L, M, and the Machine Gun Troop Were dropped from the roster of the regiment (see Appendix B). Troop D became what is now known as the First Cavalry Division Headquarters Company, while Troop H became the Second Cavalry Brigade Headquarters Troop. The Machine Gun Troop became Troop A, 2nd Machine Gun Squadron. The entire 3rd Squadron became inactive. Due to the numerous discharges at this time, the regiment was reduced to barely enough men to keep the post and animals in proper condition.

Effective September 15th—upon organization of the First Cavalry Division—the Seventh Cavalry Regiment was assigned that Division and remained as one of its organic regiments until the Army was reorganized under pentomic concepts in 1957 and the 7th Cavalry Regiment was inactivated.

The regiment won the Fort Bliss Master Trophy in the Fort Bliss Horse Show on December 3rd, by compiling a greater number of points than any other participating regiment, notwithstanding the fact that only one depleted squadron and the regimental headquarters participated in the event.

The Regimental Polo team won the First Cavalry Division Polo Tournament and trophy against all other teams of the Division. The regiment retained the 8th Corps Area Polo championship for another year since the Corps Area tournament was not held.

1922

This year was spent at Fort Bliss, Texas, performing the usual garrison and camp duties. Recruit training was carried on intensively in

order to prepare the regiment for the forthcoming maneuvers.

The regiment was inspected and reviewed by the Division Commander on January 19th and again on the 23rd in preparation for the inspection and review held for the Assistant Secretary of War and the Deputy Chief of Staff of the Army on January 25th.

On February 19th the Headquarters Detachment, 2nd Squadron, was activated and on February 27th, the Headquarters Detachment, 1st Squadron, was activated.

The regiment was reviewed by the Chief of Cavalry on March 31. *Major General Willard J. Holbrook, Chief of Cavalry from July 1, 1920 to July 23, 1924.*

During the period July 24th to 30th, the 2nd Squadron made a practice march of 153 miles.

During September Troops A, B, and C made a practice march of 54 miles, and later in the month, the entire 1st Squadron participated in a cavalry screen and communications field problem which was conducted in conjunction with airplanes. This is the first recorded use of airplanes in conjunction with the maneuvers of the regiment.

During October 2nd to 4th, 9th, 10th, and 16th to 18th, the regiment participated in extensive maneuvers with the entire First Cavalry Division. On October 26th, the regiment participated in a Division Inspection and review for General of the Armies, John J. Pershing.

1923

The regiment was stationed at Fort Bliss, Texas, performing the usual garrison duties during the entire year except for brief periods spent in maneuvers.

During the period January 21st to 30th, the 1st Squadron made a practice march of 204 miles to Marfa, Texas, and return.

On July 19th, the regiment was inspected and reviewed by Brigadier General King, Commandant of the Cavalry School.

During the period September 15th to October 3rd, the regiment marched 438 miles to Camp Marfa, Texas, and return, to participate in the Division manuevers. This was considered the most successful maneuver in the history of the regiment up to this time. The horses in particular withstood the test remarkably well which attested to the efficiency of the command.

1924

This year was spent at Fort Bliss, Texas, performing the usual camp and garrison duties. A very successful year of training was enjoyed by the regiment. Early in the year instruction of the individual soldier, the squad, the platoon, the troop, the squadron, and the regiment was completed. The saber qualification course was finished during the first quarter of the year with 99% of the regiment qualifying. The pistol qualification course, mounted and dismounted, was also finished with 99% of the regiment qualified (mounted) and 98% (dismounted). The highest score in the Chief of Cavalry Mounted Pistol Team Match was made by Troop B. Following this, regimental maneuvers were conducted involving problems in advance guard, combat (mounted and dismounted) outposts, occupation of defensive position, and dismounted attack.

Major Joel H. Eliott. Courtesy of Ed Daily.

Major (Brevet Major General) Alfred Gibbs. Courtesy of Ed Daily.

Colonel (Brevet Major General) Samuel D. Sturgis. Courtesy of Ed Daily.

Colonel (Brevet Brig. Gen.) James W. Forsyth. Courtesy of Ed Daily.

Colonel Theodore A. Baldwin. Courtesy of Ed Daily.

Major (Brevet Colonel) Louis H. Carpenter. Courtesy of Ed Daily.

Preliminary rifle instruction began in the 2nd Squadron in April preparatory to going to the Dona Ana Target Range followed by preliminary instruction in the 1st Squadron and Headquarters and Service Troops. The final results for the target season ending on June 27th showed 97% qualified with an average score of 230.46 per man. The 100% organizations were Service Troop and Troops C and F, with Troop C, Captain J.M. Lile, commanding, having the highest average score of 292.16 per man. The percent qualified in automatic rifle was 98.89 with Troop C making the highest score of 563.2 per man.

During 15 days in July, the 1st Squadron assisted in the training of the 111th Cavalry, New Mexico National Guard. From July 28th to August 26th the 2nd Squadron was engaged in conducting the Citizens Military Training Camp at Fort Bliss, Texas.

In September combat firing problems were conducted in which actual combat conditions were simulated as nearly as possible.

On October 21-22, the regiment partici-

pated with the troops of the garrison in a maneuver for the tactical inspection of the Chief of Cavalry and Major General Ernest Hinds, Commanding General, 8th Corps Area. The maneuver involved an attack at dawn across the Rio Grande River at Courcheane bridge, northwest of El Paso. *Major General Malin Craig, Chief of Cavalry from July 24, 1924 to March 21, 1926.*

During November and December the regiment held supplementary rifle and pistol practice.

During the year the regiment stood all inspections and reviews scheduled by the First Cavalry Division and the officers attended the usual schools scheduled throughout the year.

1925

This year was spent at Fort Bliss, Texas performing the usual garrison and camp duties. In June, the regiment marched 27 miles to the Dona Ana Target Range for the annual target practice.

The Regimental Basketball team made a

Colonel Edwin V. Sumner. Courtesy of Ed Daily.

Brig. Gen. Edward S. Godfrey. Courtesy of Ed Daily.

Lt. Colonel Winfield S. Edgerly. Courtesy of Ed Daily.

Colonel Charles Morton. Courtesy of Ed Daily.

Brig. Gen. William J. Nicholson. Courtesy of Ed Daily.

Brig. Gen. Frederick K. Ward. Courtesy of Ed Daily.

Colonel George K. Hunter. Courtesy of Ed Daily.

Brig. Gen. James B. Erwin. Courtesy of Ed Daily.

Lt. Colonel Francis W. Glover. U.S. Army photo.

Colonel Charles A. Hedekin. Courtesy of Ed Daily.

Colonel Selah R.H. Tompkins. Courtesy of Ed Daily.

Colonel George H. Sands. U.S. Army photo.

Colonel William A. Shunk. U.S. Army photo.

Colonel Charles J. Symmonds. Courtesy of Ed Daily.

Colonel Walter C. Short. Courtesy of Ed Daily.

Colonel Fitzhugh Lee. Courtesy of Ed Daily.

Lt. Colonel Howard R. Smalley. Courtesy of Ed Daily.

Colonel William M. Connell. Courtesy of Ed Daily.

Colonel Charles F. Martin. Courtesy of Ed Daily.

Colonel Ola W. Bell. Courtesy of Ed Daily.

Colonel William W. Gordon. U.S. Army photo.

Captain Terry de la Mesa Allen. Courtesy of Ed Daily.

Colonel Glenn Smith Finley. U.S. Army Photo

Colonel William W. West. Courtesy of Ed Daily.

Colonel Frederick Gilbreath. Courtesy of Ed Daily.

Colonel Walter E. Finnegan. U.S. Army Photo.

good showing and achieved third place in the Post League for the 1924 season which ended in January 1925. During the 1925 season there was an Inter Troop League only. This was won by Troop A which developed a crack team under the direction of Captain Paul L Singer, troop commander.

The baseball season opened on February 15 when Service and Headquarters Troops played the initial game of the Inter Troop League. Troop A carried off the honors in the Inter Troop League. A strong regimental team was entered in the Post League and for the third consecutive year the GarryOwens won the Post League championship. The team played 18 games in the league loop and lost only one game. The team crossed bats with several civilian teams including the Mescalero Indian team, carrying off the honors in each instance.

The regimental junior and senior polo teams kept up a regular schedule of practice and engaged in matches with other teams of the post during the year. Both senior and junior teams

played in the First Cavalry Division tournament held at Fort Bliss, December 3rd to 10th. In February, Captain D.S. Wood and Lieutenant Carleton Burgess of the regiment were members of the Fort Bliss team which represented Fort Bliss in the tournament at San Antonio, Texas. This team distinguished itself and was selected to represent the 8th Corps Area in the tournament at Philadelphia in the fall. The Fort Bliss team earned a national reputation at Philadelphia by scoring a win over all contenders of the 12 goal class: Fort Leavenworth, Fort Oglethorpe, Rockaway, Bryn Manor, Midwick, Chargrin Valley and Point Judith. The Fort Bliss team members were: Major, H.D. Chamberlain, 8th Cavalry; Captains L.K. Truscott, 8th Cavalry; C.E. Huthsteiner, 8th Cavalry; D.S. Wood, 7th Cavalry; and Lieutenant Carleton Burgess, 7th Cavalry.

The regiment participated in the First Cavalry Division Horse Show, April 23rd to 25th. First Sergeant M.M. Cesana, Troop B, on "Trixie," competing against an open field, won

Colonel John K. Herr. National Photo Service, San Antonio, Texas.

Colonel Thoburn K. Brown. Courtesy of Ed Daily.

the championship jump. Sergeant Cesana on the same horse also took first place in the enlisted men's jumping event. Captain R.R. Allen with "Laddie" got third place in the Officer's Private Mount jumping. Sergeant P.J. Devine with "Billie" took first place in the Pack Horse event, and third in the Auto Rifle Pack class. Captain J.M. Lili on "Cherry" won third in the officer's Light Charger class, and took second place with "Frank" in the Remount Cup event, third phase. Sergeant Kuloynski, Troop A, won third place with "Laddie" in the Handy Jumper class. Sergeant Elliot with "Frank" placed third in the enlisted men's mounts. In the Best Wheel Draft Mule event, second place went to "Red" handled by Private Day, and third place to "Slim" handled by Private Leake; while in the Escort Wagon event, second honors were attained by Private Day driving a team of bays. The mule race found "Punch" with Private Wallin second. In the Pack Mule class, Private Laske with "Chick" came second. Honors for the best Radio Section went to Headquarters Troop, and second place to the 1st Squadron, Headquarters Detachment. Second place in the Best Cavalry Horse went to "Major," 7th Cavalry. The Stick and Ball Race was won by Lieutenant F.G. Trew. In the Five Man Hunt team event, Captain R.R. Allen, on 'Laddie,' Sergeant Kuloynski on "Chief" and Lieutenant F.J. Thompson on "Komurke," won the third place. The Horse Show ended with the regiment Rough Riding Squad giving a thrilling exhibition of spectacular riding.

The Regimental Band began the concert season on February 15 trader the direction of band leader Warrant Officer Clark B. Price. During the summer months the Band gave a series of concerts at the post and in various parks in the city of El Paso, and received much praise from civilians. In August and October the band played at a fair in Roswell, New Mexico, and gave two complimentary concerts at Tularosa and at Garrizozo, New Mexico. The band also furnished music at the convention of the Chambers of Commerce of New Mexico at Ruidoso.

In November the band accompanied the good will trade excursion of the businessmen of El Paso, to Chihuahua, Mexico, where a festival was in progress.

During the year the following Sergeants were retired: First Sergeant John H. Green, Master Sergeant Edward M. Carey, Master Sergeant Samuel S. Simmonds and First Sergeant Aaron Haverstick. All had seen long service with the regiment. The usual parade and review was held by the regiment for each. Each also received a handsome gift of a gold watch and chain presented by Colonel Fitzhugh Lee on behalf of the NonCommissioned Officer's Club, and were tendered a banquet by the N.C.O. Club.

On August 3rd, 29 enlisted men, Captain D.S. Wood and Major A.D.S. McCoy, M.C., were called out with other troops of the post to aid in checking a flood at Fabens and Tornillo caused by a sudden rise in the Rio Grande River. The troops worked several days and aided materially in saving property.

On November 21st and 22nd, the Rough Riding Squad and other troops of the regiment took part in the Military Circus held in El Paso to raise funds for the Community Chest. One feature of the squad was a galloping pyramid of fifteen men on four horses, a record, perhaps, for this type of stunt.

1926

This year was spent at Fort Bliss, Texas, performing the usual garrison duties. During the month of March and April the entire regiment held intensive mounted and dismounted drill with the pistol, instructed in the prescribed course in the saber, and conducted rifle practice and record firing. Upon completion of the training period, the regiment was inspected by the 8th Corps Area Inspector.

On May 1st, a review was held for the Chief of Cavalry. *Major General Herbert B. Crosby, Chief of Cavalry from March 21, 1926 to March 20, 1930*

On June 16th, a Provisional Squadron

(Headquarters Detachment, Troops C, E, and F) departed Fort Bliss by rail for the Crow Agency, Montana, to participate in the SemiCentennial celebration of the Battle of the Little Big Horn. The Provisional Squadron returned to Fort Bliss on July 1st having traveled 1,800 miles.

Numerous division problems, inspections, and reviews were held throughout the year.

During the period October 25th to 31st, the regiment participated in the division horse show and polo tournament, again winning many trophies.

1927

The entire year was spent at Fort Bliss, Texas, performing the usual garrison duties and participating in numerous reviews, inspections, night marches and division problems.

On April 29th, a Division review was held for Major General Herbert B. Crosby, the Chief of Cavalry.

During May the Aronson Saber trophy was won by Troop B. This trophy was awarded by Mr. Charles Aronson, a local clothing store owner in El Paso, to the troop making the highest average score in saber proficiency during the training period. The troop winning the trophy was permitted to keep it until the following year. Any troop winning the trophy three years in succession was permitted to keep permanent possession of the trophy.

Two Cuban officers—1st Lieutenant Arthur Torres Y. Viera and Captain Miquel R. Llera Y Grafas—were attached to the regiment for observation and instruction during the period September 12th, 1926, to July of this year.

On July 16th the regiment held a farewell review and escort for the Regimental Commander — Colonel Fitzhugh Lee —upon his departure to attend the War College in Washington, D.C.

During the period Colonel Lee commanded the regiment it had a very high record in rifle and pistol marksmanship, and in the saber quali-

Chief "Standing Bear," Sioux Indian and graduate of Carlisle Indian School and Yale, and he was well known star in the movies. 50th Anniversary of the Battle of the Little Big Horn on June 25, 1926. U.S. Army photo.

Colonel Fitzhugh Lee with "White Man Runs Him," Crow Agency, Montant. 50th Anniversary of the Battle of the Little Big Horn. June 25, 1926. U.S. Army photo.

Colonel Fitzhugh Lee, Commander of the 7th U.S. Cavalry and Cheyene Delegation at the Crow Agency, Montana, during the 50th Anniversary of the Battle of the Little Big Horn, on June 25, 1926. U.S. Army photo.

fication course. In the year 1925, the 7th Cavalry Regiment had the highest qualification percentage of any regiment in the 8th Corps Area.

Colonel Lee took a great interest in regimental athletics, especially in baseball. Through his efforts the 7th Cavalry Regiment won the post baseball championship for four years out of five.

Colonel Lee developed the 7th Cavalry Rough Riding Squad to the point where they were renowned throughout the entire country. He also developed the 7th Cavalry band until it had achieved great popularity in the surrounding country, and requests were continuously received for the band to participate in civic activities. The following is quoted from a letter written by Lieutenant Torres, Cuban Army, then attached to the Seventh Cavalry for training, upon the departure of Colonel Lee.

"To pay a fitting tribute to Colonel Lee is beyond my ability, I do not possess the intelligence nor am I sufficiently acquainted with the language of this country.

To enumerate his merits is unnecessary; those have been under his command know them.

And viewing with sadness the departure of Colonel Lee, it is my modest opinion that we are losing a regimental commander of exceptional leadership; of rarest ability to maintain at the highest state the spirit of the regiment; a perfect gentleman; an excellent horseman; an officer of the highest sense of honor and self-sacrifice; one who thoroughly knows those under him.

I am sure that if fate would give Colonel Lee the opportunity, he would know how to give to the riders of the Seventh, fame and glory, as 'Ney' gave them to his Hussars in Wagram and

as his 'Murat' gave them to his Cuirassiers in Austerlitz.

My greatest satisfaction would be to see Colonel Lee with us again, and I say 'with us' because, although I may not be here, once a GarryOwen always a GarryOwen.

Great happiness and success to you, Colonel, in your future."

One of the most colorful ceremonies in the history of the regiment was held on July 17th, when the entire regiment participated in a Division review for the retirement of Colonel Selah R.H. "Tommy" Tompkins.

Colonel Tompkins had served with the regiment from Second Lieutenant through the rank of Colonel. His retirement brought to an end an outstanding career of an active figure in the military establishment and brought deepest regrets to officers and the rank and file of the Army in posts from Alaska to China. Colonel Tompkins probably made more friends than any officer of his day. This was apparent when the previous winter an Army truck had been required to deliver his Christmas mail. A hard-riding, hard-bitten old school cavalry soldier, Colonel "Tommy" carried on the tradition of the Indian fighting days. He believed that the Army was a place for fighters and that the nation could do without many of its military parades. He had little patience with the hair splitting niceties enforced in some of the modern Army organizations of the day. He was called the "last dragoon" and in appearance he showed little kinship with the post-World War I type of officer. With his fierce, shaggy brown and magnificent eight-inch mustachios, Colonel "Tommy" stood out in any group of military men like a cavalry patriarch.

The *El Paso Times*. El Paso, Texas, gave the following account off Colonel Tompkins' retirement ceremony. *"The finest regiment in the army — carry on our traditions — I wish you happiness — God bless you — God bless you — I thank you — God bless you — goodbye."* They came from the heart, those words, a heart overflowing with love for the boys of the regiment he served for 32 years of a long and active life.

It was Colonel Selah R.H. (Tommy) Tompkins speaking to the assembled troops of the Seventh Cavalry at the gate of the reservation [Ft. Bliss, Texas] at 12:15 p.m. yesterday.

They were his last words to his men before retirement from the army. Dramatic as the situation was—Colonel Tompkins with his long flowing beard waving in the wind sitting his horse in the little triangular park just inside the gate with the troops drawn up in the street on all sides of the park—an instant later the situation reached a climax characteristic of the old Indian fighter.

Just outside the high pillars of the reservation gate camera men were waiting with a battery of movie machines and cameras to snap the colonel as he rode through the gate, marking his exit from the army.

General E.B. Winan's (Commanding the First Cavalry Division) own car was parked just outside the entrance to pilot the retiring officer to his hotel.

Newspaper and movie men looked forward to the scene as the climax of the whole day. Colonel Tompkins had posed patiently for shots from every conceivable angle on the reviewing field a few minutes before where the Seventh went through its paces for its beloved commander.

As the old warrior ceased speaking, he removed his hat and sat with bowed head for a moment before the flag of his country. The assembled troops gave him the saber salute and he started at a gentle trot toward the gate.

The battery of cameras stared him in the face when he was 60 feet distant. Then, the heart that was pent up with emotion could stand no more. Colonel Tommy didn't want the photographic record of his exit from the army to appear in movie houses all over the country and to rest in the army files.

He leaned quickly forward. Spurs bit deep into the sides of his horse, which, by the way, was 'Fitz,' the horse that Colonel Tompkins rode into Mexico in 1916 in pursuit of Pancho Villa.

The horse gave a startled leap and at full gallop made for the gate. Camera men were just ready to start grinding when the colonel swung his horse sharply to the right and passed on the far side of the left pillar entrance so that he did not come out between the pillars where the cameras were pointed.

The fleeing soldier drew his horse up sharp beside the waiting automobile and with an agility that belied his 64 years he leaped to the ground and was in the car before the astonished news men could rush around the auto.

'Go on! go on! dammit, start this thing!' the colonel yelled to the negro chauffeur and, with eyes smarting with unshed tears, Colonel Tommy leaned out of the car as it leaped away, and to the cameramen he let loose a stream of profanity for which he had become famous.

'Fooled you that time,' he said, and followed it with a string of oaths. He was still 'cussing' as the car whisked down the hill and in a minute was lost to sight."

The following appeared in "The GarryOwen Trumpeter," and illustrates the love and respect with which Colonel Tompkins was held by all who knew him—both officer and enlisted. *The regimental newspaper published weekly between March 8, 1924 and August 3, 1927.*

Colonel Selah R.H. Tompkins who is even more proud of being a top notch cavalryman than he is of being a Colonel in the United States Cavalry, will return to his former sweetheart, GarryOwen, the Seventh Cavalry, for retirement with the colors.

'Tommy,' as he is called by his host of El Paso friends, has been transferred from his present station, Camp Stanley, Texas, to his old regiment; in view of his retirement, this transfer will be effective on or about July 10, 1927. By special permission of the War Department, Colonel Tompkins was permitted to command his old regiment from July 10, 1927, for one week before his retirement.

Almost every year since Colonel Tompkins left the Seventh Cavalry he has returned to spend the Christmas holidays with them. His heart is with his old regiment and every member will be more than glad to welcome this former Commanding Officer on his return to the GarryOwens.

First Sergeant Martin, of Troop C, Seventh Cavalry gives us the following sketch of some of his experiences while in the service with Colonel Tompkins in the past years while it was the pleasure of 'Give 'em Hell Tommy' to be the Commanding Officer of our famous regiment.

On July 1, 1912, I was transferred to Troop A. 7th Cavalry and for the first time came in contact with the 'Real Trooper of the Cavalry,' one of the the 'Old Army type' that has always been my idea of what a real Cavalryman should be—hard riding —hard fighting-cussing cavalryman—Colonel (then Major) Tommy Tompkins.

I was surprised at first at the manner in which the enlisted men idolized him; but when I came to know him better I ceased to wonder, for Colonel Tommy not only had a wonderful personality and a sense of humor, but he also had as big a heart as was ever put into an officer.

There has been much said about Tommy's swearing, but I have yet to see or hear tell of anyone taking offense at it, for swearing like Tommy's can be considered nothing less than an art the way he uses it, and he uses it in a natural inoffensive way. In fact, I heard him bawl out a man for swearing and in doing so he used at least three times as many swear words as the man himself had used, but he used them in such a manner that they were not as noticeable as the offender's.

Shortly after I joined the Seventh we went our for Squadron drill, Colonel (then Major) Tompkins in command. We took distance and did four hands to the right, four hands to the left, right about and left about, for about 15 minutes. Tommy finally raised up in his stirrups and said men, we have got the best d - - squadron in the regiment and by g - - I believe it is the best d - - squadron in the whole Army. Now pat your horses on the neck men, and show them that you

7th Cavalry Service Troop, July 1927, Fort Bliss, Texas. Courtesy of Ed Daily.

7th Cavalry Troop M passing in review, Fort Bliss, Texas. Courtesy of Ed Daily.

appreciate what they have done. Some trooper way back in the squadron came down bang, bang, on his horse's neck. Tommy threw his head up, closed one eye and growled at the trooper, 'G - D - - it, I didn't say to knock him down.'

Shortly after this we had a show down inspection. Equipment was laid out on the parade ground and Major Tommy standing opposite the center of the troop would check each article as it was called and held up by the men. Finally 'Tooth Brush' was called. Tommy let his eye run down the line but near the end was a man holding a mess knife. Tommy said: "Captain, who is that d - - fool down on the end that thinks I don't know the difference between a tooth brush and a knife? Try him and send the charges to me. No, never mind either, perhaps the d - - fool don't know the difference himself.'

Another time we were having an inspection. Tommy was riding along in front of the troops. Stepping in front of a man by the name of Dombroski, he asked him 'what he was looking so d - - mad about.' Dombroski said, 'Nothing, sir.' 'Well, d - - it, get that hard look off your face-what's your name anyway?' 'Pvt Dombroski, sir.' 'Private what?' 'Private Dombroski, sir.' 'Huh, I don't blame you a d - - bit for looking mad with a name like that' and he rode on down the line.

I wish I were capable and had the space to write all the good things I know of our Colonel but it would be a long and arduous task for even one gifted with writing ability, all I can say is that I wish I were Tommy.

To think of the shouting regiment welcoming him back and the gladness in every heart at his homecoming—what a thrill. I had the pleasure of imitating Colonel Tommy at our Christmas Parade in 1925 and no one can possibly realize how proud I felt just to have people shout 'hello there, Tommy', etc. If Tommy ever felt as proud leading his regiment as I did (as Tommy) leading that parade—well, his cup must be full.

During the period July 25th to 27th, the regiment again participated in maneuvers in conjunction with airplanes. It was during these maneuvers that Private Robert E. Griffin of Troop E was instantly killed when an airplane, flying low over the mounted column, severed his head with its landing gear. The plane, part of an attack group which was attacking the column of troops from the rear, hit an air pocket which caused the unavoidable accident.

News accounts gave the following description of the maneuvers at the time: "Cavalry-aviation war games at Ft. Bliss today took on national importance when the War Department announced that the maneuvers are a part of its program to speed up development of offensive and defensive military aviation.

Extensive anti-aircraft tests will be held at Aberdeen proving grounds in Maryland, during September and October.

Maneuvers today on the mesa back of Ft. Bliss were devoted to technical cavalry-aviation problems.

Approximately 2,000 persons saw the maneuvers today.

Planes were used by cavalry to locate and attack enemy cavalry. Cavalrymen were instructed in defensive measures.

Col. Selah R.H. Tompkins and Color Sergeant Patrick J. Devine, at Fort Bliss, Texas, July 17, 1927. Courtesy of Ed Daily.

Brig. Gen. E.B. Winans, Commanding 1st Cav. Div. and Col. Selah R.H. Tompkins reviewing the Division at col. Tompkins' retirement review, July 17, 1927, Fort Bliss, Texas. Courtesy of Ed Daily.

Col. Selah R.H. Tompkins on reviewing stand at his retirement July 17, 1927, Fort Bliss, Texas. Courtesy of Ed Daily.

Pvt. Ray Pousson, Regimental Bugler, 1927. Courtesy of Ed Daily.

7th Cavalry Regiment camp with 1st Cavalry Division maneuvers near Alimeto, Texas, 1927. Courtesy of Ed Daily.

The 1st Cavalry Division (less First Brigade), Fort Bliss, Texas, Dec. 14, 1929. Courtesy of Ed Daily.

participating in the First Cavalry Division maneuvers.

On December 2nd and 3rd, Platoon tests were conducted for Troops C and G who were competing for the Draper Trophy.

1928

The entire year was spent at Fort Bliss, Texas, performing the usual garrison duties. In January a major reorganization of the regiment took place, which reduced the regiment to a mere skeleton force.

On March 5th, a Division review was held for Major General Herbert B. Crosby, the Chief of Cavalry. On March 15th, the regiment marched 14.5 miles to Ysleta, Texas, and on March 16th, participated in a mock attack against Fort Bliss which was defended by the 8th Cavalry Regiment.

Other than the above, there were no events of significance during the year.

1929

The early part of the year was spent in. intensive recruit training and in garrison duty at Fort Bliss, Texas. Additionally, the regiment was called out to protect the border during the month of April. The following is a brief account of the activities which led up to this incident.

In early March of this year, the Escobar revolution flamed in Mexico. By March 9th, Juarez had fallen into rebel hands after five hours of fierce fighting between the rebel forces under General Agustin de la Vega and the Mexican federal troops. By mid-April American lives and property along the Mexican border adjacent to Texas, New Mexico, and Arizona were again threatened by Mexican revolutionary activities. While President Hoover had decided to support the established Mexican Government against the rebellious generals by maintaining the Coolidge Arms Embargo, which required a license for the shipment of munitions into Mexico, he did not intend to permit either side in the revolution to use American territory to launch attacks into northern Mexico, and thus involve the United States in the revolution. In order to protect the lives and property of Americans and to prevent either Mexican federal troops or the rebels from crossing the border into the United States, American troops from the entire 8th Corps Area were deployed along the border from El Paso, Texas,

The big fight will take place about one mile east of the fort. Spectators will not be allowed in the immediate vicinity of the maneuvers, as they might get in the way, officers explained.

Blank ammunition will be fired to make the fight appear realistic.

The war games will end today with a sham battle between the Seventh and Eighth Cavalry and between the 40 planes which are here from Kelly Field.

The games will start at 8:00 a.m. east of Fort Bliss. El Pasoans who wish to see the maneuvers may get their best view from a point immediately north of the wireless towers in Fort Bliss and west of the flying field in Fort Bliss.

They are warned to keep off the flying field because of the danger of a landing plane striking them.

The Seventh Cavalry will represent the 'Brown Army' and will attack Fort Bliss, which will be defended by the Eighth Cavalry, or 'White Army'.' 'White Army' cavalry and planes will be distinguishable by white hatbands and streamers.

The 'Brown Army' will have no distinguishing marks. The stunts today are expected to rival those of Monday along Newman road. Firing of blanks by artillery will add to the realistic features of the 'battle'.

During the period September 11th to October 13th, the regiment marched 183 miles while

Troop E, 7th Cavalry Regiment on 200 mile march from Fort Bliss to the Big Bend of the Rio Grande River, 1927, during 1st Cavalry Division maneuvers. Photos courtesy of Ed Daily.

At head of column is Major Louis A. O'Donnell, Executive Officer, Regimental Headquarters. Color Sergeants were Morrison and DeVine with Regimental Standards, near Van Horn, Texas, 1927, where they completed a 200 mile march.

to Douglas, Arizona, to observe all roads leading out of Mexico and to protect Americans living in the vicinity.

The 7th Cavalry Regiment began leaving Fort Bliss on April 9th, as part of the 8th Corps Area troops ordered to protect the border. The 1st Squadron left at 1:30 a.m. by rail for Hachita, New Mexico, 117 miles distant, and arrived at 7:00 a.m. on April 9th. The squadron left Hachita at 7:00 p.m. on April 11th for Culberson's Ranch, arriving about 1:30 p.m. on the following day, after a march of 52 miles. Major Terry de la Mesa Allen was in command of the squadron and preceded the column with one mounted rifle platoon. The horses were watered and fed, and a light meal served the troop, en route at Las Cienigo Ranch at about midnight on the night of April 11-12. The squadron left Culberson's Ranch at 9:15 a.m. on April 13th and marched 35 miles to Tuliva's Ranch arriving at 4:30 p.m. on the same date. The roads were very rough and full of rocks. The squadron left Tuliva's ranch at 7:45 a.m. and marched 33 miles to the San Bernardino Ranch, Arizona, arriving at 2:30 p.m. on the same date. The squadron, less Troop A which remained at the San Bernardino Ranch to relieve a detachment of the 25th Infantry, left the San Bernardino Ranch at 7:30 a.m. on April 15th and marched to Camp Harry J. Jones near Douglas, Arizona, where a permanent camp was established and patrols of three men each were sent out daily along the border.

The remainder of the regiment remained at Fort Bliss, Texas, and prepared for target practice until April 11th. On that date the regiment, less the 1st Squadron and the band, left Fort Bliss and marched 177 miles to Hachita, New Mexico, arriving at 11:30 a.m. on April 17th. On April 20th, the command, less Troop F, left Hachita at about 6:30 a.m. and marched 98 miles to Douglas, Arizona, arriving at about 11:00 a.m. on April 23rd, where it was joined by the 1st Squadron. Troop F was ordered to remain at Hachita, New Mexico.

The command rested at Douglas, Arizona, until April 25th, when it departed for Naco, Arizona, about 7:00 a.m. arriving there at about 1:30 p.m. the same date and went into permanent camp. Troop E was ordered to remain at Douglas, Arizona, and send a platoon to Slaughter's Ranch. Officer patrols were sent out each day from Naco, Arizona, and Cossack posts were

(Center seated) Lt Col. Howard R. Smalley, Commander 7th Cavalry Regiment and Staff Officers. At left of photo is Regimental mascot "Swill Can." Courtesy of Ed Daily.

established at night. The remainder of the command guarded the pump station at Naco, Arizona. The strength of the regiment at this time consisted of 32 officers and 582 enlisted men.

The entire regiment marched back to Fort Bliss, Texas, without further incident, arriving there on May 14th.

On October 11th, the entire regiment, less the band, departed for the maneuver area (vicinity of Fort Bliss) where it maneuvered as a part of the 2nd Cavalry Brigade against the 1st Cavalry Brigade until October 17th, when it returned to Fort Bliss.

The following is typical of the situation given for the maneuvers held during this period.

"The International Boundary is the boundary between two states, Brown (north) and White (south), which have recently declared war. Brown main forces are concentrating in the vicinity of Alamogordo, New Mexico (on the El Paso and Southwestern Railroad, about 80 miles northeast of El Paso), and Fort Selden, New Mexico (on the Santa Fe Railroad about 60 miles

northwest of El, Paso); and Whites in the vicinity of Ahumada, Mexico (on the Mexican Central Railroad, about 65 miles south of El Paso).

The White State, being further advanced in its preparation for war than the Brown State, is rapidly concentrating its forces in the following localities:

Organization:	Concentration Point:
10th Infantry Division	Vicinity of Monterrey, Nuevo Leon
1st Army consisting of two infantry corps	Vicinity of Ahumada, Mexico
1st Cavalry Division	Vicinity of Ahumada, Mexico

The White plan of campaign is to invade Brown territory via the Rio Grande Valley with the object of cutting transcontinental railroads, and isolating the southwestern part of the Brown State, before the latter can bring up sufficient troops to prevent it.

The 1st Cavalry Division has been ordered

7th Cavalry troopers in practice session in the snow. Courtesy of Ed Daily.

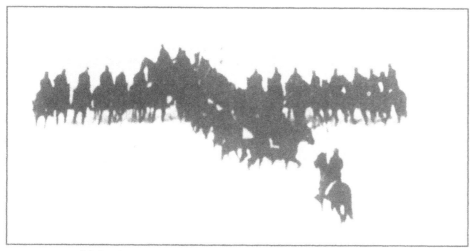

7th Cavalry troopers in practice session in the snow. Courtesy of Ed Daily.

7th Cavalry Officer showing his riding ability. Courtesy of Ed Daily.

to cover the White concentration south of Juarez, and to further the White plan of campaign, pending the readiness of White main forces, by capturing El Paso, Texas, by seizing supplies in that vicinity; and by delaying Brown concentration.

The 2nd Cavalry Brigade, reinforced by Battery C, 82nd Field Artillery Battalion (horse); one platoon, Troop A 1st Armored Car Squadron; 49th Motor Transport Company; and a detachment the 1st Medical Squadron, was ordered by the division commander to cross the Rio Grande the night of October 5th-6th, 1929; seize El Paso, Texas, including Fort Bliss, and await orders.

The 2nd Cavalry Brigade, reinforced, seized El Paso, Texas, October 6th, 1929, and on that date was in camp at Fort Bliss, awaiting orders (prepared to move on three hour notice).

Foraging parties are operating along the Southern Pacific Railroad, to the east and west of El Paso, under the instructions of the Commanding General, 1st Cavalry Division."

1930

The entire year was spent at Fort Bliss, Texas, performing the usual garrison duties. The regiment conducted its annual target firing at the Dona Ana Target Range, New Mexico, during the period June 5th to 27th. During the period October 25th to 31st, the regiment took part in Brigade maneuvers conducted in the vicinity of Fort Bliss.

1931

This year was also spent at Fort Bliss, Texas, performing the usual garrison duties. The entire regiment, less the Band, participated in the First Cavalry Division maneuvers in the vicinity of Fort Bliss during the period May 21st to 31st.

The regiment, less the Band, marched 45 miles to the Dona Ana Target Range, New Mexico, and return, to conduct annual target practice during the period August 3rd to 28th.

1932

Like the preceding two years, the regiment spent the entire year at Fort Bliss, Texas, performing the usual garrison duties. The only activities conducted during the year were participation in the First Cavalry Division maneuvers in the vicinity of Fort Bliss during the period May 9th to 20th, and the annual firing practice at the Dona Ana Target Range during the period August 3rd to 27th.

During this year, Troop E was awarded the Goodrich Trophy. This trophy was awarded annually to the cavalry troop displaying the highest standards of proficiency in every phase of cavalry drill and training. Competition was held Army-wide.

Troop E was notified in March that they were winners of the Goodrich Trophy, the most coveted and desired by all of the troops in the Cavalry Service, and the handsome trophy remained in the troop Orderly Room on display for one year. Troop E, commanded by Captain Donald A. Young, proved that it was the outstanding cavalry organization for the year 1931.

Troops and officers of the 7th Cavalry have been historically described since the organization of the regiment, and the records and activities of both individuals and troops have been followed with great interest throughout the Army.

A troop competing for the Goodrich Trophy was restricted to many technicalities and small details that were not required by non-participating organizations. It had to become a machine of high order, and the training that was necessary to pass the severe tests reveals the type of officer that commanded it. Troop E was commanded by that type of an outstanding officer whose efficiency was recognized throughout the Army—Captain Donald A. Young.

Captain Young was assigned to the Seventh Cavalry, August 15th, 1930, and was placed in command of Troop E. His troop soon became one of the best troops in the First Cavalry Division. The morale of that organization was exceedingly high. The troop won the basketball championship, Regimental League 1930-31, the baseball championship, Regimental League 1931, and the post prize for the most attractive troop area for 1930, 1931, and 1932, and the most coveted Goodrich Trophy. In the May 1931 maneuvers, Captain Young guided the regiment with attached Artillery and Trains in a night crossing of the heavily guarded Rio Grande undiscovered to a position in the enemy rear, prematurely ending the maneuver. On December 1, 1932, he was appointed Regimental Adjutant, Seventh Cavalry. In addition to that duty he has been detailed as Acting S-2 and S-3 officer during the majority of the Regimental problems and maneuvers.

The following copies of letters and commendations were received by Captain Young:

WAR DEPARTMENT
OFFICE OF
THE CHIEF OF CAVALRY
Washington, D.C., March 23, 1932
353.5/GT 1931

Subject: Goodrich Trophy Training Test.
To: Captain Donald A. Young, Commanding Troop E, 7th Cavalry, For Bliss, Texas.

Through: The Adjutant General.

To you and the members of your troop, I offer my sincere congratulations upon your winning the Goodrich Trophy Training Test for 1931. Your success may well be a matter of just pride to you and the officers and men of your troop. and one of genuine pleasure to the entire personnel of the 7th Cavalry.

(signed) GUY V. HENRY,* Chief of Cavalry
from March 22, 1930 to March 21, 1934.
Major General, U.S.A.,
Chief of Cavalry.

(Goodrich Trophy) 4th Ind. OWB/las.

HEADQUARTERS SEVENTH CAVALRY
Fort Bliss, Texas
April 6, 1932

To: Captain Donald A. Young,
7th Cavalry.

This regiment is justly proud of the honor and presitige that you and your troop has brought to it in winning the above prized trophy.

(signed) O.W. BELL,
Colonel, 7th Cavalry,
Commanding.

HEADQUARTERS FORT BLISS,
TEXAS OFFICE
OF THE POST COMMANDER

April 4, 1932

201—Young, Donald A. Off.
Subject: Commendation

TO : Captain Donald A. Young, Troop E, 7th Cavalry,
(Thru Commanding Officer, 7th Cavalry).

1. The Adjutant General under date of March twenty eighth announced Troop E, 7th Cavalry as the winner of the Nineteen Thirty One Goodrich Test.

2. It affords me much pleasure and gratification to commend you, your officers and men on this laudable victory.

3. It is such demonstrations of efficiency that enhances the reputation of the 1st Cavalry Division and adds to our pride of organization.

(signed) W.C. SHORT,
Brigadier General, U.S. Army,
Commanding.

201—Young, Donald A. (Off) 1st Ind
OWB/las

HEADQUARTERS SEVENTH CAVALRY
Fort Bliss, Texas
April 6, 1932

To: Captain Donald A.. Young, 7th Cavalry.

It is with the greatest pride and satisfaction that I transmit to you and your troop the above communication on winning the prized Goodrich Trophy. The regiment is proud of your organization and deeply appreciative of its efforts.

(signed) O.W. BELL,
Colonel, Seventh Cavalry,
Commanding.

WAR DEPARTMENT
OFFICE OF THE CHIEF OF STAFF
Washington, D.C.
May 31, 1932
Captain Donald A. Young,
Seventh Cavalry,
Fort Bliss, Texas.
My dear Captain Young:
If my name is still remembered in my old command, the First Cavalry Division, you will understand my great interest in the recent achievement of Troop E 7th Cavalry, under your command, in winning the Goodrich Trophy.

I write this letter to extend my congratulations to you and to each member of your outstanding troop. I know how difficult is the test, what amount of work goes into preparation, and how difficult it is to win the Trophy. I know, too,

how much pleasure your winning brought to my dear friend, General Short, your Division Commander.

While the Cavalry may not be much in evidence now-a-days, due to the expense of maintaining it, the Cavalry spirit is more necessary today then ever before. It is the spirit that wins the battle. It would be well if we saw more of it through civil life of the nation today.
Faithfully yours,
(signed) Geo. VAN HORN MOSELEY,
Major General, U.S. Army.

1933

This year was spent at Fort Bliss, Texas, performing the usual camp and garrison duties. On May 12th, the entire regiment, less the Band, marched 65 miles in 19 hours to the Dona Ana Target Range and return, in connection with the annual Corps Area Commanders tactical inspection.

On August 3rd, the 1st Squadron traveled 308 miles from Fort Bliss to Terlingua, Texas, to conduct the first tests of experimental horse-carrying trailers. The squadron arrized at Terlingua, Texas, on August 5th, camped there from August 6th to loth, made a mounted reconnaissance of 32 miles and returned to Fort Bliss in the same trailers, arriving there on August 12th. These trailers were to become the standard method of transporting horses for the remainder of the time that mounted units were included in the Army.

1934

This year was spent at Fort Bliss, Texas, performing the usual camp and garrison duties. The regiment, less the Band, participated in the Corps Area Commanders tactical inspection by maneuver to Newman, New Mexico, during the period May 2nd to 4th, and conducted annual target practice at the Dona Ana Range during the period August 1st to 29th.

1935

This year was spent at Fort Bliss, Texas, performing the usual camp and garrison duties; however, additional funds were provided which permitted more extensive participation in maneuvers during the year than had been the case in the previous five years.

The entire regiment, less the Band, made a 13 day practice march of 134 miles during the period April 22nd to May 3rd, marching by way of Newman, New Mexico-Orogrande, New Mexico-Valmont-Godleys Ranch—Rice Canyon—The Old CCC Camp on the Sacramento River—Sheltons Ranch, New Mexico—and Alamo Springs.

During the period July 1st to 27th, the entire regiment, less the Band, conducted its regular annual target practice and proficiencey tests at the Dona Ana Target Range, New Mexico (This range was redesignated the Fort Bliss Target Range during this year).

During the period August 13th to 16th, and August 29th to August 30th, the entire regiment was commanded by Reserve Officers in connection with their annual active duty training. During the later period of training, a provisional war strength troop was formed to provide the Reserve Officers more realistic training.

1936

The year was spent at Fort Bliss, Texas, performing the usual camp and garrison duties except for the period in which the regiment participated in the First Cavalry Division maneuvers.

On April 16th, the regiment, less the Band, departed Fort Bliss, Texas, for Marfa, Texas, to participate in the First Cavalry Division maneuvers —the most extensive maneuver participated in by the regiment up to this time. The command marched to Fabens, Texas—Fort Hancock, Texas—Wallridge Ranch—Sierra Blanca, Texas—Hot Wells, Texas—Lobo-Valentine—Ryan—Marfa, arriving there on April 24th. On April 26th, the command maneuvered from Marfa to Bishops Ranch; on April 28th from Childers Ranch, arriving at Clevelands Ranch Tank No. 27 on April 30th..The command then maneuvered from Clevelands Ranch to Fishers Ranch, Tank No. 26, having traveled 308 miles since leaving Fort Bliss.

On May 1st the command returned to Marfa, Texas, and left there on May 4th, arriving at Alexanders Well on May 5th, maneuvered to Loves Pump Station, and returned to Marfa, Texas, on May 6th. The regiment left Marfa, Texas, on May 11th for the return march to Fort Bliss, having marched an additonal 284 miles during the maneuver.

Extensive training exercises and target practice, to include anti-aircraft firing, were conducted throughout the maneuver. A report of the maneuver indicated that only $9,946 was initially alloted for the entire division maneuver. Later an additional $9,408 was provided; however, the paucity of funds precluded the Division staff from negotiating with landowners for maneuver and water rights. This resulted in the refusal of many ranchers to permit their land to be used for maneuver purposes. Observers during the maneuvers included Major General Leon B. Kromer*; Chief of Cavalry; Brigadier Vladimar A. Burzin, Soviet Army; and Major Koshiake Nishi, Imperial Japanese Army. *Chief of Cavalry, from March 26, 1934 to march 25, 1938.

While the maneuver lasted from April 1st to 25th, an excessive amount of time was spent by all troops in traveling to and from the maneuver area.

The remainder of the year was spent in extensive recruit drill and in training Reserve Officers who performed all functions of the regiment during their periods of active duty training.

1937

The entire year was spent at Fort Bliss, Texas, performing the usual camp and garrison duties.

During the period April 21st and 22nd, the entire regiment marched 67 miles to the Fort Bliss Target Range and return in connection with the annual Corps Area tactical inspection.

During the period June 10th to 28th, the entire regiment, less the Band, made a 340-mile practice march by way of Hueco, New Mexico-Ororande—Horse Mesa Camp—junction of Scott Able-Sacamenro Canyon—Cloudcroft—Silver Canyon-Tularosa Canyon-Cedar Creek—Turkey Well and return to Fort Bliss. The command traveled 60 miles on the last day of the march.

7th Cavalry Regimental Officers, Fort Bliss, Texas, 1935. Courtesy of Ed Daily.

7th Cavalry Regimental Officers, Fort Bliss, Texas, 1937. Courtesy of Ed Daily.

1938

This year was spent at Fort Bliss, Texas, performing the usual camp and garrison duties except for participating in the First Cavalry Division maneuver.

During the period March 14th to 31st, the entire regiment participated in tests being conducted for a proposed Cavalry Division.

On April 12th, the entire regiment, less the Band, departed Fort Bliss as a part of the 2nd Provisional Cavalry Regiment enroute to Toyahvale, Texas, to participate in the First Cavalry Division Maneuvers. The command marched 210 miles by way of Fabens, Texas—Fort Hancock-Finley-Sierra Blanca—Eagle Flat—Van Horn-Boracho. (On April 18th the entire command formed in a line of foragers at Wild Horse Creek to search for baggage in connection with the Frame murder case)-Levinson—Toyahvale, arriving on April 20th. The regiment experienced extremely cold weather and severe dust storms en route.

The regiment then participated in the Provisional Cavalry Division tests during the period April 23rd to May 11th, and traveled over 135 miles in connection with the tests. The command returned to Fort Bliss on May 17th, having marched a total of 540 miles during this maneuver.

During the period August 18th to 25th, the regiment, less the Band, participated in the Third Army maneuvers in the vicinity of the Fort Bliss Target Range-Las Cruces, New Mexico, and marched 181 miles in connection with this maneuver.

1939

This year was spent at Fort Bliss, Texas, performing the usual camp and garrison duties except for brief periods of maneuvers.

During the period March 16th to 18th, the regiment maneuvered to the Fort Bliss Target Range and returned, having traveled 86 miles.

During the period May 16th to 27th, the regiment, less the Band, marched 181 miles to the vicinity of Orogrande-Newman, New Mexico, and returned.

On October 2nd the regiment, less the Band, departed Fort Bliss as a part of the 2nd Cavalry Brigade to participate in the First Cavalry Division maneuvers in the vicinity of Balmorhea—Toyahvale, Texas. The command marched 200 miles by way of Fabens, Texas—Fort Hancock—Finley-Waldridge Ranch—Sierra Blanca—Eagle Flat-Van Horn—Boracho—Levison—to the 1st Cavalry Division Camp at Toyahvale. During the period October 16th to 27th, the command maneuvered in the vicinity of the Kingston Ranch and marched 191 miles during the maneuver.

On October 28th, the regiment left the camp area for its return march to Fort Bliss, arriving on November 4th—a total of 588 miles marched during the exercise.

Captain Gil C. Mudgett leads Troop E on practice march on the road from Balmorhea, Texas, 1939. Courtesy of Ed Daily.

Troop E, 7th Cavalry Regiment, charges for the benefit of Warner Brothers motion picture scenes near Fort Bliss, Texas, 1939. Courtesy of Ed Daily.

7th Cavalry Regiment's horses watering at captured earth tank, 1st Cavalry Division maneuvers, Fort Bliss, Texas, 1941. U.S. Army photo.

1940

The regiment spent the year at Fort Bliss, Texas. Training was intensified as a result of the gathering war clouds in both the Far East and Europe.

The entire regiment participated in the first of a series of maneuvers in Louisiana during the period April 26th to May 28th. This maneuver provided the troops with valuable experience in road marches and field service, but little training in cavalry tactics. Officers of the regiment learned many lessons in movement planning and the fundamentals of maneuvering large forces in the field which were to serve them well in the years ahead.

The entire regiment left Fort Bliss on August 8th by rail and arrived in Cravens, Louisiana, on August 13th for the second Louisiana maneuver. This maneuver was held in connection with National Guard Troops. The regiment returned to Fort Bliss on August 22nd.

After the Third Army maneuvers in Louisiana, the regiment assisted the First Cavalry Division in the construction of cantonments for 20,000 anti-aircraft troops at Fort Bliss and in developing the El Paso Army Air Base.

Troops C and G were reactivated in 1940.

1941

The regiment continued its intensive training at Fort Bliss as a part of the expansion of the Army, and consisted of almost 70% replacements by mid-year.

During the period August 5th to October 8th the regiment took part in the Second-Third Army maneuvers held in Louisiana—the greatest peacetime maneuvers in the history of the Army. It was during this time that the regiment, as part of the First Cavalry Division (Third Army Blue Forces), screened the advance of an armored force to an unfordable river and then established a bridgehead for the crossing of an armored division.

After a strong advance of the Blue Third Army, the Red Second Army counterattacked. To meet this counterattack the Blue Third Army used all available forces—tanks, tank destroyers, dive bombers—but what really stopped the Red Armored Force was, ironically, a Blue horse cavalry operation. The feat of fording the swollen Sabine River enabled the Blue Army to catch the Reds by surprise, capture the gasoline supply of the armored division and put them out of action. In the swampy country, with many streams and bayous, horses went where tanks

could not go; and the cavalrymen opened the way for the light motor divisions and infantry in places where heavy equipment stalled.

During the 1941 maneuvers the 7th Cavalry marched over 900 miles; tired troops and horses were obliged to march to new areas and get ready for the next phase of the maneuvers while everyone else was resting. Men would saddle their horses in driving rain, with water up to the horses' bellies, their entire equipment soaking wet; and ride forth at one, two, or three o'clock in the morning, whistling and singing. In spite of the tough going, with horses and men at times on short rations and with little sleep, the traditional quality of the cavalry soldier could be found everywhere-the urge to go on and on, no matter what the hardships were, happily and cheerfully. The many feats performed by the horse cavalry during these maneuvers would have delighted a Jeb Stuart or a Phil Sheridan; they would have warmed the heart of many a red-necked cavalryman who has been told over and over again that the armored force has made the horse obsolete.

The regiment returned to Fort Bliss from the Third Army maneuvers on October 8th as finely trained and conditioned as any unit in the Army at that time, and with the highest confidence in its own military efficiency that any unit ever enjoyed.

The news of Pearl Harbor found many members of the regiment on furlough and others back in civilian life after a year's training, but the majority of these absentees hurried to Fort Bliss from all over the United States to be with their favorite outfit when it went overseas— the GarryOwens.

Although the regiment, like the rest of the First Cavalry Division after Pearl Harbor, was champing at the bit for immediate combat, its first wartime mission was to continue its border surveillance as a component of the Southern Land Frontier of the Southern Defense Command. Shortly after the outbreak of war, plans were submitted for the conversion of the entire First Cavalry Division from horses to bantam trucks, with emphasis on the desirability of early employment in active combat.

CHAPTER IV
World War II
Islands, Jungles and
Japanese (1942-1945)
(Loss of Horses)

1942

The year dawned with the regiment stationed at Fort Bliss, Texas — apparently fated to continue in the role of border patrol which it had performed during World War I. Maintenance of the fine edge of training was assured by participation in the continuous border patrols and extensive maneuvers around Fort Bliss. Despite the extreme desire for overseas service, morale still remained high.

Headquarters 1st Squadron, and Troops A, B, and C were sent to the Cavalry School, Fort Riley, Kansas, to assist in instruction on October 4th and remained until January 23rd the following year.

1943

Routine training and border duties were being performed at Fort Bliss, Texas when orders were received in February 1943 which alerted the entire First Cavalry Division for an overseas assignment as a dismounted unit. As the dismounting procedure began, horses were transferred to the post quartermaster for public sale or other disposition, slacks were substituted for riding breeches, shoes and leggings for boots and spurs and packs for saddlebags. A training program was initiated to instruct the former cavalrymen in the ways of the foot soldier including-for the first time in the regiment's history-long foot marches without leading a horse. Transition to a dismounted status was completed well in advance of the scheduled movement date.

On June 16th the regiment departed Fort Bliss, Texas, for movement to Camp Stoneman, California, and departed the United States on July 3rd aboard the SS Monterey and the SS George Washington for Australia.

The regiment arrived at Brisbane, Queensland, Australia, at 1330 hours, July 10th, debarked and moved into bivouac near Strathpine, Queensland, Australia, the following day. A period of camp construction, physical conditioning, and intensive amphibious and jungle training as an infantry unit was carried out for the remainder of the year.

On December 15th, the regiment departed from Brisbane for movement to Cape Sudest, New Guinea. After another period of staging in New Guinea from December 25th to March 3rd, 1944, the 2nd Squadron, reinforced, departed from Cape Sudest, New Guinea, as the initial combat force of the regiment in the Admiralty campaign. Thus, after many months of anxious waiting and intensive training, the GarryOwens entered combat against the Japanese which terminated with the 2nd Squadron's triumphant entry into Tokyo many miles, many months and many casualties later.

1944

After the Allied forces had fought their way back along the New Guinea coast to Finschhafen and Saido in 1943 and early 1944, General MacArthur's island-hopping campaign was continued with the landing of the 112th Cavalry at Arawe and the 1st Marine Division at Cape Glouchester on New Britain Island. The next step was to bypass the Japanese at Rabaul and Kavieng by seizing the Admiralities. These Islands with their important airdromes would provide a springboard for future operations and serve as a base from which Japanese shipping could be prevented from reinforcing the garrisons at Rabaul and other Japanese troops stranded in the Bismark Archipelago.

Major islands of the Admiralty Islands group are Los Negros and Manus, separated by a shallow, creeklike strait extending south from Seeadler Harbor to the Bismark Sea. The islands were seized from Germany in 1914 by Australian forces and were in turn occupied by the Japanese in April 1942.

Los Negros, focal point of the Allied attack in early 1944, is a horseshoe-shaped island. The southeastern section, where Momote airdrome is situated, is generally flat, well-drained, and fertile. Elsewhere, except in the Seeadler plantation areas on the north prong of the horseshoe, the island is rugged with razorback hills covered by dense rain forests and jungle growth. Los Negros Island, prior to the operation, was devoid of roads capable of withstanding heavy motor traffic. Hills, wide streams, and lagoons were major obstacles to construction of the traffic system.

Manus is an elliptical-shaped island approximately 50 miles long and 20 miles wide with an axial mountain running its entire length. The central and western sections are heavily forested, mostly unexplored, and sparsely inhabited. The greater part of the island is covered by rain forest, with a thick mangrove growth on the foreshore, and has a veritable network of streams navigable by canoe for several miles inland. These streams are the principal routes of transportation for the natives. Such trails as exist pass through areas that are either extremely rugged or swampy. Hence, they are easily defended.

On the northeast tip of Manus sits the settlement of Lorengau looking out at Seeadler Harbor. Before the arrival of the Japanese, it was the Australian administrative seat and the only European community in the Admiralty Islands.

In planning for the seizure of the Admiralties, D-Day was originally set for April 1st, 1944. On February 23rd, however, low flying air reconnaissance of Los Negros and Manus Islands failed to provoke any enemy reaction and the pilots saw no signs of occupation. The next day, General Headquarters, Southwest Pacific Area, instructed General Walter Kreuger, Commanding General of the Alamo Force, "to prepare plans for an immediate reconnaissance in force of Los Negros Island in the vicinity of Momote airstrip, with the object of remaining in occupancy in case the area was found to be inadequately defended by the enemy; or, in case of heavy resistance, to withdraw after all possible reconnaissance had been accomplished." The force was limited to 1,025 men under the command of a brigadier general. It was recommended that the reconnaissance force be composed of one squadron of cavalry, one airborne anti-aircraft battery, one light field artillery battery, a pioneer detachment, and miscellaneous troops. The target date was designated as the earliest practicable date, but not later than February 29th. It was further directed that in event the operation succeeded, the reconnaissance force would prepare the Momote airstrip for transport planes, and that the air force units would follow at the earliest moment bringing airborne engineers to prepare the airdrome for fighter operations. (*The 1st Cavalry Division in World War II, Bertram C. Wright, 1947.*)

Thus, after many months of training and reorganization to better adapt itself to dismounted combat, elements of the First Cavalry Division received orders on February 27th to proceed to the Admiralty Islands. This marked the opening phase of hostilities for the Division and provided its baptism of fire.

The 7th Cavalry Regiment's participation in the Admiralty Operations, as a part of the Brewer Task Force, was instituted by orders received by Colonel Glen S. Finley, the regimental commander, on the evening of March 2nd. These orders directed that a full strength squadron, reinforced, prepare to embark at Cape Sudest, New Guinea, at 0430 hours on March 3rd, and proceed to Hyane Harbor of Los Negros Island to reinforce the initial Task Force, (*2nd Squadron, 5th Cavalry, reinforced, under command of Brigadier General William C. Chase*) then engaged in operations against Japanese garrison forces. The 2nd Squadron, 7th Cavalry, Lt. Colonel Robert P. Kirk, commanding, was selected and Weapons Troop, Captain Templeton, commanding, was attached, as were sufficient officers and men including the Regimental Reconnaissance Platoon, to bring the squadron to full strength. The initial combat force thus represented the regiment as a whole.

After a few hours delay, because lack of time had prevented prior planning, the reinforced squadron embarked in Landing Craft Vehicles (L.C.V.s) and Landing Craft, Mechanized (L.C.M.s), and shuttled to destroyers designated to transport troops. One unit of fire and individual equipment only was taken. All automatic weapons, mortars, and ammunition were lashed to the steel decks. At 0800 hours on March 4th, after an uneventful trip marked by the superior cooperation of naval personnel, troops were unloaded into L.C.V.s and under cover of naval and artillery gun fire made an unopposed landing on the northeast corner of the Momote Airdrome.

While Colonel Kirk reported to the Task Force Commander for instructions, the squadron was guided to an assembly position in rear of the 2nd Squadron, 5th Cavalry, whose perimeter defense it was ordered to occupy. This sector extended from the center of the airdrome's western taxiway to include the dispersal areas along its northern edge. Occasional sniper fire was received causing minor interruption during the occupation of the position. Patrolling was promptly instituted to the north and west. Troops in this sector had repulsed a suicidal counterattack the night before and the entire position was strewn with dead Japanese. Patrols returning at dusk carried two Japanese heavy machineguns and quantities of ammunition which were placed in the lines and used to good advantage that night. Sporadic sniper fire continued until dark, while during the night several light counterattacks were repulsed with an estimated enemy loss of 50 killed. Our losses were one killed and two wounded. The morning of the 5th found our men in high spirits from their initial successes in combat.

At 1200 hours the squadron received warning orders to be prepared to move north on the Mokerag Peninsula, via the Skidway, thence west to Red Beach in the Salami Plantation area, and secure a beachhead to protect the landing of the 2nd Battalion Combat Team (BCT). At 1500 the squadron moved out and immediately encountered light skirmishing fire. Once again with the aid of effective artillery and mortar support, the enemy was repulsed leaving 25 dead behind. Our casualties were 12 wounded. The squadron then continued its advance through the intolerable stench of dead Japanese who littered the entire Skidway area. Due to the lateness of the hour and because of its defensive advantages, the squadron dug in for the night on the Skidway after an advance of some 500 yards. There was considerable firing during the night from trigger happy soldiers and from minor infiltration by the Japanese. Hostile losses during the night were impossible to estimate as the entire area was littered with dead Japanese from previous action. Our losses for the night were two killed. Bulldozers and burial parties from the Task Force went to work vigorously on the morning of the 6th and bulldozer drivers were observed wearing gas masks as the stench by this time was suffocating.

At 1030 hours the squadron moved out on its assigned mission with Troop E as advance guard. The 12th Cavalry Regiment which had landed during the morning prepared to follow. The march north was through ankle-deep mud and the road, or rather trail, became heavily congested with troops and mired vehicles. Progress was delayed due to the necessity of removing many trees felled by the enemy to impede any advance. At noon Troop E was on the Salami Road two and one-half miles northwest of Momote when orders were received attaching the squadron to the 12th Cavalry and directing it to cover the northwest flank while the 12th bypassed to the west, and on the completion of this mission to revert to 12th Cavalry reserve. At 1600 hours, after an unopposed move to Salami the 12th Cavalry went into position and secured its assigned beachhead. The 2nd Squadron, 7th Cavalry Regiment, was assigned the defense of the perimeter to the north. All along the route to Red Beach the column passed Japanese arms and equipment abandoned by the enemy in his hasty retreat. Wheeled vehicles were not able to reach the beachhead perimeter although a few tanks managed to get through. Within the Red Beach area large amounts of enemy supplies were captured including five trucks and abandoned buildings containing radios, drafting equipment, charts, food and propaganda pamphlets.

There was no activity during the night of March 6th-7th. At 0800 hours on March 7th, the squadron moved several hundred yards to the north but returned to its original perimeter at 1430. Only one Japanese was slain during this action. Private First Class Floyd H. Lewis, Headquarters 2nd Squadron, later killed two Japanese in hand-to-hand combat while reconnoitering a

bunker. This was the first known instance in the regiment of physical contact with the enemy in World War II.

There was no ground activity during the night of March 7th-8th, but "Washing Machine Charlie" -the name given the enemy single engine plane which made nightly raids-dropped one bomb in the Momote area. At 1040 hours, two British Indians, waving white flags, surrendered to Troop G. Both spoke English and stated they had been captured by the Japanese in Singapore and brought to the Admiralities as labor troops. They further stated that 65 more were waiting to come in. One Indian was therefore dispatched to guide the remainder into the area-all were overjoyed at their liberation. At 1200 our vehicles began to arrive having finally conquered the muddy trail from Momote. Japanese vehicles had been inoperative during rainy weather also, and no attempt had been made to improve existing roads or trails.

At 1205 hours, orders were received to move by LCMs tinder cover of artillery and rocket fire to Lombrum Plantation and to secure a beachhead in the vicinity of Lombrum Point. "H Hour" was designated as 1420 hours. The landing was successful in the face of sporadic enemy fire which included some 20mm (millimeter) fire, and by 1430, Troops E, F, and G had established a perimeter some 100 yards in depth. Patrolling was promptly initiated but no hostile positions or personnel were encountered after the initial landing. By 1500 hours, Troop H and the Weapons Troop were disposed for action, and by 1700 the beachhead was extended to take advantage of adjacent terrain and all defensive installations were completed. Here, too, the Japanese had abandoned gas, oil and bomb dumps as well as one serviceable light machinegun, caliber 25.6, with abundant ammunition. A serviceable well was discovered within the perimeter which solved the water problem. During the night three Japanese were killed attempting to infiltrate through the lines.

The following day, March 8th, was spent mainly in rest and rehabilitation. The Reconnaissance Platoon under the Squadron S-2 patrolled the beach to Loniu Passage and reported that they had rendered two serviceable 20mm guns inoperative which were located on the beach 900 yards south of our position. Bolts and sights were removed and brought back, since ammunition was plentiful at the gun positions. A few Japanese were sighted on the patrol, one of whom fled the vicinity of the gun positions.

There was no activity the night of March 9th-10th. The Reconnaissance Platoon patrolled by LCM the following morning along the shoreline half way to Papitalai Mission. Two Japanese were killed on the beach 1,000 yards east of the squadron's position and the patrol discoverd evidence of other Japanese in that vicinity. There was no further activity that day or during the night of March 10th-11th.

On the morning of March 11th, orders were received relieving the squadron from attachment to the 12th Cavalry and it reverted to brigade control. Later that morning Lt. Colonel Kirk received verbal orders to prepare for simultaneous landings on Hauwei, Botjo, and Luo Islands on a one-hour alert notice. At 1700 hours, Troop F, with attached artillery personnel, departed by

LCM. The troop, less one reinforced platoon, landed on and secured Butjo and the platoon seized Luo. No opposition was encountered on either landing-both of which were made to secure artillery positions for further operations. Plans to land the remainder of the squadron on Hauwei were postponed until the following day.

At noon on March 12th, the 2nd Squadron, less Troop F, departed on LCMs for Hauwei with "H Hour" set at 1400 hours. A short delay due to a change in the plan for supporting fires resulted in the first wave arriving on the beach on the west end of the island at 1415. The landing was supported by naval rocket barrages and air bombardment, however, the covering fire was not accurate and most missiles fell short in the sea.

Troop E — landing on West Beach — received small arms fire and Troop G — landing on South Beach — received machine gun fire from bunker positions. A few mines activated by trip wires were successfully bypassed without casualties. The squadron then drove inland under heavy sniper fire and by 1500 hours a north-south line through the island some 300 yards inland was secured. Here the troops were temporarily pinned down by mortar, grenades and machinegun fire. By this time the entire squadron had landed and the 81mm mortars of Troop H were in position. The squadron command post was established 100 yards from the shore and telephone wire lines laid to all troops. Our casualties up to this time were three killed and ten wounded. During the next half hour Troop E continued its advance, but Troop G was pinned to the ground. The squadron commander then decided to withdraw Troop E and dig in for the night as contact between troops was being lost and ihe island was too wide for complete coverage by only two troops.

At 1600 hours, Brigadier General Verne D. Mudge, the 2nd Brigade Commander, arrived and on being advised of the situation ordered Troop C, on alert at Salami, to move at once by LCM to Hauwei. One medium tank was also altered to proceed to the island the following morning. Trop C arrived at 1800 and was placed in a support position within the perimeter.

During the night of March 13-14th, Japanese on Pityilu Island fired into the positions with 20mm weapons but caused no casualties, and the enemy's island garrison force remained quiet.

At 0730 hours on March 14th, a burst of enemy fire wounded three; at 0900 the tank arrived and the Reconnaissance Platoon designated as its close support, and Troop H displaced its weapons for better fire support.

At 1000 hours the attack was launched with three troops abreast, C-E-G from north to south, with the tank operating on the south flank. An enemy bunker, on the south shore, containing two heavy machineguns (HMGs) (type 92 JUKI 7.7mm), knee mortars, rifles and eight Japanese, was destroyed by tank fire and the troop envelopment from the north. Before being silenced this bunker withstood four direct mortar bursts and four direct hits from the tank's 75mm gun. In the center of the island a Japanese trench was enveloped and its occupants annihilated. This short trench contained HMGs (7.7mm), knee mortars, and rifles — some equipped with grenade adapters. By 1030 hours, the squadron's lines were advancing rapidly and by noon the island was completely secure. There were 43 enemy killed, while the squadron's casualties were 8 killed and 46 wounded.

In the defense of this island the Japanese had laid out fire lanes for all automatic weapons, and his sniper fire was most accurate and very harassing. The squadron's two killed and eight wounded by sniper fire all were shot in the head or chest. Bunkers were well constructed and planned to cover all avenues of approach. The Japanese had no anti-tank weapons, but accurate small arms fire smashed two telescopic sights. Captured enemy equipment on this island included two boxed generators; numerous dumps containing fuel, clothing, rations and ammunition; varied arms to include two 5-inch naval guns with the accompanying range finder. One of these guns had received a direct bomb hit and was destroyed but the other was in excellent condition and was later experimentally fired. Why this gun was not used against ships entering Seeadler Harbor will never be known as it covered the entrance thereto. The enemy garrison force consisted of naval personnel in excellent physical condition and well equipped.

That evening the squadron bivouacked on the west end of the island and the Division artillery moved in to prepare firing positions in support of future operations. The night of March 13th-14th was the first night for the squadron to sleep above ground since its initial landing at

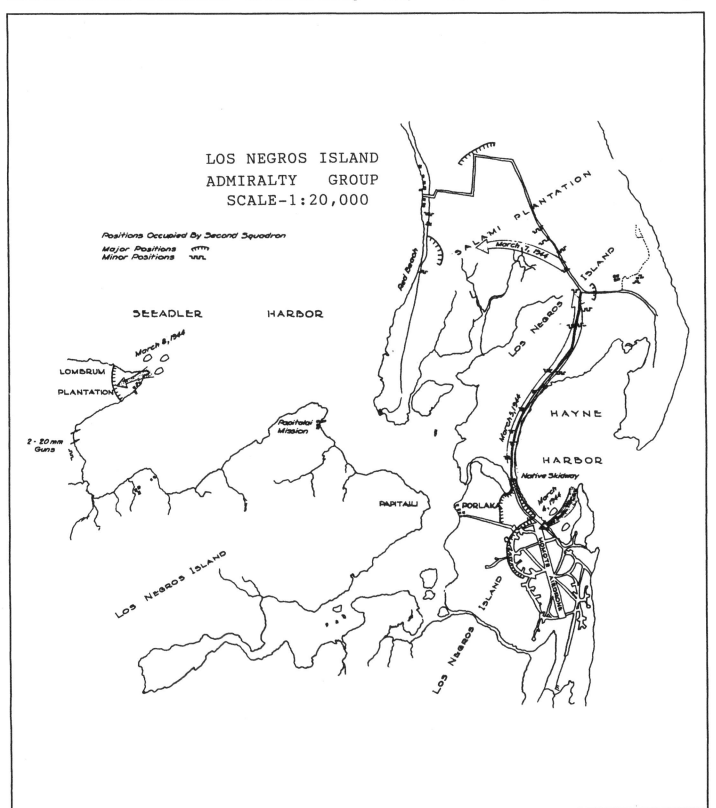

LOS NEGROS ISLAND
ADMIRALTY GROUP
SCALE-1:20,000

Positions Occupied By Second Squadron
Major Positions
Minor Positions

Hyane Harbor. On the morning of the 14th, the squadron rejoined the regiment at Salami Plantation. Personnel were badly in need of new shoes and clothing.

While the 2nd Squadron was engaged at Hyane Harbor on Los Negros Island, the remainder of the regiment was committed to action. On March 4th, the day after the departure of the 2nd Squadron, the regimental commander received orders for movement of the remainder of the regiment from Cape Sudest to the Admiralty Islands. In anticipation of a landing on hostile shores, the regiment was directed to organize a beachhead force of 560 officers and men. This force to be prepared to trans-ship to destroyers converted to Troop Transports (APDs) en route, land on Red Beach (Salami Plantation) and cover the landing of the remainder Of the 2nd Battalion Combat Team (BCT). *(A BCT consists of a battalion (squadron) reinforced by attaching tanks, artillery, and engineers in such numbers as required for a specific mission.)* After numerous detailed plans and conferences encompassing slot-loading of vehicles, the regiment boarded landing ships tank (LSTs) on the afternoon of March 6th, and sailed in convoy the following morning.

At 0800 hours on March 9th, the regimental commander trans-shipped to an LCM, picked up the commander of the 2nd BCT from a destroyer and with him led the convoy into Seeadler Harbor. It was known that there were two 3 or 5-inch Japanese guns on the eastern end of Hauwei Island and as the convoy passed through the harbor entrance there was much speculation and tension. However, no enemy, fire was delivered and several days later it was found that one of the guns was serviceable. It was not necessary to trans-ship the beachhead force as originally planned, since Red Beach had already been secured by the 12th Cavalry and the 2nd Squadron, 7th Cavalry.

The LSTs lowered their ramps at 1100 hours and immediately began discharging cargoes. The 1st Squadron remained on the beach through that night unloading the ships. Regimental Headquarters, Headquarters, and Service Troops moved into the Salami Plantation area and established a perimeter defense for the night. As vehicles were unloaded the beach road was soon turned into an impassable quagmire, completely blocking all traffic. That first night spent in the Admiralties by the troops bivouacked at Salami will long remain an unpleasant memory. Weapons and grenades were fired continuously throughout the night as it had been reported that there were still a few Japanese in the area. Fox-holes were none too deep and many troopers were sprayed with earth and grenade fragments. It was only during a two hour rain storm that any rest was enjoyed. There were no dead Japanese nor any signs of the enemy when morning came.

On March 10th, the 1st Squadron left the beach and moved to the regimental area. That afternoon Troop C patrolled to the south and west down the peninsula uncovering several enemy supply dumps but no enemy was encountered. The next two days were uneventful; however, on March 12th, Troop B patrolled south in the Native Skidway, and Troop C departed to reinforce the 2nd Squadron on Hauwei Island. March 13th and 14th were spent preparing plans and

briefing personnel for the impending operations of the 2nd BCT on Manus Island. On March 14th, the 2nd Squadron rejoined the regiment.

At 1130 hours on March 15th, the 1st Squadron embarked in LCMs from Red Beach and landed at Yellow Two Beach at 1315 to establish a beachhead perimeter in that area. The remainder of the regiment embarked from Red Beach at 1515 aboard an LST and landed on Yellow Two Beach at 1635 as the regiment was in Brigade reserve. After landing, troops forded the Lihei River, which was about waist deep, and moved to Lugos Mission where a perimeter defense covering the western half of the front was established.. Troop C established a perimeter west of the Lihei River covering that flank and two 37mm guns were also placed along Yellow One Beach. Mortars went into position and in conjunction with the artillery, placed harassing fires to the front and west flank. During the day one squadron of the 8th Cavalry Regiment moved up the road to Tingo, while the other squadron moved along the beach road to Lorengau.

The regiment remained at Lugos Mission during the morning of the 16th. The executive officer accompanied the commander of the 2nd BCT to Lorengau Air Strip at about 1200. As a result of this visit, orders were relayed to the regimental commander to move his command to the Lorengau Air Strip. At this time the 1st Squadron, 8th Cavalry, was disposed across the air strip at about midpoint, extending from the beach over the high ground to the south. They had been pinned down here by heavy enemy fire from pill boxes and bunkers located on the high ground to the front. The 7th Cavalry was then directed to relieve that portion of the 8th Cavalry (one reinforced troop) holding the position on the high ground. The regiment moved from Lugos Mission at 1400 hours in the order 1st Squadron — Provisional Squadron — 2nd Squadron, with the head of the column reaching the air strip at 1515 hours. At 1600, while the 1st Squadron was in the process of relieving Troop C, 8th Cavalry, the 1st Squadron suffered five killed, including Captain R.M. Perkins, Commanding Troop B, and 15 wounded. A portion of these casualties occurred because the 8th Cavalry troop prematurely withdrew before the 1st Squadron was firmly established in position. The remainder of the regiment established a perimeter defense behind the 1st Squadron with Troop D and the Weapons Troop mortars in position on the low ground north of the revetments. The 8th Cavalry extended the line from the north flank of the 1st Squadron across the air strip to the beach. There was little action that night. Colonel Finley had been placed in command of all forces in this area comprising the 7th Cavalry Regiment and the 1st Squadron, 8th Cavalry Regiment. During the evening of March 16th, plans were prepared for a coordinated attack to begin the next morning.

The attack was preceded by a heavy artillery concentration that blanketed the enemy positions, portions of which were only 50 yards from the front line. This was followed without interruption by a heavy mortar barrage from twenty-four 81mm mortars. During the barrage fire two 37mm guns and two light tanks fired at point blank range into enemy bunkers and pill-

boxes. As the mortar barrage ceased all automatic weapons opened up, covering the initial advance of the assaulting troops as they went over the forward slope from their position. The terrific artillery and mortar concentrations had practically wiped out all enemy resistance except for clearing the few bunkers still remaining intact. At 1033 hours when the troops came out of their fox-holes, there were numerous cries of "GarryOwen" as the 1st Squadron went into its first attack against the Japanese.

In conjunction with this attack by the 1st Squadron, the 2nd Squadron, 7th Cavalry, moved around the south flank contacting the 2nd Squadron, 8th Cavalry, then moved down the Number One Road. This closed the gap between the 7th and 8th Cavalry Regiments. At the same time the 1st Squadron, 8th Cavalry moved forward down the airstrip clearing this area of enemy opposition. After occupying the first enemy position, another artillery and mortar concentration was placed on the Japanese secondary position which again was situated on a ridge similar to the first. By 1130 hours this ridge was occupied and flamethrowers were sent forward to destroy enemy bunkers. At this time the advance regimental command post was 75 yards behind the 1st Squadron position. Throughout the above fighting, naval gun fire was placed on enemy rear installations in support of the attack. By 1300 hours, reorganization had been completed and contact established between all front line troops. Forward movement began and assault troops reached the Lorengau River at 1500 hours. Little enemy opposition was encountered on this drive, the backbone of enemy resistance having been broken at the two previous positions. Upon reaching the river the Reconnaissance Platoon was sent across and immediately drew fire from bunkers on the hills overlooking Blue Beach, whereupon it withdrew and mortar fire was placed on the bunkers which could be located. Enemy land mines were encountered in the Lorengau Area causing some casualties.

That night the 7th Cavalry and the 2nd Squadron, 8th Cavalry, formed a perimeter defense around Lorengau Township west of the Lorengau River with the 1st Squadron, 8th Cavalry, on the eastern end of the airstrip. The artillery and the navy placed harassing fires on enemy positions overlooking Blue Beach, and enemy counterattacks were not launched during the night. In spite of occasional enemy fire, Blue Beach was utilized that evening to land much needed supplies.

At 0930 hours on March 18th, the 8th Cavalry moved across the Lorengau River and established a perimeter around Blue Beach, while the 7th Cavalry spent the day cleaning weapons and equipment, reorganizing, and strengthening its position. Close in patrolling was executed on the 19th and plans were made for extensive patrolling to be initiated the following day. On March 20th, by brigade order, the following patrols were dispatched:

a. One reinforced platoon from Troop B, moving by LCM, reconnoitered the northern coastline of Manus Island to the Brundralis Mission.

b. Troop A reconnoitered down Number One Road to Drano (to be gone four days).

c. Troop F moved down the Number Two Road and reconnoitered the Warembu-Tauwo-Kelau Harbor area (to be gone three or four days).

The first two patrols were successful in carrying out their missions, but the Troop F patrol ran into considerable resistance. The remaining Japanese troops of the Lorengau area had fallen back along Number Two Road utilizing previously prepared defensive positions. At 1152 hours, the patrol reported its position as about 800 yards down the road with enemy resistance stiffening as the advance continued. Small patrols operating to the front and flanks had uncovered numerous shacks and enemy supply dumps. At about 1500 the patrol leader reported that strong enemy opposition had developed all around him and that he was trying to secure Ridge Number Three; however, the decision was made for the patrol to withdraw. In the meantime, a small enemy force had infiltrated behind the patrol and mined the road. As the artillery tractor with a one-ton trailer moved to the rear, the tractor ran over a mine and blew off a track. This blocked the road and prevented the radio jeep from getting around it. The radio was removed and the vehicles abandoned. Numerous confusing messages were received at regimental headquarters during that time. At about 1630 hours, the retrograde movement was completed with the aid of Troop E which had been sent to cover the withdrawal. The troop set up a perimeter defense on the high ground overlooking Blue Beach to hold that terrain already gained. Captain William C. Frey, the patrol leader, was wounded during the afternoon, but remained with his organization (Troop F) until it had closed behind Troop E. Regimental casualties for the operation were five killed and eleven wounded. During this severe patrol action, several men performed outstanding feats of heroism in attacking the well-protected enemy positions and wiping them out with accurate grenade and rifle fire. Among those cited for this action were: Private First Class Edward F. Covin, Private John M. Ford, Staff Sergeant Grover C. McGraw, Private First Class William T. Price and Sergeant Willie B. Randolph. Corporal James B. Anderson and Sergeant Arvel O. Treadwell went forward in a fearless manner under fire to administer first aid to wounded troopers. First Sergeant John T. Guinn, Troop F, assumed command when the troop commander was wounded and took a leading part in placing the dead and wounded aboard the tank so that they would not be left in enemy territory.

On March 21st, Troop E conducted extensive patrolling down the road and to the flanks, uncovering further supply dumps and an abandoned enemy hospital with some equipment. It was decided to send the 1st Squadron less Troop A (on patrol to Drano) down the Number Two Road the following morning. At 0830 hours on March 22nd, this force passed through the Troop E perimeter and advanced toward Old Rossum. Forward progress was slow as it was decided to destroy all bunkers encountered. As the leading elements approached the ridge, they met strong enemy opposition from machine gun and knee mortar fire. With Troops B and C abreast, the advance continued until about 300 yards from

Ridge Number Two, where heavy enemy fire was encountered and our troops pinned down. At this time Major J.A. Godwin, commanding the 1st Squadron, requested permission to withdraw, but the regimental commander ordered him to dig in on his present position and prepare a perimeter defense for the night. Troop G was then alerted to join the 1st Squadron the following morning, and arrangements were made to attach a light tank for support. Regimental casualties for this day's action were 29 wounded and 11 killed.

At 0900 hours on March 23rd, following an artillery barrage on Ridge Number Two, the squadron launched its second attack against this position with Troops B and G in the assault, and Troop C in reserve. The troops were pinned down shortly thereafter, but under cover of a mortar barrage finally reached the top of the ridge. While moving forward, the light tank ran over a mine and blew off a track and, in the meantime, the Japanese had set fire to the tractor and trailer (abandoned on the 20th). After reorganizing, the 1st Squadron again started forward, but as they reached the bottom of the slope of Ridge Number Two they met heavy resistance. After remaining in position here for a while, they withdrew to the top of the newly won Ridge Number Two where a perimeter defense was established for the night. At 1800 hours, the regimental commander and the S-3 made an inspection of the position and Lt. Colonel John B. Maxwell was placed in command of the 1st Squadron. Plans were formulated for continuation of the attack the following morning in order to secure Ridge Number One. An artillery concentration preceded by an air strike was tentatively planned in preparation for the attack. Harassing fires by the artillery during the night kept the enemy in their holes. Regimental casualties for this day's action were three killed and 20 wounded.

On the morning of the 24th, after cancellation of the air strike, the attack began at 1142 hours with Troops B and C astride the road while Troop E (brought up that morning) was to envelop around the west flank. Hundreds of rounds of 75mm artillery shells had been fired on the enemy position during the night and prior to the attack; however, the attacking troops lacked the necessary punch to capture the enemy-held bunkers and pillboxes. In a further attempt to force the enemy position, a medium tank was employed; however, it was road-bound and the tank commander refused to move forward until the preceding infantry had probed for mines — a procedure which proved extremely costly to personnel, as the tank naturally drew enemy fire. Additionally, there were no means of communicating with the tank commander except by voice through the pistol port, and at the end of the day it was generally felt that the tank had been more of a hindrance than a help.

As soon as the troops began their advance, the Japanese came out of their holes, quickly set up their automatic weapons with supporting snipers, and poured lead into our ranks. The heavy rain forest denied visibility, and after a short while considerable leadership was required to keep the troops moving forward. Troop B received the brunt of the enemy fire and Captain Roman D. Hubbell, commanding Troop B, and Lieutenant Ferguson were killed while leading

their men forward. At 1250 hours, Troop E, moving around the west flank, was pinned down by enemy heavy mortar fire, and the entire attack bogged down. At 1320 hours, the squadron commander requested permission to withdraw to Ridge Number Two to effect reorganization and to obtain artillery support. This latter request was granted and the front lines were marked by violet smoke grenades as a liaison plane of the 61st Artillery registered battalion fire on the enemy positions. An air strike by P40's was also made on this position at 1730 hours.

Two men were wounded that evening by a Japanese firing a knee mortar from a tree within the perimeter, thus bringing our casualties for the day's action to four killed and 20 wounded.

The supporting artillery kept up its fires during the night which, in addition to harassing the enemy, raised the morale of our troops. At 0900 on March 25th, the squadron withdrew 500 yards On order from the 2nd BCT. This move permitted a thorough air bombing and strafing followed by an artillery, mortar, and rocket barrage. The 1st Squadron, 8th Cavalry, then passed through our lines and in a short while captured the enemy position on Ridge Number One. Our troops returned to the regimental bivouac at Lorengau Drome and enjoyed a much-needed rest after four days of some of the most bitter fighting in the Manus Campaign. Troop B alone had lost three troop commanders in three days.

During the next four days, March 26th-29th, the regiment conducted close-in patrolling around the Lorengau area. On the 27th, local patrolling uncovered more enemy supply dumps, principally ammunition and rations, and during the same time a few Japanese were killed within the area. On the evening of the 27th, as Troop G was going into bivouac between Hiwal and Tingo, an enemy machinegun wounded both Captain J.F. Finn, the troop commander, and Lieutenant J.V. Taylor, as they were selecting positions. The troop immediately withdrew to Tingo, and sent a message asking for an ambulance to evacuate the wounded. Captain Finn later died as a result of these wounds.

In the meantime, the regiment completed plans for an attack against Pityilu Island. The attacking force to consist of the 1st Squadron, reinforced, under command of the regimental commander, as follows:

Commander of Force: Colonel Glenn S. Finley
Troops: 7th Cavalry — 1st Squadron; Weapons Troop; Anti-tank and Reconnaissance Platoons; Detachment, Regimental Headquarters; and Security Platoon
Detachment, 8th Engineers
Detachment Tanks (one light and one medium)
Detachment, 592nd Ambulance Regiment 27th Port Surgical Hospital.

Preliminary estimates placed the bulk of enemy troops and installations within the rain forest on the eastern half of Pityilu Island, while the coconut plantation was believed to be unoccupied. The only feasible landing beach was located in the center of the island on the south shore. Under cover of aerial bombardment, naval gunfire, artillery and rocket barrages, successive waves of "Buffaloes", and LCMs made an unopposed landing at 0845 hours on March

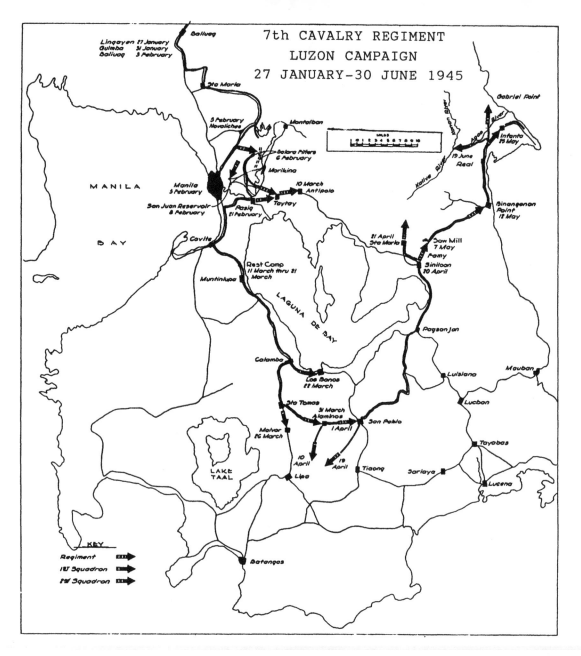

30th. A semi-circular beachhead extending to the north shore was immediately established. Troops A and B and the Reconnaissance Platoon covered the eastern sector and Troop C the western sector. Patrolling was initiated without delay with special emphasis placed on the terrain in front of the eastern sector. By 1000 hours, all patrols had returned — each reporting that enemy activity had not been observed. At 1015 with Troops A and B abreast, the 1st Squadron began its movement through the rain forest to the east.

At this same time the Reconnaissance platoon moved by "Buffaloes" to the western end of the island on a reconnaissance of that area. No evidence of enemy activity was found and the patrol returned at 1230 hours. A patrol from Troop C, moved west along the north shore and located an unoccupied trench system near an observation platform; however, neither showed evidence of recent use.

As the 1st Squadron moved forward, Troop B received fire from a bunker constructed underneath a shack. This spot had been patrolled earlier but the enemy was apparently well concealed and had withheld fire. Four Japanese with

two light machine guns were destroyed. As the advance continued, Troop B overran another group of seven enemy and at 1430, killed or captured 21 enemy troops located in a hastily constructed trench around the roots of a huge banyan tree. Upon discovery of this enemy force, located by their incessant chatter, Lt. John R. Boehme and two privates went forward to investigate. The Japanese saw them first and opened fire, wounding Lt. Boehme in the leg and slightly wounding the other two men with grenade fragments. In spite of this surprise, the two men opened fire and Pvt. Paul A. Lahman with an automatic rifle (BAR) unhesitatingly and repeatedly fired clip after clip as he moved forward. He, singlehandedly, was credited by Lt. Boehme with the destruction of practically the entire enemy force. It was found that this position had telephone communications with the first bunker encountered, and through this medium had received warning of our advance. Troop A, during its advance, ran into machine gun fire from a concealed bunker, but with the aid of the light tank the position was soon silenced and 14 enemy dead accounted for. Throughout the day's

advance all bunkers and shacks were destroyed which greatly slowed the rate of progress. At 1720 hours on March 30th, the squadron withdrew to a position on the western edge of the rain forest and established a perimeter for the night. This day's action accounted for 46 enemy killed while regimental casualties were eight killed and six wounded.

At 0730 hours on the morning of March 31st, preceded by a bombardment on the eastern end of the island, the squadron with three troops abreast completed clearing the rain forest area, and the eastern tip of the island was reached at 1225 without enemy opposition. During the return of the troops to the beach area, a bunker passed earlier that morning and on which a flame-thrower was used revealed thirteen enemy dead. Other enemy troops or installations were not found on the western half of the island which was thoroughly searched during the morning by the Anti-tank, Reconnaissance, and Security Platoons.

During the afternoon the squadron proceeded to the landing beach area and returned to Lorengau as boats became available.

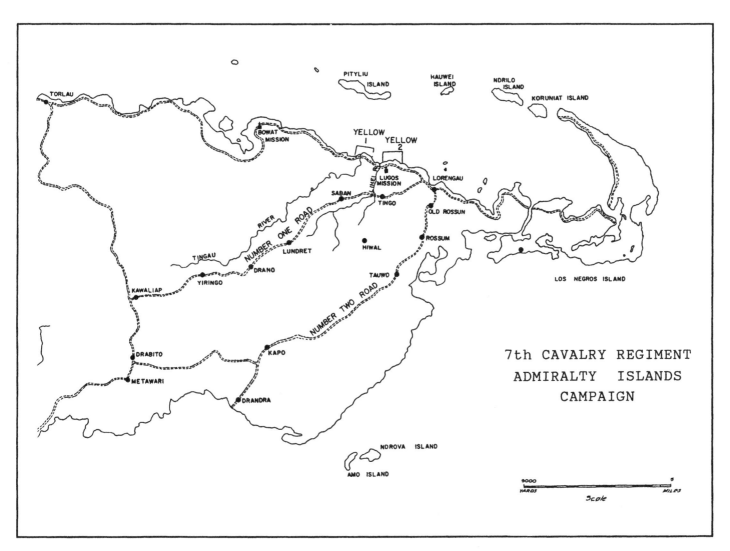

7th CAVALRY REGIMENT
ADMIRALTY ISLANDS
CAMPAIGN

Tactical missions against known organized enemy resistance were terminated in the Lorengau area on March 31st, and thereafter, mopping up operations were conducted through an extensive patrolling system.

Terrain within a four-mile radius of Lorengau was kept under close observation to prevent enemy stragglers from coming in to that area and replenishing themselves from the supply dumps which had not been removed. Approximately 20 Japanese were killed and additional supply dumps were uncovered and removed. The 1st Squadron and the Provisional Squadron supplied the necessary patrols for this period, while Troop D maintained a perimeter defense around Blue Beach and operated patrols to its front and down the Number Two Road.

On April 10th, impassable roads and unsanitary camp conditions caused by the continuous rains necessitated movement of the regimental bivouac from the Lorengau Drome to the area behind Blue Beach. On this same date the 1st Squadron moved to Lugos Mission to operate patrols from there. The Provisional Squadron — the only remaining element of the regiment — relieved Troop D and took over its mission.

On April 17th, one squad from Headquarters Troop was detailed to provide a guard for a radar installation at Satkin and was relieved on May 4th. A few nights previous, the Task Force Headquarters received a message stating that this outpost was being attacked by enemy forces and requested reinforcements. Two platoons from the 2nd Squadron under the squadron commander were dispatched in the early morning, arriving at Sarkin at 0630 hours. Patrols found no enemy or any evidence that they had been recently in the vicinity. The panic message originated between several soldiers who "thought they saw three Japs" and a radio operator who confused his code messages.

On April 19th, the regimental bivouac was moved from Blue Beach to Hauwei Island, with the 1st Squadron remaining at Lugos Mission but reverting to brigade control. This move made it possible for the regiment, less the 1st Squadron, to sleep on cots and under canvas for the first time since its arrival in the Admiralty Islands, and provided a location for the establishment of a semi-permanent camp.

Returning now to the activities of the 2nd Squadron in the Lorengau area, on April 1st, tentative plans were completed for the movement of a squadron to the Drano-Yiringo area. Supply of these troops presented a serious problem. The original plan called for the use of TD-9 (International) tractors pulling one-ton trailers as far as road conditions would permit, thence movement of supplies was by hand. Continuous rains had made the red clay Number One Road impassable to all transportation except a D-7 dozer with trailer. Beyond Tingo the road was impassable for all vehicles.

The 2nd Squadron was alerted to execute the mission and on April 2nd, Troop E moved to establish a base supply dump about 500 yards west of the Lihei River. Supplies were moved by the dozer to the east side of the river, then carried by personnel to the base dump. This involved fording the waist-deep river, then climbing a series of steep hills that were nearly impassable for foot troops carrying a load. It soon became apparent that this method of supply would not meet the demand. Reconnaissance was initiated to locate a more feasible route, and the possibility of using the Lihei River was considered. However, this means of supply offered no improvement since supplies still had to be hand-carried from the same point. In the meantime a foot bridge had been constructed across the river.

On April 8th, a route up the Tingau River was utilized and supplies were moved by "Buffalo" to a point north of Sabon. A few days later a limited number of native carriers were made available which considerably eased the burden of troop-carrying. It is interesting to note that the natives could carry a box of "K" rations weighing 41 pounds from Sabon to Yiringo in about 3 1/2 hours whereas the average soldier required from two to three days. *(This same situation was true during the Korean operation in later years; however, 7th Cavalry troopers are traditionally fighters - not porters.)*

The 2nd Squadron, less Troop E, left Lorengau on April 6th. In view of the supply

147

situation it was decided to send a reinforced troop to Yiringo to conduct patrolling from that point, and to establish each of the remaining troops along the supply route.

By the night of April 10th, troops were located as follows: Troop E at Sabon; Troop F and Squadron Headquarters at Yiringo; Troop G in the vicinity of Drano; and Troop H in the vicinity of Lundret. The intermediate troop bivouacs were selected to facilitate shuttling supplies to the base reconnaissance camp at Yiringo. These troops also conducted local patrolling and provided security for the supply route.

On April 10th, Troop F, which had arrived at Yiringo the previous night, sent two platoons to patrol the route to Kawaliap and to establish a one-day ambush at that point. During the day's movement to the objective, 13 Japanese were killed, while the troop's losses were one killed and two wounded. In order to provide rations for this mission, Troop F, less the patrol, went without food for 24 hours since resupply could not be effected. Not withstanding these hardships, an indication of the spirit which prevailed throughout the regiment is indicated in the remarks made later by Brigadier General Mudge in describing the Troop F patrol: *"You would have enjoyed the sight of one of our troops returning from patrol today. I had last seen this troop three weeks ago, after they had been out two days. On that occasion the jungle was thick, it was raining in buckets, and the mud was knee deep; the troopers were carrying four days rations and their ammunition; they had nothing but ponchos, wool-knit sweaters, and toilet articles with them in the way of comfort — but their morale was high, and there wasn't a sour face nor a grumble in the entire outfit.*

"The first. glimpse I got of the troop was as it was coming down the Lukuli River in native canoes. Never in the World was there a more picturesque sight. Of all the rough, tough, muddy, ragged troops you ever saw, they were it. Yet you have never seen a more cheerful, enthusiastic, happy bunch of men anywhere. Nor was there a set of whiskers among them; nor a rusty weapon. They were as happy as though they were headed for Coney Island. Every one of them had a grin on his face; anyone seeing them could not fail to notice that each man had achieved one of the most valuable of military qualifications — pride in himself and his troop."

On April 12th, the Kawaliap patrol returned and another platoon was sent out to reconnoiter the Kawaliap — Buyang #2 — Pundrau area. By this time rations had arrived at the base camp in sufficient quantities to properly maintain patrols. On April 14th, the squadron commander received a report that there was a small enemy concentration in the Drabko-Kandranyo area. Remaining elements of Troop F moved out that morning and arrived at Kawaliap without incident. That afternoon the platoon returned from Buyang #2 and rejoined the troop. Squadron headquarters with the necessary local protection remained at Yiringo. During the day, patrols at Drano and Bulihat each killed one Japanese.

On April 15th, Troop E patrols killed seven enemy troops south of Warrabi and three in the vicinity of Sabon. The Troop F patrol, now moving into the objective area, began contacting small enemy groups and in the Tawi-Drabito

area, 13 were killed out of four small groups encountered. At Drabko the force was split, half going to Suna to effect contact with an 8th Cavalry patrol at that point, and the remainder moving to Metawarri. This latter patrol killed two Japanese on the approach to its objective, and at the Wari River five more were accounted for as they attempted to escape in canoes. One platoon, sent to the Point where the enemy left the river bank, received hostile fire which wounded two of our men. A combination holding and flank attack broke this center of resistance and left four enemy dead. The platoon then moved to the river and a squad swam across to reconnoiter the village of Metawarri where they found and killed four Japanese. That night the squad dug in on the village side while the remainder of the platoon remained on the opposite river bank.

On April 16th, further reconnaissance of Metawarri was conducted which resulted in one Japanese killed while attempting to infiltrate our lines. The patrol sent to Suna rejoined the troop after contacting the 8th Cavalry patrol.

On April 17th, the squadron, having completed its mission, began a retrograde movement to rejoin the regiment. Troop F moved to Suna to be evacuated by boat from the south shore of Manus, and the Squadron Headquarters and Troops G and H joined Troop E at Sabon. On this same day Troop E killed three Japanese south of Warrari, and the following day moved to the mouth of the Tingua River to await boat evacuation to Hauwei Island. The remainder of the squadron moved back along the Number One Road and bivouacked at Sabon during the night. A final thrust at the enemy by Troop H resulted in six enemy dead. On the 19th, evacuation of the remaining personnel was completed and the entire squadron assembled at Hauwei Island.

Recapitulation of enemy casualties during the period April 9th-19th showed 82 killed and a large but undetermined number wounded. Regimental losses were one killed and four wounded. Skin diseases and diarrhea were the main causes for the evacuation of 74 personnel. Continuous rains and the extremely difficult movement over the muddy impassable trails were contributory causes affecting the health of the command.

While the 2nd Squadron was engaged in the Drano-Yiringo area during the period April 1st to 19th, the 1st Squadron was busily engaged in patrol activities in the Lorengau area.

When terrain conditions necessitated movement of the regiment from Lorengau Drome to Blue Beach on April 10th, the 1st Squadron was moved to Lugos Mission because of limited bivouac space in the new regimental area. Upon movement of the 2nd Cavalry Brigade from Manus Island, one squadron was to be maintained at Lugos Mission, for the purpose of providing close-in protection of the Lorengau area against possible enemy air or sea-borne attack, and to patrol the area included within the Lihei River — Hiwal — Rossum-Hamletsstern boundary of Salesia Plantation line.

The 1st Squadron took over this mission and extensive patrolling was maintained in the assigned area with patrols ranging in size from a squad to a platoon. In addition, a standing outpost was established at Tingo for the first two weeks. Only a few Japanese were contacted during this phase; however, on April 14th, a 17-man

patrol moving toward Tingo killed two Japanese. The following morning a prisoner was captured in extremely poor condition and required evacuation by litter. On April 21st, a Troop C patrol killed two Japanese at Bulihat and on the following day another patrol killed two more at Lohan.

A patrol of two squads set out for Inrim Plantation at 0430 hours on April 25th, and then moved about six miles south to the native village of Patsui. The native police boy, acting as guide for the patrol, killed four Japanese at this village. The patrol returned to Inrim that night and moved to the village of Lundret the following morning, where the Japanese had been reported. As the unit passed through Sabon it received a prisoner from the natives. Thereafter, under the direction of a native guide, the patrol established an effective ambush around Lundret where eight enemy were killed, one escaped wounded, and the remaining one, supposedly a sentry, was unaccounted for. One of the dead was identified as a naval lieutenant. All were in good physical condition and well supplied with food and arms including a knee mortar, grenades and ammunition.

On April 30th, a six-man patrol from Troop A cornered four enemy troops in a cave on the west bank of the Tingau River about one mile north of Lundret; two were captured and two killed. On May 22nd, a Troop D patrol took three prisoners at Buyang #1, one of whom was an officer.

The 1st Squadron was relieved by an 8th Cavalry squadron on May 5th, whereupon it rejoined the regiment at Hauwei Island and began work on its camp area. During the last ten days of the stay at Lugos, the squadron sent out numerous patrols under instructions from the Division at Angau. Often the mission and whereabouts of these patrols were unknown even to the squadron commander until the unit returned. Supply of the squadron was effected directly by Division agencies, since the regiment had no control and little knowledge of the squadron's activities.

Thus, after six months in Australia, followed by three months in New Guinea, the regiment entered combat against the Japanese for the first time during the Admiralty Island operation. After only one year from the time the regiment was dismounted it had met its first test of fighting as infantry, and from the viewpoint of experience, a lucrative test-ground had been supplied. Numerous errors, both of omission and commission, were made, but fortunately the nature of the enemy opposition minimized the resultant possible losses. It was the type of action that green troops hope for when thrown into their first enemy engagement — where the opposition was not too stiff, yet provided a sufficient test of the unit's mettle. The training in the swamps of Louisiana and on the sun-parched plains around Fort Bliss of previous years had paid off, and the tactical teachings, when remembered and properly employed, unfailingly brought decisive results to the GarryOwens.

The strength of the regiment when ordered into combat was 92 officers and warrant officers, and 1,895 enlisted men. Of these, 10 officers and 186 enlisted men were not present when the regiment reached the Admiralty Islands. The regiment's casualties for the operation were 43 killed, 17 died of wounds, 167 wounded, and two died of nonbattle injuries.

After a period of some five months spent in rehabilitation and extensive combat training on Hauwei Island in the Admiralty Group, the 7th Cavalry Regiment received instructions on September 25th to prepare for future operations. The regiment immediately began packing and inspecting both troops and equipment to insure that everything was in readiness for future combat. Lt. Colonel Robert P. Kirk, 2nd Squadron, was placed in vance detail which prepared a temporary staging area on Los Negros Island. On September 28th the regiment moved to Los Negros where final preparations for embarkation were made.

On October 6th, the regiment, less the 1st Squadron, preceded by an advance detachment, boarded the USS James O'Hara, for what was to be their temporary home for the next two weeks. The 1st Squadron remained on Los Negros until the night of October 9th, at which time the squadron, plus attachments, loaded on two LSTs at Red Beach. On the morning of October 10th, the 1st Squadron, under command of Major Leonard E. Smith, sailed from the Admiralties to join a larger convoy at Hollandia, Dutch New Guinea. This was the last the regiment was to see of the 1st Squadron until rejoining them on the Leyte Beach in the Philippines on October 20th.

A final farewell to the Admiralty Islands was said by every GarryOwen as the convoy steamed out of Steadier Harbor past Hauwei Island, which had been their home for so many months. But, as the Admiralties faded in the distance, all thoughts turned toward what had become the one ambition of the 7th Cavalry — "The Freedom and Revenge of the Philippines."

The early morning of October 20th found every man wide awake as this was to be the day the 7th Cavalry assaulted the beaches of Leyte Island. A final last minute check was held and the troops were given a short good luck address by Colonel Walter E. Finnegan, and with the world-famous battle cry of "GarryOwen" ringing in the ears of the men, the assault waves were lowered away. The first LVTs bearing the assault waves of the 2nd Squadron were lowered into the water from the USS O'Hara at 0812 hours. Immediately all boats formed into waves for the run to the beach. The first wave landed on White Beach at 1000, exactly on schedule. In the meantime, aboard the LSTs, the 1st Squadron loaded into LVTs and waited for the ramp to be dropped. The 1st Squadron then landed exactly on schedule on White Beach to the right of the 2nd Squadron.

The mission assigned to the 1st Squadron Combat Team was the seizure of Cataisan Point and the securing of Tacloban Airstrip. Utmost speed was necessary, as many engineer units were waiting to begin work on the airstrip. Opposition was light except in those instances where numerous pill boxes were encountered. The difficulties encountered by the troops were the swamps, the many unoccupied pill boxes — all of which had to be checked, and the many native shacks — each offering a possible place of concealment for the enemy. However, by 1400

hours, the Cataisan Peninsula was in the hands of the 1st Squadron and 31 Japanese had been killed in the conflict.

The 2nd Squadron, after a rapid reorganization on the beach, pushed ahead to secure the town of San Jose Ricardo, their first objective. As in the case of the 1st Squadron, the 2nd Squadron did not encounter heavy opposition; however, numerous buildings had to be searched for the concealed enemy. By 1230 hours, San Jose Ricado was secured and 24 Japanese had been killed. The only avenue of approach to the first night's objective was the Tacloban-San Jose Road, which was narrow, hard surfaced and literally covered with troops. The area on both sides of the road was either swampy or waist deep rice paddies, and while the troops could have pushed rapidly ahead on the road, the entire movement was necessarily slow due to these swamps. The regimental command post was established on the west side of San Jose at 1245 hours. By 1400 the 2nd Squadron had crossed the Barayan River. Although the Japanese had attempted to demolish the bridge they had succeeded only in weakening it, and several light tanks, followed by the 2nd Squadron, had crossed the bridge before it became necessary to have the engineers repair the structure to permit the crossing of the medium tanks. The repairs were finished at 1420 and the advance continued. By nightfall the regiment had pushed beyond the first day's objective. The 1st Squadron had been ordered to move overland by LVTs and join the remainder of the regiment, leaving Troop A, reinforced, to defend Cataisan Peninsula against a possible counterattack. A perimeter across the road eastward to the beach was established for the night.

A total of 60 Japanese were killed during the regiment's first day of combat in the Philippines. While the perimeter was being prepared for the night the GarryOwens played host to the first liberated Philippine natives to reach friendly lines and safety.

The first night in the Philippines, much to everyone's surprise, was very quiet as no hostile fire was received. At 0800 hours on the 21st, the 7th Cavalry resumed the advance with squadrons abreast — the 1st Squadron on the right and the 2nd Squadron on the left — with the capital city of Leyte as the objective. Terrain similar to that of the first day was encountered. The 2nd Squadron, during the advance to Hill 404D, engaged and killed 85 Japanese, while the 1st Squadron met no enemy opposition until they reached San Fernando. By 1400 hours, the 1st Squadron was in the outskirts of Tacleban and the 2nd Squadron faced the large hill mass just west of town. At this point in the operations a heavy artillery preparation was placed on both Hill 404D and on the high ground north of town. At 1500 hours, when the barrage had lifted, the advance continued. Little resistance was met in Tacloban, but the 2nd Squadron was delayed by an estimated 200 enemy troops who were well entrenched in fox holes, pill boxes, and the dense vegetation which covered the area. Murderous fire was placed on the advancing troops pinning them down. At this point the 1st Squadron was well in advance of the 2nd Squadron, and at the direction of the regimental commander, elements of the Regimental Weapons Troop and the Anti-Tank Platoon, acting as riflemen, were dis-

patched to seize the south end of the hill mass (Hill 215) opposing the 2nd Squadron. This flanking move was successful and some 20 Japanese were killed and several machineguns captured. At one time the Weapons Troop was pinned down by intense enemy fire from a bunker to the immediate front. Private First Class Kenneth W. Grove volunteered to clear the enemy from the position and cautiously worked his way through the low underbrush to the bank of the bunker, charged across the open area in front of the bunker, and succeeded in killing the four-man enemy gun crew. By 1800 hours, the southern half of the hill mass had been secured while the 1st Squadron occupied Tacloban, and the regimental command post moved to the building formerly occupied by the Leyte Intermediate School for Girls in Tacloban. *(Hill numbers throughout the text are taken from the maps used at the time of the action and indicate height in meters. Letters following the number are usually objective designations.)*

By this action the 7th Cavalry seized its objective one day ahead of schedule with an estimated 125 Japanese killed in the course of the second day's action — but at a cost to the regiment of five killed and 24 wounded.

At 0745 hours on October 22nd, an air strike was requested on the northern half of Hill 215, confronting the 2nd Squadron. This was accomplished by Navy dive-bombers with a superior display of air tactics — every bomb falling on the target area. The regiment's assault was launched at 0820 with little opposition encountered, as most of the enemy had either retreated or were killed by the aerial attack. When Hill 215 was finally taken, 335 dead enemy troops were found in the area. By 1135 the 2nd Squadron had reached the bridge across the Mangonbangan River, west of Tacloban, where junction was made with the 1st Squadron troops. The 1st Squadron continued to outpost Tacloban while the 2nd Squadron advanced through numerous rice paddies until a line just north of the road running southwest from Anibong Point was reached and contact was established with the 8th Cavalry Regiment on the left and the 12th Cavalry Regiment on the right.

At 1325 hours, five light tanks were dispatched from Tacloban to reconnoiter road and bridge conditions to the Tigbao River. This mission was accomplished at 1445 with no enemy contact being made. The road was not mined; however, the bridge across the Tigbao River was found to be in a weakened condition and not passable for military traffic. During the course of the day, the 1st Squadron patrolled Tacloban and the town was placed off-limits to all troops.

By nightfall the advance regimental command post had joined the 2nd Squadron while the rear echelon remained with the 1st Squadron. No enemy had been encountered by the 1st Squadron, however, the 2nd Squadron had accounted for 132 dead enemy troops.

At 0900 hours on the morning of the 23rd, the 2nd Squadron remained in place in 2nd Brigade reserve, while the 8th Cavalry passed through their lines and continued the advance. The 1st Squadron remained in Tacloban and spent the day cleaning equipment and preparing for future action. Colonel Finnegan, the regimental commander, made a reconnaissance of the

7th Cavalry Landing on Leyte Island, Philippine Islands, October, 1944. U.S. Army photo.

San Juanico Straits in a Landing Craft Infantry (LCI) to determine the feasibility of continued action in that direction. Upon his return at 1800 hours. it was decided that the 2nd Squadron would revert to regimental control and remain in position, while the 1st Squadron would move by LCMs to Babatngon to secure that position of the San Juanico Straits, and that the regimental command post would remain in Tacloban.

A recapitulation of casualties for the first four day period in the Philippines indicated that the Regiment had killed 428 Japanese while suffering 12 killed and 50 wounded.

On October 24th, the 1st Squadron was placed under direct control of the 2nd Cavalry Brigade. Their mission was to land at Babatngon by overwater movement and to secure the northern portion of the San Juanico Straits. At 1030 the Squadron Combat Team loaded at Tacloban Dock and set sail for Babatngon. Upon arrival, local securing patrols were dispatched and a perimeter defense established.

At 1200 hours, the regiment, less the 1st Squadron, made a combined foot and motor march to a new area near the Diit River and outposted the position.

The following day the 1st Squadron underwent an enemy air attack at Babatngon. One LCI in the harbor was the apparent target of the attack, and all casualties — 8 killed and 17 wounded-were Navy personnel. Later in the day a native reported that an unknown number of were in the town of Rizal. One platoon of Troop B was dispatched under the command of Lt. Intemann, and a second platoon was dispatched to Lukay. Negative reports were received by the squadron headquarters from both patrols.. The regiment, less the 1st Squadron, remained in position at the Diit River and Tigbao River camps.

The period of October 26th-27th was spent in active patrolling by the 1st Squadron of the Babatngon-Barugo-Carigara area. Troop A commanded by Captain Spencer reconnoitered Barugo and sent a reinforced platoon to Carigara. This platoon did not encounter any enemy in Carigara and returned to Barugo and from there to Babatngon in LCMs. The remainder of the regiment conducted local patrolling of the Diit River area.

On the 28th, Troop E, commanded by Captain Rupkey, departed the Diit River at 1300 hours by water to San Antonio on Samar Island and patrolled that area. In the meantime, Troop C, commanded by Lt. Greenbowe, had departed Babatngon to secure Barugo. Information was received by Lt. Greenbowe that there was an unknown number of Japanese in Carigara who had arrived during, the night from the direction of Jaro and Tunga. Troop C reached the outskirts of the town without meeting any opposition and began moving through the town in small patrols. After reaching a point approximately one-third of the way through town, the entire troop soon became engaged with the enemy and it soon became apparent that the enemy, far outnumbered Troop C and had the added advantage of excellent cover and concealment. Due to this situation and to the fact that Barugo had been left undefended, Lt. Greenbowe withdrew his troop back to Barugo and set up a defensive perimeter for the night on the east bank of the Minusuang River. Local Philippine guerrillas established ambushes for the night between Barugo and Carigara and succeeded in killing 63 of the enemy. Other guerrilla troops reported that Troop C had killed 74 of the enemy in their engagement at Carigara; however, the troop's casualties in this action were three killed and eight wounded.

On the following day Troop A departed Babatngon to reinforce Troop C in Barugo. The perimeter now consisted of two rifle troops as well as some heavy weapons from the Squadron Weapons Troop. The balance of the 1st Squadron patrolled the Babatngon-Santa Cruz-Rizal-Lukay.

On October 30th, the 1st Squadron, less Troop B which remained in Babatngon, closed in Barugo at 1145 hours and the 1st Battalion, 95th Infantry (Philippine Guerrila Force) was attached to the 1st Squadron, 7th Regiment. The town of Barugo was secured by a squadron perimeter while guerrilla troops outposted Canomontag, Lactusan, and Masonogon. Contact was not made by our troops; however, the guerrillas ambushed and killed 50 Japanese. Reports were received that the enemy was rapidly reinforcing Carigara.

The 1st Squadron, now in Barugo, as of October 31st, had the following troops attached: One platoon, Troop D; 1st Platoon, Company A, 85th Chemical Battalion; 1st Platoon, Company B, 8th Engineer Squadron; and 1st Platoon, Company B, 1st Collecting Troop.

At 0630 hours, the regimental command departed the Diit River camp en route to Barugo to assume command of the 1st Squadron, CT (Combat Team), the 2nd Squadron, 8th Cavalry Regiment which had joined the regiment. Later in the day the 2nd Squadron, 5th Cavalry, commanded by Lt. Colonel William E. Lobit, arrived at Barugo. The 2nd Squadron, 7th Cavalry, remained at the Diit River and engaged in local patrolling.

The command group of the assembled combat troops left Barugo at 0700 on November 1st to reconnoiter a good defensive position toward Carigara. The reconnaissance was completed by 0900 and the troops began moving to their new locations. The 1st Squadron, 7th Cavalry, established a position on the east bank of the Canomontag River, while the 2nd Squadron, 8th Cavalry, remained in Barugo. At 1130 General Hoffman, Commanding General, 2nd Cavalry Brigade, arrived and assumed command of all troops — designated as Bobolink Task Force. During the night of November 1st-2nd, many rounds of friendly artillery fire fell in the 1st Squadron's positions despite retreated efforts to have the firing halted, and at 0200 hours, one round fell on Troop Cs Command Post, killing three men, including the troop commander, and wounding four others.

The troops were scheduled to launch an attack on Carigara at 0800 hours on November 2nd, but due to the interference of friendly artillery fire, the attack was delayed until 0900. It was necessary to cross the Canomontag River in two native canoes, the onlv means available. This slowed the advance considerably; however, the crossing was completed bv 1130 and the forward elements made contact with the 24th Division attacking Carigara from the south; near San Mateo. Enemy opposition was not encountered as Highway Number 2 had evidently been evacuated in the direction of Limon. By noon the troops entered the town and established a perimeter while the 2nd Squadron, 9th Cavalry, followed closely into town and outposted the west and south sectors.

From November 3rd to 10th (both dates inclusive) the regiment, less those elements in Barugo and those engaged in patrolling, remained in Carigara. The 2nd Squadron, 7th Cavalry, closed in to Barugo on November 10th and relieved the 8th Cavalry. This period was spent in rehabilitation, local patrolling, and guarding bridges.

The regiment was then ordered to defend the seaward approaches from Barugo to Carigara to replace, with identical forces, the bridge guards on the Jaro-Capoocan Road, and to clear the area of enemy stragglers west of the Jaro Road in rear of the 1st Brigade.

To comply with this order the 2nd Squadron was ordered to maintain one troop at Jaro and one troop at Dagit while the squadron, less two troops, at Tunga was to patrol the area west of the mountains. The 1st Squadron was ordered to defend Barugo and Carigara as well as to patrol the area from Balud-Carigara west of the mountains. The Reconnaissance Platoon patrolled the area west from Capoocan-Balud and was ordered to guard the bridges within the sector. By 1600 on November 11th, all troops were in positions and Troop A was at Barugo.

From November 12th to the 17th, inclusive, an action developed which was not terminated until many days later in the Ormoc Valley. The Regimental Reconnaissance Platoon, while patrolling their assigned area, was ambushed by an enemy troop one and one half miles south of Balud. Reinforcements were sent from Troop B to develop the situation and eventually the entire 1st Squadron, less one troop, was committed. The action was fought along a sharp razor back ridge with our forces gradually forcing the enemy to retreat, step by step, from prepared positions by blasting the enemy from his holes with artillery and 81mm mortar fire.

In all, the Japanese had a total of four well-prepared positions with many pill boxes and bunkers on this ridge. Each one was up-hill from the attacking troops and well concealed by the dense undergrowth. Each time the troops were stopped by these positions they would lay down an intense barrage of artillery and 81mm mortar fire. The attack would be resumed only to find that the Japanese had withdrawn to their next position, thus causing the entire action to be repeated. It was not until the third position was taken that any enemy dead were found.

Gradually the enemy was pushed back until, on the morning of November 17th, the troops were prepared to continue the attack into the small barrio (village) of Minoro. At this time the 112th Cavalry Regiment relieved the 1st Squadron which was moved by motor to establish a camp in the Tunga area.

The regiment spent the period from November 17th to December 9th in maintaining close security patrols and guarding bridges in the Tunga-Carigara sector. During this period Troop F was ordered into the Mt. Laao sector to patrol and establish a road block in the vicinity of Lake Danao. It was also during this period that the 2nd Squadron came under control of the 112th Regimental Combat Team (RCT) and were utilized to guard the seaward defenses of Carigara and Barugo. On November 23rd, Troop F reverted to regimental control and returned to the Tunga Area. The 1st Platoon, Troop B, departed Tunga on November 25th with the mission of providing security for the radar station at Llorente, Samar Island. At 0700 on November 28th, Troop F, Regimental Weapons Troop, the Pioneer and Demolition Section and the Security Platoon of Service Troop departed from Dagot for Balud to establish a base camp and to provide labor details to maintain one and one

half miles of Highway #2 which, due to heavy rains, was practically impassable. On December 7th, Troop A moved by motor to Tacloban Airstrip to protect the strip from possible enemy airborne attack. On the same day Troop B, less one Platoon, departed from Tunga for San Miguel to reinforce the 302nd Reconnaissance Troop and to clear an estimated 100 Japanese from that Vicinity. On the following day the Regimental Reconnaissance Platoon patrolled the Borseth area. On December 11th, both Troop B and the Reconnaissance Platoon returned to the regimental area at Tunga without contacting an appreciable enemy force.

On December 9th, the 2nd Squadron began a westward movement from Carigara to relieve the 2nd Squadron, 112th Cavalry which had been stopped by bitter enemy resistance on "George" Hill situated 1,000 yards southwest of Hill 1836.

The relief was accomplished on December 10th. The action on "George" Hill proved to be one of the most difficult in the entire operation as the action was fought over a series of narrow, rugged, razor back ridges in mountains which were always rain soaked and above the clouds. Supply could be accomplished only by utilizing native carriers, as well as our own troops, packing the supplies over steep slopes that were ankle deep in mud.

Attack after attack was launched against the enemy strongpoint but the ground secured was not tenable. It was possible to make frontal assaults only, as the flanks were on $60°$ slopes and the Japanese simply rolled hand gernades down on the attacking troops. As was so often the case, it remained for the individual soldier to close with the enemy in hand-to-hand combat to gain each objective. As the troops closed in, flamethrowers were employed with devastating

Members of Troop F, about 50 yards inland on White Beach, Leyte Island. Flames are from a Japanese gas and oil dump set fire by naval shelling of the Island, October, 1944. U.S. Army photo.

Troop G moving into position west of Tacloban, October 22, 1944. U.S. Army photo.

Troop G prepares to retake Hill 215, Tacloban, October 21, 1944. U.S. Army photo.

7th Cavalry troopers with captured Japanese flag. During Battle of Leyte. Courtesy of Millard Gray.

Members of Troop E, engage with the Japanese at 100 yards inland from White Beach, Leyte Island, October 1944. U.S. Army photo.

effect. Especially noteworthy during this attack was the action of Private First Class Henry Steinbach of Troop G, who preceded the flamethrowers firing his BAR from the hip which enabled the flamethrower operators to get near enough to the enemy bunkers to finish the job.

On December 14th, Troop G, Commanded by Captain J.V. Taylor, finally penetrated the position and "George" Hill was captured. In the vicious hand-to-hand fighting, 55 enemy were killed and a total of 12 LMGs, three HMGs, nine knee mortars, one BAR, two M-I and 73 Japanese rifles were captured. Our casualties were eight killed and 15 wounded. Over 5,000 rounds of artillery fire had been placed on this position without appreciable effect. Thus, after three days of hand-to-hand fighting, Troop G completely overran the enemy stronghold. Their aggressive attack against a numerically superior enemy force marked a turning point in the fighting in the northern Ormoc Valley, and the troop was later awarded the Presidential Unit Citation for this action.

After this engagement the 2nd Squadron moved west down the mountain with the objective of securing an airdrop area in the Leyte River Valley. This was accomplished on December 17th, when the entire squadron closed in that area after killing 12 Japanese and capturing four knee Mortars en route.

During this period the regiment, less the 2nd Squadron, remained in the Tunga area and engaged in patrol and bridge guarding activities.

On December 18th the regiment departed the Tunga area, by motor, for Carigara, transshipped in LCMs to Pinamopoan, and then marched by foot to contact the 1st Squadron, 112th Cavalry, which was in the vicinity of Tolibaw. The 2nd Squadron operated on the Leyte River and received supplies while in this position, Private First Class Margarito G. Lopez of Troop E performed heroic acts for which he was awarded the Distinguished Service Cross, and gained him the reputation of being a one-man army. When a twelve-man patrol approached a well-concealed enemy emplacement,

the BAR-man was struck in the chest by a burst of machine gun fire, and seriously wounded. Lopez, unhesitatingly crawled to the side of the wounded man and succeeded in dragging him to a place of safety. He then took the wounded man's BAR and ammunition belt and launched an individual assault on the machinegun position, pouring a steady stream of fire into it as he moved forward. He killed 13 of the enemy and captured the machinegun. His action so inspired the rest of the patrol that they went forward to annihilate the remainder of the enemy position, killing 40.

At 1000 hours on the 19th, the regiment closed in an area 1,000 yards south of Tolibaw and received orders to operate on the left of the 1st Squadron, 112th Cavalry. By 1700, all units of the 1st Squadron, 7th Cavalry, were in position, while the Provisional Squadron and the regimental command post remained behind. In the meantime, at the supply drop zone, the 2nd Squadron ambushed and killed 30 enemy troops, while suffering one man wounded in this action.

Cpl. Millard Gray taking break after fighting on Leyte Island, 1944. Courtesy of Millard Gray.

At 1400 one squad from each Troop E and Troop F departed with some wounded on an evacuation mission to Limon. This group was ambushed by the Japanese resulting in five Japanese killed and five of our men wounded.

From December 20th to the 23rd, the regiment attacked south toward Lonoy with the mission of maintaining contact with the 112th RCT, to clear the assigned zone as far south as Lonoy, and to sweep the once formidable "Yamashita Line." On the night of December 20th, a group of Japanese moved into a position, recently vacated by the 1st Squadron, with mortars, machineguns, and rifles, and immediately began shelling both the 1st Squadron, 7th Cavalry, and the 1st Squadron, 112th Cavalry. Troop B, 7th Cavalry, and one platoon of Troop B, 112th Cavalry, were dispatched to attack the position and at 1745 the action was terminated with 27 Japanese killed. At 1800 hours the 1st Squadron command post received several round of enemy mortar fire resulting in three killed and six wounded. The action of Staff Sergeant Ray E Glover, Squadron Medical Detachment, in administering first aid during the disorganization and confusion is particularly noteworthy. At one point in this action, a large enemy force attempted to take a ridge line on which one section of 81mm mortars of Troop D were located. The section sergeant was wounded and left lying in an exposed position. The need for immediate rifle support became apparent and Private First Class Louis Testa voluntarily made his way through the barrage to an adjoining rifle troop and led two squads back to the mortar section. The effective rifle fire permitted the mortar section to withdraw and Private First Class Testa crawled forward and evacuated the wounded section sergeant. He then made a second trip to the forward position and dragged the two 81mm mortars from their emplacements, thus preventing their possible capture. While the command group was digging in for the night five Japanese were found in a fox hole by the S-2 section. These were killed as well as seven others when the entire area was searched by patrols.

Upon reaching Lonoy on December 23rd,

the 1st Squadron immediately sent patrols 1,000 yards west of the town but made only scattered enemy contacts. At 1000 the 2nd Squadron closed in to the regimental area, 500 yards south of Lonoy. The 1st Squadron was then assigned the mission to proceed west across the mountains to Tanguhay, and at 1200 one platoon of Troop B departed for Luperia while another platoon of Troop B headed for Agayayan. These screening patrols were followed by the remainder of the 1st Squadron and by nightfall the troops had advanced approximately 1,500 yards west of Lonoy over some of the most rugged terrain yet encountered. Twelve Japanese were killed in this movement.

The entire regiment moved west during the next two days. Many scattered enemy contacts were made and at midnight on Christmas Day, as the campaign for Leyte Island officially terminated, the regiment less the Provisional Squadron, was located in the rugged mountain terrain west of the Lonoy Road en route to Villaba on the west coast of the island. Both line squadrons closed in the vicinity of Agayayan where they were joined by the regimental commander and members of his staff accompanied by the Reconnaissance Platoon of Headquarters Troop. Up to this phase of the westward movement a total of 48 Japanese were known to have been killed and many more were killed by our supporting artillery which had been firing on large groups of enemy well to the front of our advance elements.

On December 26th, Troop C, reinforced with one platoon of Troop B, was ordered to precede the regiment to the coastal town of Villaba and develop any hostile resistance en route. Troop A, operating as advance guard for the main body of the regiment, was engaged by a well-concealed enemy group employing machinegun and rifle fire from a banana grove. 60mm mortar fire was placed on the position and the enemy was forced to withdraw, taking whatever casualties he had with him. Troop A suffered two killed and four wounded in the engagement. Troop C attacked southwest ahead of the regiment killing seven enemy during the day. All elements of the regiment received rations by airdrop, Troop C by artillery cub plane and the main body by C-47 planes. The regimental perimeter was established 7,000 yards northeast of the barrio (village) of Tanguhay while Troop C was 2,000 yards east of Pena.

On December 27th, Troop C, from a commanding position in the vicinity of Pena, observed a three mile long enemy column marching two abreast and moving west. A heavy artillery concentration was placed on the area which completely disorganized and dispersed the column. After checking the area from the air, artillery liaison pilots estimated a minimum of 100 enemy dead. By 1500 hours, the remainder of the regiment had closed on the Troop C position and established a perimeter there for the night.

During the next two days, and prior to securing Villaba, frequent contacts were made as many of the enemy were still at large. Disorganized and beaten, they clung to a vain hope of finding some escape from the relentless onslaught of the GarryOwens. Stragglers were numerous and well organized groups were encountered. The largest of these groups was engaged, initially by Troop C and subsequently by the entire 1st Squadron, with elements of the 2nd Squadron supporting, in the vicinity of Coyangian. The enemy, estimated to be upwards of 200 strong, trapped the point of Troop C on the reverse slope of a north-south ridge east of the barrio. The situation was rapidly developed and supporting artillery fire brought to bear on the enemy. Troop C killed 50 Japanese in the engagement while suffering one killed and two wounded. The following day a patrol checked the scene of the battle and counted an additional 100 enemy dead.

Concurrent with this action the 2nd Squadron, less Troop E, continued the advance on Villaba. At 1500, Troop F pushed into the town but was opposed by one enemy group which maintained a particularly stubborn resistance on the eastern extremity of the town. In this engagement, Lt. Ralph C. Conrad, commanding Troop F, was killed. Troop E was disengaged from the action near Coyangian, and joined the 2nd Squadron, assisted by the Reconnaissance Platoon, cleared the town while the remainder of the squadron cleared the outskirts. At 1830, Villaba was secured and a perimeter established on the high ground surrounding the town on the northeast and south. The entire area was vigorously patrolled from December 29th through January 1st.

The problem of supply over the difficult terrain continued to be a major problem in this phase of the Leyte campaign. Civilian pack trains protected by cavalrymen, were required to get the rations and the ammunition up to front line troops. On December 29th, Lieutenant Joseph Brauner, in command of a platoon of riflemen from Headquarters Troop and sixteen guerrilla troops, was convoying a large pack train through the enemy infested jungle when the leading elements observed three Japanese emplacing a machinegun along the trail to ambush the column. Lieutenant Brauner halted the column and, accompanied by four guerrila troops, flanked the enemy position, rushed forward, and killed the enemy with his carbine. He then sprinted across an open area to a native house where he killed four more enemy troops.

The enemy employed all the tricks of warfare in an effort to recapture the town but was repulsed in each instance with heavy losses. On the night of December 30-31st, four "Banzai" charges, each preceded by a bugle call, were hurled at the perimeter. The strongest of these was made by an estimated 200 enemy who struck the Troop F sector at 0300 hours. The enemy, worked into a frenzy by a fanatical leader, attacked from an assembly position in a coconut grove about 150 yards from the perimeter. A group of 50 rushed the perimeter and succeeded in gaining the cover of a small deftladed draw about ten yards in front of the line and from where grenades were thrown. 1st Sergeant John T. Quinn of Troop F adjusted artillery fire so close to his front line position that he received shell fragments in his fatigue blouse. With this close support and the skillful manipulation and employment of weapons, the line held and ,successfully repulsed this and subsequent attacks. An inspection of the area at daylight revealed 55 enemy bodies and evidence of possibly 100 more killed or wounded which had been removed from the area.

Major Gen. Innis P. Swift, Commander 1st Cavalry Division, Feb. 1941 — Aug. 1944. Greatly admired the 7th Cavalry Regiment. Courtesy of Ed Daily.

1945

On January 1st, acting on a report that a group of 200 Japanese carrying heavy equipment had been observed moving southeast from Hill 367 northeast of Villaba, three platoon observation posts were located on the high ground east, south, and southeast of the perimeter. Artillery fire was placed on the area and the enemy retaliated with machinegun and rifle fire forcing one of the observation posts to withdraw to a more advantageous position. Mortar fire was placed in a nearby coconut grove killing 40.

During the Leyte campaign the regiment had suffered 52 killed and 204 wounded, while inflicting 1,390 known losses on the enemy. 7th Cavalry troops killed 660 Japanese in the drive from Lonoy to Villaba alone. Besides those killed, but not physically counted, it was conservatively estimated that an additional 1,000 Japanese were killed by the regiment in this phase of the Leyte campaign.

At 0630 hours on the morning of January 2nd, the evacuation of Villaba began. Approximately 600 Philippine natives boarded the first LCMs while the troops covered the evacuation from strategic positions in and near the town. The troops were then moved to the jetty and by 1000 hours were loaded, and the convoy was underway. At 1700 the convoy arrived at Carigara, and the troops were transported by truck to the rest camp near Tunga.

Upon arrival at Tunga, the entire regiment devoted its time to establishing a camp, re-equipping, and rehabilitation. Instructions were given in the use of the flamethrowers, the new 60mm mortar, and the snooperscope and sniperscope (Telescope devices used by specially trained marksmen for both day and night firing). All new weapons were test fired on various ranges in the immediate vicinity of the camp area. On January 8th, the preliminary Embarkation Order for the Luzon campaign was received, and on January 11th, Troop B and the Pioneer and Demolition Section, departed for the assembly area at White Beach. This troop constructed storage areas for the regimental impedimenta and acted as stevedores, during the embarkation phase. No additional transportation was allocated by higher headquarters which made it necessary for the regiment to move all personnel, equipment and impedimenta from Tunga to White Beach with organic transportation. This was accomplished within the prescribed time limit by a series of shuttle movements.

On January 16th the first element of the 7th Cavalry boarded the APA "USS Leon." The Provisional Troops under Lieutenant Colonel Robert P. Kirk, shipped aboard an LST; while Troop H, under Captain Marcello W. Bordley sailed in another LST. By January 17th, all ships assigned to the 7th Cavalry were loaded and awaiting sailing orders, which were not received until the 26th. On this date the convoy formed and departed for Lingayen Gulf, Luzon Island in the Philippines.

The morning of the 27th found the 7th Cavalry in Lingayen Gulf, and at dawn the troops began debarking. An assembly area was designated for the regiment in the viciniry of Urdaneta, and on January 29th, the regiment closed there. Within a few hours the regiment moved from Urdaneta to a new assembly area near Guimba, and prepared for operations to the south and southeast.

By 0830 hours on the 30th, the entire regiment, moving by motor transportation, had closed in the Guimba area. During this movement the first action with the enemy on Luzon soil occurred. A motor serial of the 1st Squadron, commanded by Major H.W. Sheldon, moving by blackout at night, was ambushed by an unknown number of well-concealed Japanese. The Japanese fired knee mortars and rifles on the first five vehicles of the convoy and succeeded in hitting one 2-1/2 ton truck, killing one man and wounding twelve. Although mortally wounded in the action, Technical Sergeant John B. Duncan was cited for the determined manner in which he organized his platoon and eliminated this obstacle to traffic. The remainder of the men in the convoy immediately dismounted and began a search of the immediate area to locate and destroy the enemy position. The enemy withdrew to the east and the convoy was able to proceed to Guimba without further incident.

During the period of February 1st to 5th, the 7th Cavalry moved by foot and motor from Guimba to Manila, and was placed in Division reserve to guard the line of communications. This included posting bridge guards, patrolling to both flanks and road patrols. Small groups were held in reserve at strategic locations, and at one time the line of communications guarded by the regiment extended over 44 miles. It was during this action on February 4th that Lieutenant Colonel Boyd L. Branson, Regimental S-3, was awarded a Silver Star for gallantry in action when he voluntarily assumed command of the regiment's advance guard, led it across more than 40 miles of enemy infested terrain, over unreconnoitered roads, through difficult fords, and brought the regiment to its assembly area without casualties.

On February 6th, the regiment received orders to seize and secure the Manila water supply system, extending from the Novaliches Dam to the San Juan Reservoir. At 1300 hours on February 5th, in anticipation of these orders and to prevent the flooding of the line of communications, Troop G, commanded by Captain D. Berguist, departed in LVTs from Novaliches and by 1625 had secured the dam. Several land mines found in the area were defused by a Navy demolition expert.

During this period the 1st Squadron was guarding a shortened line of communications, and on February 6th was ordered to assemble in the Talipapa area to prepare for movement to the east.

In the meantime the 2nd Squadron, less Troop G, under the command of Lieutenant Colonel William L. Nash, moved by motor and foot to secure the Balara filter system, the critical element of the Manila water supply. At 1900 hours the filter plant was secured, however, the Japanese had the entire system electrically wired for demolitions and had planned to destroy the plant at 1930. Fortunately, the aggressive assault annihilated the enemy demolition crews and prevented any destruction of the system. On the following day, the entire plant was defused and over one ton of explosives was removed.

While the regiment, less the 1st Squadron, moved on Balara, the 1st Squadron protected the line of communication from Santa Maria to Novaliches Ford. Troop C established a road block at a road junction 8,000 yards north of Novaliches along the main enemy escape route from Manila to Impo. This road block was continuously in action as numerous attempts by small enemy groups to infiltrate the position were repulsed.

The following morning Troop F moved on foot to secure the San Juan reservoir. By evening the troop had thoroughly searched the surrounding area for a distance of 5,000 yards south of the filters without meeting resistance. At the same time the Regimental Reconnaissance Platoon moved 2,000 yards northeast to a hill where an estimated 200 to 300 Japanese were observed. The Reconnaissance Platoon received some machinegun and small arms fire from a well concealed enemy position to their rear. One platoon from Troop E was sent from the filters to assist in the withdrawal of the Reconnaissance Platoon which was accomplished at a cost of one killed and one wounded.

Meanwhile, the 1st Squadron arrived at Talipapa and moved at once to the Balara filters to reinforce the 2nd Squadron. This movement of the 1st Squadron enabled the 2nd Squadron, less Troop G, to assist the advance of Troop F on the San Juan Reservoir which was captured, almost intact, at 1538 hours. Shortly after the arrival of the 2nd Squadron, enemy artillery fire was received at the reservoir which destroyed the main outlet valves, but did not greatly impair the efficiency of the reservoir. During the capture of the reservoir, 56 Japanese were killed at a cost of one killed and two wounded to the regiment.

During the period February 9th to 20th, the regiment continued the mission of protecting the Manila water supply system. During this period the regiment at Balara, and Troop G, at Novaliches, were subjected to an extremely heavy volume of heavy mortar, rocket and artillery fire. The Japanese were apparently determined to destroy both the Novaliches Dam and the Balara filters. Each night attempts were made by small suicide demolition teams to infiltrate the lines, but all attempts by these enemy groups — each carrying large amounts of explosives — were repulsed. In order to secure the filter plant from small arms fire it was necessary to clear a ridge 1,000 to 1,600 yards north and northeast of the plant. It was on this commanding terrain that the Japanese had established observation posts for the heavy fire which had been falling on the Balara filter plant. The mission of clearing the ridge was given to Troop B and at 0915 hours on February 9th, an attack was launched from the west along the ridge. Initially, little opposition was encountered, but after advancing approximately 500 yards, heavy machinegun, mortar, and small arms fire was received. An 81mm mortar barrage was placed on the first Japanese position and the advance continued until 1600 hours when the commanding hill on the ridge was secured.

The attack continued on the following day as Troop C passed through the Troop B lines. The advance was slow due to the fire received from well concealed positions in the dense undergrowth. By 1500 hours on February 11th, Troop C, in conjunction with Troop E which moved along the ridge from the east, had cleared the objective of all enemy opposition. Many ammunition and clothing dumps and 21 Japanese heavy machine guns were captured, and 141 enemy troops were killed during this operation.

On February 13th, the regimental sector was extended and Troop C moved by motor to the artesian wells near the Wack Wack Country Club, and Troop G moved west of the Marikina River to establish a counter-reconnaissance screen extending from Camp Murphy to the artesian wells. At 1730 hours on February 16th, 21 Japanese trucks attempted to move through the Troop G roadblock at Calumpang. A combined artillery and 81 mm mortar barrage was placed on the trucks and all were destroyed in addition to 16 known enemy dead and five tons of Japanese explosives destroyed by the Pioneer and Demolitions Section.

During the Period February 16th to 20th, the regiment repulsed numerous suicide attacks on the Balara filters and actively patrolled and cleared the area west of the Marikina river from Bayanbayanan to the artesian wells.

On February 20th, the 7th Cavalry was relieved by elements of the 8th Infantry Division at the Manila water supply system and was ordered to assemble in the Camp Murphy area to prepare for movement to the east toward the Cainta-Taytay-Antipolo area. Troop B moved to Ugong and cleared the area of a small group of Japanese which had been raiding west of the Marikina river resulting in 28 more Japanese killed. The 2nd Squadron, in the mountains, crossed the Marikina river and secured Pasig.

The Novaliches-Balara action is filled with shining examples of gallantry, self-sacrifice and heroism. Among these were: Chaplain Thomas E. McKnight, who left his fox hole during a mortar attack to answer the call of a wounded man and was killed while administering to him; 1st Lieutenant Luther H. Adams of Troop A who also went through a mortar barrage to assist the wounded; Sergeant Althus L. Johnson of Troop A who crawled through enemy fire and dragged

four men to safety after they had fallen victims of a sniping enemy patrol; Major William A. Adams, commander of the 1st Squadron, who, while clearing the enemy from a ridge, led assaults on two machinegun positions and directed a successful attack on a concrete pillbox; Private First Class Neal H. Hultman, a machine gunner from Weapons Troop, who went to the aid of his wounded squad leader and then returned to his gun and killed two Japanese satchel-charge men; and Private First Class Melvin P. Heady, a flamethrower operator from Troop B who ran head-on through a hail of bullets to the mouth of an occupied enemy cave and drove out six Japanese who were then killed. *(McKnight Barracks which housed the Regimental Headquarters in Tokyo, Japan, during the period 1945 to 1950 was named in honor of Chaplain McKnight.)*

At noon on the 21st, the regiment began the eastward movement from Rosario with Troop C on the north and Troop F on the south with the boundary between troops the Rosario — Taytay road. By 1600 hours both troops had reached a point 600 yards north of Cainta without opposition and dug in for the night. Troop G searched the country from Calumpang south to Pasig where they joined the remainder of the 2nd Squadron. The Regimental Reconnaissance Platoon preceded the advance of the troops into Cainta and during the day encountered an estimated 50 Japanese, killing 23 of them. The following day the entire regiment closed in the Taytay area and the regimental command post was located in Cainta.

From February 23rd to March 11th, the entire regiment was employed in breaking the strongly held Japanese line west of Antipolo. This was accomplished by a series of troop actions which secured commanding terrain features

L to R: Cpl. Millard Gray receives Silver Star Medal for gallantry in action, 16 June 1945. In center is Major Gen. William Chase, Commander 1st Cavalry Division from July 1945 to 1949. Courtesy of Millard Gray.

from which the main attack was to be launched. The enemy opposed the regiment with knee mortars, heavy mortars, artillery, and rockets which-due to the accurate fire — had apparently been registered previously on the ridges and hills. Very few attempts were made by the enemy to infiltrate or counterattack as he seemed content to defend from his well concealed caves chiseled into the solid rock. These cave positions frequently were dug 85 to 90 feet into the sides of the hills, and all efforts to destroy them by mortars and artillery failed. The only solution was for demolition teams, under the protection of riflemen, to destroy each cave with explosives.

After securing a general line 2,000 yards east of Taytay, the regiment dug in and probed the enemy positions with continuous day and night patrols. Artillery and mortar observation posts placed effective counter-battery fire on all known enemy gun positions. In general, the regiment operated astride the Luzon Bus Company road and the Taytay-Antipolo roads. Numerous B-24 air strikes and Marine dive-bombing attacks were placed on known and suspected enemy positions. It was found that only 1,000 pound bombs with delay fuses could damage the well prepared Japanese caves, and then only direct hits would effectively close the caves.

On March 10th, Troop E attacked along the Taytay-Antipolo road and secured the objective area which was a high ridge dominating Antipolo from the west. This action cleared the regimental sector of enemy resistance except for one small pocket which was contained by Troops A and F. On March 11th, the 2nd Battalion, 103rd Infantry, 43rd Division, relieved the regiment in their sector and the regiment moved into an assembly area near Muntinlupa.

Of the 92 Silver Stars awarded in the First Cavalry Division for gallantry in the Antipolo engagement, 41 went to members of the 7th Cavalry Regiment. Additionally, Private First Class Calvin T. Lewis, a member of Troop B, was posthumously awarded the distinguished Service Cross for the extraordinary heroism he displayed in destroying a Japanese bunker. The platoon in which he was an automatic rifleman was stopped by enemy machine gun and rifle fire from a camouflaged bunker. After carefully searching the terrain to the front, Private First Class Lewis found the bunker, crawled forward to a point on the flank of the bunker and opened automatic fire. After placing a heavy volume of fire through the gun slits on the side of the emplacement, he moved boldly to a position in front of it. The enemy fired at him, but he returned the fire until mortally wounded and even then remained in his position engaging the enemy until all occupants of the bunker were killed.

After a period of rest and rehabilitation from March 12th to 21st, the regiment was alerted to relieve the 511th Infantry, 11th Airborne Division, and to continue patrolling toward Los Banos. This mission was given to the 1st Squadron, and the 2nd Squadron was placed in Division reserve. By 1030 hours on March 22nd, all troops of the 511th Infantry had been relieved and the 1st Squadron had established their positions 1,500 yards west of Los Banos, while the remainder of the regiment moved to Tulo.

On March 22nd, the 1st Squadron sent patrols to the east to reconnoiter hostile positions.

Small local patrol actions took place and the strong point of the enemy defense was pinpointed on a knifeback ridge overlooking a quarry about 1,000 yards southwest of Los Banos. As a result of these actions the squadron advanced 800 yards and secured an assault position. Meanwhile, the 2nd Squadron (in reserve), patrolled Mt. Bijiang, Mt. Comotes, Mr. Mabitog, Mt. Mapinggon, and Mr. Maibarara without enemy contact.

The 12th Cavalry Regiment relieved the 1st Squadron in the Los Banos area and the squadron joined the regiment south of Tulo. The 2nd Squadron then moved south following the 8th Cavalry Regiment into Santo Tomas. Troop E moved to Cabaong and established a road block protecting the flank of the main supply route from Santo Tomas to Tanauan.

On the following day, Troop C, reinforced, moved around the right flank of the 8th Cavalry at Tanauan and moved across country into Malvar, securing the town and the air field. During this movement the balance of the 1st Squadron closed in Tanauan while the 2nd Squadron remained at Santo Tomas. Troop E sent patrols southeast toward Alaminos and encountered an estimated 75 to 100 Japanese guarding a destroyed bridge about 500 yards southeast of Cabaong.

On March 27th, the regiment turned its attention toward the towns of San Pablo and Alaminos, and continued to clear and patrol the area Santo Tomas-Tanauan-Malvar. The 2nd Squadron spearheaded the attack to the southeast and by coordinated use of artillery and mortar support reached San Pablo in five days. All bridges had been destroyed and were covered by enemy fire as were all rail and road junctions.

During this phase the 1st Squadron conducted routine patrol missions and established road blocks at Malvar, San Joaquin and Santa Clara. During the early morning hours of March 29th, a column of Japanese estimated at 500,

moving from the west along the railroad track encountered the 1st Squadron road block at Malvar. According to documents and prisoners later captured, this column endeavored to reach. the main enemy forces which they believed to be in the vicinity of Tanauan. The Japanese retreated from the heavy fire from the concealed positions of the road block, and in their haste to withdraw inadvertently struck the 2nd Cavalry Brigade Command Post. This resulted in considerable confusion among the enemy troops and approximately 250 were killed, with a few casualties to our troops.

During this short but bitter engagement, Private First Class Louis Testa of Troop D fired his rifle at the advancing enemy until he had expended all his ammunition. He then took some hand grenades, rushed forward under fire and threw grenades into a deftladed enemy position along the railroad embankment. After returning to his troop's perimeter for more grenades, he advanced to within 15 feet of a Japanese mortar position where his accurate grenade throwing put the weapon out of operation by killing or driving off the mortar crew. Private First Class Testa made three additional forays with grenades against the enemy and was awarded the Distinguished Service Cross. (Private First Class Testa also heroically distinguished himself in action during the closing days of the Leyte campaign) Corporal Manuel Urenda also was awarded the Distinguished Service Cross for his heroic action in operating his light machinegun in the Troop D perimeter. Although painfully wounded four different times by mortar and rifle fire, he refused to be evacuated and kept firing his gun with devastating effect. When the assault was finally repulsed, a large quantity of weapons, ammunition, and 12 Japanese dead were found in front of his position. The actions of two other Troop D men were particularly noteworthy during this action, for which they were awarded Silver Stars. Private Paul C. Downs prevented a

L to R: Tokyo, Japan in October 1945. Boyd J. "Bull" Holland; William "Dizzy" Jean; John T. "Spade" Hindman. In front is Mindanao Pete. Courtesy of Bob "Snuffy" Gray.

Troop C slowly advances toward Japanese positions on Infanta Road, Luzon, Philippine Island, May, 1945. U.S. Army photo.

breakthrough in his section of the perimeter when he ran forward to an abandoned machinegun and placed it back into action; and Private First Class Jesus Trejo who, after receiving a painful wound in his right shoulder, continued to load a machinegun by using his left arm and refused first aid until the attack was repulsed.

Between March 28th and April 1st, troops of the 1st Squadron were busy clearing enemy stragglers in the rear areas and preparing to launch an attack on the horseshoe shaped hill mass south of Alaminos. At 1700 hours on April 1st, Troop B had secured Mapair Hill, but the advance of Troop C from Alaminos was held up by enemy opposition south of the Kauinkong river. This gorge was at least 180 feet across with sheer banks which forced the attacking troops to climb a vertical wall in the face of enemy knee mortar, machinegun, and small arms fire. Troop B, from an observation point on Mapair hill, observed continual enemy activity in and around the hills and artillery fire was placed on these enemy concentrations by the 99th Field Artillery Battalion-in direct support of the regiment.

On April 2nd, the next phase of the Luzon campaign began with the 7th Cavalry troops disposed as follows: the 1st Squadron (minus) was on the San Juan Road, 200 yards south of San Juan; Troop A was on Hill 1,228 — one of the Mapair Hills; Troop B was closing in on Hill 1,230 and was 200 yards from the top; Troop C was 500 yards south of Alaminos attempting to cross the Tarac River to patrol into the San Miguel Valley; the 2nd Squadron Command Post was located 1,500 yards west of San Pablo with Troop E at Santa Veronica on the north side of the Onipa River; Troop F was 1,000 yards south of San Pablo and on the west side of the Banedero River, and Troop G was located at the 2nd Squadron Command Post.

After heavy fighting against a dug-in enemy at the top of the steep hills, the 1st Squadron secured the Mapair hills on April 4th. En-

emy equipment left behind indicated that the hills were used as an artillery observation post for the enemy artillery located in the coconut grove in the vicinity of Santa Rosa. Troop E crossed the Tarac river and patrols made scattered contacts at the east base of the Mani hill, while Troop F crossed the Balatuin River and made a juncture with guerrilla elements on the west side of the river.

By April 5th, Troop E had moved aggressively, though hampered by difficult terrain, and secured Mani, Palindan, and the Tanza hills. By the afternoon of the 6th, Troop C had taken the Bunsulan hill and contacted Troop E elements, after killing ten Japanese in the vicinity of Santa Rosa.

When the Japanese attacked an observation post near the Mapair Hill on April 6th, Captain Urcel L. Bell and Lieutenant Raphael P. Fromm of Headquarters, 2nd Battalion, stuck to their positions and were instrumental in breaking up the assault while directing artillery fire on the attackers. Both were awarded the Silver Star for their heroic action.

This completed the mission of securing the horseshoe hill masses except for clearing the area of stragglers and snipers. Troop F travelling on level terrain, confronted by only a few snipers in the coconut groves, advanced as far south as San Bartolome — 2,000 yards north of the Onipa River.

Near Santa Rosa, Captain Wilbur P. Jackson, commanding Troop B, reconnoitered enemy territory and then led his troop in an attack. Although wounded he supervised the organizing of defenses against a counterattack for which he was awarded the Silver Star. Also awarded the Silver Star was Captain Roger O. King, commander of Troop C, who led his men in a capture of Santa Rosa and directed them as they fought their own private engagement for three days without support.

On April 7th-8th, the 1st Squadron in the

Bunsulan hills area, killed 65 Japanese who were cut off from escape across the Onipa River, and and the 2nd Squadron reached the north bank of the Onipa River on the left flank of the 1st Squadron. Thus, the regiment was spread east and west along the north bank of the Onipa River for a distance of 8,000 yards. On the south bank of the Onipa, the ground rose sharply to the 2,400 foot Mr. Mataasna peaks. A straight line was arbitrarily drawn southwest from San Gregorio to the Mr. Mataasna peak to divide the patrol missions of the two squadrons with the 1st Squadron on the right.

Initially, Major W.A. Adams, commanding the 1st Squadron, used Troop A under Lieutenant Adams to patrol south of the Onipa River while Troop C and Troop B continued to patrol the squadron rear areas. The importance of the San Miguel Valley to the Japanese was fully realized when eight 75mm guns, three 150mm howitzers, one 70mm, one 47mm anti-tank gun, and three 105mm guns, together with numerous supply dumps of ammunition, rations, and medical supplies were captured. These positions were so well camouflaged that it took several days to locate the guns in the area. Light enemy contact continued in this area until April 11th when all traces of the enemy had been eliminated.

When a patrol from Headquarters Troop approached a patch of woods near Santa Clara two men were killed and the others were pinned to the ground by a shattering burst of enemy machinegun fire from a thicket. Three men in a jeep-mounted with a machinegun — came to the rescue and set up their position in an exposed area so that they might obtain a better position from which to return the enemy fire. Private First Class John F. Copeland was the daring driver of the vehicle while Privates First Class Renaud J. Michaud and Richard T. Smith manned the machinegun. They destroyed one enemy machinegun and neutralized another, thereby relieving their beleaguered comrades and enabled the attack to proceed. Both were awarded the Silver Star for this action in which Private First Class Michaud was mortally wounded.

As the battle for Mr. Malepunyo continued, on April 12th Sergeant Jesse Riddell, of Troop F, singlehandedly attacked a concealed enemy machinegun and killed its four crew members: while Lieutenant Curtis L. Elliott, Troop E platoon commander, amid a hail of enemy bullets, directed mortar fire on one hostile machinegun, neutralized another machinegun with his rifle, and was killed trying to get a third. Both were awarded Silver Stars for their gallantry in action.

A wide, deep valley separated the regiment's forward elements from the peak of Mr. Mataasna Bundoc; therefore, further efforts were not made to actually secure the top of the peak. Organized resistance had ceased in the 7th Cavalry zone of action and the regiment proceeded to the next phase.

On April 18th, the 1st Squadron, less Troop C, moved to Lucban by motor, posting brigade guards on the Division line of communication as it proceeded from Pagsanjan to Lucban to Tayabas and east to Hauban on the coast. Troop C remained at San Pablo as an alert troop under 2nd Cavalry Brigade control, while the 2nd Squadron remained in the hills east of the Onipa

7th Cavalry Troops and Philippine Guerillas marching on the Infanta Road, Luzon, May, 1945. U.S. Army photo.

river to continue patrolling in that area and to prevent the possible escape of any Japanese that might retreat in front of the 8th Cavalry advancing from the west.

As the regiment drove on to Mt. Malepunyo, Private First Class Robert D. Underwood and Corporal Millard G. Gray of the Weapons Troop, rescued wounded under heavy fire in the vicinity of Santa Clara and were awarded Silver Stars. *(Millard G. Gray remained with the 7th Cavalry and saw combat during the Korean War 1950-51. On 12 August 1950, he was seriously wounded while serving in the most forward position as a Forward Observer, with Platoon Leader 2nd Lt., Ed Daily (Author) of Company H, 2nd Battalion, 7th Cavalry. In August 1964, he retired as a First Sergeant.)*

On April 19th, the 7th Cavalry was alerted to relieve elements of the 43rd Division in the Siniloan area. While this phase of the Luzon campaign was relatively short, the large quantity of captured enemy equipment and the number of enemy troops killed were sufficient to mark this as another successful chapter in the history of the GarryOwens. Without rest, the Mapait hills - Mt. Malepunyo phase ended and the Siniloan phase began.

On April 20th, the regiment, less one squadron, moved to Siniloan to relieve elements of the 43rd Division. The 1st Squadron (reinforced with the Weapons Troop) was detailed for this mission and was relieved by the 12th Cavalry Regiment, while the 2nd Squadron continued their mission under Brigade control. Using organic transportation plus ten 2-1/2 ton trucks attached from the Division Quartermaster, the regiment (minus) closed in the Siniloan area at 1330 hours on April 20th. The regimental command post was established on the Siniloan-Famy

road, approximately 1,000 yards north of Siniloan, while the 1st Squadron relieved elements of the 103rd RCT in place. The regimental mission was to maintain a defensive position that extended in depth from 2,000 yards east of the saw mill on the Siniloan-Infanta road to Famy where the squadron command post was located. Troop C moved to the vicinity of Santa Maria to patrol northeast in the valley, maintain liaison with the 43rd Division on the left, and to bridge the gap between the Santa Maria Valley and the Infanta road.

Until released by higher headquarters to begin a sustained drive up the Infanta road, the 7th Cavalry was to assume what was termed an "active defense".

The 1st Squadron on April 21st began patrolling to test the enemy's defenses in the saw mill area with the 99th Field Artillery Battalion in position near Famy to support their strong combat patrols. In order to keep the men fresh for the forthcoming offensive, only one third of the command was used on these daily patrols. Troop A held the most forward position on the ridgeline north of Infanta road which was used as the line of departure for the patrols. The route from Siniloan to Infanta was over a narrow, rutted, muddy trail that ran through jungle-covered mountains and was ideal for the Japanese to defend. At Famy, Technical Sergeant Howard S. Huibregtse, acting platoon leader in Troop A, was awarded a Silver Star for the skillful manner in which he shepherded his men from under a heavy enemy barrage.

Before a coordinated attack was staged on May 7th, an accurate estimate of the enemy's position had been obtained through captured documents removed from the enemy dead and from patrol reports. Patrol actions, artillery con-

centrations, and air strikes resulted in 109 enemy killed which were left behind as he withdrew from the numerous skirmishes. Estimates of the probable number of enemy killed doubled this figure while regimental losses amounted to four killed and 24 wounded.

On May 3rd, the Weapons Troop which had been guarding the main supply route from Pagsanjan to Santa Maria, and the 2nd Squadron which had been operating under brigade control on the Mt. Malepunyo sector, were released to regimental control. The Weapons Troop went into the perimeter with the regimental command post, and the 2nd Squadron was assigned the northern half of the regimental zone of action in the sawmill hill masses. Their mission was to patrol the north side of the Infanta road east to the nursery area-about 7,000 yards from Famy. This terrain — part of the dense jungle growth separated by deep gorges and rugged ridge lines — was characteristic of that found in the entire area to be covered on the regiment's forthcoming march to Infanta. By using two-day patrols, scouts were able to reach the high ground north of the nursery overlooking that area. Light opposition was encountered by the patrols thereby permitting unrestricted movement. It should be mentioned that guerrilla elements from the 45th Infantry and Rei-zar forces operated with regimental patrols and were of great help in guiding the troops through the dense growth of the terrain and in ferreting out Japanese snipers and ambushes.

One patrol sent north toward Pagus ran into an enemy holdout, one trooper was wounded and the others were forced to seek cover behind a ricepaddy dike. When the enemy prepared to attack, Private First Class, Margarito G. Lopez (awarded the Distinguished Service Cross for heroic action during the later phase of the Leyte campaign), Sergeant Earl E. Shappell and Private Delbert E. Rogers sprang from their cover and charged the enemy who was advancing nearby under the shelter of a river bank. With grenades and rifle fire they killed three Japanese soldiers and drove the rest away. All three men were awarded the Silver Star for their action.

Before passing from this phase, one other important patrol action typifying those of this period deserves special mention. On April 22nd, Lieutenant David E. Wright led a platoon reinforced with one section of light machineguns from Troop A, and a mortar forward observer from Troop D, in an attempt to find a route which would flank the enemy defensive positions on the right. The Taguhlan River which parallels the Siniloan-Infanta road on the southeast was unfordable, and any route forward had to pass between the river and the road. Lieutenant Wright's patrol departed at 0730 hours on April 22nd and reached the approach to the main hill mass where it drew heavy fire from enemy sniper positions. As the situation developed, it was realized that the resistance confronting the patrol was in reality the left flank of the enemy's defensive line. An intense fire fight ensued, climaxed by a "Banzai" charge by approximately 50 Japanese. The platoon held its ground, repulsed the attack, and killed 28 Japanese without loss to their own platoon. Due to the late hour the patrol broke contact and returned to the Troop A area.

On May 2nd at Famy, when the enemy infiltrated to within a few yards of Private First Class Earl E. Zweifel's machinegun position and threw a grenade at him, he picked up the grenade and tossed it back. It exploded just as he released it, seriously injuring both his hands; nevertheless, he continued firing his machinegun and thus enabled his comrades to make a safe withdrawal and prevented his machinegun from enemy capture. For this action he was awarded the Silver Star.

At 1400 hours on the afternoon of May 6th, squadron and troop commanders were assembled at the regimental command post by Colonel Walter E. Finnegan. Also present were liaison officers from the 947th, 61st, 82nd and 99th Field Artillery Battalions. An order was issued for a coordinated attack by combat teams on the nine distinctive knolls that formed the main hill mass southeast of the sawmill. The attack was to begin at 0730 on May 7th, preceded by an artillery preparation. The 1st Squadron was assigned the right sector of the regimental zone of action, with the 2nd Squadron on the left.

The attack was executed with the utmost precision. Taking advantage of the accurate artillery fire and Fifth Air Force bombing and strafing, the troops moved in aggressively, trapped entire enemy units in their caves, and captured the high ground, leaving scattered enemy remnants in the draws to be dealt with by reserve elements. By 1140, the first objective knolls had been secured, although the troops now exposed on bare ridges which had been cleared of growth by the repeated bombings, artillery and mortar fire, were receiving harassing small arms fire from a displaced small enemy group retreating along the high ground south of the sawmill area.

A total of 18 large caves were destroyed with scores of caves and bunkers demolished by engineer units working feverishly throughout the day using three and four satchel charges on each cave. A steady stream of native carriers brought demolitions, rations, and ammunition forward and by day's end 7th Cavalry troopers had killed 173 Japanese. Regimental losses were three killed and 15 wounded. Guerrillas who worked with our troops suffered one killed and two wounded. One field piece, which had fired sporadically and wildly during the attack, could not be found; however, it could have been hidden in one of the caves and buried when the cave was demolished.

By 1800 hours, elements of the 2nd Squadron, 8th Cavalry, attached to the regiment and held in reserve, had closed behind the 7th Cavalry Regiment and occupied the newly won ground. This freed the 2nd Squadron, 7th Cavalry, to continue its mission on the north side of the Infanta road toward the nursery and permitted the 1st Squadron to continue its advance to gain the high ground of the sawmill horseshoe and eventually close with the 2nd Squadron at the nursery.

At 0730 on May 8th, after experiencing an uneventful night, the 1st Squadron continued the assault south of the sawmill over a series of minor ridgelines containing elaborate entrenchments and caves. Troop C led the 1st Squadron advance, but the nature of the terrain caused Major Adams to broaden the squadron front by sending Troop B up on the left of Troop C. Troop

A continued to clear the rear of the squadron and protect its own line of communication. A cave that had been destroyed on the previous day was found to contain 15 enemy dead mixed in the debris. Upon examination it was found that other caves contained large stores of rice, medical supplies and clothing. Troop B patrols filtered down into the sawmill area and made a thorough search of the buildings left standing after the bombings, however, no enemy was found on this low ground as they had moved to the high ground south of the mill.

Sergeant Lonnie A. Horton, Troop A, made an important contribution to the success of the attack on the sawmill when he led his squad in a headlong rush at a Japanese pillbox, and in so doing routed 15 of the enemy.

The 2nd Squadron moved more rapidly on the north side of the road against negligible opposition and few emplacements, and by 1800 hours, leading patrols had made an advance of 2,000 yards and were looking down into the nursery area. Troop E generally followed the Infanta road, by-passed the sawmill area and established a road block approximately 600 yards beyond the sawmill. One abandoned enemy truck was found close to the road block where attempted camouflage of the vehicle had failed to hide it from strafing planes.

7th Cavalry elements killed 58 enemy troops and destroyed 30 caves while suffering only one killed during the day's action.

All resistance in the sawmill area had been broken by the morning of the 9th as the 1st Squadron drove forward to move abreast of the 2nd Squadron which had seized the nursery area. Troop E established a road block at the junction of the nursery and Infanta Roads. By 1500 hours all 1st Squadron troops had closed in the area 500 yards northeast of the road junction and were disposed around the high ground on the horseshoe, having advanced approximately 3,000 yards. Four more abandoned enemy trucks and one sedan were passed as the regiment moved along the road, and squadron patrols and local security elements killed seven Japanese.

Up to this time the Infanta road had not offered a suitable perimeter to which the necessary command post equipment could be brought forward. Frequent rains had made stretches of the main supply route impassable; however, elements of the 8th Engineer Squadron had repaired five bridges in the sawmill area, allowing the command group, along with the 99th Field Artillery Battalion, to move forward to the nursery area. The regimental Weapons Troop was posted at the sawmill and undertook the task of training newly arrived replacements.

Following the breakthrough at the sawmill, Colonel Walter E. Finnegan directed the regiment to advance in a column of squadrons, 2nd Squadron in the lead, on Infanta. Flank patrols checked each trail that branched off the main supply route for a distance of 1,000 yards. Frequent small patrol contacts resulted in 24 enemy killed, and forward elements had advanced approximately five miles toward their final objective of Infanta by May 11th. Colonel Finnegan, at the forward command post, was informed by Major William Frey that 2nd Squadron patrols had reached a destroyed bridge just ahead of the main body of the squadron, and that it was evi-

dent that the Japanese had retreated in great haste, but had destroyed several bridges which would prevent the use of the main supply route by vehicles. In addition, incessant rains west of the divide between Binangonan Point on the east coast and Siniloan, had rendered the road impassable at many points. It was then decided to move the regiment by foot to the east coast while a supporting artillery battery and a forward group moved to Mauban and by LCMs to Binangonan Point.

Each man was given three days emergency rations before departing, and on May 12th, the squadrons advanced to the coast with the 2nd Squadron in advance and the 1st Squadron in support. The only communication with the main body was by the 99th Field Artillery radios which contacted the marching troops from a small plane.

On May 12th, the 7th Cavalry command group, consisting of Colonel Finnegan, Lt. Colonel Branson, Captain Eric D. Berguist, the Regimental S-2, and a part of the S-2-3 section, moved by water to Mauban, arriving at 1800 hours. By nightfall the forward elements had reached the point where the road turns northeast from the Labayat River. Here they met their first opposition as the advance guard of the squadron clashed with the rear guard of the retreating Japanese. The advanced guard suffered five guerrilla casualties — two killed and three wounded — and one American was wounded. During the day's march, 14 Japanese had been killed.

The 7th Cavalry rear command post departed from the nursery area at 1230 hours on the 13th, and returned to their former perimeter near Siniloan. The Weapons Troop remained at the sawmill carrying out patrol missions.

On the morning of May 13th, the 2nd Squadron moved out and by 1500 hours forward elements had reached the coast. The 1st Squadron, marching behind the 2nd Squadron, moved swiftly and within 24 hours closed on the 2nd Squadron. The following day the 1st Squadron sent strong combat patrols north along the coast from Binangoan Point as far as the Kilulurom River. Patrols had minor contacts only, but the fleeing enemy had left behind eight trucks, one sedan, and seven cases of dynamite which were seized by the patrols. 2nd Squadron patrols which searched south along the coast for 2,000 yards found no evidence of an enemy retreat in that direction.

On May 15th, the regimental forward command post arrived by patrol craft at the bivouac area of the 7th Cavalry Regimental Combat Team (RCT) which had moved north from Binangoan Point some 2,000 yards. LCMs were attached and stationed at Mauban, 2-1/2 hours by water to the south.

The 2nd Squadron, which had been resupplied with rations, again took up the advance in front of the RCT and by 1300 hours had reached the south bank of the Kilulurom River. At this point the Japanese set up a small delaying action on the north bank of the river. Small arms fire from across the river caused one killed and one wounded in the 2nd Squadron. However, seven of the enemy were killed and probably four more wounded. The 2nd Squadron was unable to cross the river and moved back prior to dark. Early the next day, a Troop G patrol received small arms, machinegun, mortar, and some artillery fire from an enemy position on a ridgeline 300 yards inland from the coast. The patrol withdrew after 81mm fire had been placed on the enemy position.

On May 17th, the 1st Squadron passed through the 2nd Squadron position at the Kilulurom River with the objective of taking Real. The 7th Cavalry RCT now had in support two sections of Battery B, 99th Field Artillery Battalion, and Company A, 85th Chemical Battalion (minus). The 27th Philippine Station Hospital arrived at Binangonan Point and performed emergency operations and arranged for the more seriously wounded to be evacuated by Catalina Flying Boats. Advancing along the beach road to Real, the 1st Squadron deployed Troop A on the east of the road and assigned Troop B the mission of cleaning out the enemy which had been pin-pointed by 2nd Squadron patrols on the ridges to the west of the road. A Japanese force, estimated to be 50 to 100 men, supported by machinegun and mortar units, fought determinedly to halt the advance, but after effectively using 4.2-inch and 81mm mortar barrages, the enemy forces were gradually driven back. These engagements were marked by fierce close-in fighting, with the rugged cavalrymen using rifle grenades, bazookas and hand grenades to dislodge the enemy from the rock crevices along the beach.

It was near Real that Captain Christian Gronbeck, Jr., added to his distinguished record of bravery and self-sacrifice as a 7th Cavalry surgeon. When the advance party of his squadron was unexpectedly taken under fire at close range, two troopers were killed and a third seriously wounded. Realizing that vital time would be lost if he waited for the squadron to launch an attack so that the wounded man could be evacuated without danger, Captain Gronbeck crawled 20 yards into enemy territory to the side of the casualty. Although two enemy bullets ripped through his clothing, he remained unscathed and succeeded in dragging his patient back to safety where he administered medical care.

The next day, May 18th, three other 7th Cavalry men distinguished themselves and were later awarded Silver Stars. Private First Class Edward J. Biernacki lost his life in a gallant attempt to rescue a wounded comrade under fire, and Corporal John M. Olguin crawled 50 yards through dense underbrush with both friendly and enemy fire crashing around him to assist two wounded men to safety. He carried one and led the other back to the security of their own lines. Lieutenant Joe D. Crane, of Troop A, led his flank guard platoon in an attack against the enemy, annihilating 15 of them and capturing two machineguns and 12 rifles, thereby preventing what might have been a disaster for the troop.

On May 21st, after four days of bitter fighting, Real was captured. Once Real had been secured and patrolled, the 1st Squadron moved out on the road to Infanta. Realizing a hard-pressed enemy could not reorganize, contact was not broken and patrols again met resistance at Cawayan Creek, 1,000 yards north of Real. Troop B, after securing the peninsula north of Real, was relieved by one platoon of Troop A and joined Troop C on Cawayan Creek and, as

darkness closed in, they were still engaged at this point. During the night of May 20th-21st, an unknown number of Japanese attempted to infiltrate the Troop G perimeter, and morning revealed six enemy dead in front of their positions.

On May 22nd, Troop D led the attack toward Gumian. As this troop was consolidating a newly gained position, a Japanese force of about 150 counterattacked with mortars, machineguns, rifles, and grenades. The ferocity of the attack and the excellent concealment afforded by the dense foliage enabled the enemy to come within ten yards of the perimeter before being detected. Three men particularly distinguished themselves during this action and were later awarded Silver Stars. Technical Sergeant Pirtle H. Kennett stood erect-fully exposed to enemy view and fire — so that he could better direct the operations of his machinegunners; Private William A. Harden manned his machinegun until it was disabled by enemy fire and then held the Japanese at bay with his carbine while his assistant went to the rear and procured a new steam condensing hose to replace the one which had been shot away; and Lieutenant Charles E. Paul, who, after taking the precaution of ordering his men to remain under cover of their foxholes, returned to his observation post and directed mortar fire with such deadly close-in accuracy that the enemy was forced to withdraw and leave behind many dead and large quantities of weapons and ammunition.

On the morning of May 23rd, the 2nd Squadron took the lead, passing through the 1st Squadron at Cawayan Creek. One skirmish with the enemy near Tigbu Creek resulted in 30 enemy dead and three prisoners captured without a casualty suffered by the squadron. By 1300 hours on the 23rd, the 2nd Squadron had secured Gumjan — one more stepping stone on the road to Infanta. Here the Gumian trail led from the National road west toward the Agos river, and while the remainder of the squadron continued patrolling in the Gumjan area, Troop G, under Lieutenant Hall, probed the trail for 500 yards where they ran into an enemy trail block.

On this date, another patrol from Troop F composed mainly of new replacements who were receiving instructions in patrolling, ran into a superior enemy force and the platoon sergeant was seriously wounded. Private First Class Jack Lambert assumed command and took over the responsibility of extricating the patrol from its critical situation. Realizing that reinforcements were urgently needed, Private First Class Lambert ran through enemy fire across an open field and on to his troop where he gave information of the best route to be used in outflanking the enemy. Then, fearing that his inexperienced men might make the mistake of firing on the rescue party, he raced back across the open field and directed their actions. His calm, cool leadership permitted the wounded and the patrol to be safely withdrawn.

It was evident that the Gumian trail was being used as an enemy evacuation route, and on May 24th the remainder of the squadron swung to the left of the National road, wiped out the resistance which had halted Troop G, and continued to patrol the area west of Real to the Agos River. By nightfall, forward patrols had

cleared the enemy from this area and joined forces with the 1st Squadron elements at Comun — only 2,000 yards south of Infanta. Skirmishes with scattered pockets of Japanese added another 35 dead to the steadily mounting number of enemy casualties.

The 2nd Squadron, 8th Cavalry, following close behind this steady advance, had placed guards on bridges and established road blocks along the line of communications. One platoon from Troop C, 8th Engineer Squadron, repaired a Japanese bypass on the Pulo River and detonated two ashcantype mines the Japanese had left behind. On the morning of May 25th, forward elements of the 1st Squadron infiltrated into Infanta. Troop C was given the mission to "clean out" the city while Troop B, with guerrilla elements attached, swung south to reconnoiter Lual. When it was certain that the 1st Squadron would not need Troop A to support the attack on Infanta, this troop was dispatched to Anibong. Thus, initial efforts began to clear all enemy east of the National road to the beach. Meanwhile, 2nd Squadron elements were patrolling west and southwest of Infanta in the vicinity of Agosagos and as far north as Pamplona. Banugaw and Pilaway were also covered in patrol routes — these barrios consisting only of a few Nipa huts in which small groups of the enemy were attempting to use as hideouts. Patrol reports at the end of the day revealed that 25 Japanese had been killed.

On May 26th, 1st Squadron patrols were widespread; Troop C sent a reinforced platoon across the Agos River approximately 2,000 yards northwest of Infanta and Troop A patrolled as far as Alitas — 6,000 yards south of Infanta. Here in Alitas evidence of Japanese atrocities to the civilians was uncovered. Excited and thankful civilians who welcomed our troops reported that the Japanese had killed 200 of the total population of 300. During the day 13 prisoners were taken and 33 Japanese killed. The 2nd Squadron, from its bivouac on the south bank of the Agos River near Banugan, continued extensive patrolling south and southwest along the bank of the Agos River with only minor enemy contact.

During the period from May 26th to June 1st, an average of 25 Japanese were killed each day by the various patrols. The 1st Squadron operated generally in the Anoling area. The 2nd Squadron patrolled the San Cristobal valley area and as far south along the west bank of the Agos River as Batangan. The 2nd Squadron, 8th Cavalry, continued to hold a position on the Gumian trail and sent contact patrols to meet the 2nd Squadron, 7th Cavalry. Over what had been a long tough road from Binangonan Point to Infanta, the regiment had reached their objective — Infanta, cleared the entire Infanta area east of the Agos River and pushed the remaining Japanese west into the hills along the Agos River. It had been two weeks of hard fighting against a determined enemy who was well supplied and well fortified in previously constructed bunkers.

On June 1st, just before dawn, about 30 Japanese soldiers attacked the Troop F perimeter near Infanta. Sergeant Jessie Riddell saw one of his comrades engaged in hand-to-hand combat with a Japanese officer armed with a Samurai sword, and ran to the rescue, pausing en route to kill three of the infiltrating enemy with his rifle. He shot the officer who had narrowly missed killing his comrade by thrusting the sword through his jacket. He was awarded the Oak-leaf cluster to his Silver Star (won at Mt. Malepunyo) for this action. On the same date, a patrol from Troop B was patrolling near Gumjan when Japanese rifle fire came at them unexpectedly from nearby bushes. Private Bernis E. Stringer rushed forward firing his automatic rifle from his hip, killing one Japanese, wounding another and then reloaded his weapon in plain sight of another whom he quickly killed. He was awarded the Silver Star for this action.

The enemy had suffered 502 killed and graves uncovered by mortar barrages indicated even greater enemy losses. Most of the 66 prisoners who surrendered were Formosans. The regiment suffered 14 killed and 40 wounded while the attached guerrilla elements had 12 killed and 14 wounded.

June 1st marked what might be termed a subphase of the Siniloan-Infanta phase, in that the entire area west of the Agos River from Anoling to the north, to Real to the south, was sufficiently cleared of enemy resistance for the 7th Cavalry RCT to direct its attention to the hills west of the Agos River. The 310th Bomb Wing of the Fifth Air Froce began extensive bombing and strafing of enemy concentration areas along the Ikdan Creek, the Mr. Ashna hill mass, the Llamba Creek, and the junction formed by the confluence of the Kanan and Kaliva Rivers. The air strikes were made on the basis of intelligence reports and reconnaissance flights which located new trails clearly marked after periods of rain. Bombing and strafing continued throughout the month of June and 93 tons of bombs were dropped.

The 2nd Squadron, 8th Cavalry, was relieved.on. June 6th and did not take part in the remaining action at Infanta.

On June 5th, the Regimental Reconnaissance Platoon and Troops F and G were ordered to move by way of the Real-Binangonan Point road to report to the 2nd Cavalry Brigade upon arrival at Siniloan. The troops departed from Real at 0730 hours and on the same day the 7th Cavalry Regimental command post moved from Real to Infanta, 2,000 yards south of the Agos River and 300 yards from the coast. On June 6th, the 1st Squadron at Gumian sent Troop B under Captain Wilbur B. Jackson along the Gumian trail to what was later called "Baker Hill." This knoll blocked all enemy approaches west from the Agos valley. Major W.O. Frey, then commanding the 2nd Squadron, located his command post on the east bank of the Agos River near Pamplona and sent Captain Dorsey Barton and Troop E across the river to form a perimeter south of the Binuang River. 2nd Squadron patrols then began operating in the San Cristobal valley as far south as Batangan.

When word was received on June 7th that units from the 7th Cavalry would proceed to the junction of the Agos and Kaliva Rivers to meet elements from the 8th Cavalry coming up from the south, Colonel Finnegan, commander of the 7th Cavalry, decided to send the 1st Squadron on this mission and to leave the 2nd Squadron to patrol the Infanta and San Cristobal valley

areas. At 0700, on June 7th, Major Houck Spencer, in command of the 1st Squadron, moved his troops out on what was to prove to be three weeks of travelling over tortuous trails against an enemy fighting desperately to guard their escape route to the north. Major Spencer was forced to leave all but one 81mm mortar behind, using the other mortar crews to carry ammunition; however, batteries of the 99th Field Artillery Battalion were in direct support during the entire operation.

Leading elements of the squadron met their first resistance at Laguyang Creek, a small tributary which flows into the Agos river from the south where the Gumian trail joins the river. Three or four machinegun positions with supporting rifle men blocked the narrow trail until Troop C, led by Lieutenant John R. Boehme, cut their way south through the dense growth. The troop flanked the enemy position and killed several although a few managed to escape. This was but one of a series of encounters at each creek that the squadron crossed, namely Bisol, Mabatobato, and Quipagringan. During the nights, troop perimeters along the trail were not bothered by infiltration, but the enemy would harass the troops by firing six or seven mortar rounds in the vicinity without causing damage, while displacing their mortars from one position to another.

By the time the 1st Squadron reached Quipagringan Creek on June 16th, most of the enemy force had been engaged and broken. The last attempt was made to halt the advance of the 1st Squadron at Lusa Creek, but an observation plane spotted the enemy from the air and scattered them by directing artillery fire on their positions. 1st Squadron troops moved in quickly and engaged the fleeing enemy with machine gun and automatic rifle fire. The area around Lusa

Creek was secured on the 17th, and as the terrain opened at the mouth of the creek it was used as a drop zone for rations dropped from C-47 planes. Lusa Creek is 7,000 yards west of the National road which runs through Real. The terrain slowed the evacuation of 1st Squadron casualties to three days, which by this time had reduced the squadron to one-half of its normal combat strength. Relay stations established at Bisal Creek and Baker Hill, using Troop G and the Regimental Reconnaissance Platoon, respectively, at these positions, relieved the situation considerably as helicopters were not available.

Troops, wearied by seven months of combat, took the final objective in the Luzon campaign, on June 19th, clearing all resistance east of the Kaliva River. Up to this time the squadron had killed a total of 330 Japanese and captured several light and heavy machine guns along with other small arms along the south bank of the Agos River. Until June 26th, when the order to withdraw the 7th Cavalry RCT from the Infanta area was issued, the 1st Squadron continued to patrol in the Agos River area clearing small enemy groups still hiding in the draws and hills. All attempts to cross to the north side of the Agos River were futile due to the swift current and depth of the river. Rubber boats were dropped by small planes but could not be used in the rapids. Lieutenant Boehme, commander of Troop C, volunteered to swim across the river with a small patrol, but only two of the strongest swimmers reached the far bank, as enemy snipers on the slope across the river harassed the other men in the stream.

While the 1st Squadron was in the Agos valley, the 2nd Squadron (minus) continued to patrol in the San Cristobal valley. The complete breakdown of enemy resistance was noted by the staggering number of prisoners which sur-

Four American Leaders salute as "Old Glory" is raised above the American Embassy in Tokyo, Sept. 8, 1945. L to R: Major Gen. William C. Chase, Commander 1st Cavalry Division; Admiral William Halsey; Lt. Gen. Robert L. Eichelberger; and General of the Army Douglas MacArthur. U.S. Army photo.

Standing in prayer after the first American flag was raised over the American Embassy in Tokyo, Sept. 8, 1945. L to R front row: Admiral William Halsey; Lt. Gen. Robert L. Eichelberger; General of the Army Douglas MacArthur. U.S. Army Photo

General MacArthur's limousine in front of GHQ, Tokyo, Japan, in October 1945. Courtesy of Roy Blumenauer.

rendered to 7th Cavalry troops. Upon its return from 2nd Cavalry Brigade control, 17 June, Troop F under Lieutenant Feeley, moved to Catablingan Creek 2,000 yards north, up the coast from Agos River to receive prisoners coming in from the vicinity of Gabriel point. Captain Berguist, Regimental S-2, who had employed the services of the "trusties" in effecting the capture of many prisoners, reported 435 were taken prisoner since leaving Real, 596 Japanese had been killed and 11 wounded. The regiment's casualties during this period were 11 killed and 36 wounded, while the attached guerrillas lost five killed and 13 wounded.

The last Silver Star to be won by a member of the First Cavalry Division during the Luzon campaign was awarded to Sergeant Clyde C. Bohannon as he led a patrol from Troop B against a camouflaged enemy position in the hills near Infanta to rescue a wounded comrade from the line of fire.

On June 27th, the 1st Squadron troops departed from Infanta by LCM arriving at Mauban at 1800 hours and then proceeded by motor to the 7th Cavalry base camp near Sariaya. Between June 27th and July 28th, the 7th Cavalry RCT shuttled troops and supplies to its base camp using 32 LCMs. Elements of the 2nd Squadron remained at Infanta until July 28th to guard southeast of Infanta and by 2100 hours, the final elements of the regiment closed in Sariaya, and the Luzon campaign officially ended at 2400 on June 30th.

Lieutenant Colonel William L. Nash in command of the 7th Cavalry rear echelon, consisting of replacements and men released from the hospital, had constructed enough of the base camp to permit all of the returning men to move directly into tents with elaborate bamboo furnishings. Work was continued on camp construc-

tion and efforts were directed toward a training program for new replacements to prepare the 7th Cavalry for future operations.

During the Siniloan-Infanta phase, the 7th Cavalry had killed a total of 1,019 Japanese and captured 766. During the entire Luzon campaign (January 27th to June 30th) the regiment lost 145 killed, 37 died of wounds, 603 wounded and two missing, while inflicting 3,146 losses upon the enemy.

During the period January 27th to July 2nd the S-4 camp made 17 displacements by truck covering a total distance of 456 miles.

The entire regiment enjoyed a much-needed period of rest and rehabilitation at Sariaya until August 10th, when it entrucked at Lucena at 0730 hours and boarded the USS "Briscoe" at Canada Beach for a six-day amphibious training operation in connection with the anticipated landing in Japan.

On August 13th, a warning order was received from General MacArthur's Headquarters stating that the First Cavalry Division had been selected to accompany the Supreme Commander into Tokyo and be a part of the Eighth Army in the occupation of Japan. On August 22nd, the regiment boarded the USS "Duel" and sailed with the Division from Batangas Bay on August 25th. The following day a typhoon warning forced the convoy to make an overnight halt in Subic Bay, but on August 27th, the convoy headed out again steaming northward through the China Sea toward the Japanese homeland. On September 2nd, the long convoy steamed into Yokohama Harbor, past the big battleship, the USS "Missouri," where a little while later, General MacArthur received the Japanese surrender party.

At 1100 hours on September 2nd, the regiment made an assault landing on the beaches of Yokohama with other elements of the Division.

The big difference in this assault landing and the others of the past two years was the fact that there was no pre-invasion bombardment and no resistance was encountered. The following day the regiment moved to the Zama Military Academy nearby.

At 0800 hours on September 8th, a h1storymaking motor convoy left the Yokohama area for Tokyo. Headed by Major General William C. Chase, Commanding General of the First Cavalry Division, the party included a veteran from each troop in the Division so that all units would be represented in this historic climax of the war. Passing through Hachioji, Fuchu and Chofu, the convoy halted briefly at the Tokyo city limits. General Chase stepped across the line thereby putting the American Army officially in Tokyo and added another "First" to the record of the "First Team."

Also on September 8th, General MacArthur made his official entry into the city escorted by the 2d Squadron, 7th Cavalry Regiment, under the command of Major William W. West, III; the 302nd Reconnaissance Troop; the Division Band; and an impressive array of the Division and Regimental colors and troop guidons. At the American Embassy, General MacArthur gave the following instructions to Lieutenant General Robert L. Eichelberger, Commanding General of the Eighth Army:

"Have our country's flag unfurled and in the Tokyo sun, let it wave in its full glory as a symbol of hope for the oppressed and as a harbinger of victory for the right."

While veteran cavalrymen raised the flag atop the American Embassy building, their comrades stood at attention as the Division Band played the National Anthem. The flag was the one which had been flying over the Nation's Capitol in Washington D.C., on Pearl Harbor Day and had flown over the Battleship "Missouri" while the surrender documents were being signed. The Flag, of Liberation was also the first American flag to be flown over Rome, Italy, at the conclusion of hostilities with that country and over Berlin after VE-Day.

This flag is now in the National Capitol and was delivered to Senator Vandenberg and House Speaker Martin on April 6th, 1948, by Major General Hobart R. Gay, then commanding the First Cavalry Division.

On this same morning the remainder of the regiment moved to the Yoyogi drill field located in the Meiji Inner Shrine in Tokyo.

The Division's first mission in Tokyo was to assume control of the central portion of the city. Troops of the 7th Cavalry guarded the American Embassy where General MacArthur had taken up residence, and the Meiji Shrine, one of the most sacred areas in Japan according to Japanese belief. Daily patrols began the long task of locating, investigating and reporting all Japanese installations which had contributed to the nation's war effort. All arsenals, factories, barracks, and storage grounds had to be examined and reports made of their contents. In addition, the Division was concerned with the status of demobilization of the Japanese armed forces.

An important project during the early days of the occupation was to find adequate housing facilities for the troops. Although September was not a particularly cold month in Japan, the tent camp at Yoyogi proved unsuitable as winter quarters for troopers whose blood had been thinned by two years in the tropics. A typhoon, which damaged the camp on September 16th, emphasized the need for more permanent billets. By September 25th the entire regiment had moved into the Merchant Marine School in Tokyo.

On September 25th, a great turnover of personnel began in the regiment which continued for the next several months and added considerably to the difficulties of carrying out the occupation mission. Men with high adjusted service rating scores were transferred to the 43rd Infantry Division for shipment home and discharge. Later, as other units were inactivated or returned to the United States, many low point men were transferred to the regiment to complete their tours of duty; however these additions and the few replacements which came over directly from the United States did not equal the losses through redeployment, and by the end of the year. (Scores were computed based on the number of months in combat, months in service, decorations, etc.)

The remainder or the year was spent in occupation duties including the seizing and disposing of munitions, inventorying precious items captured by the Japanese, and conducting patrols in search of hidden Japanese implements of war.

Again the traditional American peacetime penuriousness set in and the characteristic postwar frantic demobilization of the U.S. Army left the regiment on duty in Japan with a skeleton force incapable of efficiently accomplishing its occupation mission, much less maintaining a combat capability. The atomic bomb panacea left the American public without a deep-seated urge to maintain a sharp saber and the "fat was cut" from the military budget which only resulted in hamstringing combat units throughout the Army.

About the time the regiment began to recover from the disastrous post-war demobilization, the Communist hordes invaded the Republic of Korea-South Korea. As the Red tide swept southward in Korea unabated, the regiment was frantically thrown into conflict for which it was ill prepared.

During the Korean War the regiment's desperate battles, fought amid the stinking rice paddies and barren wind-swept frozen hills of Korea, cost the regiment more than 600 killed, 3500 wounded, and 300 missing in action. Assigned with the regiment during the first year, included the gallant Greek Battalion (GEF), as part of the United Nations Forces. The Korean War ended with an Armistice Agreement on 27 July 1953. It did not end the Korean War, it only ended the fighting. The DMZ is a constant reminder that the war is not over.

The 7th Cavalry Regiment is the patriarch of the modern Army's organizational family. The modern pentomic units scattered worldwide that bear the name "7th Cavalry," have inherited a proud 128-year-old history. Throughout these years, GARRYOWEN has been synonymous with esprit de corps throughout the military profession. Today's modern Army 7th Cavalry troopers are the custodians of this esprit resulting from these years of service to Regiment and Nation.

During the Vietnam War, the 7th Cavalry was called upon to meet a new concept in warfare and tactical doctrines in the use of helicopters, which opened the way to a bold, new role in combat for the regiment.

These crack "Skytroopers," as a new Cavalry with an old spirit but young at heart, would fight heroically with determination to destroy the Communist enemy in Vietnam. Many bitter and vicious battles were hard-fought and won, creating another new chapter in the history of the 7th Cavalry Regiment and the United States Army.

Then in August 1990, the 7th Cavalry was alerted for quick deployment to Saudi Arabia for Operation Desert Storm. Again answering the call of their nation, it was a period on intense activity to meet their new task. This time to stop the oppressive enemy army of Saddam Hussein and to restore freedom to the country of Kuwait.

It was a new generation of American soldiers who were highly trained and skilled to do their jobs efficiently, with the best military weaponry in the world. In Operation Desert Storm, the 7th Cavalry used tactics by probing and jabbing with lightly armored Bradley and Cobra vehicles against the enemy positions in Iraq. This would make way and guide the MIAI tanks of the First Cavalry Division into battle.

The Persian Gulf War soon was over and the freedom of a small country preserved. Once again, it showed the world that aggression will not be tolerated. Within the Army organization, the 7th Cavalry exemplified that it always will be ready to fight, any time, any where and win. Furthermore, our Nation demands it, and our freedom depends on it. GARRYOWEN.

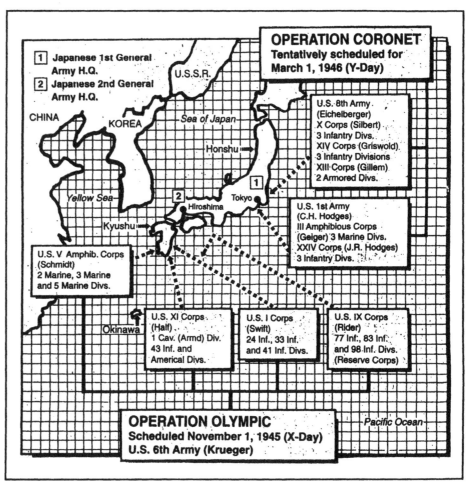

Both Olympic and Coronet Operations were under the control plans of Operation Downfall, which was the invasion of Japan during World War II. Map courtesy of the National Military Archives.

APPENDICES

Regimental Command and Organization

The following indicates the strength at the end of each year during the regiment's existance. It is interesting to note that the strength of the 7th Cavalry Regiment—as was the case with the entire American Army—fluctuated with the existing conditions of world peace. During periods of relative world calm the regiments's strength dwindled to almost cadre force while during war, or the threat of war, the strength suddenly shot upward and frequent reorganizations took place. These frequent reorganizations were due in part to the necessity for bringing the regiment to wartime strength, and in part to keeping abreast of the times as new weapons, tactics, and techniques were introduced into warfare.

The organizational changes shown include only those affecting entire units in the regiment. In addition to those shown, the regiment underwent a great number of minor organizational changes which resulted in adding or deleting a small number of personnel in different units, or in equipment changes.

Year	Regimental Strength Officer/ Enlisted	Year	Regimental Strength Officer/ Enlisted
1866	14/937	1906	50/970
1867	41/993	1907	50/1057
1868	42/787	1908	50/1088
1869	36/981	1909	50/646
1870	41/758	1910	45/905
1871	42/922	1911	49/1194
1872	43/957	1912	50/991
1873	43/743	1913	48/984
1874	41/797	1914	49/786
1875	44/1162	1915	28/934
1876	44/870	1916	52/1464
1877	43/784	1917	77/1536
1878	43/704	1918	44/863
1879	43/786	1919	35/1046
1880	43/610	1920	35/341
1881	42/696	1921	39/630
1882	42/739	1922	31/610
1883	42/764	1923	34/559
1884	42/722	1924	33/541
1885	43/594	1925	33/508
1886	43/689	1926	33/534
1887	43/743	1927	33/600
1888	43/705	1928	31/547
1889	42/616	1929	29/409
1890	43/617	1930	27/514
1891	43/616	1931	30/446
1892	43/632	1932	32/531
1893	43/645	1933	35/545
1894	43/656	1934	35/594
1895	43/630	1935	30/682
1896	45/597	1936	35/648
1897	39/1199	1937	34/655
1898	44/1053	1938	30/625
1899	46/1108	1939	54/1068
1900	49/967	1940	71/1014
1901	49/798	1941	76/1432
1902	51/749	1942	83/1881
1903	51/845	1943	101/1911
1904	49/817	1944	109/1765
1905	51/717	1945	

Organizational Change

The 7th Cavalry Regiment (consisting of the Field & Staff Troops A, B, C, D, E, F, G, H, I, K, L, and M) was constituted by Act of Congress, 28 Jul 1866, and War Department General Order 56, 1 Aug 1866, organized 1 Sep-22 Dec 1866, at Fort Riley, Kansas, War Department General Order 92, 1866

Personnel carried on the rolls of their individual companies and detailed for duty in Regimental Band were dropped from company rolls and carried on the rolls of the Regimental Field & Staff; AGO Circular 19 Apr 1870.

Troops L and M skeletonized, War Department General Order 79, 25 Jul, 1890.
Troop L filled with Indian troops, War Department General Order 28, 9 Mar 1891.

Last of Indians discharged from Troop L, 31 May 1897.

A provisional machine gun platoon appears on the strength returns for the month of September 1910.

Supply Troop, Machine Gun Troop and Headquarters Troop organized 28 Jul 1916, Act of Congress 3 Jun 1916.
Regiment was assigned to 15th Cavalry Division December 1917-May 1918. Troop C was designated as Recruit Troop and Troop 1 as Remount Troop 20 Feb 1917.
The regiment was reorganized under T/O 423P, 1920-21; assigned as an organic element of 2nd Cavalry Brigade, 1st Cavalry Division; Supply Troop redesignated Service Troop; Troop D redesignated Headquarters Troop, 1st Cavalry Brigade; Troop H redesignated Headquarters Troop, 2nd Cavalry Brigade; Troops I and K were inactive and redesignated Troops I and K, Training Center Squadron #5; Troop E was inactivated and redesignated Headquarters Detachment, Training Center Squadron #5; Troop M was disbanded, effective 15 Sep 1921, AG 320.2 (Misc. Div.), 20 Aug 1921.
Headquarters and Headquarters Detachment, 1st and 2nd Squadrons organized at Fort Bliss, Texas. Machine Gun Troop redesignated Troop A, 2nd Machine Gun Squadron, effective 14 Sep 1921, AG 320.2 (Misc. Div.), 20 Aug 1921.
As a result of these reorganizations, personnel from Troop I were transferred to the remaining lettered companies of the regiment; all personnel from Troop K were transferred to Troop C; all personnel from Troop L were transferred to Troop E; all personnel from Troop M were transferred to Troop A. Active elements upon completion of reorganization were: Headquarters and Headquarters Troop, Service Troop, Troops A, B, C, E, F, G, Headquarters and Headquarters Detachments 1st and 2nd Squadrons.
Troops I, K, and Headquarters Detachment, Training Squadron #5 redesignated Troops I, K, L, 7th Cavalry Regiment, respectively and disbanded, AG 320.2 (15 Jul 1922) Misc. Div., 17 Jul 1922.
Band, 7th Cavalry Regiment was separated from Service Troop and became a separate component, AG 322.94 (4 May 1927), 22 Jun 1927.
The regiment was reorganized under T/O 423P, 1927, effective 1 Feb 1928; Troop A, 2nd Machine Gun Squadron redesignated Machine Gun Troop, 7th Cavalry Regiment, Service Troop, Headquarters Detachment, 1st and 2nd Squadrons, Troops A, B, E & F, AG 320.2 Cav (28 Nov 1927), 15 Dec 1927.
Personnel from Headquarters Detachment and Troop C 2nd Machine Gun Squadron were transferred to various units in the regiment; personnel from Headquarters Detachment, 1st Squadron were transferred to Troops A, B, Headquarters, and Machine Gun Troop; personnel from Troop G were transferred to Troops B, E, F, Headquarters; personnel from Headquarters Detachment were transferred to Headquarters Troop and Troops B and E; personnel from Service Troop were transferred to Troops A, B, E, F, Headquarters. Personnel from Troop C were transferred to Troops A, B, Headquarters and Machine Gun. All transfers were effective

31 Jan 1928. (General Order #1, Headquarters, 1st Cavalry Division, 7 Jan 1928).

The Regiment was reorganized under T/O 2-11, 1938 Headquarters Troop redesignated Headquarters and Service Troop; Special Weapons Troop constituted and remained inactive; Headquarters Detachment, 1st and 2nd Squadrons was activated, AG 320.2 (10 Nov 1938) Misc. (Ret.), 27 Jan 1939.

The regiment was reorganized under T/O 2-11, 1940; Headquarters and Headquarters Detachment, 1st and 2nd Squadrons redesignated Headquarters, 1st and 2nd Squadrons respectively, AG 320.2 (27 Feb 1940) M (Ret.), M-C 22 Mar 1940. Special Weapons Troop was activated at Ft. Bliss, Texas, effective 1 Jul 1940, AG 320.2 (18 Jun 1940) M (Ret.) M-C, 22 Jun 1940. Medical Detachment was constituted; Troops C and G and Medical Detachment activated at Ft. Bliss, Texas, effective 1 Aug 1940, AG 320.2 (9 Jul 1940) M (Ret.) M-C, 16 Jul 1940.

The regiment was reorganized under T/O 2-11, 1942, effective 2 Oct 1942; Headquarters and Service Troop redesignated Headquarters Troop; Special Weapons Troop redesignated Weapons Troop; Machine Gun Troop redesignated Service Troop, AG 221 (3 Jun 1942) EA-M-C, 16 Jun 1942, General Order 8, 1st Cavalry Division, 18 Dec 1942, General Order 16, 1st Cavalry Division, 1 Sep 1942.

Troops D and H, 7th Cavalry Regiment were constituted effective 13 Nov 1943, AG 322 (9 Nov 1943) OB-1-GNGCT, 16 Nov 1943. Troops D and H were activated under TOE 7-18, 1943; Weapons Troop was reorganized under TOE 7-18, 1943, AG 322 (9 Nov 1943) OB-I-GNGCT-M, 13 Nov 1943. Effective 4 Dec 1943.

Troops D and H and Weapons Trop reorganized under TOE 7-18, 1944, effective 26 Jun 1944, AG 320.2 (31 Jul 1943) PE-A-M-C, 20 Aug 1943. Communications Platoon, 1st and 2nd Squadrons reorganized under TOL 7-16, 1944, effective 30 Oct 1944, AG 320.2 (31 Jul 1943) PE-A-M-C, 20 Aug 1943.

The Weapons Troop was redesignated Cannon Troop; Headquarters and Headquarters Detachment, 1st and 2nd Squadrons redesignated Headquarters and Headquarters Troop, 1st and 2nd Squadrons, AG 322 (23 Jun 1945) OB-I-GNGCT-M, 27 Jun, 1945. Effective 20 Jul, 1945, General Order 145, 6th Army, 16 Jul 1945.

Unit Citations

The following citations have been awarded the units of the 7th U.S. Cavalry Regiment for the periods indicated.

All Regimental Units:

All units are authorized the following Campaign Streamers, and when authorized, Campaign Silver Bands placed on the pike or lance of the guidon:

COMBAT PERIOD

INDIAN WARS

1867-1875
1873
1874
1876-1877
1877
November 1890-January 1891

MEXICO

1916-1917

WORLD WAR II

24 Jan 43-31 Dec 44
15 Dec 43-27 Nov 44
15 Dec 44-4 Jul 45
17 Oct 44-1 Jul 45

CAMPAIGNS AND HONORS

Comanches
Montana
Dakota
Little Big Horn
Nez Perces
Pine Ridge
Mexico
New Guinea
Bismarck Archipelago (with assault landing)
Luzon
Leyte (with assault landing)

AUTHORITY

See page 1372, Army Register, 1938; and AR 220-105
AR 220-105
WD GO 12, '46
WD GO 109, '46
DA GO 29, '48
WD GO 109, '46

In addition to the above, the following Unit Citations have been awarded all regimental units:

Extract

Department of the Army
Washington 25, D.C., 28 Dec 1950

GENERAL ORDERS
No. 47

PHILIPPINE PRESIDENTIAL UNIT CITATION
GENERAL — Section I
LIST OF UNITS — Section II

I. GENERAL: Under Paragraph 2, AR 260-15, the award of the Philippine Presidential Unit Citation to the units of the Armed Forces of the United States listed herein in recognition of the participation in the war against the Japanese Empire during the periods 7 Dec 1941, to 10 May 1942, inclusive and 17 Oct 1944 to 4 Jul 1945 inclusive is confirmed.

II. LIST OF UNITS
7th Cavalry Regiment (1st Cavalry Division).
BY ORDER OF THE SECRETARY OF THE ARMY:
J. LAWTON COLLINS
Chief of Staff, U.S. Army
Official:
Edward F. Witsell
Major General, USA
The Adjutant General

Extract

WAR DEPARTMENT
Washington 25, D.C., 19 Jul 1945

GENERAL ORDERS
No. 58

BATTLE HONORS
Citation of Units, Section VII

VII BATTLE HONORS - As authorized by Executive Order 9396 (Sec. I, WD Bul. 22, 1943), superseding Executive Order 9075 (Sec. III, WD Bul. II, 1942), under the provisions of Section IV, WD Circular 333, 1943, in the name of the President of the United States as public evidence of deserved honor and distinction:

3. Troop G, 7th Cavalry, is cited for outstanding performance of duty in action against the enemy at Leyte Province, Philippine Islands, from 12 to 18 Dec 1944. Troop G was assigned the mission of wresting from a determined and fanatic enemy a hill which was the key terrain feature in a defensive scheme preventing a junction of the forces operating in the northern Ormoc Valley. For 15 days previously a squadron had unsuccessfully assaulted the enemy stronghold,

rendered very easy to defend by the very nature of the precipitous mountain terrain and low hanging clouds that made visibility almost negligible. On 12 December, after relieving the squadron and making a thorough reconnaissance of the area, and following a heavy artillery and mortar barrage, Troop G launched its attack, but the assault echelons were stopped immediately by withering machine gun and mortar fire. For three days Troop G continued its attack, sending infiltrating parties into the enemy positions at night to locate machine gun and mortar positions, and tenaciously clinging to all ground gained. On 15 December, combining flame throwers, machine guns, grenades, and rifle fire, Troop G finally penetrated the enemy position, and three days later, after literally gouging the enemy from his positions fox hole by fox hole in a series of hand-to-hand combat engagements, Troop G completely overran the enemy stronghold, which was found to consist of 30 well constructed bunkers, 15 machine guns, 2 BARs, nine mortars and 152 rifles. After the final assault had been completed, 82 enemy dead were counted in the positions and an unknown number were sealed inside their own bunkers by demolition squads. The entrance of Troop G, 7th Cavalry, in this operation, and its determined aggressive and ruthless attack against a numerically superior enemy force enabled a juncture of our forces and marked a turning point in the fighting in the northern Ormoc Valley. (General Orders 51, Headquarters 1st Cavalry Division, 3 Apr 1945, as approved by CG, USA Forces in the Far East.)

By order of the Secretary of War:
G.C. Marshall
Chief of Staff

Official:
Edward F. Witsell
Major General
Acting The Adjutant General

Extract

War Department
Washington 25, D.C., 19 Apr 1946

GENERAL ORDERS
No. 36

BATTLE HONORS - As authorized by Executive Order 9396 (Sec. 1, WD Bul. 22, 1943), superseding Executive Order 9075 (Sec. III, WD Bul. II, 1942), citations of the following units in the general orders indicated are confirmed under the provisions of Section IV, WD Circular 333, 1943, in the name of the President of the United States as public evidence of deserved honor and distinction. The citations read as follows:

4. The 2nd Squadron, 7th Cavalry, reinforced by 2nd Section, Antitank Plat, HQ Troop, 7th Cavalry; P and D Section, Service Troop, 7th Cavalry Liaison and Forward Observers Party; 99th Field Artillery Battalion; 1st Platoon 2nd Collecting Tp, 1st Med. Sq.; Det. 603d Tank Co. is cited for extraordinary gallantry, outstanding courage, determination, and esprit de corps in cracking the Shimbu Line near Antipolo, Luzon, Philippine Islands, from 23 February to 11 Mar 1945. The squadron was assigned the mission of driving through a series of hills between Tay Tay and Antipolo and securing a high escarpment dominating the city of Antipolo and the surrounding area. All hills within the assigned sector had been systematically developed into a huge fortified zone during the Japanese occupation. No entrenchments were visible from the air, or even at close visual range, without intensive terrain study with powerful scopes. Assaulting aggressively, the squadron seized a key terrain feature and was promptly subjected to intense sniper and machine gun fire from all sides. The locations of hostile weapons were practically impossible to determine and the squadron, refusing to withdraw, dug in amid an increasing rate of casualties. That night, and for nine successive nights, the squadron was subjected to intense previously registered mortar, artillery, and rocket barrages. Supply details fought their way in and out to fortify the position and thus reduce the mounting casualty rate. Before

the position could be properly fortified, the aid station was destroyed and the squadron commander and two troop commanders were wounded. Enlisted and officer casualties mounted daily. Grimly determined to continue the assault and fulfill its mission, the squadron ranged in all directions day and night, blowing bunkers and caves and engaging in hand-to-hand fighting against infiltrating parties and counterattacking Japanese. A 47mm antitank gun was destroyed just 30 feet from the perimeter after patrols had bypassed in on three successive days. All patrols endeavoring to remain outside the perimeter in temporary entrenchments were subjected to previously registered barrages from knee mortars, 90mm and 150mm mortars and medium and heavy artillery. Tons of demolitions were utilized in sealing caves containing hostile troops and artillery and mortar positions of all types. Rocket and artillery positions were repeatedly destroyed by 37mm and 75mm guns manhandled to position within the perimeter. Hill faces were burned with white phosphorus from artillery and mortar shells and all spoil of any nature subjected to direct fire. On the 10th day the squadron moved forward, continuing a ferocious offensive plan of systematic reduction of hostile defense. On the 14th day the objective was secured and the area completely mopped up. In the reduction of this fortified area, the squadron, while sustaining over 30 per cent losses, by its aggressive, determined efforts, killed over 1,000 Japanese and destroyed more than 300 bunkers and caves containing numerous artillery, mortar, machine gun and rocket positions. In fulfilling its mission, the 2nd Squadron, 7th Cavalry, with reinforcements, contributed directly to the complete disintegration of organized defense over a wide area and the total destruction of the Shimbu Line (GO 232, HQ 1st Cav. Div., U.S. Armed Forces Pacific, 8 Dec 1945, as approved by the CinC, USA Forces Pacific.)

BY ORDER OF THE SECRETARY OF WAR:
DWIGHT D. EISENHOWER
Chief of Staff
Official:
Edward F. Whitsell
Major General
The Adjutant General

Regimental Medal Of Honor recipients (1866-1945)

The Medal of Honor (the nation's highest award for valor) has been awarded to 45 members of the 7th Cavalry Regiment. All names, organizations and citations shown herein are exactly as they appear in *The Medal of Honor of the United States Army,* published by the Government Printing Office as compiled by the Public Information Division, Department of the Army, 1 Jul 1948.

The greatest number of awards for any single battle, campaign or engagement was made for heroic action during the Battle of the Little Big Horn, 25-26 Jun 1876. However, it is sometimes forgotten that not all of the 7th U.S. Cavalry Regiment were destroyed during that battle, and that two miles away the balance of the divided force fought a three-day action under Major Marcus A. Reno against the Indians. This group not only fought the Indians, but also thirst for three days before being relieved by General Terry's column. Most of the Medals of Honor awarded during this period were made to men who volunteered to make the trips across an area swept by Indian fire in order to bring water to the wounded. The following men were awarded the Medal of Honor for their heroic action during this siege.

Private Neil Bancroft, Company A, who brought water for the wounded under a most galling fire. (Ironically Private Bancroft never actually received the medal. He was discharged from the service 20 Sep 1878, and the award was not issued until 5 Oct 1878. By the time the award was received by the regiment, Bancroft had been discharged from the service and the medal was returned to the War Department. No further attempt was made to locate Bancroft until many years later. By that time he had died, without knowing that he had been awarded the nation's highest award.)

Private Abram B. Brant, Company D, 7th Cavalry, who brought water for the wounded under a most galling fire.

Private Thomas J. Callan, Company B, 7th U.S. Cavalry, who volunteered and succeeded in obtaining water for the wounded of the command, and also displayed conspicuously good conduct in assisting to drive away the Indians.

Sergeant, Benjamin C. Criswell, Company B, 7th U.S. Cavalry, who rescued the body of Lieutenant Hodgson from within the enemy's lines; brought up ammunition and encouraged the men in the most exposed positions under heavy fire.

Corporal Charles Cunningham, Company B, 7th U.S. Cavalry, who declined to leave the line when wounded in the neck during heavy fire and fought bravely all the next day.

Private Frederick Deetline, Company D, 7th U.S. Cavalry, who voluntarily brought water to the wounded under fire.

Sergeant George Geiger, Company H, 7th U.S. Cavalry, who with three companies during the entire engagement courageously held a position that secured water for the command.

Sergeant Richard P. Hanley, Company C, 7th U.S. Cavalry, who recaptured single-handedly and without orders, within the enemy's lines and under a galling fire lasting some 20 minutes, a stampeded pack mule loaded with ammunition.

Private David W. Harris, Company A, 7th U.S. Cavalry, who brought water to the wounded, at great danger to his life under a most galling fire from the enemy.

Private William M. Harris, Company D, 7th U.S. Cavalry, who voluntarily brought water to the wounded under fire of the enemy.

Private Henry Holden, Company D, 7th U.S. Cavalry, who brought up ammunition under a galling fire from the enemy.

Sergeant Rufus D. Hutchinson, Company B, 7th U.S. Cavalry, who guarded and carried the wounded, brought water for the same, and posted and directed the men in this chare under galling fire from the enemy.

Blacksmith Henry W.B. Mechlin, Company H, 7th U.S. Cavalry, who with three comrades during the entire engagement courageously held a position that secured water for the command.

Sergeant Thomas Murray, Company B, 7th U.S. Cavalry, who brought up the pack train, and on the second day the rations, under a heavy fire from the enemy.

Private James Pym, Company B, 7th U.S. Cavalry, who voluntarily went for water and secured the same under heavy fire.

Sergeant Stanislaus Roy, Company A, 7th U.S. Cavalry, who brought water to the wounded at great danger to life and under a most galling fire of the enemy.

Private George Scott, Company D, 7th U.S. Cavalry, who voluntarily brought water to the wounded under fire.

Private Thomas W. Stevens, Company D, 7th U.S. Cavalry, who voluntarily brought water to the wounded under fire.

Private Peter Thompson, Company C, 7th U.S. Cavalry, who after having voluntarily brought water to the wounded, in which effort he was shot through the head, made two more successful trips for the same purpose notwithstanding remonstrance's of his sergeant.

Private Frank Tolan, Company D, 7th U.S. Cavalry, who voluntarily brought water to wounded under fire. Saddler Otto Voit, Company H, 7th U.S. Cavalry, for bravery in action.

Sergeant Charles H. Welch, Company D, 7th U.S. Cavalry, who voluntarily brought water to the wounded, under fire.

Private Charles Windolph, Company H, 7th U.S. Cavalry, who with three comrades, during the entire engagement, courageously held a position that secured water for the command.

Private Theodore W. Goldin, Troop G, 7th U.S. Cavalry, who was one of a party of volunteers who, under a heavy fire from the Indians, went for and brought water to the wounded.

In the action against the Nez Perce tribe on 30 Sep 1877, at Bear Paw Mountain, Montana, four companies of the 7th Cavalry along with four companies of the 2nd Cavalry under Colonel Nelson Miles forced the surrender of Chief Joseph and his band after four days of bloody siege. The following members of the regiment were awarded the Medal of Honor for their gallantry in this action:

Captain Edward S. Godfrey, 7th U.S. Cavalry, who led his command into action when he was severely wounded (see page 75).

Captain Myles Moylan, 7th U.S. Cavalry, who gallantly led his command into action against Nez Perce Indians until himself severely wounded.

The shot that set off the powder keg at Big Foots camp at Wounded Knee Creek on 29 Dec 1890, resulted in a bloody fight which raged for seven hours. There was no chance for orderly direction and each man was forced to fight on his own in the melee which followed. As a result, the following members of the regiment were awarded the Medal of Honor for their acts of heroism during this engagement:

Sergeant William G. Austin, Company E, 7th U.S. Cavalry, who while the Indians were concealed in a ravine, assisted men on the skirmish line, directing their fire, etc., and using every effort to dislodge the enemy.

Private Mosheim Feaster, Company E, 7th U.S. Cavalry, for extraordinary gallantry.

First Lieutenant Ernest A. Garlington, 7th U.S. Cavalry, for distinguished gallantry.

First Lieutenant John C. Gresham, 7th U.S. Cavalry, who voluntarily led a party into a ravine to dislodge Indians concealed therein.

Private Mathew H. Hamilton, Company G, 7th U.S. Cavalry, for bravery in action.

Private George Hobday, Company A, 7th U.S. Cavalry, for conspicuous and gallant conduct in battle.

Private George Hobday, Company A, 7th U.S. Cavalry, for conspicuous and gallant conduct in battle.

Private Marvin C. Hillock, Company B, 7th U.S. Cavalry, for distinguished bravery.

Sergeant George Loyd, Company I, 7th U.S. Cavalry, for bravery, especially after having been severely wounded through the lung.

Sergeant Albert W. McMillan, Company E, 7th U.S. Cavalry, who while engaged with Indians concealed in a ravine, assisted the men on the skirmish line, directed fire, encouraged them by example, and used every effort to dislodge the enemy.

Private Thomas Sullivan, Company E, 7th U.S. Cavalry, for conspicuous bravery in action against Indians concealed in a ravine.

First Sergeant Jacob Trautman, Company I, 7th U.S. Cavalry, who killed a hostile Indian at close quarters, and, although entitled to retirement from service, remained to close the campaign.

Sergeant James Ward, Company B, 7th U.S. Cavalry, who continued to fight after being severely wounded.

Private Hermann Ziegner, Company E, 7th U.S. Cavalry, for conspicuous bravery.

Farrier Richard J. Nolan, Company I, 7th U.S. Cavalry, for bravery.

First Sergeant Theodore Ragnar, Company K, 7th U.S. Cavalry, for bravery.

Captain Charles A. Varnum, Company B, 7th U.S. Cavalry, who, while executing an order to withdraw, seeing that a continuance of the movement would expose another troop of this regiment to being cut off and surrounded, he disregarded orders to retire, placed himself in front of his men, led a charge upon the advancing Indians, regained a commanding position that had just been vacated, and thus insured a safe withdrawal of both detachments without further loss.

Sergeant Bernhard Jetter, Company K, 7th U.S. Cavalry, for distinguished bravery.

Corporal Adam Neder, Company A, 7th U.S. Cavalry, for distinguished bravery.

Department Of The Army Lineage And Honors

7th Cavalry

Constituted by Act of Congress 28 Jul 1866
Organized 1 Sep-22 Dec 1866 at Fort Riley, Kansas
Assigned to 15th Cavalry Division December 1917 to May 1918
Assigned to 1st Cavalry Division 15 Sep 1921
Official Department of the Army Lineage and Honors, 7th Cavalry.

Regimental Commanders
27 Aug 1866-28 Feb 1946

Temporary RANK,RANK	NAME	DATES OF COMMAND
Major, Bvt. Maj. Gen.	John W. Davidson	27 Aug 1866-25 Nov 1866
Colonel, Bvt. Maj. Gen.	Andrew J. Smith*	26 Nov 1866-26 Feb 1867
Lt. Col., Bvt. Maj. Gen.	George A. Custer	26 Feb 1867-4 Mar 1867
Colonel, Bvt. Maj. Gen.	Andrew J. Smith	4-26 Mar 1867
Lt. Col., Bvt. Maj. Gen.	George A. Custer	26 Mar 1867-28 Jul 1867
Major, None	Joel H. Elliot	12 Aug 1867-15 Sep 1867
Major, Bvt. Maj. Gen.	Alfred Gibbs	15 Sep 1867-7 Oct 1868
Lt. Col., Bvt. Maj. Gen.	George A. Custer	7 Oct 1868-7 Jun 1869
Colonel, Bvt. Maj. Gen.	Samuel D. Sturgis	7 Jun 1869-20 Sep 1869
Lt. Col., Bvt. Maj. Gen.	George A. Custer	20 Sep 1869-25 Oct 1869
Colonel, Bvt. Maj. Gen.	Samuel D. Sturgis	25 Oct 1869-31 Aug 1874
Lt. Col., Bvt. Maj. Gen.	George A. Custer	16 Nov 1874-24 Sep 1875**
Major, Bvt. Colonel	Marcus A. Reno	24 Sep 1875-12 Mar 1876
Lt. Col., Bvt. Maj. Gen.	George A. Custer	12-20 Mar 1876
Major, Bvt. Colonel	Marcus A. Reno	20 Mar 1876-11 May 1876
Lt. Col.-Bvt. Maj. Gen.	George A. Custer	11 May 1876-25 Jun 1876
Major, Bvt. Colonel	Marcus A. Reno	25 Jun 1876-18 Oct 1876
Colonel, Bvt. Maj. Gen.	Samuel D. Sturgis	18 Oct 1876-8 Oct 1877***
Lt. Col., Bvt. Colonel	Elmer Otis	7 Jan 1878-28 Feb 1878
Colonel, Bvt. Maj. Gen.	Samuel D. Sturgis	28 Feb 1878-18 Sep 1878
Major, Bvt. Lt. Col.	Joseph G. Tilford	18 Sep 1878-20 Nov 1878
Colonel, Bvt. Maj. Gen.	Samuel D. Sturgis	20 Nov 1878-7 Apr 1879
Major, Bvt. Lt. Col.	Joseph G. Tilford	7 Apr 1879-8 May 1879
Colonel, Bvt. Maj. Gen.	Samuel D. Sturgis	8 May 1879-5 Jan. 1881
Lt. Col., Bvt. Colonel	Elmer Otis	6 Jan 1881-20 May 1881
Colonel, Bvt. Maj. Gen.	Samuel D. Sturgis	20 May 1881-16 Jun 1881
Major, Bvt. Lt. Col.	Joseph G. Tilford	17 Jun 1881-20 Nov 1881
Lt. Col., Bvt. Colonel	Elmer Otis	20 Nov 1881-2 Jun 1882
Major, Bvt. Lt. Col.	Joseph G. Tilford	2 Jun 1882-6 Jul 1882
Lt. Col., Bvt. Col.	Elmer Otis	6 Jul 1882-11 Apr 1883
Major, Bvt. Colonel	Lewis Merrill	12 Apr 1883-25 May 1883
Lt. Col., Bvt. Col.	Andrew W. Evans	25 May 1883-23 Sep 1883
Lt. Col., Bvt. Lt. Col.	Joseph G. Tilford	23 Sep 1883-26 Jun 1885
Colonel, Bvt. Maj. Gen.	Samuel D. Sturgis	27 Jun 1885-17 Nov 1885
Lt. Col., Bvt. Lt. Col.	Joseph G. Tilford	17 Nov 1885-10 Apr 1886
Colonel, Bvt. Maj. Gen.	Samuel D. Sturgis	10 Apr 1886-11 Jun 1886
Lt. Col., Bvt. Lt. Col.	Joseph G. Tilford	11 Jun 1886-26 Jul 1886
Colonel, Bvt. Brig. Gen.	James W. Forsyth	26 Jul 1886-6 May 1887
Lt. Col., Bvt. Lt. Col.	Joseph G. Tilford	6 May 1887-21 Apr 1888
Colonel, Bvt. Brig. Gen.	James W. Forsyth	21 Apr 1888-13 Jun 1888
Lt. Col. Bvt. Lt. Col.	Joseph G. Tilford	13 Jun 1888-16 Sep 1888
Colonel, Bvt. Brig. Gen.	James W. Forsyth	16 Sep 1888-31 May 1889
Major, Bvt. Major	John M. Bacon	31 May 1889-15 Jun 1889
Colonel, Bvt. Brig. Gen.	James W. Forsyth	15 Jun 1889-24 Jul 1889
Major, Bvt. Major	John M. Bacon	24 Jul 1889-3 Aug 1889
Colonel, Bvt. Brig. Gen.	James W. Forsyth	3 Aug 1889-24 Nov 1889
Lt. Col., Bvt. Lt. Col.	Caleb H. Carlton	24 Nov 1889-28 Dec 1889
Colonel, Bvt. Brig Gen.	James W. Forsyth	28 Dec 1889-25 Mar 1890
Lt. Col., Bvt. Lt. Col.	Caleb H. Carlton	25-29 Mar 1890
Colonel, Bvt. Brig. Gen.	James W. Forsyth	29 Mar 1890-10 Apr 1890
Lt. Col., Bvt. Lt. Col.	Caleb H. Carlton	10-30 Apr 1890
Colonel, Bvt. Brig. Gen.	James W. Forsyth	30 Apr 18909-23 Jul 1890
Lt. Col., Bvt. Lt. Col.	Caleb H. Carlton	23 Jul 1890-2 Aug 1890
Colonel, Bvt. Brig. Gen.	James W. Forsyth	2 Aug 1890-15 Oct 1890
Lt. Col., Bvt. Lt. Col.	Caleb H. Carlton	15-21 Oct 1890
Colonel, Bvt. Brig. Gen.	James W. Forsyth	21 Oct 1890-26 Jan 1891
Lt. Col., Bvt. Lt. Col.	Caleb H. Carlton	26 Jan 1891-13 Feb 1891
Colonel, Bvt. Brig. Gen.	James W. Forsyth	13-22 Feb 1891
Lt. Col., Bvt. Lt. Col.	Caleb H. Carlton	22-28 Feb 1891
Colonel, Bvt. Brig. Gen.	James W. Forsyth	28 Feb 1891-14 Mar 1891
Lt. Col., Bvt. Lt. Col.	Caleb H. Carlton	14 Mar 1891-3 May 1891
Colonel, Bvt. Brig. Gen.	James W. Forsyth	3 May 1891-16 Jul 1891
Lt. Col., Bvt. Lt. Col.	Caleb H. Carlton	16-18 Jul 1891
Colonel, Bvt. Brig. Gen.	James W. Forsyth	18 Jul 1891-23 Dec 1891
Lt. Col., Bvt. Lt. Col.	Caleb H. Carlton	23 Dec 1891-3 Jan 1892
Colonel, Bvt. Brig. Gen.	James W. Forsyth	3 Jan 1892-10 Feb 1892
Major, None	Theodore A. Baldwin	10-15 Feb 1892
Colonel, Bvt. Brig. Gen.	James W. Forsyth	15 Feb 1892-29 Dec 1892
Lt. Col., Bvt. Col.	Guy Henry	29 Dec 1892-5 Jan 1893
Colonel, Bvt. Brig. Gen.	James W. Forsyth	5 Jan 1893-19 Nov 1894
Lt. Col., Bvt. Col.	Louis H. Carpenter	19-26 Nov 1894
Colonel*	Edwin V. Sumner	27 Nov 1894-16 Dec 1894
Lt. Col.	Louis H. Carpenter	16 Dec 1894-21 Jan 1895

Colonel	Edwin V. Sumner	21 Jan 1895-26 Mar 1896
Major	Theodore A. Baldwin	26-30 Mar 1896
Colonel	Edwin V. Sumner	30 Mar 1896-20 Jun 1898
(Promoted to Brig. Gen. and assumed command of Dept. of Colorado)		
Lt. Col.	Michael Cooney	20 Jun 1898-31 May 1899
Colonel	Theodore A. Baldwin	1 Jun 1899-15 Dec 1900
Major	Edward S. Godfrey	16 Dec 1900-13 Jan 1901
Colonel	Theodore A. Baldwin	13 Jan 1901-26 Nov 1901
Lt. Col.	W.S. Edgerly	29 Oct 1901-26 Nov 1901
Colonel	Theodore A. Baldwin	26 Nov 1901-6 Oct 1902
Major	George F. Chase	6-9 Oct 1902
Colonel	Theodore A. Baldwin	10-13 Oct 1902
Lt. Col.	W.S. Edgerly	14-16 Oct 1902
Colonel	Theodore A. Baldwin	16 Oct 1902-7 May 1903
Colonel	Charles Morton	7 May 1903-15 Jul 1903
Major	Charles A. Varnum	16-22 Jul 1903
Colonel	Charles Morton	23 Jul 1903-27 Dec 1903
Major	Charles A. Varnum	28 Dec 1903-11 Jan 1904
Colonel	Charles Morton	12 Jan 1904-30 Apr 1904
Lt. Col.	S.L. Woodward	30 Apr 1904-7 May 1904
Colonel	Charles Morton	7 May 1904-12 Sep 1904
Major	W.J. Nicholson	12-30 Sep 1904
Colonel	Charles Morton	30 Sep 1904-21 Oct 1906
Major	Lloyd S. McCormick	21 Oct 1906-17 Dec 1906
Major	Edwin P. Brewer	18-21 Dec 1906
Colonel	Charles Morton	22 Dec 1906-26 Feb 1907
Major	Lloyd S. McCormick	26 Feb 1907-9 Mar 1907
Colonel	Charles Morton	9 Mar 1907-9 Apr 1907
(Promoted to Brig. General 9 Apr 1907)		
Lt. Col.	John F. Guilfoyle	9 Apr 1907-25 Jul 1907
Colonel	Frederick K. Ward	25 Jul 1907-24 Oct 1907
Lt. Col.	John F. Guilfoyle	24 Oct 1907-13 Nov 1907
Colonel	Frederick K. Ward	14 Nov 1907-24 Feb 1908
Lt. Col.	John F. Guilfoyle	24 Feb 1908-4 May 1908
Colonel	Frederick K. Ward	4-10 May 1908
Lt. Col.	John F. Guilfoyle	10-16 May 1908
Colonel	Frederick K. Ward	16 May 1908-16 Jun 1908
Lt. Col.	John F. Guilfoyle	17 Jun 1908-5 Jul 1908
Colonel	Frederick K. Ward	5 Jul 1908-5 Jan 1909
Lt. Col.	John F. Guilfoyle	5-13 Jan 1909
Colonel	Frederick K. Ward	13 Jan 1909-14 Apr 1909
Lt. Col.	John F. Guilfoyle	14-20 Apr 1909
Colonel	Frederick K. Ward	5 Jul 1908-5 Jan 1909
Lt. Col.	John F. Guilfoyle	5-13 Jan 1909
Colonel	Frederick K. Ward	13 Jan 1909-14 Apr 1909
Lt. Col.	John F. Guilfoyle	14-20 Apr 1909
Colonel	Frederick K. Ward	20-22 Apr 1909
(Promoted to Brig. Gen. 26 Feb 1910 and relieved from Regiment.)		
Lt. Col.	John F. Guilfoyle	22 Apr 1909-11 Apr 1910
Major	William J. Nicholson	11-14 Apr 1910
Colonel	George K. Hunter	14 Apr 1910-7 May 1910
Lt. Col.	John F. Guilfoyle	8-13 May 1910
Colonel	George K. Hunter	14 May 1910-19 Aug 1910
Major	William J. Nicholson	20-31 Aug 1910
Colonel	George K. Hunter	1 Sep 1910-7 Oct 1910
Major	William J. Nicholson	8 Oct 1910-3 Nov 1910
Colonel	George K. Hunter	4-16 Nov 1910
Major	William J. Nicholson	17-25 Nov 1910
Colonel	George K. Hunter	26 Nov 1910-2 Jan 1911
Major	William J. Nicholson	3-5 Jan 1911
Colonel	George K. Hunter	6 Jan 1911-17 Sep 1911
Major	Selah R.H. Tompkins	18-29 Sep 1911
Colonel	George K. Hunter	30 Sep 1911-15 Nov 1911
Major	Selah R.H. Tompkins	16 Nov 1911
Colonel	George K. Hunter	17 Nov 1911-23 Dec 1911
Major	Selah R.H. Tompkins	24-26 Dec 1911
Colonel	George K. Hunter	27 Dec 1911-15 Jan 1912
Lt. Col.	William J. Nicholson	16-22 Jan 1912
Major	Peter E. Traub	23-24 Jan 1912
Major	Selah R.H. Tompkins	25 Jan 1912
Lt. Col.	William J. Nicholson	26 Jan 1912-18 Mar 1912
Major	Selah R.H. Tompkins	19-28 Mar 1912
Lt. Col.	William J. Nicholson	29 Mar 1912-7 Apr 1912
Major	Selah R.H. Tompkins	8-25 Apr 1912
Lt. Col.	William J. Nicholson	26 Apr 1912-4 Jun 1912
Major	Selah R.H. Tompkins	5-16 Jun 1912
Lt. Col.	William J. Nicholson	17 Jun 1912-27 Sep 1912
(Promoted to Colonel 6 Sep 1912)		
Major	Selah R.H. Tompkins	24 Sep 1912-19 Oct 1912
Colonel	William J. Nicholson	20 Oct 1912-23 Dec 1912

Major	Selah R.H. Tompkins	24 Dec 1912-2 Jan 1913
Colonel	William J. Nicholson	3-7 Jan 1913
Major	Selah R.H. Tompkins	8-10 Jan 1913
Colonel	William J. Nicholson	11 Jan 1913-1 Feb 1913
Major	Selah R.H. Tompkins	2 Feb 1913-6 Mar 1913
Lt. Col.	George H. Sands	7 Mar 1913-13 May 1913
Major	Francis H. Beach	14-16 May 1913
Major	Selah R.H. Tompkins	17 May 1913
Lt. Col.	George H. Sands	18 May 1913-18 Jul 1913
Colonel	William J. Nicholson	19 Jul 1913-17 Aug 1913
Lt. Col.	George H. Sands	18-23 Aug 1913
Colonel	William J. Nicholson	24-27 Aug 1913
Major	Selah R.H. Tompkins	28 Aug 1913-24 Sep 1913
Colonel	William J. Nicholson	25 Sep 1913-8 Oct 1913
Lt. Col.	George H. Sands	9 Oct 1913-30 Nov 1913
Major	Selah R.H. Tompkins	1-2 Dec 1913
Lt. Col.	George H. Sands	3-19 Dec 1913
Major	Selah R.H. Tompkins	20 Dec 1913 -1 Jan 1914
Lt. Col.	George H. Sands	2 Jan 1914-5 Feb 1914
Major	Arthur Thayer	6-28 Feb 1914
Lt. Col.	George H. Sands	1-5 Mar 1914
Major	Farrand Sayre	6 Mar 1914
Lt. Col.	George H. Sands	7 Mar 1914-23 Apr 1914
Major	Farrand Sayre	24-26 Apr 1914
Lt. Col.	George H. Sands	27 Apr 1914-5 May 1914
Colonel	George K. Hunter	6-15 May 1914
Lt. Col.	George H. Sands	16 May 1914-4 Jun 1914
Colonel	Cunliffe H. Murray	5 Jun 1914-19 Jul 1914
Major	Peter E. Traub	20-22 Jul 1914
Colonel	Cunliffe H. Murray	23 Jul 1914-23 Aug 1914
Colonel	William A. Shunk	24-26 Aug 1914
Colonel	Cunliffe H. Murray	27 Aug 1914-14 Nov 1914
Lt. Col.	George H. Sands	15-18 Nov 1914
Colonel	Cunliffe H. Murray	19-26 Nov 1914
Captain	Joseph E. Cusack	27 Nov 1914-7 Dec 1914
Colonel	Cunliffe H. Murray	8 Dec 1914-15 Jan 1915
Colonel	William A. Shunk	16-31 Jan 1915
Colonel	Cunliffe H. Murray	1 Feb 1915-21 Apr 1915
Colonel	William A. Shunk	22 Apr 1915-3 May 1915
Colonel	Cunliffe H. Murray	4 May 1915-1 Jul 1915
Colonel	William A. Shunk	2 Jul 1915
Colonel	Cunliffe H. Murray	3 Jul 1915-2 Sep 1915
Lt. Col.	Farrand Sayre	3-8 Sep 1915
Colonel	Cunliffe H. Murray	9 Sep 1915-3 Oct 1915
Lt. Col.	Farrand Sayre	4 Oct 1915
Major	Arthur Thayer	5-8 Oct 1915
Lt. Col.	Farrand Sayre	9-27 Oct 1915
Colonel	Cunliffe H. Murray	28 Oct 1915-15 Nov 1915
Major	Edwin B. Winans	16 Nov 1915-23 Dec 1915
Colonel	James B. Erwin	24 Dec 1915-19 Feb 1916
Major	Alexander L. Dade	20-26 Feb 1916
Colonel	James B. Erwin	27 Feb 1916-4 Aug 1916
Colonel	Selah R.H. Tompkins	5 Aug 1916
Colonel	James B. Erwin	6-21 Aug 1916
Colonel	Selah R.H. Tompkins	22 Aug 1916-14 Feb 1917
Major	Edmund M. Leary	15-27 Feb 1917
Colonel	James B. Erwin	28 Feb 1917-9 Mar 1917
Major	Edmund M. Leary	10-11 Mar 1917
Colonel	James B. Erwin	12-21 Mar 1917
Major	Edmund M. Leary	22 Mar 1917-18 May 1917
Colonel	Selah R.H. Tompkins	19 May 1917-15 Jul 1917
Major	Rus H. Wells	16-20 Jul 1917
Colonel	Selah R.H. Tompkins	21 Jul 1917-30 Oct 1917
Captain	Leon M. Logan	31 Oct 1917-3 Nov 1917
Major	Francis W. Glover	4 Nov 1917-26 Dec 1917
Colonel	Selah R.H. Tompkins	27 Dec 1917-3 Apr 1918
Major	Francis W. Glover	3-7 Apr 1918
Colonel	Selah R.H. Tompkins	8 Apr 1918-19 Feb 1920
Colonel	Charles A. Hedekin	20 Feb 1920-15 Apr 1920
Colonel	Charles J. Symmonds	16 Apr 1920-Dec 1920 #
Lt. Col.	Frank T. McNarney	Dec 1920-30 Apr 1921 #
Colonel	Walter C. Short	1 May 1921-31 Aug 1921
Lt. Col.	Frank T. McNarney	1-29 Sep 1921
Colonel	Walter C. Short	30 Sep 1921-7 Jul 1923
Colonel	Fitzhugh Lee	8 Jul 1923-10 Jul 1927
Colonel	Selah R.H. Tompkins	10-17 Jul 1927
Lt. Col.	Howard R. Smalley	18 Jul 1927-Oct 1927 #
Colonel	William M. Connell	Nov 1927-30 Jun 1929 #
Lt. Col.	Charles McH.Eby	1 Jul 1929-Oct 1929 #
Major	Robert W. Strong	Oct 1929-Jan 1930 #

Colonel	Charles F. Martin	Feb 1930-17 Nov 1930 #
Lt. Col.	Frank Keller	18 Nov 1930-31 Dec 1930
Colonel	Ola W. Bell	1 Jan 1931-14 Apr 1933
Lt. Col.	William W. Gordon	15 Mar 1933-14 Apr 1933
Major	John A. Robenson	15-16 Apr 1933
Lt. Col.	William W. Gordon	17 Apr 1933-28 May 1933
Major	John A. Robenson	29-30 May 1933
Lt. Col.	William W. Gordon	31 May 1933-2 Aug 1933
MAJ	Terry de la M. Allen	3-8 Aug 1933
LTC	William W. Gordon	9 Aug 1933-2 Sep 1933
MAJ	Terry de la M. Allen	3-5 Sep 1933
LTC	William W. Gordon	6 Sep 1933-24 Oct 1933
COL	Joseph A. Baer	25 Oct 1933-8 Feb 1934
LTC	William W. Gordon	9-12 Feb 1934
COL	Joseph A. Baer	13 Feb 1934-9 Jun 1934
LTC	Herman Kobbe	10-27 Jun 1934
COL	Joseph A. Baer	28 Jun 1934-8 Aug 1934
LTC	William W. Gordon	9-25 Aug 1934
COL	Joseph A. Baer	26 Aug 1934-29 Nov 1934
LTC	Herman Kobbe	30 Nov 1934-1 Dec 1934
COL	Joseph A. Baer	2-20 Dec 1934
MAJ	Harding Polk	21-22 Dec 1934
LTC	Herman Kobbe	23-26 Dec 1934
COL	Joseph A. Baer	27 Dec 1934-16 Sep 1935
COL	John K. Herr	17 Sep 1935-26 Mar 1938
LTC	Benjamin F. Hoge	27 Mar 1938-30 Jun 1938
LTC	Harding Polk	1-19 Jul 1938
COL	William W. West	20 Jul 1938-16 Apr 1939
LTC	Benjamin F. Hoge	17 Apr 1939-14 May 1939
COL	William W. West	15-30 May 1939
LTC	Benjamin F. Hoge	31 May 1939-26 Jun 1939
COL	William W. West	27 Jun 1939-17 Jul 1940
COL	Frederick Gilbreath	18 Jul 1940-12 Mar 1941
LTC	Frederic W. Boye	13-31 Mar 1941
COL	Frederick Gilbreath	1-30 Apr 1941
LTC	Frederic W. Boye	1-15 May 1941
LTC	Thoburn K. Brown	16 May 1941-14 Nov 1941
LTC	Marion Carson	15-27 Nov 1941
LTC	Thoburn K. Brown	28 Nov 1941-6 May 1942
COL	Glenn S. Finley	7 May 1942-17 Oct 1943
MAJ	Franklin F. Wing Jr.	18-31 Oct 1943
COL	Glenn S. Finley	1 Nov 1943-29 Dec 1943
LTC	Franklin F. Wing Jr.	30 Dec 1943-10 Jan 1944
COL	Glenn S. Finley	11 Jan 1944-2 May 1944
COL	Walter E. Finnegan	3 May 1944-27 Jul 1944
LTC	Franklin F. Wing Jr.	28 Jul 1944-7 Aug 1944
COL	Walter E. Finnegan	8 Aug 1944-10 Jul 1945
LTC	W.A. Adams	11 Jul 1945-14 Sep 1945
COL	Walter E. Finnegan	15 Sep 1945-28 Feb 1946

Exact dates not shown in records.

*Remained assigned to the regiment until 6 May 1869 when he resigned from the service. He was on Detached Service from 26 Feb 1867 until the date of his resignation, commanding the Department of the Upper Arkansas and later the Department of the Missouri and was therefore not present for duty with the regiment during this period.

**Although the regimental return was signed by Lieutenant Colonel George A. Custer, the regiment was scattered during the months of September and October 1874, with each element commanded as follows:
Lieutenant Colonel George A. Custer-commanding Fort Abraham Lincoln, Dakota Territory.
Major Joseph Tilford, on detached service commanding Fort Rice, Dakota Territory.
Major Lewis Merrill, en route from the Department of the gulf.
Major Marcus Reno, absent on leave.

***Although the regimental return for the period 9 Oct 1877, to 7 Jan 1878, shows Colonel Samuel D. Sturgis, commanding, he was absent on detached service and leave of absence during the entire period. The regiment was scattered with each element commanded as follows:
Lieutenant Colonel Elmer Otis, on detached service, commanding Fort Rice, Dakota Territory.
Major Joseph Tilford, commanding, Fort Abraham Lincoln, Dakota Territory.
Major Lewis Merrill, in the field with troops.
Major Marcus Reno, in suspension for two years from 1 May 1877, per General Court-Martial Order #41, AGO, 1877.

*Brevet ranks were authorized by the Act of 6 Jul 1812, however only one brevet rank was awarded in the Army after the Civil War. General Tasker H. Bliss was awarded the Brevet Rank of General upon his retirement as Chief of Staff in 1918. Authority to award Brevet Rank was not rescinded until the revision of Title 10, U.S. Code on 10 Aug 1956.

Regimental Honors

Campaign Streamers:

INDIAN WARS
Comanches
Montana 1873
Dakota 1874
Little Big Horn
Nez Perces
Pine Ridge

MEXICO
Mexico 1916-1917

WORLD WAR II
New Guinea
Bismarck Archipelago (with arrowhead)
Leyte (with arrowhead)
Luzon

DECORATIONS:
Streamer, Philippine Presidential Unit Citation, embroidered 17 Oct 1944 to 4 Jul 1945

By Order of Wilber M. Brucker, Secretary of the Army:
R.V. Lee
Major General, United States Army
The Adjutant General

The Regimental Insignia

The designer of the regimental insignia is unknown; however, it was first proposed in 1921. The first proposal for a distinctive regimental insignia was not favorably considered as indicated in the following correspondence.

Headquarters 7th U.S. Cavalry
Camp at Fort Bliss, TX
25 Oct 1921

From: Regimental Commander, 7th Cavalry
To: C.G. 1st Cavalry Division
Subject: Regimental insignia
In compliance with Circular 244, War Department c.s. herewith submit a proposed regimental insignia for the 7th Cavalry to be worn on the collar or the blouse and olive drab shirt.
/s/ W.C. Short
Colonel, 7th Cavalry

3-Incls:
Drawings
1st Ind.
HQ 1st Cavalry Division, Fort Bliss, Texas, 24 Jun 1922, to the Adjutant General of the Army, Washington, DC.
1. Disapproved.
2. In view of the fact that a shoulder sleeve insignia for the 1st Cavalry Division has been approved by the Secretary of War and that it identifies every unit of the Division, I consider the adoption of a special collar insignia for units belonging to the division not only unnecessary but undesirable.
3. This communication has been held at Division Headquarters pending the adoption, fabrication and distribution of the shoulder sleeve insignia.
/s/ Robert L. Howze
Brigadier General, USA
Commanding
Incls. no change

AG 421.7 7th Cavalry
(10-25-21) (Miscl.) 4
2nd Ind., MC

War Department, A.G.O., 25 Jul 1922—To the Commanding General, 1st Cavalry Division, Fort Bliss, Texas.
Attention is invited to Par. 45, A.R. 600-40, under which subject to the approval of the War Department, a regiment is authorized to adopt a distinctive addition to the uniform.
In connection with the colored patches and edgings on the collar it is to be noted that the special devices are not to displace the U.S. or the crossed sabers and regimental number on the collar.
The sketches are returned for further study.
By order of the Secretary of War:
/s/ Herbert L. Collins
Adjutant General
Incls. no change

In 1924 proposals for a distinctive regimental insignia were again submitted to the War Department for approval. Pictures of these early designs are shown on the following page. The following correspondence indicates the early ideas; considerations, and final approval of the present regimental insignia:

Headquarters 7th Cavalry, Office Of The Regimental Commander

220.5   FL/LAS.
Insignia, Regtl.
Fort Bliss, Texas
9 Jan 1924
Subject: Regimental Insignia
To: The Adjutant General of the Army, War Department, DC (Thru Channels).
1. In compliance with Circular No. 244, War Department, 1921, herewith is submitted drawing in colors, specification and Blazon of proposed Regimental Insignia, 7th Cavalry.
2. It is requested that after final action on this insignia, drawing be returned to these headquarters as it is the only copy in existence at present.
/s/ Fitzhugh Lee
Commanding
3-Incls:
(1 Drawing in colors)
(2 Specifications)
(3 Blazon)
(Note: Endorsements to this correspondence omitted merely approved the preceding communication and forward it to the next high headquarters.)

Blazon of the Regimental Insignia of the 7th U.S. Cavalry, USA

A cavalry horseshoe, or, heels upward, with crease, saber, and seven nail heads, white. Above and joining the heels of the shoe, a scroll, azure, bearing the words, "GarryOwen," or.

At the base and emerging from sinister side of the shoe, a dexter arm embowed, vested azure, the hand in a buckskin gauntlet, proper, grasping an old style U.S. Army saber, or, hilted, or, blade extending to center of scroll gripe, saber threaded or.

Explanation of Design

The horseshoe is symbolic of the Cavalry. Its color, gold (yellow in heraldic tincture), is the color of the old uniform facings of the U.S. Cavalry, in existence when the Regiment was organized and is still retained as the color of the Cavalry Arm.

The words, "GarryOwen," are the title of an old Scottish (sic) war song known and used as the regimental song since the days of General Custer. Its rollicking air symbolizes the esprit de corps for which the Regiment is noted. (For many years the regimental song was accepted as being of Scottish origin; however, it has been definitely established that the song is of Irish origin.

The arm, taken from the crest of the Regimental Coat of Arms, symbolizes the spirit of the Cavalry Charge. At the time of the organization of the regiment this position of the arm and saber was known as "Raise Sabre" and was taken at the command, "Charge." The saber itself is of the old Cavalry type used in the Indian campaigns. The gauntlet is also symbolic of those times. The blue of the sleeve is the blue of the old Army uniform. The twisted emblem at toe of shoe is symbolic of Indian days.

Specifications of a Proposed Regimental Device for the 7th Cavalry, USA

THE DEVICE. To be a badge to be worn as follows:

For Officers: On each shoulder loop half way between the shoulder loop button and the insignia or rank. Also, in front of the campaign hat at the ventilating eyelet.

For Enlisted Men: On each side of the collar opening three-fourths of an inch in rear of the circumference of the standard collar insignia. Also, in front of the campaign hat at the ventilating eyelet.

THE PATTERN. To be one and one-fourths inches in vertical length, measured along the vertical median line. Other dimensions to be in the same proportions as those in the accompanying drawing.

COLORS. *The Horseshoe* to be in the standard Cavalry yellow (as represented by the felt patch mounted below the accompanying drawing). The crease of the shoe to be in black with the nail heads in white enamel.

The Scroll and Motto—Scroll to be of blue and of a shade identical with that of the doeskin formerly established as standard by the Quartermaster General for trousers of the officers of the line of the old blue uniform. Motto to be in yellow. Reverse side of Scroll to be of blue of the old Army dress coat.

Arm to be of blue and of the same shade as the reverse of scroll. Twisted emblem below hand to be alternating light blue and yellow of the same shades as the scroll and shoe.

Gauntlet to be of buckskin grey with shading of black.

Sabre to be of gold with hilt of gold. Black grip threaded with gold.

MATERIALS. Entire design to be made of enamel outlined and backed with metal. Sabre blade and guard to be of gold metal. Shading representing folds of gauntlet to be of black enamel or metal of dark coloring to give the appearance of black.

GENERAL. Attention is called to the fact that the twisted emblem below the hand is not horizontal, but forms a slight arc of nearly the same

curvature as the arc formed by the scroll above. Also, the nail heads of the shoe extend slightly beyond the sides of the crease. Badge to be slightly convex. Design to have an inner background of white enamel throughout.

FASTENING. Either a pin running the vertical length of the design originating at the top and equipped with the safety catch at the bottom, or a screw fastener from center of back. Both kinds of fastenings are desired as some men will prefer one kind and some the other.

4th Ind.
421/4138
War Department, Office, Chief of Cavalry, Washington, DC, 7 Feb 1924.
To: The Adjutant General.

1. The general design for the regimental insignia is considered very excellent and it is recommended that it be re-submitted to the Commanding Officer, 7th Cavalry, with the following defects noted:

a) The thumb should be along the back of the gripe, the end of the thumb touching the guard;

b) The coat sleeve should be of the darker blue;

c) When reproduced the size of the saber blade will be so small as to make a very weak, delicate part of the design and likely to be easily broken;

d) The scroll over the horseshoe gives the appearance of not being tied close and securely to the rest of the design. It is recommended that this be brought down, so that the points of the horseshoe touch the main band of the scroll;

e) From a manufacturing standpoint, it is doubtful whether the idea of outlining the whole in black is practicable. Even if this were done it would be of such minute fineness as to produce little if any effect. The suggestion might be made to leave out one horseshoe nail—leaving the hole pierced and open. The design would then carry seven nails indicating the number of the regiment.

For the Chief of Cavalry:
/s/ Geo. Vidmer
Executive
220.5
Insignia, Regt.
FL/LAS.
6th Ind.

HEADQUARTERS 7th CAVALRY, Fort Bliss, Texas, 24 Apr 1924.
To: The Adjutant General, Washington, DC.

1. A new design (very rough) containing pencil explanatory notes is herewith submitted. Also old designs Nos. 1 and 2 are returned.

2. A suggestion that the twisted emblem across toe of shoe could have seven sections instead of six as at present. This again would indicate the number of the regiment. It will be noted that the arm now blocks out one nail hole leaving seven.

3. The arm and saber in its present position gives slightly more length to the saber. Before, it was too short and "chunky." Also the saber is not centered. The latter should be slightly more curved than sketch shows.

4. Also it will be noted in the new design that the scroll has been brought down closer to the shoe and heels have been blunted and rounded. As in other designs heels were too sharp and long.

5. It is requested that these papers be forwarded to the Office of Chief of Cavalry, with a request that upon approval of the design, they have the manufacturer submit prices, etc., to this headquarters.

/s/ Fitzhugh Lee,
Commanding.
3-Incls.

AG 421.7 7th Cavalry
(1-9-24) (Miscl.) DMC
7th Ind.
War Department, A.G.O., 5 May 1924—To the Chief of Cavalry.

1. Each of the drawings marked #1, #2 and #3 have good points.

2. The shape of the heels of the shoe as indicated on #3 with the 4 and 3 holes showing is the best. The arm, as on #3 blotting out one nail hole is the best. Care should be taken to make the grasp of the hand and gauntlet correct. The vertical drawing of the saber on #3 is not good, the diagonal filling of the space as #1 and #2 is better artistically. The yellow and blue heraldic wreath, if used, must be of six twists. It can be omitted altogether if this is deemed advisable.

3. It is requested that another drawing be made which can be approved by the War Department without corrective notes which in the record are always liable to be misleading.

By Order of the Secretary of War:

/s/ Adjutant General

3 Incls.

421/4138

8th Ind.

War Department, Office, Chief of Cavalry, Washington, DC, 13 Jun 1924.

To: The Adjutant General.

1. The drawing requested in paragraph 3, preceding endorsement, is enclosed.

2. It is desired to emphasize the following features to be incorporated in the insignia:

(a) The words "Garry Owen" to be in enamel—cavalry yellow.

(b) The center spaces between the sides of the horseshoe to be pierced.

(c) The shoe to be of gold with the seven nail holes pierced.

(d) The saber to be of gold.

(e) The arm to be super-imposed over the shoe.

(f) The fastening to be heavy pin type with safety lock.

For the Chief of Cavalry:

/s/John B. Coulter

Executive

4 Incls. (1 added)

War Department
The Adjutant General's Office Washington

AG421.7 7th Cav.
(1-9-24) (Miscl.) D   28 Jun 1924

SUBJECT: Distinctive insignia on uniform of the 7th Cavalry, under A.R. 600-40, Par. 46.

TO: The Quartermaster General.

The Secretary of War approves the following distinctive insignia for wear as a part of the uniform of this organization:

INSIGNIA: Within a gold horseshoe showing seven nail holes, heels upward and the opening between the heels closed with a blue ribbon bearing the words "Garry Owen" in yellow letters, the crest of the regiment (on a wreath or and azure a dexter arm embowed vested azure the hand in a buckskin gauntlet proper grasping an old style United States Army saber hilted or).

The insignia will be manufactured in bright metal and enamel in one size, as the organization may select, but not in excess of one and one-fourth inches in height.

TO BE WORN:

By Officers: On the service uniform on the upper portion of the shoulder loops of coat; on the front of the service hat midway between band and crease.

On white uniform same as on service coat.

On mess jacket on both lapels above line of miniature medals.

By Enlisted Personnel: On the service uniform on both sides of the collar 3/4 of an inch in rear of the service insignia, on the front of the service hat midway between band and crease.

By Order of the Secretary of War:

/s/Adjutant General

The Regimental Coat of Arms

Regimental Coats of Arms were authorized by War Department Circulars Number 444 dated 29 Sep 1919, and Number 527 dated 25 Nov 1919. Following this authorization the late colonel (then major) and Mrs. Ben H. Dorcy, assigned to the 7th Cavalry Regiment at Fort Bliss, Texas, designed the original Coat of Arms for the 7th Cavalry Regiment.

While the exact date of authorization for the Regiment's Coat of Arms is not known, it is known that the Coat of Arms was displayed at various

The silken standard as authorized in Par. 1468, Revised U.S. Army Regulations - 1863 for all mounted regiments. The above standard was carried by the 7th Cavalry Regiment during the period 1866-1887, including the Yellow Stone Expedition, but was not with the Regiment during the Battle of the Little Big Horn.

The 7th Cavalry Regimental Standard carried in and after World War II, and during the Korean War.

regimental occasions as early as January 1920 and was officially recognized by the War Department in December of that year.

The description given the original Coat of Arms by the designers was as follows:

Blazon of the 7th Cavalry Arms
by Maj. Ben H. Dorcy

ARMS: Or, on a chevron azure, seven horseshoes of the first. In dexter chief a phoenix, rising from its ashes, proper. In sinister chief the head of a North American Indian couped at the neck, in a war bonnet, proper. In base a Yucca plant, vert.

CREST: Surmounting a Knight's helmet, a dexter arm embowed, mantled azure, gauntleted proper, holding an old style Cavalry saber, proper, at the "Charge."

MOTTO: On a scroll, azure, turned or, "The Seventh First."

It would appear that the designers—both authorities on heraldry—had some interpretations of the symbols used in the original Coat of Arms which differ from those contained in the official description of the present Coat of Arms. In the original Coat of Arms, the chevron (one of nine such lines permitted in heraldry) was intended to represent the eaves of a house supporting the roof rather than that "whose origin radition ascribes to the spur, which was formerly of that shape without rowel." The Sioux Indian Chief was intended as a reminder of the Battle of the Little Big Horn rather than to commemorate the Indian campaigns as such. The yucca plant was originally intended to commemorate the regiment's entire service and protection of the U.S. Mexican border rather than specifically the Punitive Expedition into Mexico. The original Coat of Arms was surmounted by a knight's helmet (the heraldic symbol of leadership) while the official description does not mention this symbol.

The following is the official (Department of the Army) description given the Coat of Arms of the 7th Cavalry Regiment.

SHIELD: Or on a chevron azure, between a phoenix rising from its ashes in dexter chief, the head of a North American Indian in war bonnet couped at the neck in sinister chief, all proper, and a yucca plant vert in base, seven horseshoe heels upward of the field.

CREST: On a wreath of the colors a dexter arm embowed vested azure, the hand in buckskin gauntlet proper grasping an old style United States Army saber argent hilted or.

MOTTO: The Seventh First.

The field in yellow the Cavalry color, the principal charge is a chevron whose origin tradition ascribes to the spur, which was formerly of that shape without rowel. The number of horseshoes corresponds to the numerical designation of the regiment. The phoenix symbolizes the resurrection of the regiment after its virtual extermination in the Battle of the Little Big Horn in 1876. The Indian head and yucca commemorate Indian campaigns and the Punitive Expedition of 1916 respectively. The crest shows the position of" raise saber," taken at the command "Charge" as prescribed by GO 6, AGO 1873, the arm being habited in the uniform of the period.

Shown in Figure 1 is the Coat of Arms as intended by the designers. Figure 1 shows the currently approved Department of Army design and the one generally in use today. Insofar as can be determined, changes to the more simple design shown in Figure 2 were made in May 1956 for ease of manufacture and without regard to proper heraldic significance. However, the Regimental Coat of Arms shown in Figure 1 and the following description are the most generally accepted by veteran members of the 7th Cavalry Regiment.

Blazon of the Arm of the 7th Regiment of Cavalry United States Army

ARMS: Or (Gold), on a chevron azure (blue), between a phoenix rising from its ashes in dexter chief (upper right or the shield-viewer's left), the head of a North American Indian in war bonnet, couped (cut off) at the neck, in sinister chief (upper left or shield-viewer's right), all proper (represented in natural colors, not conventional tints), and a yucca plant, vert (green), in base (at the bottom) seven horse shoes, heels upward of the field.

CREST: Surmounting a knight's helmet, a dexter (right) arm embowed (bent), vested (dressed) azure (blue), the hand in a buckskin gauntlet proper (represented in natural colors, not conventional tints), grasping an old style United States Army Saber, argent (silver), hilted or (gold).

MOTTO: The Seventh First.

Explanation of the Arms

The field of gold (yellow, in heraldic tincture) is the color of the facings of the old blue uniform of the United States Cavalry, in existence at the time of the regiment's organization and retained in the hat cords of the enlisted men.

The chevron, in the language of heraldry, is described as one of the "Honorable Ordinaries." French writers upon the subject contend that its origin was that of the spur of the knight, which was originally pointed, without a rowel.

In Egypt, Phoenix was worshipped as a god, the Sun God, Ra, and his periodical resurrection was viewed as a guaranty of the resurrection of the dead. In Arabia, the phoenix was fabled to be consumed by fire by its own act and to rise in youthful freshness from its ashes. This charge is embodied in the arms to commemorate the extermination of General Custer and Troops C, E, F, I, and L in the Battle of the Little Big Horn in 1876, and the resurrection of the regiment with its magnificent esprit de corps for which it is justly noted throughout the United States Army.

The head of the North American Indian is used in honor of a former able and valiant foe, the original native American.

The yucca plant commemorates the regiment's service in Mexico as part of the Punitive Expedition of 1916-17.

In the crest the Cavalry Charge is symbolized. At the time of the regiment's organization, this position of the arms and saber was known as "raise saber," and was taken at the command "charge."

The motto, "The Seventh First," indicates the esprit de corps of the regiment's personnel, in that all, enlisted and officer, place the good of the regiment first in their consideration.

The Regimental Guidons and Colors

Since the beginning of time military units have carried banners, flags, symbols or standards into battle as a mark of distinction, to bolster courage, to indicate the presence of the commander, or as a rallying point after the battle. The first use of such symbols goes far beyond the beginning of American history, for men have always needed symbols which represent to them that which they hold most precious at times when they are under greatest stress on the field of battle.

In the days of primitive warfare, certain tribes would carry their dead chieftains into battle with them, for security, for revenge, or for a mixture of reasons, but always with the thought that the chief somehow had the power to help them in defeating the enemy.

In the Biblical wars, David's armies carried the Ark of the Covenant into battle with them—the chest containing the laws precious to a people fighting for its existence. The Roman legions grouped around standards, each with its own numeral, each with its own esprit de corps, again pointing to the need for symbols. Napoleon gave the same type of standards, bearing eagles, to his regiments. Our own Civil War soldier fought savagely for his flag.

The earliest record of an official guidon or flag in the American Army is contained in a letter of 9 May 1808, from the Secretary of War to the Purveyor of Supplies suggesting that the "horse units will be dispersed." (Secretary of War Miscellaneous Letters, Section III 249-50, National Archives.) However, the design for such a flag was not suggested. In 1834 the guidon for the Cavalry was prescribed by the following regulations:

Extract

General Regulations for the Army—1834

ARTICLE LV
Standards and Guidons of the Cavalry
Each regiment will have a silken standard, and each company a silken guidon. The standard to bear the arms of the United States, embroidered in silk, on a blue ground, with the number and name of the regiment, in a scroll underneath the eagle. The flag of the standard to be two feet five inches wide, and two feet three inches on the lance, and to be edged with yellow silk fringe.

The flag of the guidon to be made swallow-tailed, three feet five inches from the lance to the end of the slit of the swallow-tail; 15 inches to the fork of the swallow-tail, and two feet three inches on the lance. To be half red and half white, dividing at the fork, the red above—on the red the letters U.S. in white, and on the white the letter of the company in red. The lance of the standards and guidons to be nine feet long, including spear and ferule."

Subsequent orders prescribing the size, shape and use of the guidon for mounted troops are reproduced below:

Headquarters of the Army
Adjutant General's Office
Washington, 18 Jan 1862

GENERAL ORDERS
No. 4
1. Under instructions from the Secretary of War, dated 7 Jan 1862, guidons and camp colors for the Army will be made like the United States flag, with stars and stripes.
By Command of Major General McClellan:
L. Thomas
Adjutant General

A 7th U.S. Cavalry "guidon" (30" x 40"). Each troop carried one of these swallow-tailed flags. Of the five that went down with Custer, the existence of three are known. The author was granted permission to use this photo, by Miss Claudia Nickolson, Curator of Collections of the Cultural Heritage Center, Pierre, South Dakota. A special thanks to Francis Whitebird, Commissioner of Indian Affairs, S.D., for notifying the author about the location of this historical flag.

Headquarters of the Army
Adjutant General's Office
Washington, 22 Feb 1862

GENERAL ORDERS
No. 19
The following order has been received from the War Department:

It is ordered that there shall be inscribed upon the colors or guidons of all regiments and batteries in the service of the United States the names of the battles in which they have borne a meritorious part. These names will also be placed on the Army Register at the head of the list of the officers of each regiment.

It is expected that troops so distinguished will regard their colors as representing the honor of their corps—to be lost only with their lives; and that those not yet entitled to such a distinction will not rest satisfied until they have won it by their discipline and courage.

The General Commanding the Army will, under the instruction of this Department, take the necessary steps to carry out this order.

By Command of Major General McClellan:
L. Thomas, Adjutant General

Revised U.S. Army Regulations,
1863 Standards and Guidons
of Mounted Regiments

Paragraph 1468. Each regiment will have a silken standard, and each company a silken guidon. The standard to bear the arms of the United States, embroidered in silk, on a blue ground, with the number and name of the regiment, in a scroll underneath the eagle. The flag of the standard to be two feet five inches wide, and two feet three inches on the lance, and to be edged with yellow silk fringe.

Paragraph 1469. The flag of the guidon is swallow-tailed, three feet five inches from the lance to the end of the swallow-tail, and two feet three inches on the lance. To be half red and half white, dividing at the fork, the red above. On the red, the letters U.S. in white; and on the white, the letter of the company in red. The lance of the standards and guidons to be nine feet long, including spear and ferrule.

U.S. Army Regulations, 1881
Guidons for Cavalry

Paragraph 2792. To be made of silk, with stars and stripes like the national flag; made swallow-tailed. Stars to be gilt, one and one-eighth inches in diameter from point to point.

The guidon to measure from the lance three feet five inches to the end, and 15 inches to the fork of swallow-tail, and two feet three inches on the lance. The fork of the swallow tail to be equidistant from the top and bottom of the guidon.

The letters of the company to be embroidered in yellow silk, or painted on one of the white bars of the flag.

The lance to be one and one-fourth inches in diameter, and nine feet long, including spear and ferrule.

To have a water-proof case or cover to protect the guidon when furled. (GOQM Dept.)

Headquarters of the Army
Adjutant General's Office
Washington, 4 Feb 1885

GENERAL ORDERS
No. 10

By direction of the Secretary of War paragraph 2792 of the Regulations is amended to read as follows:

Guidons For Cavalry

2792. The flag of the guidon is swallow-tailed, three feet five inches fly from the lance to the end of the swallow-tail, and two feet three inches on the lance. To be cut swallow-tailed 15 inches to the fork. To be made of silk, and to consist of two horizontal stripes, each one-half the width of the flag, the upper red and the lower white; the red to have on both sides in the center the number of the regiment in white silk, and the white to have the letter of the trop in red silk; the letter and number to be block-shaped, four and three-fourths inches high, and held in place by a border of needle-work embroidery three-sixteenths of an inch wide, of the same color. The lance to be one and one-fourth inches in diameter and nine feet long, including spear and ferrule. To have a water-proof case or cover to protect the guidon when furled.

By command of Lieutenant General Sheridan:

OFFICIAL: R.C. DRUM
Adjutant General

HEADQUARTERS OF THE ARMY
Adjutant General's Office
Washington, 13 Apr 1887

GENERAL ORDERS
No. 31

By direction of the Secretary of War paragraph 2790 of the Regulations is amended to read as follows:
Standards and Guidons for Mounted Regiments

2790. Each regiment will have a silken standard, and each troop or mounted battery a silken guidon. The standard for cavalry to be made of a single thickness of seamless yellow banner-silk, to be four feet fly and three feet on the lance. To have the coat of arms of the United States, as on the standard sample on file in the office of the Quartermaster General, and which may be described as follows: An eagle with outstretched wings; on its breast a U.S. shield; in the right talon an olive branch with red berries, and in his left 10 arrows bunched. A red scroll held in eagle's beak, with the motto, "E pluribus unum," in yellow; over a scroll a group of 13 white stars, surmounted by an arc of diverging sun rays, also in white. Below the eagle a red scroll, with the number and name of regiment in yellow, as for example "3rd U.S. Cavalry." The design, letters, and figures to be embroidered in silk, the same on both sides of the standard. The standard to be trimmed on three sides with United States silk knotted fringe two and one-half inches deep. Lance to be nine feet six inches long, including metal spear and ferrule. To have a water proof case or cover to protect the standard when furled.

By Command of Lieutenant General Sheridan:
OFFICIAL: R.C. DRUM
Adjutant General

Thus, the standards remained until 1919 when each Regiment's Coat of Arms were authorized to be superimposed on the eagle.

The Army Organization Act of 1950 prescribed "armor as a continuation of Cavalry." Section V, Department of the Army Circular 15, 1951, prescribed the armor insignia and yellow guidons for armor units of the 7th U.S. Cavalry traditionally have worn the crossed sabers and carried the red and white guidon.

Unit guidons in the 7th Cavalry, as in all other old Army units, were treated with respect and handled with care for they not only represented the unit's symbol on the field of battle, but also the banner of unit pride carried beside the troop commander. The letters on the opposite page indicate the disposition made of the unit guidons when they were declared unserviceable in the past.

Since the Battle of the Little Big Horn there have been stories, tales, accusations, and downright malicious lies as to what happened to the colors, or standard, of the 7th Cavalry Regiment. Journalists, more prone to fiction than fact, have deliberately fostered the theory that the regiment's standard, national colors, and guidons were disgracefully lost in battle and were not reissued to the regiment until many years later. There is no basis for these stories! As can be seen in the above cited authorities, Cavalry units did not carry colors (i.e. National Colors or Standards) until 1895.

Sound battle tactics would have precluded cavalry units from attracting attention when moving about in hostile country. This necessitated encasing the regimental standard and troop guidons, rather than have them fluttering in the breeze when contact with the hostile force was imminent. At the time of the Battle of the Little Big Horn, the regimental standard was cased and rolled and left with the pack train. Troop guidons were probably encased, inverted and the point of the spear inserted in the guidon boot attached to the right stirrup. The troop guidons did accompany each troop in the Battle of the Little Big Horn, and may or may not have been raised and fluttering after the troops had been sighted by the Indians; however, the regimental standard was not lost in the battle since the Pack Train was with Major Reno during the battle. The regimental standard carried with the Custer column is now on exhibit at the Custer Battlefield Museum.

Loss of the troop guidons in this instance was never considered a disgrace and the troops were never denied their return as popular stories would lead one to believe. The following are extracts of the only official Army correspondence on this subject and has been widely misquoted, misunderstood, and was not entirely factual in the beginning:

RCE-mvm
A.G. 424.5
7th Cavalry
(10-10-28) ORD
7 Nov 1928

SUBJECT: Colors of the 7th Cavalry

1. This is in further response to the inquiry contained in your letter of 10 Oct 1928, receipt of which I acknowledged 16 October.

2. Your letter having been transmitted to the Quartermaster General for his consideration, that officer informs this office that a search of the records of his office fails to disclose any information relative to a replacement of the flag of the 7th Cavalry shortly following the Battle of the Little Big Horn of 25 Jun 1876. As I have therefore informed you, nothing is found in my office bearing on the subject.

3. Inasmuch as it is commonly understood that all of the property that was with the Headquarters and five troops of the 7th Cavalry that were with the detachment of that regiment under the personal command of Lieutenant Colonel Custer on the afternoon of 25 Jun 1876, was destroyed, except the horse named Commanche which survived, it seems probable that the flag of the 7th Cavalry was permanently lost on that day and was subsequently replaced.

By order of the Secretary of War:
/s/ Adjutant General
424-7th Cavalry-G-A.
3rd Ind.

C.O. Philadelphia Quartermaster Depot, 21st Street and Oregon Ave., Phila., PA, 29 Oct 1928.

To: The Quartermaster General, Washington, DC.

1. Search of the records at this depot fails to reveal anything on this subject, therefore, this office has no information to offer.
/s/ W.S. WOOD
Colonel, QM Corps
Commanding

1 Encl.

QM 424 S-C 7th Cavalry 4th Ind.
War Department, OQMG, Washington
2 Nov 1928

To: The Adjutant General

2. The records of this office indicate that a regimental standard, Cavalry, was furnished the 7th Regiment Cavalry under date of 11 Sep 1916. (Prior to this date it was common practice for units to have their standards [and guidons] hand-made by a local seamstress.—Author) This standard contained the coat of arms of the United States. It is the understanding of this office that a regimental standard was manufactured and furnished the above organization sometime in 1921, which standard had the regimental coat of arms embroidered thereon, as illustrated on enclosed photostat of drawing No. CE 5-6-17, and which standard it is believed is still in use by the organization.

For the Quartermaster General:
/s/ F.D. SHAWN
Captain, QMC
Assistant
2 Incls.
Added: 1 Incl.—Incl. 2
Incl. 2—Photostat #CE 5-6-17

In addition to the troop guidons lost in the Battle of the Little Big Horn, General Custer carried with him his personal flag which was hand-made by Mrs. Custer. The following is an extract of a letter dated 23 Feb 1887, written by Mrs. Custer to a Colonel Hodges, and on file in the National Archives:

"My dear Colonel Hodges,

"I am sorry that I cannot give you exact proportions of my husband's personal flag but hope that you can arrive at its size from my description.

"It was a narrow swallow tail half of blue silk and half of red with white sabers of silk crossed and stitched across the flag. The sabers were the size of those used in the cavalry.

"I remember that General Custer had his flag made soon after General Sheridan designed his. They were, I think, about the same size. The reason I think so was that my husband had me make miniature models of both and used to have them standing in a little rest on the top of his gun stand. As he gave me the proportions I think they must have been right and they were both the same size in the models.

"If General Sheridan were asked for the exact proportions of his personal flag (which was blue and red with a white star on both stripes) it would render that size of my husband's quite accurately, I believe.

"I have cut a newspaper pattern of what seems to be about the size and it seems to me the flag was about two feet wide and four and one-half feet long with the swallow tail cut in about 19 inches.

"This is all guess work only I remember the silk sabers were crossed on the flag so that there was some space at the end which was fastened to the standard and a small space between the sabers and the beginning of the swallow tail.

"Very truly yours,
Elizabeth B. Custer"

The only official record of the recovery of any flag or guidon which was lost in the Battle of the Little Big Horn is contained in the Record of Events of Troop C, 3rd U.S. Cavalry for September and October (combined) 1876, as follows:

"Company left camp on Beaver Creek, D.T. 1 September and marched to Glendive Creek and Little Missouri, from thence in a southerly direction to (name of creek illegible on original record) Creek when 15 men of the company with 85 others of the Regiment under command of Captain Anson Mills, 3rd Cavalry, were detached and sent forward for rations. When on the 9th early in the morning they surprised, attacked and captured a village of 34 lodges under Chief American Horse, killing many Indians and captured about 150 ponies. Private William J. McClinton, Company C recaptured a guidon which had been taken at the massacre of General Custer's command."

The guidon was later identified as that belonging to Troop I, 7th U.S. Cavalry and is shown on the preceding page. The following certificate was rendered by Captain (then General) Anson Mills in 1898:

"This guidon belonged to Company I; 7th Cavalry (Captain Keogh), was lost with Custer at the Battle of the Little Big Horn, 25 Jun 1876, and was recaptured by my command at the Battle of Slim Buttes, then in good condition, folded up in an Indian reticule with a pair of Colonel Keogh's gauntlets marked with his name. It was loaned for several years by me to the museum of Military Service Institution on Governor's Island and from want of proper care, returned so ravaged by moths that this is the most that could be made of it." Signed Anson Mills, Brigadier General USA (RET) 22 Feb 1898.

The Saber

The saber has been a distinctive part of the Cavalry uniform and the principal weapon of mounted troops in the American Army since the first troops of Dragoons were authorized by the Continental Congress in 1877. It is hard to imagine the dashing Cavalryman of old without his saber swinging boldly for his side or raised at the "Charge" position as he galloped headlong toward the enemy. However, in 1934 the Cavalry saber was declared obsolete as an instrument of war by the following War Department letter:

War Department
The Adjutant General's Office
Washington

18 Apr 1934
AG 474.71 (2-15034)
Misc. M-D
SUBJECT: Saber
TO: Commanding Generals of all Corps Areas and Departments; Chief of War Department Arms and Services; Chief, National Guard Bureau and Assistant Chiefs of Staff, G-1, G-2, G-3, G-4, WPD.

1. The saber is hereby discontinued as an item of issue to the Cavalry. The saber is completely discarded as a Cavalry weapon.

2. Pending the publication of necessary changes in Tables of Organization and in training literature, the use of the saber, except the Officer's dress saber by officers as a badge of office only, will be discontinued at once.

3. Sabers now on hand will be stored pending further instructions.

4. The next revision of Tables of Organization and Tables of Basic Allowances for Cavalry will omit all references to the saber.

By order of the Secretary of War:
/s/ E.T. CONLEY
Brigadier General,
Acting, The Adjutant General

Thus, one of the principal weapons of defense and attack since the Medes and Persians, the Romans and Greeks, was written into the histories of warfare along with the sling David used against Goliath, Caesar's catapult, or a devastating medieval Englishmen called the long bow.

Subsequent to the above directive, the Cavalry's weapon became the automatic pistol or rifle and sabers were used only by officers as articles of military apparel.

The sword was at first a crude thrusting weapon of stone sharpened by the cave-men-ancestors of modern warriors. It developed into a striking instrument with the adoption of chain mail uniforms by the world's principal armies. And later, when plate armor was adopted as standard military dress, the sword became a light straight skewer for thrusting at open places in an adversary's covering.

The sword's decline began with the improvement in firearms in the 17th century, though until comparatively modern times it remained essential equipment, particularly for sudden thrusts by mounted troops.

With the advent of the machinegun for defense, spectacular attack formations were abandoned and the cavalry moved in a thin line with wide intervals. After the cavalry was motorized, the horse began riding in trucks or trailers. Later as the cavalryman became motorized, unhorsed, and designated Armored Corps, the saber served little purpose and would have been in the way when crawling through the open hatch of a tank. It was completely discarded even as a part of the uniform by early 1942. Nevertheless, the saber served a useful purpose in its day, and should be adopted as a colorful part of the dress uniform by the Armored Corps in today's modern Army as a reminder of its Cavalry tradition and history.

The Regiment and Music

Musical organizations in U.S. Army units date back to the fife and drummer of Revolutionary days. The 7th Cavalry Regiment is no exception, for its musical organizations have included Regimental Bands, Drum and Bugle Corps, Pipes and Drums, and Choral Groups. Each of these musical organizations has served a distinctive purpose as potent contributors to the regiment's traditional high morale and esprit de corps.

The utility of these various musical units and the esteem in which they have been held by both the personnel of the regiment and the citizens of local communities can be found throughout the history of the regiment.

In the initial organization of the regiment, a Regimental Band was not authorized. However, General Custer, being a lover of good music and recognizing the value of a band, directed his Adjutant in 1867 to organize a band "from amongst the musicians of the Regiment." These bandsmen remained assigned to their respective companies but were detailed for duty with the Regimental Adjutant to serve in the Band. They were officially transferred to the Band—on the rolls of the Regimental Field and Staff under the Adjutant—by War Department Circular dated 19 Apr 1870. Prior to that time frequent mention is made to the band in the field with the regiment, the most famous being when the band played *GarryOwen* to begin the charge at the Battle of the Washita. There is also specific mention of the band playing *GarryOwen* as the regiment left Fort Abraham Lincoln on the ill-fated Yellowstone expedition.

At the turn of the century and immediately thereafter, the regiment's history is filled with accounts of the band's participation in both military and civic functions. The social life of the Army post during the dreary depression years would not have been complete without the weekly band concert, or the Regimental Band music furnished for the officers and non-commissioned officers Saturday night dances.

The 7th Cavalry Band was established as a section in the Service Troop in 1921 and as a separate component of the regiment under command of the Regimental Adjutant on 22 Jun 1927. It was inactivated and the personnel and equipment utilized in the reorganized 1st Cavalry Division Band at Luzon, Philippines Islands on 3 Jun 1945.

Since that date several regimental commanders have attempted to organize musical groups depending upon their musical tastes and the availability of musicians within the regiment. The major problem faced in organizing such groups has been the high rate of turnover in personnel and the difficulty in obtaining the necessary equipment for a provisional organization.

Among the more successful musical groups in recent years has been the Regiment's Pipers and Drums, organized by Sergeant First Class Robert J. Scroggie in late 1954 at Camp Haugen, Japan. The pipes for this group were donated by the 7th U.S. Cavalry Association. Other equipment and the distinctive uniforms were purchased by the regiment. The unit was attired in historically significant uniforms including the blue Glengarry bonnet, the drummer's red doublet from the days when drummers led the troops to battle wearing red so that blood would not show and harm the morale of the men, the plaids and kilts of dark blue and yellow of the U.S. Cavalry, light blue to signify the present day infantry role of the cavalry, red for action and white for honor. This colorful unit participated in all regimental ceremonies and frequently performed for Japanese groups and local events thereby enhancing Japanese-American relations.

It is indeed unfortunate that unit bands cannot be authorized within the present austere budget of this impersonal space age. The contribution toward the morale and esprit of the fighting troops by Regimental Bands is historical. A unit band (even in the missile age) could engender the courage, determination, and devotion to duty in the hearts of fighting men which would enable them to achieve victory in the face of hardship, discouragement, and danger. Admittedly, these characteristics (essential for unit esprit) cannot be measured in terms of monetary values when compared with more spectacular advances in warfare.

The Regimental Song—*GarryOwen*

The origin and composer of the tune, quick march or drinking song, entitled *GarryOwen*, had been a moot question. After no little research, it was definitely established that the music is not that of Scottish strain, but without a doubt of Irish origin. (The following was taken from Keogh, Comanche and Custer, E.S. Luce, 1939, John S. Swift Company, St. Louis, Missouri, pp. 120-127.

It had been used by several Irish regiments as their quick march; the Fifth Royal Irish Lancers stationed in the suburb of Limerick called *GarryOwen* (the Gaelic word meaning Owen's Garden) used it as their drinking song. The words can hardly be called elevating, but depict the rollicking nature of the Lancers while in town on pay day in search of their peculiar style of "camaraderie." The following verses are set to the music of *GarryOwen*. (Authority; Boosey; London; [no date, presumably about 1800] *Songs of Ireland*, p. 44.)

> Let Bacchus' sons be not dismayed
> But join with me each jovial blade;
> Come boose and sing, and lend your aid,
> To help me with the chorus.
>
> Chorus:
> Instead of Spa we'll drink down ale,
> And pay the reckn'ning on the nail
> No man for debt shall go to gaol
> From GarryOwen in glory.
>
> We are the boys that take delight in
> Smashing the Limerick lights when lighting;
> Through the streets like sporters fighting
> And clearing all before us.
>
> We'll break windows, we'll break doors
> The watch knock down by threes and fours;
> Then let the doctors work their cures, And tinker up our bruises.
>
> We'll beat the bailiffs out of fun
> We'll make the mayors and sheriffs run;
> We are the boys no man dares dun,
> If he regards a whole skin.
> Our hearts so stout have got us fame
> For soon t'is known from whence we came;
> Where'er we go they dread the name,
> Of GarryOwen in glory.

The daughters of Erin—words by Thomas Moore (1779-1852). Air: GarryOwen. Edited and arranged by Granville Bantock, found in *One Hundred Folksongs of all Nations*, published by Oliver Ditson Company, Boston, MA, on pages 16 and 17—copyrighted MCMXI, by Oliver Ditson Company. In their *Notes on Songs*, page XI: No 11 *The Daughters of Erin*. Ireland. The air of *GarryOwen* to which Moore has written these words, is undoubtedly an Irish dance-tune, and, as far as we know, was first printed in a collection of Scottish dance-music, Gow's Repository of Original Scottish Dances. 1802.

It first became popular in pantomime—Harleqin Armulet—which was played in 1800, and is often used at the present day as a military quick-step. GarryOwen is a suburb of Limerick, and is said to mean Owen's Garden. Authorities: Boosey: *Songs of Ireland*, p. 44. Moffat: *Minstrely of Ireland*, p. 296. Brown and Moffat: *Characteristic Songs*, etc. p. 42. Berggreen: *Folke-Sange og Melodier*, Vol. IV, No. 35.

From Poetical Works of Thomas Moore. Printed in England at the Oxford University Press, 1856. Also in *Characteristic songs and Dances of all Nations*, by James Duff Brown, published by Bayley and Ferguson in 1901, London, England: GarryOwen is best known as a dance or military quickstep, but we have added Moore's lively words, written for the number of Irish Melodies which appeared in 1807.

Thomas Moore (1779-1852), the celebrated Irish poet, had a somewhat different idea for fitting words to the song, and in several books of music compositions dealing with Irish folksongs, we find the following words under the title of *The Daughters of Erin*.

We may roam thro' this world, like a child at a feast,
Who but sips of a sweet, and the flies to the rest;
And, when pleasure begins to grow dull in the east,
We may order our wings and be off to the west;
But if hearts that feel, and eyes that smile,
Are the dearest gifts that Heaven supplies,
We never need leave our own green isle,
For sensitive hearts, and for sun bright eyes.

Chorus:
Then remember, wherever your goblet is crown'd,
Thro' this world, whether eastward or westward you roam,
When a cup to the smile of dear woman goes round,
Oh! remember the smile which adorns her at home.

En England the garden of Beauty is kept—
By a dragon of prudery placed within call;
But so often this unamible dragon has slept,
That the garden's but carelessly watch'd after all.
Oh, they want the wild sweet-briery fence,
Which warns the touch, while winning the sense,
No charms us least when it most repels.

In France, when the heart of a woman sets sail,
On the ocean of wedlock its fortune to try,
Love seldom gets far in a vessel so frail,
But pilots her off, and the bids her good-bye.
While the daughters of Erin keep the boy,
Ever smiling beside his faithful oar,
Through billows of woe, and beams of joy,
The same as he look'd when he left the shore.

I have tried to ascertain the approximate date when this number was first introduced into this country, and when it was first used as a military quickstep by the United States Army. As far as it is known, it was most likely introduced between the years of 1861 and 1866. The first instance that we know of its use as a military quickstep by any military organization was in the early part of 1867, when it was played by the 7th U.S. Cavalry Band. It was then that the music was adopted as the regimental air by that organization.

The late Mrs. George A. Custer, wife of General Custer, several times remarked to me that she first heard her husband hum and whistle the piece a short time after the regiment was organized at Fort Riley Kansas, and that she believed the late Brevet Lieutenant Colonel (Captain) Myles W. Keogh, 7th Cavalry, was in some way connected with introducing the song to the regiment.

While this cannot be taken as an absolute fact, still, as we look further into the matter, it is not at all unlikely. Captain Keough's father was an officer in the 5th Royal Irish Lancers, and the birthplace of Captain Keough, in Orchard, Carlow County, Ireland, is but a short distance from Limerick on the banks of the River Shannon, from whence much music and poetry have emanated. When one takes into consideration the close connection between Captain Keogh and the Irish Lancers, and his companionship with Captains Henry J. Nowlan, Charles C. De Rudio of the 7th Cavalry, as well as General Coppinger and O'Keeffe, all of whom served in the Papal Guard before they came to this country and joined the Union Army in 1862, one cannot help but believe that such a boon comradeship had a very great part in bringing the song GarryOwen, to this country and to the 7th Cavalry.

The tempo and the spirit of the music is definitely comparable to the cadence of the mounted service, and instills a certain "esprit du corps" in the heart of every 7th Cavalry man.

The following quotation is from a letter written by the late Private Theodore W. Goldin, Troop "G," 7th Cavalry, a Medal of Honor man, a few days before he died. This letter was addressed to Chaplain (Major) George J. McMurry, 7th Cavalry, with reference to the Battle of the Little Big Horn River, 25 Jun 1876:

"On the day we moved out from Powder River with the pack train, the Band was posted on a knoll overlooking the river, where they played merrily while we were fording the river. After all were across and the six troops formed we took up the march towards Tongue River and the Rosebud, the Band broke into the rollicking strains of GarryOwen which, as usual, brought a hearty cheer and its notes were still ringing in our ears as we left the river bottoms, and the Band was lost to sight as we wound up a wide ravine. The strains of the old Regimental air were the last notes from the Old Band that fell on the ears of General Custer, the staff, and many officers and men of the old Regiment."

Prior to the 7th Cavalry's departure for the Philippines in 1905, Chief Musician J.O. Brockenshire, of the 7th Cavalry Band rewrote the music of GarryOwen, and also composed the stanzas and chorus.

We are the pride of the army,
And a regiment of great renown,
Our name's on the pages of history.
From sixty-six on down.
If you think we stop or falter
While into the fray we're goin'
Just watch the steps with our heads erect,
While our band plays GarryOwen.
CHORUS:
In the Fighting Seventh's the place for me,
It's the cream of all the cavalry;
No other regiment ever can claim
Its pride, honor, glory and undying fame.

We know no fear when stern duty
Calls us far away from home,
Our country's flag shall safely o'er us wave,
No matter where we roam.
"Tis the gallant 7th Cavalry
It matters not where we're going'
Such you'll surely say as we march away;
And our band plays, GarryOwen.

Then hurrah for our brave commanders!
Who lead us into the fight.
We'll do or die in our country's cause,
And battle for the right.
And when the war is o'er,
And to our home we're goin'
Just watch the step, with hour heads erect,
When our band plays, GarryOwen.

As to the origin of the tune of GarryOwen, it is believed that the following can be considered authentic.
48 Bruntsfield Gardens
Edinburgh, I.O.
Telephone 54271,
14-10-38

(THE SOCIETY OF CORRESPONDING MEMBERS OF THE ROYAL SCHOOLS OF MUSIC, LONDON) (The Royal Academy of Music and the Royal College of Music)
Captain Edward S. Luce
7th U.S. Cavalry
Fort Bliss, Texas

My Dear Sir:
Mr. John Miller, Registrar of the University of Edinburgh passed onto me your letter of 16 Sep 1938, in which you ask for information regarding "GarryOwen, your Regimental tune. I have looked the matter up with no little pleasure to myself and trust helpfulness to you!

GarryOwen (spelled GarryOwen, one word with us) is a very old Irish tune, quite traditional, as no records of its author can be found. Thomas Moore the great Irish poet wrote the words set to it, "We may roam thro' this world." It also appears in a Book of Old Irish Songs, published by John Purdie, 83 Princess St., Edinburgh, early last century to the words The Boston that Beats to a Brother's Distress. (R.A. Smith Collection)

Military Connection:

It was the Regimental Air of the Royal Irish Regiment, which is now disbanded; was also used by the 5th Royal Irish Lancers as a Quick March, Irish Guards, as a warning for parade. Royal Irish Rifles had it as their Regimental March originally, but was changed later.

The Queens Own Royal West Kent Regiment and the Durham Light Infantry also used it occasionally.

In case there may be any doubt that we are thinking of different tunes, I enclose a short musical quotation of the tune as we know in the U.K. but I expect it will be quite correct, and I trust the information I have been able to give you will suffice for your purpose.

Very sincerely yours,
Wm. Martin Hobkirk, Hon, R.C.M.
and Diploma of Raff Conservatorium
Frankfort-a-Main

Additionally, the following information pertaining to the origin of the song *GarryOwen* was furnished later ("But there were others not in the rank of ??? who at this time made a noise in the old town; and the parish of St. John in particular rang with the echoes of their wild revelry, while they caused their own name and fame to be wedded in verse to the immortal air of *GarryOwen* - an air which is heard with rapturous emotion by the Limerick man in whatever clime he may be placed, or under whatever circumstances its fond familiar tones may strike upon his ear. Not even the Ranzes des Vaches has so many charms for the Swiss exile as GarryOwen possesses for every individual who claims Limerick as his birthplace or even as his residence. The words to which this air has been wedded contain allusions not only to certain local worthies, and principally the late John O'Connell Esq. the proprietor of the Garryowen Brewery, who was deservedly much esteemed (c. 1800)

"I have been favored with another version of this favorite song written in 1811 by a soldier, a Limerick man (T.R.W.) serving at the time with the army in Portugal (during the Peninsular War) by favor Eugene O'Curry M.R.I.A. (the Gaelic Scholar) July 1862.

"GARRYOWEN" Portugal, April 1811

Let am'tous poets chaunt soft lays,
Who bask in love's meridian rays,
I sing the soul-enlivening praise
of GarryOwen a Gloria.
A theme so bold it well may fire
The heart and hand that guide the byre,
And every gallant son inspire
Of GarryOwen a Gloria.

Old GarryOwen so high renowed
Whose sons with victory's laurels crowned,
Have always made the fame resound
Of GarryOwen a Gloria.

In days of yore once proudly stood
The bulwark of the public good,
Till teach'ry, under friendships hood
Sold GarryOwen a Gloria.

In vain were Williams red-hot balls
Directed 'gainst her Royal Halls,
Her warlike sons were iron walls
Round GarryOwen a Gloria.

And though betrayed by traitors vile,
She sunk to Royal William's smile,
Received the Phoenix__??
In GarryOwen a Gloria.

Deep graven in historic page
Tradition hands from age to age,
In memory of forefathers sage,
In GarryOwen a Gloria.
Who yielded not to England's lord,
'til he had signed the Great Reward,
The glorious treaty Eirinn's guard
In GarryOwen a Gloria.

Now o'er the once embattled plains
Bright commerce holds her goodly reign
'midst rising fabrics—Eirinn's__??
Of GarryOwen a Gloria.

High raised her wealth—high raised her fame,
Wide o'er the world extends her name,
And rival cities see with shame
New GarryOwen a Gloria.

Not worked alone for lists and arms,
And souls whom kindness ever warns,
Who has not heard how beauty charms
In GarryOwen a Gloria.

Soft as the native gloves they wear,
Her daughters every heart ensnare,
Circassia's self won't stand compare
With GarryOwen a Gloria.

O *GarryOwen*, my native home,
Through parting seas between us foam,
My heart's with thee while far I roam,
Fair *GarryOwen* a Gloria.

O may thy commence prosperous thrive,
And glorious freedom long be thine,
May Eirinn's boast be richest mine
In *GarryOwen* a Gloria.

TRW

(I think 'na gloria," the genitive case of the Irish article, should be read instead of "a gloria" in these verses—? Maurice Lenihan)

"GarryOwen signifies John's Garden (Parish of St. John) a suburb of Limerick in St. John's Parish in which in these times was a public garden which the citizens were accustomed to frequent in great numbers. The opening scene of Gerald Griffin's beautiful novel of *The Collegians* is laid in GarryOwen, and from this novel Mr. Dion Bonicault has obtained materials for his famous drama of *The Colleen Bawn* (from which is derived Sr. Julius Benedict's opera *The Lily of Killarney*. The Nail here mentioned is a sort of low pillar still extant (1866) in the Town Hall upon which payments used to be made in former times. The song was translated into Latin and Greek by Thomas Stanley Troy, B.A. Scholar of Trinity College Dublin."

It will be noted that the above transcribed poem shows a considerable number of errors in spelling, and punctuation. It is possible whoever originally copied Lenihan's articles made these errors; or the papers from which they were copied, were possibly faded and torn, especially where the dashes and question marks are shown.

In the following poem the metre of the verses are practically the same and one, and it is possible that the same poet wrote both poems. In Bossey: London: (no date, presumably about 1800) *Songs of Ireland,* p. 44, this poem GarryOwen is shown, and the notation as to the composer or the music and words, merely states anonymoun.

GarryOwen C-1800

Let Bacchus' sons be not dismayed,
But join with me each jovial blade;
Come, booze and sing, and lend your aid
To help me with the chorus:

Chorus:
Instead of spa we'll drink brown ale,
And pay the reckoning on the nail,
No man for debt shall go to jail,
From GarryOwen in glory!

We are the boys that take delight in
Smashing the Limerick lamps when lighting,

Through the streets like sporters fighting
And tearing all before us.

Chorus:
We'll break windows, we'll break doors,
The watch knock down by threes and fours,
Then let the doctors work their cures,
And tinker up our bruises,

Chorus:
We'll beat the bailiffs out of fun,
We'll make the mayor and sheriffs run;
We are the boys no man dares dun,
If he regards a whole skin.

Chorus:
Our hearts so stout have got us fame,
For soon 'tis known from whence we came;
Where'er we go they dread the name
Of GarryOwen in Glory.

In the original song of *GarryOwen* (with above words) the lyrics end here. It is possible that in those days, circa 1800, they added verses to their army songs just as the Doughboys did in World War I, when the AEF sang that famous *Mesdemoiselle From Armentieres*. The following additional verses were added to *GarryOwen*, circa 1800:

Johhny Connell's tall and straight;
And in his limbs he is complete;
He'll pitch a bar of any weight
From GarryOwen to Thomand-gate.

Chorus:
GarryOwen is gone to wreck
Since Johnny Connell went to Cork
Though Harry O'Brien lept over the dock
In spite of judge and jury.

The History and Origin of Bugle Calls

Bugle calls have been synonymous with the cavalry almost since the beginning of mounted troops. It is hard to imagine a cavalry charge without being preceded by the characteristic "Charge" sounded by the bugler, usually located at the side of his commander. *Boots and Saddles* and the *Stable Call* are as well known to those who have served with "a horse outfit" as the scratchy notes from a loudspeaker sounding *Reveille* on a frosty morning are to the soldier in today's modern Army.

The origin of the bugle dates back to ancient times, with the forerunners of the present day instrument first being used for military purposes by the armies of Gideon and Saul. The military calls in present use by various nations were also used in some form or other as far back as the time of Julius Caesar. The first authenticated instance of a battle command being given by a trumpet call was at Bouvines, in 1214, when trumpets sounded the signal for the victorious French charge.

The oldest trumpet calls preserved in notations are to be found in the composition published in Antwerp in 1545—*La Bataille* describing the battle of Marignano in 1515.

The bugle calls used in the military service of the United States are the result of the contact of the Continental Army with the soldiers and armies from Europe during the Revolutionary Period. As a result, the English and French influence predominates the U.S. Army bugle calls. During this period the military signals were given by the drum and were called "beats." However, the cavalry (dragoons) used a trumpet (bugle) in a few of their mounted regiments during this time and up to and including the War of 1812. During this post-Revolutionary period many of the French (and English) calls and beats were transferred and absorbed into the United States Army.

Prior to the Civil War, both cavalry and artillery units used bugles, but the infantry continued the system of using drums for formation "calls." During the period of the Civil War, these drum calls were changed to bugle calls and remained as such until 1867. Up to this time each arm and branch of the Army had its own set of "Sound Signals"—(drum beats and

bugle calls). This system had many shortcomings and was the cause of much confusion.

In 1867, General Upton was authorized to prepare a new set of military tactics for Army instruction, embodying changes made necessary as a result of the Civil War. He requested Major Truman Seymour (later General) of the 5th U.S. Artillery, to prepare a new system of calls, the object being to provide uniformity in all arms and branches of the service. (Exceptions were specific calls peculiar to the cavalry and field artillery).

Major Seymour, a soldier of both artistic and musical tastes, did a thorough job choosing the new calls from among those then in use in the infantry and cavalry. He discarded some, revised others, and finally selected the set of calls, both practical and musical, that have remained in use up to the present time.

The following indicates the origin of those bugle calls used in today's Army:

First Call: Similar to the French Cavalry Call "Le Garde a Vous."

Reveille: Same as the French call which dates from the Crusades. (The armies of the Crusaders were amazed and frightened at the military music of the Saracens, and their instruments were captured and copied. thereafter, the European armies used music to greater advantage in both battle and ceremony.)

Assembly: The old cavalry assembly call, in use from about 1835, was replaced in 1867 by the present more martial sounding call.

Mess Call: Similar to the French call "Le Rappel."

Retreat: Same as the French call "Le Rappel."

Retreat: Same as the French Cavalry call dating from the Crusades. (See note under "Reveille.")

To the Colors (Standard): The old cavalry call "To The Standard," in use from about 1835, was replaced in 1867 by the present more military sounding call.

Tattoo: Originating during the Thirty Years War, and called the Zapfenstreich." At 9:00 p.m., when the call was sounded, all bungs (Zapfen) had to be replaced in their barrels, signifying the end of the nightly drinking bout. A chalk line (Streich) was then drawn across the bung by the guard. Thus, it could not be "tapped to" without evidence of tampering. "Tap-to" thus became "Tattoo." (See "Taps.")

In the United States Army, "Tattoo" is the longest call, consisting of 28 measures, but is still far sort of the elaborate ceremony used in the British and German services. The first section of eight measures is the same as the French call "Extinction des Feuz" (Lights Out), and was at one time used for "Taps" in our Army. this French call was composed for the Army of Napoleon, and was the Emperor's favorite. The last section of 20 measures of our "Tattoo" is taken from the British "First Post," and comes originally from an old Neapolitan Cavalry call, "Il Silencio."

Prior to the adoption of the present "Tattoo" in 1867, two other versions were in use, the first during 1835-61, and the second during the Civil War.

Taps: The origin of Taps is in itself most interesting and unique. General Daniel Butterfield of the Army of the Potomac, composed the call in July 1862, for use in his own brigade, supposedly to replace the three volleys fired at military funerals so the Confederates would not know a burial was taking place. Soon thereafter, it replaced "Tattoo" (at that time the French call "Lights Out") as the last call of the day. Its use gradually caught on and became quite popular throughout the Union Army.

When Major Seymour prepared the present set of bugle calls in 1867, he apparently did not know of General Butterfield's version, since the music was not changed to its present notation until 1874, when it first appeared in the Infantry Drill Regulations.

Reference to the word "Taps" has been found as early as 1861, and is variously explained, one version being that it originally was soldier slang for "Tap-To," as "Tattoo" was first spelled, and "Tap-To" in the infantry was sounded on a drum—thus "Taps." (See "Tattoo.")

The earliest official reference to the mandatory use of "Taps" at military funeral ceremonies is in the U.S. Army Drill Regulations of 1891. Its unofficial use as a finale to the firing salute had been customary since its inception in 1862. (In the British Army, "Last Post" has been sounded over soldiers' graves after interment since 1885, being prescribed in "Standing Orders" since that year.)

Attention: Taken from the British call "Alarm," at which time the troops turn out under arms.

Church Call: Same as the French "Church Call."

This call was one of those retained in the revision of 1867, and was taken from the "Sonneries de Chasseurs d'Orleans," promulgated in 1845.

Fire Call: Similar to certain British and French Calls.

First Sergeant's Call: This call is first mentioned in the "Martial Music of Camp Dupont," 1816, when it was a drum call sounded when the adjutant wished to summon the first sergeant. The present bugle call, used to notify all first sergeants to report to the adjutant or sergeant-major, comes from the German army.

Among the more famous cavalry bugle calls, now obsolete in the modern Army as they were used only with mounted troops, are:

Boots and Saddles: This call indicated that the formation about to follow was to be mounted. It is said to be an old British Cavalry signal although the U.S. Army call seems to be derived from the French, which is rhythmically the same, although lower in pitch.

The 7th Cavalry: The origin of this call—specifically for the 7th Cavalry—is unknown. It first appears in Appendix A, No. 60, Cavalry Drill Regulations, 1909 as follows:

Comanche

The horse "Comanche" (the private mount of Captain Miles W. Keogh) was the sole survivor found on the battlefield after the Battle of the Little Big Horn. Although some historians have stated that other horses were found on the battlefield, and there may have been some Indian ponies, records of the regiment do not indicate that any were found.

The narrative contained in this description of "Comanche" is taken from "Keogh, Comanche and Custer," by E.S. Luce, 1939, pp. 64-67.

Major Peter W. Wey was detailed by the Regimental Commander to act as Comanche's caretaker after Blacksmith Korn had been killed at the Battle of Wounded Knee Creek, 29 Dec 1890, said in a letter to the author—"he was found with one of the cheek straps of the bridle broken which permitted him to slip the bit out of his mouth but the throat latch kept the bridle on him. The saddle had turned under his belly but the blanket and pad were missing."

While the last rites for the victims were being performed on 27 June, a lone horse was observed by First Lieutenant Henry J. Nowlan, 7th Cavalry, former comrade in arms in the Pontifical Zouaves and the Civil War with Captain Keogh. Returning again and again to the field, he seemed to be seeking someone and neighed softly, as though to call some beloved master. His bewildered eyes appeared to seek familiar faces and to summon back the affection of human friends.

What harrowing experiences befell the faithful animal; what scenes he must have witnessed; what deeds of valor must have been performed that afternoon on the Little Big Horn (Comanche) the one living witness, could only express by dumb actions. The frightfulness of the Indians' attack, the grim stand of the troopers against what they must have foreseen as ultimate annihilation, have been recorded only by the mute evidence of the dead.

In the last stages of the battle, the troopers' mounts were evidently pressed into service as breastworks or parapets. From behind the bodies of their faithful dead and dying animals, the men had fought to the last. Perhaps Comanche, too, had interposed his battle-scarred body between his master and the arrows and bullets of the Sioux. When he was discovered, he was still dripping blood—many crimson blotches stained his shaggy coat, and he could hardly walk. The burial party could only guess at what he had endured.

He was so weak and emaciated that it was at first thought wise and humane to put him out of his misery. Yet the poor creature clung to life tenaciously with his ever-present stoicism. It took many hours to lead him slowly the 15 or 16 miles to the junction of the Little Horn and Big Horn rivers, where the streamer "Far West" was now moored and being loaded with the wounded men from Reno's and Benteen's commands.

Captain Grant March, of the steamer *Far West,* saw that Comanche lacked no attention, and a specially repaired stall, softly bedded with grass, was made for him at the extreme stern of the vessel. His care and welfare became the special duty of the whole boat's company on that long, yet record-breaking trip of over 950 miles to Bismark.

From there, the badly wounded animal was tenderly conveyed by wagon to Fort Lincoln, the same garrison which he had left only eight weeks before. A special "belly-band" sling was made upon which he was suspended for nearly a year. With the daily care of Veterinarian Stein, and of Blacksmith Gustave Korn and John Burkman (Old Nutriment), who were detailed on special duty as his personal attendants, Comanche was able by the spring of 1878 to move around without assistance.

Colonel Samuel D. Sturgis, then commanding the regiment, ordered that Comanche be shown every consideration. No one was permitted to ride the animal, and he was turned loose to graze and frolic as he wished. He became the "second commanding officer" of the regiment. On 10 Apr 1878, the following order was issued. It is believed that this order is the only one of its kind that has ever been issued in the service.

Headquarters, 7th U.S. Cavalry
Fort Abraham Lincoln, Dakota Territory
10 Apr 1878
General Orders No. 7

1. The horse known as "Comanche" being the only living representative of the bloody tragedy of the Little Big Horn, Montana, 25 Jun 1876, his kind treatment and comfort should be a matter of special pride and solicitude on the part of the 7th Cavalry, to the end that his life may be prolonged to the utmost limit. Though wounded and scarred, his very silence speaks in terms more eloquent than words of the desperate struggle against overwhelming odds, of the hopeless conflict, and heroic manner in which all went down that day.

2. The commanding officer of "I" troop will see that a special and comfortable stall is fitted up for Comanche. He will not be ridden by any person whatever under any circumstances, nor will he be put to any kind of work.

3. Hereafter upon all occasions of ceremony (of mounted regimental formation), Comanche, saddled, bridled, and led by a mounted trooper of Troop "I," will be paraded with the regiment.

By Command of Colonel Sturgis
/s/ Lieutenant and Adjutant
7th U.S. Cavalry

There have been reports that after the battle of Wounded Knee Creek a certain change came over Comanche. His personal attendant and friend for over 14 years, Blacksmith Gustave Korn, was killed in the battle, and it would seem that he mourned continously for him. From the date of comanche's return to Fort Riley (25 Jan 1891) he seemed to have but little interest in life. He just "didn't care." No matter what Pete Wey tried to do for him, Comanche seemed to get more morose. His "sanitary inspection" of the garbage cans became more frequent. His "sprees" at the canteen almost developed a "panhandle" status. After such "sprees" he was content to lie in his stall or mud wallows until finally on 6 Nov 1891, he passed away at the age of 29 years.

Comanche the horse died, but his spirit continued to march on. He could not be forgotten. That was the feeling of the entire regiment in which he had served for over 23 years. Professor Lewis Lindsay Dyche of the University of Kansas was called to Fort Riley, and preparations were made to mount him in his living form, as a true example or symbol of a cavalry horse.

It was originally intended that Comanche remain with the regiment, but after due deliberation this was not considered feasible, as the troops would be constantly on the move. Until a suitable place was found, the museum at the University of Kansas would suffice. Then, payment for the mounting of Comanche had to be taken into consideration.

At the time of Comanche's death, it was proposed that subscriptions from members of the regiment be taken to cover the costs of Dr. Dyche's work. Like many good intentions, this proposition vanished in thin air, and even to this day there is a certain undercurrent of feeling that the regiment had "not done right" by Comanche and had left him in "hock" with the University. This, however, is not true. Dr. Dyche was very sympathetic with the intentions of the regiment and realized that four hundred dollars was quite an item for a poorly paid body of men. It was finally decided that if the regiment would permit the exhibition of Comanche with the University of Kansas collection at the World's Fair in Chicago in 1893, the debt would be considered paid in full.

The following is a condensed descriptive list of Comanche:

Descriptive list of "Comanche"
Transferred to
Captain Henry J. Nowlan
7th Cavalry

Name: "Comanche"
Age: 6 years (25 years at date of transfer).
Height: 15 hands
Weight: 925 pounds
Color: Buckskin
Peculiar Marks: Left hind fetlock, white - black tail - black mane - white marks on back - small white star on forehead - 12 scars caused by wounds.
Condition: Unserviceable
Date of Purchase: 3 Apr 1868
By Whom: Space left blank (Major E.D. Callendar, O.D.)
Cost: $90
Purchased at: St. Louis, Missouri
Remarks: Excused from all duties per General Orders No. 7, HQs, U.S. Cavalry, dated 10 Apr 1878. Ridden by Captain Keogh in the battle of the Little Big Horn River, M.T., 25 Jun 1876.

I certify that the preceding is a correct transcript from the records of Non-Commissioned Staff and Band, 7th Cavalry.

/s/ James D. Thomas
2nd Lieutenant
7th Cavalry
Acting Adjutant
Station: Fort Meade, D.T.
Date: 25 Jul 1887

The following remarks about Comanche were taken from different historical records of the 7th Cavalry:

Arrived at Fort Leavenworth, Kansas on 10 Jun 1868 for his private mount by Captain Myles W. Keogh, 7th Cavalry, purchase price, $90.

Died at Fort Riley, Kansas, 6 Nov 1891.

Cause: Compaction of the colon; colic and general debility.

Age at time of death, about twenty-nine (29) years.

History and Origin of the Picture
"Custer's Last Fight"

One of the most famous paintings depicting General Armstrong Custer and the 7th U.S. Cavalry in that epic last stand at the Battle of the Little Big Horn is entitled "Custer's Last Fight." This painting for some 70 years has decorated barrooms and saloons from the Bowery to the Barbary Coast. The exact origin of the painting is obscure, but apparently the original was painted by an artist named Cassily Adams. A second painting almost identical, was painted by an artist named Otto Becker. A number of artists have at one time or another made claim to authorship of this famous painting while others have either tried to copy the original or have painted their own versions of the famous battle.

The original (painted by Cassily Adams some time around 1885) is the one from which the lurid lithograph, seen most commonly in barrooms, was reproduced. Little is known about Cassily Adams, but he is reputedly a Civil War veteran and the son of an Ohio lawyer who died in 1921 near Indianapolis. Becker is reported to have made his painting around 1895. The differences in the two paintings is that the Becker painting was bloodier than the Adams painting. The backgrounds are different as are the poses of many of the principal characters; for example in the Adams painting, Custer's saber is raised over his shoulder while in Becker's, he has just slashed forward with it.

Both the Adams and the Becker paintings were owned by Mr. Adolphus Busch, founder of the Anheuser-Busch Corporation of St. Louis, Missouri. The Adams painting was presented to the 7th Cavalry Regiment at Fort Riley, Kansas, around 1890, by Mr. Busch. The original 9 1/2 x 16 1/2 foot picture was painted on a wagon canvas and either displayed in a place of honor in the regiment or rolled up and stored away, depending on the cultural whims of the regimental commander at the time, until it

was destroyed by fire when the Fort Bliss Officers Mess burned in 1946. The original Becker painting is still in the possession of the Anheuser-Busch Corporation in St. Louis.

The following information collect by the Anheuser-Busch Corporation provides some insight as to the origin of the Adams painting.

"After more than 50 years had passed and after more than a million copies had been distributed since it was painted by Cassily Adams, the picture continued to fascinate people.

"The original canvas disappeared mysteriously and as mysteriously reappeared. It became the subject of some lengthy newspaper articles.

"The *El Paso Times* of 25 Oct 1931, reported that 'an original painting of historic value is laid away in a storehouse at Fort Bliss, while a correspondence, nationwide in scope, is being carried on in an endeavor to trace the source from which the painting made its way to the rafters of the old storeroom.'

"The article went on to say that no one at the Army post knew how the painting got there. It was in poor condition (the canvas cracked and the paint dirty) and funds were needed to restore it. The newspaper recounted a lot of Army red tape, culminating in a departmental request for additional data on the painting. It said that the collection of this data was in the hands of Colonel C.F. Martin, formerly commander of the historic 7th Cavalry Regiment, which was Custer's command. It added that Colonel Martin had gleaned the following facts:

From Brigadier General W.J. Nicholsen, retired:

'I remember very distinctly its arrival at Fort Riley, Kansas. It was presented to the 7th Cavalry by the Anheuser-Busch Company of St. Louis. Its value I do not know, but it was a very expensive work.'

From Charles Thompson, Junction City, Kansas, formerly an artillery man, who was present at the presentation:

'The presentation ceremony, I believe, took place in 1892. Mr. Adolphus Busch made the presentation in the Post Mess Hall. The platform was made of mess tables and on it were grouped the 7th Cavalry officers. Colonel Forsythe accepted the painting in behalf of the regiment. It was about eight or ten feet high and was between 40 and 60 feet in length. Mr. Busch said that his firm paid $35,000 for the picture, buying it outright in order to secure the right to reproduce it.'

From Anheuser-Busch:

'After buying the picture, we had it in our reception rooms for several years before presenting it to the 7th Cavalry at Fort Riley. At the outbreak of the Spanish-American War, it was sent elsewhere and we lost all sight of it until we received your letter although we had made inquiry for it through Army publications. To fix the price on the painting would be a hard thing to do because of its subject.'

From Brigadier General Ernest A. Garlington, retired, San Diego, California:

'I feel that the painting was paid for and presented to the regiment by Anheuser-Busch. I never knew the price and I have forgotten the artist. The work had considerable merit as a work of art, although the portrayal was the idea of the artist, based upon newspaper accounts of the engagement and photographs of the officers represented in the picture.'

From Brigadier General Edward S. Godfrey, Cookston, New Jersey:

'The artist's name was Adams, but I do not remember the last name.'

From the Kansas State Historical Society:

'The Custer's Last Fight picture, also known as the Adolphus Busch picture, was the work of an artist, Cassily Adams.'

'The El Paso Times said that after Colonel Martin had summed up his conclusions, he forwarded his data to the office of the adjutant general and received this reply:

'That the painting was presented to the 7th Cavalry at Fort Riley, KS, sometime near 1890 by the Anheuser-Busch Company; that the original value is unknown, but it was probably several thousands of dollars.'

One quip, undoubtedly from a sister regiment, once looked up at a copy of this famous painting hanging over a bar, raised his mug of Budweiser Beer and said, "here's to the beer that made the 7th Cavalry fameless."

Regimental Organizational Day

As noted throughout the history of the regiment, "Organization Day" has been observed on various dates depending partly upon the whims of the commander at the time, and partly as a matter of convenience to the troops. General Orders No. 31, Headquarters 1st Cavalry Division, dated 9

Dec 1948, designated 22 December as "Organization Day," while General Orders No. 29, Headquarters 1st Cavalry Division, dated 15 Jul 1949, changed the date to 23 November.

Notwithstanding these orders, the official "Organization Day" of the 7th U.S. Cavalry Regiment, and all elements thereof, was designated as 25 June, the annniversary date of the Battle of the Little Big Horn. This date-originally designated by the following correspendence and insofar as can be determined was never rescinded-was confirmed as the official "Organization Day" by 3rd Indorsement, Headquarters, Department of the Army, dated 6 Dec 1956.

Headquarters 7th U.S. Cavalry
Camp at Fort Bliss, Texas
26 Jun 1920

FROM: Commanding Office

TO: The Adjutant General of the Army
                  Washington, DC

SUBJECT: Organization Day, 7th Cavalry

1. I report that June 25th has been selected as Organization Day for this Regiment in compliance with Paragraph 7, General Orders 8, War Department, 1920.
2. Copy of Regimental General Orders attached.
/s/ CHAS. J. SYMMONDS,
Colonel 7th Cavalry
CJS/G

AO 314.73 (7th Cav)   1st Ind   FWF/TMR
Room 37
War Department, A.G.O.8 Jul 1920
To Chief of Staff
                                 /s/ FWF

                                 2nd Ind
A.G. 314/73
Rcom 37
War Department A.G.O.   14 Jul 1920
To Commanding Officer, 7th Cavalry,
Camp Fort Bliss, Texas

                  Approved.
                  By order of the Secretary of War
                  /s/ Adjutant General

Troop J

Tales as to the fate of Troop J (or Company J) have circulated throughout the Army for many years, and it is common practice for the sergeant to order the recruit to deliver a message to the Orderly Room of Company J. Hours later when the poor recruit reports to the sergeant that he cannot find Company J, he is placed on detail for his lengthy absence. Every regiment has its fantastic tales about Company J-the unit which disgraced the colors, broke and ran, lost the colors, ad infinitum. Such tales have been particularly prevalent among cavalry units in referring to the 7th Cavalry Regiment's participation in the Battle of the Little Big Horn.

The truth is that there has never been a Company (or Troop) J in the United States Army. Nothing has been found of record in the files of the Department of the Army stating the precise reason why the letter "J" was never used to designate military units. However, it is pretty well established that Colonel Charles K. Gardner, while serving as adjutant general with the rank of colonel in the Division of the North during the War of 1812, was the originator of the system of using letters to designate companies. Colonel Gardner's record contained in *A Dictionary of All Officers, Army of the United States, 1789-January 1853*, compiled by him, includes the statement: "Author of the permanent designation of companies and company books by the first letters of the alphabet." Furthermore, it is generally accepted, although no record has been found in the official files of the Army, that Colonel Gardner stated that the letter "J" was not used at the time of the establishment of the lettering system because at that time (1816)

the letters "I" and "J" were written exactly alike and that, consequently, the letter "J" was omitted to prevent confusion. Contemporary manuscripts show this to be the case. In this connection, it is customary in lettering city streets to omit the letter "J" possibly for the same reason.

The following Division Orders issued by Major General Brown, Northern Division, 22 May 1816, established the first known system of permanently designating companies by letters of the alphabet. Major General Jackson of the Divison of the South issued similar orders dated 21 Aug 1816.

(Adjutant General Office
(Brownsville 22 May 1816

Division Orders

The companies of the regiments of Light Artillery and Infantry in the Northern Division will be permanently designated by the first letters of the Alphabet-in the order in which the Captains in each regiment stand in the register, completed to the 17th instant-placing the two Light companies in the Infantry first, as follows;-A and B (for the select companies in the Infantry) C, D, E, F, G, H, I and K for the battalion companies. The sixteen companies of Artillery will also be lettered, in the order of seniority of the Captains in this Division.

These designations are never to be changed, with the change of Captains-and after a company book is opened, such company is not to be broken up. The transfer of individual men and of subalterns may be made by the Colonel, with the consent of the Captains concerned-and a transfer of Officers or Men, by the Commanding Officer of the Department, on the application of the commander of a Regiment or Battalion-except that no transfer will be made from one Battalion or Regiment to another, but by the General of the Division.

The Light companies, after being selected by the Colonel, will be permanent. They will be constantly improved, by selection from recruits, and the mode of transfer herein authorized, with as little prejudice to the battalion companies, and as little excitement of jealousy among the officers, as possible. When the vacancy of an officer occurs in a Light company it will be supplied by the Colonel's selection. *By order of Major General Brown,C.K. Gardner, Adj. Gen.*

The following are the first known published General Regulations pertaining to the lettering of companies:

General Regulations For The
United States Army
1821
(pp. 37-38)
Article 24.

Designation and Consolidation of Companies

1. At the first organization of a regiment or independent battalion, the companies will be designated by letters of the alphabet, giving the first letters to the flank companies, according to the rank of the respective captains, or, if the rank be not settled, by lottery-and the next highest letters of the alphabet to the remaining companies, on the same principle.
2. Designations so given will be as permanent as the regiment or independent battalion. A change in the relative rank of the captains will of course change the positions of the companies in the habitual order of battle, whether the captains be present or not, but will not change the letters of the companies.
3. When any company, serving with the colours, cannot be kept up to the number of twenty-eight privates, the commander will designate a recruiting party, and transfer the remainder of the company to the other companies present. In this case, the captain and the party designated and sent on the recruiting service, would retain the letter of the company, and the books and papers belonging to it-excepting such papers as ought necessarily to go with the men transferred.
4. On the return to the regiment of a company sent on the recruiting service, the colonel will, if he thinks it expedient, re-transfer to it a part of the old soldiers in lieu of as many recruits.
5. In war, the minimum strength of companies, as fixed above, may be changed, in any particular army in the field, by the commander thereof.

Troop L
7th U.S. Cavalry

Troop L of each Cavalry Regiment in the Army was skeletonized by General Order 79, dated 25 Jul 1890; however, on 9 Mar 1891 these troops were designated "Indian Troops" and filled with Indian recruits. Troop L, 7th U.S. Cavalry Regiment as organized at Fort Sill, Oklahoma Territory, and filled with Apache prisoners of war-many from the Fort Sill stockade.

These Indian troops were not Indian Scouts, but a part of the Regular military establishment designed to obtain worthwhile service from the Indian prisoners and as a means of rehabilitating them. Initially the officers and non-commissioned officers were taken from the other troops in the regiment and assigned to Troop L. It was planned to promote the Indians to non-commissioned rank when they became qualified. This experiment was not successful, partly due to the language barrier which existed between the officers and non-commissioned officers and the Indians. The following is an extract of the order activating Troop L, 7th U.S. Cavalry Regiment:

HEADQUARTERS OF THE ARMY
Adjutant General's Office
Washington, 9 Mar 1891

General Orders,
No. 28

By direction of the Secretary of War the following instructions are published for the information and guidance of all concerned:

1. The following named companies, now skeletonized under the provisions of General Orders Nos. 76 and 79, of 1890, namely, Troop L of each of the cavalry regiments (except the 9th and 10th) and Company I of each of the infantry regiments (except the 6th, 11th, 15th, 19th, 24th, and 25th), will be recruited by the enlistment of the Indians to the number of fifty-five for each troop and company. Whenever practicable, the enlistments for each regiment will be made within the department in which the regimental headquarters are located, by officers to be nominated by and under the immediate supervision of the regimental commander. When necessary, special instructions for recruiting in other localities will be given from the Headquarters for the Army, upon the recommendation of the department commander.

The officers, in making such enlistments, will be under the direction and control of the respective commanders of departments as special department recruiting officers, and will render the usual reports and returns. In general, they will be governed by existing laws and regulations, but a competent knowledge of the English language need not be considered an essential qualification, and married men not exceeding ten for each troop or company may be enlisted, with the approval of the department commander. Enlistments of Indians under the provisions of this order will be separately reported on tri-monthly reports and other returns of the recruiting service, and will be carefully distinguished from enlistments of Indian scouts.

Regimental commanders may, with the approval of the proper department commander, temporarily attach to the Indian companies such officers as are especially fitted for service therewith, and as soon as prepared to recommend officers for permanent assignment thereto, will submit their names, through the proper channel, to the Adjutant General.

Ultimately, non-commissioned officers for these companies will be supplied by the appointment of Indians in the manner indicated by Regulations, but until this is practicable, available non-commissioned officers of either of the skeleton companies of a regiment may be utilized, or, if necessary, non-commissioned officers from organized companies of the regiment may be temporarily detailed. *By Command of Major General Scofield: OFFICIAL: J. C. Kelton, Adjutant General.*

The following Report of the Secretary of War, 1897 (page 218), reports the inactivation of the Indian Troops. It is interesting to note that Troop L, 7th U.S. Cavalry Regiment, was the last of these troops to be inactivated.

Indian Enlistments

"No enlistments nor re-enlistments for the Indian contingent as made during the fiscal year ended 20 Jun 1897, but 19 Indians were enlisted or re-enlisted for duty as scouts.

The discharge, 31 May 1897, of the 53 Indians comprising Troop L, 7th Cavalry, ended the scheme-formulated by General Orders No. 28, from General Headquarters, dated 9 Mar 1891-of recruiting eight troops of cavalry and 19 companies of infantry to form an Indian contingent as part of the regular establishment. Notwithstanding strenuous and intelligent efforts on the part of the officers selected for the recruiting, command, and management of the several Indian troops and companies, the Indian contingent has reached a degree of substantial success as useful soldiers. The total number of Indian soldiers enlisted and re-enlisted since March 1891 was 1,071."

Battle Statistics For
The Battle Of The Little Big Horn
25-26 Jun 1876

There has always been some question, some speculation and considerable argument as to the losses sustained, names of survivors and participants in the Battle of the Little Big Horn.

All information shown herein is the result of many years of painstaking research by Major Edward S. Luce (Ret.), retired superintendent of the Custer Battlefield National Monument, Crow Agency, Montana, and present historian of the 7th U.S. Cavalry Association, and is used with his express permission.

The following names are taken from the *Return of Alterations and Casualties of the 7th Regiment of United States Cavalry*, 30 Jun 1876.*

———
Keogh, Comanche and Custer, E.S. Luce, 1939. John S. Swift Company, St. Louis, Missouri, pp. 92-96.

COMMISSIONED OFFICERS KILLED*

Brevet Rank	Rank	Name	Organization
Maj. Gen	Lieut. Col	George A. Custer	
Lieut. Col	1st Lieut & Adjutant	William Winer Cooke	
Lieut. Col	Captain	Myles Walter Keogh	Co. I
Lieut. Col	Captain	George W. Yates	Co. F
Lieut. Col	Captain	Thomas Ward Custer	Co. C
Lieut. Col	1st Lieut	Donald McIntosh	Co. G
Lieut. Col	1st Lieut	James Calhoun	Co. C
Captain	1st Lieut	Algernon E. Smith	Co. A
Captain	1st Leiut	James Ezekiel Porter	Co. I
Captain	2nd Lieut	Benjamin Hubert Hodgson	Co. B
Captain	2nd Lieut	Henry Moore Harrington	Co. C
Captain	2nd Lieut	James Garland Sturgis	Co. M
Captain	2nd Lieut	William Van W. Reily	Unassigned
Attached	2nd Lieut	John Jordan Crittenden	20th Infantry
Attached	Asst Surgeon	G. E. Lord	
Attached	Acting Asst Surgeon	J. M. De Wolf	

*Among the 16 officers cited in the killed column of the casualty list of the battle of the Little Big Horn, M.T., there were three whose bodies were never found, Lieutenants Porter, Sturgis and Harrington. Of the 237 enlisted men there were 14 bodies never recovered. The majority of these, most likely wounded and unable to ford the river with Reno's routed force, were drowned.

Enlisted Men Killed

Non-Commissioned Staff

Sergeant Major
William H. Sharrow

Chief Trumpeter
Henry Voss

Company "A"
Corporal
James Dalious

Privates
John Armstrong
James Drinan
James McDonald
William Moody
Richard Rollins
John Sullivan
Thomas P. Sweetzer

Company "B"
Privates
Richard Dorn
George B. Mack

Company "C"
1st Sergeant
Edwin Bobo

Sergeants
August Finckle
Jeremiah Finley

Corporals
John Foley
Henry E. French
Daniel Ryan

Trumpeters
Thomas J. Bucknell
William Kramer

Saddler
George Hawell

Farrier
John King

Privates
Fred C. Allen
John Brightfield
Christopher Criddle
George Eisemann
Gustave Engle
James Ferrand
Patrick Griffin
James Hathersall
John Lewis
August Meyer
Frederick Meyer
Edgar Phillips
John Rauter
Edward Rix
James H. Russell
Ludwick St. John
Samuel S. Shade
Jeremiah Shea
Nathan Short
Alpheus Stuart
Ignatz Stungwitz
John Thadus
Garret Van Allen
Oscar L. Warner
Willis B. Wright
Henry Wyman

Company "D"
Farrier
Vincent Charley

Privates
Patrick M. Golden
Edward Housen

Company "E"
1st Sergeant
Frederick Hohmeyer

Sergeants
William B. James
John S. Ogden

Corporals:
George C. Brown
Thomas Hagan
Henry S. Mason
Albert H. Meyer

Trumpeters
Thomas McElroy
George A. Moonie

Privates
William H. Baker
Robert Barth
Owen Boyle
James Brogan
Edward Conner
John Darris
William Davis
Richard Farrell
John Heim
John Henderson
Sykes Henderson
William Hieber
John Hiley
Andy Knecht
Herod T. Liddiard
Patrick O'Connor
William H. Rees
Edward Rood
Henry Schele
William Smallwood
Albert A. Smith
James Smith, 1st
James Smith, 2nd
Benjamin Stafford
Alexander Stella
William A. Torrey
Cornelius Van Sant
George Walker

Company "F"
1st Sergeant
Michael Kenny

Sergeants
Frederick Nursey
John Vickory
John R. Wilkinson

Corporals
John Briody
Charles Coleman
William Teeman

Farrier
Benjamin Brandon

Blacksmith
James R. Manning

Privates
Thomas Atchison
William Brady
Benjamin F. Brown
William Brown
Patrick Bruce
Lucien Burnham
James Carney
Armantheus D. Cather
Anton Dohman
Timothy Donnelly
George W. Hammond
John Kelly
Gustave Klein
Herman Knauth
William H. Lerock
Werner L. Lieman
William A. Lossee
Christian Madson
Francis E. Milton
Joseph Monroe
Sabastian Omling
Patrick Rudden
Richard Saunders
Francis W. Siefous
George A. Warren
Thomas N. Way

Company "G"
Sergeants
Edward Botzer
Martin Considine

Corporals
Otto Hagemann
James Martin

Trumpeter
Henry Dose

Farrier
Benjamin Wells

Saddler
Crawford Selby

Privates
John J. McGinniss
Andrew J. Moore
John Rapp
Benjamin F. Rogers
Henry Seafferman
Edward Stanley

Company "H"
Corporal
George Lell

Privates
Julien D. Jones
Thomas E. Meador

Company "I"
1st Sergeant
Frank E. Varden

Sergeant
James Bustard

Corporals
George C. Morris
Samuel F. Staples
John Wild

Trumpeters
John McGucker
John W. Patton

Saddler
Henry A. Bailey

Privates
John Barry
Joseph H. Broadhurst
Thomas Conners
Thomas P. Downing
Edward Driscoll
David C. Gillette
George H. Gross
Adam Hetismer
Edward P. Holcomb
Marion E. Horn
Patrick Kelley
Henry Lehman
Edward W. Lloyd
Archibald McIlhargey
John Mitchell
Jacob Noshang
John O'Bryan
John Parker
Felix James Pitter
George Post
James Quinn
William Reed
John W. Rossbury
Darwin L. Symms
James E. Troy
Charles Von Bramer
William B. Whaley

Company "K"
1st Sergeant
Dewitt Winney

Sergeant
Robert M. Hughes

Corporal
John J. Callahan

Privates
Elihu F. Clear
Julius Helmer

Company "L"
1st Sergeant
James Butler

Sergeants
William Cashan
Amos B. Warren

Corporals
William H. Gilbert
William H. Harrison
John Seiler

Trumpeter
Frederick Walsh

Blacksmith
Charles Siemon

Farrier
William H. Heath

Saddler
Charles Perkins

Privates
George E. Adams
William Andrews
Anthony Assadely
Elmer Babcock
John Burke
Ami Cheever
William B. Crisfield
John Duggan
William Dye
James J. Galvan
Charles Graham
Henry Hamilton
Weston Harrington
Louis Haugge
Francis T. Hughes
Thomas G. Kavanagh
Louis Lobering
Charles McCarthy
Peter McGue
Berthol Mahoney
Thomas E. Maxwell
John Miller
David J. O'Connell
Christian Reibold
Henry Roberts
Walter B. Rogers
Charles Schmidt
Charles Scott
Bent Siemonson
Andrew Snow
Byron Tarbox
Edward D. Tessier
Thomas S. Tweed
Michael Vetter

Company "M"
Sergeant
Miles F. O'Hara

Corporals
Henry M. Scollin
Frederick Streing

Privates
Henry Gordon
Henry Kotzbucher
George Lorentz
William D. Meyer
George E. Smith
David Summers
James J. Tanner
Henry Turley
Henry C. Voigt

Civilians

Boston Custer, brother of General Custer and Captain Custer.
Isaiah Dorman, Negro-Indian interpreter.
Mark Kellogg, newspaper reporter for *The Bismarck, North Dakota Tribune* and *The New York Herald*.
Frank C. Mann, chief packer.
Henry Armstrong Reed, nephew of General Custer.
Charley Reynolds, chief scout.

Indian Scouts

Bloody Knife — Mitch Bouyer, half-breed
Bob-Tailed Bull — Stab

The following is a roster of the survivors of the 7th United States Cavalry as of 30 Jun 1876, as taken from the Muster Rolls and Pay Rolls, Alterations and Casualties Returns, Company and Regimental Field Returns, 30 Apr to 30 Jun 1876.

Commissioned Officers

Brevet Rank	Permanent Co.	Rank	Name	Duty Status
Maj. Gen.		Colonel	Sturgis, Samuel D. Detached duty at St. Louis, MO.	
		Lt. Col.	Vacancy	
Colonel		Major	Merrill, Lewis Detached duty at Philadelphia, PA.	
Lieut. Col.		Major	Tilford, Joseph G. On leave of absence.	
Colonel		Major	Reno, Marcus A. Command regiment since June 25, 1876.	
		1st Lt.	Wallace, George D.	Adjutant.
		1st Lt.	Nowlan, Henry J. Quartermaster with Brig. Gen. Terry's staff	
	A	Captain	Moylan, Myles Comd'g Company.	
		1st Lt.	Vacancy	
		2nd Lt.	Varnum, Charles A. Comd'g Detachment of Indian Scouts.	
	B	Captain	McDougall, Thomas M. Comd'g Company.	
		1st Lt.	Craycroft, William T. Detached duty at St. Paul, MN.	
		2nd Lt.	Vacancy	
	C	Captain	Vacancy	
		1st Lt.	Vacancy	
		2nd Lt.	Vacancy	
Lieut. Col.	D	Captain	Wier, Thomas B. Comd'g Company.	
		1st Lt.	Bell, James M. Leave of Absence.	
		2nd Lt.	Edgerly, Winfield S. Duty with Company performing duties of Regt. Quartermaster.	
	E	Captain	Ilsleys, Charles S. Detached duty at Ft. Leavenworth, KS.	
		1st Lt.	DeRudio, Charles C. On temporary duty with Co. A, 7th U.S. Cavalry.	
		2nd Lt.	Vacancy	
	F	Captain	Vacancy	
		1st Lt.	Jackson, Henry DS* at Washington, DC.	
		2nd Lt.	Larned, Charles W. DS at U.S. Military Academy, West Point, NY.	
Lieut. Col.	G	Captain	Tourtellote, John E. DS as Aide-de-Camp to Gen. W.T. Sherman, Washington, DC.	
		1st Lt.	Vacancy	
		2nd Lt.	Vacancy	
Colonel	H	Captain	Benteen, Frederick W. Comd'g Company.	
		1st Lt.	Gibson, Francis M. On temporary duty comd'g Co. G, 7th U.S. Cavalry.	
		2nd Lt.	Vacancy	
	I	Captain	Vacancy	
		1st Lt.	Vacancy	
		2nd Lt.	Nave, Andrew C. Absent Sick Leave.	
	K	Captain	Hale, Owen DS at St. Louis, MO.	
		1st Lt.	Godfrey, Edward S. Comd'g Company.	
		2nd Lt.	Hare, Luther R. On duty with Co.	
Lieut. Col.	L	Captain	Sheridan, Michael V. DS as Aide-de-Camp to Lt. Gen. Philip Sheridan.	
		1st Lt.	Braden, Charles Absent Sick Leave.	
		2nd Lt.	Vacancy	
	M	Captain	French, Thomas H. Comd'g Company.	
		1st Lt.	Mathey, Edward G. Duty with Co.	
		2nd Lt.	Vacancy	
Veterinary Surgeon			Stein, C. A. Duty with Regt.	

_____

*DS - Detached Service.

The names of the enlisted men who do not have a notation after their names were on duty with their respective companies, participated in the Battle of the Little Big Horn, and were not wounded. The status of all others immediately following the battle is shown by appropriate remarks. Each note regarding duty status, etc. applies to the name immediately preceding.

Enlisted Men

Regimental Non-Commissioned Staff

Quartermaster Sergeant - Causby, Thomas
 DS Supply Base, Powder River, M.T.* 6/14/76
Saddler Sergeant - Tritten, John G.
 DS Supply Base, Powder River, M.T. 6/14/76

Band

Chief Musician - Vinatieni, Felix,
DS Supply Base, Powder River, M.T. 6/14/76
Private - Arndt, Otto
DS Supply Base, Powder River, M.T. 6/14/76
Private - Baumbach, Conrad
DS Supply Base, Powder River, M.T. 6/14/76
Private - Burlis Edmond
DS Supply Base, Powder River, M.T. 6/14/76
Private - Carter, Andrew
DS Supply Base, Powder River, M.T. 6/14/76
Private - Carroll, Joseph
DS Supply Base, Powder River, M.T. 6/14/76
Private - Eisenberger, Peter
DS Supply Base, Powder River, M.T. 6/14/76
Private - Emerich, Jacob
DS Supply Base, Powder River, M.T. 6/14/76
Private - Griesner, Julius
DS Supply Base, Powder River, M.T. 6/14/76
Private - Jungesbluth, Julius
DS Supply Base, Powder River, M.T. 6/14/76
Private - Kneubuchle, Joseph
Sick at Ft. Lincoln, D.T.** since 5/4/76
Private - Lombard, Frank
Sick at Ft. Lincoln, D.T. since 5/4/76
Private - Merritt, George A.
Sick at Ft. Lincoln, D.T. since 5/4/76
Private - O'Neill, Bernard
DS Supply Base, Powder River, M.T. 6/14/76
Private - Rudolph, George
DS Supply Base, Powder River, M.T. 6/14/76
Private - Sherbon, Thomas
DS Supply Base, Powder River, M.T. 6/14/76

Company A

1st Sergeant - Heyn, William
(Wounded)
Sergeant - Fehler, Henry
Sergeant - Alcott, Samuel
Ds Supply Base, Powder River, M.T. 6/15/76
Sergeant - McDermott, George
Sergeant - Culbertson, Ferdinand A.
Sergeant - Easley, John Thomas
Corporal - Roy, Stanislas
Corporal - King, George H.
(Wounded) Steamer Far West since 6/28/76

Trumpeter - Hardy, William G.
Trumpeter - McVeigh, David
Farrier - Bringes, John
Blacksmith - Hamilton, Andrew
Saddler - Muering, John
Private - Aller, Charles
Private - Bancroft, Neil
Private - Blair, Wilbur F.
Private - Blake, Thomas
Private - Bockerman, August
DS with Band, Powder River, M.T. 6/15/76
Private - Borter, Ludwig
Private - Bott, George
Private - Burdick, Benjamin F.
DS Suppy Base, Powder River, M.T. 6/15/76
Private - Conner, Andrew
Private - Cowley, Cornelius
Private - Diehle, Jacob
(Wounded) Steamer Far West, since 6/28/76
Private - Durselew, Otto
Private - Foster, Samuel
(Wounded) Steamer Far West, since 6/28/76
Private - Franklin, John W.
Private - Gilbert, John M.
Private - Harris, David W.
Private - Holmsted, Frederick
(Wounded) Steamer Far West, since 6/28/76
Private - Hook, Stanton
Private - Ionson, Emil O.
Private - Johnson, Samuel
Private - Keer, Dennis
DS Ft. Lincoln, D.T. since 5/5/76
Private - McClurg, William
Private - Nugent, William D.
Private - Proctor, George W.
Private - Ragsdale, John S.
DS Supply Base, Powder River, M.T. 6/16/76
Private - Reeves, Francis M.
(Wounded) Steamer Far West, since 6/28/76
Private - Seayers, Thomas
Private - Siebelder, Anton
Private - Strode, Elijah T.
(Wounded) Steamer Far West, since 6/28/76
Private - Taylor, William O.
Private - Weaver, Howard H.
Private - Weis, John
DS Ft. Lincoln, D.T. since 5/5/76

Company B

1st Sergeant - Hill, James
Sergeant - Carroll, Daniel
DS Ft. Lincoln, D.T. since 5/17/76
Sergeant - Criswell, Benjamin C.
Sergeant - Gannon, Peter
Sergeant - Hutchinson, Rufus D.
Sergeant - Murray, Thomas
Corporal - Cunningham, Charles
Corporal - Dougherty, James
Corporal - Smith, William M.
Corporal - Wetzel, Adam
Trumpeter - Connell, John
Trumpeter - Kelley, James
Blacksmith - Crump, John
Farrier - Moore, James E.
Saddler - Bailey, John E.

Private - Abos, James A.
In confinement at Ft. Richardson, Texas since 1
    May
1876
Private - Barry, Peter O.
Private - Barsantee, James F.
Private - Boam, William
Private - Bonner, Hugh
Private - Boren, Ansgarius
Private - Brainard, George
Private - Brown, James
Private - Burns, Charles
Private - Caldwell, William M.
Private - Callan, James
Private - Callan, Thomas J.
Private - Campbell, Charles A.
Private - Carmody, Thomas
Private - Carey, John J.
Private - Clark, Frank
Private - Coleman, Thomas W.
Private - Criswell, Harry
Private - Crowe, Michael
Private - Crowley, Patrick
Private - Davenport, William H.
Private - DeTourriel, Louis
Private - Devoto, Agustus L.
Private - Doll, Jacob W.
Private - Frank, William
Private - Gehrmann, Frederick H.
Private - Gray, John
Private - Keefe, John J.
Private - Klaweitter, Ferdinand
DS Ft. Lincoln, D.T. since 5/17/76
Private - Lewis, David W.
Confinement at Ft. Barrancas, FL, since 26 Apr
1876
Private - Littlefield, John L.
Private - Martin, William
Private - McCabe, John
Private - McGurn, Bernard
Private - McLaughlin, Terrence
Private - McMasters, William
Private - Morrow, William E.
Private - O'Brien, Thomas
Private - O'Neill, James
Sick at Ft. Lincoln, D.T. since 5/17/76
Private - O'Neill, John
Private - Pym, James
Private - Randall, George F.
Private - Ryan, Stephen L.
Private - Sager, Hiram W.
Private - Shea, Daniel
Private - Simons, Patrick
Private - Spinner, Philip
Private - Stout, Edward
Private - Thomas, James (alias Stowers, James)
Private - Tinkham, Henry L.
Private - Trumble, William
Private - Wallace, Richard A.
Private - Wight, Edwin B.
Private - Woods, Aaron

Company C

Sergeant - Hanley, Richard P.
Sergeant - Kanipe, Daniel A.

Sergeant - Miller, Edwin
DS Ft. Lincoln, D.T. 5/5/76
Corporal - Crandall, Charles A.
Farrier - Fitzgerald, John
Wagoner - Starck, Frank
Private - Arnold, Herbert
DS Ft. Lincoln, D.T. 5/5/76
Private - Bennett, James C.
Private - Bischoff, Charles H.
Private - Brandal, William
Private - Brennan, John
Private - Corcoran, John
In confinement at Ft. Lincoln, D.T. 5/5/76
Private - Farrer, Morris
Private - Fowler, Isaac
Private - Jordan, John
Private - Kane, William
Private - Lovett, Meredith
In confinement at Ft. Lincoln, D.T. 5/5/76
Private - Mahoney, John
Private - McCreedy, Thomas
DS Ft. Lincoln, D.T. 5/5/76
Private - McGuire, John
Private - Mullin, Martin
Private - Nitsche, Ottocar
Private - Orr, Charles M.
Private - Thompson, Peter
Private - Vahlert, Jacob
Sick in Hospital, Ft. Lincoln, D.T. 5/5/76
Private - Van Arnim, Julius
Private - Walker, Robert
Private - Watson, James
Private - Whittaker, Alfred

Company D

1st Sergeant - Martin, Michael
Sergeant - Flanagan, James
Sergeant - Harrison, Thomas W.
Sergeant - Morton, Thomas
Sick in Hospital, Ft. Lincoln, D.T. 5/5/76
Sergeant - Russell, Thomas
Corporal - Cunningham, Albert J.
DS Supply Base, Powder River, M.T. 6/15/76
Corporal - Wylie, George W.
Trumpeter - Bohner, Aloys
Saddler - Meyers, John
Blacksmith - Deitline, Frederick
Private - Alberts, James H.
Private - Ascough, John B.
Private - Brant, Abraham B.
Private - Conlan, Thomas
Private - Cowley, Stephen
DS Supply Base, Powder River, M.T. 6/15/76
Private - Cox, Thomas
Private - Dann, George
Private - Dawsey, David E.
Private - Fay, John J.
Private - Fox, Harvey A.
DS Supply Base, Powder River, M.T. 6/15/76
Private - Fox., John
Private - Green, John
DS Supply Base, Powder River, M.T. 6/15/76
Private - Green, Joseph
Private - Hall, Curtis
Private - Hall, Edward

DS Ft. Lincoln, D.T., since 5/5/76
Private - Hardden, William
Private - Harlfinger, Gustave
DS Supply Base, Powder River, M.T. 6/15/76
Private - Harris, James
Private - Harris, William M.
Private - Hayer, John
Private - Hetler, Jacob
Private - Holden, Henry
Private - Horn, George
Private - Houghtaling, Charles H.
DS Steamer Far West, since 6/29/76
Private - Hunt, George
Private - Hurd, James
Private - Kanavagh, John
Private - Keller, John
Private - Kipp, Fremont
Private - Kretchmer, Joseph
Private - Kuehl, Jesse
DS Supply Base, Powder River, M.T. 6/16/76
Private - Lewis, Uriah S.
DS Band, Supply Base, Powder River, M.T. 6/16/76
Private - Manning, David
Private - Marshall, William A.
Private - Meadwell, John
Private - Mueller, William
DS Ft. Lincoln, D.T., since 5/5/76
Private - O'Donnel, Patrick
DS Steamer Far West, since 6/29/76
Private - O'Mann, William
Private - Quinn, John
DS Supply Base, Powder River, M.T. 6/15/76
Private - Randall, William J.
Private - Reid, Elwyn S.
Private - Sadler, William
DS Supply Base, Powder River, M.T. 6/15/76
Private - Sanders, Charles
Private - Scott, George
Private - Sims, John J.
DS Supply Base, Powder River, M.T. 6/15/76
Private - Smith, Henry G.
Private - Smith, William E.
Private - Stivers, Thomas W.
Private - Tolan, Frank
Private - Welch, Charles H.
Private - Wynn, James

Company E

Sergeant - Murphy, Lawrence
Sergeant - Riley, James T.
Sergeant - Wells, John
On Furlough, Ft. Lincoln, D.T. 5/17/76
Farrier - Spencer, Abel B.
Saddler - Shields, William
Blacksmith - Miller, Henry
Private - Abbots, Harry
Private - Achison, David
Sick in Hospital, Ft. Lincoln, D.T.
Private - Berwald, Frank
Private - Bromwell, Latrobe
Private - Brumms, August
DS Ft. Lincoln, D.T. 5/17/76
Private - Gilbert, Julius
DS Ft. Lincoln, D.T. 5/17/76

Private - Howard, Frank
DS Ft. Lincoln, D.T. 5/17/76
Private - Hutter, Anton
Confinement in insane hospital at Washington, DC
since 6/19/72
Private - James, John
Private - Kimm, John G.
Private - Lang, Henry
Private - McCann, Patrick
In confinement, Ft. Lincoln, D.T. 5/17/76
Private - McKenna, John
Private - O'Toole, Francis
Private - Pandtle, Christopher
Private - Reese, William
Private - Woodruff, Jerry
DS at Ft. Lincoln, D.T. 5/17/76

Company F

Sergeant - Curtis, William A.
Sergeant - Drago, Henry
DS at Ft. Lincoln, D.T. 5/13/76
Corporal - Clyde, Edward
Saddler - Schleiper, Claus
Private - Brown, Hiram E.
Private - Butler, James W.
Private - Davern, Edward
Private - Downing, Alexander
DS at Ft. Lincoln, D.T. 5/13/76
Private - Eades, William
Private - Finnegan, Thomas J.
Private - Gregg, William J.
Private - Harris, Leonard A.
In confinement at Newport, Kentucky 5/28/75
Private - Hegner, Francis
Private - Howard, Frank
Private - Hunt, Frank
Private - Kleiner, Nicholas
DS at Ft. Lincoln, D.T. 5/13/76
Private - Lefler, Meig
Private - Lynch, Dennis
Private - Lyons, Bernard
Private - Meinike, Ernst
DS at Ft. Lincoln, D.T. 5/13/76
Private - Milton, Joseph
Private - Myers, Frank
Private - Pickard, Edwin H.
Private - Pilcher, Albert
Private - Rconey, James J.
Private - Rielley, Michael
Private - Schleifferth, Paul
Private - Shutte, Frederick
Private - Sweeney, John W.
Private - Sweeney, William
In hand of Civil Authorities at Bismarck, D.T., since 23 Jan 1876
Private - Thorp, Michael
DS at Ft. Lincoln, D.T. 5/13/76
Private - Walsh, Thomas

Company G

1st Sergeant - Garlick, Edward
On four months furlough in England since 14 Apr 1876

Sergeant - Brinkerhoff, Henry
Sergeant - Brown, Alexander
Sergeant - Cressey, Melanchton H.
DS Supply Base, Powder River, M.T. 6/15/76
Sergeant - Hammon, John E.
Sergeant - Lloyd, Frank
On DS at Ft. Lincoln, D.T. 5/15/76
Sergeant - Loyd, George
Sergeant - Northeg, Orlans
Sergeant - Wallace, John W.
Trumpeter - Carter, Cassius R.
DS Shreveport, LA since 4/19/76
Blacksmith - Taylor, Walter O.
Private - Barnet, Charles
DS Supply Base, Powder River, M.T. 6/15/76
Private - Boyle, James P.
Private - Campbell, Charles
Private - Dwyer, Edmond
Private - Flood, Philip
DS Insane Asylum, Washington, DC 4/27/75
Private - Geist, Frank J.
DS Supply Base, Powder River, M.T. 6/15/76
Private - Goldin, Theodore W.
Private - Graham, Thomas
Private - Gray, William S.
DS Supply Base, Powder River, M.T. 6/15/76
Private - Grayson, Edward
Private - Hackett, John
Private - Henderson, George W.
DS Supply Base, Powder River, M.T. 6/15/76
Private - Johnson, Benjamin
Private - Katzenmaier, Jacob
DS Supply Base, Powder River, M.T. 6/15/76
Private - Kilfoyle, Martin
DS Supply Base, Powder River, M.T. 6/15/76
Private - Laden, Joseph
DS Ft. Lincoln, D.T. 5/17/76
Private - Lattman, John
Private - Lauper, Frank
DS Supply Base, Powder River, M.T. 6/15/76
Private - Lawler, James
DS Ft. Lincoln, D.T. 5/17/76
Private - McCormick, Samuel
Private - McDonnell, John
Private - McEagan, John
Private - McGonigle, Hugh
Private - McKay, Edward J.
DS Supply Base, Powder River, M.T. 6/15/76
Private - McKee, John
DS Supply Base, Powder River, M.T. 6/15/76
Private - McVay, John
Private - Morrison, John
Private - O'Neill, Thomas
Private - Petring, Henry
Private - Reed, John A.
Private - Robb, Eldorado I.
Private - Rowland, Robert
DS Supply Base, Powder River, M.T. 6/15/76
Private - Shanahan, John
DS Supply Base, Powder River, M.T. 6/15/76
Private - Small, John R.
Private - Stephens, George W.
DS Supply Base, Powder River, M.T. 6/15/76
Private - Stevenson, Thomas
Private - Sullivan, Daniel
DS Supply Base, Powder River, M.T. 6/15/76

Private - Tulo, Joseph
DS Supply Base, Powder River, M.T. 6/15/76
Private - Weiss, Markus
Private - Williamson, Pasavan
DS Supply Base, Powder River, M.T. 6/15/76

Company H

1st Sergeant - McCurry, Joseph
Sergeant - Connelly, Patrick
Sergeant - Geiger, George
Sergeant - Maroney, Matthew
Sergeant - McLaughlin, Thomas
Sergeant - Pahl, John
(Wounded) Steamer Far West, 6/29/76
Corporal - Bishop, Alexander B.
(Wounded) Steamer Far West, 6/29/76
Corporal - Nealon, Daniel
Farrier - Marshall, John M.
Sick in Hospital, Ft. Rice, D.T. 5/5/76
Blacksmith - Mechlin, Henry W. B.
Saddler - Voit, Otto
Trumpeter - Martin, John
Trumpeter - Ramell, William
Private - Adams, Jacob
Private - Avery, Charles E.
In confinement Ft. Lincoln, D.T. 5/17/76
Private - Bishley, Henry
Private - Bishop, Charles H.
(Wounded) Steamer Far West, 6/29/76
Private - Black, Henry
Private - Channell, William
Private - Cooper, John
(Wounded) Steamer Far West, 6/29/76
Private - D'amond, Edward
Private - Day, John
Private - Dewey, John W.
Private - Farly, William
(Wounded) Steamer Far West, 6/29/76
Private - George, William
Private - Glease, George W.
Private - Haack, Henry
Private - Haley, Timothy
Private - Hood, Charles M.
Sick, Ft. Lincoln, D.T. since 5/17/76
Private - Hughes, Thomas
Private - Hunt, John
Private - Kelly, George
Private - Kelly, James
Private - Lambertin, Frank
Sick, Ft. Lincoln, D.T. since 5/17/76
Private - Lawhorn, Thomas
Private - Maller, Jan
Private - McDermott, Thomas
Private - McNamara, James
Private - McWilliams, David
Private - Muller, John
Confinement, Columbus Bks., Ohio since 12/22/75
Private - Nees, Elder
Private - Nicholas, Joshua S.
Private - O'Ryan, William
Private - Phillips, John
(Wounded) Steamer Far West, 6/29/76
Private - Pinkston, John S.
Private - Pittet, Francis

Sick in hospital, Ft. Rice, D.T. 5/5/76
Private - Severs, Samuel
(Wounded) Steamer Far West, 6/29/76
Private - Tably, David
Sick in hospital, Ft. Rice, D.T. 5/5/76
Private - Walsh, Michael J.
Confinement, New Orleans, LA since 5/10/76
Private - Walter, Aloyse L.
DS Supply Base, Powder River, M.T. 6/16/76
Private - Williams, William C.
Private - Windolph, Charles (alias Charles
    Wrangel)

Company I

Sergeant - Caddle, Michael
DS Supply Base, Powder River, M.T. 6/15/76
Sergeant - DeLacy, Milton J.
Sergeant -Gaffney, George
Sergeant -Murphy, Robert L.
Corporal - McCall, Joseph
DS Ft. Lincoln, D.T. since 5/17/76
Farrier - Rivers, John
DS Supply Base, Powder River, M.T. 6/15/76
Saddler - Haywood, George
Sick in hospital, Ft. Lincoln, D.T. 5/17/76
Private - Brown, Franz C.
Private - Cooney, David
(Wounded) Steamer Far West, 6/29/76
Private - Farber, Conrad
DS Dept-Headquarters, St. Paul, MN 6/1/76
Private - Fox, Frederick
DS at Ft. Lincoln, D.T. 5/17/76
Private - Geesbacher, Gabriel
DS Supply Base, Powder River, M.T. 6/15/76
Private - Grimes, Andrew
DS at Ft. Lincoln, D.T. 5/17/76
Private - Haack, Charles L.
Sick in hospital, Ft. Lincoln, D.T. 5/17/76
Private - Johnson, Francis
Private - Jones, Henry P.
Private - Korn, Gustave
Private - Lee, Mark E.
DS attending wounded on Far West, 6/26/76
Private - Lynch, Patrick
Private - McGinnis, John
Sick in hospital, Ft. Lincoln, D.T. 5/17/76
Private - McNally, James P.
Private - McShane, John
Private - Miller, William E.
Sick in hospital, Ft. Lincoln, D.T. 5/17/76
Private - Myers, Fred
DS Supply Base, Powder River, M.T. 6/15/76
Private - Owens, N. G.
Private - Porter, John
Confinement Columbus Bks., Ohio, 6/1/76
Private - Ramsey, Charles
Private - Saas, William
DS Ft. Lincoln, D.T. 5/17/76
Private - Thomas, Herbert P.
DS Ft. Lincoln, D.T. 5/17/76

Company K

Sergeant - Campbell, Jeremiah
Sergeant - Frederick, Andrew

Sergeant - Hose, George
Sergeant - Madden, Michael P.
(Wounded) Steamer Far West, 6/28/76
Sergeant - Rafter, John
Sergeant - Rott, Louis
Corporal - Murray, Henry
DS Supply Base, Powder River, M.T. 6/15/76
Corporal - Nolan, John
DS Supply Base, Powder River, M.T. 6/15/76
Trumpeter - Penwell, George B.
Trumpeter - Schlafer, Christian
Farrier - Steintker, John R.
Blacksmith - Burke, Edmund H.
Saddler - Boissen, Christian
Wagoner - Whytenfield, Albert
DS Supply Base, Powder River, M.T. 6/15/76
Private - Ackerman, Charles
DS Supply Base, Powder River, M.T. 6/15/76
Private - Anderson, George
DS Ft. Lincoln, D.T. since 5/17/76
Private - Bauer, Jacob
Sick in hospital, Ft. Lincoln, D.T. 5/17/76
Private - Blair, James E.
DS Ft. Lincoln, D.T. since 5/17/76
Private - Blunt, George
Private - Bresnahan, Cornelius
Private - Brown, Joseph
Private - Burgdorf, Charles J.
DS Supply Base, Powder River, M.T. 6/15/76
Private - Burkhardt, Charles
Private - Chesterwood, Charles (alias John C.
    Creighton)
Private - Coakley, Patrick
Private - Corcoran, Patrick
(Wounded) Steamer Far West, 6/28/76
Private - Crawford, William L.
DS Supply Base, Powder River, M.T. 6/15/76
Private - Delaney, Michael
DS Supply Base, Powder River, M.T. 6/15/76
Private - Donohue, John
Private - Dooley, Patrick
Sick in hospital, Ft. Lincoln, D.T. 5/17/76
Private - Fisher, Charles
DS Supply Base, Powder River, M.T. 6/15/76
Private - Foley, John
Private - Gibbs, William
Private - Gordon, Thomas A.
Private - Green, Thomas
DS Supply Base, Powder River, M.T. 6/15/76
Private - Gunther, Julius
Sick in hospital, Ft. Lincoln, D.T. 5/17/76
Private - Holohan, Andrew
DS Supply Base, Powder River, M.T. 6/15/76
Private - Horner, Jacob
DS Supply Base, Powder River, M.T. 6/15/76
Private - Hoyt, Walter
DS Supply Base, Powder River, M.T. 6/15/76
Private - Jennys, Alonzo
Private - Lasley, William W.
Private - Liberman, Andrew
DS Ft. Lincoln, D.T. 5/17/76
Private - Lyons, Daniel
DS Supply Base, Powder River, M.T. 6/15/76
Private - McConnell, Wilson
Private - McCue, Martin
Private - Mielke, Max

(Wounded) Steamer Far West, 6/28/76
Private - Murphy, Michael
Private - Murphy, Thomas
Private - Ragan, Michael
DS Supply Base, Powder River, M.T. 6/15/76
Private - Raichel, Henry W.
Private - Reilly, Michael
DS Supply Base, Powder River, M.T. 6/15/76
Private - Robert, Jonathan
Private - Roth, Francis
DS Supply Base, Powder River, M.T. 6/15/76
Private - Schauer, John
Private - Schwerer, John
Private - Seifert, August
Private - Smith, Frederick
DS Supply Base, Powder River, M.T. 6/15/76
Private - Taube, Emil
Private - Van Pelt, William A.
DS Supply Base, Powder River, M.T. 6/15/76
Private - Wasmus, Ernest
Private - Whitlow, William
Private - Wilson, George A.
DS Supply Base, Powder River, M.T. 6/15/76
Private - Witt, Henry
DS Supply Base, Powder River, M.T. 6/15/76

Company L

Sergeant - Bender, Henry
DS Supply Base, Powder River, M.T. 6/15/76
Sergeant - Findersen, Hugo
DS Ft. Lincoln, D.T. 5/17/76
Sergeant - Mullen, John (alias James Hughes)
Corporal - Nunan, John
DS Supply Base, Powder River, M.T. 6/15/76
Private - Abrams, William G.
Private - Banks, Charles
Private - Brown, Nathan J.
Private - Burkman, John
Private - Colwell, John R.
DS sick in hospital, Ft. Lincoln, D.T. 5/17/76
Private - Conlan, Michael
DS Ft. Lincoln, D.T. 5/17/76
Private - Etzler, William
Private - Hoehn, Max
DS Supply Base, Powder River, M.T. 6/15/76
Private - Keegan, Michael
DS Supply Base, Powder River, M.T. 6/15/76
Private - Lepper, Frederick
Sick Supply Base, Powder River, M.T. 6/15/76
Private - Logue, William S.
Private - Marshall, Jasper
(Wounded) Steamer Far West, 6/26/76
Private - McHugh, Philip
Private - McPeak, Alexander
DS Supply Base, Powder River, M.T. 6/15/76
Private - Moore, Lansing A.
Private - Rose, Peter E.
Private - Sprague, Otto
DS Ft. Lincoln, D.T. 5/17/76
Private - Stoffel, Henry
Private - Sullivan, Timothy

Company M

1st Sergeant - Ryan, John M.

Sergeant - Capes, William
DS Supply Base, Powder River, M.T. 6/15/76
Sergeant - Carey, Patrick
Sergeant - McGlone, John
Segeant - White, Charles
Corporal - Lalor, William
Trumpeter - Fisher, Charles
Trumpeter - Weaver, Henry C.
Farrier - Wood, William M.
DS Ft. Rice, D.T. 5/5/76
Saddler - Donahue, John
Wagoner - Ricketts, Joseph
DS Supply Base, Powder River, M.T. 6/15/76
Private - Bates, John
Private - Bowers, Frank
Confinement, Ft. Wayne, Michigan, 2/14/76
Private - Braun, Frank
Private - Cain, Morris
Private - Davis, Harrison
Private - Dolan, John
DS Supply Base, Powder River, M.T. 6/15/76
Private - Gallenne, Jean B. D.
Private - Golden, Bernard
Private - Heid, George
Private - Kavannagh, Charles
Private - Mahoney, Daniel
Private - McConnell, James
DS Supply Base, Powder River, M.T. 6/15/76
Private - Meier, John H.
Private - Moore, Hugh N.
Private - Moore, William E.
Private - Neeley, Frank
Private - Newell, Daniel
Private - Pigford, Edward
Private - Robinson, William
Private - Rutten, Roman
Private - Ryder, Hobart
Private - Rye, William W.
Private - Seamans, John
Private - Senn, Robert
Private - Severs, John
Private - Sivertsen, John
Private - Slapper, William
Private - Sniffin, Frank
Private - Sterland, Walter S.
DS Supply Base, Powder River, M.T. 6/15/76
Private - Stratton, Frank
Private - Thornberry, Levi
Private - Thorpe, Rollins L.
Private - Varner, Thomas B.
Private - Weaver, George
Private - Weeks, James
Private - Widmayer, Ferdinand
DS Supply Base, Powder River, M.T. 6/15/76
Private - Wiedman, Charles G.
Private - Whisten, John
Private - Wilbur, James
Private - Williams, Charles
Private - Zametzer, John

_____
*Montana Territory
**Dakota Territory

The following is the Muster Roll of Lieutenant James H. Bradley, 7th Infantry, Company of the Crow Indian Scouts enlisted for the campaign, from the first day of May 1876, when last mustered to the 30th day of June 1876.

Name	Rank	Enlisted	When By Whom	Remarks
1. Shows His Ear	Pvt.	Apr. 10/76	Lt Bradley	AWOL since June 26/76
2. Mountain That Shows	"	at Crow	"	AWOL since June 26/76
3. Big Nose, alias Bernard Bravo	"	Agency, MT	"	AWOL since June 26/76
4. One Ahead, alias Goes Ahead	"	"	"	On DS with Major Reno since 6/21/76
5. Corner of the Mouth	"	"	"	AWOL since June 26/76
6. Elk	"	"	"	AWOL since June 26/76
7. Show His Face	"	"	"	AWOL since June 26/76
8. Little Face	"	"	"	AWOL since June 26/76
9. Jack Rabbit Bull	"	"	"	DS since 29/76
10. Horserider, alias Tom LaForgey	"	"	"	Absent sick at Ft. Pease, since 6/24/76
11. Half Yellow Face	"	"	"	DS with Maj. Reno
12. Grandmother's Knife	"	"	"	AWOL since June 26/76
13. Runner	"	"	"	AWOL since June 26/76
14. Spotted Bird	"	"	"	AWOL since June 26/76
15. White Swan	"	"	"	Severely wounded in fight with Sioux Indians with Maj. Reno DS since 6/21 with Maj. Reno
16. White Man Runs Him	"	"	"	AWOL since June 26/76
17. Buffalo Calf	"	"	"	AWOL since June 26/76
18. Horses Head	"	"	"	AWOL since June 26/76
19. Shoves, alias Push	"	"	"	AWOL since June 26/76
20. Hairy Moccasin	"	"	"	DS 6/21/76, Maj. Reno
21. Curly	"	"	"	AWOL since June 26/76
22. Wolf	"	"	"	AWOL since June 26/76
23. Young Yellow Wolf	"	"	"	AWOL since June 26/76
24. Two Whistle	"	"	"	AWOL since June 26/76
25. Dirty Faced Fox	"	"	"	AWOL since June 26/76

The following is the Muster Roll of Lieutenant Charles A. Varnum, Detachment of Indian Scouts, from the 30th day of April 1876 to the 30th Day of June 1876.

Name	Rank	Enlisted When (All Deserted on Battlefield, June 25, 1876)	Where	By Whom	Period
1. Bear Comes Out	Pvt.	Feb. 3	Ft. Lincoln, MT	Lt. Cooke	6 months
2. Bear Running in the Timber	"	May 11	"	Lt. Varnum	"
3. Black Calf	"	April 26	"	Lt. Cooke	"
4. Black Fox	"	May 9	"	Lt. Varnum	"
5. Bull	"	May 9	"	Lt. Varnum	"
6. Bull in the Water	"	May 9	"	Lt. Varnum	"
7. Bush	"	April 26	"	Lt. Cooke	"
8. Cross, William	"	April 17	"	Lt. Cooke	"
9. Good Elk	"	May 13	"	Lt. Varnum	"
10. Good Face	"	May 9	"	Lt. Varnum	"
11. One Feather	"	May 9	"	Lt. Varnum	"
12. Round Woody Cloud	"	March 31	"	Lt. Cooke	"
13. Rushing Bull	"	May 9	"	Lt. Varnum	"
14. Soldier	"	April 26	"	Lt. Cooke	"
15. Sioux	"	Feb. 3	"	Lt. Cooke	"
16. Strikes Two	"	May 9	"	Lt. Varnum	"
17. White Cloud	"	May 14	"	Lt. Varnum	"
18. White Eagle	"	May 9	"	Lt. Varnum	"

Note: Three additional names are obliterated on the Muster Roll and cannot be read.

On a separate Muster Roll of 1st Lieutenant J.M. Burns, 17th Infantry Detachment of Indian Scouts, it appears that five additional Indian Scouts-Bears Eyes, Horn in Front, Laying Down, Left Hand, Sioux and One Horn-were also turned over to Gen. Custer's troops on 21 June, and were with him or Major Reno.

The Indian Scouts names above deserted before the battle began. The Arikara Indians returned to Mandan, North Dakota, and the Crow Indians returned to their reservation near Columbus, Montana.

The following is a report of persons and articles employed and hired by the expedition in the field, stationed at the mouth of Powder River, M.T. during the month of June 1876, by 1st Lieutenant H.J. Nowlan, Regimental Quartermaster, 7th Cavalry, A.A.Q.M., U.S.A., June 1876.

Name	Designation and Occupation	Rate of Hire or Compensaion per month (dollars)	Date of Contract or Entry into Service	Remarks
1. Abbot, Frederick S.B.	Gen. Supt.	$ 75.00	4-28-76	In office of Expedition QM
2. Custer, Boston	Guide	100.00	3-03-76	Employed by CO Killed 6-25-76 by Indians at Battle of Little Big Horn River
3. Reynolds, Charles	Guide	100.00	3-03-76	Employed by CO Killed 6-25-76 by Indians at Battle of Little Big Horn River
4. Bloody Knife	Guide	50.00	3-03-76	Employed by CO Killed 6-25-76 by Indians at Battle of Little Big Horn River
5. Gerard, F. F.	Interpreter	75.00	5-12-76	
6. Doran, Isaiah	Interpreter	75.00	5-15-76	Killed in Battle of Little Big Horn River
7. Borowsky, Charles	Master Mech.	100.00	5-01-76	Charge of Mechanical
8. Macy, George	Blacksmith	60.00	4-24-76	Repairing of Transp.
9. Hickey, Patrick	Blacksmith	60.00	5-16-76	Repairing of Transp.
10. Treshman, George	Wheelwright	60.00	5-01-76	Repairing of Transp.
11. Hutchins, H. C.	Wheelwright	60.00	5-15-76	Repairing of Transp.
12. Thomas, Thomas	Saddler	60.00	3-12-76	Repairing of Transp.
13. Wagoner, J. C.	Chief Packer	100.00	3-01-76	Charge Packtrain
14. Loeser, C.	Packer	50.00	3-26-76	Packing of Public Animals
15. Lawless, William	Packer	50.00	4-01-76	Packing of Public Animals
16. Fretts, John	Packer	50.00	4-17-76	Packing of Public Animals
17. Alexander, William	Packer	50.00	4-17-76	Packing of Public Animals
18. McBratney, H.	Packer	50.00	4-17-76	Packing of Public Animals
19. Mann, Frank C.	Packer	50.00	4-17-76	(Killed 6-25-76)
20. Flink, Moses	Packer	50.00	5-16-76	Packing Animals
21. Lainplough, John	Packer	50.00	5-02-76	Packing Animals
22. Moore, E. L.	Packer	50.00	5-13-76	Packing Animals
23. Brown, Charles	Mstr/Transp.	100.00	3-11-76	In Charge of Train
24. Meuson, John	Asst. Wagonmaster	45.00	3-11-76	In Charge of 25 Teams
25. Hadley, Orange	Asst. Wagonmaster	45.00	5-16-76	In Charge of 25 Teams
26. Welsch, Oscar	Asst. Wagonmaster	45.00	5-16-76	In Charge of 25 Teams
27. Slack, J. H.	Asst. Wagonmaster	45.00	5-16-76	In Charge of 25 Teams
28. McGee, James	Asst. Wagonmaster	45.00	5-20-76	In Charge of 25 Teams
29. Campbell, Gordon	Asst. Wagonmaster	45.00	5-16-76	In Charge of 25 Teams Discharged 6-10-76
30. French, Charles	Asst. Wagonmaster	45.00	3-27-76	In Charge of 25 Teams
31. Allen, Charles	Teamster	30.00	4-09-76	Driving Teams
32. Aldermann, John	Teamster	30.00	4-08-76	Driving Teams
33. Aslen, Isaac	Teamster	30.00	4-09-76	Driving Teams
34. Allen, George	Teamster	30.00	4-22-76	Driving Teams
35. Acty, Herrmann	Teamster	30.00	5-20-76	Driving Teams
36. Bunker, Fred	Teamster	30.00	4-11-76	Driving Teams
37. Briner, J. H.	Teamster	30.00	4-11-76	Driving Teams
38. Brown, Charles	Teamster	30.00	4-14-76	Driving Teams
39. Bruer, Samuel	Teamster	30.00	4-17-76	Driving Teams
40. Beal, John	Teamster	30.00	4-23-76	Driving Teams
41. Bostwick, Louis	Teamster	30.00	4-23-76	Driving Teams
42. Boutiette, Edward	Teamster	30.00	3-11-76	Driving Teams
43. Bartholomew, J. R.	Teamster	30.00	3-11-76	Driving Teams
44. Blackbird, Eugene	Teamster	30.00	3-14-76	Driving Teams
45. Bushea, I.	Teamster	30.00	4-01-76	Driving Teams
46. Bennett, James	Teamster	30.00	5-05-76	Driving Teams
47. Boyken, William	Teamster	30.00	6-25-76	Driving Teams
48. Connelley, James	Teamster	30.00	5-11-76	Driving Teams
49. Cassidy, C. W.	Teamster	30.00	5-16-76	Driving Teams
50. Commonford, J. C.	Teamster	30.00	4-11-76	Driving Teams
51. Churchill, R. C.	Teamster	30.00	4-17-76	Driving Teams
52. Carter, George	Teamster	30.00	10-17-74	Driving Teams
53. Case, George	Teamster	30.00	3-15-76	Driving Teams
54. Childs, Charles	Teamster	30.00	4-09-76	Driving Teams
55. Cosgrove, Michael	Teamster	30.00	4-09-76	Driving Teams
56. Close, W. A.	Teamster	30.00	4-22-76	Driving Teams
57. Clark, Thomas	Teamster	30.00	5-07-76	Driving Teams
58. Crawford, Carlton	Teamster	30.00	5-08-76	Driving Teams
59. Cochran, James	Teamster	30.00	6-22-76	Driving Teams
60. Crimble, Charles	Teamster	30.00	5-14-76	Driving Teams
61. Dermott, John J.	Teamster	30.00	4-01-76	Driving Teams
62. DeMules, Alfred	Teamster	30.00	4-01-76	Driving Teams
63. Drew, James	Teamster	30.00	4-17-76	Driving Teams

64. Devrant, John	Teamster	30.00	4-18-76		Driving Teams
65. Demules, Gilbert	Teamster	30.00	3-11-76		Driving Teams
66. Darling, Joseph	Teamster	30.00	4-15-76		Driving Teams
67. Dean, George	Teamster	30.00	4-22-76		Driving Teams
68. Doris, Andrew	Teamster	30.00	5-08-76		Driving Teams
69. Davy, Charles	Teamster	30.00	5-01-76		Driving Teams
70. Edwards, George	Teamster	30.00	4-01-76		Driving Teams
71. Egan, John	Teamster	30.00	3-28-76		Driving Teams
72. Ferguson, William	Teamster	30.00	3-18-76		Driving Teams
73. Franklin, Ed	Teamster	30.00	4-02-76		Driving Teams
74. Ford, William	Teamster	30.00	4-22-76		Driving Teams
75. Folts, Warren	Teamster	30.00	5-08-76		Driving Teams
76. Finn, James	Teamster	30.00	5-06-76		Driving Teams
77. Fowler, Edward	Teamster	30.00	5-08-76		Driving Teams
78. French, Charles	Teamster	30.00	5-14-76		Driving Teams
79. Gutgesell, R. D.	Teamster	30.00	6-01-76		Driving Teams
80. Gruenwald, William	Teamster	30.00	3-12-76		Driving Teams
81. Granns, Frank	Teamster	30.00	3-14-76		Driving Teams
82. Glynn, Pat	Teamster	30.00	3-27-76		Driving Teams
83. Griffin, John	Teamster	30.00	5-07-76		Driving Teams
84. Goodrich, William	Teamster	30.00	5-12-76		Driving Teams
85. Campbell, Gordon	Teamster	30.00	6-12-76		Driving Teams
86. Hegarty, William	Teamster	30.00	4-01-76		Driving Teams
87. Hempton, Edward	Teamster	30.00	4-18-76		Driving Teams
88. Hart, Charles	Teamster	30.00	11-10-75		Driving Teams
89. Howard, Frank	Teamster	30.00	3-12-76		Driving Teams
90. Hoffman, John	Teamster	30.00	4-09-76		Driving Teams
91. Hill, Philip	Teamster	30.00	5-01-76		Driving Teams
92. Hartsgrove, Charles	Teamster	30.00	5-12-76		Driving Teams
93. Henderson, Frank	Teamster	30.00	5-08-76		Driving Teams
94. Karney, James	Teamster	30.00	5-16-76		Driving Teams
95. Kelley, Martin (1st)	Teamster	30.00	4-18-76		Driving Teams
96. Kelley, Martin (2nd)	Teamster	30.00	6-25-76		Driving Teams
97. Lafarge, M.	Teamster	30.00	4-17-76		Driving Teams
98. Logan, Austin	Teamster	30.00	4-22-76		Driving Teams
99. Louis, Augustus	Teamster	30.00	3-11-76		Driving Teams
100. Levere, Joseph	Teamster	30.00	3-15-76		Driving Teams
101. Lowe, C. H.	Teamster	30.00	3-15-76		Driving Teams
102. Kincaid, George	Teamster	30.00	8-09-76		Driving Teams
103. Kincaid, B. F.	Teamster	30.00	3-11-76		Driving Teams
104. Kennedy, L.	Teamster	30.00	5-13-76		Driving Teams
105. Keefe, Thomas	Teamster	30.00	5-14-76		Driving Teams
106. Leahy, Con	Teamster	30.00	4-09-76		Driving Teams
107. Lanning, Thomas	Teamster	30.00	4-21-76		Driving Teams
108. Lander, Ben	Teamster	30.00	6-07-76		Driving Teams
109. Lee, Edward	Teamster	30.00	5-12-76		Driving Teams
110. Meyer, T. B.	Teamster	30.00	4-11-76		Driving Teams
111. McCullom, John	Teamster	30.00	4-11-76		Driving Teams
112. McPherson, David	Teamster	30.00	4-19-76		Driving Teams
113. Muzzy, Frank	Teamster	30.00	3-11-76		Driving Teams
114. McKusick, Charles	Teamster	30.00	3-28-76		Driving Teams
115. Marlow, Samuel	Teamster	30.00	4-15-76		Driving Teams
116. Maxwell, Harry	Teamster	30.00	4-15-76		Driving Teams
117. Mason, Frank	Teamster	30.00	4-03-76		Driving Teams
118. Martel, Anderson	Teamster	30.00	4-01-76		Driving Teams
119. Mooney, Thomas	Teamster	30.00	5-01-76		Driving Teams
120. McGovern, A.	Teamster	30.00	5-12-76		Driving Teams
121. Myers, George	Teamster	30.00	5-12-76		Driving Teams
122. Miller, John	Teamster	30.00	5-15-76		Driving Teams
123. Noyes, Wilber	Teamster	30.00	4-11-76		Driving Teams
124. Niering, Robert	Teamster	30.00	4-22-76		Driving Teams
125. Pearson, Isaac	Teamster	30.00	4-01-76		Driving Teams
126. Page, Runn	Teamster	30.00	3-11-76		Driving Teams
127. Parens, Fred	Teamster	30.00	3-13-76		Driving Teams
128. Phups, I.	Teamster	30.00	4-08-76		Driving Teams
129. Roberts, Robert	Teamster	30.00	5-11-76		Driving Teams
130. Richardson, D.	Teamster	30.00	4-01-76		Driving Teams
131. Riley, John (1st)	Teamster	30.00	9-29-74		Driving Teams
132. Ryan, Thomas	Teamster	30.00	4-15-76		Driving Teams
133. Reese, William	Teamster	30.00	4-24-76		Driving Teams
134. Riley, John (2nd)	Teamster	30.00	4-01-76		Driving Teams
135. Rounnsavelle, Frank	Teamster	30.00	3-11-76		Driving Teams

136. Ryland, Henry	Teamster	30.00	4-21-76		Driving Teams
137. Rosengreem, Olez	Teamster	30.00	5-01-76		Driving Teams
138. Riley, James	Teamster	30.00	5-14-76		Driving Teams
139. Smith, Charles	Teamster	30.00	4-01-76		Driving Teams
140. Smith, D. L.	Teamster	30.00	6-19-75		Driving Teams
141. Smullins, Pat	Teamser	30.00	11-10-75		Driving Teams
142. Sinks, Oscar	Teamster	30.00	2-05-76		Driving Teams
143. Stoning, E.C.	Teamster	30.00	3-12-76		Driving Teams
144. Slew, W. C.	Teamster	30.00	3-12-76		Driving Teams
145. Shields, William	Teamster	30.00	3-15-76		Driving Teams
146. Stone, James	Teamster	30.00	3-27-76		Driving Teams
147. Sevins, Oliver	Teamster	30.00	4-01-76		Driving Teams
148. Smith, David	Teamster	30.00	4-09-76		Driving Teams
149. Sullivan, Henry	Teamster	30.00	5-01-76		Driving Teams
150. Tomarto, H. R.	Teamster	30.00	4-08-76		Driving Teams
151. Thomas, Joseph	Teamster	30.00	4-09-76		Driving Teams
152. Victory, James	Teamster	30.00	4-15-76		Driving Teams
153. York, Peter	Teamster	30.00	4-01-76		Driving Teams
154. Yuba, Charles	Teamster	30.00	4-22-76		Driving Teams
155. Young, Francis	Teamster	30.00	5-09-76		Driving Teams
156. Warren, William	Teamster	30.00	4-08-76		Driving Teams
157. Warren, Henry	Teamster	30.00	4-08-76		Driving Teams
158. Walker, William	Teamster	30.00	5-08-76		Driving Teams
159. Whipple, William	Teamster	30.00	5-14-76		Driving Teams
160. Willis, Gilbert	Teamster	30.00	5-14-76		Driving Teams
161. Jones, John	Teamster	30.00	5-17-76		Driving Teams
162. Herendeen, George B.	Scout (Job)	100.00	6-25-76		Scouting Job

Note: At the bottom of this form it shows: Amount of rent and hire during the month...$20,248.00; Total amount due and remaining unpaid...$4,265.81.

Additional pertinent information on these pay roll forms:
26 two-horse teams and wagons hauling supplies at $4.95 per day
10 two-horse teams and wagons hauling supplies at $5.00 per day
John A. McLean-$3,861.00 for hauling supplies for expedition, 1-30 Jun 1876
N. P. Clark-$1,500.00 for hauling supplies for expedition, 1-30 Jun 1876
Total for rental of teams and wagons and teamsters for 1-30 Jun 1876, $11,003.48
Total from 1-20 Apr 1876, due and remaining unpaid for expedition, $21,476.31
The above information pertaining to the employment of persons and articles was obtained from the expedition accounts and papers on file in the General Accounting Office, Washington, DC, by Edward S. Luce, superintendent, Custer Battlefield National Monument, Crow Agency, Montana, 30 Jan 1956.

ROSTER OF THE 7TH U.S. CAVALRY

Abbey, John P.
Abell, Richard
Abshear, James R. "Jim"
Ackerman, Richard R.
Ackiss, Jr., Alton J. "John"
Adamcazk, Bernard
Adams, Beverly H.
Adams, Harry
Adams, Russell E.
Adams, Warren E.
Adams, William A.
Aemisegger, Darven B.
Albrecht, Jeffery L.
Alcon, David
Alevizakos, Spyridon
Alexander, William
Alicea, Ronald H.
Allen, John P.
Allen, Louis
Allen, Roy E.
Alligood, Danny S.
Allison, Benjamin W.
Allison, John E.
Almy, Frank H.
Alva, Jose "Joe"
Alvarez-Perez, Wilfredo
Alves, Jr., Walter L.
Ament, Arthur R.
Ammons, Terry
Anderson, Ashley C.
Anderson, Elray R.
Anderson, Howard P.
Anderson, James A.
Anderson, Joe E.
Anderson, Robert J.
Anderson, Robert V.
Anderson, Jr., Robert P.

Andrews, Louis W. "Andy"
Apple, Gary L.
Apple, James D.
Applegate, James H. "Jim"
Arbasetti, Robert "Bob"
Arendt, Orville R.
Arnoldt, Robert P.
Atkins, Jerry S.
Back, James Daniel
Back, Wendy Mae
Baer, Ralph
Bafs, Carl J.
Bagdasarian, Douglas G.D.
Baker, James R. "Leprechaun"
Baker, William E.
Balicki, Robert R.
Ballard, Henry E., Jr.
Bamesberger, John G.
Banko, III, Stephen T.
Bannister, Harold R.
Barber, Junio-Omar
Barca, Joseph S.
Barrow, Ronald
Bartlett, Perry
Barton, John H.
Bates, Donald E.
Baylock, Francis A. "Frank"
Beard, John Richard
Bearden, Hall
Beauliey, Keith W.
Beck, Bill
Becker, Virgil H.
Bell, Edwin
Bell, Urcel L.
Benn, Edmond B.
Bentley, Jr., Mack
Benton, Ronald H.

Bents, Reinhold A.
Berberich, James G.
Berendsen, Henry E.
Berge, Gregory S.
Bernotas, Ralph G.
Berry, Bill S.
Berube, George E.
Besch, Eric
Bess, Guy F.
Bevington, Nicholas
Bijesse, Albert "Al"
Birkel, Jr., Anthony A.
Black, Dave L.
Blanc, Harold
Blankenbeckler, Paul N. "BB"
Blessing, Dennis D.
Blockhus, Christopher L.
Bloss, Robert W.
Blume, William F.
Blumenauer, Roy C.
Bodnar, Mike
Bohlender, Otto R.
Boland, John F.
Boldt, Glenn M.
Bollinger, Royal D.
Bondurant, Mildred C.
Bookwalter, Thomas E.
Bornstein, Herman
Bosse, Donald John
Bouterse, Robert A.
Bower, Robert J.
Bowman, Arnold Jimmy
Bowman, Perry A.
Bowman, Robert
Boyd, Margaret Ann
Boyd, Richard T.
Boyd, Thomas E.

Boyle, Jr., Richard A.
Bracewell, Robert E.L. "Bob"
Bradbury, Richard E.
Bradley, Thomas E.
Braunstein, Ralph E.
Breen, Joseph B.
Bremer, Charles L. "Chuck"
Brennan, Donna L.
Brennan, Joseph F.
Brennan, Michael J., M.D.
Briley, William H.
Brister, Alan A.
Britton, Richard T. "Dick"
Brofer, Duane R. "Brof"
Brookover, Jesse
Brooks, Paul E.
Brostrom, Gerhard
Brown, Raymond H.
Browning, IV, John W.
Bruce, Robert B.
Bruner, Sr., Vincent G.
Buchanan, Crawford
Bucholtz, Sr., Robert "Bob"
Buck, Paul Ray
Bugher, James D.
Buhr, Herman H.
Bumgarner, Glen G.
Bunting, William A.
Burditt, Elijah F.
Burnett, Ed
Burnett, Thomas R.
Burns, Billy D.
Burton, Jonathan R.
Burton, Joseph J.
Busho, Sr., Waylen G.
Butler, Joseph C.
Butler, Sir-Nathaniel

Byron, Milton
Cable, Rick
Caffey, Robert I.
Calabrese, Dennis J.
Caldwell, David
Calhoun, Guy R.
Callaway, John W.
Campbell, Donald D.
Campbell, Richard W.
Cancelliere, Francis P.
Cangro, Peter V.
Caper, Lamont
Carlson, Donald T.
Carnahan, Douglas E.
Carney, Clarence A.
Caro, Arthur "Art"
Carroll, John F.
Carroll, Robert M.
Cash, John A.
Castleberry, Jack
Cauley, John E.
Chacon, Joseph L.
Chance, Rayford E. "Ray"
Chaney, Jr., Leroy
Chatham, Mary Lou
Chi, Hyung Jae
Childs, W.F. "Jack"
Chirchill, Richard S.
Christensen, Kurt A.
Christian, Eugene A.
Cisson, Kenneth
Clainos, Peter D.
Clair, Alfred B.
Clair, Rosemary "Rosey"
Clark, Danny D.
Clark, Harold J.
Clark, John P.

Clark, Orval D.
Clarke, Timothy M.
Clear, Charles C.
Cleary, Doris J.
Clutts, Robert E.
Coblentz, Richard L.
Cochran, Bill D.
Cochren, Rowland E.
Coiner, Benjamin W.
Colburn, James R.
Cole, Peter C.
Coleman, James
Collins, William T.
Comer, James C.
Conlon, Robert
Conlon, Jr., John J.
Connor, William M.
Cook, Robert W.
Cooper, Robert "Bob"
Cooper, Robert M.
Cope, William C. "Bill"
Copeland, Everett L.
Copello, C.L.
Copulos, George A.
Corbett, Richard Lee "Bull"
Cordero, Jr., Mauricio F.
Cordon, Steven C.
Cotterell, Jr., John
Couch, Jack L.
Court, James V. "Jim"
Cox, Robert E. "Bob"
Cox, Terry
Craig, Raymond "Lee"
Creamer, George T.
Creazzo, Dominick
Creekmore, Harry S.
Crews, Robert R.
Crist, Junior E. "Edward"
Crocker, John R.
Cross, Jr., Joseph H.
Culley, Harriet
Cullings, Donavan A.
Cumbow, Elliott R.
Cummings, James F.
Cummings, Michael L.
Curram, James W. "Jim"
Cyr, Michael P.
Dahl, Stanley
Daily, Edward L.
Daly, James E.
Daly, James R.
Daly, John E.
Dandy, Kevin M.
Dandy, Matthew W.
Daniel, Marvin C.
Dashner, Jr., Charles A.
Daugherty, Francis "Pancho"
Daujatas, Donald
Davidson, David S.
Davie, Robert M. "Bob"
Davis, Bennie F.
Davis, Charles M.
Davis, Claude L.
Davis, Jr., James C.
De Maine, John
Deal, Dennis J.
Deal, Stephen R.
DeFino, Frank
DeHart, Bill
DeLao, Robert
DeLeon, Dimas
Della Ripa, John
Dempewolf, Vincent M.
Dempsey, Philip
Dennigan, James J.
Depriest, James L.
Detty, Raymond M.
Dewitt, Allen E.
Deyoe, William A.
Diaz, Justo M.
Dicaprio, Jr., Raymond
Dillon, Dana B. "Horse"
Distad, Eric A.
Doak, William C., Jr.
Doerner, John A.
Doherty, John C.
Dohle, Richard
Donnelly, David A.
Donnelly, Donald R.
Dowd, John J.
Dowell, Richard K.
Down, Donlad, D.
Downs, Jr., James Lewis
Draper, Steven C.
Dubrowa, Dennis J.
Dudley, Halford M.
Dunkleberger, Jonathan K.
Dunlow, Garry
Duranty, Edward T.
Durham, Melvin A.

Dutram, John H.
Duty, Chirls S. "Charly"
Duve, Fred A.
Dyson, Johnie M.
Early, Earl
Eason, Emory Allen
Eastham, Kenneth G.
Eckert, Michael G.
Edens, Jackie C.
Edmunds, Guy M.
Edwards, Woodrow P.
Elia, Charles A.
Elkins, James
Elliott, Lewis E. "Lew"
Elliott, Sara
Ellis, Ester H.
English, Arnold R.
Enos, James
Enos, Julie
Ernst, Louis
Erwin, Ira "Ike"
Etts, Larry Eugene
Etts, Sandra Jean
Eubanks, Hal D.
Euteneuer, David G. "Ike"
Evans, Brent
Evans, Thomas J.
Fairly, Kenneth W.
Fallon, Joseph E.
Fantino, Sam P.
Farinelli, Richard J.
Farrell, James E. "Jim"
Farrelly, Peter T.
Feldman, Donald
Fels, Eugene
Ferguson, Denver C.
Ferraro, Ron
Ferwerda, Merle
Fetter, L. David
Fillmore, C. Mike
Fillmore, Margaret
Finch, Ellen R.
Finley, Allison R.
Fischer, Clifford D.
Fisher, Joe M.
Fitch, Robert K.
Fitzgerald, William T.
Flanders, Sherman C.
Fleck, Charles H.
Flesch, Joseph E.
Fleury, Kathy L.
Flick, Jack R.
Flierl, Leroy H.
Flynn, Ronald B.
Foley, Thomas C.
Fonder, Russell C.
Ford, Buford W.
Fowler, Kenneth D.
Fox, Allen G.
Fox, Victor L.
Francioni, George F.
Frank, Jr., Timothy Jay
Franklin, William W. "Bill"
French, Michael L.
Frisbie, Robert
Fry, William D.
Fullam, Edward R.
Fuller, Charles A.
Fuller, Thomas W.
Funderburk, Earl F.
Fuselier, John
Gaborsky, Jr., Joseph
Galloway, Joseph L.
Galloway, Roger
Galvin, Thomas P.
Gambone, Joseph W.
Game, Henry Erio
Gange, Joseph W.
Gargis, Paul
Garrett, Jerry
Garvin, James E.
Garza, Homer Miguel
Gast, Gerald L.
Gavin, Martin T.
Gehling, Duane W.
Gemelli, Bernard N. "Barry"
Genz, Marilyn
Geoghegan, Camille
George, Robert P.
Gerrits, Paul
Gersten, Roy
Gibbs, Lyle R.
Giedeman, Gregory W.
Gigandet, Francis V.
Gilbert, Lawrence R.
Gilreath, Larry M.
Girard, Terrance P.
Gish, Frank D.
Glasco, Anthony D.
Glass, Charles R.

Glass, Rexford L.
Glodowski, Conrad "Duke"
Glover, Reece M.
Glowiak, Raymond P. "Ray"
Goerlitz, Delbert "Del"
Goetze, Arnold A.
Gonzalez, Enrique G. "Hank"
Gooden, James H.
Goodrich, Horace Gideon
Goodwin, Lynn R.H.
Gottesman, Harold
Gourley, Daniel F.
Graham, Chong Suk Lee
Graml, Otto A.
Graumann, Otto G.
Gray, Carolyn J.
Gray, Earl G. "Gene"
Gray, Millard G.
Gray, Robert C. "Snuffy"
Green, William E.
Greenway, Thomas J.
Gregory, Melvin L.
Greiner, John W.
Grider, Edgar L.
Griebel, Ronald J. "Ron"
Griepp, Frank R.
Griffin, Jr., Joseph T.
Griffiths, Don
Grimsby, Roger
Groft, Edward S.
Grohowski, Jerry
Guarnieri, Jr., Albert
Guffey, Paul D.
Guyer, Kenny
Gwin, Jr., S. Lawrence
Hackett, James F. "Jim"
Haddle, Brian
Hagood, Jr., Samuel
Haight, Sherman P.
Hale, Stephen D.
Hall, Dillard R.
Hall, Ibby
Hall, James W.
Hall, Kerry D.
Hallden, Charles H.
Hanell, John C.
Hanlen, Don f.
Hanson, Douglas G.
Hardy, Douglas C.
Hardy, Jr., Robert W.
Hargrove, Lawrence E.
Harman, Charles W.
Harris, James
Harris, Ralph N.
Harris, Stephen R.
Harris, Thomas Pressley
Harrison, Ari
Harry, Curtis E.
Hart, Donald "Shorty"
Hart, L. Dean
Hartin, Thomas E.
Harwood, Thomas P. "Tommy"
Haskell, John "Jack"
Hasson, Alain Victor M.
Hatch, Gardner
Hatfield, Emsley
Haugerud, Howard E.
Hawksby, Richard
Hayes, Douglas
Hazen, Robert D.
Hedges, L. Wesley
Hedley, William
Heflin, John
Heis, June
Heismann, Steven H.
Heiter, James A. "Tony"
Heltsley, Nancy Bernice
Henry, Larry P.
Herman, Jeffrey B.
Hernandez, Andrew M.
Hernandez, Cesar A.
Herren, John D.
Herrera, Gilbert A. "Gil"
Hibbler, Jr., Virgie
Hickey, Pennell "Joe"
Hill, Carl M.
Hill, Jacque
Hillegas, Samuel R. "Richard"
Hindman, John T.
Hines, Sr., Woodrow N.
Hlavacek, Conrad "Groundhog"
Hobbs, Michael C.
Hockenberry, Richard A. "Hock"
Hoffman, Christopher
Hoffman, William H.
Hogans, Darius N.
Holbrook, Elizabeth K.
Holland, Theron
Hollingworth, Roy
Horn, Charles R. "Chuck"

Horn, Roland E.
Hoskins, Robert
Hoskins, Jr., Clayton
Houf, Thomas A.
Hough, Robert M.
Howard, John R.
Howard, Lee E.
Howden, John M.
Howell, Donald, S. "Don"
Howell, Robert M.
Howley, Carlos W.
Huerta, Sal Vic
Huff, Jack
Huggins, Otis L.
Hughes, Richard G.
Hughes, Thomas M.
Hume, Mark
Hume, Shannon S.
Humphrey, Floyd R.
Hunt, George L.
Hunt, Henry C.
Hunter, Art
Hursh, John
Hurtt, Thomas Leroy
Hutson, Frank Lee
Hyde, Charles V.
Ingley, Stephen J.
Inka, Dennis
Jackson, Bobby J.
Jackson, Clyde E.
Jackson, George "Bob"
Jackson, John M., M.D.
Jacobson, Lyle W.
Jelten, Stephen A. "Al"
Jennings, George W.
Johns, Barbara
Johnson, Dale N.
Johnson, Delores
Johnson, Elmer R.
Johnson, Gregory W.
Johnson, Harlen
Johsnon, Kenneth D.
Johnson, Robert D.
Johnson, Robert W.
Johnson, Thomas L.
Johnston, E. Bruce
Johnston, Robert J.
Jones, Alzalkie C.
Jones, Robert D.
Jones, Ronald S.
Jordan, Dwight E.
Julian, Casey H.
Kahrs, Jr., Donald H.
Kang, Theophile
Karhohs, Fred E.
Kaufman, David X.
Keane, Patrick J.
Keck, Dennis
Keeton, Douglas W.
Kelley, Donna Kay
Kennedy, II, Glenn A.
Kennemore, Jr., Charles M.
Kerecz, James J.
Kesterke, Katrina A.
Kesterson, William J.
Kidd, Gary R.
Kiernan, John P.
Kieslar, John D.
Kietzman, Gerald R.
Kilduff, Thomas C.
Kincaid, Charles E. "Bob"
Kinder, Robert E.
King, C.
King, Daniel J.W.
King, Jr., Charles F.
Kinnard, Harry W.O.
Kinney, Michael L.
Kinser, Todd J.
Klein, Alfred A.
Klincke, Matilda
Kluever, E. Kent
Kluever, Patty
Knight, Wylie "Gus"
Kofman, Edmunde
Korry, Julius
Kosinski, John E.
Krachinski, Roger W.
Kral, Daniel R.
Krampien, Robert F.
Kritzman, George
Kruske, Richard T.
Krysik, John
Ksepka, John G. "Shorty"
Kuykendall, Anthony
Kvidt, Reuben D.
Lacey, Richard S.
Lacey, William J.
Lacey, William J., Sr.
Lajeunesse, Robert W. "Bob"
Lajoie, Daniel G.

Landis, Tim
Lane, James L. "Jim"
Langevin, Joseph
Larsen, Clifford "Swede"
Larson, Bobby D.
Larson, Todd A.
Larzalere, Robert "Larz"
Lasater, R.C.
Laws, Bill R.
Layne, George W.
Leary, Michael C.
Lee, Edgar J.
Lee, Jesse F.
Lee, Richard C.
Lee, W. Suey
Legocki, Richard W.
Lehigh, Laura C.
Lenon, Helen
Lenon, Jr., James E.
Lent, Thomas D.
Lewis, Charles E.
Lewis, Ernest R. "Ray"
Lewis, George
Lewis, Robert D.
Linver, Sidney L. "Sid"
Lippincott, John C.
Lippincott, Kevin A.
Litle, Jr., Robert F. "Bob"
Little, J. Patrick
Little Big Horn Association
Litton, James "Larry"
Logan, Terry L.
Lommerse, Rutgerus M. "Rudy"
Long, Thomas R.
Lovell, William C. "Bill"
Lowry, James M. "Jim"
Lucas, Jennifer
Lucero, Richard L.
Ludke, Tammy A.
Lukes, Frank J.
Lute, Douglas E.
Lutz, Roger
Luxton, Charles
Lynch, James H.
Lynch, Timothy D.
Lynd, Allyn David
Lynn, Sr., John R.
Mac Farland, Donald J.
Mace, Herman A.
Mack, Theodore
MacMillan, IV, William D.
Madigan, James C.
Maize, Gerald L. "Dr."
Mancini, Daniel P.
Mapp, Bill
Mapson, Betty
Maruhncik, Andrew G.
Mariotti, Peter J. "Pete"
Marks, Frank L.
Marm, Walter "Joe"
Martin, Calvin
Martin, Lewis
Martin, Randall D.
Martin, Robert "Bob"
Martinez, Robert V.
Martino, Julius A.
Marahnich, John
Massey, Gary L.
Masterson, Michael J.
Matichak, William
Mattes, Charles W.
Matthews, John A.
Matthews, John D.
Matthias, Henry N.
Mauger, Robert N.
Maxwell, M. Donald
Maybury, Richard E.
Mayer, Christopher T.
Mayse, Jack H.
Mazza, Emilio A.
McAleer, Charles A.
McAnany, Joseph "Joe"
McBride, Jack E.
McBride, John P.
McBride, Norman L. "Doc"
McBroom, Richard C.
McCarey, Edward J.
McClung, Jr., William
McClure, James A.
McClure, Robert M.
McComas, Clyde W. "Mac"
McCray, Catherine Metsker
McDonald, Jr., George J.
McElhannon, Paul
McGregor, Michael
McIlroy, David A.
McKenzie, James A.
McKeon, Thomas L.
McKinley, Russell "Russ"
McKinney, John J.

McKnight, Thomas L.
McKown, Rick
McKown, William N. "Bill"
McManus, Francis W.
McNaney, Phillip J.
McQuistion, Jeffrey D.
Mead, John P.
Mears, Leland R.
Meeker, Jeffery L.
Mehl, Louis S. "Lou"
Melander, Robert J.
Menalo, Frank M.
Menard, C. Jack
Menard, William E.
Menser, Kent D.
Mercer, William R. "Bill"
Merchant, Richard "Dick"
Metheny, Pat
Metrando, Andrew J. "Doc"
Meyer, John J.
Meyers, Christopher Shawn
Meyers, David E.
Migut, Ronald J.
Millar, Tim
Miller, Dall H.
Miller, Frank L.
Miller, Frederick E.
Miller, Paul V.
Miller, Robert E.
Miller, Vernon L.
Milliner, William K.
Millis, Michael Edward
Milum, Hank
Miner, Norval M.
Mingus, Robert A.
Minnick, Walter D.
Mione, Saluatore
Mitchell, Charles F.
Mitchell, Charles J.
Mitchell, Richard N.
Mitchell, Jr., Tommie L.
Moffat, David L.
Mohr, Jerry A.
Molinari, Robert J. "Bob"
Molloy, E.A. "Mike"
Montean, Carl R.
Montgomery, William
Mooney, William T. "Bill"
Moore, Curtis G.
Moore, Gary L.
Moore, Harold G. "Hal"
Moore, James R.
Moore, William F.
Moran, Ray J.
Moreland, H. Boyd
Morelli, James
Morgan, Robert Dwight
Morton, Richard L.
Moser, Marsha
Mote, Robert G.
Moyer, John K.
Moyers, Ann B.
Mrochek, Jeffery A.
Murphy, Charles U.
Murphy, Dennis J.
Murphy, George N.
Murphy, Isaac
Murphy, Jim
Murphy, Thomas L.
Muskevitsch, Patrick W.
Myers, Charles W.
Myers, Jacob C.
Nacke, Albert
Nadal, II, Ramon A. "Tony"
Nardi, Patrick
Natale, Gil
Naumann, Michael E.
Neill, Marion C.
Nelms, Lindsey C. "Buddy"
Nelson, Charles W.
Nelson, David C.
Nelson, Tommy A.
Nelson, Jr., Edward I.
Nemec, Alice
Nemetsky, Howard A.
Newhouse, Gregory A.
Ngiralmau, Godwin S.
Nichols, Claude V.
Niemeyer, Walter A.
Niles, David P.
Niles, Guy Richard
Nock, Thomas C.
Nonnweller, Edward P.
Norman, Donald W.
Norris, Billie P.
Norris, Else R.
Norris, Roland E.
O'Brien, John
O'Brien, William E.
O'Donnell, Robert

Oakes, Thomas J.
Odems, Paul
Oden, Charles B.
Ogden, Lawrence J.
Oggs, Dennis I.
Olivier, George A.
Olivio, Grank J.
Olson, Lewland
Oneal, Lewis John
Oresick, Andrew
Orr, Thomas R.
Ortiz, Guillermo C.
Ortiz, Nelson
Osborn, George M.
Osterby, Norman R.
Osterby, Peggy
Ouellette, Robert P.
Owen, Joseph K.
Palmer, Fred L.
Parker, Larry B.
Parkinson, George T.
Parle, John J.
Particelli, J. David "Dave"
Parton, Joey N.
Passos, Connie
Passos, Ignacio "Nash"
Paterno, Edward F.
Paterson, Steven J.
Patterson, Charles W.
Patterson, Howard D.
Pauley, Sr., Henry John
Paulsen, James G.
Peck, Wendell R.
Pellerito, Andrew P. "Andy"
Pelot, Marguerite
Pelot, Mell S.
Pelow, John J. "Jack"
Penczar, David W.
Penczar, Walter A.
Pennison, Forrest J.
Penny, John R.
Perales, Frank J.
Perkins, James D. "David"
Perozek, Charles J.
Peter, David M.
Peterson, Merle J.
Pethel, Charles G. "Charlie"
Peyser, Daniel B.
Phillips, Christopher L.
Phillips, Ronald W.
Pickett, Earl E.
Pignatona, George
Piscal, Richard G.
Pittman, Donald R.
Plaisance, Jr., Ecton J.
Pless, Paul E.
Plumley, Basil L.
Poley, Clinton
Pomeroy, William B.
Pool, James C.
Porche, Stanley E.
Post, Alton G.
Potts, John O.
Powers, Jimmy C.
Poznansky, Jack
Presgraves, Donald C.
Preslan, Robert S. "Bob"
Prue, Pearl,
Przepiora, David
Pujals, Enrique V.
Rabchenia, Nick J.
Raisner, Walter T.
Ramirez, John M.
Ramsey, Alberta
Ramsey, Willie L.
Randall, Vernon C.
Randazzo, George
Randel, Jr., Herbert R.
Randell, Thomas E.
Rangel, Jr., John
Ransome, John G.
Rasmussen, Michael R.
Reece, David N.
Reed, Brian L.
Reed, Cliff V.
Reeves, Scott E.
Reigle, Kenneth
Rescorla, Richard
Reyes, Roy c.
Reynolds, Pamela
Rhea, Samuel G.
Richard, Emile
Richards, Jerry R.
Richardson, Eva
Richardson, Francis H. "Frank"
Richardson, Harold L.
Richardson, Robert D.
Richardson, William A.
Rivera, Mary T.
Roberts, Kaylon E.

Roberts, William H.
Roberts, Sr., Charles R.
Robey, James E.
Robinson, Dan
Robinson, J. Paul
Robinson, John B.
Robinson, Robert E.
Rodgers, Martin A. "Marty"
Rodriguez, Jose N.
Rodriqueg, Jr., Sebastain
Rolf, Oliver E.
Rosado, Ed
Rose, James K.
Rosinski, Sr., Adam J.
Ross, Billy R.
Ross, Donald S.
Ross, Mary A.
Ross, Nadean
Ross, William L.
Roth, Pauline S.
Rottenberg, Marvin
Roulhac, Jerome L.
Rourke, John C., M.D.
Rowley, Ada Ruth
Rowley, Glenn W.
Royer, Rowland M. "Sam"
Rozanski, Gordon P.
Rudel, Karen Metsker
Rulon, Hurley
Runnion, Lewis R.
Runyon, Myron D.
Rupert, Robert B.
Russ, Marion T.
Russell, Robert G.
Ryan, Frank L.
Ryland, Richard C.
Ryland, William "Bill"
Rylant, Timothy M.
Sack, Thomas A.
Sagerhorn, James
Saldana, Rafael
Sales, James M.
Samaniego, Jr., Pedro "Pete"
Sammons, Kenneth R.
Sammons, Robert B.
Sanders, Glen H.
Sandidge, Donovan B.
Santry, Robert M.
Savoie, Phil
Scarlato, Louis
Schaaff, Fred
Schild, James "Jim"
Schleusner, C.R.
Schlieve, Gregory A.
Schmitz, Charles R.
Schoelch, Frank F.
Schrank, Walter C.
Schwietert, Clinton L.
Scott, James A.
Screws, Eldon D.
Sebranek, David C.
Selber, Eric A.
Self, Jimmy R.
Self, Robert T. "TJ"
Selley, Harold V.
Serge, Michael L.
Serri, Domenico P.
Setelin, John I.
Severson, Gordon J.
Sewak, Steven Michael
Shackelford, Ray
Shannon, Robert A.
Sharp, Stephen E.
Sharp, Walter L.
Sheldon, Harrison W. "Bill"
Shields, Richard J.
Shingler, John
Shipley, Don
Shipman, Charles C.
Shirah, James L.
Short, Lawrence J.
Shutt, Don "Doc"
Silber, III, Carl H.
Simmeth, Harry G., Jr.
Simmons, Milton E.
Simpson, Darrell D.
Simpson, Homer D.
Sinegar, James M.
Sisson, Robert D.
Sleeis, Ronald G.
Slusser, James F.
Smith, Arthur D.
Smith, Barton M.
Smith, David C.
Smith, Jack P.
Smith, James C.
Smith, James R.
Smith, John P. "Jack"
Smith, Joseph M.
Smith, Leo B.

Smith, Raymond J.
Smith, Timothy J.
Smith, Toni
Smith, Wilbur J.
Smith, William D.
Smolick, Vincent Wm.
Snow, Tommy A., Jr.
Snyder, Jesse M.
Snyder, John H.
Snyder, Nevin D.
Soeldner, Robert M. "Bob"
Sollenberger, Earl W.
Sowder, Jo
Sowers, Michael R.
Sparrow, James A.
Spencer, Stephen P.
Sprayberry, James M.
Spriggs, Montie F.
St. Martin, Robert D.
Stahl, Earnest L.
Stallman, Donald L.
Stanley, Jr., Arthur J.
Stanton, Billy
Stark, PhD, Louisa
Stausmire, John W.
Steffen, Jan P.
Stern, Roy
Stevens, Sr., Fred
Stewart, Billy
Stewart, William J.
Sticken, Robert J.
Stillman, Jr., Frank E.
Stockton, Carlos J. "Jay"
Stokes, Sr., William
Stone, Jr., Thomas H.
Stone, Jr., Willie W.
Stopper, Larry E.
Stoutland, Fredrick A.
Stover, Lynn "Gordon"
Streeter, William T.
Stripling, Carrol D.
Strowder, Edward H.
Stump, Vallie H.
Sugdinis, Joel E.
Sulcer, James R.
Sullivan, Bradley C.
Sullivan, Kenneth G.
Sunde, Eiven
Sutton, Becky
Swain, Richard A.
Swan, William H. "Bill"
Sweet, Clarence A.
Swillinger, Ralph "Rusty"
Swoyer, David L.
Szymczak, Edward J.
Talavera, III, Jose M-Toso
Tallau, Howard G.
Talley, Jack H.
Tanner, Ray E.
Tapia, Peter Genaro
Tardiff, Chris
Tarpey, William R.
Tasker, Kenneth Rodger
Tavean, IV, Horatio Sprague
Templeton, Robert L.
Terrell, Jr., Ernest P.
Theall, Frank
Thiel, Todd V.
Thoele, Evelyn
Thomas, John W.
Thompson, James W.
Thompson, Jr., William R.
Thorn, Thomas H.
Thorpe, Jr., Henry B. "Hank"
Tichenor, J. Edward
Tilelli, Jeanne M.
Tilelli, John
Tilelli, Margaret A.
Toborg, Robert H. "Bob"
Torres, Jr., Frank G.
Toskas, Anthony L.
Towles, Robert L.
Treanor, Michael E.
Trevino, Noe S.
Trout, Jr., Donald F.
Trowbridge, Gordon P.
Tucci, Jerry
Tucker, Frank
Tucker, Terry L.
Turner, Dave
Tuzzolino, Paul L.
Tyree, Elzie
Umpherville, Kenneth R.
Valane, Peter "Pete"
Vallier, Emery A.
Valliere, Ronald B.
Van Dyke, Sherman M.
Van Hoff, Jr., Vincent
Vassalotti, Michael J.
Velarde, Mike A.

Villacres, Edward J.
Visor, Rick L., M.D.
Vivieros, Thomas J.
Von Ruedgisch, Margarete
Vosmeir, Leonard F. "Bud"
Votaw, E.L. "Chip"
Wagner, William D.
Wagner, Frank Hall, M.D.
Wagnild, Edward
Walker, Jr., Lawrence Bayne
Walker, Jr., Robert E.
Walks Over Ice, Loreen
Wallace, Owen C.
Wallace, William C.
Wallenius, Jon W.
Walsh, William J.
Wamble, James
Ward, Daniel G.
Ward, Greg
Ward, Richard J.
Wares, Jr., William M.
Watkins, William D.
Webb, Jr., William L.
Weber, William E.
Webster, Albert A.
Weichmann, Jack
Weinstein, Stanley A.
Welch, Charles Alfred
Wenger, Craig W.
Werner, Jr., Floyd S.
Wernsing, Merrill
Wertman, Millard W.
Wertzler, Karl I.
Wessels, Jr., Herman J.
West, Gene
West, Robert D.
West, William W.
White, Jerome P. "Georgia Boy"
White, Richard
White, William J.
Whitebird, Francis G.
Whitright III, Chauncey F.
Wickham, Jr., John A.
Widener, Larry E.
Wiestruk, Cliff
Wigant, Harold M.
Wigle, David C.
Willen, Charles J.
Williams, Charles J.
Williams, Donald T.
Williams, Herman D.
Williams, Howard M.
Williams, James D.
Williams, John R.
Williams, Lonnie D. "Bandit"
Williams, Nevin R. "Pete"
Williams, II, Nevin R.
Williamson, Barry L.
Williamson, Richard M.
Wilson, James A.
Wilson, Robert J.
Wilson, Wes
Wilson, Jr., David E.
Wiltshire, Clifford R. "Bucky"
Wing, Jr., Franklin F.
Winter, Peter J.
Withorne, Steven L.
Witte, Peter N.
Wolfe, Robert H.
Wols, Donald K.
Womach, T. Eugene "Gene"
Wood, James P.
Woodall, Harold L.
Woodley, Clinton A.
Woodrow, William W.
Woods, Avon Eugene
Woods, William J.
Wyeth, Philip M.
Wyosnick, Kathleen Cronan
Young, Chester D. "Chet"
Younger, Edwin William
Youts, Jr., Robert B.
Zadell, Joe
Zallen, Jerald D. "Jack"
Zanoni, Scott A.
Zent, Larry D.
Zook, Phillip M.
Zook, William E. "Bill"

ACKNOWLEDGEMENTS

I wish to express a special thanks to those individuals who assisted the author along the way, and to the recognition of that dedicated support by those members of the 7th U.S. Cavalry and 1st Cavalry Division Associations. Also, I realize that I cannot thank each one separately, then it is with hope that this book will serve as their reward.

Special Recognition

General Charles D. Palmer (Ret.), U.S. Army: To an excellent General who always was tough-minded with a fighting stance, and former 1st Cavalry Division Commander during the Korean War 1950-51.

General John H. Tilelli, Jr., Asst. Chief of Staff, Department of the Army; Thanks John for your continued effort in keeping the American Army the finest in the world, and to his lovely wife, Valerie, and daughters, Christine, Margaret, and Jeanne.

Lieutenant General Harold "Hal" Moore (Ret.), U.S. Army: Thanks for your continued loyalty to the 7th U.S. Cavalry and 1st Cavalry Division Associations; and to his lovely wife Julie who always expresses her dedication to the 7th U.S. Cavalry Association, and a special thanks for your support to the history of the 7th Cavalry Regiment in your book, "*We Were Soldiers Once...And young.*" Note: (General Moore is the HONORARY COLONEL of the 7th Cavalry Regiment.)

Lt. General Wesley K. Clark, Former Commander, 1st Cavalry Division, Fort Hood, Texas, and to his lovely wife Gert: My sincere gratitude and appreciation for your support of various projects for the 7th U.S. Cavalry and 1st Cavalry Division Associations, and a special thanks for keeping the "FIRST TEAM" spirit and legacy alive.

Major General Eric K. Shinseki, Commander, 1st Cavalry Division, Fort Hood, Texas, and to his lovely wife Patty. Best wishes as the new Commander of the "First Team."

Brigadier General Art Junot (Ret.), U.S. Army, presently, the executive director, 1st Cavalry Division Association: Thanks, Art, for your continued support, and sincere thanks goes to his lovely wife, Nan.

Colonel Robert F. Litle (Ret.), U.S. Army, former 2nd Battalion Commander, 7th Cavalry Regiment, 1st Cavalry Division (Vietnam), immediate past executive director and current program director, 1st Cavalry Division Association: Thanks, Colonel Bob, for your continued support, and sincere thanks goes to his lovely wife Linda.

Colonel John W. Callaway (Ret.), U.S. Army, former 2nd Battalion commander, 7th Cavalry Regiment, 1st Cavalry Division, Korean War 1950-51: My most humble thanks, Colonel John, and lovely wife Lynn, for your loyalty and dedication to the Korean War Veterans Chapter of the 7th U.S. Cavalry Association.

Lieutenant Colonel Douglas Lute, former commander, 1st Squadron, 7th Cavalry Regiment, 1st Cavalry Division, Fort Hood, Texas, and to his lovely wife Meg, and daughter Amy: My sincere thanks for keeping the spirit and legacy alive in the 7th Cavalry Regiment.

Lieutenant Colonel Robert "Rob" Soeldner, Commander, 1st Squadron, 7th Cavalry, 1st Cavalry Division, Fort Hood, Texas; and to his lovely wife Mary, and sons Max and Jake. My sincere thanks for keeping the spirit and legacy alive in the 7th Cavalry Regiment.

Lieutenant Colonel Timothy D. Lynch, commander, 2nd Battalion, 7th Cavalry Regiment, 1st Cavalry Division, Fort Hood, Texas, and to his lovely wife Sheryl, daughter Elizabeth, and sons David and Steven: My sincere thanks for keeping the spirit and legacy alive in the 7th Cavalry Regiment.

Command Sergeant Major James L. DePriest, 1st Squadron, 7th Cavalry Regiment, Fort Hood, Texas, and to his lovely wife Nancy: A special thanks for keeping the spirit and legacy alive in the 7th Cavalry Regiment.

Major Robert "Snuffy" Gray (Ret.), U.S. Army, former sergeant and officer, 2nd Battalion, 7th Cavalry Regiment, 1st Cavalry Division, Korean War 1950-51, and to his lovely wife Pauline: Our friendship goes back prior to the Korean War in 1949, during Occupation Duty. We shared that bond of brotherhood during the many struggles and hardships of combat, which were experienced within the Korean War 1950-51. Sincere thanks, my friend, for your support of this book project and for the loyalty and dedication to the 7th U.S. Cavalry Association.

Jesse Brown, Secretary of Veterans Affairs - please continue your great work effort and thanks for your support, and dedication to the needs of all veterans of all wars.

Sherman Haight, Chairman, The Foundation, 1st Cavalry Division Association. Thanks Sherm for your sincere dedication and support to the 1st Cavalry Division, and 7th U.S. Cavalry Association.

Richard Boylan, Assistant Chief, Military Field Branch, Military Archives, Washington, D.C.; Thanks Richard Boylan for your personal help and assistance in the research of military records and documents.

Steven L. Withorne, Commissioner, Office of Indian Affairs, State of South Dakota and to office personnel, Kathy L. Fleury and Pearl Stone: Sincere thanks for your friendship, support and help.

Said Sultan Al-Busaidi, his entire family and to the Sultanate of Oman. My sincere thanks for the many years of your devoted friendship.

Dr. Dewey Dunn, Dr. Dave Shepard and Mary Woodward Smith - many thanks to each of you for your dedication to the medical profession and for trying to care and help with the special needs of all veterans at the Nashville VA Medical Center.

Lorinda Stout, Editor-Office Manager, 1st Cavalry Division Association - many thanks to you for your continued friendship, support and help.

Becky Sutton, Director, Fort Meade Cavalry Museum, Sturgis, SD: Thanks for your friendship, support and help to the Lakota Nation and 7th U.S. Cavalry.

Mrs. Vera Chandler (widow of Lt. Col. Melbourne C. Chandler), for permitting the author to use invaluable material from the book, *Of Garryowen In Glory*; and associate member of the 7th U.S. Cavalry Association. I extend my most sincere thanks and appreciation.

James Chandler (son of the late Melbourne C. Chandler), his wife Suzanne, and son Christopher: Thanks, Jim, for your continued support.

Fred and Lois Carlen of Carlen's Free-Lance Photography: Many thanks for your continued support and excellent photo service within this book.

To all former GARRYOWEN officers, non-commissioned officers and enlisted troopers who previously served in the 7th Cavalry Regiment: I salute all of you! Their names are not listed due to the limited space in this book. (Please refer to the roster of the 7th U.S. Cavalry Association in this book.)

In Memory

In memory of Douglas MacArthur, General of the Army, U.S. Army, former Allied Supreme Commander, Far East Command.

In memory of Matthew B. Ridgway, General, U.S. Army, former Commander-in-Chief of the United Nations Forces during the Korean War.

In memory of William H. Harris, Major General, U.S. Army, former Regimental Commander, 7th Cavalry Regiment, 1st Cavalry Division, Korean War 1950-51.

In memory of Peter "Pete" Clainos, Colonel, U.S. Army, former Commander of the 1st & 3rd Battalions, 7th Cavalry Regiment, 1st Cavalry Division, Korean War 1950-51.

In memory of Melbourne C. Chandler, Lieutenant Colonel, U.S. Army, former Company Commander, Executive Officer, and Battalion Commander (after Callaway), 2nd Battalion, 7th Cavalry Regiment, 1st Cavalry Division, Korean War 1950-51.

In memory of John McCamley, Command Sergeant Major, U.S. Army (Ret.), former Honorary Sergeant Major of the 7th Cavalry Regiment.

In memory of William H. Kreischer, former President of the 7th U.S. Cavalry Association and recently installed President of the 1st Cavalry Division Association, who passed away on December 24, 1994.

In memory of all those GARRYOWEN officers, non-commissioned officers and enlisted troopers of the 7th Cavalry Regiment who served with relentless courage and dauntless bravery and who made the supreme sacrifice-their names are not listed due to space limits. This book, however, is a tribute to them and their families.

In memory of those Native Americans, men, women and children, who made the supreme sacrifice with their lives during the Indian Wars.

In memory of those Native Americans, the officers, non-commissioned officers and troopers of the 7th Cavalry Regiment, 1st Cavalry Division, who served with relentless courage and dauntless bravery and who made the supreme sacrifice with their lives. Their names are not listed due to space limits. This book, however, is a tribute to them and their families.

Interesting Comments

History is history, we can't change it! We need to make sure it is told as accurately as it can be. We need to go on and deal with issues today that will help our citizens and future generations to come.

Deborah Painte, an Arikara tribal member from New Town, SD, and executive director of the North Dakota Indian Affairs Commission said, *"We need to lay the animosities to rest!"*

Chauncey Whitright III, a Lakota Sioux from Montana's Fort Peck Reservation and chairman of the Strong Heart Society said, *"We need to get out from under all the blaming and get on with it, and go forward and strengthen this country. I'm doing this for my kids and my family, my people, myself, and my non-Indian friends!"* *"Peace Through Unity, will stand as an important symbol for mankind,"* he said.

My thoughts and love to all my immediate family and relatives. To my dear Mother, Mrs. Zelma Daily, who always gives me her support, kindness and love. To my son Eddie and daughter-in-law, Mary, and especially to my grandsons, Eddie III an Patrick, and my granddaughter, Julie. *Edward L. Daily, Clarksville, TN*

Custer To MacArthur - 7th U. S. Cavalry 1866-1945

Sources

Richard Boylan, Assistant Chief, Military Field Branch, Military Archives, Washington, DC 20409

Of Garryowen In Glory, Lt. Col. Melbourne C. Chandler, author, *The Turnpike Press*, Annandale, VA

American History Illustrated, Volume V, Number 10, The National Historical Society, Box 1831, Harrisburg, PA 17105

Research Review, Volume 3, Number 1, Little Big Horn Associates, 2415 McKinley #24, El Paso, TX 79930

The Custer Album, Lawrence A. Frost, author, University of Oklahoma Press, Norman, OK

Greasy Grass, Volume 6, Custer Battlefield Historical and Museum Association, P. O. Box 39, Crow Agency, MT 59022

Son of the Morning Star, Evan S. Connell, author, Harper Collins Publishers, 10 East 53rd St., New York, NY 10022

Warpath, Stanley Vestal, author, University of Nebraska Press, Lincoln, NE

Black Hills/White Justice, Edward Lazarus, author, Harper Collins Publishers, 10 East 53rd St., New York, NY 10022

My Friend the Indian, John McLaughlin, author, Houghton Misslin Publishing Co., 1910

Printed in the USA
CPSIA information can be obtained
at www.ICGtesting.com
JSHW060053150824
68134JS00032B/2721